Signs of Change

Contemporary Studies in Philosophy and Literature 4
Hugh J. Silverman, Editor

Signs of Change

Premodern → Modern → Postmodern

Edited by

Stephen Barker

State University of New York Press

Production by Ruth Fisher
Marketing by Fran Keneston

Published by
State University of New York Press, Albany

Printed in the United States of America

For information, address the State University of New York Press,
State University Plaza, Albany, NY 12246

Library of Congress Cataloging-in-Publication Data

Signs of Change : premodern-->modern-->postmodern / edited by Stephen Barker
p. cm. — (Contemporary studies in philosophy and literature ; 4)
Selected papers, most revised, from the Sixteenth Annual Conference of the International Association for Philosophy and Literature (IAPL), held May 1991 at the Université de Montréal, in collaboration with Concordia University and other institutions.
Includes bibliographical references and index.
ISBN 0-7914-2433-2 (CH). —ISBN 0-7914-2434-0 (PB)
1. Literature—Philosophy—Congresses. 2. Literature—History and criticism—Theory, etc.—Congresses. I. Barker, Stephen, 1946– . II. International Association for Philosophy and Literature. Meeting (16th : 1991 : Université de Montréal) III. Series.
PN45.S418 1996
801—dc20 94-25974
CIP

10 9 8 7 6 5 4 3 2 1

Contents

Acknowledgments

The essays in this volume were selected from those given at the sixteenth annual conference of the International Association for Philosophy and Literature (IAPL), held at the Université de Montréal, in collaboration with the Concordia University, McGill University, the Université de Québec à Montréal, and the Centre Canadien d'Architecture, under the direction of Professor Christie McDonald. The pieces included here have been reworked since their delivery at the conference, but only to allow for their authors' subsequent thinking; no effort has been made to shape them into a coherent whole for this volume. Rather, their integrity as separate entities has been assiduously maintained, for reasons thematically connected with the conference and the volume. The conference theme was "Penser le Changement: Art/Politique/Science." The twenty essays are here framed within a six-part structure devised by the editor after the fact and are further structured by the editor with a general introductory essay and specific introductions to each of the volume's sub-topics.

Thanks to Executive Director Hugh Silverman and the IAPL executive board for the opportunity to realize this project.

The University of California at Irvine has contributed valuable resources to the volume's production. The time, effort, and logistical strategies of Barbara Thibodeau and Dale Short of the Drama department in the School of The Arts, without which the volume could only have been assembled with great difficulty, are gratefully acknowledged.

Able assistance from Barry Cavin and Jon Eckfeld, in the latter stages of editing and in formulating the index, resulted in helpful support and good suggestions for improvement as well as a much speedier conclusion for the project.

To Topher, Jon, and Jeremy, I can only say thanks for understanding on those days and nights when I was hidden behind stacks of paper and couldn't extricate myself. As always, Dr. Michelle Barker's constant support has provided ongoing proof of the most wonderful aspects of "plus ça change. . ."

Introduction

> Nothing endures but change.
>
> —Heraclitus[1]

> Rien au monde ne dure
> Qu'un éternel changement.
>
> —Honorat de Bueil, Marquis de Racan[2]

Penser le changement (the thought of change) is so ubiquitously a part of our—indeed of global—culture that we find it problematic to conceive of or discuss the thought of change as such, so bound are we by our understood notions of it. Change is assumed to be an unchanging condition of life, human and otherwise. Indeed we say, after Heraclitus, that nothing in the world endures save eternal change; the familiar conundrum has been repeated throughout history to mark the dialectical threshold between being and becoming, essence and existence. Change is our fear and our hope for life.

Only since the advent of philosophical thought has change been conceived of in the human community as any kind of problem; only through the philosopher's lens is change, as such, susceptible to conceptualization—the process by which it could in fact become a "problem." For prephilosophic Greek thought, for example, the concept of change seems to have taken the form of dithyrambic, poetic acknowledgement of the power of the turning seasons and the hopes and fears generated by a dawning awareness of the forces these unchanging changes contained. For early Greek philosophy, change was an ubiquitous and grounding condition of the world and thus of philosophy. For Thales, Anaximander, and Anaximenes the world evolved from simpler states to more complex ones, moving through stages of development in a dense ambiance of change. For Anaximander, different (opposite) substances could be seen to grow into ever more complex and discrete states out of a primordial, undifferentiated, and ubiquitously indefinite matrix (chaos); for these thinkers, the process of *metabole* was responsible, so to speak, for the evolution of the world in its plenitude. *Metabole*, however defined, was a given.

The Pythagorean notion that the cosmos is unlimited and that only cosmology itself sets the limits by which we "know" it offered another, in some respects quite modern, turn to the consideration of change: Pythagoras's central idea concerning change, that the evolution from the unknown unlimited to the known limited marks and defines the world as we perceive it, contains within it a perspectivism we can easily recognize and which we might find familiar and even comfortable today.

It was Heraclitus, however, and Parmenides in response to his conception of change, who established the dialectical tone for all ensuing discussion not only of change, but of the *thought* of change. Indeed we are still, and have been ever since, working within their dialectical sense of the "problem" of change. In the post-Cartesian evolution of philosophy we can see clearly distinct shadings of this ancient discussion: for example, the tenets of idealism, with Kant's notion of the creative mind, and Hegel's image of the unfolding of reality through stages of reasoned thought, and romanticism, with its dynamism and evolutionary nature. In the plethora of philosophic schools vying for legitimacy in the twentieth century, the dialogue between ideal changeless forms, at some level, and an "actualism" that ostensibly denies such static grounding is clearly in evidence.

But since this introductory discussion begins with a mythic citation from Heraclitus, it is important to ground this twenty-part discussion of the thought of change in that first discussion, to look at Heraclitus's thought of change and some of its implications, and to see how and why for Parmenides the Heraclitan notion is unacceptable. For Heraclitus, change, *metabole*, is a fundamental quality of the *logos* (which for Heraclitus meant something like "formula") of the world, particularly since the grounding condition of that world, in its right and normal state, is one of strife. Since strife takes place within a structure of polar opposites, and is indeed the product of the necessary balance of these opposites (since without this balance all proportion would be destroyed and strife itself would cease to exist), all things—to use Heraclitus's oxymoronic concept—constantly change. One of the most disturbing and fascinating ramifications of this anti-state of "cosmic flux," with its continuous alteration of all things, is epistemological: whatever is perpetually changing is, logically, not susceptible to knowledge, since knowledge is concerned with what *is*, and thus must remain unknown. Thus, no concerted and structured view of the world, no thought connected to thing or thingness, no actual knowledge of process or product is possible. And further, since any so-called fact is simply not available in a world of ubiquitous change, only opinion can be formed with regard to the "actual" Heraclitan world. It follows that the basis for the polar disparity between rhetoric, as the study of the forceful presentation of that which is not susceptible to proof, and dialectic, as the study of that which can be proved factually—a distinction so clearly marked by Aristotle—is born in Heraclitus, within the context of the theme of change.

Heraclitus himself, of course, is famous for his fidelity to the ramifications of his own theory, having devised the most elliptical and mysterious, aphoristic philosophy that indeed is not susceptible to systematization. The remnants, shards, and ancient references we call "Heraclitus" represent the most radical anti-substantialism of Greek thought: since all change is contradictory, contradiction (as the simultaneous maintenance and unity of opposites) is the very essence of reality.[3]

Parmenides, responding directly and by name to Heraclitus in asking the most salient question of early philosophy, "what is the nature of real being?" and secondarily its epistemological corollary "how do we know?" sets up rhetorical conditions from which only one answer can be derived. Because the goal is *knowledge* of the real world, and since knowledge can only be had of stable things, change *cannot* exist. Parmenides's rejection of change and the thought of change grounds itself in an oxymoronic rhetoric of ontology: "what is not" is not knowable, not even thinkable. Since any concept of change involves the alteration of an "is" containing an "is not" which then becomes an "is" containing an "is not," etc., it follows for Parmenides that the Heraclitan world (in which constant reference to the "is not" is required) is a world of pure illusion—a world of nonsense. For Parmenides, the only logical conclusion concerning the thought of change is that since for thought a nothing or void is impossible, since "nothing" cannot *be thought*, change itself is not possible.

More importantly, in his attempts to show the static nature of all things, Parmenides claims that only the mind can reach beyond the world of appearance, of empirical reality that seems to change, to the immutable and static homogeneity behind it. Indeed, only in this mental realm is static and constant reality perceivable; thus in Parmenides do we see the beginning not only of the abstract thought on which Socratic tradition will build to establish philosophic tradition, particularly the Aristotelian notion of immanent form "beneath" the flux encountered by the senses, but also the joining of the argument about *penser le changement* and the concomitant conventions of change, out of which are derived conventions of philosophy such as Plato's paideic cosmos and Aristotle's *dynamis*, claiming that "where there is better there must be best," that things tend toward their own completion and so, being deprived of that *telos* must move in a certain direction toward it. Despite the obviously Parmenidean element in Plato, the Heraclitan thought of change can be seen to be reflected in Plato's *Timaeus*, with its contrast between that which always is and has no becoming, on the one hand, and that which is always becoming and never is, on the other. Plato's (Heraclitan) conclusion: one can have no knowledge of the world of change, only opinion; since no "science" can be based on mere opinion, no true science of the physical world can exist. In consequence, we find Aristotle conceiving of the immutable Being or inherent Form "behind" the mutable physical world the eternalized nature of matter that legitimizes the marriage of knowledge and material alterity.

It might be said that all subsequent philosophy is produced in the shadow of that Heraclitan/Parmenidean dialectic concerning conventions of change. The Heraclitan notion of contradiction as the essence of reality, and the Parmenidean one rejecting change as itself contradictory and therefore not real,[4] confront each other from Plato to Plotinus to Kant to Sartre to Derrida. To cite just a few examples of this pervasive influence: Plotinus's synthesis of change and stasis, resultant from ideas of "emanation" and "*dynamis*," is brought about by the Divine Intellect that alone can grasp the immutable nature of Being, while all lesser souls, in their benighted striving, find themselves in a condition of partial comprehension and desperate striving to understand; change is thus the result of the human inability to grasp everything at once (Plotinus would understand Heideggerian Being in this regard). Plotinus's thought on change leads us to two seemingly contradictory contemporary conventions of change: time is an infirmity of the human mind preventing us from seeing things as they are in their eternal immutability, and mentality and temporality enjoy a close correlation. Thus do we again confront physical/metaphysical differentiation inherent in Plato and Aristotle, Bruno and Bradley, Spinoza and Sartre. Kantian monadic idealism continues this structural thought: for Kant, time is a form of sensibility that applies only to phenomena, not to the "intelligible world." Thus also Fichte's "Absolute Ego," for which everything is at once and time exists only in the imagination, is atemporal. Hegel agrees with Heraclitus that reality is "historical" and that the world is constructed of opposites, but "Absolute Idea," central to the Hegelian worldview, is atemporal/metaphysical. Again and again in contemporary philosophy we confront this dialectical association of the physical—the "lived"—with the metaphysical, and thus of time with timelessness and change with changelessness. In the twentieth century, post-Newtonian physics has altered our view of physical change profoundly, working increasingly closer to a Heraclitan notion of ubiquitous and dynamic, vehicleless change, interpreted by contemporary philosophy as a dialectic between determinism and indeterminism. According to the Heraclitus/Parmenides dialogue, which has seemingly just begun, the former has had the upper hand in the last century or so, the latter more power in the longer-term. Current philosophy is concerned with the psychology (existentialism, essentialism, etc.) and politics (Marxism, feminism, etc.) of human existence, within the context of the conventions of both philosophy and change.

Change, then, is a function of time, space, and the conventions of traditional self-reflection, a phenomenological marker or figure for temporality and therefore, as conception and figure, is perpetually caught in the discourse of reality and illusion. The fall into time is the fall into change, since to know one is to know the other. Since all knowledge is built on difference, since differentiation is thus required to establish *nomos*, and because language (i.e., differentiation) is required for knowledge, knowledge requires change. The very idea of change is impossible—as both Heraclitus and Parmenides discovered—without a sense of identity, of stasis, and of the relative play of dialectical opposition and difference. This is inherent in the very words we use for the phenomenon (or non-phenomenon) of change. *Metabole*, to throw or glance across, contains within it the clear sense both of action and substance. *Change*, from the Latin *cambiare* (to exchange or barter), out of the Celtic base *kamb* (to bend or crook), indicates both the economic root of the idea of change, in the sense of its being based on exchange of something for something, and the swerving or willful (out of Epicurus and then Lucretius) sense of deviation from a normative or rigid direction. Change, in its very linguistic roots, has to do with a strategic deviation from an identifiable convention or position; change and the thought of change, even while aculturally normative, are always a potential disruption or disturbance of equilibrium and of convention.

In our own current cultural atmosphere, *penser le changement* consists of and entails normative and transgressive thinking, temporally oriented within an evolving cultural milieu of premodern, modern, and postmodern signs. Since Nietzsche, we have had to realize that the thought of change requires us to collate philosophy with psychology, and to make adjustments in the abstractions, absolutes, and conventions on which philosophic thought works to accommodate human (i.e., self-interested) *telos* and its psychological constraints. I mention Nietzsche here because the crux of the normative/transgressive issue in philosophy, certainly with regard to change, can be traced to Nietzsche's reconsideration of the Heraclitus/Parmenides dialogue. After *The Birth of Tragedy*, Nietzsche's motto became *Los Vom Mythos*, "away from myth!" And once away from myth (as if he ever was), Nietzsche fabricated the "tragic philosophy" of Becoming and the Will to Power, grounded in self-overcoming through development of the apocryphal *Übermensch* and thus to the Zarathustra phenomenon, that most ironic and parodic of transgressive estrangements.[5] According to Nietzsche, the philosopher of tragic *Erkenntnis*

> restrains the uncontrolled drive toward knowledge, but not through a new metaphysis. He does not set up a new faith. He feels the vanishing of the metaphysical ground as a tragic event and cannot find a satisfying compensation for it in the motley spiralling of the sciences. (X 118)

Ironically for Nietzsche, this embracing of tragic insight leads directly to his deep interest in change, and thus in the philosophy of Heraclitus:

> I set apart with high reverence the name of Heraclitus. When the rest of the philosopher crowd rejected the evidence of the senses because these showed plurality and change, he rejected their evidence because they showed things as if they possessed duration and unity. . . . Insofar as the senses show becoming, passing away, change, they do not lie. (Nietzsche, F., *Twilight of the Twilight*, "Reason" in Philosophy, 2)

Later in the same section of *Twilight of the Idols*, the interrogation of "reason" reaches its apex in the declaration that

> Change, mutation, becoming in general were formerly taken as proof of appearance, as a sign of the presence of something which led us astray. Today [1889], on the contrary, we see ourselves as it were entangled in error, *necessitated* to error, to precisely the extent that our prejudice in favor of reason compels us to posit unity, identity, duration, substance, cause, materiality, being; however sure we may be, on the basis of a strict reckoning, that error is to be found here. (5)

The error, according to Nietzsche, is to place language and its effects, "reason" and "being," at the core of creation; since being, so-called, is a creation of ego, it is always a function of both philosophy and psychology, which for Nietzsche creates a loop in which concepts—signs—labor to convince us of their substance and authority, always with our complicity. Not spiralling into the sciences but still anticipating Heisenberg, Nietzsche declares that "at any precise moment of a force, the absolute conditionality of a new distribution of all its forces is given: it cannot stand still. 'Change' belongs to the essence, and therefore also to temporality: with this, however, the necessity of change has only been posited once more conceptually" (*The Will to Power* 1064). The constitutive and creative notion of change, and by extension becoming, stands as the sign of a reading of the world free of the insidious errors of both progress and stasis.

It is within this pivotal Nietzschean context that this volume is conceived, and like a constellation of unlike stars arranged by their various forces around an empty center that the essays in the volume have been gathered together and juxtaposed. The essays in this volume approach the theme of change, and *penser le changement*, from widely various standpoints. No attempt has been made to lessen their rhetorical or thematic differences; indeed, their divergences and the eclecticism of their overall effect are themselves signs of change, in the sense that such signs always must mark difference, must form a dialectical relationship based on difference. The theme of change is thus approached in the volume precisely, and not always directly, by its signs. "Signs of change" are not change, any more than becoming is being. But signs of change mark the boundaries of evolution of the culture in which we live, and those markers guide us toward worldviews of disturbing and provocative complexity. In a postmodern age (and surely no sign or marker has received more diverse treatment than this "postmodern" age), the mapping of a tendentious route to the postmodern is one of the chief pastimes, avocations, and vocations of critic, theorist, philosopher, and pundit. This activity, itself a cultural normative, like the IAPL gathering at which it was a central consideration, requires for its carrying out the establishing of a grounding concept, a convention from which to operate. "Convention," the word and its denotative mark, is a sign for the static, for a fixed mode or structure of operation; what is conventional is (for the present) unchanged and eternal. Conventions are the laws by which regulation and regularization are (trans)fixed. Thus, conventions are always subject to the law and may not, as Derrida has shown, produce insights beyond the law. This is itself, of course, a postmodern insight, and is thus "outside the frame" from the point of view of the premodern. The volume's subtitle, with its evolutionary structure, exhibits the postmodern irony of suggesting that the so-called premodern, no more nor less than the time of the establishment of conventions and normatives, "causes" or "paves the way for" the modernist revolt that itself contains and yet "causes" the postmodern. All of these familiar strategic worldviews consist of self-identifying conventions, and all are signs—something "representing something for someone," as Lacan says[6]—and thus the indices of differences and divisions. This volume is a reminder of those divisions and the condition of change within which they are manifest.

Indeed, this volume concerns itself not only with conventions of change, but with a convention on change: the sixteenth annual convention of the International Association for Philosophy and Literature, held in Montréal in May, 1991, explored this complex and provocative issue from remarkably diverse points of view. Because of the IAPL's unique nature, the conventions of philosophy, literature, and literary theory discourse with one another in intense and fruitful debate. While the volume does not attempt to represent, nor to be a sign for, that convention nor for the conventional, it emerges from both so as to engage the thought of change in such a way as to attempt an interrogation (which is of course itself a sign) and a provocation. If, since Derrida—since Nietzsche?—since Erasmus?—the provocative has been an increasingly strained meta-strategy for inquiry and the questioning of culture, its value and centrality is not lessened but rather heightened in the postmodern, which is quite literally a strategy of provocation. Perhaps this volume will have been at the cusp of that postmodern interrogation of cultural convention, its provocation a catalyst for a turn of the epistemological wheel.

As has become conventional in IAPL volumes, this one is subdivided into areas of thematic coagulation. No attempt is made to be comprehensive in these divisions, to (re)present a thorough investigation of the theme of change/signs of change, nor to track some inevitable course from the Premodern to the postmodern in each section or overall. Some of the essays in the volume draw broad theoretical strokes; some are quite specific in their application of theory to a particular thinker or artist, body of work, or text. The desired effect of a close reading of the volume in its entirety is both a cacophonous and an orchestrated one. The volume's six subdivisions do, however, trace an abbreviated path through some considerations of the theme of change. It would be possible to construct a logical sequence out of the constituent parts, beginning with the semiotic, semantic, and hermeneutic conditions on which any system of signs must be predicated (Part 1); then introducing the spatial dimension of change and the cognition of change through a consideration of the topographical and the broader topological, focusing here on the concrete evidence by which change is gauged and measured (Part 2); then, in the central section of the volume, taking up the temporal core of change in a double sequence of essays exploring the historical and the historiographic, followed by a discussion of the nature of (dis)closure as a function of history (Parts 3 and 4); then, within this spatial and temporal context, to a consideration of the politics of change (Part 5); and finally, to a concluding and re-framing discourse in which the more directly strategic aspects of the theme of change are considered (Part 6). It would also be possible to consider the volume, as I did often during its construction, from numerous other points of view, and in light of numerous other arrangements and disarrangements. Ideally, in some respects, the volume, like some of those in Borges's apocryphal library, would continuously permute through a series of differing orders, never settling on any "right" one. Since in the linear, codex form of the book (and the same will still be true of the CD-ROM form of the book, and every other form that requires linear reading as we know it now) some structural organization is necessary, here is one. As with Nietzsche's strings and clusters of aphorisms in his more allusive later writings, significant thematic connections may be felt more strongly and clearly laterally, between (parts of) uncontiguous essays in disparate sections of the volume, than between those grouped together under the sign of an organizing and organicizing rubric. Further, in some of the volume's twenty essays, the theme of change is addressed directly, as a theoretical or cultural marker, and in some it is merely alluded to as a component of the work or works being assessed. Yet change and the thought of change are centrally the driving themes behind each of the collected essays assembled here.

By a similar token, the volume plays with notions of the "modern" and its more formal critical construction, the "Modern" (along with that most evanescent and intractable of constructs, the "Postmodern"), without attempting definition, explanation, or juxtaposition. The volume is content to be at work and play in the general environment of these conceptualizations without being defined nor controlled by them.

If the following pieces as a whole, or any them as separate or constituent elements, engender thought on the part of the reader concerning the power and complexity inherent in the nature of change in its myriad aspects, then the volume will have accomplished its goals.

Part One

Semantics/Semiotics/ Hermeneutics

> Semiotics attempts to make explicit the implicit knowledge which enables signs to have meaning, so it needs the reader not as a person but as a function: the repository of the codes which account for the intelligibility of the text.
>
> —Jonathan Culler, *The Pursuit of Signs* 38

> Language has turned on us.
>
> —Gary Shapiro, *After the Future* xviii

Within the context of both the directly textual and the indirectly textual world of events, we have seen how the mechanisms of memory, time, space, and identity—not to mention language itself—have served historically as signs of change. Though Culler's distinction between "implicit" and "explicit" knowledge has a distinctly modern, if not indeed a downright premodern, ring, his attention to the syntactic connection between these kinds of knowledge is a useful reminder of the theatricality of the semiotic enterprise. Culler's declaration can be taken in several ways: mechanistically, he declares the automatic cause-response relationship between sent and received information, as though that simple distinction could still be made; semiotically, the Aristotelian, reader-response implication of the dynamic in Culler's statement implies a pact between reader (as functionary) and read (as textual, whether written or not), a relationship that can blossom into the densest thicket of cross-meanings and covert agendas with only the slightest attention.

And, of course, this dialectical dynamic itself, in its very form, entails change: it can be seen in the development of a hermeneutic system, as part of a culture or sub-culture at a given time; in the establishment of semiotic "languages" within cultures as diachronic structures. In fact, it is not empty semantics to declare that change is itself a semiotic marker. As a number of essays in ensuing sections will indicate, history and signs, politics and signs, space and signs are fundamentally enmeshed. Thus the volume might be seen to begin with semantics, semiotics, hermeneutics: activities of structuration and interpretation, and of the inscription of meaning.

To begin at the end, as Gary Shapiro so tersely points out in his introduction to *After the Future*, language (in the postmodern) has turned on us. But if it has done so, it had, as such, always done so, and its turns are the most fundamental signs of change we can know.

The terms gathered together for some kind of mutual consideration here show forth this complex relationship to change: *semantics*, as the investigation of contextual meaning; *semiotics*, as the structuration of code and sign systems and their implementation; *hermeneutics*, as the discovery of meaning through exegesis—the triangulation of these terms is itself a semiotic and conceptual orchestration. The notion of signs for things can be traced back at least to the cave walls at Lascaux, and separately to the origins of writing itself in the recording of bills of lading for goods exchanged and accounted for by systems of marks, and though these notions are closely linked to the systematization of the hermeneutic enterprise in its links to the earliest religions, and the philosophic activity of semiotics to the roots of the philosophic enterprise—certainly in the metaphorical pre-Socratic philosophy of a Heraclitus or a Parmenides. Idealist philosophy is necessarily and indigenously marked by semiotics (Plato's cave, for example, is a dense semiotic network or images and concepts, and conceived as such, within the context of a language that is always turning on us), and the more pragmatic philosophy of Aristotle is pervaded by an awareness of the dangers and powers of semiosis (the *Poetics* and the *Rhetoric* come instantly to mind). That semiotics as a self-reflexive activity is a phenomenon of the twentieth century, emerging indirectly through the work of Russell, Freud (*The Interpretation of Dreams*), Cassirer, Heidegger, and others, and more directly through the work of Peirce and Saussure, and coming to fuller fruition after the middle of the century through the structural anthropology of Lévi-Strauss, shows how pervasive has been our century's obsession with relationality and affinity, difference and estrangement. Semiotics, like psychoanalysis, is a function of the twentieth century. And yet unlike psychoanalysis, semiotics is "nomadic," always subject to the ambiguities not only of interpretation but of language and enculturation as well. Where semiotics is concerned, there are no facts, only interpretations.

Though semiotics is the middle term in designation of Part One, its investigation forms the core of the first and fourth essays in the section. In an abjectly secular age, hermeneutics and semiotics become virtually identical. All four of the section's essays investigate the tension between the metaphysics of hermeneutic applications to texts and non-texts, and all four address the structural poetics of semantics. Nonetheless, a look at premodern, modern, and postmodern semiotics is finally the essays' chief nourishment.

Ib Johansen works with the chronological evolution of the treatment of laughter in his essay. Starting from the premise that laughter is the chief sign of culture (and thus of change itself), that it is always a semiotic marker that in its vicissitudes marks the evolution of cultural attitudes and moods, Johansen evokes Bakhtin's notion of laughter as the synchronic, parodic underminer of authority that has undergone a "degradation" in the postmodern world, but that is still a "totalizing semiosis" covering all aspects of the "carnival" of society—laughter is from this point of view cultural, not psychological. Johansen tracks the history of laughter from the medieval to the postmodern, showing for example how its denigration in medieval thought results in its reinscription and reintellectualization in the Renaissance turn to reasoned laughter. Whereas for John Donne laughter presents an epistemological critique of wisdom and folly, for Baudelaire and the early modernists Donne is reversed—now the wise man is afraid of laughter. Whereas for Foucault laughter is "aporetic," for Cixous feminine laughter, linked to the body but still a social and political force, heralds the breakdown of patriarchal hegemony. Johansen's tracking of the hermeneutic evolution of this single semiotic marker opens many potentially fruitful interpretive possibilities.

Erdmann Waniek takes a close and thoughtful look at another singular marker—silence, in the more limited context of selected twentieth-century German poetry. He explores the relationship between silence and language, always remembering the essential ambiguity of silence as such, declaring that the initiatory power of silence is immense: "it is as if for us, the language animal, the world opens only upon the loss of language." Treating more than half a dozen poets from Hofmannsthal to Christa Wolf, Waniek focuses on Brecht's acknowledgement that silence is a "*trockenlegung des weiten Prasensumpfes*," particularly in light of the enormity of twentieth-century German social and political dynamics. Brecht, it is clear, meant *linguistic* silence (Kattrin in *Mother Courage* loses her life as a result of being herself mute but certainly and fatally not silent), asking whether silence makes one an accomplice in a time of political injustice. Brecht's double desire is to be free of such questions, but not to avoid them where necessary. The poet, according to Brecht, can only become a witness to injustice by writing/speaking of it; to witness without speaking is not to witness (this theme resonates provocatively with recent work by Derrida on the nature of the witness, who must speak to be legitimate but who cannot, in speaking, witness for those who did not witness). Waniek explores various responses to Brecht's question, specifically related to the Holocaust: Brecht knew that "easy silence" had to be lifted, Célan (whose suicide stands as a final silence in the face of the immensity of witness) knew that language veils the truth. Waniek's treatment of the symbol-systems of silence and speaking/writing alight on fascinating imagery, such as Brecht's use of the tree about which the poet would like to speak purely aesthetically but cannot, since doing so would entail denying larger issues demanding attention.

Waniek's plotting of the curve of poets' attitudes toward silence reveals a fascinating relationship between ideas of the poet as advocate and as aesthete. The evolution from Brecht to Célan to Enzensberger to Fritz and then to Christa Wolf can be seen, Waniek shows, as one from "an aesthetics of resistance to an aesthetics of silence to a renewed but muted aesthetics of resistance, with less hope and certainty," the question of silence bringing up the ancillary one of the place of beauty in the social *locus*. Finally, for Wolf, silence acts as a healing agent, a pastoral escape from city noises, but this silence leads to the final question: is beauty "silent about and detached from the real world"? As he takes us through a series of powerful and poignant examples of the poetic use of silence, Waniek explores the changes in an attitude toward the sign of silence and its relation to its signifieds, and asks how silence is implicated in poetic and social change.

Echoing this social theme, Elinor Fuchs addresses postmodern nostalgia within a Debordian context, as the erasure of the past by democratic mass society, employing the "before theatre/after theatre" model of cultural change. Fuchs uses the sign of the theatrical to show how the postmodern establishes itself as a great "leveller of differences" and then, as the repository of resistance, as the agent of change. She invokes the connections between the aesthetic postmodern and the architectural to show how Western culture is "constructed around the protean image of the theatrical." Fuchs then traces the idea of theatre through the work of a series of (male) postmodern theorists from Debord to Derrida to Foucault to Deleuze/Guattari to Baudrillard, linking history and semiosis. Particularly interesting in this developmental analysis is her treatment of Derrida's notion of a non-imitative writing not preceded by speech, an imitation of nothing, in which "we enter the de-ontologized world of simulacra through the . . . *hymen* of theatre"—the theatre is the post-metaphysical world. Baudrillard, according to Fuchs, presents the furthest extension of antiontological simulation of the theatricality.

But Fuchs's is a dialectical strategy: after her treatment of postmodern theory in Baudrillard, she turns her attention to a feminist theatre semiotics, showing how theatre can be seen as the "patriarchal Other," the "ubiquitous theatre of male representation" (Françoise Collin) feminists must evade. Fuchs then presents several strategies for accomplishing this, for example in Cixous and Irigaray. In Irigaray, Fuchs finds the most systematic demonstration of the "feminine-as-performance" confronting patriarchal theatre. For Fuchs, the postmodern is "that moment in culture when the last ontological defenses crumble into theatre"; thus, theatre-as-marker is a vital sign of change.

John Johnston summarizes contemporary semiotic notions of change by chronicling and exploring the historical structuralism of Baudrillard and Deleuze-Guattari and their systems of simulacra. Since no referent is a "given," but is always produced by a sign system and a "reader," Johnston shows how these theorists critique respective "regimes of signs," never forgetting that framing historical references in semiotic terms means that of course critical theory is itself situated within a regime of signs subject to the same critique. Johnston shows how in Baudrillard even "history" is now simulated existence engendered to justify certain discourses, and that for Deleuze-Guattari history is a "universalization" mae possible by capitalism's abstracting, deterritorializing process. Even (or perhaps particularly) in the postmodern, the role of the critic, theorist, or intellectual is still that of interpreter.

1

The Semiotics of Laughter

Ib Johansen

INTRODUCTION

In his book on Rabelais, Mikhail Bakhtin has tried to trace some of the changes undergone by the attitude to laughter in the Western world since the Middle Ages and the Renaissance period. With regard to the Middle Ages—and in particular the medieval use of parody—Bakhtin stresses "laughter's universal character"[1]: "Laughter was as universal as seriousness; it was directed at the whole world, at history, at all societies, at ideology."[2] Furthermore, laughter is associated with a number of grotesque and "carnivalesque" elements, and it has profound links with a subversive folk tradition. In this perspective laughter represents "the defeat of divine and human power, of authoritarian commandments and prohibitions . . . ,"[3] insofar as "The people play with terror and laugh at it; the awesome becomes a comic monster."[4] This anti-authoritarian and anti-terrorist ethos seems to prevail in the premodern and in the early modern period, but later it undergoes a number of revisions, and Bakhtin summarizes the history of laughter in the last three or four hundred years as "this process of laughter's *degradation*."[5] What has happened to laughter in the modern—or to pursue the transformation a little further—in the *post*modern world?

I propose here to investigate a number of literary and philosophical texts that may be brought to bear on this question. I shall concentrate on three texts: a paradox, a short story, and a novel; i.e., John Donne's paradox VII, "That a wise man is knowne by much Laughinge," the English surrealist Leonora Carrington's story "The Skeleton's Holiday," and Angela Carter's "carnivalistic" novel *Nights at the Circus*. My discussion of the semiotics of laughter will thus be based on an early modern

(Renaissance) and two contemporary or near-contemporary texts. But I shall also offer cursory comments on a few other texts that I consider relevant in the present context.

First, I want to contextualize my discussion concerning laughter. In his book on Rabelais, Bakhtin seems to philosophize on laughter in an inclusive sense—what he has in mind is neither laughter as a physical utterance nor as a response to a specific social situation, comprising a particular "psychological" set-up, such as it appears to be, e.g., in Henri Bergson's definition when he states that "our laughter is always the laughter of a group";[6] to Bakhtin laughter is rather a comic perspective on the world as a whole, a total and a totalizing semiosis covering all aspects of what Bakhtin has termed "carnival." That is, in Bakhtinian theory laughter is no longer a purely psychological, but basically a cultural phenomenon.

As far as its theoretical status is concerned, laughter proves to be a somewhat slippery term. In Julia Kristeva's essay on Bakhtin, "Word, Dialogue, and Novel," the attempts to limit the "scope" of the word—or to subject it to some kind of reflective control—appear to be just as futile as in Bakhtin's case. Laughter has become an extremely evasive, "sliding" signifier. According to Kristeva, "The laughter of the carnival is not simply parodic; it is no more comic than tragic; it is both at once, one might say that it is *serious*," but at the same time modern writing seems to possess special qualities as far as the "omnified scene" of carnival is concerned, and here the subversive power of laughter is suddenly toned down: " . . . *laughter* is silenced because it is not parody but *murder* and *revolution* (Antonin Artaud)."[7] There seems to be a revolutionary as well as a nonrevolutionary type of laughter, the former associated with the subversive language and hyperbolic theatricality of carnival culture, the latter a purely literary phenomenon.

LAUGHTER AND DISMEMBERMENT

In a number of premodern cultures laughter turns out to be an extremely powerful force, in terms of its creative as well as its destructive potential. It may be linked up with the "death" and the symbolic resurrection of a neophyte undergoing a shamanistic ceremony of initiation, such as it is the case in the following example from Melanesia, quoted by Mircea Eliade in his *Shamanism: Archaic Techniques of Ecstasy* (1951, 1972, 1974); here a medicine man is initiating his nephew into the secrets of his "art":

> Then he said to his nephew: "Come here. Lie down on this leaf," and the youth lay down on it. Then the Bwili made himself a bamboo knife and

> cutting off one of the young man's arms, placed it on two of the leaves. And he laughed at his nephew and the youth laughed back. Then he cut off the other arm and placed it on the leaves beside the first. And he came back and they both laughed again . . . [he cuts off the legs, too] . . . Lastly he cut off the head, held it out before him. And he laughed, and the head laughed, too.
>
> Then he put the head back in its place and took the arms and legs that he had taken off and put them all back in their places.[8]

In this case magical mutilation and magical "healing" have been perfected to such a degree that nothing can apparently go wrong—the shaman or "Bwili" is in control of everything. Even if the "sacrificial" role of the nephew implies dismemberment and death, it is accompanied by laughter. This is not the heroic laughter of the Christian martyr vis-à-vis the executioner, but rather a laughter that signalizes a secret understanding or agreement between the two persons. One's laughter mirrors that of the other, and thus "The worst returnes to laughter" (*King Lear*).[9]

In *Rabelais and His World* Bakhtin focuses on the carnivalistic "rending of the human body"[10] and analyzes a number of episodes involving "dismemberment" in Rabelais' *oeuvre*.[11] Occasionally we may also come across such an "anatomization" of the human body in the tradition of "Easter laughter" (*risus paschalis*). This clerical custom is explained in the following way in Bakhtin's book: "The priest could tell amusing stories and jokes from the pulpit . . . . The jokes and the stories concerned especially material bodily life, and were of a carnival type."[12] In the Protestant clergyman's *M. Johann Mathesius Leben Dr. Martin Luthers in siebzehn Predigten*, published shortly after the Reformation, the theologian alludes to the tradition of the *risus paschalis* and recapitulates a story he heard in his youth:

> When the Son of God came to Limbo and made a forward stroke with his cross, tho devils put forth their long noses as bolts. But when Christ knocked, so that door and hinges were by main force opened, he struck off the noses of the two devils.[13]

The *Ostermährlein* just quoted is clearly concerned with a carnivalesque inversion, an "anatomization" of the Prince of Darkness and of Hell! Sacred history is turned into a humorous anecdote, and the Harrowing of Hell—a metaphysical project of the first water—is eclipsed by the grotesque dismemberment of two of the Devil's helpmates. In this fashion the magical and/or archaic aspects of the concept of ritual dismemberment are downgraded and the latter is submitted to a carnivalistic "turn."

THE PARADOXES OF RENAISSANCE LAUGHTER

During the Renaissance laughter may be said to undergo a process of intellectualization. According to Bakhtin, "The lower genres begin to penetrate the higher levels of literature . . . The culture of laughter begins to break through the narrow walls of festivities and to enter into all spheres of ideological life."[14] But this cultural change involves a certain paradoxical risk, for the intellectual as *eiron* gradually turns out to master what he/she derides, and this may be characterized as a kind of Foucauldian "turn," more or less identical to the takeover of madness and/or folly by its opposite, i.e., by critical reflection or "reason," in Renaissance humanism. When the scholar (Erasmus) hides behind the mask of Dame Folly, it appears to be a strategic operation that, in a wider perspective, inaugurates the final victory of reason—or Cartesian subjectivity.[15]

According to Montaigne in his essay on Heraclitus and Democritus, laughter circumscribes the human condition, and we have no way of escaping from it: "Our owne condition is as ridiculous, as risible; as much to be laught at, as able to laugh."[16] In this connection we notice that in Montaigne's essay laughter has very little to do with the pleasure principle, but is rather based on a certain blasé contempt for the world: it is better to laugh than to weep, because "We are not so miserable, as base and abject."[17] First and foremost, the ability to laugh signalizes the spiritual agility of the reflecting subject, the "superior" position of the "wise man" vis-à-vis his surroundings, and thus the subject-object split may be said to be installed at the heart of laughter, affecting its very mode of being.

In John Donne's paradox VII, "That a wise man is knowne by much Laughinge" (written sometime in the early 1590s?),[18] the superiority of the laughing subject is asserted expressly by the text and contrasted with the alleged inferiority of the object of laughter. At the same time categories such as wisdom and folly—universal themes in Renaissance literature and philosophy—are submitted to quasi-serious reflection as well as rhetorical manipulation in Donne's text. What is at stake in Donne's paradox is precisely the epistemological position of folly or madness as well as reason or wisdom.

One of the characteristics of the Renaissance paradox as a literary genre is its pseudo-dialogical character. The reader is challenged to find arguments against it, and, according to A. E. Malloch, the paradoxes "do not become themselves until they are overthrown. They are written to be refuted, and unless they are refuted their true nature is hidden."[19] By appealing to the active cooperation—or rather *counter*operation—of the reader, the writer of the paradox in a certain sense deliberately belittles his own rhetorical or argumentative power, thereby adopting the stance of the *eiron*, i.e., the man who, in Northrop Frye's phrase, "deprecates himself,"[20] and in this way opposes the comic antagonist, i.e., the *alazon* or impostor. These stock characters also make their appearance in Donne's paradox, but the problem seems to be that it is very difficult to pinpoint the exact position of the agents of the text. Where is the laugher and where is the laughing-stock, where the *eiron* and where the *alazon*? It turns out to be nearly impossible to come up with plausible answers to these questions.

At first sight Donne carries out a strategic transfer of laughter from the realm of folly to the realm of wisdom in his paradox—simply by interpreting a common saying against the grain or turning it upside down:

> I allwayes did and shall
> understand that Adage,
> *per risum multum possis cognoscere stultum,*
> that by much laughing thou mayst know there is a foole, not
> that the laughers are fooles, but that amongst them ther is
> some foole at whom wise men laugh.[21]

At this point the festive space of carnival—or "the gay and free laughing aspect of the world" (Bakhtin)[22]—seems to be left behind, insofar as the Fool is excommunicated from good society and relegated to a negative role as *the Other of his community*. The Fool has been reduced *ad absurdum*, insofar as the privilege of laughter has been taken from him, "For fooles are the most laughd at, and laugh least themselves of any."[23]

In his paradox Donne uses paralogical argumentation as well as literary allusion to drive home his points. He opens his paradox with a quotation from Martial: "Laugh, if you are wise, O girl, laugh."[24] Actually, Martial is quoting Ovid—even if the passage cannot be found in his extant works—and Martial's whole epigram is used to disprove his literary colleague's statement or injunction, for the woman Martial addresses has only got "three teeth" and would be better off looking dead serious all the time. Therefore, Martial ends his epigram with a counter-injunction: " . . . weep, if you are wise, O girl, weep."[25] Obviously, Donne is playing around with the signifiers, when he uses this passage from Martial to support his argument "against common opinion,"[26] "That a wise man is knowne by much Laughinge."

But Donne has a further surprise in store for us at the very end of his paradox. Here the categories tend to break down altogether when his *persona* refers to a certain overrefinement of manners as characteristic of contemporary society, where "allmost every man affects an humor of / jeasting" and is even satisfied to "become foole" to "give his wise companions occasion to laughe, and to shew / themselves / wise."[27] Apparently the process of civilization has led to this deplorable result, but the whole argumentation is given a further twist when Donne turns the laughter in the direction of the speaker himself:

> Which promptnes of laughing is so great in wise men, that I thinke all wise men (yf any wise men do read this paradox) will laugh both at it and me.[28]

What we are confronted with is an infinite regression, where the wise man (*alias* the reader) is supposed to laugh at the suggestion that he should laugh at the suggestion that he should laugh, etc., etc. The rhetorical paradox is turned into a logical paradox. For if the wise man actually laughs "at *it*," he confirms the essential truth-value of its statements, thus making the latter more than mere trifling laughing-matter. According to the text itself, we "laugh both at witty and absurd things,"[29] but in either case it should be hard to find truth in the paradox—of course, there is more truth in "witty" than in "absurd" things, but the moot point is that "wit" is based on linguistic skill rather than an earnest search for truth. Furthermore, the *persona* himself at the end of his paradox intimates that he has "become foole" in order to satisfy his wise companions' need for a laughing-stock. But in this case his statements are no longer reliable, and if his readers affirm his thesis by laughing at his text (and himself), the fool has outwitted his superiors. An atmosphere of "*joyful relativity*" (Bakhtin)[30] thus qualifies the whole rhetorical operation.

But, on the other hand, a laughter that has been anticipated or "prescribed" by someone else, in this case the *persona* or the writer of the paradox, no longer possesses its original impetus. A spontaneous reaction on the part of the reader has been rendered impossible, and laughter itself has been intellectualized to such an extent that it has more or less lost its "festive" aspect. Anyway, it has been submitted to a kind of rhetorical overkill, similar to what we find in Burton's "Democritus Junior to the Reader": " . . . we have now need of a Democritus to laugh at Democritus'; one jester to flout at another . . . : a great stentorian Democritus, as big as that Rhodian Colossus. For now as Sarisburiensis said in his time, *totus mundus agit histrionem*, the whole world plays the fool . . ."[31]

MODERNISM AND ITS DISCONTENTS

On the whole, the project of Enlightenment seems to be hostile to laughter, and it may be regarded as symptomatic of that trend that "Easter laughter" was actually forbidden by the authorities in the eighteenth century.[32] In Hobbes's *Leviathan* (1651) laughter is already reinterpreted in accordance with a narrowly defined egotistical *ethos* and represented in blatantly "mechanistic" terms as an automatic response to stimuli, modified by a biased self: "*Sudden glory*, is the passion which maketh those *Grimaces* called LAUGHTER"; it is described as a purely self-congratulatory act on the part of the laughing subject.[33] Laughter belongs to the private sphere, and its links with the carnival crowd seem to be severed.

During the Romantic period various attempts were made to recuperate laughter or to reinvest it with some of its old powers. Thus William Blake in his "Laughing Song" in *Songs of Innocence* (1789) tries to (re)universalize laughter by inviting everyone to take part in his mirth: "Come live & be merry and join with me, / To sing the sweet chorus of Ha, Ha, He."[34] But this carefree celebration of the pleasure principle is undermined in various ways in other poems in the *Songs of Innocence*. In "The Ecchoing Green," the *melancholy* laughter of an old man under the village oak relativizes or problematizes the merriment of the children: "Old John with white hair / Does laugh away care, / Sitting under the oak / Among the old folk."[35] At the end of the poem darkness prevails and envelops everybody, and the "sport" of the children is "no more seen."[36] Thus laughter is coupled with a mournful contemplation of the transitoriness of human existence. It is no longer true that present mirth has present laughter, for the gaze of the spectator(s) is turned towards an inaccessible past, a missing referent.

In modernism laughter tends to develop a number of anxiety-provoking or "demonic" features, summarized by Baudelaire in his "L'Héautontimorouménos," when he characterizes himself as "Un de ces grands abandonnés / Au rire éternel condamnés, / Et qui ne peuvent plus sourire!"[37] The laugher has become a *poète maudit*. In a famous essay, "De l'Essence du Rire" (1855), Baudelaire has elaborated on the "satanic" character of laughter, echoing perhaps Hobbes's definition:

> Laughter originates in the idea of one's own superiority. A satanic idea if ever there was any such! Pride and aberration! But it is noteworthy that all the lunatics in the hospitals have developed the idea of their own superiority beyond all measure. . . . Observe that laughter is one of the most frequent and most numerous expressions of madness.[38]

And Baudelaire turns Donne's argument in his paradox VII upside down, for he asserts that "The wise man is afraid of laughter, just as he is afraid of worldly spectacles and concupiscence."[39]

Furthermore, laughter is associated with a divided self, with man's separation from his own body as well as other people's bodies, for only a philosopher is capable of laughing at himself falling.[40]

In Lewis Carroll's *Alice in Wonderland* (1865), laughter is also associated with madness, and its links with the human body—or with the ancestral body of carnival[41]—have been intercepted. The Cheshire Cat represents precisely this lack of materiality on the part of the laughing subject, vanishing "quite slowly" to the heroine's great astonishment, but leaving behind its grin for a while ("A grin without a cat! It's the most curious thing I ever saw in all my life!").[42] After this strange episode everything is ready for the mad tea-party!

THE LAUGH OF THE MEDUSA

In what way or ways may the Bakhtinian notion of carnival be linked to sexual politics? In a recent essay Clair Wills points out that the carnivalesque may take on a different meaning in women's texts: the question she asks is "whether some women's texts may not have a more productive relationship to carnival, leading to a closer connection between literary transgression and cultural transformation."[43] Another feminist critic, Mary Russo, notices that "In terms strikingly similar to Bakhtin's formulation of the grotesque body as continuous process, Hélène Cixous calls . . . [the female] body 'the body without beginning and without end.'"[44] According to Mary Russo, Bakhtin has neglected to perceive the position of the feminine as a problem when he discusses the characteristics of carnival as a festive practice: "Significantly, Bakhtin finds his concept of the grotesque embodied in the Kerch terracotta figurines of senile, pregnant hags."[45] Moreover, according to Bakhtin, "The old hags are *laughing*."[46] According to Mary Russo, however, Bakhtin's "notion of the Female Grotesque remains, in all directions, repressed and undeveloped."[47]

In her article "Castration or Decapitation?" (1976, 1981), Hélène Cixous explicitly links up female laughter with the breakdown of patriarchal hegemony: "Culturally speaking, women have wept a great deal, but once the tears are shed, there will be endless laughter instead."[48] Furthermore, Cixous associates this comic turn with "a humor that sees man much further away than he has ever been seen,"[49] i.e., with a kind of philosophical distancing device. In an earlier article, "The Laugh of the Medusa" (1975, 1976), Cixous demystifies the terroristic attributes of the said mythological being: "You only have to look at the Medusa straight on to see her. And she's not deadly. She's beautiful and she's *laughing*."[50] The recuperation of femininity—and female autonomy—is thus synonymous with a recuperation of laughter, i.e., a laughter linked to the body and (omni)present as a social and political force.

The male hero in the British-Mexican surrealist Leonora Carrington's story "The Skeleton's Holiday" (written in 1938 or 1939) is similarly seen at a much greater distance "than he has ever been seen" (Cixous); he has undergone a thorough uncrowning by being disinvested of his flesh, his *materiality*: "The skeleton was as happy as a madman whose straight-jacket had been taken off. He felt liberated at being able to walk without flesh . . . He was neither hungry nor thirsty, hot nor cold. He was far from the lizard of love. . . ."[51] Death itself has lost all its terror(s) in Leonora Carrington's text. The writer's death jokes in "The Skeleton's Holiday" may recall the abundant supply of *calaveras*—skulls or skeletons—around the Day of the Dead in Mexico (2 November), characterized by what has been called "the average Mexican's stoic, but far from humorless, view of death."[52]

The death-world itself merely provokes "a pleasant and invisible smile"[53] on the part of the protagonist, i.e., the skeleton, in Leonora Carrington's story, but on the other hand he is also fond of practical jokes. Thus he "went into a joke shop and bought himself a supply of those Parisian pleasantries, imitation turds." And he shocks his servant by putting some of these turds "in his chamber pot."[54] The skeleton carries out the good joke-work long after his death, and the *simulacrum* (the "imitation turds") turns out to be capable of replacing "the material bodily lower stratum" (Bakhtin)[55] in the economy of carnivalistic expenditure—as far as *the labour of laughter* is concerned.

The real threat in Leonora Carrington's text is *eros*, or the sexual drive. Thus the skeleton manages to lead a cannibalistic persecutor astray by "letting fall a young zeppelin bone, on which the professor pounced, reciting chemical hymns and covering the bone with hot kisses"![56] But although the skeleton himself has been liberated from the slippery "lizard of love," he nevertheless cannot do without some kind of support from a female character. When he is terrified by the appearance of a profusion of (biblical?) frogs in one of his own drawings—signalizing the fact that even this death-world is teeming with life—he sets off to "see a fortune-teller" (in the French version she is explicitly female: "une cartomancienne").[57] There is something that cannot be mastered or subordinated to the routines of the skeleton's ordinary middle-class life-style, and in order to come to terms with this "chaotic" force the skeleton simply has to draw on the resources of a powerful, "occult" femininity.

In other texts written by Leonora Carrington laughter undergoes a further *feminization*. In "The Happy Corpse Story" (1971) a female cadaver takes her son on a guided tour through the Otherworld and makes him give up an amorous pursuit, after which she "dissolved into ashes, and laughing heartily," returns to her tree.[58] Death itself is uncrowned in a bout of laughter. And in her novel *The Hearing Trumpet* (1977), Leonora Carrington lets her heroine, the ninety-two-year-old Marian Leatherby, take part in a kind of witches' sabbath in an old ladies' home, joining "in the shrill laughter" of her fellow crones after having undergone a process of magical rejuvenation in "a great iron cauldron."[59] Marian Leatherby may be compared to the "senile, pregnant hags," celebrating the comic aspect of life through their laughter; in Bakhtin's comment on the grotesque body they are characterized by the oxymoronic reference to a "pregnant death, a death that gives birth."[60]

Angela Carter's *Nights at the Circus* (1984) is a strange mixture of a picaresque novel, a Gothic fantasy, a Marx Brothers movie script, a circus extravaganza, and a feminist utopia. It falls into three sections, set in Victorian London, Imperial Petersburg, and Siberia, respectively, its fantastic and cataclysmic events taking place around the turn of the century. The career of the heroine, the winged woman Fevvers, traces a downward curve—until she finally reassumes control over her own life in the very moment when her love-affair with the globe-trotting American journalist Jack Walser reaches its consummation and (literal) climax. As a new century begins, time has come for the appearance of the New Woman—after Fevvers has proved that women can fly. And Jack Walser is the "Candide" or *ingénu* of the novel who must be initiated into the secrets of female sexuality as well as female aviation—casting off once and for all his fear of flying.

In part one laughter is linked up with the huge, monstrous or "gargantuan" proportions of the (female) body and represented primarily by Fevvers's hearty guffaw. In part two it is associated with madness and death, i.e., with the Master Clown, Buffo the Great's, "convulsive self-dismemberment"[61] in the arena of the circus—after a bout of more than heavy drinking the demented Buffo comes close to killing the Human Chicken alias Jack Walser and has to be taken to a madhouse after this final act. But the audience is unaware of the seriousness of his condition and accompanies all his homicidal exertions with "howls of delight!"[62] Catastrophe or the universal breakdown of rationality and order is thus applauded by an enthusiastic crowd, which may recall a famous anecdote in Kierkegaard's *Either-Or* (1843), according to the personal papers of the writer referring to an episode taking place in "Petersburg" (!):

> It happened that a fire broke out backstage in a theater. The clown came out to inform the public. They thought it was a jest and applauded. He repeated his warning, they shouted even louder. So I think the world will come to an end amid general applause from all the wits, who believe that it is a joke.[63]

Finally, in the third part of Angela Carter's novel laughter takes on a "utopian" dimension, as it is unleashed by the heroine in a sudden fit of unconquerable mirth, when she discovers to what extent she has fooled her lover. At this point the sad remnants of Colonel Kearney's circus troupe have been derailed and dispersed in faraway Siberia, and Fevvers has broken her wing. Nevertheless, her "endless laughter" (Cixous) seems to have regained its universal validity; it has become an irresistible cosmic force:

> The spiralling tornado of Fevvers' laughter began to twist and shudder across the entire globe, as if a spontaneous response to the giant comedy that endlessly unfolded beneath it, until everything that lived and breathed, everywhere, was laughing. Or so it seemed to the deceived husband, who found himself laughing too, even is he was not quite sure whether or not he might be the butt of the joke . . .[64]

The wheel has come full circle. From the premodern "guffaw" of part one through the modernist death-throes of Clown Alley in part two and on to the final, *post*modern celebration of a comic ethos in part three, where the "spiralling tornado of . . . laughter" is turned into a global, earth-shaking event. In this context it is paradoxical that the geographical itinerary of the characters traces a trajectory in the opposite direction: from the modern metropolis (London) through a late feudal setting (Petersburg) to a region "outside" the civilized world and its discontents, inhabited by Siberian bears and shamạns and considered to be ruled by *magic* (Siberia).

POSTMODERN LAUGHING-MATTER

In modernism laughter tends to be situated in some kind of anxiety-provoking context, associated with "satanic" merriment or a horrible *novum*; according to Renate Jurzik in her *Der Stoff des Lachens* (*Laughing-matter*, 1985) "all sorts of catastrophes of motion" ("Bewegungs-katastrophen aller Art") find their outlet and are submitted to a kind of hyperbolization in the silent film comedies of the 1920s, where the Sunday stroll of the bourgeois "through a process of speeding-up develops into a race involving all and sundry."[65] During this period Buster Keaton becomes "the White Clown of the Screen in the Catastrophic Age of Technology";[66] his Great Stone Face bears witness to the disastrous costs and consequences of the process of modernization: annihilation is now so close at hand and such an all-enveloping reality that it no longer provokes any facial response in the terrified spectator. The dry, ascetic laughter of Samuel Beckett's anti-heroes similarly points in the direction of a tragic contingency, in this case associated with a destabilized, *post*apocalyptic world.

Postmodernism may be said to question the ontological status of laughter. What is there to laugh at? Is there anything to laugh at? Or can you laugh at anything? In one of the episodes in the British television series "Monty Python's Flying Circus" a city gent is turned into a universal laughing-stock—whatever he says or does, however trivial it may seem, immediately makes his surroundings "collapse" with mirth, and apparently for no reason whatsoever![67] There is no longer any obvious relationship between laughter and its object.

In a post*structuralist* setting laughter has also acquired a high degree of symbolic—and theoretical—power. Derrida has been called "the laughing rabbi,"[68] and scholars have commented on Foucault's laughing habits, i.e., on "that laugh, which was so distinctive of the man" (Bernauer and Rasmussen).[69] In the famous preface to Foucault's *The Order of Things* (1966, 1970) laughter takes on a characteristically aporetic function in the context of his reading of a passage in Borges' *Other Inquisitions* (1937–1952, 1964): "That passage from Borges kept me laughing a long time, though not without a certain uneasiness that I found hard to shake off."[70] *In casu* Foucault's uneasy laughter is called forth by the literary representation of an impossible taxonomy, allegedly to be found in a certain "Chinese encyclopaedia" and spread out by purely linguistic means "in an unthinkable space."[71] But in the introduction to Foucault's next book, *The Archaeology of Knowledge* (1969, 1972), laughter signalizes the permanent instability of the text and the signifier in Foucault's *oeuvre*; according to his imaginary interlocutor, Foucault is apparently always already somewhere else, "laughing at" his reader.[72]

An American avant-garde rock group has composed another "Laughing Song," in many respects very different from that of William Blake—or, for that matter, his beat interpreter Allen Ginsberg who set Blake to music in the 1960s.[73] *The Residents* have written their own text, accompanying its nonsensical words with electronically processed laughter, closer to barking than to anything produced by the human voice. The song deconstructs romantic love (Burns) as well as American commercialism in its return to the animality of the "carnivalesque" body: "A red red rose saw a big pig pose/On the edge of a silver dollar./The end of his tail/ Was a long-necked nail./ In place of his face was a scholar."[74] Certainly, at this point the theoretical subject—alias the "scholar"—no longer masters anything; he seems to be no more than a transparent front for the "swinish multitude," emanating from the world of carnival, where according to Peter Stallybrass and Allon White, "the pig was celebrated."[75] The "ontological flicker" of the postmodern world (McHale)[76] makes all his grand schemes crumble—invariably the academic subject seems to be, like Jack Walser in *Nights at the Circus*, "the butt of the joke."

2

Silence and the Rehabilitation of Beauty: Twentieth-Century German Perspectives on the Poet's Task

Erdmann Waniek

Quien calla, otorga.

In an age of ever-present noise and ubiquitous communication, silence is rare. Correspondingly our need for restorative silence has intensified.[1] But, of course, not all silence is soothing. While a rose may indeed be a rose, silence is never just silence; it is essentially ambiguous. Silence constitutes a void that beckons to be interpreted, and if it is personal silence, its motivation must be clarified. The Spanish proverb used as a motto for this essay suggests that silence may be viewed as agreement, but we are also familiar with silence as a stringent form of disapproval or ostracism. Silence may take hold in stubborn defense or clear defiance; it may be rooted in contemplation and trustworthy loyalty, or signal utter destitution and emptiness.

The silence of writers, specifically, does not always or only originate from a dearth of inspiration, never to be rekindled, or from postmodern exhaustion beyond replenishing. Instances come readily to mind and range from Valéry's or Rilke's patient and intense silence of gestation, which bore fruit in some of their greatest poems, to the various descents into silence of Rimbaud, Robert Walser, Georg Trakl, Samuel Beckett, Wolfgang Hildesheimer, or Johannes Kühn. Frequently the silence of writers is charged with protest or saturated with an overwhelming sense of the unsayable.[2] The literary portrayal of silence is equally prominent, whether almost archetypically in certain fairy tales, in some of Kafka's ominous incantations, in Kroetz's *Wunschkonzert*, Turrini's *Sauschlachten*, or in Kosinski's *The Painted Bird*. Kosinski's muted child does not permit any latitude in interpretation. Here, silence rises from unspeakable terror, which, in turn, may be aided by silence. It was acquiescent individual and collective silence that helped to make possible the atrocities of the Third Reich. Survivors such as Primo Levi have tried to dispel the silence about their experience with accurate words of memory, words that are intended to overcome the silence of death. Dan Pagis evokes and recreates this silence of the victims, which is a loud and most disquieting cry. It is a silence that belies the viability of words or language:

> "Written in Pencil in a Sealed Boxcar"
> here in this transport
> I am Eve
> with Abel my son
> if you see my older son
> Cain son of Adam
> tell him that I[3]

In silence the relation between language and the world is suspended, if not violated or disrupted. This relation, or the analogous, broader one between art and reality, has never been easy. Nineteenth-century efforts directed at narrowing the gap, namely realism and naturalism, could be sustained only for a limited time and actually resulted in an increased emphasis on the difference between artefact and life, and in a tendency to exploit that difference. Frequently twentieth-century avant-garde movements such as Dada or Surrealism jettisoned and denounced any and all allegiance to mimesis or to surface verisimilitude, and insisted on their radical newness. Writers who did not join those movements were also forced to come to terms with the shortcomings of the realist experiment, which were immeasurably exacerbated by the awareness that on occasion events of this century offered a reality seemingly beyond the reach of language and any traditional aesthetic of imitation or *Widerspiegelung*. Abandoning older models of writing but unwilling to fall silent, authors such as Heinrich Mann or Hermann Broch had to rethink literature and its place in the world, given a deeply disturbing reality and the limitations of language.

At the beginning of this century Hugo von Hofmannsthal's *Ein Brief* (1902)[4] responds, as it were, to both Mauthner's seminal critique of language, published one year earlier, and to Mallarmé's celebration of the liberated word. *Ein Brief* also records one possible alternative, and its consequences, to the experiment in realism. The purported author of the letter, Lord Chandos, chronicles his development from an existence in the rich and unquestioned fullness of language to a state of wordless paralysis, or rather from a retreat into an aesthetic realm to unaccountable and inexpressible encounters with reality that are fortuitous moments full of involuntary wonder, moments of epiphany.[5] It is as if for us, the language animal, the world opens only upon the loss of language. The aggressive counter-point to this tentative exit from the dead end of self-absorbed aestheticism was advocated by Hofmannsthal's contemporary, Karl Kraus, who criticized not only Hofmannsthal's later war poems but his literary efforts in general as sadly and objectionably incommensurate with reality, especially the reality of World War One.

Word-conscious and language-hungry as any young Lord Chandos, Karl Kraus was neither overwhelmed by the possible inadequacies and pitfalls of language, nor silenced by any disjunction between language and reality. On the contrary, he optimistically began his work with the explicit purpose of the *Trockenlegung des weiten Phrasensumpfes*[6] that characterizes public language use. It provided him with unlimited grist in a singular career of dissecting faulty thinking and warped morals. Yet the horrors of World War One and the patriotic cant accompanying it like a mad chorus drained even Kraus's belligerent stamina, and for a time he was stunned into a silence of protest only to realize that if his words had neither routed injustice nor squelched stupidity, his silence would not vanquish inhumanity. Kraus resumed his fight and continued it throughout the twenties, but he fully despaired at the rise of Hitler and fell silent for good. He was taken to task for his seemingly cheap, gratuitous capitulation at such a critical, unparalleled moment that arguably posed the most formidable challenge of his career, but at least one poet, Bertolt Brecht,[7] understood this silence in context as a desperate, not to say the ultimate outcry against Hitler. It was a measure of this evil that Karl Kraus, of all writers, had no words for it.

Early in the century Hofmannsthal and Kraus thus articulated exemplary options between language, silence, poetry, and politically responsible writing, options that had to be weighed anew by subsequent generations of authors. In broad yet vital terms they are options faced by everybody, namely the choice between silence, whether in protest or agreement, and participation, spelled out in words or actions. If Hofmannsthal and Kraus circumscribe fundamental positions, it is Brecht who formulated the choice perhaps most memorably in lines that have become famous in twentieth-century German poetry: "Was sind das für Zeiten, wo / Ein Gespräch über Bäume fast ein Verbrechen ist / Weil es ein Schweigen über so viele Untaten einschließt!" (IV, 723). The numerous echoes and responses to these lines[8] sketch a history *in nuce* of political and literary change. The highpoints are documented in the answers by Paul Célan, Hans Magnus Enzensberger, and Walter Helmut Fritz. Pointedly enough the trajectory of change that emerges is anchored in silence, its virtues and shortcomings.

Written in Danish exile in 1938, Brecht's exclamation is part of a long poem in free verse, *An die Nachgeborenen,* an elegy about the present that is suffused with hope for the future. The lines give succinct expression to an intolerable set of conditions. The tone of quiet restraint and the somewhat odd choice of a potentially trifling *Gespräch über Bäume* as a barometer for the political climate should not mislead us into trivializing the situation. Its monstrosity is precisely underscored by the juxtaposition of an innocuous *Gespräch über Bäume* with crime and silence. A specious solution would be to give up seemingly unnecessary "talk about trees." But of course this would not lift the silence that infests every conversation not directly addressing injustice, the injustice done to our neighbour. In the name of truth the poet cannot avert his eyes and pretend to be blinded by beauty; he must try to see and spell out the truth. While sympathetic to Kraus's outcry of silence, Brecht was acutely uneasy about the ambivalence, not to say guaranteed futility, of silence, and thus chose a different path. With clearsighted intensity Brecht took up the poet's task of resistance as it is mandated by the conviction that in time of injustice, which resound with the cries of the persecuted, the silence of those spared becomes almost a crime.

Brecht was not always that severe. In one of his stories about Mr. Keuner, *Maßnahmen gegen die Gewalt* (V, 375f.), he honors silence as a prudent, calculated subterfuge against force, and in a poem from 1932 he condones silence when he proclaims that it is better to be a coward than to be dead (IV, 469). At the same time Brecht chastises Thomas Mann for writing *The Magic Mountain* and keeping silent about the state of the republic (IV, 472), a charge, we may add, that overlooks Thomas Mann's numerous public statements for Weimar and against the Nazis. Brecht's ambiguous appraisal of silence continues in *Mother Courage* with the figure of Kattrin who, though mute, offers vociferous resistance to the enemy by playing a drum, yelling as it were, in a language of her devising. Returning to the lines quoted, we realize that Brecht is not as much censuring silence as he is burdened by the need to speak out against daily inhumanity that thoroughly destroys all innocence.

We can legitimately enlarge Brecht's *Gespräch über Bäume* to mean poetry about nature and apolitical art in general.[9] In a different poem, *Schlechte Zeit für Lyrik* (IV, 743), Brecht deplores the fact that instead of the *Begeisterung* for a blooming apple tree, it is the *Entsetzen* about Hitler that moves him to work at his desk. Reaching back to the eighteenth century, *Begeisterung* is highly charged notion, opposed to reason, in poetics. It postulates inspiration as the source of aesthetic creation and implies the enthusiastic embrace of this world as it is—or once was—instead of a critical appraisal of what the world ought to be. *Begeisterung* cannot be governed and legislated, but the concomitant desire to praise also cannot and indeed must not motivate poetry when outrage prevails. *Entsetzen* forces out *Begeisterung*. Yet while Brecht is determined to place his own efforts in the public service of change, he nonetheless insists that *Begeisterung* ought to have free range for its expression. He is appalled—and wants us to be—that the times do not allow for the enjoyment of pastoral beauty, let alone for the privilege of private, purposeless poetry that remains silent about the overtly political realm.

Though the poet's task is guided, if not fully determined, by the times and their crises, Brecht does not propose to silence the *Gespräch über Bäume*. A different public atmosphere that would liberate such conversations from invidious incriminations is unquestionably preferable. Adamant advocate of change and committed writer, Brecht in fact wants to preserve a space that is free of politics or, more accurately, wants to create a political space that does not compromise *Begeisterung* and conversations about trees. It is among Brecht's most acute and disturbing insights that the order of the Third Reich eradicates any and all seemingly acceptable exceptions to its inhumanity. There is no asylum, no enclave, that is not thoroughly infected by the crimes of the Nazis. A case in point is the silence of the *innere Emigration*, which created but an illusion of distance and untainted separateness. In a sense Brecht's project was the recuperation of *Begeisterung*, and the reactions to Brecht inevitably weigh the choice between *Begeisterung* and *Entsetzen* as the motivating force for writing.

Brecht raised a strong voice against a blanket of silence where there should have been a storm of protest. Many of Brecht's poems are proof of his conviction as stated in his *Fünf Schwierigkeiten beim Schreiben der Wahrheit* (VIII, 222ff.), that the true word exists. Making it public was a matter both of political acumen and cunning, and of courage and integrity. In *Deutschland*, Brecht states: "Aber die Wahrheit/Muß schweigen," only to add immediately: "Ist es so?" (IV, 488). The right words, even of pathos and suffering, are available, a conviction, to be sure, that did not inoculate Brecht against writing Stalinist propaganda poems permeated by, at best, wishful thinking. More uncompromisingly so than Brecht with his political agenda and allegiances, the *Nachgeborenen* whom he addressed in his poem, having learned from him, have made it part of their credo to speak out against all injustice, regardless of its provenance. This credo is neither softened by the knowledge that silence, as Karl Kraus showed, need not be acquiescent, nor shaken by a loss of trust in the power of the word to represent and move. Silence is ambivalent and invites suspicion, and whether silence inescapably makes us accomplices remains a guilt-provoking question that is, after all, not laid to rest with the defeat of the Third Reich.

Brecht never reached the point of despair at which Kraus faltered. He upheld the notion of the poet as an outspoken witness who is shaping his times. If the task of doing justice to this notion is less plagued by Brecht's question, how the poet can reconcile the times and *Begeisterung*, it is deeply affected by an even more intractable one, namely, how can the poet speak, with a flawed language nonetheless, about the unsayable of the Holocaust? The crucial point of reference, the catalyst for reaction, has changed from the general injustice of the Third Reich to its most heinous crime. Brecht's successors after 1945 do not need to fear reprisals for writing the truth, yet doing so seems more difficult than Brecht imagined.

The Holocaust tended to disappear in a black abyss of silence, opened by shame or a desire to forget, or indeed by denial. Deepening, if not legitimating, the silence was a consensus that, in the words of George Steiner, "the world of Auschwitz lies outside speech as it lies outside reason."[10] Most cruelly survivors like Primo Levi or Paul Célan suffered from and, as if forced into the next torture for survival, struggled against the fissure between language and their experience. The consequence of that fissure was succinctly and harshly formulated by Adorno when he proclaimed that it is barbarous to write poems after Auschwitz, a claim that derives its power from the central place in our lives of beauty and that is implicitly confirmed by Primo Levi's practice of writing. Yet silence after and about the reality of Auschwitz is equally unbearable and not, it would seem, a prudent, even triumphant, strategy for survival as in Mr. Keuner's parable about force. Silence would validate and extend the success of the murderers who prevail in silencing even the survivors. In a very different mode from Primo Levi, Paul Célan searched for a language commensurate with the burden of memory and the task of bearing witness. He expressed the inherent and insoluble paradox with unsurpassed clarity in five extraordinary lines pointedly dedicated to Bertolt Brecht. The opposition has shifted from *Gespräch über Bäume* and *Untaten* with silence as the common denominator, to one of *Gespräch* and *Gesagtes*. Once more the common denominator, and the link to Brecht, is silence. Célan does not name that denominator:

> Ein Blatt, baumlos,
> für Bertolt Brecht:
>
> Was sind das für Zeiten,
> wo ein Gespräch
> beinah ein Verbrechen ist,
> weil es soviel Gesagtes
> mit einschließt?[11]

Despite Célan's intermittent confidence in the German language, gleaned from a speech from 1958 or his work in general, for him all language and every *Gespräch* is always and ineluctably contaminated, not by silence but by *Gesagtes*. On the one hand, it would seem the poet's supreme task to purify language of *Gesagtes* and to write the poem that might be *Gespräch* instead of being "the hundred- / tongued pseudo— / poem, the noem."[12] On the other hand, Célan's careful rearrangement of Brecht's opposition, changing it only minimally but crucially, precludes the realization of a true *Gespräch*, and the poem implicitly invokes silence as an alternative. Brecht knew that the cover of easy silence could and ought to be lifted: truth could be given a voice; for Célan indisputable truth can only be approximated in silence. Language actually veils the truth. His claim, an echo of Adorno's, for the modern poem, namely that it shows a tendency to fall silent, characterizes above all his own work in which this poem is a distinct exception with respect to clarity. His need and struggle to coin words and expand a language so that it might express the unsayable, culminate or rather fade away in silence, not the least because they leave his readers at a loss for words fitting to continue the *Gespräch*. Célan's daunting efforts, born out of agonizing as well as insidious silence, have charted a unique, paradoxical, and inimitable path between cry, poetry, and silence. Brecht could not have envisioned it as an alternative to his experience of silence, which he felt capable of breaking cleanly.[13]

The temptation to interpret Célan's suicide as either climax or negation of his poetic career is odious, yet in a desperate sense his falling silent gives credence to Adorno's diagnosis of the difficulty of writing poetry after Auschwitz. The devastating corollary of that diagnosis was bluntly put by Hans Magnus Enzensberger: "Wenn wir weiterleben wollen, muß dieser Satz widerlegt werden."[14] Enzensberger speaks *pro domo*, as it were, and unencumbered by any guilt about (poetic) beauty. His aggressive and combative poetry does not grow out of certainty about what constitutes the truth, as does much of Brecht's work. It is instead enlivened by the core knowledge that silence, even when enforced—and dignified—by suffering beyond words, can never be accepted as an answer to injustice. The following poem is a response to both Brecht and Célan:

> Zwei Fehler
>
> Ich gebe zu, seinerzeit
> habe ich mit Spatzen auf Kanonen geschossen.
>
> Daß das keine Volltreffer gab,
> sehe ich ein.

Dagegen habe ich nie behauptet,
nun gelte es ganz zu schweigen.

Schlafen, Luftholen, Dichten:
das ist fast kein Verbrechen.

Ganz zu schweigen
von dem berühmten Gespräch über Bäume.

Kanonen auf Spatzen, das hieße doch
in den umgekehrten Fehler verfallen.[15]

Brecht's aspirations for the political effectiveness of the poet were inflated, and Enzensberger concedes that literature does not change reality, but that is no reason for the poet to be quiet. On various occasions Enzensberger, ever quick-witted, has amplified his position, as when he submits that a *Murmeln* is preferable to complete silence,[16] or when a character in his *Der Untergang der Titanic* exclaims: "Ich schwimme und heule . . . weiter."[17] Any reaction, even crying, is better than silence, which can always be (mis-)understood as acquiescence.

In 1968 Enzensberger wondered about the "death" of "literature." Here he dismisses the move towards silence as a possible choice for the writer and goes one step further. With a wicked sleight-of-hand he dramatically radicalizes and extends the original accusation against the apolitical poet. Along with sleeping and breathing, writing poetry is claimed to be life-sustaining, yet it is declared to be *almost no crime*. In other words, in social conditions of unlimited exploitation and full interdependence there is no longer any activity exempt from guilt: all aspects of our lives are implicated. The sense of injustice potentially motivating the writer has reached global dimensions indeed, and more insistently perhaps than ever engenders the perception that an engaged literature not based on (private) *Begeisterung* and aiming at beauty is needed.

Enzensberger was spared an experience of suffering comparable to that motivating Célan's writings, and he refuses to create for himself a bedrock of political convictions that might imprison him as they did Brecht. Nonetheless, he insists on the specific task of critical poetry in the face of systemic injustice, namely to point out to the readers their participation in it. He is keenly conscious of the fact that language is a flawed tool of enlightenment, but he does not grant this problem any sway over his own writings. While poetry may not produce great effects, it still is nobly motivated by a notion of public responsibility. This is not to say that there are no doubts about the poet's task and work. They surface quite strongly for example in *Der Untergang der Titanic*, where

Enzensberger names an insurmountable obstacle to truth: poets inescapably lie, "weil es also ein anderer ist, / immer ein anderer, / der da redet, / und weil der, / von dem da die Rede ist, / schweigt."[18] This general insight poignantly applies to the victims of the Holocaust, as Primo Levi and Paul Célan felt and knew, but it would be wrong to appropriate it as an alibi for silence. Poetry, understood as deputyship, bars the flight into silence. In fact, Enzensberger's observation may better be interpreted as an irreducible definition of the poet's task and responsibility, namely to speak for those who do not have a voice.

The following poem by Walter Helmut Fritz does that in a surprising framework:

Bäume

Wieder hat man in der Stadt,
um Parkplätze zu schaffen,
Platanen gefällt.
Sie wußten viel.
Wenn wir in ihrer Nähe waren,
begrüßten wir sie als Freunde.
Inzwischen ist es fast
zu einem Verbrechen geworden,
nicht über Bäume zu sprechen,
ihre Wurzeln,
den Wind, die Vögel,
die sich in ihnen niederlassen,
den Frieden,
an den sie uns erinnern.[19]

Across decades the poem could be addressing Lord Chandos's language crisis. Hofmannsthal's Lord Chandos stopped writing since neither English nor Latin had words to capture his encounters with the wordless world of things and events. He can only surmise what the language might be "*in welcher die stummen Dinge zu mir sprechen.*"[20] It is the premise for Fritz's endeavour in various poems, namely to understand and translate into our language the language of things. One of his poems is programmatically entitled: *Gib den Dingen das Wort.*[21] In doing so the poem selected here broadens what Célan with reference to Kropotkin's anti-Darwinian *Mutual Aid* called the *Gegenwart des Menschlichen* (III, 190), and establishes it as an attitude of respect for the other, which does not extol the human at the expense of the non-human world. This respect proceeds from the unity of (life in) this world, and correspondingly the poem casts in simple words as a potential and soothing experience that which shattered Lord Chandos. The Lord's mystic notion and wordless epiphany of all-unity is transformed into a measured embrace of the world on the basis of its interconnectedness. The poem is silent about the Holocaust; for Enzensberger and Fritz, who have attempted poems about the Third Reich, the crimes of the Nazis have sunken below the horizon not of memory but of the present with its threats for a future. The emphasis has shifted from the historical time coordinate to the ecological one. This poem is a timely *Gespräch über Bäume,* unfortunately not growing out of *Begeisterung* and not in peaceful praise as Brecht wished for.

Unassuming as the poem is, it is one of protest and resistance, and as with Brecht's conversation about trees the specific, seemingly negligible occasion should not cause us to take lightly the impliclations. We are so inundated by and accustomed to supposedly unstoppable progress that the poem may almost seem quixotic in its unabashed affirmation of a different world, of peace and harmony with nature. But can we afford to render a soft voice like this ineffective, not to say silent, by labelling these reactions to a common and truly minor incident, the removal of trees for a parking lot, as nostalgia and anachronistic romanticism? Enzensberger writes in the shadow ot the big catastrophes; Fritz sees them in the small one. His poem was written under duress and with the conviction that not talking about trees—once again understood as metonymy—makes us accomplices in the daily terror leading towards a fatally silent nature. The view is the opposite of Brecht's, who regretted the fact that a *Gespräch über Bäume* had been tainted by the times. Walter Helmut Fritz asserts that now such a *Gespräch* is necessary, if not already too late. His poem is neither straightforwardly political nor didactic, nor explicitly concerned with capturing or presenting beauty; it restores as the source of writing, if not *Begeisterung* then the observed and experienced moment, the recognition of its wider significance, and the intention of communicating both to the reader.

The difference between Brecht and Fritz is less pronounced than might be suspected. In some regards their positions are remarkably close. Broadly speaking we can outline the changes from Brecht, to Célan, Enzensberger, and Fritz, as a move from an aesthetics of resistance (Peter Weiss) to an aesthetics of silence (Susan Sontag), or an *Ästhetik des Abschieds,*[22] to a renewed, but muted, aesthetics of resistance, now without Brecht's ideological certainty about and real hope for the future. If Enzensberger and Fritz share with Brecht the basis of an aesthetics of resistance, it is in their cases tempered, in different ways, by intimations of catastrophe and apocalypse, of silence and *Abschied,* intimations that are subdued, though not unknown, in Brecht. Fritz's poetry is one of wistfulness and rehabilitation. The *Bäume* of his poem are not accidentally *Platanen*, the classical tree of poets under which to seek inspiration and to write. By virtue of contiguity Fritz's poem is also about the precarious place of poetry in a time of parking lots victorious. Indirectly the place of beauty is, once again, in question as it has been not only since Hofmannsthal's Lord Chandos letter and his half-hearted critique of aestheticism.

This critique, stemming from and reinforcing the traditional bad conscience of the artist, gained considerable force as the century advanced and the social and political problems deepened. It forms the backdrop in the search for politically responsible literature, especially in the Weimar Republic,[23] and it was repeated, with significant variations, in Brecht's opposition to culinary art, or in the interdictions in the 1940s of such different writers as Thomas Mann or Hermann Broch against beauty and the beautiful work, against the so-called purely aesthetic. Arguably this tension between aesthetic appreciation and public responsibility reached a new level with the Third Reich, and was refocused with unforgiving sharpness in Adorno's verdict about poetry after Auschwitz. It was also the need to resolve this tension that lead in 1968 to Enzensberger's symptomatic and fanciful projection of the "death" of "literature."[24] Beauty seemed blighted beyond recovery, its enjoyment no longer anti-bourgeois protest or eccentricity, but criminal.

Fritz's poem makes manifest in one instance the efforts to leave the shadow cast by these verdicts and proclamations, efforts in which an unsuspected comrade is Christa Wolf. In her writings most of the aspects discussed so far converge and perhaps culminate. With changing emphasis her work is distinctly preoccupied with the familiar issues of politically responsible writing, issues that come to the fore especially in *Kindheitsmuster*.[25] The novel, a record of a journey in 1971 into the narrator's childhood in the 30s and 40s, addresses the difficulty of not being guilty in these times: "Es geht wohl über die Kraft eines Menschen, heute zu leben und nicht mitschuldig zu werden" (231); it knows the difference between writing and action, between distancing description and engaged interference (215); it copes with the impression of questionable legitimacy, reminiscent of Enzensberger: "O über diese Zeit, da der Schreibende, ehe er zur Beschreibung fremder Wunden übergehen darf, die Wunde seines eigenen Unrechts vorweisen muß" (232). The novel echoes and intensifies Brecht when it submits "daß es im Zeitalter des Argwohns das aufrichtige Wort nicht gibt" (484), and while taking into account the degradation of many words (239), and in general "die Grenzen des Sagbaren" (549), the stated impetus is to go against Wittgenstein's well-known dictum by insisting: "Wovon man nicht sprechen kann, darüber muß man allmählich zu schweigen aufhören"

(242). Assuming that the reality of Auschwitz cannot be described (430), the book takes up the search for *Aufrichtigkeit* and, similar to Célan, tries to practice a literature that avoids the choice between silence and "'Pseudo'"-talk (504; cf. 301). If in *Kindheitsmuster* aestheticism is not a viable option the book nevertheless poses a suspicious question, namely why knowledge as a guiding force replacing faith has so far produced so little beauty (453). Beauty is not necessarily the fetish of the aesthete, but encapsulates as a measure of harmony the utopian goal of peace.

Wolf's central concern, that is the search for the right language and home, and for "das wirkliche Leben,"[26] also dominates her more recent *Sommerstück*. Without inhibition this novel circles around the simple life and conjures the real, if slightly miraculous and short-lived, possibility of an idyll of peaceful harmony and enriching beauty. As if written in response to Fritz's evocation of the peace of which the trees remind us, *Sommerstück* is the story of a retreat from the city world to one of the few remaining *heile Flecken* (138), to a countryside, which, impossibly, still knows a *große Stille* (23). As not only the extreme example of Luisa shows, silence in this world can be an effective healing agent.

Wavering between mild forms of nostalgia and apocalypse, the novel skirts and thus provokes the question of the appropriate direction of writing after Auschwitz. This novel as a matter of fact leaves aside past as well as current atrocities and instead singles out the embarrassed denial and rejection of an aesthetic attitude as an indication of the times present and future. Anticipating the objections against her story of a beautiful summer, the narrator chooses to name the problem in its smallest manifestation: "Ist Schönheit beschreibenswert? Eine vernichtende Frage. Was bleibt zu hoffen für eine Zeit, die von Hohn auf Schönheit gezeichnet ist? In der eine vertrackte Art von Mut dazu gehört, von einer gewissen Baumgruppe . . . zu behaupten und zu wiederholen, sie seien [!] schön."[27] It is a plea for beauty, indeed for a conversation about trees that is neither protest nor alibi but grounded in aesthetic appreciation. To see the beauty of a tree does not blind us to human injustice, it rather reminds us of the limits of purposeful rationality.

Wolf raises the case against destructive rationality at its most critical point, our perception of beauty in nature. A society that reveres nothing but the rule of rationality, and a period that insists on the usefulness of the artist's contribution—"Ist Schönheit beschreibenswert?"—are not prepared, in a lapse into what would be false consciousness, to consider a tree an aesthetic object. Lord Chandos's epiphanies could be triggered by a dog, a rat, or "ein verkümmerter Apfelbaum;"[28] Brecht's *Begeisterung* was sparked by a blooming apple tree and dutifully supressed; here a "Kirschbaum in seinem unvernünftigen [!] Blütentaumel" (8), an image of *Begeisterung*, leaves an indelible impression on Ellen, the writer-character. In this epiphany the distance between silent nature and art meant to communicate collapses, and the bad conscience about nature and beauty—both silent about *Untaten*, as Brecht knew—might be cleansed. Yet the costs of this kind of epiphany are characteristically high. It results in a *Gefühl von Unwirklichkeit* (21) in a world where silence is either threatened or needs to be broken, and where the experience of beauty is at best a fragile moment.

If the creation of beauty is no longer the unquestioned task of the artist, its perception and appreciation have become everyone's domain, not to say responsibility. Similar to the Lord Chandos letter—and to another document of modernism, Rilke's *Notebooks of Malte Laurids Brigge*—Christa Wolf's *Sommerstück* is also about learning to see, but different from them it is specifically about learning to see beauty. Shunning outright references to beauty, Fritz buttressed his appeal for a life with trees by evoking the world that they—and poetry—preserve. Wolf divests her defense of those aspects; she narrows and intensifies the perception of nature and its objects to an almost religious appreciation of their distinct aesthetic impact, and shows it in the lives of some of her characters. If nothing else, an aesthetic attitude, discredited as indifference and routinely subordinated to practical considerations, might teach us to see and listen, to appreciate and respect, rather than to subjugate, consume, and discard. We destroy less (!) readily what we know and what we consider beautiful. Continuing the line from Hofmannsthal and Rilke to Fritz, Wolf's narrator shatters the silence with an expressionist cry: "So schrien die Dinge uns um Erlösung an" (8). Rilke's "Du mußt dein Leben ändern" now reads: "Ich glaube, wir müßten anders leben. Ganz anders." (24).

The changing assessments of aesthetic appreciation, silence, and responsibility have for very good reasons favored the latter, whereas in *Sommerstück* Christa Wolf portrays aesthetic appreciation in a positive light that seemed to be extinguished, if not by Lord Chandos, or Brecht, and Adorno, then by the rule of economic calculations. Why do we, even if not persuaded by the latter, retain our reservations about such an attempt to rehabilitate beauty, if not art and aestheticism?[29] Are any reservations just proof of the strength of prevailing misgivings that beauty is silent about and detached from the real world, misgivings that Camus in *The Plague* embodies in the portrait of the pathetic poet Grand? Or is the credibility of such attempts called in to question by competing and renewed claims about the death of literature caused now more plausibly than in 1968 by a media revolution with ramifications for all the arts? It may also be that aesthetic appreciation continues to be too passive, not to say silent, an attitude with which to break the aggressive domination of usefulness in our lives. Above all, the shadow of Auschwitz lingers, and neither silence nor the appreciation of beauty were weapons against it.

* * * *

> Und die Schönheit ist schön, und wenn sie bis
> zum Hals in der Jauche steht.

Brecht (IV, 554)

3

Postmodernism and the Scene of Theatre

Elinor Fuchs

> "The spectacle does not realize philosophy, it philosophizes reality."
>
> Guy Debord, *Society of the Spectacle*

In its twenty-year spasm, postmodernism has had more "moments" than Hegel's history of the spirit. Its first incarnation was celebratory and utopian, liberationist in its ideology of play, indeterminacy, and pure difference. But the question arose, was this actually "post-" modernism, or a version of the old avant-gardes recycled through late modernism? The real postmodernism, we were told, especially in the popular press, was about flight from modernism: a revival of the classical, the figurative, the decorative. Postmodernism was inherently backward-looking and nostalgic.

But nostalgia, to students of the emerging field of cultural studies, was not really about the past but about its erasure by democratic mass society. Postmodernism was the great leveler of differences, horizontally across culture, vertically within history. This same identification between mass culture and postmodernism was made by neo-Marxist critics, but less tolerantly: postmodernism was the cultural "dominant" of late capitalism, commodity-driven, and fundamentally reactionary.

Perhaps this moment could or should have been its last, but through a clever graft with materialist feminism and other theories of the margin, postmodernism suddenly acquired, or reacquired, a politics of resistance. The multiple subversions of narrative, realism, centering and closure, earlier criticized by Anglo-American feminist critics and others as leading to a paralytic relativism, were now seen as political when used for the "right" ends in the "right" hands. And this moment was then extended into a range of multicultural studies, some of whose devotees would like to forget the politically ambiguous postmodern route that took them there.

Like a hologram that produces three-dimensional objects through a mysterious transformation of two-dimensional images, postmodernism has been an elusive story of now-you-see-it, now-you-don't. Many of its defenders experienced quasi-religious conversions as they suddenly glimpsed its paradigm shifts, but to some it was always an elaborate renaming trick, a kind of intellectual magic show with smoke and mirrors. This is the postmodernism I want to take up here: not the truth claims of its moments, but the ontological ground on which they have been played out.

To introduce my own intervention in the waning discourse of postmodernism, that of the theater critic, I want first to tell two brief stories. Both are derived from the field in which postmodernism was early and most unequivocally identified, architecture. Story one: Reading architectural critic Charles Jencks's *What is Post-Modernism?*, I come across a passage that delivers a stirring contrast between the heroic modernism of LeCorbusier in 1927 and the classical "Post-Modernism" represented at the 1980 Venice Biennale of Architecture, which Jencks helped to organize around the theme "The Presence of the Past."[1] One of Jencks's favorite entries was "Strada Novissima," an architectural installation consisting of twenty facades designed by leading postmodern architects. These facades show renewed interest, Jencks says, in "ornament, symbolism and other taboos," a return he describes as a "Counter-Reformation" to the "Protestant" disruption of modernism. Under the segment of the Strada that appears in color illustration 31 of this little book, Jencks inserts the legend, "The Strada illustrates the 'return to architecture,' to polychromy, ornament and above all to the notion of the street as an urban type." But two pages later Jencks lets drop the otherwise unremarked bit of information that the installation was "based on a Renaissance stage-set."[2]

On a Renaissance stage-set? Jencks' central thesis is that all postmodern art proceeds by double coding, in this case the revaluing of the past and its simultaneous dislocation through the use of modernist stratagems. But here is a third element, not accounted for in Jencks's scheme: both resurgent classicism and modernist ironies are deployed not in the obvious way through the creation and installation of a model street, but through resort to the forced perspective of a theatrical stage setting standing in for a street. The double coding is itself pre-encoded with a theatrical strategy that makes both the recouping of the classical past and the modernist commentary appear strangely weightless. The structure that is supposed to represent the recontextualization of architecture into the street and into history itself gives the impression that the street is poised in air, precisely lacking historical contextualization. Its organizing principle is not community, history, the long tradition of architectural design: these are all seen to be subsidiary to the conventions, albeit historical conventions, of theatrical design.

Story two: At Emory University, where I taught for some years, the Atlanta hotel architect and favorite son John Portman was invited to enhance the campus by remodeling a 1927 neo-high Renaissance dining hall designed by Atlanta's then leading historicist architect, Lewis Edmund Crook. The crowning glory of the building was its entrance: a magnificent sweep of steps framed by voluted scrolls and crowned by an elegant portico and an imposing Tuscan doorway, the whole faced in a white Georgia marble. The new building was to become the university student center.

The usual architectural solution to such a problem—apart from tearing down and replacing the building—is to build adjacent to, above, or behind the original structure, attaching to the old face a new body with added height or depth. Portman did just the opposite. In one of the loopy outside-in/inside-out gestures favored by postmodern architects, he incorporated the old building, including its marble front wall, into the interior of the new edifice. Building forward from the old classical, or classicizing, structure, he left the facade of the building intact, but enclosed it within a large hemispherical atrium, through which one now enters the building. Standing inside the atrium with one's back to the old exterior wall, one faces a series of ascending, semicircular balconies fitted out with tables and chairs to service a food concession. Reversing perspective, one gazes down from these balconies to the atrium floor below. The eye travels to the marble portico of the original Crook building as if to a stage. Indeed, one cannot escape the impression that one has become a spectator in a classically-inspired theatrical space. The old facade has become the "scaenae frons," the atrium floor the "orchestra," and the balconies complete the invocation of both an ancient amphitheater and its Renaissance imitations.[3]

These two architectural "theater pieces" occupy an interesting boundary between actual theater and what we might think of as "cultural theater." Portman seems to deploy the stage as mediator, common ground, or transition between traditional and contemporary architectural forms. Yet beware the stability of the image "transition," for the stage in this case is not some third intervening element between epochs, but rather a transformation of the historical into stage, the contemporary into auditorium. Their interface becomes, *eo ipso*, a theater, struck off by the force of cultural collision. Alternatively, the Strada Novissima is, I take it, *novissima* not because old and new meet at the point of the theatrical, but because the Strada subsumes or perhaps consumes old and new in the sign of the theatrical. On the Strada Novissima, nothing stands outside the theatrical. To rewrite Derrida, *Il n'y a pas de hors-théâtral*.[4]

I introduce the stagings embedded in these postmodern architectural narratives as a visual transition to the historical/cultural theatrical "spaces" that are the subject of this essay. These spaces emerge from the theatrical metaphors that appear with surprising frequency in the post-structuralist texts—semiotic, deconstructive, neo-Marxist, feminist—that have retrospectively served as both anticipation and explication of the postmodern paradigm shift. If theory and theater—from the same etymological root—were once in competition for the right to dominate the "place of seeing" (as the long anti-theatrical tradition in western metaphysics might suggest), they seem almost to merge in this contemporary body of writing, in which trajectories of western culture, or theories of such trajectories, have been constructed around the protean image of the theatrical.[5]

In the 1960s, the spectacle and the scene ubiquitously appeared as units of currency in the post-Marxist/Freudian/Saussurean discourses that laid the groundwork for the cultural and literary theory of postmodernism. The chief "spectaclist" of the 1960's was Guy Debord, filmmaker and leading theorist of the international Situationist movement, best known for his 1967 volume *Society of the Spectacle*. Debord presents a series of 221 numbered sections, aphoristic fragments staked on the far edge of commodity aesthetics. He argues that the spectacle is "the main *production* of present-day society,"[6] the chief and entirely malign consequence of which is the dehistoricization of culture:

> The spectacle, as the present social organization of the paralysis of history and memory, of the abandonment of history built on the foundation of historical time, is the *false consciousness of time*. . . . The irreducibly biological element which remains in labor, both in the dependence on the natural cycle of waking and sleep and in the existence of irreversible time in the expenditure of an individual life, [becomes] a mere *accessory*. . . .[7]

Before industrialization, says Debord, there was natural time, measured cyclically by the operations of natural forces and human biology. Natural time was humanized and socialized into historical time. But this culturally produced time, still related to natural time, was subsequently alienated, artifically broken into dehumanized work on the one hand, and spectacularized leisure on the other. Human consciousness in societies where modern conditions of production prevail is "immobilized in the falsified center of the movement of its world." Everything "that was directly lived has moved away into a representation."[8]

Debord creates a narrative of the development of human culture in which hegemonic spectacle provides an almost apocalyptic finale. His vision of history moves from the natural, human, social, and realistic, and from the consciousness of the historical itself as a category within history, to the alienated realm of total theater. Debord can only counter this movement with a despondent late Marxism, an over-convinced call for educated cadres pursuing an "historical mission of installing truth in the world."[9]

If Debord follows Marx to arrive at the spectacle, Derrida reads Freud and attends to the "scene." "Freud and the Scene of Writing" evidences the subtle attraction that theater and its terms hold for Derrida, as do three other of the eleven essays in *Writing and Difference*, the two on Artaud and the meditation on "play"—"Structure, Sign and Play in the Discourse of the Human Sciences." In its insistence on the substitution of elusive maskings and unmaskings for unequivocal textual identities, Derrida's notion of play may be seen as inherently theatrical. His philosophical world, in which heroic figures of the metaphysical tradition, such as Rousseau, are ironically confounded by the mysterious, uncontrollable, quasi-personified force of writing, has a distinctly tragic, Sophoclean cast. In "The Double Session," however, Derrida moves beyond the theatrical metaphor or suggestion to strikingly connect his central notion of writing and play with actual theater. The piece owes its title (selected not by Derrida but by his 1970 *Tel Quel* editors) to a series of two lectures conducted by Derrida in early 1969 at the *Groupe d'Études théoriques*.[10] Each seminar student was given a sheet of paper on which appeared two statements, one from the *Philebus* of Plato and one from Mallarmé's *Mimique*. Through these quotations Derrida chases the theme of mimesis.

In the *Philebus*, Derrida says, the soul is compared to a book. Within the soul is the *doxa*, a natural upwelling of truth, or an attempt at truth. The *doxa* should emerge into dialogue with another, but alternatively may emerge dialogically into the book, figured as an externalization of internal speech. The book as presented by Plato, he says, is thus one face of a binary model of mimesis, which splits into the image and the thing imaged. Derrida stresses the doubleness: "First there is what is, 'reality' the thing itself, in flesh and blood as the phenomenologists say; then there is, imitating these, the painting, the portrait, the zographeme, the inscriptions or transcription of the thing itself."[11] Order consists of the discernable distinction between imitator and imitated.

As in so many other of his texts, Derrida has once again made a demonstration of the binary form of thought within the closure of the metaphysical tradition, with all its attendant relations of inside to outside, prior to latter, originary to alienated. But there is another model of mimesis, Derrida goes on to say, a model that consists of a non-imitative writing, behind which no originating moment hovers as a standard of truth. And where does Derrida find this radical model of a writing not preceded by, thus not separated from, speech, this destabilizing writing capable of bringing down a millenium and a half of metaphysics? He finds it in the theater.

The passage from Mallarmé recounts the poet's experience of reading a small book by the mime Paul Margueritte, based on his own stage performance, "Pierrot Murderer of his Wife." Derrida points to the seeming paradox that the mimodrama in question, in which the "text" emerges from the performer, who himself becomes the blank sheet on which it is written, exists neither in an originary present, nor as an imitation of a prior originating moment. On the one hand, "There is no imitation. The Mime imitates nothing. And to begin with, he doesn't imitate. There is nothing prior to the writing of his gestures. His movements form a figure that no speech anticipates or accompanied."[12] Yet the absence of an "original" from which the performance is an "imitation" or copy does not make the performance itself the "original" of which the book Mallarmé has read is a copy. On the contrary, "*There is* mimicry. Mallarmé sets great store by it. . . . We are faced then with mimicry imitating nothing; faced, so to speak with a double that doubles no simple."[13] This Mallarmean non-mimetic mimesis takes us into a *verkehrte Welt* in which "[T]his imitator having in the last instance no imitated . . . this sign having in the last instance no referent, their operation is no longer comprehended within the process of truth but on the contrary comprehends it. . . ."

I lay aside the obvious query raised by the undissolved binary "logos" of male/female embedded in the story of a Pierrot who tickles his wife to death (!), to join the deconstructive logic of Derrida's analysis. Among the many doublings laced through the "double session," one is clearly the structure suggested by the two texts, ancient and modern, which might be seen as representing two moments in western culture. This pair of doubles lends itself, like many Derridean analyses, to an implied historical, or historicized, structure, a before and an after. In the "before" we accepted the logic of the logos; in the "after," the logos loses its stability and begins to dance with doubt and undecideability. In "the Double Session" a transitional term between before and after can be abstracted: it is theater.

Before theater/after theater: in the narrative suggested by this pair, Plato not only initiates but stands in for the entire tradition of western metaphysics. Truth is still an achievable goal, the model/copy binary inherent in the Platonic view of writing functioning as its guarantee. (Plato's known suspicion of art will perhaps help to support the view that the Platonic example occurs "before theater.") But then, in this implied Derridean "history," the Platonic tradition of writing-as-truth is interrupted by a new type of writing in the form of stage performance. Within this new writing the entire metaphysical apparatus of "truth" is subsumed, relativized, and aestheticized; instead of truth it offers "reality-effects."[14] It is not by chance that we pass into this de-ontologized world of simulacra through the medium, or—Derrida's more complex and problematical word, adopted by Mallarmé from the traditional Pierrot vocabulary—through the *hymen* of theater.[15] No better medium can be found (and here I am adding my own words to Derrida's) than theater, with its undecideable play of model and copy, presence and absence, to suggest the new post-metaphysical world that, so to speak, cries havoc and lets slip the dogs of writing. But theater is not merely the model of that world, or the exemplary transition into that world. It is, with its perpetual mysterious *mise-en-scène* of emerging inscription, *in itself* that world.

Thus from two seemingly quite different ideological starting points in the 1960s, Debord and Derrida describe great historical trajectories that suppose a culture moving from stability—whether rooted in reality or in illusion universally accepted as actuality—towards and into a new instability of which theater becomes both model and agent.

This before theater/after theater model of cultural change may be found in many post-structuralist texts of the 1970's. The theatricalist move beyond metaphysics was bruited by Foucault in *The Archeology of Knowledge* (1969), where Foucault debates the status of texts in a post-logocentric world and substitutes an Austinian standard of "performance" for the older, more stable standard of "competence."[16] Foucault doesn't merely advance the criterion of performance, but to some degree enacts it, splitting his voice in two, in the conclusion to the *Archeology*, to stage a dialogue with himself. His argument for an archeological and performative standard instead of an historical, truth-seeking standard in the evaluation of texts, itself moves towards a self-performance that recapitulates the suggestion of a before theater/after theater scheme of cultural change. Foucault makes this shift explicit in "Theatrum Philosophicum," a 1970 essay on books by Deleuze. He greets Deleuze's *Logique du sens* as a watershed in western philosophy, ushering in an era beyond traditional metaphysics of play and the mask. Using the by then current Derridean terms of the simulacrum and of mime ("repetition without a model"), Foucault concludes that Deleuze writes "philosophy not as thought, but as theater."[17]

In their 1972 *Anti-Oedipus*, Deleuze and Guattari move so decisively towards the theatrical pole of the before/after cultural binary I have been examining, that the theatrical has been shifted to the historical position. The book unfolds a carnivalesque social psychology, "schizoanalysis," to supercede the "classical theater" of Oedipus, Freud, and capitalism. Theater, a site for the dangerous loosing of the forces of play, sexuality, irreality to traditional anti-theatricalists like Augustine and Rousseau, becomes itself the agent of repression in Deleuze and Guattari. Freud's procrustean primal scene has turned all psychoanalysts into "directors for a private theater": "Shit on your whole mortifying, imaginary and symbolic theater," they exclaim.[18] And this Freudian/capitalist theater is "not even an avant-garde theater, such as existed in Freud's day," they say, alluding to Wedekind's theater of "natural" sexuality, "but the classical theater, the classical order of representation."[19]

In their trajectory of western culture, Deleuze and Guattari place theater not in a terminal but in an intermediate position. The artificiality and false consciousness of the capitalist/Freudian theater is already being destroyed, they believe, by late capitalism itself. However, it will be succeeded by a "real" that is far from the space of stability and rootedness that Debord hankers after and that Baudrillard, as we shall see in a moment, projects back onto western culture. Their real is a burning, Artaudian eruption of "desiring-machines"—"wild production and explosive desire"—which, pushed by the force of exchange itself, will crack through the social controls produced by nuclear family triangulation.[20]

Jean Baudrillard, the last of the male theorists in this discussion, returns us full circle to Debord's theory of the spectacle, which Baudrillard extends and sophisticates. Baudrillard's critique of Marx's theory of production is constellated around the theatrical notion of mimesis, inherent in the central image of the mirror.[21] On one side of Baudrillard's "mirror of production" is the "real" of labor and use value; mirrored back is an aestheticized economy of exchange dominated by a code of self-referential signifiers. Baudrillard sees these two worlds not merely as sides of a contemporary reality, but as stages in an implied history of culture, moving (as in Debord) from the real to the "irreal," the ontologically grounded to the emptily spectacular.

By the 80s, Baudrillard casts off the Marxist anchor of production value (last vestige of a reality-principle in his social analysis) and floats through the looking-glass into the late capitalist world of "simulation." In this world the "scenodrama" of contemporary culture does not imitate reality, but simulates it in an effort to disguise its disappearance. Even the old labor "scenario" of work and strikes is but one more instance of a "collective dramaturgy upon the empty stage of the social."[22] To express his revulsion against the spectacle of the metastatic exchange of meaning, Baudrillard reaches for extreme, trans-theatrical language. He sees a world so intensely theatrical that theater has passed over into itself:

> [T]he whole newsreel of "the present" gives the sinister impression of kitsch, retro and porno all at the same time. . . . The reality of simulation is unendurable—more cruel than Artaud's Theatre of Cruelty, which was still an attempt at a dramaturgy of life, the last flickering of an ideal of the body. . . . For us the trick has been played. All dramaturgy . . . has disappeared. Simulation is master. . . .[23]

Baudrillard follows, in the most extreme form yet encountered, the historico-cultural trajectory already familiar from Debord. Once there were cause and effect, he says, subject and object, ends and means. "All of western faith and good faith was engaged in this wager on representation: that a sign . . . could exchange for meaning, and that something could guarantee this exchange." But now we live "under the ecstatic sign of the technico-luminous cinematic space of total spatio-dynamic theatre."[24] Here, indeed, is the contemporary social spectacle as Wagnerian *Gesamkunstwerk*.

In these texts, theater becomes not simply a metaphor but a structural element in a series of world-cultural narratives. Debord wishes to turn western culture back from the spectacle to a criterion of truth. Derrida dispassionately exposes the theatrical undecideability underlying, or superseding, metaphysical truth claims. Baudrillard contemplates the movement of society from a stable real to a final and negative hypertheatre. Only Deleuze and Guattari construe theater as a form of falsely imposed order, instead of a disintegrative disorder. But the schizoanalytic future they depict has much in common with the continuous spectacular seen by Baudrillard. Yet in all these schemas, theater, or more properly, theatricalized society, emerges as a late, and sometimes terminal and tragic, phase of western culture.

Threaded through the writings of various feminist theorists of the 1970s, theater appears once more as a central image in a schematic history of culture. The cultural narrative theater is employed to advance, however, differs radically from those of the male writers just examined. Here theater sometimes appears as an absolute patriarchal Other to the (literally) *grounded* work of feminists, as in this statement by the Belgian feminist activist Françoise Collin, editor of *Les Cahiers du Grif*, who turns radically against all "show":

> As soon as we speak or write; as soon as we open a restaurant, a women's centre, a library; as soon as we organize a party, produce a film, a show, a book, a journal, a newspaper . . . as soon as we are seen and let ourselves

> be seen, we become part of this "theatrical society." . . . It is as if a revolutionary existence is only possible in absolute secrecy, underground.

To evade the ubiquitous theater of male representation, Collin concludes, women must become "ants that eat away at the earth."[25]

In her 1975 essay, "The Laugh of the Medusa," Hélène Cixous calls for the insertion of the female body into writing, and female writing into history; she envisions woman's "shattering entry into history" and the beginning of a "new history" that would emerge with that entry.[26] In Cixous's mythology, this utopian vision will mark an end to the "false theater of phallocentric representationalism." Within that theater, the Freudian/Lacanian "drama manglingly restaged" of Lack, this "oldest of farces," must finally be discarded.[27] In an encapsulated scene in the essay she actually stages this farce with characters and dialogue:

> Oh what pwetty eyes, you pwetty little girl. Here, buy my glasses and you'll see the Truth-Me-Myself tell you everything you should know. . . . You see? No? Wait, you'll have everything explained to you, and you'll know at last which sort of neurosis you're related to.[28]

As in this last passage, the new female order revealed by French feminist writing of the 1970s often uses a kind of guerilla performance to counter what it presents as the hegemonic "classical" theater of male power/male writing. Carnivalistic scenes erupt in the texts of the Clement and Cixous collaboration, *The Newly-Born Woman*. In "The Guilty One," for instance, Clement's two protagonists, the Sorceress and the Hysteric, appear in a "Theater of the Body" and in several "scenes" of seduction.[29] But it is the Cixous-Clement "exchange" in the final part of the book that most reveals the multi-vocal performativity embodied in their vision of a new female writing. Unlike Deleuze and Guattari, whose collaboration speaks with a single voice, Cixous and Clement open up the text to expose their own differences, and further double their dialogue by running beneath their split pages an intermittent dialogue with Brecht, Engels, Freud, and with Cixous's own text on the Dora case.[30] Thus theater occupies a double-edged position in Cixous and Clement. On the one hand, the theatrical is projected back onto history as the patriarchal mode. But on the other, this theater can only be countered by a more adroit, guerilla theater, performing satiric skits or feats of dialogic expansion in the unexamined or forbidden spaces of the patriarchal model.

This notion of the feminine-as-performance to counter the theater of patriarchy is nowhere more systematically carried out than in Luce Irigaray's essay on Freud and female sexuality in *The Speculum of the Other Woman*. Irigaray doesn't only see scenes, she makes scenes. She plays all the parts: ventriloquizes Freud, then rips off the Freud mask and taunts "you men," now takes herself offstage to join an audience of superior but indulgent women ("Let us continue to listen without impatience"), and finally distances the entire performance with periodic comments about woman's relation to the stage.[31] Calling to mind Joan Riviere's brilliant female academic patient of the 1920s (not as tragedy but as farce), Irigaray masquerades the masquerade of femininity.[32]

In "Plato's *Hystera*," Irigaray deepens the theatrical structure. She constructs a world-historical narrative that could be seen as a reversal of Derrida's reading of Plato in "The Double Session." Instead of moving from the firm representationalism of the metaphysical tradition towards the modernist instability of the theatrical, Irigaray depicts a western metaphysics deluded by theater at its inception. Deep in the cave of *The Republic*, woman both provides the stage for, and at another level is entrapped in, the male show. The cave is, after all, her *hystera*, her womb, but on the "stage" of male oblivion, she is decor for the male "stage setup," the "magic show." Men enact a false "process of mimesis" without ever knowing how the "parts [are] being cast", or what or who is behind the "dazzling *trompe l'oeil*" projected "within the symmetrical enclosure of this theater."[33]

Outside the shadowy phallic theater in the cave Plato locates another world, and this he takes, or according to Irigaray, mistakes, for unconditioned reality. But the Sun and the Good it stands for represent only another kind of show, another mind of mimesis. The "reflections" of this "spectacle above," are "guaranteed not by the cunning, the magic practices, the spells of the magicians—since these can result only in 'opinions'—but by nature."[34] To Irigaray, the great binary of Plato's parable—illusion/reality—is no opposition at all; in both cases, below and above, there are still only shadows, reflections, representations, the Idea. Both shows take place within something else which cannot be seen at all, "the earth, the mother, the *hystera*."[35] "He who has never dwelled within the mother will always already have seen the light of day," writes Irigaray.

> The oblivion of incarceration in the shadow and the water of the mother's cave, room, womb, that immemorial home, the blindness shrouding the memory, blocking reminiscence, that inoperable leucoma covering the eye (of the soul)—all this the Father vows to do away with by dazzling you with an endless day. [But] . . . *Forgetting you have forgotten* requires a long and methodical initiation. Some time must elapse, some distance must be covered, some turns managed, mimes enacted. . . . Scenographies which precede and prepare the possible re-inscription of ideal forms.[36]

Irigaray indicts the metaphysical tradition at its root as an elaborate system of theater, a dazzling *trompe l'oeil* constructed in air and lacking a grounding that—with Heidegger—Irigaray locates precisely in and with the ground, the earth. In her epistemic narrative, there is a primary female principle outside the masculinist play of mirrors, manipulatively erased from consciousness in the male epoch of theater and spectacle. Finally, by implication, the principle of the *hystera* will be restored to consciousness in a new epistemology with the unmasking of the Platonic "show." The account of western culture implied in Irigaray could almost be said to turn Baudrillard upside down. In Irigaray, the metaphysical tradition begins where his leaves off, in spectacle and simulation, in his fourth and final stage of representation, where the image forgets all reference to the real.[37]

The male theorists I have considered place the image of theater at a late stage in their accounts of culture. Some cannot envision culture beyond theater; it is a wholly degenerative symptom. Irigaray, Cixous, and Clement place theater much earlier, at the fount of the patriarchal order. They contemplate a way through the crisis in representation to new grounding in a semiotics of the body, sexuality, and writing gendered female. But it would be naive and over-essentializing to claim that the women present a simple anti-theatrical utopia in contrast to the male theatrical anti-utopia. Rather, their essays usher from a cultural moment that is full of promise precisely in its ungroundedness, a moment in which theater can also be used to explode and dismantle, and especially to experiment, through play, with new voices and subject positions in an emerging feminist discourse.[38]

Both the male and the female writers I have looked at enter the scene of theater, it seems, when grounding principles fall away; when—as Saroyan's philosophical Arab mutters in *The Time of Your Life*—"No foundation. All the way down the line."[39] For the generation of theorists I discuss here, this is a sobering issue. Lyotard identifies the failure of the master western narratives of legitimation as the principal source of the postmodern paradigm shift. The male theorists mourn their passing (Debord and Baudrillard), or project the present moment of doubt both backward and forward onto origins and destinations (Derrida), or adopt a rebellious stance that promises a future of even more radical delegitimation (Deleuze and Guattari). From the point of view of feminist writers, these "metanarratives" themselves are exposed as fundamentally flawed and illusory. In both cases the figure of theater becomes a kind of lifeboat for those who are jumping metaphysics. In this sense, the scene of theater appears to be transitional. It arrives just after, or just before, some general quality these writers appear to regard as "virtue." To test this notion, yet half as a joke, I opened at random Alisdair MacIntyre's study of the decline of western moral philosophy, entitled *After Virtue*, to read "To a disturbing extent our [contemporary] morality will be disclosed as a theatre of illusions." And elsewhere, in his discussion of the importance of "characters" in modern society, I came across MacIntyre's insistence that he "intend[s] this dramatic metaphor with some seriousness."[40]

For the theater critic contemplating the spectacle of theory, yet another definition of postmodernism now presents itself: postmodernism is that moment in culture when the last ontological defenses crumble into theater. It is in that space, in that *scene*, that a poststructuralism that risks giving up politics in order to jettison metaphysical binaries coincides with a feminism throwing over the patriarchal binary in order to make a new politics. It is the intersection where once more the Sphinx and "man" confront each other.

If theater comes after virtue, what comes after theater? We all want to get on with it. We are bored with all these gestures. Bored with Baudrillard's fascinated horror. Bored with Deleuze's giddy release. Bored even with Derrida's infinitely discriminating canniness. We would like with Cixous to see a new history, a new epistemology. But will it come? Are we already in it? How can we know? Perhaps theater itself, the actual theater of material practice, can help us here. The idea that when the meta-narratives begin to slide theater appears in their place has after all been foreshadowed by the practice of modern theater itself. A theater critic could even make the not entirely far-fetched argument that the theatrically self-conscious theater of modernism, in a reverse mimesis, is the modernism that postmodernism is post.

The idea of the *theatrum mundi*, the theatrically irreal nature of the world, to which the theatricalist strain of modernist theater is indebted, can be traced to the Stoics. In the Middle Ages the concept became a commonplace of medieval homily. It entered theater practice in the English Renaissance, but found its purest form later in the seventeenth century in Calderon's *Great Theater of the World*. There God the Author—director, spectator, and fixed guarantor of eternal values—sits on his golden globe in heaven and surveys the transitory and tragic human scene, where the human actors perform their momentary worldly roles. The idea of the *theatrum mundi* has waxed and waned on the western stage since the Renaissance. In the modern period it reappears with a vengeance, and strangely transfigured, as perhaps may be seen by compressing a complex history into one recognizable example, Pirandello's *Six Characters in Search of an Author*.

In *Six Characters*, Pirandello's obsessional figments long to be released from the purgatory of their single narrative. The actors who attempt to portray them are just the opposite; continuously in search of a text, they seem miscellaneous and underimagined in their offstage personalities. Both require the theater for actualization, and it is only through theatrical enactment that they meet. Theater becomes a kind of security zone between non-cohering realms, the threshhold between the twin problematics of the playwright's imagination and the materiality of the world.

"I have gathered it [the scene] up again into my own fantasy without removing it from the spectator's eyes," Pirandello wrote in his preface to the play. "That is, I have shown them, instead of the stage, my own fantasy in the act of creating—my own fantasy in the form of this same stage."[41] The liminal function of theater is even deeper in the play's structure than his words suggest. In *Six Characters*, theater is the "as if" space that permits actors and characters each to approach the other, to engage in ideological contestation, to assay their narratives. It is the space from which they *act*. In short—and this gesture is replicated in every modernist theatricalist play—theater itself has become the best substitute contemporary "advanced" culture can muster for the fixed point, what I call the "guarantee," once provided by God on his golden globe in Calderon's *Great Theater of the World*. In *Six Characters* it is Pirandello's version of the real. It may have assumed this function as well for the generation of theorists I discuss here.

The day before I read an abridged form of this essay at a conference in Montreal, this conclusion—that theater functions in much contemporary discourse as a form of "grounding principle"—was handily reenacted at the conference itself.[42] Professor Nancy Miller, in an address to a plenary session, described the development of feminist thought from the 1960s on, both in theoretical terms and in the anecdotal terms of her own personal history. Miller explained that she had begun to write herself into the story of changes in feminist theory only in the late 1980s, when she perceived that the theoretical explosion of the past three decades of feminism was drawing to a close. From now on, she feared, feminist criticism would be submerged in simpler thought—thought so simple that it will "have a beat and you can dance to it." As Miller attached an intimate personal story to each phase of feminist theoretical awakening, it was clear that what was formerly an objective and progressive linear history had dissolved for her into a species of auto-performance. Here was a recapitulation in miniature of the first type of cultural trajectory described above: when certainty in the survival of the linear narrative ebbs for Miller, theater takes its place.

The respondent to Miller's talk, the Italian feminist Rosi Braidotti, was even more interested in performance than Miller herself. Her narrative was inseparable from theater at the outset. Braidotti did not accept Miller's sense of a decaying linearity. For her this same history, and "history" in general, needed to be rethought as multi-vocal, multi-directional, and performative at its core. Braidotti rendered her account of the same decades Miller addressed, the 1960s, '70s, and '80s, by playing tapes of songs performed by a succession of female pop stars. The performers and their lyrics constituted a feminist history in practice, seen from a radically populist perspective. Without question, Braidotti rejoined, "It has a beat and you can dance to it." Some members of the eminent academic assemblage clapped along. Braidotti gave us not history mutating into performance, but history *as* performance, and performance itself as history. Braidotti is willing to throw grounding principles to the wind—they were only an illusion anyway—and pull back the curtains to reveal that the most reliable version of reality is theatrical and performative.

In 1967, in a now famous, some would say notorious, essay in *Artforum*, "Art and Objecthood," Michael Fried made the claim that "theater and theatricality are at war today, not simply with modernist painting . . . but with art as such . . . with modernist sensibility as such." His dire prophecy continued, "The success, even the survival of the arts has come increasingly to depend on their ability to defeat theater."[43] Postmodern practices have remarkably confirmed Fried's prediction of the turn towards theater, if not of the demise of art. In the decades since Fried staged this last-ditch effort, not only art but seemingly all of culture and society in late capitalism have defeated presentness, in Fried's sense, to embrace the performative. The very theoretical texts that we have read for the past twenty years to help us understand the changes that Fried sought so vehemently to stave off in art themselves construct cultural narratives to which the theatrical is central. Postmodern art and culture have not only aspired to the condition of theater, but have normalized and even celebrated the spectacle of spectacular society.

Contemporary social practice of all kinds, especially since 1980, has seemed to confirm the insight of theater as grounding principle in a period of conflicting or dissolving truths. The theatrical is where we improvise—culture, politics, ethics; it is what we have while we wait to find out, with Portman and his Emory University student center, whether theater is a phase the culture will pass through en route to new forms, or whether, with Jencks and the *Strada Novissima*, theater has become the enabling form—not only the way to the new, but the very scene itself.

4

Theoretical Invention and the Contingency of Critique: The Example of Postmodern Semiotics

John Johnston

While there is nothing inherently "postmodern" about semiotics—indeed, we find examples of sign theory in Stoic philosophy, Saint Augustine, and other premoderns—semiotics would seem to offer a theoretical vantage point for investigating postmodernism if we assume that the latter can be characterized as an intensive "problematization" of the referent, or as a condition in which not only all stable referents but indeed all referential finalities are put into question. Since semiotics assumes from the outset that no referent is ever simply "given" but always produced by a specific sign system, it would seem ideally suited to help us grasp what is distinctive about postmodern processes of signification. With this aim in mind, I want to contrast the semiotic models developed in the work of Jean Baudrillard, on the one hand, and Gilles Deleuze and Félix Guattari on the other. Both models give us four distinguishable orders or "regimes of signs," which follow one another in a loosely historical sequence. And while Baudrillard's model tends to privilege the object world, Deleuze/Guattari's concentrates more specifically on the formation of subjects. This is not to suggest, however, that these theories are complementary; on the contrary, they are radically incompatible. Nevertheless, despite their obvious differences, these two models reveal an underlying commonality: by framing historical differences in semiotic terms, they situate critical theory and its representational logic within a specific regime of signs. As a consequence, both declare the historical contingency of "critique" and the necessity of inventing or constantly re-inventing, new roles for theory.

II

In *L'échange symbolique et le mort*, published in 1976, Baudrillard sets out three "orders of simulacra" that correspond to three mutations in the law of value that regulates the way signs function.[1] However, since Baudrillard begins with the feudal order as background against which the first order appears, his analysis actually includes four orders in all. In the chronologically first order, the medieval or feudal hierarchy, signs are transparent and limited in number and serve primarily to mark rank and social position, and to designate the social and cosmic values that fix the social structure in an immutable hierarchy. Furthermore, these signs assume their full value only as an interdiction; that is, they define a reciprocal obligation between castes, clans, or persons. For this reason, Baudrillard asserts, these signs are "cruel": they are never "arbitrary" but function as part of a "strong" symbolic order (*S*, p. 84). Clothing, speech, emblems, religious and social iconography—all appearance is governed by a clarity of signs designating order, rank, and obligation.

With the destructuring of the feudal order and the dissolution of the social bond of obligation by the historically emergent bourgeoisie, these fixed and limited signs are emancipated. As Baudrillard puts it, "the arbitrary sign begins when, instead of linking two persons in an unbreakable reciprocity, the signifier starts referring back to the disenchanted universe of the signified common denominator of the real world toward which no one has any obligation" (*S*, p. 85). Having been detached from the divinely sanctioned cosmic order of feudalism, the sign is first grounded in "nature" and the "natural order." This relationship, however, is not so much guaranteed as "simulated," for the emancipated sign is really a counterfeit of the feudal sign of obligation; not because it corrupts an "original," but because it extends in every direction a process of signification whose former efficacy depended upon its very restriction of the domain of reference. Baudrillard explains:

> Non-discriminating (it is now only competitive), unburdened of all constraint, universally available, the modern sign still simulates necessity by giving itself as somehow linked to the world. The modern sign dreams of the signs of the past and would very much like, with its reference to the real, to again find an *obligation*; but it finds only a *reason*: this referential reason, this real, this "natural" off which it will live. But this bond of designation is only the simulacrum of symbolic obligation: it produces neutral values only, that can be exchanged in an objective world. The sign here suffers the same destiny as work. The "free" worker is free only to produce equivalents—the "free and emancipated" sign is free only to produce the signs of equivalence. (*S*, 86)

Because the modern sign now finds its value in a simulacrum of "nature," it gives rise to an entire problematic of the "natural," to appearance and reality, and consequently to the dominance of theater as the basic formal principle in architecture and public life. At the same time this new order of the counterfeit eliminates all difference in blood, rank, or caste under the sign of bourgeois values based on "natural rights," and brings into existence fashion and competitive democracy; but above all it inaugurates a new metaphysics revealed in the ambitions of a "worldly demiurge" to transform and synthesize all of nature into a single substance. This is how Baudrillard understands the bourgeoisie's obsession with the imitation of nature, most visibly in the proliferation of stucco as a simulacrum of "natural" substance:

> In the churches and palaces stucco is wed to all forms, imitates everything: velvet curtains, wooden corniches, charnel swelling of the flesh. Stucco exorcizes the unlikely confusion of matter into a single new substance, a sort of general equivalence of all the others, and is prestigious theatrically because it is itself a representative substance, a mirror of all the others. (*S*, 88)

Similarly, Baudrillard understands the Jesuit ambition to reunify the scattered world after the Reformation under the aegis of a homogeneous doctrine and to universalize both the old and new world under a single language as the imposition of an order that is at once worldly and spiritual, but also a counterfeit of the state. Hence the clerkly magnificence and theater of the cardinals and grey eminences, their entire apparatus of organization and training.

The era of the counterfeit, as a dominant scheme of appearances that constitutes the first order of simulacra, extends from the "classic" period of the Renaissance to the Industrial Revolution. Baudrillard introduces the second order of simulacra, the dominant scheme of which is production, by considering the differences between two artificial beings, the automaton and the robot. The automaton is a theatrical counterfeit; it plays on the difference in appearance between a human being and its mechanical simulacrum according to the principle of analogy and the effects of resemblance. With the entry of the robot, however, we leave the theater or drawing room for the factory, for the robot, above all, is a worker defined by its mechanical efficiency. If the automaton is the human being's analogon, the robot is his or her equivalent, and annexes her to itself in the unity of the operational processes of work and production. Essentially, then, the first-order simulacrum never abolishes the small difference between semblance and reality in which "all the charm of the automaton" resides. The robot, on the contrary, as a simulacrum of the second order, absorbs this small difference, or liquidates it. It signals a new era in which the entire principle of theatrical illusion and the metaphysical oppositions it expresses become irrelevant, and give way to an entirely different logic of operational rationality and industrial production.

Thus what Baudrillard calls the "industrial simulacrum" encompasses a whole new order of appearance based on production, and especially the assembly-line production of nearly identical objects by nearly identical subjects (identical, that is, in their function as workers). Just as the robot "absorbs" the small difference between the real and its simulation in the automaton, so industrial production absorbs the difference between the natural and the counterfeit, replacing the metaphysical opposition between appearance and reality with the more "objective" finalities of political economy. The latter inaugurates a new order of signs—without tradition, without origin, indeed without reference, at least in the sense these words had for the previous order. Borne of technique and serial production, these signs have to one another only a relationship of equivalency and indifference. And just as the previous era, that of the counterfeit, "played on" the natural law of value, so the era of production plays on the commodity law of value, which, as Marx demonstrated, functions as a generalized law of equivalence regulating labor-value, capital, and production.

The world presided over by the commodity law of value—the industrialized western world of the nineteenth and early twentieth centuries—is thus a world that calls for "critique," since, as Marx saw clearly, the bourgeoisie did not push its revolution all the way but stopped short and reified its own historical position into a "natural order." However, what Marx didn't realize, as Walter Benjamin and Marshal McLuhan did (according to Baudrillard), is how the era of production, marked by its prodigious expansion of technique, industry, and political economy into all areas of life, slides inevitably into an era of reproduction. Benjamin saw that reproduction absorbs the process of production, changing its finalities and altering the status of product and producer. Thus Benjamin (and McLuhan even more) understood technique not as a "productive force" in the Marxist sense, but as a medium, as form and principle of a whole new generation of sense. This seems obvious to us today, since it is now at the level of reproduction—fashion, media, advertising, information and communication, that is, in what for Marx were the nonessential sectors of capital—that the global processes of capitalist production receive their objective finality. Benjamin and McLuhan thus implicitly sensed an imminent reversal of the industrial simulacrum's origin and finality: "for all the forms change [Baudrillard states] once they are not so much mechanically reproduced but even conceived from the point-of-view of their very reproducibility, diffracted from a generating nucleus we call the model" (*S*, 100).

At this point of reversal, we enter the present era of simulation, defined by the presence of third-order simulacra, which play not on the commodity law of value but on what Baudrillard calls the structural law of value, that is, a code of structured differences and binary oppositions. Now we no longer find counterfeits of an original, nor identical items in a pure series, but models that generate forms according to modulations of their differences. In his earlier analyses of consumer society, Baudrillard had shown that consumption in modern industrial society is not regulated by need, utility, or use value—indeed, the latter only function as an alibi or rationale for a semiotic mechanism that delivers the consumer object as a sign-form. What are consumed are not so much materials but objects as signs.[2] Subsequently, Baudrillard argued that the Marxist productivist model and its fetishizing of work only mirror capitalism's own assumptions, since Marxism and capitalism alike unconsciously assume a metaphorical system that imposes itself as a principle of reality. But now the "mirror of production" must be broken by a historical theory of sign structures, and the concept of mode of production must be replaced by that of mode of signification.[3] From the perspective of the latter, human society begins not with the act of producing food but with the outstretched hand offering food; that is, with a sign.

This is precisely the perspective from which Baudrillard addresses us. What allows him to situate both capitalism and Marxism within the same historically defined semiotic regime—one that presupposes a referential reason based on political economy—is simply the fact that we have passed to another regime, one of operational simulation based on indeterminacy and a structural code. As Baudrillard summarily declares : "After the metaphysics of being and appearance, after that of energy and determination, comes that of indeterminacy and the code. Cybernetic control, generation from model, differential modulation, feedback, question-answer, etc., such is the new *operational* configuration (industrial simulacra are only *operative*). Digitality is its metaphysical principle (the god of Leibnitz), and DNA its prophet" (*S*, 103). Yet what makes the "passage" from the industrial era of serial production to the current one of simulation and the generation of objects and signs according to modular differences nearly invisible is that instead of disappearing the previous era of industrial production is now simulated (just as formerly the bourgeois or counterfeit order simulated its predecessor the feudal order). Thus the entire world of political economy, with its reality principle based on production and the oppression of the working class—hence the exigencies not only of critique but of social revolution—now constitute only a phantom referential domain or simulation effect (no longer simulating "nature" but "political" or "economic" reality). What regulates the present social system are not the exigencies of production but the operationality of a giant cybernetic machine. In *The Postmodern Condition*, Jean-François Lyotard describes the present Western political/ economic system in similar terms, as a cybernetic machine based on performativity, but for Baudrillard what most fully characterizes this system is not its redefinition of knowledge as information but its hyperreality.[4]

First and foremost, it is the simultaneous duplication of the sign and suspension of its referent that brings about its hyperrealization. For Baudrillard, the fact that there are two World Trade Towers in Manhattan "signifies the end of all competition, the end of all original reference"(*S*, 136). The Twin Trade Towers both hyperrealize and bring to an end the competition displayed in the New York skyline, which, thanks to the Towers, can no longer be read as columns of a statistical graph that mimic capitalist competition. Similarly, Warhol's multiple replicas of Marilyn's face declare "at the same time the death of the original and the end of representation" (*S*, 136). Photorealist painting, in which the painter copies photographic reproductions in order to convey signs of our objective world with a meticulous but eerily unreal accuracy, operates according to this same logic of hyperreality. Perhaps Baudrillard's most compelling single example of hyperreality however is Disneyland: its simulacra—pirates, the frontier, the future world—no doubt function ideologically, he says, as "a digest of the American way of life, a panegyric to American values, [an] idealized transposition of a contradictory reality" (S, 24), but these simulacra also conceal the fact that America itself is the real Disneyland, just as modern prisons conceal the fact that the social fabric itself, in its "banal omnipresence," has become carceral: "Disneyland is presented as an imaginary order in order to make us believe that the real is real, when in fact all of Los Angeles and the America surrounding it are no longer real, but of the order of the hyperreal and of simulation. It is no longer a question of a false representation of reality (ideology), but of concealing the fact that the real is no longer real, and thus of saving the reality principle" (S, 25).5 Finding itself in this "last stage of the image," in which the image neither reflects, perverts, or masks the absence of an underlying reality, but instead generates a "reality-effect" through simulation, contemporary American culture is relentlessly driven to produce the real, to make everything "more real than the real." The result, instead, is an increasing hyperrealization and attendant loss of the real.

In the hyperreality produced by the dominance of third-order simulacra and simulation models the opposition between appearance and reality is evacuated, their differences drained away. We see this in the opinion poll, which is a simulation of public consensus that reduces response to the terms of a binary code. Of course no one really believes in these polls (except perhaps politicians and newscasters), but belief is irrelevant since the opposition between what people actually think and what is reflected in the poll is displaced by the efficacy of the simulation. The same digitality operates in the current democratic two-party system, which now only "simulates" political opposition. According to Baudrillard, the system's "duopoly" form is the final stage of monopoly, for power now tends to become absolute by diffracting itself into various equivalents. In the era of the Cold War, Baudrillard declares, "you need two superpowers to keep the universe under control." But control is maintained through deterrence, which suspends war as a possible finality by duplicating and stockpiling nuclear weapons far too devastating ever to be used (thus the Bomb becomes a frightful, hyperreal sign). What is at stake in any confrontation, therefore, must be sought at another level.

Thus Baudrillard sees the Vietnam war as really about the United States' normalization of relations with China; Watergate was the system's simulation of scandal, an attempt to regenerate itself, to re-inject—like a hormonal treatment—the "reality" of politics into a system that derealizes politics by its very nature. The fact that media simulations cannot be contested by pointing to "realities" defined by an earlier semiotic order reveals the media's true power, since such demonstrations only serve the ends of the system, which needs to "re-inject realness and referentiality everywhere, in order to convince us of the reality of the social, of the gravity of the economy and the finalities of production"(S, 42). Thus the media only represent and keep in circulation forms of content that serve as a countervailing ballast weight against what otherwise would be experienced as a massive loss of reality: "all media and the official news service only exist to maintain the illusion of actuality—of the reality of the stakes, of the objectivity of the facts" (S, 71). Consequently, the events reported must always be read in reverse, "having exhausted their meaning long in advance and only surviving on an artificial effervescence of signs. . . ." These signs assume a cardinal importance, however, since it is through them that the media can promote itself—in every sense of the word—through a displacement of a reality that it has already volatilized. Hence "all these events follow on illogically from one to another, with a total equanimity towards the greatest inconsistencies, with a profound indifference to their consequences (but this is because there is none any more: they burn out in their spectacular promotion)—thus the whole newsreel of 'the present' gives the sinister impression of kitsch, retro and porno at the same time" (S, 72).

For Baudrillard, then, there is only one conclusion to be drawn: the conditions from within which a "critique" or critical perspective could be elaborated no longer effectively exist; in the place of the critical scene there are now only networks of communication and circulation within which the subject functions primarily as a monitor or screen. Thus, if formerly the scene and mirror of critique provided the means of reflexive transcendence, today there is only "a nonreflecting surface, an immanent surface where operations unfold—the smooth operational surface of communication."[6] Without this possibility of critical, reflective transcendence, we now live in a state of what Baudrillard calls the "obscene ecstasy of communication." How can theory respond, now that it can no longer simply describe or reflect the real, nor enter into a relationship with it of negative critique? For Baudrillard, since these approaches simply conspire with the given, what is necessary is to imagine or invent a new role for theory. Henceforth, theory must refuse to mirror the real and must instead offer itself as a symbolic challenge to the real. A *défi* or raising of the stakes, theory must surpass the limits of the real by being more objective, more ironic, more seductive, more excessive than the real ever could be.

III

For Gilles Deleuze and Félix Guattari, theory plays a somewhat different role: it serves to reveal the various ways in which "reality" as a social construction is always in the process of re-confirming itself (reterritorialization) and, simultaneously, exceeding its own limits (deterritorialization). In their conception, the coding, overcoding, and decoding of social reality always takes place in relation to specific referential "territories" defined by different "regimes of signs." In *A Thousand Plateaus*, published in 1980, they analyze four such "regimes of signs" by which material is coded semiotically and thereby given recognizable social meaning and significance.[7] In the *pre-signifying regime*, which is usually found in primitive social organizations and pre-literate societies, the coding is inscribed on the body, in dance, ritual, and myth in multiple and nonhierarchical forms, and takes as its ultimate referent the body of the earth itself. In the *signifying or semiotic regime*, certain signs or signifiers are singled out and undergo a "paranoid" reorganization, as they are "overcoded" into highly formalized systems, which constantly require interpretation in order to insure the privileging of certain signs over others. Centered on the face of a despot as the ultimate reference, this regime corresponds to despotic social organizations that insure and maintain the unity and coherence of their formalized semiotic system through constant interpretation by a priest or some other professional class. Opposed to this regime, the *counter-signifying* regime subverts such over-coding by generating numerical and spatial multiplicities; it corresponds to nomadic and marginal groups who refuse or undermine the imperial and state bureaucracies of the despotic regime. Finally, the *post-signifying regime* allows modern forms of subjectivity to appear; it emerges in the simultaneous double process of a betrayal or "turning away" from the despotic, semiotic regime and the formation of a "point of subjectification" that splits the subject into a subject of the utterance (*énonciation*) and a subject of the statement (*énoncé*).

Deleuze and Guattari admit that their typology is not exhaustive and that individual "regimes of signs" often combine in multiple ways. Mixtures, they say, can appear "in a history of confrontation and intermingling of peoples . . . in languages in which there are several competing functions, or in a psychiatric hospital in which different forms of insanity coexist among the patients or even combine in a single patient; or in an ordinary conversation in which people are speaking the same tongue but different languages (all of a sudden a fragment of an unexpected semiotic surfaces)" (*TP*, 119). What assures that one regime will assume predominance over another is the fact that all semiotic systems function as part of what Deleuze and Guattari call "collective assemblages of enunciation." The latter, in turn, exist only in a state of reciprocal determination with "machinic assemblages," or the disposition and possible interactions of bodies in a given social field.

To illustrate how a single regime of signs operates, let us focus on the post-signifying regime, the regime responsible for the production of modern forms of subjectivity, or what Deleuze and Guattari call "subjectification." However, since the post-signifying regime can only be understood in relation to the semiotic or signifying regime from which it derives, we must consider the latter first. As its designation suggests, the signifying regime privileges the sign (or signifier), which in its proliferation and infinite circularity (signs always and only refer to other signs) always seems both excessively meaningful and lacking in precise meaning. To a perceiver these signs appear to be organized in circles that radiate outward from a center of significance, much like a particular religious form of organization, that of the despot-god at the center surrounded by interpretive-priests. (Actually, this "model" is one specific form taken by this particular "regime of signs"; another is the delusional system that psychiatrists call "paranoia.") The interpreter-priests function not as a supplement but as an essential part of the system, since they "must provide the center with more signifier to overcome the entropy inherent in the system and to make new circles blossom or replenish the old" (*TP*, 114). Signs themselves being inherently ambiguous, the priests do this by isolating a portion of the signified, which is then made to correspond to a sign or group of signs "for which that signified has been deemed suitable, thus making it knowable." More specifically, through their acts of interpretation the priests add to the syntagmatic axis of the sign (along which signs refer to other signs) a second, paradigmatic axis, along which a "suitable signified" or "meaning" is continually fashioned and refashioned. In this way the priests attempt to overcome the "inadequation" between signifier and signified inherent to any signifying system.[8] Furthermore, since the system is closed upon itself, and all signs must ultimately be made to refer back to the despot-god at the center, a certain deception (that of the priests), in addition to a high state of redundancy, is inherent to the system. Deleuze and Guattari explain as follows:

> Interpretation is carried to infinity and never encounters anything to interpret that is not already itself an interpretation. The signified constantly re-imparts signifier, recharges it or produces more of it. The form always comes from the signifier. The ultimate signified is therefore the signifier itself, in its redundancy or "excess." It is perfectly futile to claim to transcend interpretation or even communication through the production of the signifier, because communication and interpretation are what always serve to reproduce and produce signifiers. (*TP*, 114)

Thus, in this regime, one can never escape from the vicious circle of signs and the functional, operative necessity of interpretation; for this reason, Deleuze and Guattari call the latter "interpretosis," and liken it to a disease.

At the very center of the system, the face of the despot "crystallizes all redundancies . . . emits and receives, releases and captures signifying signs" (*TP*, 114). The despot's face therefore forms the "substance of expression," or what allows the whole system of deterritorialized signs to be reterritorialized in a circular feedback system constantly recharged by the mediating interpreter/priests. Moreover, because the voice emanates from the face, the signifying regime always retains an "oral or non-book character." However, a potential for change and transformation of this regime resides in the existence of a scapegoat on the outside or outer circle of the system, a faceless figure who is always opposed to the despot at the center as the latter's negative mirror-image. This faceless figure of the scapegoat is linked to the despot as a kind of "counter-body" with whom he communicates, but whose own body is tortured, humiliated, subjected to exile and exclusion. At the same time, as a source of disorder and noise emanating from the periphery of the system, the scapegoat threatens the very organization of the latter, according to which all signs refer to and revolve about a master signifier in the person of the despot:

> In the signifying regime, the scapegoat represents a new form of increasing entropy in the system of signs: it is charged with everything that was "bad" in a given period, that is, everything that resisted signifying signs, everything that eluded the referral from sign to sign through the different circles; it also assumes everything that was unable to recharge the signifier at its center and carries off everything that spills beyond the outermost circle. Finally, and especially, it incarnates that line of flight the signifying regime cannot tolerate, in other words, an absolute deterritorialization; the regime must block a line of this kind or define it in an entirely negative fashion precisely because it exceeds the degree of deterritorialization of the signifying sign, however high it may be. (*TP*, 116)

The scapegoat thus functions both as the system's limit and as a point around which the signs that cannot be recharged and cycled back through the system by interpretation will gravitate. Eventually, these "negative" signs will accumulate until they must be discharged and expelled out of the system along a "negative line of flight" in a ritual purification. But with this "negative line of flight" the stage is set for a transformation into another regime of signs, the "post-signifying regime," which will come about when the negative valence of the line of flight reverses into a positive one. The result will be a mode of "subjectification" in which all the variables of enunciation—including interpretation—will assume a different functional value.

In order to explain the transformation from the semiotic or signifying regime to the post-signifying regime, Deleuze and Guattari consider three seemingly unrelated events: the Jewish exodus from the despotic Egyptian empire, the creation of a doubled subject in the first modern philosophy of Descartes, and the distinction essential to nineteenth-century psychiatry between ideational delusion (like paranoia) and subjective or passional delusion (like erotomania). Since these three "events" are combined and synthesized in the logic of the post-signifying regime of signs, they both explain and illustrate its distinctive features.

In their exodus from the despotic Egyptian empire, the Hebrew people embraced the scapegoat's negative line of flight and converted it into their own divinely inspired course of destiny. Essential to this conversion is the role of the prophet. Unlike the despotic priest who interprets signs of the despot-god, the prophet is possessed or overwhelmed by God; his relationship to God is "passionate and authoritarian rather than despotic and signifying." Instead of the radiating network of signs, signs are now detached and gathered into a bundle, forming a portable packet that the Hebrews can carry along with them: the covenant, the ark, but above all the sacred written Book, whose first form is the inscribed stone tablets God gives to Moses. The deception inherent in the interpretation of signs now gives way to a recurrent betrayal; however, the betrayal works both ways: God refuses to reveal his face to Moses, who also turns away in veritable fear of God. Many stories in the Bible—Cain, Jonah, even Jesus on the Cross—illustrate this "double turning away" that replaces the radiating full-face visage of the despot. Semiotically, the double turning away transforms the negative line of flight into a linear trial or proceeding, an ever-renewed series of segments that form a straight line. Thus the Promised Land at the end is constantly deferred, leaving the Jewish people living out a state of indefinite postponement or "existence under reprieve."

Deleuze and Guattari call the point at which this segmental line commences "the point of subjectification." (It replaces the center of significance in the semiotic or signifying regime.) Almost anything can function as a point of subjectification: for the Jews it was God, for the Cartesian *cogito* it is the idea of infinity, for an anorexic it is food, for a fetishist it can be a shoe or item of underwear, for someone in love a facial trait, and so on. What matters in each case is that in relation to this point of subjectification the subject is split or doubled into a subject of the utterance (*énonciation*) and the subject of the statement (*énoncé*). This doubling in turn produces an anchoring or recoiling of one subject onto the other or a relay back and forth between a mental reality produced by the speaking subject and the dominant reality referred to by the subject of the statement. In short, it produces a deterritorialization that sweeps the subject down a "line of flight." In the instance of the Jewish exodus, "Moses is the subject of enunciation, constituted on the basis of the tablets of God that replace the face; the Jewish people constitute the subject of the statement, for betrayal as well as for new land, and enter an ever-renewed covenant or linear 'proceeding' rather than a circular expansion" (*TP*, 128).

In the splitting of the subject into an empirical and a transcendental subject in modern philosophy we witness a striking example of this semiotic doubling. In Descartes's philosophy, for example,

> [t]he Cogito, consciousness, the "I think" is the subject of the enunciation that reflects its own use and conceives of itself following a line of deterritorialization represented by methodical doubt. The subject of the statement is the union of the soul and the body, or feeling, guaranteed in a complex way by the cogito, and performs the necessary reterritorializations. The cogito is a proceeding that must always be recommenced, haunted by the possibility of betrayal, a deceitful god, and an evil genius [*Malin Génie*]. When Descartes says, I can infer "I think therefore I am" but not "I walk therefore I am," he is initiating the distinction between the two subjects. . . . (*TP*, 130)

This doubling of the subject is a "strange invention," however, since the subject seems to appear as both cause and effect of its own statements. Instead of a signifying despot, we have the paradox of the self-legislating subject:

> The more you obey the statements of the dominant reality, the more in command you are as subject of enunciation in mental reality, for in the end you are only obeying yourself! You are the one in command, in your capacity as a rational being. A new form of slavery is invented, namely being [a] slave to oneself, or to pure "reason," the Cogito. Is there anything more passional than pure reason? Is there a colder, more extreme, more self-interested passion than the Cogito? (*TP*, 130)

Needless to add, it is precisely this split or doubled subject that provides the condition of possibility of "critique" from Kant, Hegel, and Marx to the Frankfurt School.[9]

Despite its apparently "intellectual" nature, the post-signifying regime is a fundamentally "passional" regime. The term "passional" derives from the work of the nineteenth-century psychiatrist Gatian Clerambault, whose distinction between a paranoid, interpretive delusion and what Clerambault calls "passional delusion" (querulousness or seeking redress, jealousy, erotomania) became crucial to the development of psychiatry, since it formed the basis for two distinct but problematic groupings of "the mad": those like Judge Schreber who seem obviously crazy but are usually quite harmless and even capable of managing their own affairs, and those who outwardly appear quite normal but who suddenly erupt into dangerous and violent acts. Clerambault also found that in passional delusion the subject must follow a segment or linear proceeding through to the end before it can begin another, whereas in paranoia the delusion forms an endless, self-adjusting network developing in all directions. Thus Clerambault's work confirms and further clarifies the distinctions between the signifying regime and the subjectifying, post-signifying regime.

Just as the signifying regime has two axes—signs referring to other signs along a syntagmatic axis, and signifiers referring to a signified along the paradigmatic axis—so too the post-signifying or passional regime has two axes or lines of subjectification: consciousness as passion and love as passion. These two "figures" of doubling define two ways in which the subject of the enunciation can recoil upon the subject of the statement: "the syntagmatic figure of consciousness, or the consciousness-related double, relating to form (self = self); and the paradigmatic figure of the couple, or the passional double, relating to substance (Man = Woman, where the double is immediately the difference between the sexes)" (*TP*, 132). Whereas Cartesian philosophy provides the example *par excellence* of thought-consciousness, Western literature is replete with examples of love-passion: Adam and Eve, Richard III and Lady Anne, Tristan and Isolde, Klossowski's host and the latter's wife, but above all Strindberg's hateful couples, who raise domestic bickering to the intensity of a veritable semiotic regime. In fact, Deleuze and Guattari suggest that there is more than just a complementary relation between an over intense thought and an over-feverish couple: they are both figures of the same passional regime. As the authors somewhat humorously assert, "passional love is a cogito built for two, just as the cogito is a passion for the self alone" (*TP*, 131).

Whereas the signifying regime brings about a certain uniformity in every act of signification (since all signs refer ultimately to the despot), the post-signifying regime brings about a subjectification, and thus an individuation, that can be individual or collective, or both at once. And because there are always multiple points of subjectification in any social or historical field, these coexistent points give rise to distinct and usually incompatible linear proceedings (thus "betrayal" is an inherent feature of this regime). Indeed, the various forms of education or "normalization" imposed upon the individual subject consist in making him or her change points of subjectification, always bringing the subject closer to conformity with some supposed ideal.

The final, most important difference between the signifying and post-signifying regimes concerns the comparative degrees of deterritorialization possible in the respective systems. This difference is ultimately a function of the sign's internal redundancy. In the signifying regime, redundancy is a matter of the *objective frequency* of signs or signifiers in relation to other signs. In effect, this means that the regime develops a kind of "wall" on which signs are inscribed. In the post-signifying regime, the redundancy is one of *subjective resonance* involving linguistic shifters, personal pronouns, and proper nouns. As we should expect, Deleuze and Guattari specify two forms of subjective resonance, one a reflexive form involving the maximum resonance of self-consciousness (self = self), the other a comparative resonance of names (Tristan . . . Isolde . . .) that defines the intensity of the couple-in-love. Both forms of subjective resonance bring about a new danger, however, for in the post-signifying regime "there is no longer a wall upon which the frequency is tallied but instead a black hole attracting consciousness and passion and in which they resonate. Tristan calls Isolde, Isolde calls Tristan, both drawn toward the black hole of a self-consciousness, carried by the tide toward death" (*TP*, 133).

This new danger inherent to subjectivity follows from the difference in potential for deterritorialization within the two regimes. In the signifying regime, where signs refer only to other signs and the set of all signs to the master signifier, the line of flight, as we have seen, is negative, and thus the overall deterritorialization of the regime is relative. In the post-signifying regime, in which "the sign breaks its relation of significance with other signs and sets off racing down a positive line of flight, it attains an *absolute* deterritorialization expressed in the black hole of consciousness and passion." However, this potential for the absolute deterritorialization of the cogito also contains intrinsic limits, owing to the fact that the line of flight essentially constitutes a series of finite linear proceedings, one of which ends before the next begins:

> Thus the cogito is always recommenced, a passion or grievance is always recapitulated. Every consciousness pursues its own death, every love-passion its own end, attracted by a black hole, and all the black holes resonate together. Thus subjectification imposes on the line of flight a segmentarity that is forever repudiating that line, and upon absolute deterritorialization a point of abolition that is forever blocking that deterritorialization or diverting it. (*TP*, 133–34)

As a consequence, the post-signifying regime of subjectification is at once inherently segmentary (which, as Deleuze-Guattari show, makes the subject highly susceptible to binary coding; e.g., child/adult, male/female, white/black, etc.), and yet still allows desire to attain to such a degree of excess and unloosening that it can annihilate itself.

To reach the extremes made possible by the post-signifying regime involves great risks, risks that Deleuze and Guattari nonetheless advocate by exhorting us to make consciousness an "experimentation in life" and by using love and passion to "abolish subjectification." Although they supply no details for a specific program, it is clear what this abolition would mean: "to get out of the black hole of subjectivity, of consciousness and memory, of the couple and conjugality" through a transformation of identity. In the chapter or plateau entitled "1730: Becoming-Intense, Becoming-Animal, Becoming-Imperceptible . . . ," we see how the flight from dominant schemes of signification always entails some kind of "becoming other": becoming-woman, becoming-animal, and becoming-imperceptible are the basic forms, but the possibilities seem endless, as the array of examples drawn from literature, cinema and myth suggests. The becoming-whale of Melville's Ahab; D. H. Lawrence's becoming-turtle; the various becomings of dog, bear, or woman in Kleist's plays; Kafka's becoming-insect; the becoming horse of Little Hans in Freud's case study; the becoming-rat in the Hollywood film *Willard;* the becoming-Jewish in Joseph Losey's film *Mr. Klein;* metamorphoses like those of the werewolf and the sorcerer in mythology and folklore; numerous instances of becoming-child and becoming-woman—all these transformations of identity occur through strange alliances that form a double and reciprocal relay that tears the solitary subject away from self-identity and launches him or her on a trajectory of becoming. These becomings are neither an imitation or copying—"becoming animal" does not mean becoming like an animal—nor an allegorical or symbolic figuration, but experimentations with identity conducted along a line of flight or escape towards the unknown.

IV

For both Baudrillard and Deleuze-Guattari, a semiotic model reveals how different orders of appearance (or referential domains) are linked to meaning (or meaningfulness, significance) within the context of a social order. Where these theoreticians perhaps differ most visibly is in their response to historical process. For Baudrillard, history presents a succession of neo-Hegelian, self-contained semiotic stages or orders, with the previous order functioning as a phantom or simulated referent for the current order. But we have arrived, Baudrillard argues, at the end of history, and attained a utopia of sorts. "History" itself now possesses only a simulated existence and serves primarily as a justification for certain types of discourse. Arguing for the loss of history not only as a referent but also as a mode of understanding, Baudrillard is thus very much a post-historical thinker whose theory of simulation and hyperreality is essentially an attempt to account for our current sense of "reality loss." For Deleuze and Guattari, on the other hand, "reality" is always a social construction, made and re-made in accordance with various "regimes of signs." They view history as the process of "universalization" made possible by and ultimately indistinguishable from the abstracting, deterritorializing processes of capitalism. However, any historical juncture, our own included, is always comprised of a mixture of different "semiotic regimes." One regime will usually dominate, but it will always contain "lines of flight" or escape along a gradient of deterritorialization towards an undefinable and uncodable "outside." Built into Deleuze and Guattari's theory, then, is not only a theory of "reality-construction" but also a theory of "reality-escape," or means by which the limits of the dominant regimes of signification have been and can be surpassed.

From Deleuze and Guattari's point of view, Baudrillard's theory fails to account for the appearance or invention of singularities, and only allows the infinite replication of simulacra according to the exigencies of the code in an airless, hyperreal universe. In such a space all forms of political or critical resistance are out-of-date and short-circuited in advance precisely because they presuppose a scene of dramatic struggle and confrontation where now there is only *ob*scene transparency. From

Baudrillard's point of view, Deleuze and Guattari's theory is problematic for the same reason as Michel Foucault's: whether it is the micro-politics of power (Foucault) or desire (Deleuze-Guattari), what is unquestioned in both cases is the reality of this ultimate referent.[10] For Baudrillard, then, concepts like power and desire, even when redefined to operate at the micro-cellular level of networks, grids, and assemblages, do not engage the current system in its essential functioning. By defining power as a relationship of forces manifest in and through institutional discourses, practices, and strategies, Foucault misses the scene of power's most efficacious effects: in media signs and simulations, in their effect as seduction. Since in our society power and desire operate primarily through signs of power and desire, the referential finality or ultimate reality of what these signs point to can no longer be simply assumed. Finally, Baudrillard insists on a contradiction in Foucault's and Deleuze-Guattari's theories of "molecular" power and desire. In both, power or the law is geared down or miniaturized to a "microphysical" level, where it suddenly and unaccountably becomes "resistance" in Foucault and "revolutionary desire" in Deleuze and Guattari. In both cases Baudrillard senses a "complicity with cybernetics" and remains suspicious of a theory that would find freedom and resistance ("the molecular revolution") in a space that the cyberneticists describe precisely as a matrix of coding and control.

I take it for granted, however, that both of these semiotic models are attractive in different ways: Baudrillard's theory provides a new and useful description of the present object world and its unreality, and within the latter's baleful enchantments he discovers new forms of "objective irony"[11]; Deleuze and Guattari provide a new semiotic understanding of the form of modern subjectivity, all while elaborating means to escape "subjectification" for essentially political reasons. Must we choose between them? In his book *Legislators and Interpreters*, Zygmunt Bauman points out that current western society operates simultaneously according to two very different means of order: one based on seduction, the other on repression.[12] But as we have seen, seduction and repression turn out to be the subjective and objective finalities in response to which Baudrillard and Deleuze-Guattari respectively work out their theories. Furthermore, if our society both seduces and represses, and does so according to two very different semiotic mechanisms, it would seem that neither theory alone would be adequate for understanding and resistance. Finally, and perhaps important, Bauman's argument that postmodernism must be seen in relation to a mutation in the role of the intellectual—from "legislator" to "interpreter"—throws further light on how both Baudrillard and Deleuze/Guattari are postmodern in their conceptions of theory.

Bauman defines "the postmodern view of the world" as "one of an unlimited number of models of order, each one generated by a relatively autonomous set of practices." He goes on to explain:

> Order does not precede practices and hence cannot serve as an outside measure of their validity. Each of the many models of order makes sense solely in terms of the practices which validate it. In each case, validation brings in criteria which are developed within a particular tradition; they are upheld by the habits and beliefs of a "community of meanings" and admit of no other tests of legitimacy. Criteria described . . . as "typically modern" are no exception to this general rule; they are ultimately validated by one of the many possible "local traditions," and their historical fate depends on the fortunes of the tradition in which they reside. There are no criteria for evaluating local practices which are situated outside traditions, outside "localities." Systems of knowledge may only be evaluated from "inside" their respective traditions. If, from the modern point of view, relativism of knowledge was a problem to be struggled against and eventually overcome in theory and in practice, from the postmodern point of view relativity of knowledge (that is, its "embeddedness" in its own communally supported tradition) is a lasting feature of the world.[13]

From this perspective Bauman argues that the role of the modern intellectual as legislator has been surpassed by the postmodern intellectual as interpreter. More specifically, in the cultural arena the modern legislator's role amounts to defining and arbitrating among criteria of taste, judgment, and value, etc., whereas in the political/economic arena it means bestowing legitimacy or authority on policies by virtue of the modern intellectual's superior objective knowledge. In contrast, the postmodern intellectual's role is that of an interpreter:

> It consists of translating statements, made within one communally based tradition, so that they can be understood within the system of knowledge based on another tradition. Instead of being orientated towards selecting the best social order, this strategy is aimed at facilitating communication between autonomous (sovereign) participants. It is concerned with preventing the distortion of meaning in the process of communication. For this purpose, it promotes the need to penetrate deeply the alien system of knowledge from which the translation is to be made (for example, Geertz's "thick description"), and the need to maintain the delicate balance between the two conversing traditions necessary for the message to be both undistorted (regarding the meaning invested by the sender) and understood (by the recipient).[14]

In describing the coded indeterminacies and aleatory modulations of our current simulational society, Baudrillard confirms Bauman's argument that the modern intellectual's role as legislator is outmoded, and no longer effective. On the other hand, the patchwork, constructivist, inventive method of Deleuze/Guattari, which draws on many local traditions of knowledge without ever trying to totalize or universalize the results—indeed, they argue that such efforts can only play into the hands of the dominant power structure—provide an exemplary instance of the postmodern intellectual's role of "interpretation" and translation, or of what Deleuze and Guattari would call transcoding. Finally, and most important, in neither instance—Baudrillard or Deleuze/Guattari—is theory driven by the motor of critique.

In a recent contribution to a colloquium entitled *Après le sujet, qui vient?*, Deleuze made the following remark: "A concept only dies insofar as new functions in new fields render it obsolete. This is also why it is never very interesting to criticize a concept: it is better to build the new functions and discover the new fields which make it useless or inadequate."[15] Deleuze's explicit appeal to the creative or inventive power of theory over its critical function serves to point up the imbalance that has reigned in our largely pragmatic and empirically biased reception of continental theory. For while the poststructuralist legacy in America has of course been widespread and complex, most of its influence has manifested itself in one or another form of "critique": deconstructive literary readings, gender analysis, the politics of cultural representation, not to mention the "critiques" of theory itself. In short, the tendency either to "apply" or "critique" theory has by and large held sway. Little surprise, then, that as the eighties drew to an end one often heard that poststructuralism had run its course, that its energies had guttered out in various "returns"—to history, 'straight' philosophy, and ethical questions—or had diffused themselves across the vaguer terrain of postmodernism. Moreover, and this is the point to which Deleuze's remark is addressed, in demanding that theory first be held accountable in the high courts of critique, whether of left- or right-wing politics, ethics, pragmatics, or deconstructive analysis, do we not deny in advance the possibility that the concepts that new theory inevitably invents may render these accountings irrelevant or even nugatory, and lead instead to new structures of thought and perception?

The debates surrounding postmodernism provide an especially visible instance. Where one would expect to find a range of "theories" of postmodernism, one encounters instead a proliferation of "critiques." Presumably the latter arise from postmodernism's allegedly scandalous indifference to the pieties that today define a serious and responsible (i.e., critical) attitude. Such "critiques," mistakenly in my view, tend to identify postmodernism with today's highly eclectic and consumerist-defined media culture, instead of seeing the latter as only the former's visible "surface." Like the term "modernism" before it, which when applied to art usually functioned as a counter-term to "modernization," the term "postmodernism" can also designate the production of singularities—aesthetic, epistemological, methodological—which have become visible within postmodern culture, but which are not reducible to or fully accountable within the terms the latter provides. In order to theorize this now postmodern field of functions and variables, we shall have to draw not only upon the critical but above all upon the creative or inventive side of poststructuralism's legacy.

Part Two

Topography/Topology/ Concretions of Change

Having introduced the themes of *chronos* as history, and *logos* as language and sign to the discussion of change as ontological entity and as construct, it is necessary to turn attention to *topos*, since place, as space, object, and construct, is a vital dialectical index of change. From the opening of the debate on change, topology (and the sense and evidence of the concrete as objects in space) has been a vital element in its composition. Philosophers have from the beginning been unable to resist incorporating a theory of space and objects into their notions.

Place, as such, and place in the formal sense of decorum as pertaining to an order of things into which one fits, in the sense of "one's place in the scheme of things," have been at the center of philosophy, and of literature and literary theory, from the outset. Even more provocatively, philosophy has at least since the dialectical sparring of Heraclitus and Parmenides concerned itself with *images* of change as rooted in place and object. Since then, philosophy has seen as one of its central tasks the job of addressing the physical existence of things, their relation to images or ideas of them, and the theme of objects as semiotic markers. Place and object are always functions of assignment, planning, designation, and mapping. The three essays in the following section explore specific aspects of these phenomena.

Roger Bell, in his "From Wittgenstein's House to Morphosis: Deconstructing 'Forms of Life,'" construes the notion of *topos* in terms of the relation between philosophy and architecture, specifically in Wittgenstein's combining of the two in his professional life and the result of that admixture. Bell explores the juxtaposition of an exhibition entitled "*Morphosis*" at the San Francisco Museum of Modern Art with a display of Wittgenstein's house designs, contending that "Wittgenstein's architecture is the space ('*topos*') for the most famous *change* in twentieth-century philosophy, within the context of the link between architecture, art, and philosophy." Wittgenstein's architectural genius, Bell claims, was to create a space that "transcended its place, occupants, and designer"; that is, that overcomes subjectivity. The formal, cool, calculated, and isolating nature of Wittgenstein's house designs leads, according to Bell, after 1930, to the phenomenological questioning of space itself; Bell relates this to the dialogue within Wittgenstein concerning the *parergon*, the frame by which any construction is "known." Beginning with the claim that his plain, simple architectural style is reminiscent of sentences in the *Tractatus*, Bell goes on to show how relations of space, geometry, and measurement are common to both architecture and philosophy for Wittgenstein, as can be seen in the *Philosophical Remarks*, and finally that the application of measurement to visual space, of the practice of architecture to building is a "basic *topos* of the *Investigations*." Wittgenstein offers a consistent challenge to the notion of "personal identity," particularly in the relation between thought and reality. The blueprint acts for Wittgenstein as a "focus for the difficulties of representation," and is in this regard a performative.

Bell provides his own dialectical *parergon* to Wittgenstein's architectural philosophy in the form of extensive, "parallel" notes in which he lays out parenthetically the philosophical and architectural complexities of the Wittgenstinian transformation, particularly—given the early link between postmodern architecture and literary theory—with regard to Derrida and deconstruction. The essay is a particularly rich investigation of the tensions between idea and image, place and sign, in a rapidly-evolving world of signs.

On quite a different tack, Eva Geulen explores in "Nietzsche's Trees—and Where They Grow" tree imagery as an emblem for philosophy and other disciplines as least as far back as Descartes (and incidentally continues the volume's *leitmotif* of tree-imagery; see Erdmann Waniek's extensive discussion of trees in Brecht and Célan in Part Two). Here, in the context of Nietzsche's trees, the emphasis is on the tree as an emblem of unity, systematicity, totalization; Geulen shows how the tree is philosophy's image for itself, and how this image denotes the desire for unity. Geulen's contention starts in Nietzsche's urging for an awareness of concretion, evolving out of a rich history of the relations between things themselves and "similes of things." While for Descartes the tree is a simile for all of philosophy, for Kant it is a metaphor as truncated simile, since at the "root" of any metaphor is metaphoricity itself. This inherent duality produces an ever-greater desire for the "full tree," which comes back through Fichte and Hegel. Geulen shows an alternative discourse in Johan Georg Hamann's non-unitary, anti-Kantian, anti-Hegelian tree, which suggests a grounding in dialectics: "the tree with two roots—one up in the air, the other down in the ground," with this contradiction unsolved by any synthetic. This doubled tree leads to Nietzsche's.

Geulen then goes on to point out how in Nietzsche a new kind of totality appears, marked by the images of the tree of knowledge and the tree of life. In his "final argument about history," Nietzsche replaces any concept of origin with an originary concept of the critique of origin; for Nietzsche, the tree metaphor stands for the cultural/metaphysical development not of topology and physicality, but of historiography—from a new *topos* outside history as such. Investigating Nietzsche's notion of the "*Jahresringe*," Geulen shows that for Nietzsche the "tree of metaphysics" must be cut down before it can be analyzed. This eternal dichotomy between the tree of knowledge and the tree of life (one must be destroyed in order to study the other) leads Nietzsche to his ultimate "terrible truth": strength of life over strength of knowledge. Since we cannot truly investigate the tree of life, because we are inscribed in it and thus can investigate only the tree of knowledge, "the tree is not—it is becoming." In this regard, the tree acts as one of Nietzsche's "metametaphors of metaphoricity as that mode of articulation which has given up the claims to universality and instead bespeaks its own becoming in the form of metaphorical chains or displacements." Thus the tree ceases to be a concretion and becomes, in Nietzsche's radically ironic gesture, an emblem of becoming and of desire, a changing sign of a thing.

Bruno Bosteels's "Misreading the Map" takes on directly the topographic theme in philosophy and theory; indeed, according to Bosteels, theory today is characterized by its strategy of "courting the map." Mapping itself is a theoretical activity, so the contemporary emphasis on theory produces a kind of "cartophilia" within which the constant danger, according to Bosteels, is a misreading of the map, a misunderstanding of the map and the nature of topography. Maps, even in the postmodern, are utopian structurations, potentially linking world and earth (in the Heideggerian sense) and ideological phenomena, embodying both the real and the imaginary. Bosteels's desire is to chart the emergent interaction of the postmodern from the premodern and the modern, and their dialogue with Marxism; consequently the essay excavates a good deal of Jameson's work on Marxism, maps, and totality, and the undesirability of any map of social totalization. This critique leads to a consideration of Borges's map-puzzles, concluding that the mapped realm of totality is an "autodestructive nightmare," in that the inscription of the total, all-encompassing map contains its own death: in relinquishing its power as sign, by exactly corresponding to the "real," it renders itself useless. Maps always reveal the inevitable incompleteness of the mapped (including modernity itself). Thus the idea of the postmodern map is particularly provocative, since such a notion contains an inherent subversion or denial of the totalizing urge. Poststructural analyses of maps confront the map metaphor, always interrogating and denying its mimetic or representational role.

Bosteels moves from Borges to a reading of Foucault and the map, Guattari and the map, Baudrillard and the map, claiming that for poststructuralists "the cartographic activity engenders the territory to which it refers"—the map constructs its subject. This idea applies to cognitive maps as well as real ones, Bosteels shows, as far back as C. S. Peirce, for whom mental diagrams are constructed in an "abductive" process. For Guattari, the idea of the map actually constructs the unconscious, thus rendering "obsolete" the difference between map and thing mapped. Contemporary spatialization of thought and the process of thought is increasingly putting "cartography itself back on the map." Our perpetual desire for some apocryphal wholeness is the map's great danger; we must be wary of any definition of the map that makes it "akin to God" or any other "unmappable yet omnipresent transcendence," including the "postmodern." Bosteels's is a (pre)cautionary note deconstructing the map and our desire for and satisfaction in it.

In the cultural shifts from the premodern to the modern to the postmodern, itself an embedded process of mapping (with all of its satisfactions and dangers—how many MLA and APA sessions have been devoted to defining the postmodern?), the dialogue between change and stasis is continually re-energized. Each of the essays in this section contributes to our participation in that ineluctable process.

5

From Wittgenstein's House to Morphosis: Deconstructing "Forms of Life"

Roger Bell

I.

This journey actually began in San Francisco, at San Francisco Museum of Modern Art's (SFMOMA) installation of *Morphosis: Three Houses* (the second in the series *Architecture Tomorrow* organized by the Walker Art Center). The museum's billing as an exhibit, architectural, of three houses by the Los Angeles firm whose work I wasn't unfamiliar with (the "alley" additions in Venice, starting with the *2-4-6-8 House* in 1979, each exquisitely detailed grammatical explorations of surface, structure, and form), didn't prepare me for the complexities and difficulties of reading found within the familiar atrium space of SFMOMA's fourth floor. Holding forth under the skylite space appeared first but the remains of architecture, elements scattered across the floor, an uninhibited display of the resistance of bringing architecture indoors (as art?). For in or out, one expects, at the least, to be able to read architecture, to envision through models and drawings the inhabited dimensions of these three houses. Morphosis, it would appear, asks us to suspend, defer such habits, to rethink the automatic judgments by which seeing reads the presence or absence of its comforts, its inhabitations. Such exhibitionism installed against our inhibitedness to read otherwise tends to keep even the unwary museum-goer at the threshold, on the other side of its door(s). And it was here that I was reminded of Wittgenstein.

In another show across the hall, entitled *New Work: a New Generation*, an oversize photograph (9' x 4') by Gunther Forg, "Villa Wittgenstein, Wien," caught my attention, reminding me that Wittgenstein had been an architect. Perhaps it was also the line in Mayne and Rotondi's state-

Figure 1: Morphosis's Venice III. (Courtesy of *Morphosis*)

ment afixed to their installation: "Our interest in indeterminacy parallels our interests in formal language." Yet this photograph of Wittgenstein's house, of a view looking out through a series of interior glass doors, depicted a dark and dismal interior. Documented in this photograph scaled as a painting appeared the demise of modernism. No longer a force of inspiration for the arts, now just another collection of artifacts, relics, in need of preservation. This would appear to be the message of this "new generation" of artists, found within the representatives of Forg's images, the empty interior of the house that the noted philosopher Ludwig Wittgenstein designed for his sister Marguerite Stonborough-Wittgenstein.

Figure 2: Villa Wittgenstein, Wien. (Drawings from Paul Wijdeveld, Ludwig Wittgenstein, Architect, courtesy "The Pepin Press, Amsterdam")

"Villa Wittgenstein, Wien," then, uniquely prefigured the dimensions of the problem Morphosis con-figures. Wittgenstein, a painter "tells" us, was an architect, and I needed to be reminded of this fact. The museum, it seemed, was suggesting a matrix for architecture located between the old rivals philosophy and art, hanging Wittgenstein's house as a clue to the difficulties of reading Morphosis's work, but how?

II.

This house, built between 1926 and 1928, marked the end of the transition period in Wittgenstein's life between the wars and his return to philosophy and Cambridge in 1929 (see Figure 2). While most often his teaching experience in Austrian schools during this period is given as the context for his philosophical turn from the earlier work of the *Tractatus* to the language games and therapies of the *Investigations*, it is my contention that his experience in architecture was the punctuating moment and provides an important *topos* for the most famous change in twentieth century philosophy.

After separating reality from myth it turns out Wittgenstein was primarily responsible for the interior details of the house, for instance the layout and design of the windows, doors, certain engineering features: elevator, radiators, part of the electrical and heating systems, etc. The basic design of the house had been set by his friend (and student of Adolf Loos) Paul Engelmann in exchange with his sister Marguerite. Wittgenstein's entrance into the project was late and to a great extent involved overseeing the construction phase. But as in the *Investigations*, where he insists that "we must focus on the details" (*PI* I, 51), a great deal can be learned of Wittgenstein's architectural sensibility from these details and their important contribution to the overall design of the house.

The philosopher George Henrik von Wright, following generally accepted opinion, in a biographical sketch writes of the Wittgenstein house:

> The building is his work down to the smallest detail and is highly characteristic of its creator. It is free from all decoration and marked by a severe exactitude in measure and proportion. Its beauty is of the same simple and static kind that belongs to the sentences of the *Tractatus*.[1]

Does von Wright suggest here that the building's freedom from decoration is a condition of such exactitude of proportion? Is this a stripping away of the ornamental, then, according to a logic, it turns out, different than of Adolf Loos? How are we to get clear about the creative genius of this mythical figure within the recent traditions of professionalized philosophy with regards to just this coincidence between architectural beauty and his writing, as von Wright suggests exists with the *Tractatus*? But more importantly how are we to understand the connection between his philosophy, at this moment of transition, and architecture as more than mere coincidence?

To answer these questions we must examine the house's interior, for it is on the inside that Wittgenstein's hand, at once both architectural and philosophical in manner, must be detected.[2] Equally important, with respect to the obvious indebtedness of the house to Loos, it provides a comparison to Loos's interiors, which he always privileged in the design process: "building from the inside out."[3] Following Loos's precedent one would expect to find within Wittgenstein's house that intimacy that derives from the rule "the building should be dumb on the outside and reveal its wealth only on the inside."[4]

Bernhard Leitner, who leads the way here,[5] retains the formulation of the inner/outer distinction that builds the wall through the oppositional force of the sacred (private) and the profane (public). His reading gives the interior a transcendent significance (far beyond the personal idiosyncratic of even bad taste allowed by Loos) as seen in the statement:

> The building is an intellectual process; an individual attempts to overcome subjectivity and succeeds through the force of his extraordinary intellect. Ultimately the building becomes depersonalized and anonymous; great architecture.[6]

This is an interior that contrasts with the exterior, the contingent, historical, public facade, revealing an anonymous, universal truth. Wittgenstein's skill, then, as an architect (Leitner's claim[7]) was, through his strength of intellect, to create a space that transcended its place, occupants, and designer. In stark contrast to Loos's understanding of the interior and the importance of intimacy, Leitner attributes to Wittgenstein an interior space that achieves a formality of essence quite beyond subjective presence, inhabitation.[8] Possibly this depersonalization motivated Wittgenstein's older sister Hermine to say of it: "It seemed to me much more a dwelling for the gods than for a small mortal like me, and at first I even had to overcome a faint inner opposition to this 'house turned logic' as I called it, to this perfection and monumentality."[9] Possibly her criticism derives from this opposition between the sacred and the profane by which Leitner praises the house as "great architecture." For it is a house, one to be occupied by his sister nonetheless, and not a temple of the gods. As for a place to "overcome subjectivity," to find the anonymity that Wittgenstein himself reportedly sought from his aristocratic origins, the interpretation is all too nicely psychoanalytic. Leitner's generalizations read as epitaphs to the abandoned ruin of Wittgenstein's legend found with the remains of modernity, not unlike its dark, empty representation in Gunther Forg's photograph. Could this really have been the reality from the beginning and not the mark of age? Let's look closer at this interior space turned logic.

Other than the floor plan, the primary features are dark floors, dull, grey, light colored walls and ceilings, very pale ochre-yellow metal doors and windows, naked light bulbs, an absence of carpets, chandeliers, and curtains. The surfaces then are plaster, a prefabricated, artificial stone flooring, steel, and glass. The austerity and simplicity of the interior is derived from the materials, the colors, and the absence of furnishings.[10] The floor plan was designed to provide aligned, framed views through multiple glass-doored entranceways and foyers. In fact, against the starkness of these materials and finishes the proportionate placing and scaling of apertures in the walls, interior and exterior, Wittgenstein's use of "window doors," gives the building's interior its one source of elegance.

Let's begin with Wittgenstein's doors! They seem to have captured most strongly the imagination of his followers into the building's interior, especially, one must add, the glazed doors. And here the attraction is precisely the illogicality of their design, their lack of any middle rail to provide the structural integrity needed for the required flatness of such large doors. Wittgenstein's persistence with respect to overcoming this obstacle, finding a manufacturer willing and able finally to deliver such doors, made with a standard bottom rail, a very narrow top rail, and three narrow vertical styles (only one out of eight firms contacted agreeing to accept the commission), counts as an important contribution to the house. The vertical emphasis derived, especially as repeated throughout the house, would not have been otherwise achieved and provides an elegant, light quality. These are the doors that Wittgenstein's sister Hermine remembers: "While I am writing this, a great yearning comes over me to see again these noble doors, in which one would be able to recognize their creator's spirit, even if the rest of the house were to be destroyed."[11] Yet the irony of the doors, then, is that entrance to the spirit of this interior is gained through material contingent skill and not, as we have been led to believe, that formal, essential thinking likened to the *Tractatus*.

The "logical and rigorous reasoning" that Leitner ascribes to Wittgenstein's interior, where "nothing is left to a speculative aesthetic judgment,"[12] is really simply a measured, calculated use of proportion. Perfection is represented primarily through centering of windows and doors with respect to walls, hallways, entrances, a perfection of symmetry. An example that Leitner gives is the solid door between the hall and the salon. This door, taller than other adjoining doors, stands at the hall's axial end, framed by half and quarter columns on the sides and an exposed beam at the top. Wittgenstein, who Leitner reports "made a drawing of each separate door and window in order to determine proportions according to the surrounding wall, the size, and the purpose of the specific room,"[13] indeed calls attention to the wall through his centered scaling of the door and its dark color contrasting to the light painted wall. However, the design strategy is unique and uncompromising only if one is limited to standard sized doors, a limitation that, of course, today we are more used to.[14] In actuality the design is trivial. Wittgenstein merely made the double door half as wide as the framing wall it is set in and determined its height by providing an equal border at its top as on its sides. The doorway is framed by the exposed structural members, and the wall becomes the intermediate border matting. In fact, even the design employed derives from the picture framer where the bottom margin most often gives of itself to allow the top and sides equidistance. Here one sees Wittgenstein's doors doing the same thing, its dark surface rising up from the equally dark floor into the contrasting light wall. In French (and these are French doors, after all) the wall becomes the *passe-partout*, the frame within the frame, often cut with a bevel on the inside edge, a touch which Wittgenstein omits, also the master-key, the adage that money opens most doors. But these are questions that Wittgenstein's design, borrowing from the framer's idiom, does not address. The wall, as Leitner points out, calls attention to itself through the proportioning of the door, but without asking the question of its purpose, the wall's, of asking the question of the action of the *passe-partout*, in any of its different meanings.[15] Precisely at the end of the hall on the ground floor, at the entrance to the salon, to the reception and sociality of the occupants, at this very juncture of the door, Wittgenstein's architecture remains silent, and not a sublime silence but an empty silence.[16]

This silence is easily contrasted to the idiosyncratic design moves employed by Loos in his Moller house of the same period, whereby his interiors are made to speak in intimacy. This house, the interior of which has been described as probably influenced by Wittgenstein's house, seen in an emptying of the interior, remains, however, strikingly different.[17] From the entrance, which from the outside is defined symmetrically, on the inside one moves upward in a complex ascent through ninety-degree turns and across different levels until reaching the heart of the house on the second floor (see Figure 3). One arrives at a living room, which is complicated by being spilt-level and linking all corners of the house.[18] The most intimate adjoining space is the raised sitting room reached by five steps, set in the rectangular protrusion that forms the nose of the

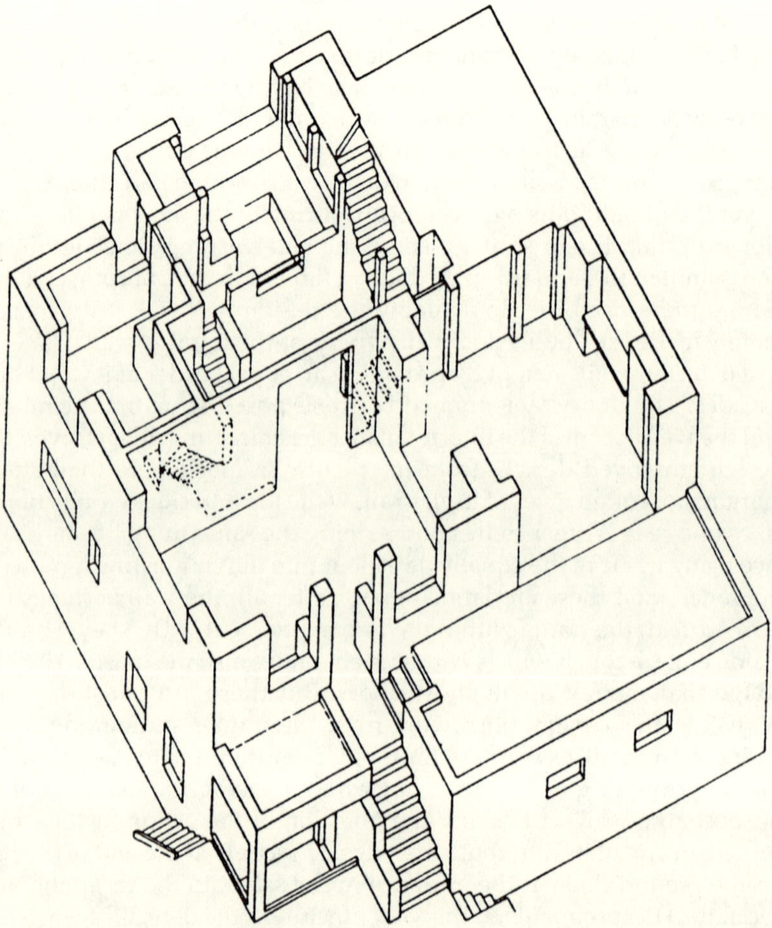

Figure 3: Loos' Moller House (Courtesy of Rizzoli International Publications)

facade cantilevered over the entrance. Unlike Wittgenstein's floor plan Loos's links each adjoining room in an important and unusual manner. Upon entering the interior of the house one feels the relationships between its spaces, not left to the absolute closure of the doors by which Wittgenstein isolated the individual within the domain of each room. This is due not only to the use of split level, creating ceilings of 3.2 meters and 2.5 meters for more formal and more private spaces, but more importantly to the manner and lengths to which Loos went in opening the rooms up to each other structurally and visually.[19] If one looks at Wittgenstein's floor one notices a transverse orientedness of the salon, defined by the symmetrical placement of doors opposite the important

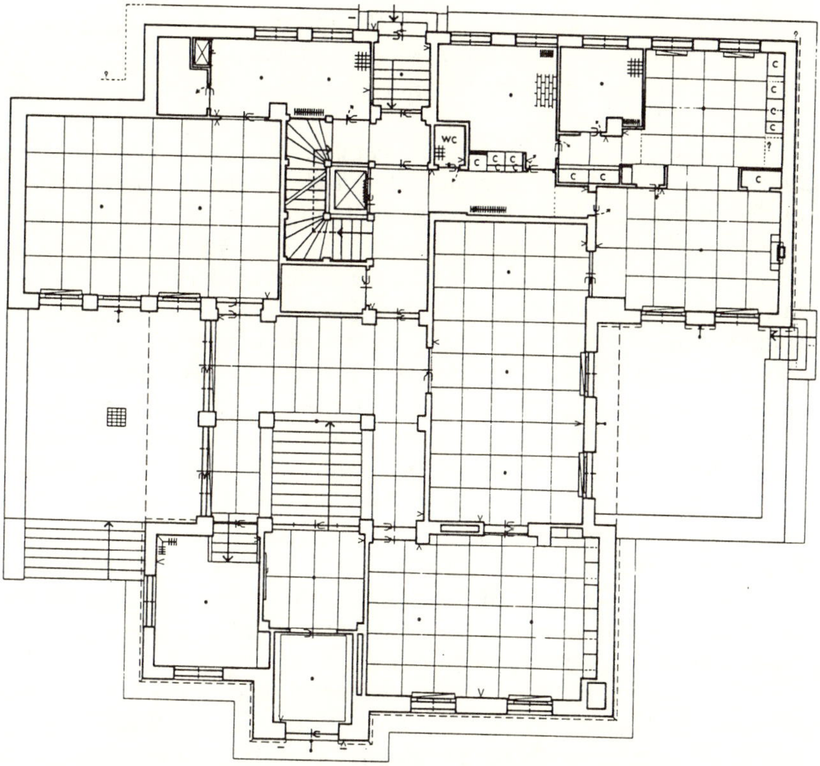

Figure 4: Villa Wittgenstein, plan. (Drawing from Paul Wijdeveld, *Ludwig Wittgenstein, Architect*, courtesy The Pepin Press, Amsterdam)

entrance door from the hall (see Figure 4). Upon entering one's eye is immediately caught by the view to the terrace through the opposing door/window that, with the entrance, bisects the room. The southern door to the living room remains diminutive and distant from this axis of entrance. In a way the salon functions like the hall except more confined; even the dimensions suggest this: 4.80 x 9.32 m. And, indeed, this center of the house functions more as a waiting room to serve access to the living room or to Marguerite's quarters (which she evidently used as a living room during the day) than as a room within which one would want to remain. The interior, rather than opening up to progressively enlarged and complex spatial views, as in Loos's Moller house, displays but neatly placed steel doors and narrow views down blind corners. Any possibility of intimacy, as achieved in the spatial treatment of Loos's interiors, giving views of secluded seating niches, etc., is prevented. Wittgenstein's spaces are containers, and exchange between rooms is always by way of narrow openings. Produced is a labyrinthine quality always by way of narrow openings. Produced is a labyrinthine quality to these interior spaces, despite the aligned, symmetrical views of the corridors, best seen in the narrow corridor that follows the outer, northwestern wall of the salon.

To contrast these different logics applied to the spatial relation between adjoining rooms compare Wittgenstein's narrow door at the end of the salon connecting it to the main living room with the analogous junction in Loos's Moller house between the music room and the dining room. Here Loos has employed a very wide sliding door to enable opening the adjoining wall up 3.2 meters, this with rooms scaled a great deal smaller than Wittgenstein's. But the further radicality of Loos's design move here is that the two rooms are at different levels (floor levels, the same ceiling levels), giving the more intimate low ceiling to the dining room. So the sliding doors open the possibility of movement between these rooms that the absence of any stairs negates. The rooms remain somehow disconnected from each other, although there is a hidden foldout ladder in the base that can be used to get up the seventy-centimeter discrepancy. With regard to doors that serve as entrances to rooms, they are placed off-center, leaving the room's central space free from the demands of circulation (in contrast to the placement and consequent demands on space of Wittgenstein's salon).

With this Dadaist intervention that opens the rooms to each other (the device was actually first employed in the Tzara house, 1926) the wall itself is put in question, developing a spatial logic or plan (Loos's *Raumplan*)[20] that retains his quest for intimacy. Gained is a psychological subtlety, even through such radicality of invention, that is lacking in the measured Wittgenstein house. Loos recognizes the wall as a *passe-partout* by which the importance of space, as the creation of the good architect, is framed. In a quote from as early as 1898 Loos writes:

> At the beginning there was finishing. There are architects who proceed differently. Their imagination does not create rooms but wall structures. The rooms are a by-product of the wall structures. And only afterwards will the architect choose the surface finish which he considers most suitable. The artist, however—the real architect—thinks first of the effect he wants to achieve and sees with his mind's eyes the rooms that he wants to create.[21]

Wittgenstein's house was clearly laid out according to facade and floor plan, delineating rooms through the placement of the walls in contrast to Loos's privileging of the section, a space plan.[22] The step in the design to which so much attention is paid (most notably in Leitner's analysis) is the secondary arrangement of breaks in the surfaces of these defining walls: the window and door apertures.[23] While Wittgenstein made calculations for symmetry, Loos was imaginatively envisioned the space of his interiors, eliminating or adding walls or partitions. Working according to his *Raumplan*, from the interior to the exterior, Loos rethinks the house, pushing the material limits of building (the language of materials providing the only true grammar of building),[24] inadvertently (he argues) discovering possibilities, spaces that undermine the popular distinction between new and tradition.

Loos, with his attention to grammar, leaves us with the question of this "frame" itself, of the work of the wall as the framing of the question (of structural integrity, of entry, of a view, of light, etc.). This question, the question of the *parergon*, the work of the frame, Wittgenstein does not raise, neither by the end of the *Tractatus*, nor in his house with its centered framing of windows and doors.[25] Interestingly, the *parergonal* (defined as the subordinate, ornamental accessory, that outside the work, on the frame as an embellishment, etc.) is no longer seen as frivolous in Loos's handling of architectural grammar. The *parergonal* is integral to the spatial orientation of designing according to his *Raumplan*.[26] However, for Wittgenstein this importance of the grammar of ornamentation is lost, as in modernism. Yet, in the *Tractatus* he wrote:

> My propositions serve as elucidations in the following way: anyone who understands me eventually recognizes them as nonsensical, when he has used them—as steps—to climb up beyond them. (He must, so to speak, throw away the ladder after he has climbed up it.) (*T* 6, 54)

Is this prophetic of his view of his sister's house and the steps it provided in returning him to philosophy and recanting his views of the *Tractatus*?[27] By the time of the *Investigations* ornamentation is likened to our desires for definitions in philosophy: "Remember that we sometimes demand definitions for the sake not of their content, but of their form. Our requirement is an architectural one; the definition is a kind of ornamental coping that supports nothing" (*PI* I, 217).

III.

In a remark from the collection *Culture and Value*, dated 1940, Wittgenstein makes his most explicit criticism of the house:

> Within all great art there is a WILD animal: *tamed*. Not with Mendelssohn, for example. All great art has man's primitive drives as its groundbase. They are not the *melody* (as they are with Wagner, perhaps) but they are what gives the melody its *depth* and power.
>
> In *this* sense: the house I built for Gretl is the product of a decidedly sensitive ear and *good* manners, an expression of great *understanding* (of a

> culture, etc.). But *primordial* life, wild life striving to erupt into the open—that is lacking. And so you could say it isn't *healthy* (Kierkegaard). (Hothouse plant.) (*C & V*, 37–39)[28]

While Wittgenstein identifies Kierkegaard with this lack of "health" of the design, the critique itself is decidedly Nietzschean.[29] It is drawn from that period of the latter half of the nineteenth century about which an earlier remark, also from *Culture and Value* (1929, the year he returned to philosophy after completing Marguerite's house), mentions he "left out" in arriving at his "cultural ideal," the ideal, that is, of the *Tractatus*. This lapse, which he termed "a purely instinctive development . . . not the result of reflection" (*C & V*, 2), now appears to form the basis of a new critique situated within the space of his design for his sister's house.

This "primordial, wild life" that he calls for, something to which his well-mannered, civilized design doesn't address, returns us to Loos's theoretical injunctions against such a threat to culture, what he calls the degeneration of art. In the above lines has Wittgenstein embraced the erotic dimensions of art which Loos sought to transcend? At the very least he differed with Loos in maintaining that architecture is an art. The "primordial," the "wild," reminds one of key figures of the phenomenological tradition: Husserl, Heidegger, and especially Merleau-Ponty, the wild being of a brute ontology interrogated in his *The Visible and the Invisible*, to which Wittgenstein's relation has always been clouded.[30] Identifying such dimensions of life as lacking in his house admits new architectural possibilities and challenges, even beyond Loos's critique caught between the successionists and the modernists. Likewise, the interpretation of the full philosophical challenge signaled in his recanting of the house would fall on deaf ears, which were then (and to such an extent remain today) positivist in their adherence to an objectivist, scientific truth.[31] The proprietary ownership of Wittgenstein's corpus by the Anglo-American analytic tradition that inherits this positivism, despite Wittgenstein's continental origins, further serves to hide the full context of this difficult question, tending to lump both Wittgenstein's house and Loos together with modernism in general, which would fit with the Bauhaus's positivist leanings.[32] Yet Wittgenstein himself provides the clue, a question of ears, Nietzsche's question as Derrida has reminded us,[33] the labyrinthine structure that cannot be closed: "a product of a decidedly sensitive ear and *good* manners."

IV.

Wittgenstein's *Philosophical Remarks* (1930), the first text following his reentry into philosophy, is his most phenomenological. Here the discussion of the relationship between space, geometry, and measurement is particularity relevant to Wittgenstein's experience in architecture. A critique of his house's formal, logical rigor would sensibly follow a phenomenological approach, reconsidering the question of space and its contingent grammatical possibilities, criticisms that bring Wittgenstein closer to Loos's approach. The architectural *topos* serves as both example and the experiential background within which Wittgenstein's inquiry can be seen shifting from a formal logic to essential possibilities, as in the grammatical forms of a house by which life would open outward to its primordial, wild being: a building of *Lebensform*, the articulation of the problem reached by 1940. Such a building is now proposed, not from the logical, measured "good manners" of his sister's house, but from a phenomenological questioning of space itself. The failure of his house lies in its attempted embodiment of formal law in a logical space (the aptness of his sister Hermine's comment: a "house turned logic"), a law for living that presumes to have explained life, rather than a grammatical exploration of architectural possibilities, a description of life's possibilities: the work of Loos's *Raumplan*. Wittgenstein asks the pertinent question in section XVI of the *Remarks*: "The question is, in what sense can the results of measurement tells us something concerning that which we also see" (*PR*, 178).

Wittgenstein's problem, one exemplified by his house, is "how to explain certain contradictions that arise when we apply the methods of inference used in Euclidean space to visual space" (*PR*, 210). That is, how is the "expansible sign" of even analytic geometry to escape these contradictions, to represent the "multiplicity and properties of space"? Analytic geometry, a geometry not of proofs and demonstrations, but of constructions, even more aptly evidences the contradiction.[34] Wittgenstein continues in the *Remarks*:

> The moment we try to apply exact concepts of measurement to immediate experience, we come up against a peculiar vagueness in this experience. But that only means a vagueness relative to these concepts of measurement. And, now, it seems to me that this vagueness isn't something provisional, to be eliminated later on by more precise knowledge, but that this is a characteristic logical peculiarity. (*PR*, 211)

Is the picture theory of propositions here becoming blurred, giving way to the later systems of use?[35] The comparison of systems of propositions and rulers of measurement dates from the conversations of 1929 and 1930 with members of the Vienna Circle, and this section in the *Remarks*, bringing the comparison to the logic of colors and space, also involves language: how "expansible" the sign system must be. What is this "vagueness relative to measurement," that is, to our representational systems?

How is it to be understood as an inherent characteristic of the logic of experience itself?[36] This intermingling of the themes of language and visual space within the context of this question certainly returns the architectural theme (and Loos' emphasis upon the importance of studying grammar). As for Wittgenstein, the realization, definitely phenomenological, leads him to the categorical statement "In visual space there is no measurement" (*PR*, 212). But how, then, is this to be applied to the practice of architecture, to building (a basic *topos* of the *Investigations*), that is, to ensure the designing of visual spaces? Mustn't architecture always involve the use of some signifying system, even in the case of modernist minimalism, a system which at bottom must comply with the many measured scales of the building codes? That is, the designing of spaces, Loos' ultimate goal and Wittgenstein's recognition of the 40s, must base itself in the material technologies of measurement.

In the final aphorism of chapter XX Wittgenstein again restates the dilemma, this time with an apt example for architecture:

> We might think that the right model for visual space would be a Euclidean drawing-board with its ideally fine constructions which we make vibrate so that all the constructions are to a certain extent blurred (further, the surface vibrates equally in all directions lying in it). We could in fact say: it is to be vibrated precisely as far as it can without its yet being noticeable, and then its physical geometry will be a picture of our phenomenological geometry.
>
> But the big question is: Can you translate the "blurredness" of phenomena into an imprecision in the drawing? It seems to me that you can't.
>
> It is, for instance, impossible to represent the imprecision of what is immediately seen by thick strokes and dots in the drawing. (*PR*, 217)

What, then, remains of this impossibility of representation, a residual of spatiality, which the architect can resuscitate in rebuilding the environment such that "primordial," "wild" life might erupt from its centered coordinates, as Wittgenstein comes to hope? What answers can be found to this pessimism regarding "translation," to the "imprecision of what is immediately seen" that always escapes the draftsman's pen? The drawings Wittgenstein made of the window and door placements for his house provided the means by which the proportions were determined. As evidenced in the notorious raised ceiling of the salon (a 3-cm correction), these drawings were meant to determine exact dimensions and placement, determinations which were made according to geometric procedures in two-dimensional representations prior to all construction. The relation between such working drawings and the constructed architecture was not questioned by Wittgenstein. Here I am immediately reminded of the difficult drawings found within the Morphosis exhibit, of drawings made after the project was built, drawings that question the standard architectural delineation of distinct phases of the project: design, drawings, and, then, construction. Wittgenstein's blurred drawing board seems to hint at what has just arrived: a "deconstructivist" architecture that nevertheless builds, and builds with an eye to formal language. Must one have (which Wittgenstein didn't) a CAD station instead of a Euclidean drawing board, even one automatically, indecipherably blurred, with an interestingly productive virus in the program?[37] But these *Remarks* are still only the beginning of the middle period, just the immediate aftereffects of Wittgenstein's sojourn within architecture.

V.

Later in 1947 Wittgenstein addresses a series of written remarks[38] to the faculty of taste and within them mentions the limitations of his house. Described is the function of taste, its role within art and any creative activity. The series begins:

> The faculty of "taste" cannot create a new structure, it can only make adjustments to one that already exists. Taste loosens and tightens screws, it does not build a new piece of machinery.
>
> Taste makes adjustments. Giving birth is not its affair.
> Taste makes things ACCEPTABLE.
>
> (For this reason I believe that a great creator has no need of taste; his child is born into the world fully formed.)
>
> *Sometimes* polishing is a function of taste, but sometimes not. I have taste. (*C & V*, 59)

Taste is described as changing the picture ever so slightly. If taste "makes things acceptable," "sometimes polishes," is a "refinement of sensitivity," then perception's grammatical possibilities, as they are incorporated in architectural possibilities, are not immune to history's vicissitudes. The orientation of the earlier *Philosophical Remarks* in "having a perspicuous view of the foundation of possible buildings," has shifted from this foundational orientation to one skeptical of any such origins. Design is now seen to involve the risk of possibly not getting things just right, so as to expose the concealing garments of mere vogue and taste. Through such exposure, its openness to desires, a greater complexity of the architectural and philosophical task can be assessed. Wittgenstein's assumption of "correctness" can be seen to gradually shift from its early foundationalist formulation to being a property of a particular, historically situated language game, recognizable within what he calls a "form of life." The question, however, regarding the fuzziness of such pictures remains, translating into the later framework of discourse, philosophic and architectural.

The series expands:

> Even the *most refined* taste has nothing to do with creative power.
>
> Taste is a refinement of sensitivity; but sensitivity does not *do* anything, it is purely receptive.
>
> I am *not* able to judge whether taste is all I have, or whether I have originality too. The former I can see quite clearly but not the other, or only quite indistinctly. And perhaps this is how it has to be, and you can only see what you *have*, not what you are. Someone who does not lie is already original enough. Because, after all, any originality worth wishing for could not be a sort of clever trick, or a personal peculiarity, be it as distinctive as you like.
>
> In fact the beginnings of good originality are already there if you do not want to be something you are not. And all this has been said before much better by other people.
>
> Taste can be charming, but not gripping. (*C & V*, 60)

To do something, to be creative, then, would indeed have to be "indistinct" to the one whose originality necessarily is put in question in the doing. Such would be the logic of anything that exceeded good taste. Creativity's test, then, always remains historical, often marked precisely by its distance from taste and the mannered imitations of the time. In the process the rules of discourse must gradually transform according to the activity of such new uses, effecting new standards of taste, without full knowledge, contingently. Originality, for Wittgenstein, requires a recognition of one's taste as distinct from one's culture; it must be found within that difficult personal dialectic between what one first takes oneself to be (most often dictated by culture's mannered possibilities) and the desire to not be what one consequently is not. The reference of the question of correctness goes to the individual user, the designer, the artist who transforms the language through a particular use: morphosis, derivative forms, but with a difference. Turning to his own example, Wittgenstein continues:

> An old style can be translated, as it were, into a newer language; it can, one might say, be performed afresh at a tempo appropriate to our own times. To do this is really only to reproduce. That is what my building work amounted to.
>
> But what I mean is not giving an old style a fresh trim. No, you are really speaking the old language, perhaps without realizing it, but you are

> speaking it in a way that is appropriate to the modern world, without on that account necessarily being in accordance with its taste. (*C & V*, 60)

Wittgenstein's house, then, is a translation, a reproduction of an old style in a newer language adjusted more to the times. The metaphor is musical interpretation: performance, tempo. "[A]ppropriate to the times" in this case entails precisely one's ear. Wittgenstein's recanting, then, challenges ears and taste to new uses of language, uses which seek not universal reserves, but personal identities, not an expressivity, but the transformational possibilities of what was to become philosophy's therapeutic identity. One is still speaking the old language, appropriateness survives, but without that speaking necessarily accorded the standards of taste. One language is not translated into another language, according to Wittgenstein, rather the language is made to render new forms, new uses, new capabilities.[39] And not giving the house "fresh trim," enhancing the details, but formal, structural shifts that alter the language games themselves. As if there might be a doubt about this important shift in Wittgenstein, the series ends with the following aphorism, which addresses tolerance and our inability to know what drives a society, the laws of its development.

> A man reacts *like this*: he says "No, I *won't* tolerate that!"—and resists it. Perhaps this brings about an equally intolerable situation and perhaps by then strength for any further revolt is exhausted. People say: "If *he* hadn't done *that*, the evil would have been avoided." But what justifies this? Who knows the laws according to which society develops. I am quite sure they are a closed book even to the cleverest of men. If you fight, you fight. If you hope, you hope.
>
> You can fight, hope and even believe without believing *scientifically*. (*C & V*, 60)

A scientific approach to the question of laws cannot be justified. Wittgenstein simply leaves us to fight, to hope, to believe, that is, to improvise changes in the language, to modify one's use and consequently oneself. The structure of these modifications, its modes of creativity must always remain indistinct, unknown to its practitioner, just as the very language so retained, in avoiding mere translation, its naive sense, most often becomes hidden behind these changes.

VI.

So in contrast to the skepticism of the transitional work of the *Philosophical Remarks;* Wittgenstein by 1947 holds that such depiction is a problem of style: "to invent a style of painting capable of depicting what is, in this way, fuzzy" (*C & V*, 68). Borrowing from the example of the painter, this would be a style, of line, form, and color, which can represent the richness of detail within the borders of a contingent frame without recourse to architectonic composition. As Wittgenstein had already confessed in 1931 in an aphorism: "I really do think with my pen, because my head often knows nothing about what my hand is writing" (*C & V*, 17). The possibilities of thinking, limits again, are traced out initially in a writing, or a drawing, that comes to reflectively recognize its own style, and this style must resist the temptation to fill itself out in a self-possessed meaning or significance.

The *Philosophical Remarks'* problem of the drawing-board, and of language in general, as to representing phenomena, the constructions by which such representations are projected, recalls one particular drawing in the Morphosis exhibit for "Venice III, a composite really, depicting the puzzling reactions, for architecture, between models, artistic renderings, plan and elevations, cross-sections, axonometrics, exploded views, and the working blueprints (see Figure 1). The exploded view, seen as an abstracted model sitting on its base with the blueprints draped underneath and across the edge, is projected against a grey wall upon which is already attached with stick pins the artistic rendering, all of this aligned by the grid of fiducials, which show their displacement by a shadow. When one looks closely a model is to be found in the rendering sitting upon a table, the image of which is captured in a mirror conveniently leaning against the nearest wall. Morphosis, again in keeping with their name, asks us to question the congruence of these modes of representation by which the project is defined and not the building. The picture is puzzling, and the final document of the project, which testifies to the building's adherence to the codes (the only drawing that requires signature), the working drawings, themselves blueprints, never originals, are blurred. Morphosis places these drawings, upon which the building according to its method of construction is based, closest to our eye, in the foreground, but indecipherably blurred.

In response to the difficulties of the Euclidean drawing-board ("translating the 'blurredness' of phenomena into an impression in the drawing"), Morphosis's drawing depicts the uncertain displacements by which each mode of representation affects the other in the process of the project, continuing through the construction phase (the exploded axonometric here representing the building process, during which the blueprints are given interpretation). Morphosis's work, in fact, takes Wittgenstein's difficulty regarding the drawing-board, the place of design, quite seriously, returning to it after the project has been completed in hopes of bringing the finished structure in closer dialogue with the design phase, seeking at once both a better means of depicting the inherent fuzziness of the architectural project and the direction and limitations of a firm's manner and style of working.[40]

Wittgenstein himself addressed this specific difficulty again in more architecturally explicit terms six years after the *Philosophical Remarks*, an extended note from the *Nachlass* appended to the text of the *Philosophical Grammar*. Here the use of the blueprint provides the focus for the difficulties of representation, i.e., the linking of thought and reality. Quoting at length:

> What gives us the idea that there is a kind of agreement between thought and reality?—Instead of "agreement" here one might say with a clear conscience "pictorial character."
>
> But is this pictorial character an agreement? In the *Tractatus Logico-philosophicus* I said something like: it is an agreement of form. But that is an error.
>
> First of all, "picture" here is ambiguous. One wants to say that an order is the picture of the action which was carried out on the order; but also, a picture of the action which *is to be* carried out as an order.
>
> We may say: a blueprint *serves as a picture* of the object which the workman is to make from it.
>
> And here we might call the way in which the workman turns such a drawing into an artefact "the method of projection." We might now express ourselves thus: the method of projection mediates between the drawing and the object, it reaches from the drawing to the artefact. Here we are comparing the method of projection with projection lines which go from one figure to another. But if the method of projection is a bridge, it is a bridge which isn't built until the application is made. This comparison conceals the fact that the picture plus the projection lines leaves open various methods of application; it makes it look as if what is depicted, even if it does not exist in fact, is determined by the picture and the projection lines in an ethereal manner; every bit is determined, that is to say, as if it did exist. (It is "determined give or take a yes or no.") In that case what we may call "picture" is the blueprint plus the method of its application. And we now imagine the method as something which is attached to the blueprint whether or not it is used. (One can "*describe*" an application even if it doesn't exist.)
>
> Now I would like to ask "How can the blueprint be used as a representation, unless there is already an agreement with what is to be made?"—But what does that mean? Well, perhaps this: how could I play the notes in the score on the piano if they didn't already have a relationship to particular types of movement of the hand? Of course such a relationship *sometimes* consists in a certain agreement, but sometimes not in any agreement, but merely in our having learnt to apply the signs in a particular way. What the comparison between the method of projection and the projection lines

> connecting the picture with the object does is to make all these cases alike—because *that* is what attracts us. You may say: I count the projection lines as part of the picture—but not the method of projection.
>
> You may of course also say: I count a *description* of a method of projection as part of the picture.
>
> So I am imagining that the difference between propositions and reality is ironed out by the lines of projection belonging to the picture, the thought, and that no further room is left for a method of application, but only for agreement and disagreement. (*PG*, 212)

Placing Morphosis's drawing opposite this remark suggests that indeed Wittgenstein is imagining things when it comes to "ironing out" the differences between propositions and reality. Locating the "lines of projection" of an efficient analytic geometry between the elements of Morphosis's drawing is not self-evident. Expressed is precisely the lack of congruence and the difficulty of translation between the three modes of representation used in architecture. Of course, following a strategy that Wittgenstein makes legend in the *Investigations*, we can read his lesson as oriented by the assumption that buildings are indeed constructed from such blueprints. In other words, that which stands to be learned from Wittgenstein's examples regards the inherent puzzles of how we come to see our methods of representation when we set them aside from their use.[41] This is why Wittgenstein emphasizes from the start the picture's futural projection: "a picture of the action which is to be carried out as an order." Blueprints, then, are performatives, borrowing Austin's terminology. Yet Morphosis's picture, their practice, is made and used after the construction phase, indicating not a performative but representing a completed performance, questioning in turn both the lines and methods of projection as they were implied by the drawing stage. To speak of "agreement" between the blueprint and the artefact is precisely the attractive simplification that Morphosis challenges in their practice, looking back to the drawings precisely to locate the manner of morphosis or departure occasioned inevitably by construction. Wittgenstein's suggestion that agreement can be located in "having learnt to apply the signs in a particular way" is deconstructed by an architecture that designs according to a grammar operating upon the contingent material signifier. Morphosis's practice deconstructs the conventional agreements and protocols that seek to hold together expression and content, the regional building codes prescribing only a small part of the required linkages of signs. Morphosis demythologizes the architectural plan, the project that locates a future in the representational present. Wittgenstein's analysis here, in the mid-thirties, can be seen falling to the temptation to simplify that he comes to resist only a few years later in the *Investigations*:

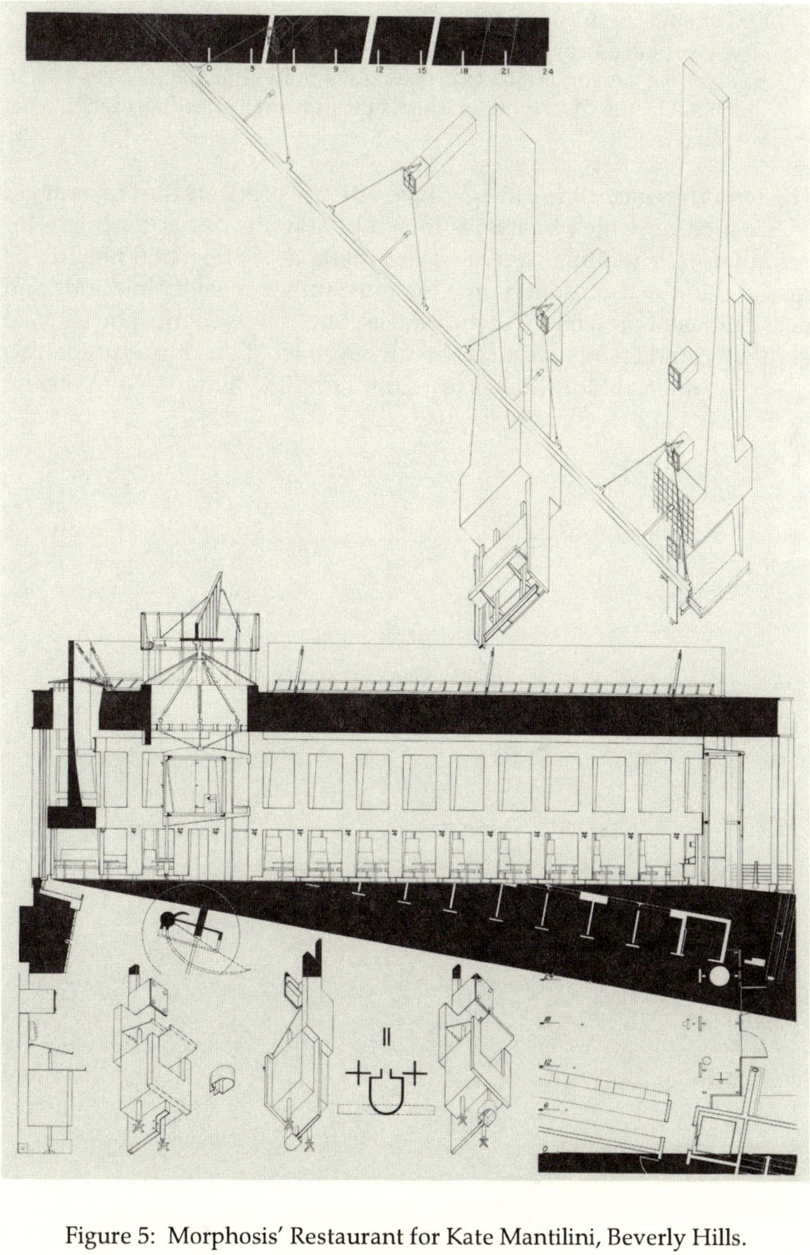

Figure 5: Morphosis' Restaurant for Kate Mantilini, Beverly Hills.
(Courtesy of *Morphosis*)

> One might say that the concept "game" is a concept with blurred edges. "But is a blurred concept a concept at all?"-Is an indistinct photograph a picture of a person at all? Is it even always an advantage to replace an indistinct picture by a sharp one? Isn't the indistinct one often exactly what we need? (*PI*, 71)[42]

The wrinkles that he imagines "ironed out" are precisely the blurredness of the picture, which he comes to accept and view as appropriate for certain uses. The projection lines and method of projection needn't be resolved in the representation. One must rather speak of methods and possibilities of projection, of morphosis. Such a lesson must be learned gradually, and I really didn't see it fully until I had the opportunity for a leisurely lunch at Morphosis's restaurant for Kate Mantilini on Wilshire in Beverly Hills (see Figure 5).

6

Nietzsche's Trees—And Where They Grow

Eva Geulen

Da stieg ein Baum. O reine Übersteigung!
[There rose a tree. O pure transcendence!]

(R. M. Rilke)

Ich stieg eine Böschung hinan und legte mich unter einen Baum. Der Baum war eine Pappel oder eine Erle. Warum ich seine Gattung nicht behalten habe? Weil, während ich ins Laubwerk sah und seiner Bewegung folgte, mit einmal in mir die Sprache dergestalt von ihm ergriffen wurde, daß sie augenblicklich die uralte Vermählung mit dem Baum in meinem Beisein noch einmal vollzog. [. . .] Ein leiser Wind spielte zur Hochzeit auf und trug alsbald die schnell entsprossenen Kinder dieses Betts als Bilderrede unter alle Welt.

[I climbed a slope and lied down under a tree. The tree was a poplar or an alder. Why I do not remember its kind? Because, while looking up into the foliage and following its movements, the language in me was seized by the tree in such a way that it instantaneously performed the age-old marriage with the tree once again. [. . .] A quiet wind played for the wedding and soon it carried the quickly born children of this bridal bed as image-discourse into the world.]

(W. Benjamin)

für e.

I.

The original title cover of Descartes' *Discourse on Method* (1637) bears a printer's mark depicting a man who digs up the ground to plant a tree. In his *Principles of Philosophy* (1644) Descartes explains what the tree is to philosophy:

> Thus the whole of philosophy is like a tree. The roots are metaphysics, the trunk is physics and the branches emerging from the trunk are all the other sciences [. . .].[1]

As one of the most generic philosophical images, the tree has weathered historical changes with the proverbial endurance and persistence of its species. Thus philosophy's trees certainly belong to those metaphors of which Nietzsche famously remarked that we have forgotten their metaphorical status long ago.[2] Indeed, so deeply rooted is the tree imagery, even in everyday language, so widely do its implications for thought and knowledge branch out, that any attempt to fully exfoliate its signifying possiblities in order to determine the extent to which all knowledge is perhaps rooted in the tree would quickly find itself at a proverbial—or better, arboreal—end: One no longer sees the forest for all the trees, which is to say, the wealth of available material, the ubiquitous presence of trees in philosophical discourse has already undermined the stability and specificity that an analysis of a particular instance of tree-imagery would require. Yet these empirical difficulties of an account of philosophical trees reflect back on the tree's very function in philosophy. To the extent that the tree signifies philosophy's claim to unity, systematicity, and totality in general, the more fundamental question must be raised if the very project of a continuous, systematic, and, ideally, exhaustive account of all trees could even hope to escape the all-encompassing shadow cast by the tree's image. Whether with the intent of systematizing the forest of philosophical trees or along the lines of a genealogical account (as a family tree of the tree), all methods of subjecting the tree to an order or a system will inevitably remain within the realm of thought delimited by the very tree itself. The universal validity of trees is intrinsically related to the claims to universality represented by the tree.

That the philosophical tree is indeed not one image among others in philosophy but philosophy's preferred image of itself, its claims, intentions, and self-understanding is evident even in those cases where the tree appears in the seemingly less pretentious fashion of a marginal example. In one of his essays on technology, and thus in a context where the tree must seem particularly archaic or anachronistic, Martin Heidegger refers to trees in order to illustrate that metaphysical thinking of essence which his own thought attempts to break away from:

> In the academic language of philosophy, 'essence' is *what* something is, in Latin *quid*. *Quidditas*, whatness, provides the answer to the question concerning essence. For example, what pertains to all kinds of trees—oaks, beeches, birches, firs—is the same treeness. Under this inclusive genus—the 'universal'—fall all real and possible trees.[3]

Heidegger, who was probably aware of trees in the philosophical tradition, selected the 'tree' as a telling emblem of the traditional understanding of essence: The tree is never just *a* tree but always *the* tree, the generic tree, the genus and the genre of philosophy proper—or at least of academic philosophy, as Heidegger hastens to add.

For this very reason, the tree—whose history would only be another tree—also does not lend itself easily to "metaphorology" in the sense developed by Hans Blumenberg's studies on the role of metaphors in philosophical discourse. The persistency, essential selfsameness and universality of the tree across philosophical schools and changing times seems to defy metaphorology's interest in the reinscriptions and transformations of metaphors. Though the tree is not an object of investigation in Blumenberg's work, it is no surprise to learn that a tree should figure as the metaphor of metaphorology itself. In the case of Blumenberg, the tree attests to its special status precisely where it functions as the metaphor of metaphorology's meta-theory.[4]

Whether the tree symbolizes the unity of part and whole as in Descartes or demarcates the life-worldly origins of metaphor as in Blumenberg, the tree has aspired to a meta-theoretical status throughout the tradition. Thus, it is all the more important to point out another equally persistent dimension of philosophical tree imagery. There always seem to exist at least two different and even opposed trees. The effects of the sharp line drawn in the biblical description of the paradisiacal garden between the Tree of Life and the Tree of Knowledge are palpable throughout the tradition. Already Augustine speculated on the two trees and their relationship when he rendered the course of sacred history as the movement from one tree to the other, from the Tree of the Knowledge of Good and Evil to the Tree of Life symbolized by Christ on the wooden Cross.[5] The opposition of these two trees continued to be important; Given that a tree originally marks a site of seduction and stands, so to speak, at the beginning of shame and sexuality, it is not surprising to find that the opposition of the two trees often appears to be associated with gender differences and sexual union.[6]

II

Before Descartes planted his tree of philosophy, the trees of knowledge functioned primarily as a mnemotechnical device, a place system for locating data. In this context, the tree is of equal significance as the other two cosmological images: the Great Chain of Being[7] and Jacob's Ladder.[8] Among the many trees of cosmical unity in medieval texts, the Arbor Scientiae of Ramon Lull merits special attention for its unusually complex structure and innovative features. Influenced by cabalistic meditations based on numerical and letter syntheses, the Spanish philosopher developed the tree as a combinatory system. In his tree, the strictly theological aspects of the cosmic tree (represented by the Divine names that form the basis of his chart) are linked to a cosmological and elemental basis. This double foundation of his tree led Lull to argue that his logic was more "natural" and thus superior to the dominant scholastic variant.[9]

But only in Descartes is the theological hierarchy implied and posited by the tree radically displaced. In his philosophy the purely systematizing function of the tree recedes into the background and a new conceptualization of hierarchy emerges. It is no longer based on either cosmological order or theological considerations but rests on the foundational principles of human knowledge. A little later, due to the influence of British Sensualism, Locke in particular, the French Encyclopedists' tree of knowledge evidences their desire for ordering newly founded disciplines and of presenting the new data in a systematic fashion. Descartes' rather static tree is replaced by a tree designed to allow for the integration of new and previously unexpected material. To a certain extent, the tree becomes once more a mnemotechnical device in the hands of the philosopher who surveys the growth of knowledge. In the *Preliminary Discourse* concerning the Encyclopedia of 1751, d'Alembert speaks of

> placing the philosopher at the vantage point, so to speak, high above this vast labyrinth, whence he can perceive the principal sciences and arts simultaneously [. . .] It is a kind of world map which is to show the principle countries, their position and their mutual dependence, the road that leads directly from one to the other. This road is often cut by a thousand obstacles, which are known in each country only to the inhabitants or to travelers, and which cannot be represented except in individual, highly detailed

> maps. These individual maps will be the different articles of the *Encyclopedia* and the Tree or Systematic chart will be its world map.[10]

Of the three old images, the Great Chain of Being, Jacob's Ladder and the Tree, only the tree could adjust to the changed philosophical landscape. By virtue of being a naturally growing organism, it alone was able to accommodate the newly emerging temporal index of knowledge. The threat of an ever-growing mass of new data that would eventually outgrow the systems designed to accommodate them was answered by the increasing temporalization of knowledge which culminated in Darwin's theory of evolution.[11]

Given its formal character and transcendental scope, Kant's philosophy would not appear to have room for any such trees. Since his interest lies neither in the systematization nor in the hierarchization of data or principles but rather in accounting for the conditions of their possibility, he wishes to postpone any tree planting until such time as the grounds are ready for trees, grounds which currently bear neither fruit nor trees. In the preface to the *Critique of Pure Reason* Kant casts himself as the gardener of philosophy whose task it is "to clear and level totally overgrown grounds".[12] As it turns out, the cleared grounds will never be suitable for trees of knowledge in the older sense of the early enlightenment because the conditions of possibility of philosophy turn out to be such that there are only "two stems" [or "trunks" which is the other meaning of the German *Stämme*], "of knowledge, namely *sensibility* and *understanding*, which perhaps spring from a common, but to us unknown root."[13] Kant's successful gardening procedures uproot the tree of knowledge before it can be planted. The price for having anchored human knowledge in the transcendental principles is the impossibility of philosophy ever existing as one whole, which is to say, the impossibility of philosophy's existence as the tree. For Descartes, the tree was a simile corresponding in all respects to philosophy, and for the Encylopedists, it was a mnemotechnical chart or, in their own words, a world map. Kant, however, reduces the tree to a metaphor in the proper sense: nothing is left of the majestic tree but a truncated simile, that is—a metaphor.

This truncated nature of Kantian philosophy, presumably scared by an intrinsic dualism or a 'gap,' became the focal point of post-Kantian speculative idealism up to and including Hegel. The German Idealists, most strikingly and most convincingly Hegel, sought to restore the whole of the tree. The emergence of decidedly organicistic and historicizing thought allowed for this reappropriation of the tree imagery. Already in the philosophical and literary work preceding Kant's Copernican revolution, the static tree of knowledge had begun to exhibit increasingly dynamic qualities. The theoretical texts of the so-called Storm and Stress

Period are a particularly rich source of this tree interpretation. Among the initiators of these new tree metaphors belongs, for example, Johann Gottfried Herder whose prose is often literally overgrown by entire thickets of trees. One of many examples of the affinity between the tree and the new method of a genetic and historical approach can be found in Herder's *Auch eine Philosophie der Geschichte* [Also a Philosophy of History] in which the "eternal tree- and patriarch life" is cast as a necessary condition "to root and ground humanity in its first tendencies and institutions."[14] Thus the trees come to signify how this original state is preserved and developed throughout the course of history:

> All around hundreds of young blossoming trees, a beautiful forest of posterity and eternity. But see, the old cedar tree continues to blossom and it carries the whole young forest with the sap and strength of its roots.[15]

The tree increasingly comes to signify the desire for a unity in which systematicity and organic development are no longer separated. In the same vein, Fichte in his *Wissenschaftslehre* describes the originary unity and synthetic nature of consciousness by opposing the organic power of a tree to its various parts such as blossoms, trunk and roots:

> Thus the *Wißenschaftslehre* is organic and discursive. It contains only syntheses. The present synthesis is the fundamental one in which discursive thought first develops. The tree, for example, consists in an organic energy and not in blossom, bark, stem. Thus it is here with consciousness. Thinking in time [. . .] is not the innermost of consciousness. It is, so to speak, only leaves, blossoms and fruit; the innermost is originally one.[16]

Hegel finally achieved the systematic unfolding of this original unity, which in his eyes had remained purely posited in Fichte's philosophy. In his early writings on Christianity, Hegel describes the nature of the philosophical concept in the following manner:

> The concept constitutes the beginning in philosophical treatment too. But here it is the substance of the thing, like the seed from which the whole tree unfolds. The seed contains all of its characteristics, the entire nature of the tree: the type of sap, the pattern of its branches etc. However, these are not preformed, so that if one took a microscope, one would see the twigs and the leaves in miniature, but they are instead enveloped in a spiritual manner [. . .]. This enveloped being of the tree's nature, this simple seed is the product or result of the entire life of this tree.[17]

Hegel's tree-seed is the beginning that is the "Aufhebung" of all trees in philosophy and the "Aufhebung" of the tree itself.

There is one notable exception to this dominant function of the tree in post-Kantian thought. It is all the more remarkable since it anticipates to a certain degree Nietzsche's powerful rewriting of the tree's tradition: Johann Georg Hamann was one of the very first to respond to the publication of Kant's *Critique* when he published a brief review, entitled *Metakritik*, in 1784. In Hamann's short and enigmatic text, the tree appears for the first time not as an image of philosophy but explicitly as an indication of philosophy's precarious relationship to tropological language in general and metaphoricity in particular. In these few pages, for the most part an ingenious montage of quotations from Kant, Hamann takes up the metaphorical residue of the two trunks of knowledge in the context of his thematization of the eclipse of language in Kant's project. Kant's philosophy, Hamann argues, presumes what can never exist, a universally valid language which remains unaffected by and distinct from its designations. Kant could convince himself of having "solved reason's misunderstanding with itself"[18] because he based his solution on the purification of reason from language—the subtitle of Hamann's review is "purismum of reason"—: "The third, the highest and so to speak empirical Purismum concerns language, the first and last organon and criterion of reason, without any credit other than tradition and usum."[19] This last, the Kantian purification is, according to Hamann, not only illegitimate but, at the source, it is doubly impure: "Receptivity of language and spontaneity of concepts! From this double source of ambiguity pure reason draws all elements of its dogmatism, its dubious desire to doubt [. . .]."[20] Because words have, according to Hamann, logical *and* aesthetic faculties, language must remain the site of reason's self-misunderstanding. Hamann argues for the "genealogical priority of language before the seven sacred functions of logical propositions and conclusions."[21] In the presentation of these arguments, Hamann not only plays with the prefix -meta, as in metaphor and metaphysics, but he also rewrites the two Kantian stems of knowledge:

> If "sensibilitys" and "understanding" are the two stems of the one root of human knowledge [. . .] why is there need for such a violent, illegitimate and stubborn separation of what nature has united. Will not both trunks whither from the dichotomy at their common root? Is not one single trunk with two roots, one upper in the air and one lower in the earth, a more appropriate image of our knowledge?"[22]

A strictly theological reading of this passage, based on the notion of God's condescendence (with which Hamann was very familiar), and the ensuing double nature of humanity which participates in both the transcendent and the earthly sphere, will not suffice here. Insofar as Hamann displaces the hierarchy of root and trunk, he emphasizes the moments of noncorrespondence. In contradistinction to his contemporaries, Hamann obviously has no intention of reconciling what Kant has split apart. Quite on the contrary, he locates the contradiction at and as the root itself. Once the root has been doubled, so that it extends into two different and contradictory directions, it no longer corresponds to itself and the concept of root as origin ceases to be self-identical.

While Hegel can be said to have solved the contradictions by dissolving them into the law of dialectics, it is Nietzsche, as the philosopher of style and language in many ways akin to Hamann, who begins where Hamann left off. In a passage of *Thus spoke Zarathustra* entitled "The Tree at the Mountain," the growth of the roots upward and downward into depths of evil are two necessary and self-contradictory factors of self-knowledge: "— Aber es ist mit dem Menschen wie mit dem Baume. Je mehr er hinauf die die Höhe und Helle will, um so stärker streben seine Wurzeln erdwärts, abwärts . . . [— But it is with humans as with the tree. The more they strive towards height and light, the stronger their roots strive towards the earth, downward . . .]" (IV, 51).

III

It has become a tradition by now to mark the breakdown of all claims to totality and universality by Nietzsche's thought of language and his radical problematization of subjectivity. Accordingly, a naive understanding of Nietzsche's revolutionizing thinking would have to assume the total absence of an image as overdetermined as the tree by the very tradition Nietzsche criticizes. And even a more sophisticated acknowledgement of the tree as an image of genealogy would still have to demonstrate the impossible, namely that the genealogical tree is entirely free from all organicistic overtones.

As used by Nietzsche, the tree undeniably points to a qualitatively new and different type of unity, distinct from and critical of systematicity and organicism alike. Radical genealogy no longer takes recourse to the root as primary origin but instead it excavates or traces the various stages of concepts such as origin, totality, or identity. Nothing has its origin in itself and all origins are other than what became. That is why Nietzsche can sum up his genealogical inquiry into the roots of the phenomenon of the *intellectuales Gewissen* [intellectual conscience] with the words: "So ist auch hier etwas Moralisches höchster Gattung aus einer Schwarzwurzel herausgeblüht. [Thus here too something moral of the highest kind has blossomed forth from a black root]" (II,391). These kinds of roots are not to be mistaken for historical origins. Rather history as the sort of historicism practiced by his contemporaries is described by Nietzsche as a "metaphysischer Nachtrieb [a late branch of metaphysics]."[23]

On several occasions, Nietzsche refers to the study of a tree's "Jahresringe [annual rings]" (II,244) as a model of understanding historically constructed phenomena. In short, the manner of a tree's growth cannot be determined on the basis of its roots but it has to be read off the *Jahresringe*. Their exposure always requires the scission that destroys the tree in question.

The law of evolution, according to which nature makes no jumps, prescribes also the philosopher's task as genealogist who subjects all claims to stable concepts and truths to a rigorous critique which demonstrates they *are* not but have become:

> Wenn der Mensch sich noch so stark fortentwickelt und aus einem Gegensatz in den anderen überzuspringen scheint: bei genaueren Beobachtungen wird man doch die *Verzahnungen* auffinden, wo das neue Gebäude aus dem älteren herauswächst. Diess ist die Aufgabe des Biographen: er muss nach dem Grundsatze über das Leben denken, dass keine Natur Sprünge macht.
>
> [However strongly humans develop and appear to jump from one contradiction to the next: more precise observation will reveal the *links* where the new edifice has grown out of the new. Such is the task of the biographer: he has to think about life according to the maxim that no nature makes jumps]" (II, 640).

For Nietzsche, there can be no mutually exclusive oppositions, only gradual differences. Opposites come into existence only on the basis of neglecting those differences.

But one constitutive opposition seems to be exempt from this rule, the undeniable opposition between Nietzsche's genealogy and the biologistic tendencies that often function as a last resort where thought fails, or, in other words, the opposition between the tree of knowledge and the tree of life. In this sense, the tree would be the site where Nietzsche's organicism lingers. But this would be the case only if Nietzsche had indeed maintained the incompatibility of life and knowledge so that the tree as the image shared by both could be understood as the indicator of their secret complicity. Yet life and knowledge are by no means linked by the tree alone. Since the *Birth of Tragedy,* Nietzsche has been working with the notion of *terrible truth.* The amount of truth someone can afford to bear is proportionately related to the strength of life. All truth, all knowledge threatens life. Under the dead knowledge of historicism, for example, life withers. The economy of strength and weakness that structures Nietzsche's concept of life—although strictly speaking it is not a concept but rather the determining borderline of all conceptuality, which does not itself ever become a concept—is frequently associated with trees:

> Prüfet das Leben der besten und fruchtbarsten Menschen und Völker und fragt euch, ob ein Baum, der stolz in die Höhe wachsen soll, des schlechten Wetters und der Stürme entbehren könnte [. . .]. Das Gift, an dem die schwächere Natur zu Grunde geht, ist für den Starken Stärkung - und er nennt es auch nicht Gift.
>
> [Examine the lives of the best and most fertile humans and peoples and ask yourselves, whether a tree that wants to grow proudly upward could do without bad weather and the storms [. . .]. The poison which brings down the weaker gives strength to the strong—and he does not call it poison, either] (III, 390).

Given the interdependency of life and knowledge, the tree is obviously not simply the last troublesome remainder of biologism in Nietzsche's thought. Instead, the necessary interrelation of the two trees is accounted for by nothing other than the tree itself which is capable of signifying a necessary yet contradictory and ultimately unresolvable, antagonistic relationship. In a reflection on radical evil, Nietzsche proposes that we should, for the sake of argument, try to think man as radically evil. Radically thinking radical evil means to think the root of the root—radical comes from the latin *radix* = root —. Nietzsche quickly adds that the assumption of radical evil is just as false as its opposite, radical good, but he insists on the necessity of thinking the root because "ihre Wurzeln haben sich bis in uns und unsere Zeit verästet [the roots have branched out into us and our time]" (II,75). That the roots are not only present but we ourselves are the roots points to the fundamental problem of genealogy: the impossibility of assuming a standpoint outside, beyond, or in any other way distinct from what it investigates. The tree of knowledge can never be distinguished from the tree of life because we are ourselves the branches. No knowledge of roots is itself without roots. Nietzsche's genealogy does not stop short of the subject of such inquiry; the genealogical truth is subject to the same law of genealogy: which is to say, we *are not* but we *became* and we are still becoming. No concept, no image can endure because "im Werdenden kann sich ein Werdendes nicht als fest und dauernd, nicht als ein "Das" spiegeln [in what is becoming cannot something that is (itself) becoming cannot reflect itself as stable and enduring, cannot reflect itself as a "that"]" (II,387). Any stable antagonism between life and knowledge is thus revealed as inappropriate by the very tree that is not only an image of becoming, but, by virtue of its different manifestations in Nietzsche and in the philosophical tradition, it also accounts for the becoming of images. The tree would then be one of the meta-metaphors of metaphoricity as that mode of articulation which has given up the claims to universality and instead bespeaks its own becoming in form of metaphorical chains. And indeed, Nietzsche's theory of metaphoricity as the human drive produce metaphors as elaborated in *On Good and Evil in an extramoral sense* is very much informed by the metaphorical register of drives/branches.[24] His example of conceptualization on the basis of metaphorical leaps is, of course, a leaf.[25]

And yet: even if the contradictory directions of the tree imagery are philosophically relevant in light of the problem of subjectivity and the law of becoming, then why does Nietzsche insist, over and over again, that knowledge is never life, life never knowledge? Why does he quote Byron with such enthusiasm: "the tree of knowledge is not that of life" (II,108)? And on another occasion he writes under the heading *Vom Baum der Erkenntnis* [Of the Tree of Knowledge]:

> Wahrscheinlichkeit, aber keine Wahrheit: Freischeinlichkeit, aber keine Freiheit, - diese beiden Früchte sind es, derentwegen der Baum der Erkenntnis nicht mit dem Baum des Lebens verwechselt werden kann"
>
> [The appearance of truth, but no truth, the appearance of freedom but no freedom. It is because of these two fruits that the tree of knowledge can never be mistaken for the tree of life] (II, 540.)

While the *Schein*-character of all fruits of knowledge is obvious, it is less obvious why this should be the reason for the impossibility of ever mistaking one tree for the other. Is the true life, after all and in the final instance, indeed the one and only, the whole truth? Nietzsche gives an answer under the heading *Wir Unverständlichen* [We the Ununderstandables]:

> Man verwechselt uns—das macht, wir selbst wachsen, wir wechseln fortwährend, wir stossen alte Rinden ab, wir häuten uns mit jedem Frühjahre noch, wir werden immer jünger, zukünftiger, höher, stärker, wir treiben unsre Wurzeln immer mächtiger in die Tiefe - in's Böse, während wir zugleich den Himmel immer liebevoller, immer breiter umarmen und sein Licht immer durstiger mit allen unsren Zweigen in uns hineinsaugen. Wir wachsen wie Bäume—das ist schwer zu verstehen wie alles Leben! - nicht an Einer Stelle, sondern überall, nicht in Einer Richtung, sondern ebenso hinauf, hinaus wie hinein und hinunter, - unsre Kraft treibt zugleich in Stamm, Aesten und Wurzeln, es steht uns gar nicht mehr frei, etwas Einzelnes noch zu *sein*.

> [One mistakes us (*verwechselt*). That is because we change (*wechseln*) constantly, we grow (*wachsen*), we shed old barks, we still shed our skins every spring, we become ever more younger, become more becoming, become higher, stronger, we drive our roots ever more powerful into the depth,—evil, while we also embrace the sky ever more lovingly and more broadly and suck in its light ever more thirstily with all of our branches. We grow like trees—that is difficult to understand like all life! - not in one place, but all over, not in one direction, but upward and downward as much as in and out - our strength sprouts simultaneously in trunk, branches and roots, we are no longer free *to be* something singular] (III, 623).

The reason why the tree of life cannot be mistaken for the tree of knowledge is that both are constantly becoming, displacing, replacing each other so rapidly that neither of them ever remains in the same position long enough to be mistaken for the other. The tree is not our image because we are the tree. If we are the tree, the tree is itself not an image, not a metaphor but it marks the impossibility of ever arresting the movement of metaphorical displacement. Thus Nietzsche can describe the philosopher as the curious researcher who wanders among people as if they were trees "und [er] nimmt sich selber als ein Phänomen wahr, welches nur seinen erkennenden Trieb stark anregt [and he perceives himself as a phenomenon which strongly excites his drive for knowledge]" (II, 210).

The tree *is not*, it is becoming. Under the section *Der Baum der Menschheit und die Vernunft* [The tree of humanity and reason], Nietzsche writes:

> die Menschheit soll einmal ein Baum werden, der die ganze Erde überschattet, mit vielen Millarden von Blüthen, die alle neben einander Früchte werden sollen [. . .]. Die Aufgabe ist unsäglich gross und kühn: wir Alle wollen dazu thun, dass dieser Baum nicht vor der Zeit verfaule! [. . .] Wir müssen vielmehr der grossen Aufgabe *in's Gesicht sehen*, die Erde für ein Gewächs der grössten und freudigsten Fruchtbarkeit *vorzubereiten*, - eine Aufgabe der Vernunft für die Vernunft!
>
> [Humanity shall one day become a tree that gives shadow to the whole earth, with billions of blossoms which shall all become fruits next to each other [. . .]. The task is unspeakably large and daring: we all want to contribute that the tree does not decay before its time! [. . .] Rather we have to *face* the large task, to *prepare* this plant for the greatest and most joyful fertility, - a task of reason for reason!] (II, 636).

But who we? We trees.

7

A Misreading of Maps: The Politics of Cartography in Marxism and Poststructuralism

Bruno Bosteels

The following considerations regarding the omnipresence of "cartography" in contemporary critical and theoretical discourse might be read in contrast with a passage from Cervantes in which Don Quixote radically opposes the recourse of maps. Only the "courtiers," or *caballeros andantes* of the Court, says Don Quixote, travel all over the earth merely by looking at a map, whereas the "real" errant knights, who are exposed night and day to the inclemencies of the weather, take the measure of the entire globe with their feet without looking at *niñerías* or childish trifles.[1] Closer to Quixote's courtier, in this respect, than to the real errant knight, critical and theoretical discourses today hardly "trifle" with cartography; the concept of the "map" and the process of "mapping" contemporary—modern or postmodern—intellectual history on the contrary meet with increasingly enthusiastic approval.

What thus currently seems to be taking place in some of the most fertile fields of literary, cultural, and philosophical studies is a gradual yet thorough displacement from text to territory.[2] Abandoning the rhetoric of temporality, critical and theoretical inquiries today are increasingly moving toward the politics of spatiality.[3] From a textual analysis of "writing" modeled upon the ontological analysis of "being" (i.e., upon the "event" of temporality, in the Heideggerian sense), the emphasis is shifting toward the cultural study of literary, artistic, and ideological forms of "mapping" (i.e., toward the "locus" of an event, to use Michel Foucault's expression).[4] Opening a recent new series of books called "Mapping" with a collection of representative articles under the title

Mapping Ideology is in this sense a significant and almost redundant gesture, typical of the current cartographic turn.[5]

Less recent examples of this trend include "Mapping the Postmodern," in which Andreas Huyssen describes how he will "simply start from the *Selbstverständnis* of the postmodern as it has shaped various discourses since the 1960s" so as to provide "something like a large-scale map of the postmodern."[6] A similar project receives a more theoretical and political treatment in Fredric Jameson's celebrated essay "Postmodernism, or The Cultural Logic of Late Capitalism." Pleading ardently for "an aesthetic of *cognitive mapping*" in an effort to surmount our present inability "to map the great global multinational and decentered communicational network in which we find ourselves caught as individual subjects," Jameson concludes that "the political form of postmodernism, if there is any, will have as its vocation the invention and projection of a global cognitive mapping, on a social as well as a spatial scale."[7]

In the short article "Mapping the European Mind" a literary critic presents an equally ambitious project that involves no less than a definition of "Europeanness," for which the author pulls out of his high hat "neither a chronology nor an atlas, but a mapping out of major symbolic landmarks," fulfilling his quest for "places of European consciousness in the 1990s, places that are grounded historically and have modern or postmodern aura."[8] In Europe itself, then, a group of scholars proposes to counter the growing fragmentation of intellectual life with the projection of global "maps" or "world-pictures" that would be "comparable to the work performed by cartographers in Antiquity and the Middle Ages."[9] To compose an "atlas," on the other hand, is the aim of a French philosopher who thus justifies his latest book, which includes a summary of his entire work, as a full-blown cartographic project.[10]

There would be virtually no end to a list of every artist, literary critic, critical theorist, art historian, sociologist, or philosopher who globally or locally "maps out" the contemporary cultural landscape. Instead of merely continuing this enumeration, however, I shall situate the debate within a larger theoretical and political context to interpret the ascendancy of the cartographic metaphor as one instance of a wider cultural phenomenon. What I particularly wish to study is neither the increased interest in maps appearing in literary and artistic works—from Thomas More to Italo Calvino to Mahasweka Devi and from *La Carte du Tendre* to Jasper Johns to Guillermo Kuitca—nor the tiresome use of the term "mapping" as a mere synonym for "describing," but, rather, the explicit interpretation of cartography as an exemplary cultural activity with a seemingly intrinsic critical and often utopian potential.[11]

Especially among contemporary marxists and poststructuralists a predilection for maps demands comment. This commentary will here take the form of a confrontation of prominent marxist and poststructuralist models of cartography in an attempt to answer the following questions: How did cartography emerge as such a powerful notion in contemporary theoretical discourse? Why does cartography exert such a strong pull on the imagination, among others, of marxists and poststructuralists? How do marxism and poststructuralism describe the semiotics of mapmaking? And, most importantly, how do these modes of understanding affect the formal and theoretical as well as the practical and political evaluations of cartography?

A fruitful way of answering this last question in particular is to compare the ways in which marxist and poststructuralist authors—Jean-François Lyotard, Fredric Jameson, Michel Foucault, Gilles Deleuze, and Guy Debord—interpret two texts on cartography by Jorge Luis Borges. What thereby becomes apparent is that models of marxist and poststructuralist cartography, irrespective of specific antagonisms, all critically engage a similar set of presuppositions underlying the possibility and impossibility of representation. This set roughly coincides with the constellation of rules that govern mimetic representation which Jacques Derrida for example describes.[12] The various readings, or misreadings, of Borges's maps, however, not only lead to a critique or deconstruction of the mimetic model of cartography, they also commit the reader to consider the extent to which this critical-deconstructive gesture requires another, more positively redefined model of cartography. In addition to the presentation of the cartographic models derived from marxism and poststructuralism, I will therefore lay the tentative groundwork for a semiotic model of mapmaking—not coincidentally influenced by thinkers who exceed the admittedly restrictive rubrics of marxism or poststructuralism, namely Jean Baudrillard, Umberto Eco, and Félix Guattari—which is poietic rather than either mimetic or antimimetic, in a sense the following pages shall specify.

I

Before considering hypotheses about the fascination which the specific image of the map exerts, the reader should take into account how the last decades have seen a general proliferation of geographical and topological concepts and metaphors as part of a widespread spatialization of contemporary thought. This spatial turn occurs first and foremost in reaction to nineteenth-century historicism and to the model of historical continuity implied in eschatological and dialectical philosophies of history.

The grand narratives of the "world-process" of history in Hegel and Marx for example are the object of vehement criticisms both at the close of the historicist century, for instance in Nietzsche's second *Untimely Meditation*, and in our century, with regard to the repeated "end of history" debate. To the "historical malady," however, Nietzsche opposes primarily the "suprahistorical" forces of art and religion, whereas the "end of history" usually leads either to some sort of "posthistoire" or to a situation without memory which Nietzsche calls the "unhistorical."[13]

Whether suprahistorical, unhistorical, or posthistorical, these answers do not altogether relinquish the problematic of temporality and historicity. In fact, they continue to operate within the historicist mindset and the philosophical devaluation of spatiality which Foucault diagnoses: "Space was treated as the dead, the fixed, the undialectical, the immobile. Time, on the contrary, was richness, fecundity, life, dialectic."[14] In recent decades, however, critics of historicism have also radically turned to "space" for nearly everything "time" once offered: richness, fecundity, life—even, indeed, the dialectic.

This turn is not altogether surprising if the reader recalls that Hegel's philosophy of history, which concerns itself only with "that which has been and that which is," cannot help relegating the future (including "America," which for Hegel is "the Land of the Future") to a section on geography.[15] In what might then appear to be a mere reversal, the rejection of Hegelian dialectics by contemporary authors like Gilles Deleuze and Félix Guattari also leads to a rediscovery of the problematics of space and geography (a rediscovery not surprisingly at one with a utopian celebration of both cartography and "America"). If for Hegel space lies outside a history with "no future," today the future seems to lie inside a geography with "no history."

"Time" and "space" thus appear to trade positions, as witnessed in a statement by Susan Sontag which reverses Foucault's diagnosis of historicism: "Time does not give us much leeway: it thrusts us forward from behind, blows us through the narrow funnel of the present into the future. But space is black, teeming with possibilities, positions, intersections, passages, detours, U-turns, dead ends, one-way streets."[16] However, this shift in emphasis from time to space, which incites some commentators to speak of a veritable paradigm change, is not merely the result of a mechanical swing of the pendulum.[17] Nor should a statement like Sontag's or, for that matter, the celebration of cartography in marxism and poststructuralism be considered a mere reversal of the hegemony of time and history. Rather, space and geopolitics are themselves ever more determining in the administration of contemporary industrial societies. Capitalist social formations today are at the end of a long process by which, in the words of Georg Lukács, "time sheds its qualitative, variable, flowing nature; it freezes into an exactly delimited, quantifiable continuum filled with quantifiable 'things' (the reified, mechanically objectified 'performance' of the worker, wholly separated from his total human personality): in short, it becomes space."[18]

Contemporary social and cultural theories must therefore increasingly add a spatial dimension to the more traditional—temporal and historical—analysis of society and culture under capitalism. Marxists like Henri Lefebvre and Edward Soja have thus requested that materialism be both historical and geographical to allow for a "socio-spatial dialectic."[19] Similarly, Foucault uses spatial and geographical metaphors primarily to articulate the relations of force between discursive formations and tactic or strategic power formations into an "imaginary geopolitics."[20]

With or without the dialectic, the key shift from time to space, or from historiography to geography, is critical to both marxism and poststructuralism, and partly explains their heightened interest in "cartography." Soja for example invokes the metaphor in the name of a new social praxis: "A new 'cognitive mapping' must be developed, a new way of seeing through the gratuitous veils of both reactionary postmodernism and late modern historicism to encourage the creation of a politicized spatial consciousness and a radical spatial praxis."[21] Whether in the words of Soja or Jameson, this program of "cognitive mapping" presents substantial overlaps with the "principle of cartography" central to the works of Foucault and Deleuze. At least in this respect marxism and poststructuralism are not as incompatible as they sometimes appear to be. In both cases an awareness of decisively spatial developments in contemporary social formations leads to a politics of mapmaking.

II

And yet, to explain how "cartography," specifically, arises as a root-metaphor in contemporary social and cultural theory, another factor must also be taken into account, aside from the spatial turn, namely the historical process by which the "map" becomes a metaphor to begin with. This process describes the paradoxical acculturation of cartography.

Over the last fifty years, on the one hand, a number of technological developments (including satellite imagery, digital cartography, and remote sensing) have increasingly eliminated some of the most daunting empirical problems of cartography and facilitated both the measurement of territories and the manipulation and graphic display of data. The science of cartography in the strict sense has thereby become progressively less burdened by what Jameson considers "the unresolvable (well-nigh Heisenbergian) dilemma of the transfer of curved space to flat charts."[22] On the other hand, however, the concept of mapmaking has also been transposed to a growing number of social and cultural fields outside of the strictly geographical, land-based territories of traditional cartography.

This intensified cultural interest in the activity of mapmaking not only leads to a rising success of cartographic images generally, but also draws critical attention to the political and ideological aspects of all kinds of maps. As a result geographers who, often under the direct influence of thinkers like Foucault, have become ever more sensitive to these political and ideological issues, also demand that new, culturally reoriented "maps" be incorporated into the discipline of cartography.[23] The process of acculturation thereby turns paradoxical insofar as the cultural expansion of cartography, which technological advances in part make possible, also entails a critical repudiation of the positivistic assumptions strengthened by these same technologies. History thereby repeats the struggle between the ideal of cartography as a science and cartography as an art, between empirical self-confidence and cultural self-consciousness.

Thus, the "map" has in recent decades traveled back and forth across disciplinary boundaries, with each use of the image outside the field of land-based cartography adding one more layer of signification to the rapidly mutating concept. The image spread for example from geography and strict cartographic science to social and cultural theory, crisscrossing through the fields of genetics, neurobiology, and psychology, where the respective concepts of "genome map" or "DNA map," "brainmapping," and "cognitive mapping" are now widely in use.[24] Other examples include the concept of a "map" referring to diagrammatic representations, articulated in psychological and psychoanalytical theories, which attempt to capture the topological structure of the human mind and the unconscious.[25] Another "map of the mind" represents "the relationships between human beings and their geographic environment," which are the object of "psychogeography."[26] In theory and philosophy, finally, evaluations of the metaphor of the "map" belong to a mode of thinking that Deleuze and Guattari have most recently labeled "geophilosophy": the study of philosophical issues in terms of an economy between "earth" (*terre*) and "territory" (*territoire*).[27]

Several of these developments in the acculturation of cartography have had a lasting impact on marxist and poststructuralist models of cartography. Psychogeography, for example, not only pervades the everyday practices of the Situationist International but must also be linked, no doubt through the latter, to Jameson's proposal of "cognitive mapping."[28] Here I do not wish to disentangle the complex relations of influence behind these developments. Suffice it to conclude that, taken together, the general turn of contemporary social and cultural thinking toward questions of space and the concomitant acculturation of maps delimit the genealogical horizon in which the marxist and poststructuralist politics of cartography emerge.

III

Historical factors—the new global space and the acculturation of cartography—are in themselves nonetheless insufficient to explain the remarkable seductiveness of the image of the "map" for contemporary theoretical discourse. The explanation must also foreground the tangle of connotations that adhere to the image with something of the aura previously attached to the mediations of the "concept," a notion which as the preeminent site of intellectual activity has itself in recent decades been eclipsed by "sign" and "text." If today "mapping," or "charting," is a seductive and persuasive answer to old and new problems of representation, to the point of competing with "signifying" and "writing," then the analysis should at least briefly consider the intricacies of the semiotic process of cartography as part of the explanation.

To account for the appeal of cartographic semiosis in contemporary discourse, useful preliminary insights can still be culled from the distinction between "map" and "territory," established by the semanticist Alfred Korzybski and recently popularized, among others, by Gregory Bateson.[29] Originally Korzybski's famous slogan, "The map *is not* the territory," has the value of a therapeutic reminder expressing the central premise of his general semantics: "A word *is not* the thing it represents." With cartography as an analogon for language Korzybski thus argues time and again against the application of the "is" of identity to the relationship between the levels of objectivity and linguisticality. This negative premise does not entail that there is no connection whatsoever between "map" and "territory," but what positively defines this relation is structural similarity rather than identity: "A map *is not* the territory it represents, but, if correct, it has a *similar structure* to the territory, which accounts for its usefulness."[30]

Leaving aside the problem of similarity, the main lesson which the reader may draw for the moment from Korzybski's argument relates to the structural interdependence of "map" and "territory." Part of the appeal of the image of the "map" for contemporary cultural studies indeed hinges upon the way the semantic and pragmatic play between "map" and "territory" is implicated, if not theoretically then at least figuratively, within cartography as a complex term. In this sense a "map" may be the only way today to approximate the older ideal of a book of nature: a sign folding the material and the semiotic, the raw and the cooked, into a multiplicity in which both sides reciprocally presuppose one another to the point of being inseparable.

Cartography for example resists the split of the geographical discipline into human and physical geography. What is a "map" indeed if not the embodiment of a middle ground through which human beings bestow meaning upon their material environment at the interface between "nature" and "culture," "earth" and "territory"? Cartography thereby summons within a multilayered sign the facts of a natural landscape or *Urlandschaft* and the values of a human-made landscape or *Kulturlandschaft*.[31] To use slightly different terms, what is inscribed in the "map" is the indissoluble counterplay and reciprocal presupposition between the "earth" (*Erde*) and the "world" (*Welt*), which for Heidegger defines the origin of the work of art.[32]

The master dichotomies of "nature" and "culture," "earth" and "world," etc., may seem to lead us far astray from the topic of this section—the reasons behind the seductiveness of cartography for marxism and poststructuralism. Moreover, the description of cartography in binary terms is one of the main obstacles for anyone who wishes to avoid the pitfalls of the traditional reflective and mimetic views of mapmaking. At the same time, however, what should be clear is the vast potential, for both marxism and poststructuralism, of any notion involving stakes as sizeable as the relations between the material and the semiotic, nature (*physis*) and culture (*tekhnè*): relations most often understood metaphysically but also, for that very reason, in dire need of a critical reinterpretation.

The structural interdependence of "map" and "territory" explains for example why "cartography" presents considerable advantages over other notions prevalent in contemporary social and cultural theories, including the "sign" and the "text." As opposed to the latter, the "map" is unimaginable without at least some "territory" as the signified or referent of the semiotic construct. In other words, given a definition of cartographic semiosis as a three-tiered function, with the "map" as signifier, the "territory" as signified, and the "earth" as referent, the reciprocal presupposition of "map" and "territory" impedes the reduction of cartography to a mere play of signifiers—a reduction unfortunately still quite frequent and tediously difficult to avoid in discussions of the "sign" and the "text."

The seductive emergence of the "map" in contemporary critical and theoretical discourse must therefore be related to a heightened interest in the semantic and pragmatic, and, thus, socio-historical and political aspects of cultural forms. In the heydays of formalism and structuralism, these situational aspects were bracketed in a welcome effort to establish the study of cultural signs as a formal science. Today, however, semiology as a paradigm for cultural studies may partially have been superseded by the metaphorical model of cartography. Developments in contemporary marxism and poststructuralism thus suggest that with the "map" the study of the semiotics and politics of cultural forms encounters a model at once thicker and more dynamic than "sign" or "text," the most intimately related notion being Foucault's "discourse," of which the "map" is then a metaphorical equivalent.[33]

IV

The counterplay between "map" and "territory" helps not only to explain the success of cartography today, but also to outline the most general differences between marxist and poststructuralist models of cartography. The dynamics of cartographic semiosis, however, cannot be described functionally with the Saussurean vocabulary, relying as it does on a set of oppositions (sign-referent, signifier-signified) which risks to reinforce a static and mimetic interpretation of representation. In Peirce's model of semiosis, by contrast, the terms involved (sign or "representamen," "object," and "interpretant") function dynamically within a series of rotating triangles.

The semiotics of cartography might thus be described in Peircean terms as follows: The "map" is a *representamen* which stands for an *object*, the "earth" (Peirce's *dynamic object*) and the "territory" (Peirce's *immediate object*), by determining a third term or *interpretant* (the term lacking in Saussure's semiology), which can be defined as the "legend" of the map in the broadest sense of the term, as the sign or series of signs to which the mapping process gives way and which can in turn become the "earth" or "territory" of another "map," and so on endlessly.

With these rather basic distinctions, a further analysis can define the difference between marxist and poststructuralist models of cartography in terms of Peirce's well-known description of three possible relations between object and representamen. Cartography can thus be defined as predominantly iconic, indexical, or symbolical.[34] Schematically, a marxist model of cartography in the final instance stresses the *indexical* causal relations between the "map" and the "raw" materials worked upon, namely, real social contradictions. A poststructuralist model on the other hand stresses the *symbolical* relation between "map" and "territory," a relation defined by an unlimited play of differences. Both contemporary marxist and poststructuralist models of mapping, finally, imply a rejection of the common *iconic* interpretation of cartography according to which a relation of similarity defines the "map" merely as a reflection or mimetic imitation of a pre-given "territory."

In a marxist analysis of culture, cognitive mapping becomes instrumental above all to underline "the materialist perspective of the conditioning of life and thought by objective nature."[35] Jameson, for example, presents cartography as an eminent model of cultural production, i.e., the formation of imaginary solutions to real social and political contradictions. As a code word for class-consciousness, cognitive mapping is an ideal model for the study of cultural and ideological processes, which are themselves forms of mapping, insofar as the concept conveys the definition of "ideology" from Louis Althusser: "A 'Representation' of the Imaginary Relationship of Individuals to their Real Conditions of Existence."[36] This "Real," of course, is what a marxist critique of ideology must uncover by tracking the leakages, as it were, from codes of information and representation to modes of production. In this manner cognitive mapping promises an overcoming of one of the central difficulties facing marxism in an age dominated by the media, "the difficulty of articulating cultural and informational commodities with the labor theory of value."[37] To manage this difficulty, the cognitive map functions for Jameson as a mediator which through the multiple layers of allegorical and symbolical meaning in the final instance relates the "imaginary" solutions to the causally determining "real" conditions of existence. The most lively debates thereby still center upon the kinds of causality—reflective, expressive, or structural—established between base and superstructure.

A marxist model of cartography thus foregrounds above all the "indexical" constituent of cartography which like the finger or arrow on a map strategically points toward particular social and historical contexts or situations, which are the sites of an event. Pointing toward some "objective nature" or "territory," a marxist "map" repeats the typical cartographic gesture of telling the reader: "You Are Here!" Or, as Althusser writes: "The real this way!"[38]

A poststructuralist model of cartography on the contrary reveals the extent to which the projection of all kinds of maps is inextricably bound up with the rules, codes, and conventions defining what Peirce calls a "symbol." Between "map" and "territory" poststructuralism not only finds a relation of arbitrariness rather than of natural resemblance but, over and against Saussure, this arbitrariness works itself out only through an unlimited play of differences. So much so that the "territory" becomes an "effect" and an "alibi" of this play of differences instead of being a pre-given entity which lies in wait behind the veil of cartography, fully to be recovered by a hermeneutical interpretation. In fact, the poststructuralist definition of the relationship between object and representamen as difference (*différance* or *signifiance*) is a critical-deconstructive gesture which unmasks precisely the ideological assumption of an autonomous "map" standing over an equally autonomous "territory" in a relation of "pure" resemblance or "direct" indexicality.

Similar discussions have recently taken place in the field of cartography in the nonmetaphorical sense where map-historians have unmasked apparently value-neutral cartographic representations to uncover instead a series of ideologically and historically determined conventions and constraints (this also entails blurring the difference between the metaphorical and the nonmetaphorical sense of "cartography"). For instance, behind the projection invented four centuries ago by the Flemish cartographer Mercator and still used today in most schools and handbooks, a Eurocentrist bias is at work, as Mercator pushes the Equator down in the bottom half of the map, giving more proportional weight to the North than to the South. And even for as simple yet important a convention as the positioning of the Northern hemisphere at the top of the map, no "natural" or "scientific" justification is present at hand.[39]

Thus, often directly influenced by poststructuralist theories of representation, current criticisms of cartography highlight less the "index" of reality, whose self-presence might turn out to be an ideological mystification, than the degree to which a map as "symbol" acquires meaning only differentially through an open set of conventional and contextual rules or interpretants. Among the elements typical of cartographic semiosis, in other words, a poststructuralist model does not stress the pointing finger or arrow as much as the "legend," in the etymological sense of the term: "To be read."

And yet, the "map" is still commonly interpreted as a purely "iconic" sign: the mimetic representation of a geographical environment without further conventional, political, or ideological encumbrances. Consider for example the amount of maps floating around on a daily basis in newspapers and textbooks like the "empty" signifiers waiting to be colored by children in primary school. Something of this familiarity which contemporary readers and TV viewers quickly learn to appreciate in maps of all colors and kinds certainly adds to the seductive power of cartography in contemporary theoretical discourse.

Stressing either the indexical or the symbolical constituents of cartography, however, runs counter to this traditional iconic concept of cartographic and other kinds of representation. To accept iconicity as the only ground of cartography means closing off the political and ideological struggles which have given substance and form to maps ever since the inception of cartography. By contrast, the two injunctions deriving from a marxist and a poststructuralist cartography, i.e., "You Are Here!" and "To Be Read!," serve the critical purpose of disrupting, questioning, and ideally changing the ideological mystifications that support interpretations of the "map" as a value-indifferent representation grounded in a relation of simple resemblance to the "territory." The pointing arrow and the legend, the two elements of cartographic semiosis preponderant in contemporary marxism and poststructuralism, are thus central to a politics of cartography which revolves around the surplus (or lack) of meaning and difference that makes the "map" always already more (or less) than just a copy of the original "territory."

V

While the preceding considerations necessarily remain preliminary, how semiotics describes cartography also decisively affects the ways in which marxism and poststructuralism evaluate the most divisive issue of the debate over mapping. This issue centers upon a notion fiercely beleaguered by poststructuralists yet indispensable to marxists, namely, the representability or knowability of "totality" as the promise if not also the premise of any critical-utopian project. Martin Jay for example opens his monumental overview of this concept with an introduction, "The Topography of Western Marxism," oriented by the very metaphor of a "map" of totality.[40] Moreover, while this link between marxism, cartography, and totality might at first appear capricious or arbitrary, the opposite is in fact true. As Jameson remarks: "An aesthetic of cognitive mapping is an integral part of any socialist political model"; and cognitive mapping "obviously stands or falls with the conception of some (unrepresentable, imaginary) global social totality that was to have been mapped."[41]

This conception of cartography implies that the totality of society, though unrepresentable, must somehow be knowable. However, is not the invocation by knowledge of a totality before or beyond representation one of the main objects of criticism in poststructuralism? Can poststructuralism accept the premise of any rigid distinction between knowledge and representation to begin with? Is the ideal of a map of totality then merely another version of the metaphysical ideal of knowledge untainted by representation, or does marxism offer modes of representation capable of circumventing this type of logocentrism?

These are only a few of the questions that most decisively oppose marxism and poststructuralism in a debate over the mappability of totality (whereby the term "mappability" remains neutral as to the distinction between knowledge and representation). To discuss both the formal and the political arguments of this debate, I would like to take two texts by Jorge Luis Borges as my central point of reference. In "On Rigor in Science," on the one hand, Borges unveils the ruins of an impossible cartographic project to draw a total map, on the scale of a mile to a mile, of an unnamed Empire:

> . . . In that Empire, the Art of Cartography reached such Perfection that the map of one Province alone took up the whole of a City, and the map of the Empire, the whole of a Province. In time, those Unconscionable Maps did not satisfy and the Colleges of Cartographers set up a Map of the Empire which had the size of the Empire itself and coincided with it point by point. Less Addicted to the Study of Cartography, Succeeding Generations

> understood that this Widespread Map was Useless and not without Impiety they abandoned it to the Inclemencies of the Sun and of the Winters. In the deserts of the West some mangled Ruins of the Map last on, inhabited by Animals and Beggars; in the whole Country there are no other relics of the Disciplines of Geography.
>
> Suárez Miranda: *Viajes de Varones Prudentes*, Book Four, Chapter XLV, Lérida, 1658.[42]

On the other hand, in a fragment from "Partial Enchantments of the *Quixote*," Borges illustrates another aporia of cartography with the paraphrase of a passage from Josiah Royce's *The World and the Individual* also mentioned by Korzybski and Peirce:

> . . . let us suppose, if you please, that a portion of the surface of England is perfectly levelled and smoothed, and is then devoted to the production of our precise map of England. . . . But now suppose that this our resemblance is to be made absolutely exact, in the sense previously defined. A map of England, contained within England, is to represent, down to the minutest detail, every contour and marking, natural or artificial, that occurs upon the surface of England. . . . For the map, in order to be complete, according to the rule given, will have to contain, as a part of itself, a representation of its own contour and contents. In order that this representation should be constructed, the representation itself will have to contain once more, as a part of itself, a representation of its own contour and contents; and this representation, in order to be exact, will have once more to contain an image of itself; and so on without limit.[43]

Commentators of "the famous Borges map" often obfuscate the fundamental difference between these two texts. Yet while the first parable exemplifies the paradox of complete mimesis which leads to tautological perfection, the second fragment discusses the very different paradox of self-reflexive mimesis which leads to aporetic embedding or nesting. Borges thereby reduces the cartographic ideal of mimetic representation to an alternative between tautology and infinity. To the futility of a completely mimetic map on the scale of a mile to a mile, he juxtaposes the endlessness of an exactly mimetic map on a scale other than 1:1. From a formal vantage point, in other words, Borges's texts put a double check on the project of mapping a totality. Whenever a map *is* the territory, cartography is useless or, in any case, without semiotic value as a sign.[44] Yet no sooner do cartographers abandon the futile ideal of full-scale representation than the rigor of an exact map implodes into infinity. The dream of total mimesis then becomes a self-destructive nightmare. At bottom the birth of a total map imprisons its own death; the "rigor" of Mercator's science, when taken to extremes, comes dangerously close to its "rigor mortis."

Cartography as mimesis not only collapses into an infinitely smaller map within the map in an endless series of self-embedded representations. A logic of supplementarity also impedes cartographers to step beyond the borders of the map in order to contain the territorial totality from an exterior Archimedean point of view. A map of totality is susceptible to Derrida's statement to the effect that "no border is guaranteed, inside or out."[45] Aside from opening up a bottomless pit at the center of the map, Borges tells us that cartographers can never reach a bird's eye perspective sufficiently elevated to embrace both the entire territory and their own map. Even if a rigorous map of the entire territory were drawn on a scale other than the impossible and futile 1:1, this map would fail to represent itself accurately, *en abyme*, within its own structure, so that an ever higher and more encompassing form of cartography or meta-cartography would be required, and so on, *ad infinitum*.

Here the reader may remotely detect echoes of Kurt Gödel's theorem of incompleteness, in which a certain "mapping" ironically also plays a fundamental role.[46] Jean-François Lyotard, for example, discusses "On Rigor in Science" at the heart of *The Postmodern Condition* as a "layman's version" of Gödel's theorem, interpreted generally as "the de facto impossibility of ever achieving a complete measure of any given state of a system."[47] Surprisingly, though, the importance of this reference to Borges in *The Postmodern Condition*—the only literary example in a book pervaded by the theme of narrative—has scarcely been taken into account.

Lyotard invokes Borges's impossible cartographic project as an illustration of why postmodern societies fail to legitimize the scientific pursuit of knowledge. No longer supported by modern metanarratives of emancipation or epistemological metadiscourses, a scientific endeavor is considered legitimate in the postmodern condition, according to Lyotard, merely on account of a good "performance," namely, whenever the output exceeds the input. Yet what "On Rigor in Science" illustrates for Lyotard is the fact that "a complete definition of the initial state of a system . . . would require an expenditure of energy at least equivalent to that consumed by the system to be defined."[48] Borges's map thus indicates that performance as the postmodern criterion of legitimacy is no less bound to failure than traditional metanarratives, since the energy absorbed in circumscribing the input equals or exceeds the amount of energy producible by way of output. To phrase this aporia in the words of a recent cartographer: "Every survey we do seems to contain a structure as big as the survey."[49]

Faced with totality, mimetic representations inevitably run aground and produce the "mangled ruins" of Borges's parable which, from Lyotard's viewpoint, appear as the remainders or "relics" of an excessive expenditure of energy that keeps every cartographic representation from being rigorously accurate and adequate to the territory. Borges's "beggars" and "animals" on the other hand not incidentally evoke "unproductive" and "inhuman" forces which a system of pure production, exchange, and consumption cannot put to "meaningful" use (beggars are in this sense more radically "unproductive" for example than Walter Benjamin's ragpickers, who still have the capitalist function "to subject even rubbish to exchange value"[50]). In short, Borges's "ruins," "beggars" and "relics" disrupt the very logic of production and reproduction supporting the mimetic ideal of mapping a totality. Hence, while Lyotard's interpretation of "On Rigor in Science" may strike the reader as overly formal, Borges's map poses theoretical problems with regard to the ideals of mimesis and closure which even a marxist politics of cognitive mapping must address, especially when this implies the idea of a global social totality.

A first, largely unsuccessful attempt on the part of marxism to overcome the structural limits of the representation of totality engages an often-quoted metaphorical description of deconstruction from the hand of Terry Eagleton. In *Against the Grain* Eagleton writes that "to deconstruct" is "so to speak, to reverse the imposing tapestry in order to expose in all its unglamorously dishevelled tangle the threads constituting the well-heeled image it presents to the world."[51] While this lyrical passage promises to reconcile poststructuralism with the kind of materialist reversal typical of a marxist critique of ideology, Eagleton's gesture clearly fails when applied to the representation of totality. As a matter of fact, adherents of deconstruction would be the first to point out that this gesture of reversal presupposes a representation of totality which from an alleged outsider's point of view is simply a mirage and, from within the totality, at best an aberration.[52] To expose what Borges in the poem "Things" calls "the other side of the tapestry" or "the reverse of the dreary mappamundi" ("The things which no one sees, except for Berkeley's God"), Eagleton would not only be pulling the magic rug from under his own feet. To map a totality marxism also has to ignore Borges's aporias which keep cartography, like any other reflecting representation, as Derrida remarks, "from folding back upon itself or reproducing itself within itself in perfect self-correspondence, from dominating or including itself, tautologically, from translating itself into its own totality."[53]

Formal criticisms against cartography and the representation of totality, however, apply only to reflective or mimetic models of representation. Yet contemporary marxism seeks to bypass traditional reflection theories of representation as much as poststructuralism aims at deconstructing classical mimetologism. Jameson for example argues that "the cognitive map is not exactly mimetic, in that older sense; indeed, the theoretical issues it poses allow us to renew the analysis of representation on a higher and much more complex level."[54] While Jameson cannot yet satisfactorily describe this higher and more complex analysis of representation, which would require revolutionary social changes, his readings do achieve impressive results by transforming the onerous issues of totality and incompleteness into problems to be answered historically and dialectically rather than formally. Throughout his works Jameson thus provides the reader with the elements necessary for a dialectical-materialist interpretation of "On Rigor in Science" in which formal arguments against the representation of totality in the final instance no longer work as a hindrance. Rather, they will be helpful and historically illuminating precisely to the extent that they hinder representation.

First, as mentioned earlier, Jameson defines cartography or cognitive mapping with Althusser's Lacanian formula as "a 'Representation' of the Imaginary relationship of individuals to their Real conditions of existence." Second and most important, Jameson also follows Lacan by defining the "real" as "what resists symbolization absolutely."[55] Together these two premises enable a marxist ideological analysis to avoid the pitfalls of classical models of representation in which every superstructural element (or "map") is merely a mimetic "reflection" or homologous "expression" of an objective and positively given socio-historical totality (or "territory"). To the contrary, marxism here approaches the "real" only negatively or asymptotically in the understanding that, though structurally inaccessible, the socio-historical totality is approachable as an absent cause through its effects. Without presupposing an impossible gesture of total reversal, Jameson thus captures a glimpse of "the dark underside" of the tapestry so as to unearth "the presence beneath ideology and appearance of that labor which produces and reproduces the world itself, and which, like the attention of God in Berkeleyan idealism, sustains the whole fabric of reality continuously in being."[56]

Marxism thereby acknowledges and dialectically exploits the structural incompleteness of cartography while at the same time grounding the aporias of Borges's texts in a social and historical context. The "ruins" of the Emperor's map then not only, or primarily, confirm a formal theorem which flatly denies the possibility of total representation. Rather, they constitute blind spots or unresolved social contradictions which resist the ideological formations and thereby register the historical effects of the "real." Now Borges's "ruins" in other words form the locus where the "raw" materials of history burst through ideology—tearing up the rugged surface of the imperial map with the disclosure of social struggles, here alluded to in the name of the outcast "beggars."

Regarding the formal side of the debate about the mappability of totality, in sum, Lyotard and Jameson both start from the premise of an inevitable gap between "map" and "territory." This gap or incommensurability in principle excludes both the mimetic ideal of identity and the ideal of one-to-one correspondence, as Borges's examples respectively illustrate. From a poststructuralist vantage, however, this gap is due to the fact that the "map" proliferates into a signifying chain which inevitably exceeds the "territory." Classical mimesis thus collapses in the face of "the irreducible excess of the syntactic over the semantic,"[57] while Lyotard's analysis attests to "the incommensurable excess of the Idea before the real."[58] Through this signifying excess the entropic expenditure of energy dispels the possibility of an immediate and positive access to the "real" or to the "totality" of meaning. This is also the sense in which a poststructuralist model stresses the ineradicable "symbolical" aspects of cartographic semiosis which constitute the so-called autonomy and primacy of the "symbolical order" (the differences between the Peircean and the Lacanian sense of "symbolical" here being negligeable).

From a marxist vantage point, by contrast, the gap between "map" and "territory" is at least for Jameson due to the fact that "content" ultimately resists "form": a typically Hegelian view which Jameson transcodes in terms of Lacan as the "real" that resists the formation of "imaginary" solutions. Yet this content, which disrupts and breaks through the formations of ideology, registers the dynamic effects of history as an absent cause, or absent totality. A marxist model thereby safeguards, in part by acknowledging Lacanian poststructuralist theory, the "indexical" function of cartography to point toward that ultimate bedrock of reality which a radical poststructuralist critique of mimesis might have tossed like the proverbial baby with the bath-water.[59]

VI

With Jameson's answer the debate about the mappability of totality moves away from strictly formal and theoretical matters into the political and ideological arena. Here, at last, readers turn to what is obviously the most striking aspect of Borges's texts, namely the way in which "On Rigor in Science," especially, draws upon the suspicion that "cartography" bears the stigmata of political structures of domination and exploitation, particularly imperialism—a suspicion for which the history of cartography provides ample data.[60] Since Borges partially invents his allegory in light of the passage from Josiah Royce, the reader may even conjecture that the mention of "England" is suppressed in "On Rigor in Science," which leaves behind only a generic deictic reference to "that Empire" (as in Franz Kafka's parable "An Imperial Message").

Even without the presence of the British Empire, though, Borges's small text invites a political interpretation in which the mimetic ideal of a "map" coinciding point for point with the "territory" is seen as a supreme form of cultural imperialism.[61]

Discovering similar intrinsic or historical links between "representation" (semiology) and "power" (political economy) is often, though not always with great subtlety, thought to be the trademark of French critical theory. Foucault especially is one of the most perspicuous cartographers of the semiology of power-relations, most notably in *Discipline and Punish: The Birth of the Prison* (a book which Deleuze studies in a chapter of his *Foucault* under the title "A New Cartographer").[62] The work of Foucault thereby seems to have given "cartography" the decisively pejorative political slant of "a tendency towards a more finely tuned justice, towards a closer penal mapping of the social body," which would ideally "make the punishment and repression of illegalities a regular function, coextensive with society."[63] For Foucault, the "map" or "diagram" indeed seems exclusively a disciplinary instrument of surveillance to establish "a whole penal, administrative, geographical hierarchy"; the Panopticon for example is "the diagram of a mechanism of power reduced to its ideal form," which reflects "a change of quantitative scale in the groups to be supervised."[64] In this sense Foucault's work might confirm the bleak view that "the 'mind' as a surface of inscription, with semiology as its tool," produces a cartographic apparatus that belongs to an arsenal of stealth weapons worthy of Big Brother.[65] The cartographic metaphor would then run the risk of being incorporated into the dictionary of Orwellian Newspeak. Maps are indeed drawn not merely to represent the shifted battlelines once the smoke of fire clears up; they are also a tool in battles fought without fire that are intimately tied to what Foucault calls the microphysics of power. "Cartographers manufacture power: they create a spatial panopticon."[66]

The reader might object that "Empire" and "Big Brother" no longer adequately describe the capitalist world system today, when multinational and neo-colonial forms of accumulation mask and subsume the exploitation of imperialist and totalitarian regimes. To overcome the panopticism of cartography, however, more is necessary than a claim that "On Rigor in Science" stands just for an imperialist stage of capitalism allegedly overcome; nor does Foucault's "mapping" stand simply for a gridlike space typical of the earlier stage of market capitalism, as Jameson wants his readers to believe.[67] To the contrary, Borges's story of scientific rigor and Foucault's study of disciplinary surveillance are equally cogent today in what is variously labeled late capitalism, the media age, or the society of the image. As a matter of fact, when Guy Debord explains in *The Society of the Spectacle* how capitalism raises the level of accumulation to the point where the entire world becomes a "spectacle" wholly independent from the producers, he describes this process unsurprisingly in terms of a cartography akin to Borges's imperial map: "The spectacle is the map of this new world—a map drawn to the scale of the territory itself."[68]

Thus, whether from the perspective of discipline, imperialism, or the spectacle, the chances of transforming a cartography of totality into a viable form of political practice, let alone a value to pursue, appear rather grim. What is more, the previous conclusions of the formal and theoretical debate must now be put on their head. For Foucault and Debord the chief problem is not that a cognitive map of the social whole is theoretically impossible, but that this map is practically undesirable yet risks to have been achieved in the society of the spectacle or modern discipline. Particularly with regard to the mappability of totality, therefore, the politics of cartography in marxism and poststructuralism must be approached with the utmost caution, since neither current is simply pro or contra.

"Local" cartographies, however, have in recent years been forming a forceful political alternative to the historically and ideologically tainted ideal of "total" mapping. The political practice of local and oppositional mapping in fact transforms the dilemma—the tension between the theoretical impossibility and the undesirable practical reality of a cartography of totality—into a political instrument of delegitimation. The structural incompleteness of cartography, logically derivable from formal arguments like Gödel's theorem, thereby functions as a powerful means to uncover and eventually undo the sham completeness of hegemonic cartographies.

If indeed the representation of totality is in principle impossible, then the various forms in which the whole social process is in fact mapped out and legitimized as a seamless totality must necessarily remain at bottom incomplete—or complete only on the surface, masking strategies of exclusion and repression, separation and discursive saturation. Against such strategies as the disciplinary and spectacular organization of society, various oppositional practices today unfold local and critical forms of cartography in an endeavor to situate forgotten and excluded territories back on the map. The "ruins," "beggars," and "relics" of Borges's Empire may have been renamed or silenced today, but a "mapping of the ruins," or what might also be called "a writing of the ruins, micrologies, grafitti," appears more necessary than ever.[69]

Thus, Houston Baker pleads fervently for "the mapping of local territories" as part and parcel of "a rigorous local pedagogy designed for the twenty-first century," while Toni Morrison begins *Playing in the Dark* with the proposal "to draw a map, so to speak, of a critical geography and use that map to open as much space for discovery, intellectual adventure, and close exploration as did the original charting of the New World—without the mandate for conquest."[70] These are only two prominent examples among numerous other contemporary artists, writers, critics, and theorists who propose forms of local, critical, and countercultural mapmaking, for example in postcolonialism and feminism,[71] not only in the United States but also, and above all, in Canada, Australia, and Latin-America.[72]

Two remarks are important here. First, some critics argue that without a view of the social whole, local practices run the risk of systematic isolation and cooptation.[73] Yet local cartographies require a thorough revision of the entire debate concerning the mappability of totality. Far from promoting a simple opposition between total and local mapmaking, oppositional cartographies with regard to race, gender, or class point to the need to rethink the general conception of cartography itself. If they were merely to replace the ideal of totality with local forms of resistance, the aporias of representation would inevitably resurface on smaller scales. To answer the pressure of totalizing cartographies, in other words, "it will not suffice to shift one's labor from system building to micrological mappings of local historical functions."[74] What is needed, as Toni Morrison suggests, is rather a form of cartography "without the mandate for conquest," which means that the quantitative opposition should entail a qualitative reconsideration of the very logic of mapmaking—a reconsideration which will perhaps no longer preclude the possibility of mapping the global social totality.

A second remark concerns the place of poststructuralism in this debate. Here, too, the issue requires greater subtlety as oppositional cartographies contradict the purely negative view by suggesting that poststructuralist criticisms of representation remain compatible with a viable mapping practice.[75] In addition to the critical-deconstructive interpretation of the "map" as a mimetic and panoptic form of representation, poststructuralism must thus entail some critical-utopian form of cartography. And while the latter will already be familiar to readers of Deleuze and Guattari, here too the case of Foucault is more complex than first appears. Again the issue is not merely to decide whether poststructuralism rejects or embraces the ideal of local or total mapmaking, but to sharpen the qualitative description of cartographic semiosis.

Foucault, to begin with, never uses the metaphor of the "map" in the French original of *Discipline and Punish*. In the English version, however, a single cartographic metaphor translates two quite different French terms. On the one hand Foucault uses the term *quadrillage* critically to describe forms of panopticism, as in the aforementioned case of "a closer penal mapping of the social body." On the other hand, however, "mapping" also translates the term *repérage* with which Foucault repeatedly, even to the point of monotony, characterizes his own discourse especially in opposition to the classical historical approach.[76]

This is no mere technical matter of correct or incorrect translation. To be sure, the conflation of *quadrillage* and *repérage* in one cartographic metaphor appears to be an unfortunate oversight which easily will have led the English-speaking reader to obliterate the qualitative difference between the objects and the method of Foucault's discourse. Yet the translation also undeniably has its merits and enables the reader to capture a glimpse of significant ambiguities present both in Foucault's work and in other poststructuralist cartographies.

Not only is the possibility of obfuscating the difference between object (*quadrillage*) and method (*repérage*) confirmed by the trend of Foucault's own discourse to become, as Jean Baudrillard remarks, "a mirror of the powers it describes."[77] The decision to translate both concepts with the particular cartographic metaphor is also justified by Foucault's own work to the extent that the "map," as Deleuze points out, constitutes a central though largely implicit aspect of *Discipline and Punish.* Finally, the translation offers a key to unravel the enigma of Foucault's cartography by revealing the point where the views of Baudrillard and Deleuze actually complement each other. That is, precisely insofar as the confusion between object and method is not just a translator's mistake but marks a deeper ambiguity of Foucault's own discourse, the possibility and even the obligation arises to offer a more explicit and rigorous description of the qualitative differences between "mapping" as *quadrillage* and "mapping" as *repérage.* What will thereby become evident is that Baudrillard judges Foucault exclusively from the point of view of cartography as a panopticon (*quadrillage*), whereas Deleuze honors Foucault primarily with regard to the utopian dimension of cartography as a rhizome (*repérage*).

Without a redefinition of the differences in kind between these modalities of cartography, the debate will revert to the false question of deciding "whether deconstruction provides us with a *better* map of the way things are or offers a *critique* of 'map.'"[78] In fact, while the first half of this question—the notorious moment of reinscription—is frequently overlooked, there can be no critique or deconstruction of cartographic mimetologism which would not also presuppose a critical-utopian reinterpretation of cartography, just as Derrida counters the Platonic-Hegelian model of mimesis with a gloss on the performance of the mime in Mallarmé's *Mimique.* Likewise, marxism cannot surmount the mechanical determinism of its classical view of representation without also offering an alternative for the traditional reflective and expressive theories of language—precisely the kind of alternative Jameson describes as "mapping" and "transcoding." With regard to cartography, however, no one offers a more explicit and rigorous account of the differences between the critical-deconstructive and critical-utopian views than Deleuze and Guattari.

Central to Deleuze and Guattari's rhizomatic thinking is the "principle of cartography and decalcomania."[79] Thus, aside from occasionally reiterating Foucault's opposition between *repérage* and *quadrillage*, Deleuze and Guattari explicitly distinguish the "map" (*carte*) from what they call the "tracing" (*calque*).[80] The latter roughly corresponds to the view of cartography formally and politically deconstructable as mimetic and panoptic. The former instead is a rhizomatic form of cartography comparable to recent developments in hypertextuality and non-linear mapping, namely, "a map that must be produced, constructed, a map that is always detachable, connectable, reversible, modifiable, and has multiple entryways and exits and its own lines of flight."[81]

The qualitative differences between "mapping" and "tracing," unlike Foucault's opposition between *repérage* and *quadrillage*, cut across the epistemological distinction between method and object. In psychoanalysis, for example, a "cartographic" object like a child's dream can become the object of a discourse typically marked by "calcomania" ("Look at what happened to Little Hans already, an example of child psychoanalysis at its purest: they kept on BREAKING HIS RHIZOME and BLOTCHING HIS MAP").[82] The description of a "tracing" like the Panopticon, on the other hand, does not in turn have to become a "tracing" (as is the case for Baudrillard in Foucault's discourse) but can itself form a "map" (as Deleuze argues).

Deleuze thus describes the change in perspective from Foucault's *The Order of Things* and *The Archaeology of Knowledge* to *Discipline and Punish* as a shift from the "archive" (the forms and strata of knowledge) to the "diagram" (the forces and strategies of power), while comparing the latter to a "map": "The *diagram* is no longer the auditory or visual archive, but a map, a cartography that is coextensive with the entire social field."[83] In this passage as elsewhere Deleuze presupposes that even a "map" coextensive with the entire "territory" need not be rejected as panoptic but has the potential of opening up rhizomatic lines of flight. "Thus there is no diagram that does not also include, besides the points which it connects up, certain relatively free or unbound points, points of creativity, change and resistance, and it is perhaps with these that we ought to begin in order to understand the whole picture."[84] Kafka's *Amerika*, for example, follows such lines of flight, resistance, and creativity, "in projecting the photo of the father onto the map of the world."[85] That is, while the paternal photo remains locked onto the territorial patterns of a "tracing" (the Oedipal family-romance), the journey through the land of America projects an issue out of this grid by inventing a "map" (a network of lines of flight). As Deleuze says: "To flee is to trace a line, lines, a whole cartography."[86]

A purely nominal distinction between *calque* (or *quadrillage*) and *carte* (or *repérage*) certainly does not yet amount to a full theory of the qualitative differences between the deconstructive and utopian interpretations of cartography, which would also entail a redefinition of the semiotics of mapmaking. Before discussing these differences in detail, however, I should briefly clarify the implications of Deleuze and Guattari's principle of cartography and decalcomania for the debate over totality.

Time and again, Deleuze and Guattari in fact underscore the possibility of "mapping" a totality. Rather than being indicted, once and for all, as either formally impossible or politically undesirable, the coextensivity between a "map" and the whole social "territory" appears to have utopian potential in rhizomatic thinking. What they reject, however, are the deterministic and overcoded "tracings" of totality by which dialectical philosophies of history, for instance, project the social whole back onto a lost mythical origin or a pre-established emancipatory future.

Thus Deleuze and Guattari write in *A Thousand Plateaus*: "We no longer believe in a primordial totality that once existed, or in a final totality that awaits us at some future date. . . . We believe only in totalities that are peripheral [*à côté*]."[87] For Deleuze and Guattari, in short, the truth no longer firmly lies in the whole, but wanders about at the periphery, in the adjacency of that which, from a dialectical or metaphysical vantage point, appears to be *à côté*, peripheral, or beside the point—like the nomadism of Borges's beggars, wandering amidst the ruins of the Empire in the deserts of the West.

What does it mean, however, to believe only in peripheral and adjacent totalities? Or, rather, since the authors of *Anti-Oedipus* no longer seek to pose the question of meaning, how does rhizomatic thinking go about "mapping" rather than "tracing" a totality? Beyond the terminological subtleties of Deleuze and Guattari's text, these questions constitute the crux of the debate about cartography. Not only do Deleuze and Guattari explicitly indicate the differences in kind between a deconstructive and a utopian view of cartography by opposing a rhizomatic "map" to the panoptic and mimetic "tracing." But, by offering a more flexible account of the mappability of totality, they also stake out a possible meeting-ground for the cartographic models typically found in marxism and poststructuralism.

At first Deleuze and Guattari again foster the illusion that the "mapping" of adjacent totalities implies a "local" cartography as the mere displacement from center to periphery, from the global to the local. Such a displacement from the whole to its parts would resemble Nietzsche's strategy, for example, with regard to classical philosophy: "The philosopher believes that the value of his philosophy lies in the whole, in the building: posterity discovers it in the bricks with which he built and which are then often used again for better building: in the fact, that is to say, that that building can be destroyed and *nonetheless* possesses value as material."[88] Likewise, when "philosophy as architecture is ruined, but a writing of the ruins, micrologies, graffiti can still be done," as Lyotard claims, then this "writing of the ruins" might mean only "to deconstruct," or "to assemble by disassembling."[89]

"Mapping," as Deleuze and Guattari seem to understand it, however, involves not merely destroying and reassembling (an operation which, like graffiti on a government building, risks to leave the founding principles untouched, even aside from facilitating exactly the kind of rampant urban planning that razes old patrimony to the ground to erect new shopping malls), but rethinking the entire conceptual edifice, from large-scale groundplans to the most elementary bricks and building blocks. "Mapping" in other words twists out of the mimetic and panoptic predicament of the "tracing" only if it entails, not just a change of scale, but a radically different understanding of the semiotics of cartography. The latter, I repeat, is in fact a necessary presupposition in every formal and political deconstruction of cartography as iconic mimesis. Only rendering explicit this tacit presupposition, what follows is then a semiotic rethinking of cartography no longer as mimesis but as poiesis.

VII

"Poiesis" here summarily indicates a general trend in contemporary thinking toward an affirmative redefinition of representation. This trend, for which "mapping" is often a code word, appears under many, sometimes almost imperceptible guises: for example, as a shift in emphasis from constative toward performative speech-acts, or as the displacement from a Platonic-Hegelian toward an Aristotelian understanding of mimesis.[90] In what follows, though, I will limit myself to the works of Baudrillard, Guattari, and Eco in order to present an interpretation of cartography which, while no doubt entailing a strong misreading of Borges's texts, promises to reformulate, if not to answer, some of the representational problems that contemporary marxism and poststructuralism still grapple with.

Simulation is the key to Baudrillard's treatment of Borges. The opening pages of *Simulacra and Simulation* are in this sense as fundamental to the understanding of cartography as Foucault's prefatory remarks about Borges's laughter are to *The Order of Things*—a project of which "The Order of Simulacra," in Baudrillard's earlier book *Symbolic Exchange and*

Death, in many ways constitutes a provocative counterpart.[91] Between these two books, however, Baudrillard's positions undergo a drastic transformation, not only in defusing the potential of symbolic exchange as a radical alternative to capitalist production and accumulation, but also with respect to the place of "On Rigor in Science" in his theory of simulation.

In "The Order of Simulacra," Baudrillard applies his rough brushes to paint a brief history of three orders of simulacra: counterfeits, reproductions, and simulations. Though without mentioning Borges, a footnote then appears to situate "On Rigor in Science" at the turning point where, with the vanishing of reality into the hyperreal, the whole second order of production and representation also collapses into third-order simulacra: "The coefficient of reality is proportionate to the reserve of the imaginary that gives it its specific weight. This is true of terrestrial as well as space exploration: when there is no more virgin territory, and thus one available to the imaginary, when the map covers the whole territory, something like the reality principle disappears."[92] Simulation would thus begin when the older mimetic ideal of reproduction reaches the point of absolute identity between map and territory, between medium and message. "'The Medium is the Message' is even the formula of the political economy of the sign when it leads on to third-order simulation. A distinction of the medium from the message remains characteristic of second-order signification."[93]

Soon after *Symbolic Exchange and Death*, however, Baudrillard abandons this implicit juxtaposition of simulation with Borges's cartographic tautology. Only a year later, he writes for example in *The Beaubourg Effect*: "Gone even the Borgesian utopia, of the map coextensive with the territory and doubling it in its entirety: today the simulacrum no longer goes by way of the double and of duplication, but by way of genetic miniaturization."[94] Finally, in the overture of *Simulacra and Simulation*, Baudrillard explains at length why the Borges fable no longer is "the most beautiful allegory of simulation," but "possesses nothing but the discrete charm of second-order simulacra."[95]

What now defines simulation is not the total coextensivity of map and territory so much as the generation of the one by the other in an aleatory and circulatory process. "The territory no longer precedes the map, nor does it survive it. It is nevertheless the map that precedes the territory—*precession of simulacra*—the map engenders the territory, and if one must return to the fable, today it is the territory whose shreds slowly rot across the extent of the map."[96] Simulation in fact no longer permits any differentiation whatsoever between antagonistic poles. Instead, under the modeling pressure of a genetic or cybernetic code, both map and territory dissolve into a general state of Möbian indifference and indeterminacy: "A single *model*, whose efficacy is immediate, simultaneously generates the message, the medium, and the real."[97] How different is this description, by the way, from one of Derrida's rare positive statements in his reading of *Mimique*: "At once page and quill, Pierrot is both passive and active, matter and form, the author, the means, and the raw material of his mimodrama"?[98]

Perhaps even more patently than before, Borges's case thus forms an exemplary turning-point in the history of simulacra, at the threshold between the absurd perfection of mimetic reproductions and the threatening implosion of cybernetic simulations. Regardless of whether "On Rigor in Science" marks the culmination and consummation of the former or in a strong misreading already exemplifies the latter, however, does this alternative exhaust the possibilities for cultural cartography today? Apart from the retro mode of lost referentials, which everybody these days knows how to deconstruct so well, is simulation the only solution waiting at the end of the long road currently being traveled by critics of mimetic representation?

The consequences of a positive answer to these questions, while being as exasperating as they seem exhilarating in the eyes of Baudrillard, would obviously be fateful for marxism and poststructuralism. In fact Baudrillard integrally undermines the Lacanian-Althusserian legacy which still supports the practice of cartography for all of the authors above, when he defines the real as that which *never* resists symbolization: "The very definition of the real is *that of which it is possible to provide an equivalent reproduction*," so that, ultimately, "the real is not only that which can be reproduced, but *that which is always already reproduced*: the hyperreal."[99] Simulation thus also erases the single most important premise for contemporary marxist and poststructuralist cartographies: the minimal difference between map and territory which alone leaves room for critical projection.

The entire fields of critical theory and cultural studies today could in this sense be seen as split among the melancholy admirers of McLuhan, for whom *the medium is the message*, and the hopeful followers of Korzybski, for whom *the map is not the territory*. Yet the irreconciliation of both positions is perhaps only a lure, as such inseparable from the kind of semiology for which radical alternatives are also available. Perhaps Baudrillard's descriptions of simulation should then be reread in light of a different semiotic framework altogether. After all, his remarks about the implosion of meaning in the media, and vice-versa, are provocative only for someone who at the same time stubbornly clings to the whole phantom set of polar oppositions behind the ideals of mimetic reproduction and meaningful representation, which the theorist of simulation then so giddily undercuts in the name of genetics and cybernetics.

At bottom Baudrillard does hardly more than to define simulation in terms of a negation, or reversion, of resemblance: "Representation stems from the principle of the equivalence of the sign and the real (even if this equivalence is utopian, it is a fundamental axiom). Simulation, on the contrary, stems from the utopia of the principle of equivalence, from the radical negation of the sign as value, from the sign as the reversion and death sentence of every reference."[100] The same is unfortunately also true, I believe, for someone like Derrida, whose gloss on the simulacrum of Mallarmé's mime is for the most part merely negative as well: "The operation, which no longer belongs to the system of truth, does not manifest, produce, or unveil any presence; nor does it constitute any conformity, resemblance, or adequation between a presence and a representation."[101] Such authors as Guattari and Eco, by contrast, allow a positive redefinition of cartographic practices without the mimetic principles of presence, equivalence and correspondence, thanks to an entirely different tradition, namely, Peirce's semiotics and Louis Hjelmslev's glossematics.[102]

At first Guattari would seem to confirm Baudrillard's analysis. In *Schizoanalytical Cartographies*, for instance, he too cancels out the polar opposition between map and territory: "Not only does the map start referring indefinitely to its own cartography, as Alfred Korzybski has well noted, but it is the distinction between the map and the territory (the map and 'the thing mapped') which tends to disappear."[103] At two different moments, moreover, Guattari alludes to Borges's example, which he interprets not only as "a map which exactly covers a territory," but also, in a strong misreading, as "a cartographic activity which engenders the territory to which it refers."[104] These statements, however, are identical to Baudrillard's only in appearance, since they presuppose a semiotics of cartography which is triadic and poietic rather than dyadic, and hence irreducible even to the implosive model of simulation.

Thus, especially in his collections *Molecular Revolution* and *The Machinic Unconscious*, Guattari elaborates Hjelmslev's model of the stratification of language into an a-signifying diagrammatic regime of signs, which will dominate the entire semiotic component of *A Thousand Plateaus*.[105] Most relevant here is the role of "matter" or "purport" (Hjelmslev's *mening*), which constitutes the "amorphous continuum, on which boundaries are laid by the formative action of the languages."[106] Both the plane of content and the plane of expression, in the vocabulary of glossematics, stratically unfold according to three rather than only two layers: form, substance, and purport. To use Hjelmslev's eloquent metaphor, language produces formed substances "by the form being projected on to the purport, just as an open net casts its shadow down on an undivided surface."[107] In this triple metaphor, the "open net" stands for the forms, the "undivided surface" for the purport, and the "shadow" for the formed substances, that is, in cartographic terms: the map, the earth, and the territory respectively. Here a comparison with Baudrillard's medium, the real, and the message already indicates that a semiotics of cartography need not submit to sheer indeterminacy, as long as the description also abandons the binary framework as the only reasonable alternative.

This model of stratification then allows Guattari to oppose what he labels a-signifying semiotics to signifying semiologies. The latter, including the Saussurean model of the sign as well as the Derridean model of the text, operate exclusively with signifiers and/or signifieds, that is, with already semiotically formed substances of expression and content, which are furthermore overcoded in poststructuralism by the instance of the letter, to the detriment of other substances of expression. A-signifying semiotics, on the contrary, exceed the double articulation of both content and expression; they work flush with the real, beneath the relations of signification and representation, and have direct purchase on the continuum of material flows in the purport. "Mapping" then occurs whenever, beyond the two planes of formed substances, a diagram connects figures of content and expression to a plane of consistency at the level of abstract matter or purport, which a concrete assemblage articulates into applicable forms and strata.

With this definition of a diagrammatic axis, in addition to the syntagmatic and paradigmatic pair, Guattari did undoubtedly assign the practice of cartography a specific place of activity. To account for the concrete process of cartographic semiosis, however, the Hjelmslevian model of stratification alone lacks dynamic force. An exhaustive explanation as to how exactly a map engenders the territory to which it refers should also pass through the Peircean concept of abduction, which Eco compares to an inventive kind of code-making or mapping. Instead of a simulation, then, the poietic alternative to the aporias of mimetic cartography will entail an abduction.

On the continuum of modes of sign production, which appears in *A Theory of Semiotics*, Eco situates the process of "mapping" at the most creative pole of "invention" and at the complete opposite of the "replica."[108] Evidently this presentation runs counter to common sense insofar as cartography typically stands for an imitative view of sign production.[109] For Eco, however, the mimetic logic of equivalence fully applies only to the replica, which is in this sense similar to Deleuze and Guattari's tracing. The activity of mapping, on the contrary, highlights the general fact that a sign "appears to be based upon pure equivalence simply because we do not recognize in it a 'sleeping' inference."[110] Unlike Baudrillard and Derrida, in other words, Eco proposes a positive alternative to the mimetic principle of equivalence. Neither a play of difference and deference nor a game of indifference and deterrence, what defines the relation between map, earth, and territory is an active principle of inference. Especially helpful here is the type of hypothetical inference for which Peirce coined the term of abduction.

Abduction, briefly put, is an inference from a *result* and a *rule* to a *case*.[111] Confronted with some surprising fact or *result* (e.g., "These beans are white"), we hypothetically suppose a general *rule* ("All the beans from this bag are white") which would explain the result as a *case* of that rule ("These beans are from this bag"). Depending upon whether this rule or code (a) existed already but had to be applied to this particular instance, (b) is the combination of two or more previous hypotheses, or (c) had to be invented, Eco then further distinguishes between (a) overcoded, (b) undercoded, and (c) uncoded or creative abductions. This third and most radical instance involves a situation whereby the subject "delves directly into the as yet unshaped continuum, mapping his perception as he organizes it."[112] Creative abduction, in other words, is "a mode of production whereby the producer of the sign-function chooses a new material continuum not yet segmented for that purpose and proposes a new way of organizing (of giving form to) it in order *to map* within it the formal element of a content-type."[113] Cartography thus entails a creative activity of code-making *simultaneous* to the application of that generic code to a singular result. As a character from *Foucault's Pendulum* exclaims: "This isn't a map, then; it's a design for a machine to produce variations of maps, until the right map is found!"[114]

Thus, in the face of an as yet uncharted land or unfamiliar earth (the continuum or purport) as those which today are the metaphorical object of cultural studies, a cartographer has to invent the very legend (the forms, rules or codes) with which to interpret and map out the land or earth as territory (as semiotically formed substances). Cultural, ideological, and political landscapes are thus not given blank spots out there waiting to be discovered, but even to be perceived as territories, they have to be mapped, named, and semioticized, that is, engendered. Nor are maps and legends out there, waiting to be projected onto a stark territory. Rather, map, earth and territory mutually constitute one another in the process of hypothetical inferences, the joint product of which forms the realm "we" live in, and "us" as well, insofar as "the map of semiosis, as defined at a given stage of historical development (with the debris carried over from previous semiosis), tells us who we are and what (or how) we think."[115]

A recent multimedia project, for example, commemorates an abandoned section of New York City's canal zone with an artistic map combining distorted photographic and cartographic images with literary subtitles from Calvino's *Invisible Cities*. With this project, *Angst: Cartography*, the authors wish to express their conviction that "the cartographer both replicates and conceives," a conviction for which they find confirmation in "the wisdom of the seven-year old who intuitively understood that because the line of the equator has been drawn by the cartographer, a new reality has been inscribed."[116] To account for this youthful wisdom, as I have tried to show, neither writing nor simulating are satisfactory answers. Putting the mimetic principles of presence, correspondence and equivalence under erasure, or pushing them toward their reversion into death, by no means explains how it is that a cartographer both replicates and conceives. Only if criticisms of mimesis also yield positive redefinitions of poiesis, namely, if the philosophy of difference leads to an affirmative rethinking of inference, will the current shift from textuality to territoriality be able actively to take up the motto of *A Thousand Plateaus*: "Writing has nothing to do with signifying. It has to do with surveying, mapping, even realms that are yet to come."[117]

Part Three

History/Historicity/ Historiography

According to Ortega y Gasset (after Dilthey), we have no nature, but only a history. Aside from the negative implications for any "universal laws" of existence, this distinction itself initiates us into the arena of change. Without the thought of change, no thought of history can exist; indeed, the thought of change *is* historical thought, and the concept of change is itself historiographic. The activity of mapping cultural evolution, privileging and deprivileging discourses, and mechanizing the orchestration of terrestrial relationships, within the context of temporal structure, is the plotting of change at the macrocosmic level. Conceptualizations of history and historical process rely fundamentally on change, at minimum as a dialectical agent.

Within the context of history and historiographic change, the fundamental questions of human existence are framed. How can we and should we see ourselves, individually and collectively? How are we to see ourselves relative to the nonhuman world? How do historical conceptions manifest themselves conceptually? How do language, memory, metaphor work as contributors to a treatment of history and culture?

Since history, and any mapping of history's legitimation, involve fundamental questions of broader (and more specific) cultural legitimation, this first section addresses historical grounding in change.

History and historiography, in their very nature, are functions and signs of change. Taking into account questions of both space and time, historical and historiographic discourse continues the Heraclitan/Parmenidean dialogue of change, as well as the Aristotelian question of evolutionary teleology. If Freud is right, and all culture is in fact a repetition compulsion, then the "historical will" must contain and exhibit the great issues of stasis and lack of stasis in culture and the individual. It is repetition, in that it is marked by the recurrence of an object (physical or non-physical) in time.

In addition, culture and history are constructed conceptually in a language system that is itself always caught between stasis and movement, always within the context of change. Linguistically, history is an index of the mechanical processes of change.

Acknowledging that the very concept of history entails change, the essays in this section by Beehler, Chaney, and Calefato explore, within a very widely diverging subject matter, the centrality of a connection between the concepts of history, the mapping of history in historiography, and of change. Immediately reversing the temporal order of the volume's subtitle, Michael Beehler exposes the postmodern idea of the "crossing of two traces" in any (historical) writing: that of the no longer and that of the not yet. Grounding his historiography in de Certeau's *Heterologies* and *Writing of History*, Beehler demonstrates the relation of historiography to time and to writing themselves, showing how it is an attempt to erase time and its relation to time. The "law" of writing is that identity is never one, but two: it is and another, in the form of a sign. Writing is the loss of unified existence and the opening and acknowledgement of difference. Writing desires that we forget this originary difference, and that the "amnesia of the representation of all—and certainly of historical—texts" is necessary for the establishment of the authority of history and text alike.

Interestingly, Beehler's concentration on de Certeau's reading of Freud's Moses brings to light the "speaking for [the] nothing" of any historically oriented text. According to Beehler and de Certeau, all narrative, including historical discourse, "speaks for nothing" successfully when it suppresses the real conditions of its production. This amnesia is essentially historical. Calling up the theatricality of writing, Beehler (like de Certeau) makes repeated use of performative metaphors such as the *mise en scène* and the *trompe l'oeil* of writing to show its representational nature. Beehler, through de Certeau and Freud, sets up conditions for reading any historical text that casts the shadow of the postmodern back across the modern and premodern. Beehler's essay sets into motion a series of questions about the nature of the relationship between (historical) writing and change that will pervade the discussion to follow.

In a provocative, if more direct, historical reading reframed in light of issues Beehler's essay has raised, Joseph Chaney's essay takes up the theme of repetition and its relationship to change, within the context of the history of rhetoric and the relationship between metaphor and science, specifically in the age of the New Science of Bacon and the rhetoric of his time. This discussion at that historical juncture is particularly interesting, Chaney points out, because within the context of the tendency toward epistemological convergence of science in general and the New Science in particular and the inherent divergence of metaphoricity, the origins of the tropic are to be found. Metaphoricity begins, Chaney shows, at the very point of the excess of language. The "metaphoricity of proper meaning," traced through the history of rhetoric since Cicero, is itself re-metaphorized as clothing: metaphor as the "dress" of rhetoric. The rise of the New Science in the seventeenth century prompted a return to the discussion of the legitimation of language and to the notion of the empirical, direct language/world link lost in metaphor and "indirect" or clothed language. Ironically, though the New Science called for a legitimation of *new* pre-metaphorical language, its rise did not change rhetorical styles of the time: the desired return to the "plain style" of speech and writing simply was not practiced by its advocates, as Chaney shows.

History, by extension, is a function of the re-regulation of language, intended to unmask or undress it, a return to the supposed (and desired) facticity "behind" or "below" rhetorical figurality. Chaney traces the development of the notion of the plain style through John Locke's acknowledgement of language as empty signifier, a turn that inadvertently paves the way for the shift into contemporary notions of language and history. Chaney's case is closely observed evidence of, and a demonstrated evolution in the view of, change in the historical treatment of language and of history itself.

In her analysis of the relationships between memory, discourse in general, and historical discourse, focusing on an investigation of Marguerite Yourcenar's historical novel *Mémoires d'Hadrien*, Patrizia Calefato re-orients the temporal and the historical in Bakhtinian terms. She refers to historical "distance" as historiographic and non-chronological, Bakhtin's "great time," the very condition of discourse and literary experience. Calefato establishes a triangulated theoretical matrix in which historical views of Bakhtin, Barthes, Foucault, Nietzsche, and Benjamin confront each other in order to explore the discourse of history. According to Barthes, the difference between the literary and the historical is "the ideological character of the production of 'effects of the real,'" in which sign systems for history are never merely verbal, but relate to the world of experience. The discourse of history entails taking possession of the "inner world," but finding "there" that "outside otherness and distance self has no sense." Calefato's conclusion is that we cannot transform experience into any assertion, that experience is itself a passage from non-signs to signs.

This approach entails a change in the nature of meaning and its relation to language and time, predicated on a "differential" or "generative" temporality in which values and experience are created. In this model, history is a process of the actual construction of sense and of memory. Calefato shows how, as in Benjamin, history is a dissociation of the microcosmic and the macrocosmic, an exploding of any homogeneous course of event and historical treatment of the event. This is particularly provocative in Calefato's treatment because of her choice of subject matter: Yourcenar's in a historical novel, the meeting of literary text and historical discourse that tests assumptions about both.

In the relationships between the specific treatments found in each of the essays in this section and the more general issues raised therein are found the fundamental questions about change and human discourse within whose orbit all texts operate.

8

Speaking for Nothing: Michel de Certeau on Narrative and Historical Time

Michael Beehler

[For Joseph Riddel]

> To speak for nothing is not: not to speak.
> Above all, it is not to speak to no one.
>
> —Jacques Derrida, "How to Avoid Speaking: Denials"

What takes place in historiography's encounter with psychoanalysis? The works of Michel de Certeau reflect upon this question by staging a continual face-off between the disciplines' two ways of writing about time, their two rhetorical strategies of temporality. According to de Certeau, historiography's strategy relies upon a spatialization of time that posits a "clean break between the past and the present" (*Heterologies*, 4). This break, "taken for granted everywhere by the [historiographic] text," allows for the distribution of time into two distinct places: an "over here," the present text itself, and an "over there," the past that the text takes as a mute object calling for analysis and explanation (*Writing of History*, 218). Historiography then conceives of the relationship between these separate temporal sites as a hierarchy of knowledge and power in which the silence of the past is given speech by a present discourse that is "supposed to have knowledge" (*Heterologies*, 31). In other words, the "historical," as de Certeau defines it, is "the analysis which considers its materials as effects of symptoms (economic, social, political, ideological, etc.) and which aims at elucidating the temporal operations (causality, intersection, inversion, coalescence, etc.) which were able to produce such effects" (*Heterologies*, 21). Driven by a "will to objectivity," it thus understands its project as one of diagnosis and revelation, and relies upon the spatializing gesture that places the past always beside the present in relations de Certeau characterizes as "succession . . . , correlation . . . , cause and effect . . . , or disjunction" (*Heterologies*, 4). What historiography cannot conceive of, however, is the past and the present "both at the same time": not the past *beside* the present, but the "past *in* the present." This relationship, excluded from the conceptual field of historiography, is what psychoanalysis "recognizes" and remembers. Where historiography, as de Certeau explains it, spatializes time by conceiving a radical and discernible difference between present and past, psychoanalysis, he suggests, temporalizes space by bringing together in one textual moment an "'own' (the present of this historiography) and an 'other' (the 'past' under study)" whose differences cannot be readily distinguished or spaced out. In the strategy of time characteristic of psychoanalysis, the relationships of past and present are those of

> imbrication (one in the place of the other), of repetition (one reproduces the other in another form), of the equivocal and of the *quid pro quo* (What "takes the place" of what? Everywhere, there are games of masking, reversal, and ambiguity). (*Heterologies*, 4)

Seeking to determine what takes place at the intersection of historiographic and psychoanalytic time, and at the crossing of the one's "clean breaks" with the other's "imbrications," de Certeau frequently turns to Freud himself.

His analysis of what he calls "the Freudian novel," and particularly of *Moses and Monotheism*, is a calculation of this taking place. De Certeau is drawn to Freud's theoretical explanation of the origins of monotheism because it "is situated at this intersection of history and fiction" and continually poses as a question Freud's "own relation to writing" (pp. 308–09). What is most important for de Certeau about this crossroads narrative is not only the way in which it puts forward a "theory of analytical (or scientific) narrativity," but also its confession that it must do so in the form of a fantasy, in a story that is at once a fiction of theory and a theory of fiction (*Writing of History*, 309). As an "elucidation [that] does not escape what it is elucidating," it is a disclosure of the fabricated origins of legend that nevertheless admits its own status as legendary fabrication. De Certeau's essays are explorations of this imbrication of fictional narrative and historical object. He finds Freud's text dancing over this ambiguous crossing, "swaying left and right . . . [like] a dancer who is in unstable equilibrium wherever she tips her toes," performing (at) the intersection of an historiographic and a psychoanalytic rhetoric of time (*Writing of History*, 308). The performance of an unstable, doubled writing, Freud's text elucidates what de Certeau translates into principles of writing in general, principles articulated through the Freudian notions of repression and mourning, and shared by both "historiographic" and "fictional" rhetorical strategies. Neither simply history nor simply fiction, and yet both history and fiction, *Moses and Monotheism*, "changes the scientific and didactic discourse of history into a 'displaced' writing (displaced both in itself and in respect to the 'discipline'), that is, into a novel" (*Writing of History*, 343). What takes place at the crossing marked by *Moses and Monotheism*, in other words, is displacement itself, an oscillation between two strategies of time and, we might also say, between the constative and the performative registers of writing: between what the text says and what it does. This oscillation, for de Certeau and for his reading of Freud, brings to light a certain law of writing.

De Certeau's reading of Freud's "novel" zeroes in on its display of the "inherent structure of the scriptural experience" and on the mutual interferences between historical, scientific method, and psychoanalytic doubt (*Writing of History*, 317). *Moses and Monotheism* is a stratification and a mixture of these two rhetorical registers, and a reintroduction of the ambiguities of time, memory, and writing into the stable spaces of conventional historiography, which Freud slips into like a "thief of a legitimacy." Where the Moses legend provides Jewish monotheism with a secure point of origin, a legitimizing place that orders its subsequent displacements and wanderings, Freud, with his "'Egyptian Moses, . . . initiates a 'dis-order' in the very place protected by the legend" (*Writing of History*, 334). Where it speaks of an initial identity, Freud "brings forth the returns of an initiating division," of an originating cut, repression, or murder, that de Certeau reads as the necessary structure of all scriptural practice (*Writing of History*, 335). In this manner Freud's fantasy becomes an account of "his own relation to writing," a suspicious reflection on its own historicity and on the process of fabrication that enables and directs its historical elucidations. It thus "initiates a play . . . between the object under study and the discourse performing the analysis . . . between the labor that constructs and the ruse that would 'make us believe' in the fiction—a mixed terrain of production and lure" (*Writing of History*, 309). This mixed terrain of writing—which cannot avoid bearing the trace of a praxis always disguised and forgotten by the illuminating knowledge it produces—"leads us back to a march of time" that, "no matter what it reveals or conceals . . . loses nothing." This infinitely retentive time "contradicts the illusory stabilities of space" (*Writing of History*, 335), and in it the past—as a scriptural praxis whose repetition is irrecusable—cannot be simply objectified as that which is beside a discursive present that explains it, but rather appears in that present as that which leaves there its haunting, destabilizing trace. Freudian time, for de Certeau, is the time of memory—it is anamnesic—and of the ghostly return of writing's enabling repression.

What de Certeau reads in Freud is thus a story recounting "the principle of writing, of analysis (which is division, decomposition), and of history": namely, that "identity is not one, but two. One and the other. In the beginning, there is the plural" (*Writing of History*, 314). It is this original duality or cleavage, this identity in pieces, that the legend of Moses both substitutes for and repeats through the movement de Certeau characterizes as the *quid pro quo*. Following Freud, he argues that "the murder of Moses marks the initial division and represents within the vocabulary of an inherited tradition . . . the event that cannot be written . . . , the invisible bloodstain whence the text is generated." The Moses of Jewish legend takes the place of this initial duality, replacing it with the myth of an originating—but purely scriptural—identity, while not being able to completely efface the murder that enables this displacement. In this manner, Freud's story of the murder of Moses becomes de Certeau's story of writing and of the structural quid pro quo that oversees its practice. As de Certeau reads the Freudian analysis of the Jewish legend, "death is something outside of the text of the legend; it conditions discursive production. Within the text, the quid pro quo is the effect of the text's functioning as the figure tricking death." But the trick never completely works, for it is the taking place of this quid pro quo movement, repeated by all writing as its enabling praxis, that destabilizes scripture itself, making of its self-identity a "discourse of fragments" (*Writing of History*, 316). Freud's text is so powerful for de Certeau because, unlike the historiographic writing he often criticizes, it "deals precisely with what historiographers presuppose and place outside of their field of inquiry when they attempt to comprehend various figures (economic, social, mental) established as distinct units" (*Writing of History*, 315): namely, the practices that behind their backs organize and direct their discourses of knowledge. Freud, on the other hand, narrates these practices while playing them out ("The *quid pro quo* is at once the statement and operation of theory" [*Writing of History*, 331]): in his texts, "the uncertainty of place, or division, is not what must be eliminated so that discourse can be organized." Rather, division, rupture, and doubt are admitted as

> the postulate of the construction (*Konstruction*) and the element within which the discourse is produced. The doubt and the method imply one another. . . . Writing is born and treats of admitted doubt, of explicit division; in sum, of the impossibility of its own place" (*Writing of History*, 320).

The *beside-ness* of doubt and method is crossed, for de Certeau, by the Freudian imbrication of doubt and method, of the one and the other at play in the same place and within the same text that, for this reason, cannot fail to be wounded.

De Certeau reads Freud's text as both explaining and demonstrating this wound. It tells of how "the disappearance of Moses allowed for the appearance of the Mosaic saga," and of how the experience of such a disappearance structures writing in general, making of it the inevitable site of sacrifice and mourning (*Writing of History*, 324). What disappears so that writing can take place is, for de Certeau, "a presence" or a legitimizing "place" that, "as it vanishes, founds the obligation of writing" (*Writing of History*, 325). Writing, then—like Freud's story of the origin of the Moses legend—bears the trace of this withdrawal and of the sacrifice—the "loss of existence"—that must have taken place for there to have been a scriptural replacement: that is, the legend or the text itself (*Writing of History*, 324). Writing bases itself on this loss, and thus opens itself as (in) the inscription of a gaping wound, or as the articulation of a debt that "must be traced relentlessly" (*Writing of History*, 325). This enabling wound or debt can only be repeated. Never can it be healed or made good, since each repetition, each event of writing, "articulates the constantly initial fact that the subject [and the text] is *never authorized* by a place," and hence "begins with an exodus" (*Writing of History*, 320, 319). "*Mourning this* [authorizing] *presence* and giving it up as lost" is, for de Certeau, "equivalent to writing" (*Writing of History*, 324), which is thus generated by "this loss and this obligation" (*Writing of History*, 320).

The labor of mourning that marks writing's beginning-in-displacement, and hence its exilic and nomadic character, cannot be made the object of a traditionally historiographic or scientific elucidation, since the "moral of [Freud's] story"—namely, that "one must die in the body before writing can be born"—is for de Certeau "not proven by dint of a system of knowledge." It is, rather, "merely narrated," repeated as a fantasy or story, a fiction "built on the 'nothing' of past existence from which nothing (*nichts*) subsists" (*Writing of History*, 322, 324). Narrative speaks for this nothing and admits to what the explanatory strategies of historiography repress: that is, the fact that the game of writing is "organized by a loss," that it "has no hereditary soil," and that it "cannot forget the misfortune [the departure and the debt] from which its necessity springs" (*Writing of History*, 319). Freud wagers in *Moses and Monotheism*, as de Certeau reads it, that through the reintroduction of narrative, fiction, and fantasy into the amnesic place of historiographic seriousness, into the very "*law of* [the authorizing] *place*" that historical discourse takes for granted—through, that is, an anamnesic rhetorical strategy that is the "memory of a forgotten separation" (*Writing of History*, 323)—the praxes that organize and direct this writing can be clarified, and the didactic power of such "scientific" discourses can be diminished. *Moses and Monotheism* narrates the return of the repressed (the Egyptian Moses) to the place of identity and authority (Moses's name), and, in a similar manner, according to de Certeau, it also enacts the return of the repressed (narrative, fiction, fantasy) to the authoritative rhetoric of historiography, changing it into an "historical novel," an unstable duality and a "science fiction" that oscillates between its two registers (*Writing of History*, 347). For Freud, "Moses" names the imbrication, the site of the uncanny "*one and the other*—the occupant and the ghost," the intersection marking the two-in-one-place that historiography, by placing the past beside the present, or "history" beside "fiction," seeks not to know (*Writing of History*, 346).

Where historiography spatializes, distinguishing between the here and the there, the past and the present, narrative temporalizes and "states the inverse of what is founded by spatial structure" (*Writing of History*, 333). In the place of knowledge, the place of discrimination and of the self-identity of discrete places, it recalls the repression—the scriptural and psychological praxes—that originally produces and therefore from the beginning divides, wounds, and destabilizes these historiographic legends. Narrative marks the operation of a memory beyond intentionality: it is the trace of the practices—of the very historicity of its writing—that oversee historiography's productions but about which it can never directly speak. This past unsettles the present of knowledge and writing, returning to haunt it as an uncanny familiarity, the ghost of what is both present in and absent from every present. Freud's historical narratives, for de Certeau, are a way of getting at this past, of making it reappear in the place of historical knowledge, and thereby effecting in that place an "epistemological rupture" that "excludes the possibility of closure" (*Writing of History*, 299).

Throughout his writings, de Certeau understands historiography as an "action directed against [this] past" and as a rhetorical strategy aiming at "erasing its own relation to time" (*Heterologies*, 3; *Writing of History*, 323). In "History: Science and Fiction," he explores in detail how this desire to forget temporality itself is connected to representation and to the knowledge of the "past" produced by the historiographic text. There are for him two "reals" in such a text: a past "as represented by historiography" and a "real" that determines the production of this representation. These two "reals" do not "correspond." Rather, like the Mosaic legend of Freud's text, historiography "hides behind the picture of a past the present that produces and organizes it." This "*mise en scène* of a (past) actuality" disguises what makes possible its taking place: namely, the "present" time of its own productive practices (*Heterologies*, 203). This is substitution and replacement par excellence, what for de Certeau constitutes the enabling condition—the primal murder, the general law of loss and debt—of writing itself: the *trompe l'oeil* of the text whose "representation of historical realities is itself the means by which the real conditions of its own production are camouflaged" (*Heterologies*, 206). Historical representations, in pretending to remember another past that legitimizes them, are in fact the instruments of an active forgetting of their own past and of their status as exiled performatives. Since they gain authority "only if they are successful in obliterating any memory of the conditions under which they were produced," they must be seen to "speak in the name of the 'real,'" and by the ruse of this trompe l'oeil, which makes representation appear to speak for something, forgetting takes place (*Heterologies*, 208).

This fundamental amnesia, which by its very occurrence is the trace of a "return of the past in the present discourse," constitutes for de Certeau the "essence of the historical" (*Heterologies*, 214). This past, to which the present text of knowledge is infinitely indebted, is the obscene that takes place within historiography's *mise en scènes* as their excluded other and as the focus of their amnesic, repressive gestures. It is the performative register of the *mise en scène* without which any scene of "knowledge"—structured in advance as the substitution of representation for praxis; of spaced-out, historical difference for temporal, narrative imbrication—could not take place. The fact that this "'off-stage' (ob-scene) of language" (*Heterologies*, 160), this unrepresentable "other," is "already there, in place" (*Heterologies*, 217) in every scene of representation, divides that scene from the beginning, wounding it with the trace of an "elsewhere" of discourse within discourse (*Writing of History*, 251). This elsewhere within—what Emmanuel Lévinas might term "the proximate"—is, for de Certeau, the mark of time itself, the "very mode through which time insinuates itself" into the discursive present (*Heterologies*, 217). When he argues that it is "necessary today to 'repoliticize' the sciences" and to "make explicit" their "internal and prevailing relationship to power," he is outlining the need for an historical discourse of the proximate and the obscene, one that will "bring to light those 'shameful' aspects that historiography believes it must keep hidden" (*Heterologies*, 215, 214). Not unlike a Freudian novel, which narrates the doubling of the place of identity with the return of the uncanny other—recalling that, behind the stability of the one lies the instability of the two—such an anamnesic discourse would articulate "temporal experience as the "impossibility of an identity fixed by a place," and thus be the remembrance of the "ambivalence that affects the place from which it speaks and . . . the ambiguity of place as the work of time within the space of knowledge itself" (*Heterologies*, 218, 217). It would be a fiction, as that term begins to re-emerge in Freud with "another logic" as the site "where the other insinuates itself in the place of the 'subject of knowledge'" (*Heterologies*, 219). It would be the narrative of the obscene—the obscenity of narrative in the "scientific *mise en scènes* of historiography—and of the unrepresentable praxes that both produce those scenes of representation and knowledge, and leave in them an ambiguous trace that marks them as a "work of time." In the post-psychoanalytic age de Certeau's works inhabit, the writing of history shares with the writing of fiction its character of producing a "knowledge jeopardized and wounded by [an] otherness" that is the trace of temporality itself (*Heterologies*, 27). Like a "myth," historiography comes to be seen by him as a "story permeated by social practices . . . that are at once absent from its narrative and yet oversee it" (*Heterologies*, 220).

Thus the work of time as the trace of the performative de-legitimizes, as an obscene internal necessity, knowledge's *mise en scènes*. To make this trace explicit is to reopen the wound camouflaged by historiography's representations and thereby to prevent historiography from creating simulacra that, by "assuming the guise of a scientific autonomy, . . . would have the effect of eliminating any serious treatment of the relationship that a language of sense or of communication maintains with a network of forces" (*Heterologies*, 215). It is to make explicit writing's exilic character and the "nothing" upon which it constructs the masks of its scenic displays. Time as trace, in short, brings to light a certain temporal beat, a "cadenced repetition" (*Heterologies*, 99) or scriptural rhythm by which writing oscillates between the assertion of its legitimacy—as a representation of a real past—and the denial of this legitimacy: between, that is, the scene of representation authorized and countersigned by a past actuality, and the confession of the counterfeiting by which that signature is produced. This oscillation between scenic display and temporal performance—between historiographic spacing and narrative time—accounts for the double game of "science fiction" and for writing's irrepressibly dual identity. When de Certeau takes up the question of Freud's use, in *Moses and Monotheism*, of a fragment of a Schiller poem, he makes us hear this scriptural rhythm of writing. The appearance of this poetic aphorism ("What will live of the poem's immortal / must darken in this life") at a "decisive moment of Freud's project" brings to light the "nothingness ('*rien*') on which 'the writing of history' is constructed." It is a confession demonstrating that the truth of this writing is finally poetic: that it speaks for nothing and is authorized, countersigned, and "supported by nothing other than writing's relationship to itself, its beauty" (*Heterologies*, 29). For de Certeau, such a confession "rejects the authority of the fact," "transgresses the social convention which demands that the 'real' be law," "opposes social conventions with its own nothingness," and inverts the "project of historiography," which functions to "obscure nothingness, to suppress the void, to fill the gap." The return of the obscene, poetic confession to the place of knowledge makes it impossible for historiography to obey the first commandment of the scientific: namely, that "the absence or loss at the origin of its construct must not be unveiled" (*Heterologies*, 31). De Certeau's probings of the intersection of psychoanalysis and historiography bring to light this irrecusable transgression and the double negative of a writing that cannot not unveil the nothing "at the origin."

But if Freud's appeal to poetry explicates the double negative of the scriptural rhythm, it must do so, as de Certeau makes clear, only by producing another scenic disguise. Thus not only can writing not *not* be an unveiling of "nothing," it also cannot *be* this unveiling. That is to say, the obscene of writing can be "brought to light" only in an additional *mise en scène* of representational lucidity, another fiction of place or identity that substitutes itself for the temporal praxes that produce it. Hence the double bind that constitutes the double imperative of writing's two-step dance, the impossible demand that it at once must and must not reveal, make explicit, elucidate, unveil, and remember; and at once must and must not displace, substitute, repress, hide, and forget. Freud's historical novels are no less a problematic response to this re-doubled demand than is the historiography they de-legitimize. As de Certeau puts it,

> There is present in the process of writing itself a duality which allows it to work (as well as the analyst) at times as a cast-off excluded from reality, an illusion of knowledge, a dejection of science, and at times as a voracious authority and a dominating institution. (*Heterologies*, 29)

This is even the case with Freud's quotation of Schiller, which de Certeau notes changes, through its inscription in Freud's text, from a "poem . . . presented in the visibility of its unknowing" to a sign of Freud's own credibility, authority, and knowledge: "From this point of view, Freudian discourse again makes a poetic gesture, all the while institutionalizing this gesture. It thereby gains legitimation, while the poem is the text which nothing authorizes" (*Heterologies*, 30–31). The Schiller poem becomes for Freud a symptom countersigning Freud's own insight into the "nothing" at writing's origin. Its quotation is the trick by which Freud displaces this "nothing" with his knowledge-of-nothing, the way in which he silences "nothing" by making it explicit, by speaking of and for it, thereby submitting himself to the law of repression and substitution, all the while acknowledging and confessing that this is what he must do. For de Certeau, what Freud's texts do (i.e., submit to a law of writing they cannot avoid) is evidence of Freud's own insightful cleverness ("Cleverly, he maneuvers between the 'nothing' of writing and the 'authority' that the institution furnishes the text" [*Heterologies*, 33]) and of the legitimacy of what his texts say: namely, that all writing (including and most especially his own) is inevitably the symptom of the repression that structures it.

De Certeau's readings of Freud share the same kind of cleverness he attributes to Freud and produce similar kinds of effects. For example, he prefaces his discussion of Moses and Monotheism with the following caveat. It is worth quoting in full:

> But in constructing this history in which the text plays the role of a hero among adversaries, passing through trials to a final disclosure, what am I indeed doing, if not effacing the rupture operative everywhere in the text and taking a chronological continuity for granted, where the various withdrawals from and returns to the "work" are arranged in order? I am building in turn a "legend" of the text. Through my narrative, I am obliterating the rift which was marked from the beginning, which organizes the form of this text disseminated in small fragments, and which is repeated within its content with the obsessive mention of "lacunae," with the scrutiny of contradictions from which it is developed . . . , or with the imbroglio into which it sinks further and further as it advances. I am taking this text back to a linearity which betrays it. I am putting the ersatz of my history (a connected series or known facts) in the place of this writing which is a novel by dint of its avowed relations with its other. (*Writing of History*, 311)

By confessing to the strategy by which he will replace Freud's ruptured "writing" with his own *mise en scène* or *ersatz* history, de Certeau acknowledges his debt to the law of the *quid pro quo* that his essay will explicate through Freud's text and offers his own work as a symptom of this general logic. His text thus confirms what he knows to be true about all writing, a calculation that explains for him in advance what will have already been the fate of his own writing, which then becomes a discourse about, of, or on this fate. Because of this pre-scriptural certainty, it would appear that nothing could surprise de Certeau (or, for that matter, Freud himself, since nothing can escape the structural necessity de Certeau is dedicated to explaining). His "discourse on the other" provides us with a meta-commentary that accounts for the function of the "other" within the positivities of scientific and historiographic rhetoric, describing the repressed "other" ("the discourse's mode of relation to its own historicity," as Wlad Godzich puts it [*Heterologies*, xx]) that "returns" to these discourses as what has always already been there in them. This discourse on the heterological in discourse, and on the logic of the always already there that irrecusably haunts writing, foresees the future of any writing as the return of its past. It thereby calculates and determines the function and significance of the heterological, circumscribing any "other" within the anticipatory horizon of its own meta-commentary. De Certeau's self-reflective confessions that this meta-commentary is simply another *ersatz* substitute for a past (Freud's text) it must murder or repress in order to take its place does not wound the knowledge that his text produces: rather, it confirms it in its honesty and apparently clairvoyant lucidity. From this perspective, de Certeau's writings determine the "other" as an alterity whose return has been always already anticipated in a foresight it is the function of their caveats and self-accusations to mark. In making explicit a logic of this return, in thematizing the "other" in a discourse on the other, they utilize a form of address that would seem to foreclose the possibility of change and the thinking of a different future: that is, of the future as the site of the unforeseeable "itself." Making the heterological foreseeable, inscribing the "other" within their own anticipatory horizon, they would seem to deny any chance for such thinking.

And yet, a brief parenthetical comment at the end of "The Fiction of History" suggests a different mode of address, one that gives the unforeseeable a chance by maintaining a place for it within the clairvoyance of the present discourse. There de Certeau expounds on the theory of science fiction and its relation to Defoe and Kafka, both of whom are for him writers (like Freud) in whose works the law of the return of the repressed—of "death" and "doubt"—is reiterated, and the logic of the quid pro quo is most clearly demonstrated. Interrupting his elaboration of this general logic, de Certeau parenthetically notes, "but we must speak with discretion about what we do not know" (*Writing of History*, 347). How might this speech be possible? what must we do to speak of what we do not know? If we speak about what we do not know—even if we speak circumspectly, with caution and discretion—do we not in fact bring what we do not know into the realm of what we do know, since, by so speaking, we explain that we know that we do not know, and thereby determine and delimit our lack of knowledge? Such speech, like de Certeau's caveats and self-accusations, simply extends and confirms its clairvoyance and lucidity, leaving in it no place for the experience of another not already qualified by being foreseen. And yet "we *must* speak" (with or without caution and discretion), and it is this "must," this call to speech, that leaves the trace of its withdrawal in our responses to that call: in, that is, the *mise en scènes* of what we speak. And not only must we speak, but "we must speak *about*" something: as Derrida notes in another context, "there cannot be an absolutely negative discourse: a *logos* necessarily speaks about something; it cannot avoid speaking of something; it is impossible to refer to nothing" ("How to Avoid Speaking" 34). For de Certeau, this speaking about, which betrays the other and puts otherness itself at risk, is what we must do; it is "what must be said if something else is to be understood" (*Heterologies*, 326). It is only thanks to this speaking—itself the trace of a call that infinitely precedes it—that this "something else" takes place as the extra, excessive trace of *that which has yet to take place*, of the unforeseeable itself, and of that which remains "to be understood" in some unspecified future. Speech for de Certeau is the crossing of these two traces: the trace left in the present by the passing of the no longer present, and the trace opened in the present by the unforeseeable futurity of the not yet present. It is the taking place of the place where nothing takes place, a nothing that, as the site of a play of traces—an intersection of the no longer and the not yet—marks the "taking place" of time itself. Through his writings, de Certeau speaks for the nothing of this crossing, making it explicit not by speaking about it, but by speaking at all, by addressing himself to it as to another that remains other, in a mode of address that is both the trace of "what is lacking" and the "making a place for a future" (*Writing of History*, 85). His is a speech "for the sake of speaking, to experience what happens to speech through speech *itself*" (Derrida, 5), and in the experiencing of this indefinite passivity, is a speaking for nothing.

9

The Revolution of a Trope: The Rise of the New Science and the Divestment of Rhetoric in the Seventeenth Century

Joseph Chaney

FIRST CLOTHING: CICERO

In *De Oratore*, Cicero suggests that metaphor was originally nothing other (and nothing less) than catachresis.[1] It "sprang [*genuit*] from necessity due to the pressure of poverty and deficiency" (3.38, 155). Originally, then, metaphor was not a substitute for ordinary usage. Instead, it supplied a want, supplementing an essential lack of words—a lack which, according to the logic of Cicero's claim, originally had been total. The first word was a metaphor, the translation to a new context of a term properly belonging to another place. But in this case, in the first linguistic instance, the term was transferred from nowhere to nowhere, with the effect that the second nowhere had now become a somewhere. Creation out of nothing. Here is the myth of the divine power of language, specifically of metaphor. Metaphor as the discovery of substance, the genesis of the first substantive. And the history of a positive science that would have language refer directly to substances or to ideas will be, in part, the history of the denial, forgetting, covering-up, and veiling of this impossible origin of signification.

In this, the formal rhetorics are complicit. As we shall see, the forgetfulness that is the possibility of science is already operative in Cicero's *De Oratore* and in all of the rhetorics that follow the classical model. Not surprisingly, Bacon, Descartes, and their followers would never be able to acknowledge the manner in which the discipline of rhetoric, against which they so meaningfully reacted, paved the way and cleared a space for science. The Ciceronians and Ramists of the sixteenth century each did their part. But first let us attend to Cicero himself.

According to Cicero, once the original linguistic lack presumably had been supplied by metaphor, metaphor could at last function stylistically. Figurative language then came into popular use due to its "agreeable and entertaining quality." At this point Cicero introduces the analogy of clothing to explain the origin of rhetoric:

> For just as clothes were first invented to protect us against cold and afterwards began to be used for the sake of [bodily] adornment and dignity as well, so the metaphorical employment of words was begun because of poverty, but was brought into common use for the sake of entertainment (*delectationis*). (3.38, 155)

In other words, having been born of linguistic necessity, metaphor was later (for the sake of pleasure and dignity) extended to common use, as a semantically superfluous substitute within an already sufficient lexicon. But here the analogy to clothing in fact exposes (even as it conceals) the semantically constitutive function of metaphor. For the idea of ornamentation as an extension of metaphor beyond its original, necessary usage preserves the catachretic function of metaphor as its essence. The decorative, dignifying metaphor, which is secondary and defined by its nonessential quality, is said to be founded upon a prior metaphorical (i.e., catachretic) language. Clothing replaces clothing, the same clothing, with the effect that the first clothing is now proper and essential—in effect, barely clothing at all. The difference consists in the repetition of the same. Rhetoric, pleasure, dignity, culture are the effect of a repetition that conceals repetition *per se*.

One wonders what place the primary, catachretic metaphor could possibly have in a rhetoric of which it would be the condition of possibility. As is well known, classical rhetoric answers this difficulty by itself supplying the term *catachresis*, or *abusio*, and giving it a place within an exhaustive catalog of tropes, as one trope among others. In a moment of purposeful forgetfulness, the linguistically generative function of metaphor is termed an abuse of language and is injected as such into a rhetoric. It is worth remarking that (according to this model) only after the natural languages had been made virtually replete with proper meanings could metaphor (as metaphor and as catachresis) properly take its place in an art of rhetoric, or could rhetoric properly be a place. In that place, the source of places is degraded. In the service of an instituted language, catachresis—the barest of metaphors—is now conceived as language at its most improperly excessive. That which in the myth of the origin of language was proper, necessary, and fundamental to humanity—as requisite as clothing—henceforth defines what is improper in languages. At the same time, this same clothing worn against the cold, the proper-improper origin of language and of substances, is (con)fused with, or incorporated into, the natural body and made to don the ornamental and dignifying clothing of rhetoric. Buried, shrouded in rhetoric, the original, generative metaphor is presumably "dead"; as representational language, not as rhetoric, it henceforth constitutes the proper or the usual. The cold is forgotten. Nevertheless, as we shall see with regard to the history of language theory, what is dead also has a life of its own.

For Cicero the concept of similitude authorizes a representational epistemology only after catachretic metaphor is consigned to a catalog of tropes and its generative function masked by the concept of "borrowing." Cicero completes the movement of this masking:

> For even country people [say, "the vines are gemming," "the grass is extravagant," "the crops are happy"].[2] The explanation is that when something that can scarcely be conveyed by the proper term (*verbo proprio*) is expressed metaphorically, the meaning we desire to convey is made clear by the resemblance of the thing that we have expressed by the word that does not belong (alieno verbo). Consequently the metaphors in which you take what you have not got from somewhere else are a sort of borrowing. . . . (3.38, 155–6).

Here subsuming catachresis under the term *metaphor*, Cicero assumes that resemblance authorizes the metaphor, which appears, therefore, as a more or less appropriate application of an alien word.[3] The borrowed term is, in this case, the appropriately improper. It pays a linguistic debt only. As Cicero would have it, there is no essential shortfall; for already present in the linguistically impoverished place is some "thing" the appearance of which may be properly represented by the alien word—that is, represented differently, although perhaps presented for the first time—but nevertheless re-presented as the same. The borrowed term becomes an instrument, not of invention or disclosure or even of dissimulation, but of representation and of truth—a paradoxically transparent medium, revealing in its proper place, making clear, even by means of otherness, the meaning that was always evident there.

The same would hold true *a fortiori* in cases in which metaphors substitute for proper words. In the representational system defined by the concept of metaphor-as-borrowing, rhetoric operates (epistemologically) according to a tropic logic: words are like things; things like words. But the things are metaphysically prior. Or, more precisely, the like-ness, the principle of resemblance (which is the archeotropic meaning that links things and words) takes up residence in things and authorizes names. But where does meaning itself originate? Cicero's narrative ultimately denies what it at once confesses, namely that meaning is a metaphorical effect. The rhetorical metaphor displaces an original metaphor, thereby effecting the propriety of the prior metaphor; and this effect of propriety, in turn, masks the metaphoricity of proper meaning. This logic holds even when there is no prior metaphor in evidence. Even Cicero, then, denies the metaphoricity of knowledge.

It is already clear how the advocates of the new science had their work cut out for them by the rhetoricians. By means of a rhetoric founded on resemblance, words had been defined by proper meanings corresponding to things. Figurative language might overlay the proper or, as sometimes in the case of catachresis, abusively disrupt it. But already the principle of substitution and secondarity prevented any formal rhetoric from speaking of a clothed body as though the body were defined by its clothing.[4]

THE NOBLE DRESS OF ELOQUENCE: WILSON AND PUTTENHAM

In the rhetorical treatises of the sixteenth century the social value of eloquence is regularly represented in terms of the classical sartorial metaphor of metaphor. For rhetoricians such as Thomas Wilson and George Puttenham, eloquence comes to authorize knowledge, guaranteeing representational truth, while also marking social distinctions. Let us here examine the ideology of rhetoric as it was given to Bacon (without yet bothering about the propriety of that inheritance), noting its sociopolitical as well as its metaphysical significance. Below, in the third section, we shall inquire how the advocates of the new science come to terms with the metaphorics of this ideology of language, which is at the same time aristocratic in principle and scientifically conservative.

We should first recall that the epistemological devaluation of metaphor begins within the discipline of rhetoric proper. In the Ciceronian rhetoric and in the reforms of Pierre de la Ramee (Peter Ramus), the way was already paved for scientific positivism. The crux of Ramus's reform in the 1540s and 50s was the division of classical rhetoric into the art of speaking (rhetoric) and the art of thinking (dialectic, or logic).[5] Invention and arrangement, the first two parts of the traditional rhetoric, were now joined under the heading of *logic*, the discipline most valued by Ramus, and the scope of rhetoric thereby reduced to considerations of style and delivery. The English Ramists, for instance Harvey, Fenner, and Fraunce, take for granted this reduction. The Ramist rhetorical treatise becomes, at best, an aid to argumentation and, at worst, an anatomical commentary on poetic uses of ornament.[6]

Ramus's reforms were made possible, if not necessary, by the Ciceronians themselves, who already viewed metaphor as semantically superfluous. Epistemologically, the substitution theory of metaphor privileged referential language and essentialized the "natural" things to which language referred. Thus, even in the *Arte of Rhetorique* (1553) by the Ciceronian Thomas Wilson, we find, in connection with a censuring of affected speech and of the immoderate use of tropes and "foreign" words, an assertion of the primacy of "things." Words are used aptly, Wilson writes, when they "properly agree unto that thyng, whiche thei signifie, and plainly expresse the nature of the same" (332).[7] Although after Bacon such a statement could be read as a prescription for scientific language, Wilson writes as a teacher of oratory. For him, tropes are nevertheless essential to the presentation of knowledge.

Tropes are not valued for their capacity to "express" things; they do not convey knowledge, but rather, "beautifie the sentence, as precious stones are set in a ryng, to commende the golde" (332). Jewels function paradoxically to supplement and praise the beauty of their own setting. In Wilson's analogy, the matter of speech or writing is, like gold, fundamental. Gold, the paradigmatic substance, refers to things. The jewel makes gold appear more properly gold-like (i.e., appear *as such*). Tropes draw proper attention to proper speech. By a supplementary gesture, tropes are reinscribed within the language of propriety as a surplus value. Their presence in discourse comes to signify linguistic propriety and to authorize knowledge. Knowledge is in the place of gold; the wealth of ornament discloses or displays wealth in general, knowledge in general. The knowledge of ornamentation is the knowledge of how wealth and knowledge properly disclose themselves, appear as such, and assume authority. This association of tropes, wealth, knowledge, spectacle, and authority is not accidental. For Wilson, figurative speech is aristocratic.

Wilson seems to be aware of an emerging merchant class from which a mastery of rhetoric may assist the aristocracy and the learned in distinguishing themselves culturally. Although he addresses much of his advice to learned "clerks" (or because he addresses himself to fellow social climbers), his language and imagery constantly promote aristocratic values. And, indeed, in an attempt to secure patronage, he addresses himself first of all to the nobility in the person of the younger John Dudley, Earl of Warwick, whose father, the Duke of Northumberland, was, after 1549, the most powerful man in England. In his dedication, Wilson suggests that his *Rhetorique* may raise to perfection Dudley's already superior oratorical skills:

> Consideringe therfore your Lordshyps hyghe estate, and worthy callyng, I knowe nothyng more fittynge wyth your honoure, then to the gyfte of good reason and understandynge, wherwith we see you notably endued, to join the perfection of Eloquente utteraunce. (6)

Dudley, already naturally endued with, or dressed in, the skills of invention and arrangement, will, by the artificial addition of eloquence, be made a complete orator. In the third book of the *Rhetorique*, on elocution, having already treated of invention and arrangement, Wilson describes the same relationship between reason and eloquence, but this time compares the latter to clothing:[8]

> For whereas Invencion, helpeth to finde matter, and Disposicion serveth to place argumentes: Elocucion getteth wordes to set furthe invencion, and with such beautie commendeth the matter, that reason semeth to bee clad in purple, walkyng afore, bothe bare and naked. (323)

Elocution is both potent and noble. Wilson's metaphors are strangely mixed. Elocution fathers forth ("getteth") purple words with which to clothe reason in nobility. Invention and disposition or arrangement (the two parts of what will become the Ramist logic, and the natural parts Wilson attributes to Dudley), go without beauty, bare and naked, until elocution sets them forth in princely raiments. The Earl of Warwick appears to be deficient. Bare reason and natural intelligence, although good in themselves, are unpresentable, ineffective culturally. Reason is made into a king by eloquence.

The learned clerk may be ennobled by eloquence as well. At one point in the *Rhetorique*, Wilson rebukes learned but ill-spoken men for failing to display their knowledge:

> I much marvail that so many seke the only knowlege of thynges, without any mynd to commende or set furthe their entendement: seyng none can knowe either what thei are, or what thei have, without the gift of utterance. Yea, bryng them to speake their mynd, and enter in talke with suche as are said to be learned, and you shal finde in them suche lacke of utterance, that if you judge theim by their tongue, and expressyng of their mynde, you must nedes saie thei have no learnyng. Wherin me thinkes thei do, like some riche snudges, that havyng great wealth, go with their hose out at heeles, their shoes out at toes, and their cotes out at bothe elbowes. For who can tell, if suche men are worth a grote, when their apparel is so homely, and al their behavior so base? (324)

Clearly Wilson never doubts that these people nevertheless are what they are, and do have knowledge, although they may not know how to demonstrate it. In fact, they may not even know what they know until eloquence discloses their knowledge. Wilson would teach the miserly rich men, the snudges, to acknowledge and display their wealth. Eloquence bestows upon the learned man dignity and authority, dresses his knowledge to look like knowledge. Wilson is concerned with social self-representation, with the value of appearing to be, in speech and aspect, the rich person one is in fact. Rhetoric represents the internal self; like clothing, it distinguishes the rich from the poor, the noble from the common.

Wilson's analogies nevertheless admit the possibility that alien, metaphorical language, intervening in the place of familiar things, produces the self-sameness of representational truth. For knowledge (or nobility) by itself lacks the authority and force of knowledge. In the name of representation, eloquence produces the effect of an essence. Wilson elides the suggestion that the rich clothing of eloquence may ennoble the man only in effect. As the successful social climber knows (and Wilson was one of the most successful), practically speaking, rhetorically speaking, effect is sometimes everything. But Wilson would have noble dress signal a nobleman, would have the effect of knowledge correspond to an actual essence. For Wilson, the value of metaphor consists in its ability to pass away as metaphor and, in the service of a knowledge that is social and not yet scientific, reveal the truth. The showy jewel shows the gold; loud clothing announces the nobleman; eloquence bespeaks knowledge.[9]

George Puttenham, in *The Arte of English Poesie* (1589), takes to its logical conclusion the argument that rhetoric lends social value to speech. The argument in favor of rhetoric leads ultimately to the paradoxical conclusion that figurative language is socially necessary because it is logically unnecessary. Early modern science begins as an exploitation of this breach between figurative language and representational language, which is opened up by the rhetoricians themselves. But in Puttenham the gap remains a passage between rhetoric and representation, even if this passage permits a crossing on the part of rhetoric only, in the sense that figurative language is allowed the capacity to represent or even produce the truth, while putative statements of fact are still accredited the ideal status of transparent revelatory instruments.

Puttenham gives to rhetoric the work of establishing social reality. He writes explicitly for the benefit of courtiers, especially new courtiers, for whom his *Arte* "may serve as a principall good lesson":

> that being now lately become a Courtier he shew not himself a crafts man, & merit to be digraded, & with scorne sent back againe to the shop, or other place of his first facultie and calling, but that so wisely & discreetly he behave himselfe as he may worthily retaine the credit of his place, and

> posession of a very Courtier, which is in plaine termes, cunningly to be able to dissemble. (299)

The new courtier must learn rhetoric, which is the art of discretion, secrecy, disguise, dissembling. This art will not only mask the former craftsman, but will disguise the present courtier as well. The courtier cuts a figure among men. Unlike the craftsman, he is a dissembler by nature. Disguise is proper to the courtier, who is what he is only insofar as he doesn't appear to be what he is. Figurative language is the same. Defined by, and even as figurative language,[10] the courtier is by virtue of seeming other, by representing what he is not—which is not to say that he is any less himself, or any less natural, from Puttenham's perspective. And it goes without saying: if the courtier, secret, discreet, hiding what ought not to be known, conceals only the absence of a secret at the heart of the aristocracy, he is nonetheless the keeper of a secret—perhaps the most fundamental secret, that of dissembling, concealing.

Although the *Arte* treats mainly of poetry, Book III, "Of Ornament," follows the conventions of a Ciceronian rhetoric with its catalog of tropes and figures. And the catalog is prefaced by several chapters on the appropriate use of figurative language in oratory as well as in poetry. The argument of chapter two, for instance, is "How our writing and speaches publike ought to be figurative, and if they be not doe greatly disgrace the cause and purpose of the speaker and writer" (p. 138). Puttenham praises the beauties of aristocratic discourse. He writes in chapter one that the purpose of ornament is to

> delight and allure as well the mynde as the eare of the hearers with a certaine noveltie and strange maner of conveyance, disguising it no litle from the ordinary and accustomed: neverthelesse making it nothing the more unseemely or misbecomming, but rather decenter and more agreable to any civill eare and understanding. (137)

What sometimes deceives the ear and mind also pleases them. The deception no doubt follows from the pleasure, but the latter is not essentially tainted by the former, and the plain style is not therefore to be preferred. Depending on circumstances, a strange usage may be more seemly than an accustomed.

Puttenham finds no reason absolutely to prefer one style above another. At times he commends plainness, as though language could achieve transparency of meaning. But his tendency is to say that customary, ordinary, and merely instrumental speech ought not to appear nakedly. It seems that the sophisticated "strangeness" of ornamental language raises speech above "the common course of ordinary speach and capacitie of the vulgar judgement" (137–8). This stylistic elevation involves the judgment in a higher art that is precisely not common but aristocratic. Puttenham compares poetic ornament to the fashionable adornments of the "great Madames of honour." These ladies may be very beautiful in "personage" and yet would be "halfe ashamed or greatly out of countenaunce" to go without their "courtly habillements." Poetry is similar:

> Even so cannot our vulgar Poesie shew it selfe either gallant or gorgious, if any lymme be left naked and bare and not clad in his kindly clothes and colours, such as may convey them somwhat out of sight. . . . (137)[11]

Clothes and colours are, in their own way, "kindly," or natural. Propriety, and perhaps nature itself, demands that the natural body be removed "somwhat out of sight" by artificial adornment.[12] Where culture is concerned, the merely natural is the vulgar, the common, the ordinary. Common speech, like the unadorned female body, no doubt has its proper place; but in poetry and oratory—public arts—the natural and the plain are improper. Of any bare limb of poetry, it may be said that "being artificially handled must needs yeld it much more bewtie and commendation" (138).

There is in this conceit an implied ideology of aristocratic privilege. By associating linguistic ornamentation with the bodily adornments of the cultured nobility, Puttenham, in the tradition of Wilson and others, accords the highest social value to tropes and figures, and thus to rhetoric itself.[13] One thinks of certain portraits of Queen Elizabeth (for instance, the woodcut portrait that faces the opening of Book I and which, in the words of the Cambridge editors, "seems to have constituted Puttenham's dedication to the *Arte*"), in which the queen's physical body is concealed beneath a spectacle of rich finery that gives to her form a purely symbolic significance. Puttenham's distinction between poetic and ordinary language finds its sociopolitical analogue in the dress codes of the period. Just as clothing ennobles a person by concealing the ordinary body, figures ennoble and perfect speech by repressing all that is vulgar and "natural" about ordinary language. The same logic organizes both activities toward a single political aim. For what pleases the "civill eare and understanding" of courtiers also mystifies and pleasantly deceives the minds of commoners. Just as domestic political power during the reign of Elizabeth was, to a significant degree, a matter of persuasion by means of spectacle, so eloquence can be presumed to derive its cultural force from the entire noble pageantry which its conventions adumbrate.

In this respect, Puttenham typifies the kind of rhetorical theorist scorned by seventeenth-century advocates of the new science. But here we should caution against hasty simplification. The disapprobation with which Puttenham views what he considers real abuses of figurative language in chapter seven, "Of Figures and Figurative speaches," seems to rival that of the Baconians. With regard to forensic oratory, Puttenham writes:

> As figures be the instruments of ornament in every language, so be they also in a sorte abuses or rather trespasses in speach, because they passe the ordinary limits of common utterance, and be occupied of purpose to deceive the eare and also the minde, drawing it from plainnesse and simplicitie to a certaine doublenesse, whereby our talke is the more guilefull & abusing, for what els is your Metaphor but an inversion of sence by transport . . . seeking to inveigle and appassionate the mind. . . . (154)

Puttenham's censure is almost always contextual. The same figures, when not spoken by "wresters of upright judgement" to impassion "the straite and upright mind of a Judge," but instead by the poet "in the eare of princely dames, yong ladies, gentlewomen and courtiers," are "not in truth to be accompted vices but for vertues in the poetical science very commendable" (154–55).

The point seems simple: serious matters, such as the search for truth, demand the plain style, whereas poetry may aspire to ornamental usage. Nothing could be more Baconian. The difference is that Puttenham maintains an ambivalence regarding the epistemological value of figurative language, whereas the new scientists will wish to decide that value once and for all. Decorum establishes a double standard. Judges ought not to be deceived, but commoners and women may be. Throughout the *Arte,* two sets of roughly synonymous terms correspond to proper and improper language. On the one side we find terms such as *commendable, pleasant, sweet, civil, discreet, decency, beauty, harmony, dignity, custom, proportion, measure, decorum,* and their variants; and on the other, *foul, excessive, disordered, defective, vicious, uncivil, barbarous, foreign, inconvenience, disproportion, deformity, indecency, abuse, heresy of language, trespasses in speech, ill or vicious manners of speech,* and so forth. The distinction is crucial. For Puttenham, literary style, social behavior, and dress are all equally subject to "decorum," which he defines in terms of a natural hierarchy. In chapter twenty-four ("Of decencie in behaviour which also belongs to the consideration of the Poet or maker"), we find the following commentary on dress:

> And in the use of apparell there is no litle decency and undecencie to be perceived, as well for the fashion as the stuffe, for it is comely that every estate and vocation should be knowen by the differences of their habit: a clarke from a lay man: a gentleman from a yeoman: a souldier from a citi-

> zen, and the chiefe of every degree from their inferiours, because in confusion and disorder there is no manner of decencie. (283)

Puttenham believes that clothing, like speech, functions to maintain the social order, keeping people in their proper places. At the same time, however, he is unable (and even unwilling) to conceal the manner in which rhetoric systematically disrupts the linguistic order. For, relative to this binary, hierarchical scheme, figurative language is defined not so much by one set of terms or the other, as by a capacity to cross from one to the other: from the figure's proper place in the improper, to the place of propriety, which may be rendered paradoxically all the more proper and commendable by such a trespass. This is the skill of the courtier, even the courtier who was lately a craftsman. And the good orator, careful of context, is able to make "now and then very vice goe for a formal vertue in the exercise of this Arte" (155). In the mouths of the eloquent, tropes and figures are virtuous vices, excess is sufficient, foul is fair.

In chapters twenty-one and twenty-two Puttenham discusses the unequivocal "vices" of speech, the affected, barbarous, or superfluous figures. He finds that these notorious vices are on occasion excusable. Moreover, a number of Puttenham's vernacular terms for the commendable tropes and figures connote transgression or disorder, as, for instance, the misnamer (metonymy), the overreacher or loud liar (hyperbole), the trespasser (hyperbaton), and the straggler (parecbasis: "by allusion to the souldier that marches out of his array, or by those that keep no order in their march" [233]). By translation and neology, Puttenham remetaphorizes the Greek terms, virtually personifying the various figures and animating language with dozens of individual agents of elocution, some ostensibly proper and virtuous, others improper and vicious, but all of them licensed, under the regulation of decorum, to participate in speech. Language itself assumes the lively appearance of a society in need of law. In Puttenham's text, decorum performs a constant and arbitrary policing, for it occasionally inscribes within formal unlawfulness a line of difference that renders impropriety provisionally proper.

Because Puttenham conceives the problem of representation in terms primarily moral and practical rather than formal, the improprieties of rhetoric never vitiate those persons who would distinguish themselves from the crowd: the poets, the courtiers, and the prince. Rather, rhetorical vice originates in the bad intentions of the deceptive commoner, the false courtier, the hypocrite, the pretender, each recognizable by his failure at dissembling.[14] By implication, abuses are not abuses when performed successfully by legitimate noblemen. And legitimacy acquired after the fact is still legitimacy. The good speaker converts the vices of language into virtues. The clerk thereby converts himself into a prime minister. In this manner, rhetoric escapes the responsibility of representational truth at the same moment that it claims that truth as an ideal.

The transgression of figurative language is in principle unlimited. The forgotten lesson of rhetoric (and thus of science) in the early modern period is that "representational" meaning is infinitely manipulable because it is figuratively constituted. Even in the *Arte* this lesson is not allowed. Puttenham makes decorum regulate rhetoric in accordance with a representational ideal whereby the truth of language corresponds to the truth of given things. A knowledge of the fundamental duplicity of figurative language (by the admitted separation of word and thing or of word and idea) would perhaps undermine the received principle of representation were it not that figurative language, under the regulation of decorum, acts to conceal duplicity at the level of proper and usual words.[15] By means of figures, rhetoric preserves representational language at the same time that it goes beyond it; it preserves it precisely by going beyond it. Representation, and indeed truth itself in the classical sense, depends on the reduction of metaphor and the other semantic figures to the function of decoration, linguistic clothing. During the early modern period this reduction made possible not only the formal rhetorics themselves, but also the codified inscription of social distinctions in speech. A scientific theory of language that would seek to "strip" language of its figures for the sake of representational truth would therefore implicitly threaten the social order such a rhetoric helps to maintain. For science attempts to see the craftsman in every courtier. This practice promises social revolution, despite the conservative politics often espoused by the theorists themselves for the purpose of ensuring the perpetuation of their research (if for no other reason). But the linguistic reduction is not revolutionary in the fundamental metaphysical sense that animates the dream of a language of science.

NAKED SCIENCE: BACON AND AFTER

The Baconians of the seventeenth century worked implicitly, and perhaps unconsciously, to reduce the social value of rhetoric; but they labored purposefully to limit the authority of rhetoric as a discipline concerned with truth. Their aim was to legitimate the "new," and to some extent competing, discipline of science. In practical terms, it is not surprising that they wished to improve the instrumental quality of language by ridding it of the redundancies that the rhetoricians themselves seemed to acknowledge.[16] Nor is it surprising that their crusade against rhetoric should itself have been productive of so much figurative language, although the irony is worth noting. But as Brian Vickers remarks in "The

Royal Society and English Prose Style," the apparent contradiction is accounted for largely by the simple fact that it is "difficult . . . to express a strong opinion or evaluation of anything without resorting to metaphor" (21).[17]

The new scientists did not oppose rhetoric absolutely. Vickers warns against confusing conceptual and stylistic issues. He points out that "Bacon made a clear distinction between the language of scientific method and the communication of experiment, and other language, in which an appeal to the imagination was legitimate" (14). Vickers finds fault with the influential views of Richard Foster Jones, who argued that the "stylistic ideal" of a purely denotative language, espoused by Royal Society polemicists such as Thomas Sprat, "was reflected in the scientific writings of its members" (quoted in Vickers, 17).[18] Vickers demonstrates the impossibility of distinguishing among camps of writers in the seventeenth century on the basis of use or nonuse of metaphor (21). English prose style remained unchanged, and in practice rhetoric was not abandoned by the new scientists.

With regard to the history of science, Jones misapplies both Sprat's and Bacon's statements against rhetoric, wrongly assuming that such writers are anti-rhetorical rather than opposed specifically to the use of excessive figurative language in works of science. As Vickers demonstrates, many ostensible attacks on rhetoric were aimed against heterodox factions, scientific and religious: the alchemists, for example, and the various nonconformists. Among apologists of science after the advent of the Royal Society, an opponent's mere use of metaphor became increasingly a target of attack.[19] The Conformist scientists of the Restoration denigrated their opponents' language as metaphorical in order to portray their opponents as irrational, effeminate, and fanciful. Conversely, the new scientists privileged the plain style (which they associated with masculinity and reason), disingenuously claimed it for themselves as the proper language of science, and, with equal dishonesty, projected that style onto the homiletics of the Church of England as well.

Prose style in England, even among the new scientists, appears not to have undergone a revolution. What concerns us here is rather the rhetoric of science as it engages questions of rhetoric, truth, and power. In the polemics of the new scientists, the plain style, which had always (since Aristotle) been associated conventionally with truth and sincerity, is at last linked to political power and made to triumph over eloquence itself. In discourses concerned with the foundation and origin of knowledge a persistent rhetoric of linguistic stripping and nakedness characterizes the defense of the new science as, in part, a polemic against the discipline of rhetoric. In these discourses eloquence is represented as an obstructing veil of superfluous verbiage.

We see the beginning of the scientific critique of rhetoric in the works of Bacon. In *The Advancement of Learning* (1605), Bacon's stated goal is to lay a new scientific foundation upon new principles—primarily inductive reasoning and experimentation subject to repeatability. In the field of scientific philosophy Bacon does, however, value figurative language when it is used sometimes to "clothe and adorn" obscurity with "sensible and plausible elocution" in discourses and counsels for the purpose of transmitting knowledge (284). That is, he values *enargia*, or vividness, as an aid to conceptualization. But "in the severe inquisition of truth" figurative language can become a hindrance that quenches our desire to pursue further knowledge before we reach the end.

In Book I Bacon partly attributes the decline of substantial learning to the rise of the kind of "delicate learning" associated with rhetorical training. He notes in Luther a recognition of the "necessity" of rhetoric for purposes of persuading the vulgar masses: it was the "fittest and forciblest access into the capacity of the vulgar sort" (283). Although Augustine held much the same view, Bacon's causal analysis places the decline at the beginning of the Reformation, when (Bacon believes) the renewed study of the classical authors developed into a kind of idolatry.

> So that these four causes concurring, the admiration of ancient authors, the hate of the schoolmen, the exact study of languages, and the efficacy of preaching, did bring in an affectionate study of eloquence and copie of speech, which then began to flourish. (283)

During the sixteenth century this study "grew speedily to an excess; for men began to hunt more after words than matter. . . ." The whole tendency of those times, Bacon claims, was "rather towards copie than weight" (p. 284). In traditional rhetorical fashion, men were taught to repeat and vary old knowledge rather than discover new knowledge. Bacon emphasizes the decorative function of the modern rhetoric in connection with the old science. Works of this "delicate" kind, he says, are "like the first letter of a patent or limned book; which though it hath large flourishes, yet it is but a letter" (284). From Bacon's point of view, the history of knowledge up through his own day has been, like rhetoric itself, an excrescence, an excess growth upon the bare letter of truth.

In the name of ridding science of the influence of the rhetorical tradition—in the very act of attempting to do so—Bacon employs a series of metaphors and similes the logic of which motivates the new science. The central motivation is not so much the advancement of learning as the desire to return to an origin. In *The Great Instauration* Bacon compares the beginning of the new science and his own role in it, to God's carefully planned creation of the world (12). The true source of knowledge is not human tradition but nature itself. In the "Epistle Dedicatory" to *The Great Instauration*, Bacon writes to King James that his works "are quite new, totally new in their very kind: and yet they are copied from a very ancient model, even the world itself and the nature of things and of the mind. . . ." (5). In introducing the arguments of the several parts of the Instauration, Bacon states that his "design" is "to set everything forth, as far as may be, plainly and perspicuously," and adds the parenthetical explanation that "nakedness of the mind is still, as nakedness of the body once was, the companion of innocence and simplicity" (17). Here the classical sartorial metaphor takes a negative form in the metaphor of "nakedness," but this metaphor still refers to metaphor itself (or its absence), as the stylistic reference to plainness and perspicuity testifies. The clear language is not so much transparent as stripped of the obscurity of rhetoric. By a curious circularity of figure, metaphor strips language of metaphor. This trope permits Bacon to associate plainness of style (the language of science) with the language of Adam, who named the creatures "according to their propriety" (15). The "pure and uncorrupted natural knowledge" of Adam did not "[give] occasion to the fall," which was instead caused by "the ambitious and proud desire of moral knowledge to judge of good and evil." Thus, natural knowledge may be restored to its original and perfect state. In the "Proem" to *The Great Instauration* Bacon says of the scientific project that "all trial should be made, whether that commerce between the mind of man and the nature of things [. . .] might by any means be restored to its perfect and original condition" (3).[20]

Although it is certainly the case that Bacon is concerned partly with disarming those authorities who might perceive his project as a threat to religion, he establishes in these foundational works the program for the public devaluation of rhetoric among the new scientists. And Bacon does at times confuse conceptual and stylistic issues. In his "Natural and Experimental History," he proposes a "history" of arts and experimentation—a kind of catalog of scientific observations of nature under the influence of human activity. In Aphorism 5 he argues that such activity is especially valuable, because it has the effect of "tak[ing] off the mask and veil from natural objects, which are commonly concealed and obscured under the variety of shapes and external appearances":

> The vexations of art [i.e., the manipulation of nature for human purposes] are certainly as the bounds and handcuffs of Proteus, which betray the ultimate struggles and efforts of matter. For bodies will not be destroyed or annihilated; rather than that they will turn themselves into various forms.

> Upon this history therefore, mechanical and illiberal [i.e., not intellectual; involving manual activities] as it may seem (all fineness and daintiness set aside) the greatest diligence must be bestowed. (29)[21]

Experimental science is the occult study of the rhetoric of nature. The scientist is an Aristaeus who violates the cave of nature and captures protean matter, unmasking it and forcing it to disclose its truths. Rhetoric allegedly conceals knowledge and even participates in the deceptiveness of the external appearance of natural objects, for such objects operate like rhetoric to veil the truth. Physical matter is structured like the matter of speech in a classical rhetoric: its meaning is internal; its external shapes deceptive and substitutive. The rhetoric of nature is, like rhetoric in the usual sense, copious and obscure. Setting aside all "fineness and daintiness" (eloquence), the scientist is to pursue knowledge in the permutations of matter, rather in the manner of a rhetorical critic.

By a process of displacement, Bacon manages to preserve rhetoric in phenomena. Thus rhetoric (figurative language, eloquence) is made secretly to support a sense of the concealment of truth that is essential to the scientific positivist ideology of "discovery." The rhetoric of science veils itself. The metaphor of a language stripped of metaphor gives birth to what will henceforth deny it. Those who follow Bacon—Sprat, Wilkins, Locke, and others, repeat the gesture, tirelessly or exuberantly. It is a heady proposition. Sixty years later Thomas Sprat, for instance, seems to repeat Bacon when he writes in his *History of the Royal Society* that the intention of the enterprise of the English academy is not, like the French, "the Artifice of Words, but a bare knowledge of things" (40). He is, on the one hand, merely elevating the English scientists above the French; but the terms of the comparison form a dichotomy between words and things, which, although simplistic as a description of science, does repeat more broadly a common Baconian gesture. Sprat writes, in a famous passage, that the members of the Royal Society have

> a constant Resolution, to reject all the amplifications, digressions, and swellings of style: to return back to primitive purity, and shortness, when men diliver'd so many *things*, almost in an equal number of *words*. They have exacted from all their members a close, naked, natural way of speaking; positive expressions; clear senses; a native easiness: bringing all things as near the Mathematical plainness, as they can: and preferring the language of Artizans, Countrymen, and Merchants, before that, of Wits, or Scholars. (113)

Sprat's discourse is programmed throughout by a rhetoric of origins, primitive purity, original clarity of language, nakedness of expression. Science requires a reduction of ambiguity. In a reversal of the rhetoricians' figure, Sprat writes that truth is to be "cloth'd with Bodies," so as "to bring *Knowledg* back again to our very senses, from whence it was at first deriv'd to our understandings" (112). In other words, the bodies are to be stripped of their artificial clothing in order to become the first, true clothing of essential nature, a true representation of truth. Scientific progress is imagined as essentially a return to an origin by means of the elimination of corrupt secondary growth.[22] This "Adamic" notion corresponds to the social division between the presumably more primitive artisans, country people, and merchants, and the sophisticated, derivative, and therefore superfluous class of wits and scholars.

Sprat's suggestion regarding actual prose style is of course patently false.[23] But this ideological inversion, what Vickers calls "the myth of plainness" (45), ought not to be passed over as a mere ploy. We should not fail to consider the extent to which the Baconians may have been persuaded by their own arguments, mystified by their own myths.[24] The movement from clothed to naked language involves a single metaphor that unites even as it distinguishes. Whereas the new scientists represent rhetoric as an enemy of science, that which should be banished—eliminated from the field, defeated in the name of knowledge—they really only encrypt it, and thereby preserve it, keep it pure. They publicly deny metaphor, only to give it the secret function of programming science. Moreover, rhetoric (and its tradition; and language in general, insofar as metaphor is constitutive of language) provides the seductive clothing of things and ideas, the obstruction science desires to strip away. Hinting at an underlying nakedness, this opaque surface suggests the need for penetration, discovery.

Bacon suggests that figurative language is useful in the explanation and communication but not in the discovery of knowledge. Robert Boyle's essay, "A Free Enquiry into the Vulgarly Received Notion of Nature," may stand as an example of the way in which metaphor in fact constitutes knowledge. In an essay in which he takes great pains to eliminate the ambiguity of the word *nature*, especially by censuring figurative notions, Boyle arrives at a definition of the universe that is itself figurative and ambiguous:

> According to the foregoing hypothesis, I consider the frame of the world, already made, as a great and, if I may so speak, pregnant *automaton*, that, like a *woman* with twins in her womb, or a *ship* furnished with pumps, ordinance, &c., is such an engine as comprises or consists of several lesser engines. And this compound *machine*, in conjunction with the *laws of motion* freely established and still maintained by God among its parts, I look upon as a *complex principle*, whence results the settled order or course of things corporeal. (191)

The figure of the "pregnant automaton" contradicts, to some degree, that of the ship, for the former suggests the possibility of progressive creation. It is also, of course, an organic model. At any rate, what the formulation communicates depends on the imagination of the reader. Such figures are constitutive of knowledge rather than merely supplementary and explanatory, because they produce a precise (if complex and somewhat ambiguous) structure whose qualities would not otherwise be perceptible. Furthermore, the notion of a universe that is structured like a complex machine produces new directions of speculation and new contexts of observation. The "discovery" of the workings of the universe cannot be known before it is formulated in language. New knowledge will always depend for its generation upon catachresis. In the works of Boyle, as in those of Aristotle himself, we find a tendency to explain nature in terms of art. (The great clock of Strasbourg is his central model.) And, as in Aristotle, this relationship between art and nature is not merely expositive (i.e., representative of truths external to the representations themselves), but is in fact programmatic and determinative of the truth of "nature" Boyle posits.

Boyle is no theorist of language. For a systematic treatment of language from a philosophical or scientific point of view we need to turn to Locke's *Essay Concerning Human Understanding*. There we find the concept of the "naked idea," a fundamentally Baconian notion but based firmly on the linguistic theory of the arbitrary sign. Locke's insistence that a philosophical language be founded on "usual" (as opposed to proper) words—that is, words about which scientists may arrive at a common understanding that renders them useful rather than true—corresponds (I would argue) to a faith in dead metaphors. Locke's work includes, in Book IV, an attack on the traditional rhetorical logic of the syllogism. Locke discusses the proper means of discovering the logical fallacies "that are often concealed in florid, witty, or involved discourses." Rejecting the syllogism as itself a kind of figure, he proposes "to strip" each argument of its "superfluous ideas,"

> which, blended and confounded with those on which the inference depends, seem to show a connexion where there is none; or at least to hinder the discovery of the want of it; and then to lay the naked ideas on which the force of the argumentation depends in their due order. . . . (397)

Locke's view is not anti-rhetorical, strictly speaking. He wishes to reduce rhetoric to arrangement and clarity for purposes of scientific communication. Only when the ideas are arranged before us stripped of their rhetorical form, and thus of their accidental associations, can we determine their true merit. The "naked idea" is the idea displayed by a dead metaphor, which is a de-metaphorized term that suggests nothing beyond its common meaning, and in fact does so by suggesting nothing of itself. Locke would not have us consider that the "naked idea" lacks something analogous to clothing. In the case of the phrase "naked idea" itself, he would not want us to "associate," in an accidental manner, the naked and the cold, the exposed, the impoverished, the sensual, the seductive—associations that threaten to invoke the entire history of rhetoric. To revive the metaphor would be to destroy its instrumental quality. And yet, isn't it already alive, more alive than ever, in the discourse of Locke? Certainly there is something seductive about the naked idea. One might say that the idea of the naked idea must remain a naked idea or all is given over again to rhetoric. But it is always already too late.

Ultimately, the practice of science cannot be divorced from the rhetoric of its polemics. Even if the new scientists could (or wanted to) banish metaphor from scientific discourse, they would need to employ it in their apologies. The new scientists, in their attempt to avoid, circumvent, control, or neutralize metaphor, would need, at the very least, this metaphor of metaphor (here, by implication, that of clothing), which is itself (whether in the form of clothing or nakedness) uncontrollable. Taking the form of an open denial, an active argument, the "naked idea" harbors in its metaphoricity precisely what it would keep out of philosophy. It keeps the secret of the metaphoricity that generates philosophical concepts; that is, it preserves it by concealing it. Inevitably it exceeds its use.

The metaphor of clothing/nakedness is a master trope in the history of rhetoric and of science. Although neither of the two disciplines precisely turns on a trope at the beginning of the seventeenth century, the readable history of each is nevertheless tropological, even where it is concerned with "hard" facts. Science, also, is a rhetoric, and its operative tropes define its ideological enterprise and determine the scope of its practice at any stage of its history. The founding tropes of the new science of the seventeenth century place science in a privileged position vis-a-vis the truth. The institution of this relationship is made possible within the discourse of science by a denial (inaccurate but effective) of the function of metaphor in the production of knowledge. Metaphor is instead given the supplementary function of an explanatory aid in the communication of knowledge. The overwhelming success of this early rhetoric of science remains evident today.

10

Memory, History, Discourse

Patrizia Calefato

THE CONCEPT OF "DISTANCE" IN YOURCENAR'S *MÉMOIRES D'HADRIEN*

In "Carnet de notes", following *Mémoires d'Hadrien*, Yourcenar calls attention to the concept of distance, which in her novel she both establishes and bridges. The concept of "distance" may be classified into three orders: first the distance between the writer and Hadrien, whom she searches for in biographies, pictures, portraits, in the books of his library (*"L'une des meilleurs manières de recréer la pensée d'une homme: reconstituer sa bibliotèque,"* 327), or, indirectly, in Antinoüs's portraits and statues (Antinoüs was the young man whom Hadrien loved).

Second, there is the distance between Yourcenar and her memories of the places where Hadrien lived, from Villa Adriana to Asia Minor, which she visited at different times. In this connection Yourcenar writes:

> Pour que je pusse utiliser ces souvenirs, qui sont miens, il a fallu qu'ils devinnsent aussi éloignés de moi que le IIe siècle (322).

Finally, there is a distance within the writer herself, in the time of writing: from the first drafts of her novel, written between the ages of twenty and twenty-five, to the torn pages, from the condensation of her work in a single night, to delays lasting years.

Chronological time has nothing to do with these three orders of distance. The distance we are concerned with concerns what Bakhtin calls "great time," which is both the measure and condition of discourse and of literary experience.

The first order of distance concerns the historical past as it emerges through documents and records. The second order concerns memory.

The third order concerns an interior experience of time. We may add a fourth order: the distance between Hadrien and his own memories; that is, his time recovered from the experience of the approaching of death. Yourcenar writes that had finally found the point of view for her novel in one of the first utterances she had Hadrien pronounce: "Je commence à apercevoir le profil de ma mort" (322).

Historical time, memory, and interior experience of time are three forms of constructing both narrative and historical events in discourse. In *Mémoires d'Hadrien*, analogies and relations between historical discourse and literary discourse are easily recognized, for *Mémoires d'Hadrien* is canonically considered a "historical novel." Yourcenar writes:

> Le roman dévore aujourd'hui toutes les formes; on est à peu près forcé d'en passer par lui. Cette étude sur la destinée d'un homme qui s'est nommè Hadrien eût été une tragédie au XVIIe siècle; c'eût été un essai à l'époque de la Renaissance. (340)

However, analogous forms in the production of historical events on the one hand and literary events on the other can be traced through consideration of the so-called "semiotic modalities" of the temporal construction of discourse.

ANALOGIES BETWEEN HISTORICAL DISCOURSE AND LITERARY DISCOURSE ACCORDING TO ROLAND BARTHES

In "Le discours de l'histoire" (1969), Barthes points to analogies between historical discourse and literary discourse. Such analogies concern the conditions of the utterance (*énonciation*, 2), the units of enuntiatum (*énoncé*), 3), and signification (*signification*).

Concerning the utterance of historical discourse, Barthes recalls the "shifters" that enable the historian to designate his own act of utterance. These are mostly "listening" shifters (*d'écoute*) and "discourse organizing" shifters (*organisateurs du discours*).

The historical enuntiatum is made of units of content, which may be existences, occurrences, objects or values of narration; and classes of content units, such as signs and clues recalling metaphorical meaning, syllogisms and enthymemes, and function of the tale (in Propp's sense).

In relation to signification, Barthes writes that historical discourse is always ideological discourse; therefore, historical facts exist linguistically and textually and expect to faithfully represent extra-textual existence; that is, "reality."

According to Barthes, the main difference between historical discourse (*historia rerum gestarum*) and literary narration consists in the ideological character of the production of the "effect of the real" or "referential illusion" in the *res gestae*, while at the narrative level there are many deep relationships that connect these two types of discourse. Barthes examines a historiographical *corpus* covering Herodotus, Machiavelli, Bossuet, and Michelet; he refers to Flaubert and Michelet with regard to the effect of the real in history and literature; May, 1968, in France is for him an example of the "writing of the event," that is, of the interaction among "three writings"—word, symbol; and violence—which produced the event of May, 1968, "semiotically" in its historical originality.

Barthes was a pioneer because he worked in the field of historical discourse when, during the 1960s, it was not yet considered by semioticians. Nevertheless, the heterogeneity of the corpus he choses to work on produces a sort of levelling of the genre called historical discourse. In fact, Barthes doesn't take into account the existence of many historical discourses that describe the conditions of the production of their own genre. Moreover, Barthes considers ideology as a linguistic system. While it is true that history is discourse and that facts are interpretations, discourse, interpretation, and, more generally, ideology, though analysable semiotically, are not made of verbal or sign elements alone. It was in the same 1960s that the Italian philosopher Ferruccio Rossi-Landi (1921-1985) introduced the notion of sign systems as "pieces of reality" and "forms of social planning." We may say that the concepts of "sign system" and "discourse" are similar, but they are not verbal systems only. In fact, sign systems do not exhaust those objects, bodies, and situations that, as Rossi-Landi writes, are not sign elements in themselves, though they may become such at any time.

OTHERNESS AND MEMORY

The experience of time is distance in Yourcenar's sense, a distance that empties and fills itself with memory and that produces self through continuous interaction between verbal and nonverbal signs. This kind of temporality is exemplarily present in literature, but we may also find it in history if we consider the latter as discourse, or, as Rossi-Landi would say, if we consider history in terms of the social reproduction of sign systems.

To paraphrase Yourcenar, who refers her words to the so-called "historical novel," the discourse of history is no more than the taking possession of an inner world. "Inner world" is experience, not something reified and separate from an "external world," but something that exists through both the perception and discourse of temporality.

To speak of experience is to speak of the singularity and of the absolute uniqueness of "stories" which can paradoxically exist only for others and in relation to others. Yourcenar writes:

> Ma propre existence, si j'avais à l'écrire, serait reconstituée par moi du dehors, péniblement, comme celle d'un autre; j'aurais à me adresser à des lettres, aux souvenirs d'autrui, pour fixer ces flottantes mémoires. (331)

The experience of time is set up in a dialogic context. Outside otherness and distance self has no sense. "Mon cher Marc" is the *incipit* of *Mémoires d'Hadrien*: memory makes space for another; the past emerges for another time. In fact, Marc (Marcus Aurelius) is still a child when Yourcenar has the emperor Hadrien write his memories, as we discover at the end of the novel. The expression "Mon cher Marc" seems to condense an idea of dedication.

The possessive "my" is a sign of memory. It introduces memory *in absentia*, that is, memory of the relations between Hadrien and his own "memories."

The possessive recalls personal pronouns: both substitute individual bodies for verbal signs. In this sense the human body is transformed into a sign, though not totally because the body also survives in itself as an "extrasign residue," as Rossi-Landi would say. The concept of "residue" is crucial from the viewpoint of temporality in the process of the body's transformation into a sign, and vice-versa. In fact, such transformation produces cyclic time open to returns, interruptions, and suspensions.

Hadrien the hero (in Bakhtin's sense) lives among many "voices": his (hi)story lives in a time without an equivalent, that is, in the time of incommensurable experience. Let us remember, for example, the pages in the novel dedicated to Antinoüs's death and funerals. In these pages the mourning celebrations serve to defer the event of death itself.

Memory conceived as the experience of otherness exceeds history conceived as a linear narration: memory shows itself, whereas narration hides its generative mechanisms. Barthes writes that there is a homology between historical discourse and realistic literary discourse: each both levels and confuses referent and meaning. This is true with regard to historical discourse conceived as cumulative narration or as a necessary and finalistic temporal relation between cause and effect.

On the contrary, we cannot transform experience into an assertion: with regard to experience we cannot pronounce the statement "it is true" and make it become meaning. Experience is a generation of sense, a passage from non-signs to signs and vice-versa in the light of a dialogic conception of time.

HISTORICAL DISCOURSE AND GENDER

Historical discourse brings to the fore the question of gender, that is, the question of the "passage" between sex as nature and gender as a category of sense and culture. It is not our intention to search for cumulative narrations or their gendered masters or mistresses; on the contrary we are concerned with those polyphonic values, meanings, sentiments through which the self interacts with the world and with others.

Concerning her choice of the "narrative self"—Hadrien of the male gender, Yourcenar says:

> Impossibilité aussi de prendre pour figure centrale un personnage féminin, de donner, par example, pour axe à mon récit, au lieu d'Hadrien, Plotine. La vie des femmes est trop limitée, ou trop secrète. (329)

In Yourcenar's extraordinary work, the viewpoint of the male hero is not neutral. The writer has created something of another and invisible point of view in which awareness of gender is assumed as a kind of corner mirror where two beams of light are reflected and meet in the place of writing.

Experience conceived as experience of time and gender may be defined through Rossi-Landi's notions of "initial meanings" and "additional meanings." Though both of these notions refer to language, and precisely to the methodics of "common speech," the relations connecting these two kinds of meanings do not belong to the linguistic field alone, but also concern ideologies and values.

In Rossi-Landi's opinion, "initial meanings" may be classified as direct, immediate, explicit, literal, near, present, main, primary, and conscious. On the other hand, "additional meanings" may be defined as indirect, mediate, implicit, metaphorical, remote, absent, latent, accessory, secondary, and unconscious. Meaning is defined as "initial" or "additional" with reference to the context of interpretation and not on the grounds of incontestable necessity. The temporal relation between these two kinds of meaning is not casual and subsequent, though the notions themselves of "initial" and "additional" meanings may induce one to think of a temporal consequence. Rossi-Landi believes that chronological temporality is "irrelevant," while underlying the importance of relations among the various "universes of discourse" to which each meaning belongs.

This may be defined as a "differential" kind of temporality, in which values generate behaviors, preferences, habits, and sentiments. Gender emerges in this temporal relation among meanings: what is immediately conceived as sex (initial meaning) becomes *gender* (additional meaning), that is, becomes a value conceived as the ideological sense of the meaning. We may reverse the "arrow" of time: values may "filter" initial meanings and give them a structure in their immediacy and presumed objectivity. In this sense, "natural" and "biological" sexual difference is mediated by the dominant cultural and ideological value of such concepts as male and female. In this context gender is the semiotic category that can condense and explain cyclicity and temporal co-occurrence linking initial and additional meanings.

Such a conception of time may be defined as "generative temporality." Semiotics has often considered time in the light of similar conceptions, especially in relation to literature, but in the field of common sense there is still a clear separation between literary fiction and historical reality.

SEMIOTICS AND HISTORY

Contributions by the School of Tartu (Lotman, Uspensky) to the semiotics of history are extremely interesting because they stress the question of perception of time. According to Uspensky, history is essentially the attribution of sense to the past, and historical experience consists of the relations of cause and effect identifiable from the viewpoint of what is actual at a given moment. In this sense, the historical importance of the present is essential for consciousness, and the movements of time are linked by both perception and interpretation.

Uspensky compares history to dreams from the viewpoint of the perception of time and of the attribution of sense. He maintains that in our dreams as well as in history we are able to perceive an external event as a relevant sign event, and we are able to give it a global sense that determines the course of the dream itself in a backwards temporal movement. For example, we could perceive the banging of a door, give it the sense of a pistol shot, and thus determine the very sense of our dream: the story of a murder.

In Uspensky's opinion, the historical process is conceived as a communicative process in which new pieces of information cause different reactions in the social addressee. The *communicative model* of the historical process needs a code, in this case a "language" (in a broad sense), which determines the perception of both real and potential facts in the historical-cultural context.

In this way "facts" can signify: the text of events is read by society. In Uspensky's view, the semiotics of history is founded on a double level: the first is connected with *facts*, that is, with the "propositions" of the historical text with its internal, self-descriptive point of view; the second is connected with the transformation of non-signs into signs and of non-history into history, that is, with the historian's external point of view. Therefore, history is conceived as a process of sense construction following a double temporal movement: from the past to the present (events of described reality), and from the present to the past (historical consciousness). It is in this movement that the idea of the future is also built.

In this conception we find a sort of dualism between history conceived as a "fact" in its "reality" and history conceived as the sense given to the fact itself. Such dualism is part of the "semiotics of communication," which runs the risk of reifying either the "fact" in itself or the subject of interpretation, though reduced to a "point of view."

Historical experience is experience of time: in this sense, the historian himself, who interprets the signs of the past, has a historical experience. "The past" does not look at the historian as something in its objectivity, but as a complex of signs and non-signs that interact, are transformed, and determine the very eyes looking at them.

Yourcenar writes:

> Le sorcier qui se taillade la pouce au moment d'évoquer les ombres sait qu'elles n'obéiront à son appel que parce qu'elles lapent son propre sang. Il sait aussi, ou devrait savoir, que les voix qui lui parlent sont plus sages et plus dignes d'attention que ses propres cris. (341)

That something happened at a certain point in time constitutes the "initial" meaning of history; that this something is interpreted, and even before this is singled out as interpretable, constitutes the shift of sense towards additional meaning. This "something" is perceived as a sensible event in the present, and such social perceptions and interpretations constitute the discourse of history.

Broadly speaking, we may identify two conceptions of temporality in discourse:

1. A finalistic, cumulative, linear temporality that follows the course of narration. Historical discourse conceived as the order of discourse (in Foucault's sense) is organized according to this kind of temporality. We may ascribe de Certeau's judgment on historiography to this temporal movement: "historiography is a contemporary way of celebrating mourning." In de Certeau's opinion, the writing of historiographers begins from an absence; by writing they repeat the act that produced that absence, for they deal with time as a mere instrument for classifying regularities.
2. A temporality connected with experience, with production of sense and subjects, with otherness.

DISCOURSE AND GENEALOGY

We cannot avoid connecting this second type of temporality with the philosophical and semiotic discussion of the concept of "discourse" in some of its various accepted meanings. Foucault's conception of "discourse" is inscribed in the wide universe of the institution of beliefs, cognitions, and interdictions, which produce and reproduce what we call "knowledge" and "subject," and which in the past was called "truth" and "reason", as opposed to "falseness" and "madness." In this sense, a "theory of discourse" may contribute to outlining a genealogy and a critique, as Foucault himself would say. Genealogy and critique are two concepts that Foucault owes to Nietzsche.

Foucault writes that genealogy requires the minutia of knowledge, a great deal of accumulated materials, and patience:

> To trace the singularity of events outside monotonous finality; to spy them where they are least expected and in what passes as being without history—sentiments, love, consciousness, instinct; to capture their return, not in order to trace the slow curve of an evolution, but to rediscover the different roles; to define also the instance of their absence, the moment in which they did not take place (Plato did not become Mahomet in Syracuse) (Foucault, "Nietzsche, la génealogie, l'histoire").

This is the task of genealogy, according to Foucault's comment on Nietzsche. For Foucault, the genealogical sense of history is inseparable from its critical sense. Such a position involves three "uses" of history that contrast, point by point, the modalities of history as envisaged by Plato. They include: 1) a parodical and clownesque use as opposed to history conceived in terms of reminiscence and recognition; such a use represents the ironical upsetting of what Nietzsche called "monumental history" in the second of his "Unzeitgemässe Betrachtungen"; 2) a dissociative use, destroyer of identities; such a use opposes history conceived as continuity and tradition; it opposes what Nietzsche called "antiquarian history"; 3) a "sacrifical" use, destroyer of truth; such a use resumes Nietzsche's concept of "critical" history and upsets its sense: criticism is not conceived in the name of a present truth, but in the name of the modalities of the sacrifice of the knowing subject. In Foucault's opinion (in current knowledge, that is), the will to know calls us to experience of ourselves.

At this point we may consider the semiotic point of view. Obviously we do not intend semiotics here as a "science of regularities" (as historiography in de Certeau's opinion). On the contrary, our reference is to an interpretative, genealogical, and critical semiotics. On the one side, it is addressed to singularities, repetitions, interruptions, feelings, passions, experiences insofar as they generate senses, subjects, and values. On the other side, following Foucault's "uses," it is addressed: 1) to the genesis of memory, included literary memory, conceived as a parody of the "monument"; 2) to temporal discontinuities; 3) to the critique of what Rossi-Landi called "linguistic alienation" and that we may define more broadly as "sign alienation," inborn in the order of discourse.

In his "Geschichtsphilosophische Thesen," Benjamin writes that history is the object of a construction whose site isn't homogeneous and empty time full of actuality (*Jetztzeit*). In Benjamin's opinion this *Jetztzeit*, this present is time "in suspense," a time perceived and conceived as a standstill, as a historical monad. What Benjamin calls the "historically comprised" is the possibility of dissociating an epoch from the homogeneous course of history, a given life from an a epoch, and finally a specific work from a whole work.

The categories of singularity and discontinuity introduced by Benjamin and Foucault may be interpreted in the light of a theory of discourse. As we may understand from what has been said so far, by "discourse" we intend the procedures of representation and self-representation of social reproduction. The concept itself of "discourse" is, then, strongly ambivalent, and this is particularly evident from the point of view of temporality.

On the one hand, discourse comprehends what Foucault calls "order" and that time defined by Benjamin as the "homogeneous and empty time" of "universe history." On the other hand, discourse produces a "suspended time," as Benjamin would say, a present that is not subject to the passage from past to future.

RETURN

Hadrien writes:

> Je m'efforce de reparcourir ma vie pour y trouver un plan, y suivre une veine de plomb ou d'or, ou l'écoulement d'une rivière souterraine, mais ce plan tout factice n'est qu'un trompe-l'oeil du souvenir. (33)

Memory conceived as the search for the same, *in* and *of* discourse, cannot but break against its very own project.

> Je ne suis pas de ceux qui disent que leurs actions ne leur ressemblent pas. Il faut bien qu'elles le fassent, puisq'elles sont ma seule mesure, et le seul moyen de me dessiner dans la mémoire des hommes, ou même dans la mienne propre. (33)

Memory contains the time of experience insofar as it contains discontinuity, uniqueness, and even amnesia.

> Les trois quarts de ma vie échappent d'ailleurs à cette définition par les actes: la masse de mes velléités, de mes désirs, de mes projets même, demeure aussi nébuleuse et aussi fuyante qu'un fantôme. . . . J'ai ma chronologie bien à moi, impossibile à accorder avec celle qui se base sur la fondation de Rome, ou avec l'ère des Olympiades. Quinze ans aux armées ont duré moins qu'un matin d'Athènes; il y a des gens que j'ai fréquentés toute ma vie et que je ne reconnaitrai pas aux Enfers. (34)

Lived experience takes on value when experienced for others: this is not intended as the exhibition of one and the same lived experience, but rather in the sense that the uniqueness of experience and temporal incommensurability render lived experience simultaneously absolutely distant and extremely near, for others and for ourselves.

The last chapter of *Mémoires d'Hadrien* is entitled "Patientia," as if to evoke that "profile of death" that constitutes the point of view of the novel. Hadrien foresees and lives this profile with patience, with a sense of dilation and of expectancy of an ending that, as Hadrien says, was "lentement élaborée au fond de mes artères" (303).

"Tout reste à faire" (304), goes on Hadrien; he has exceeded the hour of impatience and the wish to anticipate his own death through suicide. Patience evokes slowness, and slowness evokes a return. The end of the novel returns to its beginning: Hadrien returns to the first lines of his *Mémoires*, that is, to the day when he was visited, presumably for the last time, by his physician Hermogenes. The final dedication to Hadrien's successor, Antoninus, is also a return to the beginning, for it is the rival project of the initial "Mon cher Marc."

Similarly to the establishment of a psychoanalytic setting, time has both advanced in the narration and withdrawn in the course of memory. Time now stops upon two "symptoms" that recall otherness—two dedications.

[I am grateful to Susan Petrilli for her help in translation from the Italian.]

Part Four

The Ends of History: Life/Death/(Dis)Closure

Change is a matter of life and death: life as a process marked, in its animation, by the fact of change; absence of change as the rigidity of death (though even in death there is change). The life and death of culture(s), people(s), idea(s), language(s), all gather in evidence of the historical imperative. Following from the previous section, this group of essays explores the limits, the boundaries, and the structures of change inherent in the harmonics of culture and discourse.

Otherwise stated, among the most telling dialectical markers of change is that of gain and loss. The constant dynamic interplay between these polarities produces our sense of stasis and action, of history, and again of life and death; the sense of balance, or lack of it, we experience results from the constant and ubiquitous changes that occur along the axis of gain and loss. The sense of value life has for us is plotted across the economy of gain and loss, and its relation to cultural history and the always-tendentious human future. Indeed, this pervasive dialectical theme constitutes the life and death of change, as it exists for us individually and collectively.

Further, history is a nexus of *(dis)closure.* As in history, in this (post) modern word, "(dis)closure," its enigmatic "dis" suspended at a purgatorial distance, the closure of meaning and value is reversed and subverted by the very writing process by which it comes into being. History is the play of repression and subversion, in language and in culture. The closure of history, which occurs in the discourse of history, is always at the same time a disclosure, at least of that repression. As a discourse of logical determinism, the critique of history denies the life and death about which it speaks, even while it acts as its chronicle. This subtle process of subsumption and transmutation, of life and death into historical discourse, prosaic or poetic, is itself a disclosure of the tendentiousness of historicity that pervades the premodern, the modern, and in its way the postmodern; historicity's tendentiousness is a structural constant that in its strategies produces signs of change.

In this section, three essays further explore some aspects of this issue's dense texture. The ends of history, in the sense of both finitude and teleology, take very different forms here but return, each by a different route, to a grounding in historical discourses ranging from the political to the poetic, from the notion of loss to that of shame and redemption.

In "The Loss of Language Within Imperial Liberalism," Steve Martinot starts with the assumption that political language is often designed to silence itself, through the creation of a kind of senseless or absurd envelope, to enter which is to engage in the absurd whether one supports particular politics or not. For Martinot, the absurd consists of the radical slippage of political language, no longer even remotely connected with what it means in a social context (his example is the "stop Hussein" rhetoric during the Gulf War). The result is a certain inarticulability, what he calls "the loss of language," that is at once obscurantist and highly strategic within a secularized, monolithic, consumerist, American capitalism, within which there are no real alternative socialist or ideological voices. Analyzing Norman Birnbaum's *The Radical Renewal,* Martinot explores the American 1960s as a time during which an attempt was made to undo a prior political silence and during which the secularization of social theory became universal, during which no American socialism nor other alternative arose in a dialectic with consumer-oriented capitalist rule, and which saw the dissolution of political language (and by extension of language in general). Martinot asserts that during the 1960s, in the final solidification of consumerism, the American Protestant agenda became equivalent to American consumerism through its strategy of social fragmentation, and that the public's misunderstanding of this fragmentation has meant that no successful effort to overcome the instrumentality of this rhetoric has been made. In this framework, "society as a whole," along with any collective sense of citizenship, become impossible, and in the absence of a "public," a pervasive social aporia develops in which language is radically disempowered in an environment of empty critical thought: "in the ideology of consumerism, class is indistinguishable from career—disguised by individualist preference," resulting through the myth of progress in solipsistic self-defense and the obsolescence of citizenship. Grounding institutions of social structuration—church, union, community—no longer mediate between the (lost) public and the institutions of representation—advertisers, politicians, media—through which failed language is disseminated, producing a shift into the area of Lyotard's differend, an incommensurable systemic aporia in which a fragmented social perspective leads to an inability to share a social discourse, and of which the inevitable by-product is social injustice. Injustice is subsumed within the differend; as the "public" disappears into consumer demographics, so does any recourse or redress against the system: "American society itself is a differend."

This loss, Martinot points out, stems from a dilemma of participation and representation. In the former, individuals have a place in the evolution of culture and society; in the latter, they are detached and disempowered. People participate in "movements," but are merely represented in typical governmental structures. To join a political party is to be co-opted by representation and to be excluded from the discourse of social interaction, and this "degradation" of language, and of value, is a rhetoric of exclusion. Indeed, the production and perpetuation of a differend is always a strategy of "exclusion, deferral, and silencing." In practice in America, the slippage of reality "out from under the ability to understand it" has resulted in a political paradigm of subjugation of an other that lies at the heart of all political institutions, a paradigm we must overcome to regenerate social discourse. But we insidiously comply with this system of exploitation in our language-lives at present. American social and political discourse has changed, Martinot concludes, but from full to empty, from living to dead, and this has had a pervasive effect on our lives. Dominant (consumerist) discourse shapes and alters all discourse, neutralizing opposition and eviscerating language. In such an environment, to choose to engage in social and political dialogue is to obey the rules of co-option imposed by this lost language—to disappear into it. This shift represents a radical social change as well as a fundamental change in the relations between language and culture.

Sharon Meagher, in her study of the evolution of Roland Barthes's rhetorical strategies, implicitly suggests a strategic antidote to Martinot's thesis. "Searching for the Barthian corpus" through the various stages of Barthes's development, Meagher concludes that Barthes's "position" on. language and the body cannot be rationalized, but remains a series of inconsistencies. But while the changes from early to late Barthes, in terms of the development of an ethics of the body, seem to portray a growing hedonism "on the grave" of commitment, and a return to absolute difference, the death of the author eventuates in the birth of a new ethics of writing. Meagher shows how Barthes's theory of commitment emerges from Sartre's, but that the early ethic of commitment is lost in the late Barthes. Two tenets seem to underpin Barthes's development: writing is not transparent, and an ethic of writing is not certain. Responding to Sartre's condemnation of modernist writing since Flaubert as having failed in a commitment to ethics, morality, and any "principle of engagement" with the reader, Barthes declares that modernist writing must be seen as an evisceration of the text, containing no "subject," no commitment, but a "flow of empty signs" whose movements are, nonetheless, significant. It is precisely in this flow that *écriture*, as a locus of commitment, gains meaning.

For Barthes and Meagher, the premodern (here, prior to the midnineteenth century) is characterized by a single mode of writing in a given epoch; since the advent of modernism, we have been awash in a sea of forms, each demanding and being accorded significance. For the Modernist, to choose a mode of writing is to place oneself in society. As in Steve Martinot's presentation, for Sharon Meagher this theme of loss and gain has to do with the appearance and disappearance of the subject in literature and writing. Further, for Barthes, the loss of simple hegemonic writing codes is a gain rather than a loss, so long as it is accompanied by a commitment of the body. Echoing Martinot's distinction between participation and representation, Meagher presents Barthes's case against an "intellectual [Sartrean] writing" that "can lead only to complicity or impotence, which means, in either case, to alienation." As writing "enters history," its responsibility is transformed.

But writing, especially the ideal, mode-less writing Barthes calls writing-degree-zero, is inherently the destruction of any origin; texts are places not of *plaisir* but of *jouissance*, the loss of identity rather than its comfortable discovery. In the writerly social environment, both author and reader are fictional constructions, hence, as for Martinot, the commitment to the body, and to its "value." Barthes' notion of *jouissance* juxtaposes body and value without synthesizing them in a closed dialectical process, but leaving them as dialectical tensions: ethical commitment versus pleasure. Meagher's assertion concerning Barthes's strategy for writing in the modern/postmodern age is that it is not the grave of commitment, but the (re)birth of an ethic or morality of the body. As Meagher says, this freer writing is a rewriting of the old, but with a remainder unincorporated in previous social forms of writing. The ends of history, for a postmodern age in which ends are ubiquitous and impossible and history is "the dead hand of the past," require a bodily commitment to the pleasure of the text.

The ends of history are, for James Hatley in his treatment of Célan's poetry, addressed to a history of annihilation and the annihilated, in which the "injustice" Martinot isolates in Lyotard's differend infuses the world of the Shoah and its subsequent treatment. The question for Célan, of course, is one of silencing the Shoah or finding a way to speak of and about it; at the same time, Célan looks for a change in history to a dimension in which the wish for confidence in a just future can be considered real. History, as Célan's poetry addresses it, neglects the dead. Only survivors have a voice, but as survivors they cannot and do not speak for the dead. Only in "prophetic" history, which is not a record of achievements but the "ethical critique" of a people's responsibility, are the dead remembered. Since silence and a "withdrawal" of existence mark corpses' entry into history, it becomes a haunting, and a memory of loss and violation. For Célan, this sense of historical loss breeds shame, in a world permeated by injustice and in which no consolation exists for the irreversible and unplacatable suffering of which the Shoah consists-one can only be faithful to its memory. For Célan, God is as implicated in the shame of history as are humans, since Shoah threatens all justice, all expectations of compassion. The only possible strategic response to history and to Shoah, for the voice of the victim, is the *gegenwort*, the word of resistance, Célan offers in his poems. Célan, by inspiring shame, permits Shoahs victims to resist their history. However powerless this resistance might be, particularly to the voices of history, it is imperative to the victim and to the memory of the victim. This resistance is intended to produce a grave disturbance in those who face the Shoah and who realize that while adopting the victim's history is abhorrent and unethical, the adoption of the dead becomes the victim's identity. As both Martinot and Meagher assert as well, identity is subsumed into the writing of history, incorporated into the "life-projects" of survivors and thus into the "profitable" ethics of the survivors. As Levinas points out, when the dead are identified by their works or their words, "ipseity" (particularity) is lost. The danger of historicity, in this regard, is that the reasoned construction of history sublates alterity itself, what is "resistant to appropriation." Indeed, the particularity of historical beings requires differentiating them from their sense of history and from their works. Célan's, like Barthes's degree-zero, is an alterative to historicity and historiography, but unlike Barthes's mode-less writing, Célan's history returns the dead from alienated third person to a second person association with the living poet and poem. If reinscription of the Shoah cannot change historicity, it can certainly change history and its tendency to subsume and neutralize.

The three powerful essays in this section, which acts as a dialectical continuation and conclusion (without closure) of the previous section, all address questions of ethics, morality, and responsibility in the context of a history that is immensely powerful and in need of resistance.

11

The Loss of Language within Imperial Liberalism: The United States' Political Structure as Differend

Steve Martinot

The example of Ben Tre, once extreme, now only seems (since the bombing of Iraqi civilian populations) prototypical. Ben Tre was a Vietnamese town of 15,000 inhabitants obliterated by Air Force bombing in 1968, after which an Air Force officer made the (in)famous statement, "We had to destroy it to save it." It is possible to discount this statement as public relations hypocrisy, but it bespoke a foreign policy in which Americans were both complicit and excluded precisely by such rhetorical senselessness. In the invasion of Grenada, likewise, all the rationales given were shown to be hypocritical (e.g., to avenge a socialist revolutionary's murder by his "comrades") or false. Reagan extolled the invasion by saying "we don't like thugs," but in employing this to excuse the world's most powerful nation mugging a small island, he revealed a messianism, a pretended legitimation, a permission given to the impermissible that does not leave us unscathed. Even raw opposition to these statements means granting them a certain sense, and any attempt to make sense of these statements is an abdication to them. In other words, refusal to be the victims of senselessness engenders support for the senseless. We are left speechless. In Iraq, a culture, a social infrastructure. and hundreds of thousands of civilians were destroyed in order to (quote) "stop Hussein" (a mere slogan about a run-of-the-mill dictator who was first armed and employed by the United States against Iran and then enticed into a sting operation in Kuwait, and who, in any other context [Guatemala, for instance], would be considered a bastion of the free world). The issue of what "stopping Hussein" meant was buried beneath the slogan's use; it became a derogatory term rather than a rallying cry. And ultimately, the senselessness of such political rhetoric can no longer be considered simply "public relations"; we must recognize it as strategy. It marks situations designed to silence themselves (and us) through a dissolution of language itself.

This theme of a loss of language is one that threads itself subtly through Norman Birnbaum's recent book *The Radical Renewal*, published in 1988.[1] I begin with these examples because at one point in his book, while correlating an apparent dissolution of citizenship in America with power centralization, Birnbaum remarks that "we face a situation for which no rhetoric prepares us" (114). This is a somewhat startling statement for a social scientist or intellectual historian to make. But, in fact, Birnbaum succeeds in demonstrating, in part against his will, that the problem is more general than one might perhaps think. The structure of this inarticulability, as an absence that he essentially silhouettes with his exposition, is what I want to discuss here.

I find four major motifs in Birnbaum's book. The first is that the 1960s were a fulcrum, a transition point, an attempt to undo a prior silence. The second is that the same period saw what Birnbaum calls a "secularization of social theory." Third, Birnbaum expresses an emphatic desire to understand why there is no American socialism, no native alternative to capitalist rule emerging from the plentiful cultural and political critique one finds in America. And the fourth is the question already broached: the dissolution of language. I will consider the first three briefly and address the last more fully.[2]

For Birnbaum, there were three main dimensions to the upheavals of the 1960s: a revolt against the culture of Protestantism, a refusal of empire, and a demand for participation rather than representation. In this I think he is correct—and indeed, it is refreshing to read a nondenigratory account of that period. He recognizes that the movements of the 60s were not a "convulsive and ignorant attack on impregnable cultural traditions and social institutions" (11–12). Nor were they simply a middle-class phenomenon; working class opposition to the war surpassed that of the educated middle class (36), though, significantly, not at the "point of production." But the period's three "fronts" were never successfully integrated, and in that regard it failed to delegitimize the authority it contested.

For Birnbaum, the "culture of Protestantism" embraces a spectrum of constraints (from psychological puritanism to the "work ethic") that functions as a force for social fragmentation. It sets each radically individualized person in isolated relationship to a distant standard. He points out that modern consumerism, as one's sense of becoming who one is through entry into the market, is itself a contemporary representation of Protestantism. One weakness of the 60s' revolt was its failure to understand this. In consequence, intellectual entry into "the marketplace of ideas"—which for Birnbaum is not a metaphor—resulted in a fragmentation of thought that, tied to the cultural fragmentation and impotence socially engendered by consumerism, looked natural. For example, he recounts the inverse fates of maverick social critics like C. Wright Mills and of the avant-garde in art. If the former were commercialized and ignored by university discourse, the latter, whose modernism was courted and absorbed by the university, were also commercialized and divested of political content. Both were effectively separated from their respective communities, spaces where they might have swung some sociopolitical weight. In its failure to understand the exile and social fragmentation incurred in consumerism, the attack on the "culture of Protestantism" ran aground.

On the other hand, Birnbaum sees empire as a force for homogenization. Empire consists of the "unimpeded access to cheap raw materials, protected markets, and possibilities for investment in much of the world" (31). The problem for empire is the difficulty of arriving at policy decisions in a democracy; that is, the problem of empire is how to rule, as an imperial state, while maintaining the appearance of democratic structure. The answer is a politics of consensus, which is a euphemism for the accommodation of domestic politics to domination by foreign policy. Originally engineered by the New Deal (by the center liberals rather than the right), after the McCarthy era consensus was promoted under the rubric of "national security," a politics whose ideological content not only included paranoia, but also a conception of America as an exportable political system whose responsibility was to "bestow" itself upon the world's people. In other words, it constituted a conflation of messianic nationalism and xenophobia. This kind of nationalism, Birnbaum remarks, is unlike European nationalism; not rooted in common cultural and historical experiences, it is rather an "acquired taste" (37).

Against the intellectual homogenization of consensus, the refusal of empire sought to effect itself ethically and politically in the marketplace of ideas. But it miscalculated the depths to which consumerism constituted the life's blood of empire (not only in commodities, but drugs, images, and consensus itself). If each aspect could be intellectually apprehended, they could not be collectively addressed ideologically. In effect, in the confluence of cultural revolt and political refusal, and the very desire for participation, radicalism trapped itself in the incommensurability of homogenization and fragmentation. Its refusals of social institutions contained within itself a "refusal to believe that human institutions could be different" (194).

In his second motif, the "secularization of social theory," Birnbaum reveals a different dimension of this same incommensurability. In general, for Birnbaum, "social theory is the effort of a social group to reflect upon itself" (13). To claim it has been secularized implies that social theory had been in some sense religious. Traditionally, he points out, American social science had tended in practice to constitute a "legitimating ideology" for the American "experiment." In abandoning a certain "hauteur" after the war, it transformed itself into an instrumentality—for use by government, bureaucracy, and corporation (14). A classic example is its insistence that the term *class* really means "income group," thus obviating the possible apprehension of contradictory political and economic interests (14). In this way, as an intervention in mass culture, it functioned to prevent real conflicts from engaging public consciousness (15). But, in that case, something other than secularization is at work, or at stake. If, rather than self-awareness, social theory has the effect of generating the culture and social ethos it describes, then it functions more like a religious *a priori*: it becomes the lens that simultaneously engenders the world seen. Rather than be secularized, social science underwent a transformation from myth to ecclesiastic doctrine.

For Birnbaum, two things were actually desacralized in the process, however: first, the former non-recognition of empire; and second, the ethos of consumerism. The first had originally been hidden behind nationalism, and the second behind the notion of progress. "Empire" had been only a topic for Marxism, and a strategy rhetoricized in messianism, prior to World War Two; after that war, from which the United States emerged as the only unscathed industrial nation, it was recognized as a political reality, a control structure toward client, comprador, and "alliance-ed" states. Empire finally emerged into public consciousness through radical opposition to the Vietnam War, though rarely as more than moral critique. One reason was that it revealed itself from behind nationalism only by continually providing proofs of empire's character: endless facts and figures on its particular activities and operations. These particulars had to be settled before the class relations of empire could be made real. Thus, the critique of empire found itself awash in minutiae, and in discourses on the colonial referent (in the marketplace of ideas), rather than in contention on the political stage. Consumerism had likewise emerged from its former disguise and transformed itself from the myth of progress to the real pragmatics of internal economic stability.

Absorbed in the ethos of consumerism, the critique of empire became an end in itself. In effect, it got caught between the consumerism it attempted to use and the empire it attempted to refuse.

The effect (Birnbaum's third motif: the absence of an American socialism, of an alternate vision of society) was a dual process of withdrawal: first, a withdrawal of political thought and social criticism (whether academic or popular) from engaging the public, and thus from providing that public with a medium or framework for a discourse of alternatives; second, a withdrawal of the public toward disinvolvement, amounting to a reduction of public sovereignty and public space (18). With respect to the second, he points out that people are "unwilling to venture into a public sphere" because "they see no connection between it and their own lives" (187). Politics then ceases to be a way in which one's life is made public. Or, to put it more forcefully, in holding onto "terrain they now possess," people "interpret suggestions for change as threats of eviction" (178). In effect, a defense of one's space as a citizen calls in question the notion of citizenship altogether. Birnbaum suggests that one can trace, throughout American history, a progression toward greater and greater disinvolvement, a gradual reduction of public sovereignty and public space (18). Ultimately, he points out, such a retreat from, or abandonment of, public space makes it very difficult to retain an idea of society altogether (92). "Society as a whole" becomes conceptually unconstructable (175).

With respect to the first, the withdrawal of social critique, an even larger absence is produced. Birnbaum gives the examples of environmentalism and individual health. The medical profession is unprepared to engage in an ideological critique of itself that might bridge the gap between public submission (which includes a rejection) to an artificially esoteric expertise, and medicine's own specialization (fragmentation) as a form of market commodification. Conversely, ecological ideology is unprepared to extend its recognition of the unity of critique and public participation from the level of individual and industrial use of the environment as raw material to a critique of industrialism itself. The ideological inertia exemplified in both these fields constitutes, for Birnbaum, a "shrinkage of social thought" (176); it becomes like a "black hole" at the center of our intellectual universe (153). The withdrawal of social critique from the public expresses not only the fragmentation of social and public thought, but "the immensity of the ideological transformation" needed even to consider social change (176). Social discourse defaults to a language of pollsters and newsweekly publicists (174). With the technological promotion and blackout of information around the bombing of Iraq, one could say social discourse stopped altogether. Furthermore, the recurrent sectarianism of radical thinkers reflects both the inarticulability of the whole and the default of language in the particular; sectarianism signifies a forfeiture to familiar rhetorical formulations, which simultaneously undermines the ability to muster sufficient "rhetorical conviction" to make an alternative real.

This demise of citizenship in the abandonment of both public space and social critique results in what Birnbaum marks as the absence of a *polis*, of a public which is, in itself, the very arena in which that public can practice politics. Without a polis, critical thought becomes empty. The dissolution of the polis constitutes the central aporia in which language has been disempowered, dissolved. It creates a problem insolvable by critical or programmatic means. For an alternative to make sense, for Birnbaum, a public must be reinvented. This is Birnbaum's main point, and in it I think he is correct. But if he projects that a polis must be reinvented, he is also suggesting that the source of dissolution of the polis is to be sought in the realm of social discourses rather than in historical processes. Birnbaum has demonstrated that the public becomes blurred or undecidable within the very terms of reference that a public would use to constitute itself. Thus, our situation is an aporia of a loss of language within the very discourses with which we would hope to grasp our situation. In other words, certain sociopolitical realities, as discourses, silence themselves and us as soon as we address them.

Birnbaum does not say it this way, nor does he follow the logic of his argument out to this juncture; but the aporia of language re-emerges again and again in his essay, like a whale in mid-ocean. To grasp the significance of this, we must see how it happens in his own examples. Ultimately, the examples he gives cease to be examples, and re-submerge into the "black hole" that lurks at the center of his text, silhouetted by the incommensurability of fragmentation and homogeneity.

One important example is the question of class: the discourse of class does not become problematic simply because its articulation has been rendered sociological. The notion of exploitation central to class relations has also been rendered self-contradictory with respect to colonial domination (in Latin America, for instance). In particular, the exploitation by United States society as a whole of the colonial system in general obstructs the working class internationalism that would make (US) domestic class relations, as internal exploitation, intelligible. Instead, a self-reinforcing conflict of irreconcilable nationalist ideologies (protectionism, liberalism, anticommunism) become hegemonic and obfuscating at the same time. Furthermore, within an oligopolized American economy, market operations no longer provide an index to the exchange of labor power. Instead, oligopoly creates the possibility for itself of reversing (and thus ignoring) the law of supply and demand. The exchange of commodities ceases to be self-regulating and becomes both governed and unbalanced. Thus, the market categories upon which exploitation could be articulated slip out from under it. In a high-tech economy, with its decline of skilled labor, decommodification of computer labor, automation of clerical work, and commodification of information and information circulation, even Marxism has had to question the political and economic boundaries of what is meant by the "working class." The characteristics of a working class become absorbed into an employee market paradigm (as the contemporary arena in which self-definition and individuation occur); it devolves to a mixture of "class position, educational attainment, occupation, and political preference" (57). In the ideology of consumerism, class is indistinguishable from career—disguised by individualist preference or lost in chronic unemployment. The overall effect is a dispersion (even an undefinability) of the rhetoric of classes—which in turn fulfills the needs of consensus (homogeneity).

The unions are symptomatic. Though aware of themselves as organizations of social reform (50); they restrict themselves to "bread-and-butter" issues; thus, they trap themselves in the market both economically and consensually. When the government declares class warfare from above (e.g., in the suppression of the air traffic controllers' strike, or continual pressure for contract rollbacks), it does so as the main advocate of the culture of consumption. The rhetoric of working class interest is both coopted and rendered empty; the market demands of workers are not heard as political opposition, and ideological or ethical opposition to empire finds no relevant articulation within the program of workers' economic demands. For the working class, the culture of consumption and consensus engenders the ultimate fragmentation: silence. Though an exploited class has not ceased to exist theoretically (115), its existence and its power of self-definition have been pitted against each other.

The boundaries of the capitalist class have become similarly ambiguous. One could list corporatism itself, or the functionlessness of financial speculation, or the extreme decentralization of new industry (such as technologized service, or industrial software) (115) as instances of the separation of control and ownership. But with transnationalism and the remapping of the economic world by runaway shops, the sources of real economic decision retreat into an indiscernible distance; a class of people (capitalist) is replaced by a list of structures to which agency cannot be given. Birnbaum points out that while the imperial state preempts the decision-making process (from social structures of representation), "those who command the imperial state have in turn been preempted by the internationalization of economic decision" (114). That is, if representative democracy has become but a mask for the imperial state, the imperial state has in turn become a mask (rather than a steering committee, à la Lenin) for the elite. Political power still exists in relation to economic interest and decision in an understandable way, but approaches to that power no longer have a means of expressing themselves in the discourse of that relation. In total, the language of classes destructures itself because the reality articulated by that language continually escapes it, and the reality to be described produces a language that disguises that reality. The bombing of Iraq exemplified this destructuring in the political realm; its ferociousness produced a multilayered impossibility of discourse, and the absence of apparent economic interest (for the United States) made the singling out of Iraq from a host of similar cases unintelligible. In effect. one bought the package or not; political discourse was displaced by the question of support.

In sum, the rhetoric of classes has become mute. The seeming separation of empire and consumerism, and their actual inseparability, place consumerism at the core of a deconstruction of class itself. This is not a dialectic; dialectical negation and process occur in terms of commensurables. The incommensurability of the factors involved constitutes that deconstruction. (Perhaps this explains why Marxists, seemingly no longer a threat, are being courted by university humanities programs.)

Politics within the imperial state becomes destructured and undecidable. Birnbaum points out that the social structures on which representation is ostensibly founded, such as church, union, community (which have traditionally been the centers of popular self-definition), have become irrelevant because they too now "proceed on criteria of power enhancement and profit accumulation" (114). If they had once been the mediations between the public and the institutions of representation (the legislatures, etc.), that role is lost. This loss of mediation sets both the imperial state (demanding uniformity) and representative government (the arena of "diversity") out of reach in the distance. Beyond public involvement (though not beyond public interference), the elite functions as if the state were democratic, and the representative structures function as if they were the elite. Democratic procedure becomes the excuse for misrepresenting power, and power becomes the excuse for misrepresenting democratic procedure. To contest the imperial state in traditional terms means to be deflected back to the traditional "centers of decision," and absorbed in the market, while politically contesting the traditional centers of decision means deflection back toward the imperial state. That is, there is a deferral of government.

How is one to proceed? Birnbaum, having delineated the skewing of language to its own referent, has no way out of the dilemma; in fact, there is an undercurrent of despair in his text. He recognizes that no solution lies in the arena of program, for that would only return us to a language that has already failed. And an invention of a language is not a possibility. The question that confronts him, and us, is how to structure this destructuring of American thought, in order to "speak of our situation."

Lyotard has described a structure characterized by silencing, aporia, and destructuring, which he has called a "differend."[3] *Differend* is a French legal term referring to a dispute or difference of value. It marks the conflict between two incommensurable discourses, in which one side remains essentially outside the other, incomprehensible, unheard. Lyotard gives the example of a native of Martinique who, as a French citizen, has legal rights and protections against injury, but has no protection or rights against the injury he suffers as a French citizen; such injury is not heard in the discourse of French courts in Martinique. Similarly, the worker who argues for his humanity, who claims there is more at stake than a market exchange between his labor power and his wage, will not be heard within the capitalist discourse of market relations; he is paid by the hour as a commodity exchange, and that is that. The victim of injustice is rendered mute, without representation within the discourse or idiom in which the injustice occurs. It is, in fact, the very nature of injustice that it occurs at the hands of a discourse that does not permit that injustice as a referent.

One example of this, in contemporary political history, is the dispute between those who are willing to sacrifice the Bill of Rights to international goals and those who aren't; i.e., between nationalist and pluralist positions. If, for one side, the "free world" must not be sacrificed for liberal freedoms and niceties, for the other, the internal democratic structure must not be sacrificed to the export of a (United States modelled) power structure. These are two separate discourses in which the same statement ("We must not sacrifice democracy in defense of democracy") has two inverse and incommensurable meanings. In each discourse, the others' values and vision of power relationships become indiscernible. Neither can hear the other, nor grasp the idea that both are founded essentially on empire and consumerism. In fact, the very question of empire gets trapped within the realm of civil liberties issues. If the rhetoric of consensus is nationalism, and the rhetoric of democracy is pluralism, each becomes the form in which the other disappears.

The differend, as a structure of injustice, returns us to the examples given in the introduction. In the Air Force colonel's statement, two clearly recognizable discourses (of war and messianism) have been pitted against each other, revealing their incommensurability. Because the attempt to make sense of them entails complicity, we are subjected to them without recourse. The very demand for intelligibility renders us victims. A similar relation can be drawn for the structures addressed in Birnbaum's motifs. For instance, if the American social structure cancels public existence, then voting becomes a ratification of silencing, an acceptance of exclusion; for those who vote, however, the discourse of voting does not permit it to be seen as an emptiness, indeed, as an injustice. Though the emptying of public space cancels the content of critical political thought, for critical thinkers, restriction to certain given political rhetorics is not seen as an injustice, but a state of the political world. The very questions of why there is no American socialism, and that a public must be reinvented, belong to a discourse in which the political structures that engender those manifestions (through its forms of exclusion, atomization, absorption) remain inarticulable. Thus the ability to articulate a humane alternative to fragmentation, empire, and consumerism can only appear dreamlike, beyond a horizon, illusory, a moment of eternal disappearance. Only those wholly outside the system can see the injustices signified by those emptinesses, or absences; but they can speak of them only from afar. In sum, as a political process without a public, a democratic structure in which critical thought cannot be heard, American society itself is a differend.

The final question is, does political activity also fall prey to this differend? After all, even though very little of "our social life is rendered public by politics" (186), political activity at any level would seem to constitute the realm in which situations are changed, especially activity engaged in by "the movements." But in the relations between political parties and movements, a differend asserts itself with great concreteness. Birnbaum argues that American political parties, even third parties, are not mass organizations, but "loose coalitions of local elites, lobbies, and specific interest groups" (61). They reflect, and thus are unable to overcome, a prevailing absence of community—the absent community whose presence would have re-energized the polis and its "centers of decision." It is indeed the absence of community in party activity, and the necessity of community for political activity in general, that calls movements into existence. Even in the case of so-called single-issue movements, a substratum of philosophical and critical dialogue already constitutes a community of discourse. The pro-choice movement, a single-issue activity, could not have existed without the women's movement, i.e. without the women's community and its extended process of consciousness raising.

But though movements arise in order to provide what parties lack, and to demand participation rather than representation, they nevertheless operate in the context of party politics. To engage in discourse at the party level, they must also denature their differences with the parties. This means developing specific (issue-oriented) programs and presenting themselves as special interests. In effect, their attempt to unify a "citizenry" contributes again to its fragmentation, and they end up operating outside their own critical discourse. Where, on the one hand, real community gets dissolved through cooptation by artificial party activity, a movement, on the other, substitutes artificial community ("an acquired taste") for a real political public.

To the extent that movements are even marginally successful (from the parties' perspective), they effect a confrontation between participation and party democracy (especially at the local level). The traditional party attitude toward issue-oriented movements is that they are not "engaging" democratic practice because their goals pertain not to representation but to program, to a change of policy through a change in popular social outlook. Because this occurs outside the party framework, movements are seen by the parties as corrupting the democratic process, and as reflecting a "recalcitrance . . . to treat elites with deference" (62). Rather than deference, there is deferral to immediate popular involvement. The result is a differend in practice. This means that, for a movement to join party activity, it would have to dissolve the community it reflects and give itself up to representation; i.e., become other than it is, or can be. Yet, not to join party activity is to be excluded from discourse with organizations whose activity the movement is supplementing.

If we think of racism, or sexism, or patriarchy as a whole, we realize that this last scenario is familiar, in terms of a structural congruence. And I would like to use this congruence, in conclusion, as a way of broadening the consideration of both the differend and of an understanding of the political structure itself. Let me posit a structure of chauvinism in general, whose operation we can then begin to describe. Chauvinism (whether sexism, racism, patriotism, etc.) first discriminates another through the definition of a difference and then reduces or degrades the Other in terms of that discrimination, producing a subordinate status that appears to have generated the original discrimination. In this way, the Other is refused access to the defining discourse, and the Other's own statements are not heard; the Other's subjectivity has already ceased to exist as a referent in this discursive inversion. That is, through an *a priori* definition, chauvinism generates an other who is then dealt with as having produced the *a priori*.[4] The white man who walks up to a black man and says: "Apologize for being in my way, or I'll hurt you," is an example. The Other is noticed, and approached, only to be so addressed. To respond, "You walked up to me; I wasn't in your way," is to have made a meaningless statement within the chauvinist discourse. Thus, the other is placed wholly outside the chauvinist's experience, precisely in order to be replaced by, or absorbed as, abstract otherness. In the political discourses in question, parties denigrate movements precisely in order to charge them with standing outside the "democratic" process.

The chauvinist then makes two impossible demands on the victims:

first, that they differ from the difference imposed upon them (a priori), which means that they exclude themselves even from being who they are constructed to be, and second, that they be like (identical to) the chauvinist in the face of that exclusion. The wife who is attacked by her husband for not understanding (presaging or foreseeing) his feeling of not being understood (foreseen) by her, is attacked both for not being him and not being who she is supposed to be (one who foresees his emotional states); in effect, she is attacked for her very existence.

In other words, as a referent (of the chauvinist discourse), the victim doesn't exist, other than as the *a priori*; the victim's claim to selfhood becomes speech that is not heard. Under such conditions, the victim becomes "a referent," an "other" for himself/herself as well. Or, as Sartre would say, one becomes an object for oneself in the other's eternal and unseen look; one becomes an element of one's own external situation.[5] Chauvinism is thus an imposed, and enforced, differend. It is not one that arises from the nature of a dispute in discourse, but it is a discourse whose purpose and strategy is a differend, with its exclusion, deferral, and silencing.

With respect to party-movement relations, the demand that the movement speak the language of representation, address issues within that purview, and give deference to it effectively demands that the movement become other than it is, a demand for a silence through exclusion and deferral. Silence becomes the condition of speech. But this, then, suggests that the earlier polis was illusory, a political public identifiable only through the existence of an excluded other (race, ethnic, or gender difference), which dissolved in the wake of an assault on those internal boundaries (by the many anti-chauvinist movements—feminist, black, Chicano, gay, lesbian, anti-imperialist, environmentalist, etc.). In posing the structure of chauvinism as I have, I am suggesting that the dissolution of the polis, which Birnbaum has noticed and decried, is the logical political extension of a centrality of chauvinist operations to American political life. That is, it is precisely the chauvinist form as manifested in the political aporias Birnbaum describes—a relation he himself does not see. This implies that surpassing and dissolving chauvinist relations in their particular forms as racism, sexism, classism, etc., must be the central aspect of reconstituting a polis.

Like chauvinism, party politics is a discourse designed to empty all alternate discourses of meaning. Within the party paradigm, participation is not considered politics; only the bestowal of representation, or proxyism, is. More generally, however, as suggested above, for the imperial state, a public can be an entity only in order to be a nonentity; i.e., it must both be the imperial state and not exist at the same time, both be the nation and be silently what the nation (state) represents *a priori*. In the case of the bombing of Libya, or the invasion of Grenada, the exclusion of non-supporters from public consciousness, attention, and information is already grounded in *a prior* silencing of the discourse of non-support. (Actually, support for the bombing was also another form of exclusion, but that is a different discussion, addressing certain specific political economic processes at work in the world as a whole.)

In effect, in American politics, we confront structures that "speak" the syntax of chauvinism. If the citizenship Birnbaum is looking for equals public space and the use of it, it is chauvinism that usurps that space as it is cleared, and denudes it of growth. We are faced with the necessity of overcoming the chauvinist paradigm that underlies all American political institutions, if we are to regenerate a language that will once again permit political discourse. To the extent that Birnbaum points out and recognizes the slippage of American reality from underneath the ability to understand it, one that continues to leave empire untouchable, and consumerism the only community permitted, he only delineates the central dilemma; chauvinism persists as it does in part because it engenders a situation in which the mere desire not to be a victim oneself of its differend places one in support of it. That is, part of chauvinism's tenacity is its continual generation of insidious complicity.

It might be reasonable to expect that a critique such as this would conclude on a programmatic note, if it were not to succumb to pessimism. But, as suggested above, program, at this point, could only be articulated in the language already implicated in the problematic, and which is thus suspect. We cannot fall back upon political procedure just because it has a certain stability, a certain defined *modus operandi* extant. We would have to question that stability: stability for whom or for what, and who is excluded by it? Indeed, as soon as one specifies the limits or boundaries of a differend, or defines it discursively as a disparity with a particular form or content, rather than as an interstice in discourses itself, one has already fallen into a liberalism in which one simply champions the "rights" of the silenced. In the name of individual rights, or social justice, or any other universalization, one would simply have stretched the boundaries of the universalization to a different point, a procedure that calls in question neither the authority behind the differend nor the continued exclusions constructed by universalization itself. "Solving" the differend will not reveal how it empowers chauvinism through its imposition.

If a language is required in which to make sense of, or to articulate intelligibly, the political situation we are in, it must arise from communities that themselves address and embrace multiple subjective cultural being. Movements are already communities of sorts, precisely because they generate a language that is both the effect and the dynamic of survival against multiple forms of domination. But the language of a radical renewal must itself be multiple, and fluid, if it is not to become simply another differend, another exclusion, within a political structure that lives on exclusions. But communities, and their languages, cannot be built programmatically—though political communities are all built in part upon a critique. And central to this process is always the development of a literature (which also cannot be engendered programmatically) as the site at which new languages are constructed.

12

Spinning Ethics in Its Grave: Tradition and Rupture in the Theory of Roland Barthes

Sharon Meagher

PREFACE: EARLY BARTHES/LATE BARTHES

Is it possible to capture Barthes's writing on writing? If Barthes is at all successful at his project, if his (later) texts are texts of *jouissance*, then it cannot be possible to capture Barthes: he remains the elusive outlaw.[1] The writer/reader of Barthes is plagued with the task of trying to make sense of (which generally means to *systematize*) the Barthian corpus. This might seem easy enough: after all, the work is complete, insofar as Barthes is dead and can write no more. Very often critics then organize the work of an author as a whole with some reference to a chronology, usually that of the author's biography. Such is the case with the Barthian text, which is often discussed with the aid of a number of dichotomous categories: early Barthes/late Barthes, structuralist Barthes/post-structuralist Barthes, texts of pleasure/texts of *jouissance*, living Barthes/dead Barthes. But these dichotomies have only marginal utility. They help us create a myth that might give us a momentary, fragmented glimpse of the Barthian corpus.

In the writing of this paper a chronology that parallels Barthes's life has been imposed in an attempt to present the development of a Barthian ethic of writing. The story begins with Barthes's concept of an ethic of commitment, which stems from his critique of Sartre's theory of literature and commitment. But with "The Death of the Author" there appears a shift away from authorial commitment, followed by a move toward pleasure in "From Work to Text." This concept of pleasure is further developed and refined in Barthes's later texts, *Pleasure of the Text* and *Roland Barthes by Roland Barthes*, where the concepts of *plaisir* and *jouissance* are unfolded.

This chronology, this order, gives us a way of elucidating the meaning of Barthian texts by viewing their operation within the context of other texts. But this order slips away from us too, for in *jouissance* we find a turning of early Barthes upon late Barthes: an ethic of commitment is not abandoned, only lost (in the sense of displaced).[2] *Jouissance* derives from the pursuit of the playful outlaw, and from the terror of the prospect of lurking spirits. The more we chase Barthes, the faster his spirit chases us. We are caught in a whirlwind, a tailspin.

We need the figure of Barthes; it is a way for us as readers to make sense of it all.[3] But the "it all" always slips away from us; we cannot systematize the whole body of texts that bear the signature *Roland Barthes*. Barthes cannot function as the place where the multiplicity of meanings gathers; only the reader can serve as that locus.

As reader/writer of Barthes's *writerly* texts, then, one can only hope to inscribe some mythic Barthes. Any exercise or attempt to capture Barthes's intentions or THE REAL BARTHES is fruitless. At best the reader/writer of Barthes can hope to manage the text by playing in a similar spirit, by striking a chord that gets in tune with the Barthian text.

INTRODUCTION

Poststructuralist literary theory has called for a rethinking of previous paradigms of literary analysis. In part this has seemed a matter of necessity: previous paradigms seemed no longer adequate to what was being analyzed. Under traditional ethical approaches to literature, modernist literature could only suffer condemnation. But perhaps, argues Roland Barthes in *Writing Degree Zero*,[4] this is not the fault of modernist literature; perhaps it is the case that ethical approaches to literature such as that espoused by Sartre in *What is Literature?*[5] are simply no longer relevant.

Barthes's riposte to Sartre does not entail an outright rejection of an ethics of writing, but rather a rethinking (and a rewriting) of the question "What is Writing?".[6] The point of re-asking this question is not to find a solution, but to find the problem.

> Although Barthes agrees with Sartre that the writer's vocation has an ethical imperative, he insists on its complexity and ambiguity. Sartre appeals to the morality of ends. Barthes invokes "the morality of form,"—what makes literature a problem rather than a solution; what makes literature. . . . For Barthes, it is not the commitment that writing makes to something outside

> of itself (to a social or moral goal) that makes literature an instrument of opposition and subversion but a certain practice of writing itself.[7]

Writing is not (and can no longer be considered as) transparent; an ethic of writing is not (and can no longer be considered as) certain.

EARLY BARTHES (*WRITING DEGREE ZERO*, 1956): CRITIQUE OF SARTRE'S *WHAT IS LITERATURE?*

An analysis of Barthes and Sartre will illustrate how Barthes throws these two matters into question, thus opening up the possibility for later "poststructuralist" approaches. Barthes criticizes Sartre's phenomenological approach to writing, which sought to explicate literary meaning by focusing on "the activity of the individual subject who constitutes the literary work and its meaning."[8] Sartre is primarily concerned with writing that is significative, i.e., prose-writing. His concern lies not with the poets' interest in the physical properties and density of words, or in language as object. Rather, his concern lies with language as communication, or with words "which are first of all not objects but designations for objects" (Sartre, 20). Prose-writing achieves the goal of talking about something, or communicating.

Sartre writes that

> Prose is, in essence, utilitarian. I would readily define the prose-writer as a man who *makes use* of words . . . The writer is a *speaker*; he designates, demonstrates, orders, refuses, interpolates, begs, insults, persuades, insinuates (Sartre, 19).

This quotation captures two important elements of Sartre's theory of literature. First, the prose-writer is one who acts; she or he chooses whether to write, what to write, how to write, and to whom to write. Second, Sartre equates prose-writing with speech.

The writer tells thoughts to others. This necessitates a value judgment, a decision as to whether a thought is worth communicating.[9] The translation of thoughts to words takes time and care. During this process of translation, the spoken or named is transformed. "Anything which one names is already no longer quite the same; it has lost its innocence" (Sartre, 22). In this sense writing both creates and reflects the world. The words reveal one's thoughts to others so that they exist for us (author and reader) and affect our relationship to the world.

"To write is to make an appeal to the reader that he lead into objective existence the revelation which I have undertaken by means of language . . . the writer appeals to the reader's freedom to collaborate in the production of his work" (Sartre, 46). The aim of writing is the encouragement of self-consciousness. The "engaged" writer is one who makes choices (regarding style and subject) that will ensure that this goal is achieved. The choice of subject is the choice of what to disclose or change; the choice of style is the choice of how to disclose the subject. As such, the choice of style should be made with the choice of subject in mind. Style is valuable, in that it determines the quality and effectiveness of the prose.

This in short is Sartre's theory of writing. Sartre's theory of writing and his conception of an ethics of writing are intimately bound up with one another. According to Sartre, writing conveys meaning; literature is bound to the task of communicating. "The writer is (potentially) a giver of consciousness, a liberator. His medium, language, confers on him an ethical obligation: to aid in the project of bringing liberty to *all* men—and this ethical criterion must be the foundation of any sound literary judgment."[10] Literature is valued by Sartre; it has moral utility. The good author is one who recognizes and commits to a language-instrument. Thus Sartre condemns the modernist writer (beginning with Flaubert) for failing to recognize this responsibility, for rejecting the principle of engagement. There is no way then, Sartre claims, of liberating one's consciousness, of making one aware of one's historical circumstance, and therefore of clearing the path for revolution.

Barthes's critique and revision of Sartre's theory of writing saves modernist literature from this utter condemnation. Barthes claims that modernist writing, unlike classic bourgeois literature, is not communication and is distinguishable from speech. Whereas speech is intentional and communicative, writing "is nothing but a flow of empty signs, the movement of which alone is significant" (Zero, 19). Language for Barthes is opaque, not transparent as it is for Sartre.

While Sartre analyzed literature in terms of two major categories, language and style, Barthes introduces a third category, *écriture*. In this way Barthes is able to take into consideration both writing as production (the function of writing) and the product of writing. Barthes's concept of language does not differ much from that of Sartre. Barthes rejects, however, Sartre's concept of style as a matter of authorial choice at the service of the writing's content. According to Barthes,

> A language is . . . a horizon, and style a vertical dimension, which together map out for the writer a Nature, since he does not choose either. The language functions negatively, as the initial limit of the possible, style is a Necessity which binds the writer's humor to his form of expression (*Zero*, 13).

Both language and style are different dimensions of Form, both of which are given to the writer.

> Now every Form is also a Value, which is why there is room, between a language and a style, for another formal reality: writing (*écriture*). Within any literary form there is a choice of tone, of ethos, if you like, and this is precisely where the writer shows himself clearly as an individual because this is where he commits himself (*Zero*, 13).

Écriture is best translated into English as "mode of writing." It is the third dimension of form, and it serves as the locus of commitment.

Unlike Sartre, Barthes does not think the effects of writing are worthy of ethical consideration, since they are always bound to, and determined by, history. Barthes's ethics of writing is focused upon *écriture*, which he also calls "the morality of form." Barthes's answer to the question "What is writing?" yields a more complicated, ambiguous answer (which is an answer only insofar as it opens up the problem of writing). This in turn requires a more complicated conception of an ethics of literature. Since writing for Barthes is simply a "flow of empty signs," any value of writing lies within its form, its flow, rather than with the signified. Only within *écriture* can the author make any choice or commitment, and so take any ethical responsibility.

The modernist, for example, whom Sartre criticizes for destroying literature, cannot, according to Barthes, be held culpable for a situation which is not of his making. According to Barthes, the only responsibility that the author has is to be true to his or her historical circumstance. The extent of that responsibility varies with history. The modern situation is unique in that for the first time in history, the writer is confronted with a circumstance in which all modes of writing have been exhausted. "The multiplication of modes of writing is a modern phenomenon which forces a choice upon the writer, making form a kind of behavior and giving rise to an ethic of writing" (*Zero*, 84). Prior to the modern period, there existed only one mode of writing for each epoch. In bourgeois society, which gives rise to an *écriture*, only a single mode of writing developed because there was a unified ideology. The writer's consciousness or thought was identical to that of society. The paradox of the modern situation is that the ethos of this culture is one in which universal consciousness is denied. Modern writers find themselves in situations in which there is no one form specific to that historical, cultural situation, but rather a plurality of forms. A choice of form must be made from all those given throughout history (i.e., in past writings). Each choice has political significance, because each form is connected to a specific political historical circumstance. "Writing is thus essentially the ethic of form, the choice of the social domain within which the writer decides to situate the Nature of his language. But this social area is by no means that of an actual consumption. It is not a question for the writer of choosing the social group for which he is to write. . . . " (*Zero*, 15). Barthes argues that the choice is "a way of conceiving literature," rather than a choice of political ends or social audience, as Sartre thinks it is.

In choosing a mode of writing, the writer chooses a place in society; it is a way of reconciling the writer's vocation with society.

> This specialized language, the use of which gives the writer a glorious but nonetheless superintended function, evinces a kind of servitude, invisible at first, which characterizes any responsibility. Writing, free in its beginnings, is finally the bond which links the writer to a History which is itself in chains: society stamps upon him the unmistakable signs of art so as to draw him along the more inescapably in its own process of alienation (*Zero*, 40).

Écriture is "a suspension between moment and duration, instance and history . . . it opens a dichotomy between the individual writer's gesture of free will and the historical determination that engulfs him" (Ray, 171). It saves the writer from alienation, albeit temporarily.

Modernist writers should not be condemned for recognizing the failure, or rather the impossibility, of a lasting commitment. The intellectual mode of writing that Sartre chooses, with its obsession with political commitment, "can lead only to complicity or impotence, which means, in either case, to alienation" (*Zero*, 28). The possibilities open to the writer are restricted to those made available to him or her through past writings (*Zero*, 15–16). And at the instant that the choice is made, it too is swept into history. It is not that the modernist writer is irresponsible, or that an ethic of commitment is denied, but rather that this responsibility and commitment is transformed. Given this transformation, the most responsible action that a writer might take is to try to approximate the ideal of a "mode-less" writing (zero-degree writing). "An author's true responsibility is to support literature as a failed commitment. . . ."[11] This paradoxically requires commitment, but of a different sort than Sartre demanded.

THE DEATH OF THE AUTHOR

In *Writing Degree Zero*, the Sartrean concept of an ethic of commitment is put into question. Barthes redefines the problem of writing and authorial commitment. Barthes's claims regarding *écriture* and the density of language suggest that writing is more problematic and ambiguous than Sartre thought. Barthes does not propose a solution to this problem, except to say that this process of questioning must continue if writing is to be possible at all.

Fifteen years later, in his 1968 essay "The Death of the Author," Barthes continues this interrogation of the author's responsibility and commitment. Here Barthes leads the poststructuralists in announcing the death of the author.[12] Barthes argues that the notion of an author is a bourgeois construct that arose as a result of capitalist ideology. The rise of the concept of modern individualism turned the readers' (and critics') attention to the person of the author as a way of understanding the literary work. But in avant-garde writing the text is transformed by removing the author, that is, by subverting the possibility of reading the work through an analysis of the person of the author. Such an analysis fails to understand the complexity of writing. The writer does not create *ex nihilo*. Literary expression is possible only through language, and language is already given. "It is language that speaks, not the author."[13]

The question "Who is speaking?" a question that echoes from "The Death of the Author," is repeated throughout Barthes's later text, *S/Z* (1970).[14] This question is always unanswerable in the given context, or rather, no one answer is correct, because "writing is the destruction of every voice, of every point of origin."[15] The force of such inquiry is to make the author die. Barthes calls the author "that somewhat decrepit deity of the old criticism."[16]

Barthes uses the term *scriptor* to denote the person who mixes writing—the social being who inscribes his/her mother tongue (social language). Unlike the author, the scriptor is neither a creator nor an immortal being; the scriptor comes to life simultaneously with the text, and its existence is coterminous with that text. Having buried the author, the scriptor can no longer believe in the idea of writing as self-expression. The author is the embodiment of the origin of the text's meaning, but this is not true for the scriptor. Barthes avoids the word *author*, since to assign the text an author is to impose an artificial limit on the text. The concept of author furnishes the text with a final signified. That is, it is to read that text as if there is one correct interpretation, that which the author intended. Such a reading denies the play of the signifier, restricting the multiplicity of meanings in the text.[17] It privileges signification over *signifiance*:

> [W]hen the text is read (or written) as a moving play of signifiers, without any possible reference to one or some fixed signifieds, it becomes necessary to distinguish signification, which belongs to the plane of the product, of the enounced, of communication, and the work of the signifier, which belongs to the plane of the production, of enunciation, of symbolization—this work being called *signifiance* . . . Contrary to signification, *signifiance* cannot be reduced, therefore, to communication, representation, expression: it places the subject (writer, reader) in the text not as a projection . . . but as a "loss," a "disappearance".[18]

Signifiance characterizes the avant-garde writings that Sartre condemns. It is that which makes a writing a "text" as opposed to a "work." Works are "readerly" texts, "what can be read, but not written."[19] There is a closure of signification, so that there is nothing left for the subject (writer or reader) to do but consume the cultural codes as they have been inscribed. These are what we call classic texts. In the "writerly" text, on the other hand, we find the play of the signifier and a subversion of cultural codes because no particular code or law is communicated.

In *From Work to Text* (1971), Barthes poses what he calls a "hedonistic aesthetics" as an approach to the text. There is also a pleasure of the work. "But this pleasure, no matter how keen and even when free from all prejudice, remains in part (unless by some exceptional critical effort) a pleasure of consumption."[20] There is pleasure in the "readerly" text, but it is the pleasure of consuming (since the text cannot be "rewritten" by the reader). It is the comfort gained from the security of staying within the law, or "curling up" with it (as one does with a "good book"). It is the pleasure felt when a reader is at one with the culture as it is codified in the work.

The text, however, is marked by the death of the author. With the death of the author comes the birth of the "reader," that is, a construct, or place, where the multiplicity of the text is focused. The reader is the producer of the text, insofar as the reader constructs and destructs each intertext. The pleasure of the text, then, is not a pleasure of consumption. The text is

> bound to *jouissance*, that is to a pleasure without separation . . . the Text achieves, if not the transparency of social relations, that at least of language relations: the Text is that space where no language has a hold over any other, where languages circulate (keeping the circular sense of the term).[21]

Jouissance, unlike *plaisir*, is marked by loss of cultural identity. The capitalist economy (and ideology) that marks our culture is perverted; the social relations are upset.

LATE BARTHES (*THE PLEASURE OF THE TEXT*, 1973): PLEASURE/*JOUISSANCE*

Pleasure and *jouissance* are explored, developed, and woven in Barthes's later writings, *The Pleasure of the Text* and *Roland Barthes by Roland Barthes*. The announcement of the death of the author is also repeated in these writings:

> As institution, the author is dead: his civil status, his biographical person have disappeared; dispossessed, they no longer exercise over his work the formidable paternity whose account literary history, teaching, and public opinion had the responsibility of establishing and renewing; but in the

> text, in a way I *desire* the author: I need his figure (which is neither his representation nor his projection), as he needs mine.[22]

In writing we desire that brush with the law, the figure of the author, the name: some *structure* that we can "play off."[23] Otherwise the construction and destruction of the text is not possible.

We can no longer pretend to know the person of the author, any more than the scriptor can pretend to know that of the reader. Both author and reader are fictitious constructions, a collection of connotations and stereotypes, which aid in the production and destruction of the text.

Roland Barthes declares the death of the author and kills his own authorship in his texts, even in his autobiography. Barthes's autobiography does not create a place for Barthes. In fact, he wiggles out of the "pigeonholes" in which he has been placed by carving new niches and destroying them too. Every effort is made to block the reader's attempt to psychoanalyze Barthes or his texts. Inscribed in the prefacing page to *Roland Barthes by Roland Barthes* are the following words: "It must all be considered as if spoken by a character in a novel." [24] Yet this death of the author is neither murder nor suicide, for it is not Roland Barthes who does this, but writing itself.

But what then has happened to the concept of authorial commitment? Does it die with the author? After *Writing Degree Zero*, the concept of authorial commitment "disappears," just as does the author. An ethics of commitment is buried in the later Barthian texts. But it is buried in a shallow grave, and its slightly decomposed remains are left exposed. In the later Barthian writings, both author and authorial commitment are displaced. They are superficial levels of meaning, which must be buried so that new possibilities for an ethics of writing can be unearthed. As the reader spins new meanings, it becomes possible to spin ethics in its grave. In this way old, conventionalized codes are twisted (and possibly broken). A code is a culturally delineated system of meaning. A break in that system is achieved by a play[25] on the multiplicity of meaning. "The plural of the text depends . . . on its weave of signifiers."[26]

FOR(E) PLAY: THE EROTICISM OF MULTIPLICITY

In his autobiography, Barthes writes about amphibologies, "In general the context forces us to choose one of the two meanings and to forget the other. Each time he encounters one of these double words, R. B., on the contrary, insists on keeping both meanings. . . . "(Barthes, 72). Two words that keep cropping up (and slipping away) in the Barthian text are *body* and *value*. By unravelling and reweaving the meanings of these two words, an ethics can be spun as well. This seems a viable strategy, since what is desired here is to pursue *jouissance*. But such a chase cannot follow a direct path, but must weave in and out of the web.

Body

Barthes plays[27] on the meanings of the word *body*, and relatedly, *corpus* and *corporeal*. The eroticism of the body is personal/social, as well as biological/cultural. By playing on the plurality of the meanings of *body* we can focus on the tension between the individual and the social. Body is both irreducible difference and the principle of structuration. For example, Barthes writes about his colleagues at *Tel Quel* who expect him to speak a common incorporeal language, yet it is a language that must be spoken with one's own body (*Barthes*, 175). Here the body is a distinguishing principle, that which makes one's own language different from others. Yet all, to a certain degree, share the same body of language, that is, the same corpus of texts.

Body can mean biological body, erotic body, social body, body politic, a lived body, a dead body, a collectivity, a consistency, a shape. At times the context of Barthes's writing allows us to choose among various meanings of *body*, while at other times the ambiguity in meaning is enforced.[28] Similarly this occurs with the use of the words *corporeal* (of or pertaining to the body; of a material nature) and *corpus* (body, especially when dead; anatomy, a structure constituting the main part of an organ; principal or capital; a large collection of writings of a specific kind or on a specific subject).[29]

This tension is maintained not only by playing with the referents, but by writing a "writerly text" in which one can lose his/her body to the body of the text while taking pleasure in the texture, the consistency of the text, the materiality of the play of the signifier. There is a temporary suspension of the conventionalized codes that normally control and maintain the relationship between individual subject and text.

In this multiplicity of the meanings of *body* there is a focus on the tension between dichotomies that have traditionally had a place in ethics of writing: individual/social, content/form. The choices that are made in a Sartrean ethic of commitment (the priority of the individual over the social; the priority of content over form) are subverted.

But this emphasis on body is also significant for ethics because in the text of *jouissance*, value is shifted from the signified to the signifier (*PT*, p. 65). The text is valued according to pleasure, rather than old standards of good and bad (*PT*, 13). "How does the word become value? At the level of the body" (*Barthes*, 130).

Value

What is this value? Economics, aesthetics, and ethics are all embodied in the word *value*. To think of writing as both process (production) and product is to value it, at least in an economic sense. But value means so many things: there are, of course, the economic connotations of the term—value as monetary worth, as material worth, as equivalent worth. Value can also describe that which has utility or merit. Value can denote a desirable standard, whether in ethics or aesthetics. And value can also mean precise meaning or import.[30]

The evaluation of the text is at once ethical and semantic (*Barthes*, 154). "Value (and with it, meaning) thus unceasingly oscillates" (*Barthes*, 139). The text is always a play of and with meaning. In the text there is a tension between the "historically bound *act*," the act of inscription, and the "permanent textual *fact*, embodied in a word or series of words whose meaning transcends particular volition and can be apprehended in its structure by any individual possessed of the language."[31] Yet the tension between instance and system, between what "I mean" and what the word means, is subordinated in Barthes's later writings to the tension between meanings. It is the latter tension that Barthes ultimately seems to value.[32] Let us then examine the other meanings of the word *value* that are played off one another.

Value means worth (monetary, material, equivalent). These economic connotations are important and multiple. A morality of the body is one that is concerned with the material. Signs are exchanged—hence, equivalent worth. And there are frequent references to monetary worth, economic transaction. The capitalist exchange relations are turned and overturned. The contract that is celebrated as the model contract is the contract of prostitution (*Barthes*, 59). And "the positive value par excellence [is] the praxis, the perverse expenditure ('for nothing')" (*Barthes*, 62).

Both of these allusions to economics double back so that, for example, *expenditure* denotes both economic and erotic function. Such a doubling of meaning simultaneously constructs and destructs bourgeois values. Barthes reveals an eroticism in the capitalist exchange system that gave birth to the bourgeoisie and its values. In this way their values are perverted—and decomposed.

A particular bourgeois value that finds itself in the grasp of Barthes's play is the value of usefulness or utility. This is a value that is so valuable to the bourgeoisie that it can be connoted by the very word *value*. The value of the text reveals bourgeois society's own perversion.

> It is the text's very uselessness that is useful, as a potlatch. In other words, society lives according to a cleavage: here a sublime, disinterested text,

> there a mercantile object, whose value is . . . the gratuitousness of this object. But society has no notion of this split: *it is ignorant of its own perversion* (*PT*, 24).

Once bourgeois values are perverted and uprooted, Barthes's own values (and perversions) are overturned and exposed. The standard that Barthes desires is one that is newly unearthed, over and over again. Barthes calls himself a "hedonist"; he makes use of this name. And a name "is an instrument of exchange: it permits the substitution of a nominal unity for a collection of traits by positing a relationship of equivalence between the sign and the sum" (*S/Z*, 95). But naming is not simply an act of closure; it functions simultaneously "as an act of closure and reopening, and as a process, it restates the history latent in textuality."[33]

> To read is to find meanings, and to find meanings is to name them; but these named meanings are swept away towards further names; names invoke each other, come together, and their conglomeration calls out to be named anew; I name; I unname: thus passes the text: it is a nomination in the becoming, a tireless approximation, a metonymic project (*S/Z*, 17–18).

The process of naming, a process only possible in the realm of aesthetics, thus allows us to be both inside and outside the system (the economic, the ethical/political, and the aesthetic).

The names *body* and *value* sum up a collectivity of meanings. These unities are unravelled (by calling many things or traits by the same name) and then rewoven. There is a spinning of meaning. An interweaving of the multiple meanings of *body* and an interweaving of the multiple meanings of *value* simultaneously serves to bury a bourgeois ethics and to unearth new possibilities.

JOUISSANCE

Jouissance is a name that captures multiple meanings in such a way that it eludes renaming (translation). In *Pleasure of the Text*, Richard Miller translates *jouissance* as "bliss," but this English word does not carry the range of meaning that the French word *jouissance* does. *Jouissance* has sexual, spiritual, physical, and conceptual connotations. It can mean enjoyment, in the sense of enjoying a legal or social possession, pleasure, bliss, and/or coming (the pleasure of sexual climax).[34] There is also a pun at play: *jouissance* = *j'ouis sense* = I heard meaning.[35] The word *jouissance* can be found in the texts of Lacan, Barthes, and Kristeva. In all three cases, a certain pleasure is taken in the slippage of meaning of *jouissance*. All meanings of the word simultaneously come together.

Perhaps nowhere do we experience *jouissance* more fully than in the reading of texts that are of and about *jouissance*.

As noted earlier, Barthes sets up an opposition between *plaisir* (cultural enjoyment and identity) and *jouissance* (shattering, dissipating, losing cultural identity) in *Pleasure of the Text*.[36] This distinction (*plaisir/jouissance*) is confused, contradicted, made ambiguous and overcome when the reader takes in the slippage of meaning of body, value, and ultimately, *jouissance*. It is important to note the meaning of *jouissance* that denotes the bourgeois notion of property rights. This meaning illustrates the way in which *jouissance* carries with it *plaisir*, that is, the enjoyment of the values of the culture, without succumbing to it. The multiplicity of meaning, the infinite advance of the symbol, allows for the brush with the law so that one is both in and out of it. *Jouissance*, then, is not absolute anarchy, but a temporary suspension of the law.

Body and value both come to play in *jouissance*. But *jouissance* cannot be read as a synthesizing term between "body" and "value." In the first place, "body" and "value" are not opposites. Each word gives the reader access to a fuller understanding of *jouissance* and its implications for an ethics of writing. They are multi-stranded threads, both of which are woven into the fabric of *jouissance*, but there are remnants, leftovers. And this is the second point: *jouissance* is not a synthesizing term because there is not a closed, dialectical process at work.[37]

In *jouissance* the multiple meanings of "body" and "value" are gathered and dispersed. There is an economy of language; one word captures and disseminates many meanings. The materiality that both "body" and "value" connote, for example, are found in the texture of *jouissance*. *Jouissance* does refer to body and bodily function in the literal sense. And the pleasure that is experienced in coming is a desirable standard (a value). Yet *jouissance* has its costs: it is no coincidence that the Victorians had another name for coming: spending. Whenever we come there is a loss—a loss of self (self-suspension), a loss of Other (Other disappears as the two bodies come together), a loss of bodily fluid. But what is this Other? It is body, but there are so many bodies—and it is all of them—lover, social body, text. There is no privileging of one meaning over any other; all signifiers are woven together.

This is not a dialectical process of overcoming, but a process of spinning. Dichotomies are spun (woven/turned) so that similarities and differences become (at least momentarily) a blur, and then rupture. This is *jouissance*; and this is the subversive move. It gathers and disseminates dichotomies: content/form, individual/social, theory/practice, private/public, ethics/politics.

Roland Barthes desires and values disruption—breaks in the capitalist ideology (in hopes that these fissures will erode ideology and eventually cause its collapse).[38] This break cannot be achieved by simply burying a conception of individual ethics of responsibility (a conception that is both marked and legitimized by the capital exchange). Simple rejection of old concepts is not a workable strategy. The residue of that dead concept sticks everywhere, especially on the underside of its newly erected opposite. Complete erasure, as Barthes knows, is not possible.

If Barthes buries one term of a binomial (ethical commitment) and then erects the other term (pleasure) on the grave, it is only so that that term can then be buried and the other unearthed. The shift from one term to another is merely a tremor, a foreshadowing of the rupture to come. Nothing is permanently lost. Rather, it is a perpetual cycle of death and resurrection. There is no standing on solid ground. The reader is set adrift (*PT*, 18, 23).

TURNING BARTHES UPON BARTHES

The question asked earlier is now asked again: what has happened to an ethic of commitment? This question cannot be answered by simply reading the categories developed in Barthes's later texts back into early Barthes. Indeed, much of the early Barthes stubbornly resists inclusion in the later texts. There is, for example, no way of translating the threefold distinction of language, style, and *écriture* developed in *Writing Degree Zero* into the language of *jouissance* without some remainder. Similarly, there is a close parallel between the concepts of commitment and *plaisir*, since both are concerned with the bond to cultural codes.

The disruption of cultural codes does not occur when the opposition between hedonism and commitment (or *jouissance* and *plaisir*) is struck, but rather when this opposition is diverted and altered. This diversion, this alteration, takes place in the play on "body" and "value," and is ultimately captured (and released) in *jouissance* itself. The texts of *jouissance*, then, allow for a turning of Barthes upon Barthes. The distinctions discussed in the preface of this paper: early Barthes/late Barthes, structuralist Barthes/poststructuralist Barthes, and so forth, provide a structure (through a certain economy of words) that continually reopens itself.

A Barthian ethics of writing should not be construed as a hedonism erected on the grave of commitment, but as a (re)turn (a comeback) to a new ethic—a morality of the body—every body. The grave is spun. This spinning does not take the form of a circle, but rather that of a spiral. The spiral is "a kind of circle distended to infinity . . . on the spiral things recur but *at another level*: there is a return in difference, not repetition in identity."[39] This is the "way to escape the alienation of today's society: to retreat ahead of it" (*PT*, 40). There is a continual rewriting of the old, although something is always left over. There is some loose change, some room for an ethics of writing. This is the place of revolution.

POSTSCRIPT(OR)

Eulogy:

> Like all great aesthetes, Barthes was an expert at having it both ways. Thus he identifies writing both with a generous relation to the world (writing as "perpetual production") and with a defiant relation (writing as "perpetual revolution of languages," outside the bounds of power). He wants a politics and an anti-politics, a critical relation to the world and one beyond moral criticism.[40]

(This politics/anti-politics is Barthes's *jouissance*, and that desire for pleasure can never die—it is perpetually renewed, continually spun.)

Epitaph: "It is evident that the object of all his work is a morality of the sign" (*Barthes*, 97).

Barthes(s') remains: gay in-law/elusive (playful) outlaw

13

Célan's Poetics of Address: How the Dead Resist Their History

James Hatley

CÉLAN'S PROPHETIC LYRICISM

In their tortured yet insistent address of the annihilated of the Shoah,[1] Paul Célan's poems, especially those of *Die Niemandrose,* would give witness concerning the plight of beings who no longer live, who no longer are. Being acts of memory directed to and speaking for a time that no longer is, the poems are more consciously historical than one would expect of the modern lyric, a genre whose capabilities seem more suited to a complexly emotional, intensely personal, and self-consciously imaginative voice. Such a voice easily becomes enamored with its own artfulness and pathos; not unexpectedly, the modern lyric shows a tendency to adopt an attitude of diffidence or even hermetic indifference toward the forces at play in a historical world lying outside the imaginative world of the poem.[2] But Célan's poems counter this tendency to discount the historical by invoking a lyricism reminiscent of Biblical prophecy, in which the pathetic reaction of the speaker to the victimization of actual persons leads the poem to challenge directly the logic of a history in which such victimization occurs. As Célan himself expressed it, his poems would give "a *Gegenwort,*" a "word of resistance," which "rends the wire," which "bows down no more before the 'do-nothings and show-horses' of history."[3] Such a word resists those who would use their power to grasp the world for themselves, even as they forget the suffering of those who succumb to violence in the wake of their domination.

Thus, in spite of its deeply personal tone, Célan's prophetic lyricism is essentially an historical rather than personal writing, insofar as it questions the affective meaning of historical events. Such a writing is to be distinguished from a more straightforwardly historical writing that puts itself in the service of heralding the accomplishments of history's greatest actors.[4] Levinas has argued that these latter accounts, which he terms "historiographies," are written primarily for the sake of history's "survivors," those for whom the past means nothing more than a series of achievements that now justify and benefit the expectations of the living.[5] History, in its obsession with the works of the dead that are passed on to the living, neglects the dead themselves. But from the prophetic viewpoint, history is not so much the record of a personality's or a civilization's achievements as it is the ethical critique of whether a people have been responsible to their own and other peoples. The failure of a people to become responsible inevitably results in the victimization of human beings, an event to which the pathetic voice of the prophet, a voice that not only heralds the achievements of history but remembers their victims, is uniquely capable of responding.

THE SHAMEFULNESS OF VOCATIVE MEMORY

But Célan's resolve to give a prophetic *Gegenwort*, which would resist "the show-horses of history," is no easy matter and involves far more than a self-righteous moral outrage at the barbarity of any perpetrator, of victimization. Such an outrage can all too easily forget the real moral outrage, namely that some particular human has suffered at the hands of such perpetrators, and in this suffering has lost the capability of speaking for him- or herself. The more extreme this suffering, the more extreme is the muffling of the voice of the victim, and the more difficult it is for those who lie outside the scope of the other's suffering to attend to its meaning. But it is precisely the meaning of the victim's suffering that the Célanian *Gegenwort* would bring into memory. Thus one is called upon to confront history in a gesture of resistance that addresses those who have been victimized.

For example, in the poem *Radix Matrix*,[6] Célan summons the dead of the Holocaust through his act of writing. He addresses, even questions these dead:

> Who
> Who was it, that
> lineage, the murdered, that looms
> black into the sky:
> rod and bulb—?

Here the familiar and the familial is evoked against the background of the helplessly murdered, those dispossessed of their history. The poet, within the vocative mood, calls out to the corpses, to the dead. Their answer is no work of historiography, no heroic account of a civilization's achievements. Rather, the dead enter into the poem in the very disruption of the poem's address. Paradoxically their entrance into history, their becoming historical, is marked, as a gravestone marks a tomb, in the silence, the withdrawal of their once-having-been. Their hollow of absence plays through the body of the poet. His hand becomes the hand of the dead writing out their own reticence in the wake of the living's questioning.

> Yes
> as one speaks to stone, as
> you
> with my hands grope into there,
> and into nothing, such
> is what is here:

The poem enacts the haunting of the living by the dead. The poet's hand is opened to the hands of the dead—they too grope into the poem, into this "nothing" that serves as a memorial to the loss of an earlier generation. In Célan's poems history moves from the descriptive to the vocative mode, a move which would have memory speak toward the dead rather than about them. Indeed, for Célan, historical memory is vocative—it calls out to those who lie beyond one's own voice and one's own time and place in such a manner that one continually seeks to respond to the uniqueness of these other sufferings and deaths.

But to address and be addressed by the persecuted, the murdered, the annihilated is to expose oneself to the way in which their suffering was a violation, a degradation of their own human integrity. Thus the memory of historical suffering becomes the memory of a loss of voice, of face, of self. To turn in memory toward this loss is profoundly disturbing to the living, since it requires that they encounter the other at precisely that moment when he or she was utterly exposed to the violence of those who would use her or him as nothing more than a means to an end. This nakedness of the victim to historical violence is in itself shameful and constitutes one of the most disturbing aspects of victimization.

In its address of the victimized, the Célanian voice discovers its utter incapability of reversing the course of a time already past, of undoing an unjust harm already suffered by another person. The loss to which the victim is submitted is discovered to exceed any possible restitution that might be given for it. Thus the shame of the victim is contagious and infects the memory of any survivor who would respond to the victim as victim. Those who would remember the other vocatively come to inherit the finality of the other's suffering, its irremediableness in time.[7] In such an inheritance, the cathartic moment of Aristotelian poetics is interminably delayed, since the shame of the other's historical victimization is impossible to appropriate as if it were one's own. Precisely the fact that one did not share the "fate" of victimization but instead flourishes in its aftermath becomes its own shame, which signals the impossibility of one's cleansing oneself from a history permeated with crimes against the weak. Indeed, the refusal of catharsis becomes another sort of climactic moment for Célan's poems in which the annihilated of the Shoah awaken both the poet and the reader to an ethical humility before the voice of loss as well as an outrage at the loss of voice.

CÉLAN'S *GEGENWORT*: AN EXAMPLE

Although Célan himself never speaks directly of the pathos of shame in his theoretical writings, other have made much of it. Adorno, for example, argues that Célan's poems are "permeated by a sense of shame stemming from the fact that art is unable either to experience or to sublimate suffering."[8] It is my contention that this affective tonality of shame characterizes Célan's prophetic response to historical loss, particularly in his volume of poems entitled *Die Niemandrose*. For example, in the poem *Hinausgekrönt* (Crowned Out),[9] the shamefulness of the other's suffering infects the voice of the poet as he addresses those who have disappeared in the death camps.

These victims are initially referred to as those who have been "crowned out,/spewed out into night," an elliptical allusion to the smoke of their burning corpses as it rises at night toward the stars overhead. This style of elliptical and condensed reference permeates the poem's language and leads to a fragmented series of images and allusions whose meanings resist a consistent interpretation, precisely because the disorientation that the poem embodies is not merely feigned but real. The disorientation occurs as the voice's attempt to address reverently the dead of the Shoah is inevitably contaminated with the shamefulness of their victimization. Thus the poet speaks of plaiting and unplaiting and plaiting yet again the strands of "Berenice's head of hair," an image that juxtaposes the intimate and tactile gestures of a lover to his beloved with that shameful ascent toward the constellation *Comus Berenice* of the beloved's cremated body in columns of smoke that wreathe and unwreathe. Troubling the juxtaposition of these two allusions is yet another image, that of the hair shorn from each Jewish woman before she was gassed and cremated. To remember the dead, so goes the subliminal association made in the poem, is to submit to fingering this hair, to plaiting and unplaiting it, even as the person to whom it belonged is annihilated. In such a gesture of submission, the poet acknowledges the shamefulness of the other's victimization, a suffering that he cannot prevent, even as he remains faithful to its memory.

This repeated action of doing and undoing and doing yet again characterizes a disturbed memory, one that refuses catharsis, one that is distrustful of its own efforts even as it embraces a responsibility to continue its encounter with what cannot in principle be resolved. In taking up the impossible task of remembering those who have disappeared in the Shoah, Célan's lyric voice inevitably adopts a tone of lament that refuses consolation, precisely because whatever might be offered as consolation has proven ineffective in undoing the monstrosity of what has occurred. In this refusal of consolation, the Célanian voice exceeds the outrage of that prophetic voice that would emphasize the shame of history in order to justify the righteousness of a G-d transcending history. In counter-distinction to such a viewpoint, Célan's voice finds G-d is as much implicated in the shamefulness of history as any of G-d's creatures. Thus, *Hinausgekrönt* deflates the grandeur of G-d by willfully juxtaposing a Cabalistic image for G-d ("Blue Chasm") with a whore upon whom the poet's remembrance of the victims of the Shoah would then sexually advance with both "curses and prayer." Such a gesture of taking G-d for one's harlot inverts the more traditional gesture of shame that a righteous G-d expresses concerning humans when he commands Hosea to "take to yourself a wife of Harlotry, for the land commits great harlotry by forsaking the Lord" (*Hosea*, 1: 2).

For Célan, the violence of the Shoah so threatens all expectations that history might become just, that humans might be treated with compassion, that the poet is left with no other alternative than to let the disturbance of such a threat itself become the meaning of the victim's suffering. In this manner, the poem indicates that prayer has become shameful, but that shame itself remains a sort of prayer that continues to indicate the failure of history to renounce a violence that annihilates its victims. In such an allegiance to the shame of the victim's suffering is the *Gegenwort* that would resist the "show-horses" of history, precisely those who would forget such shame in the heralding of their victories. The lips singing such a *Gegenwort*, as suggested in the penultimate verse of *Hinausgekrönt*, would be "reedy," thin with starvation, and would direct their voice into "tundra-ears," the ears of a history bent upon the repression of the *Gegenwort*.

The allegiance of the poetic voice to the shameful memory of the other's victimization is an absurd gesture, one lacking entirely in the power to erect a civilization, to give orders that will be followed, to dictate the meaning of its accomplishments. Yet this poetic voice opens up a responsibility to an other whose difference from oneself utterly transcends the glory of such achievements. In this transcendence is given the possibility of a judgment of history in which those who inherit its violence resist succumbing to its logic, i.e., to a logic in which might makes right, in which only the survivors of history have a voice in its writing. Thus, the final lines of *HINAUSGEKRÖNT* state

> And an earth rises up, ours,
> this one.
> And we'll send
> none of our people down
> to you,
> Babel.

Here the dead are given a voice, one held in solidarity with the poet's and one that refuses succumbing to a history of victimization.

Yet such a gesture of resistance is permeated with irony; the new earth referred to here is "this one," i.e., precisely the gesture of the poem itself. Such a gesture is not the establishment of a heavenly city beyond the boundaries of time, as if eternity was another place beyond history. Such an alternative has already been rejected by the poem's earlier accusation that the majesty of G-d was vulnerable to the shame of history. For Célan, the turn to the Divine makes the suffering of history even more problematic, even more shameful, since G-d's transcendence is no longer defined in terms of an omnipotent manipulation of history from outside of its boundaries but in terms of an ethical command articulated from within historical life to human beings that they care for one another. Such a command is helpless before the Other, who may or may not choose to submit to it. Thus, the danger of history's succumbing to the forces that drive victimization is real. The logic of victimization that strives to become the final law of history must be resisted here and now. There is no guarantee that eternity will undo the shame of history. As Célan has stated, one must raise "the claim of infinity" but "grasped through time, through time to the end (*durch sie hindurch*), not over it and away (*über sie hinweg*)."[10]

Thus, Marlies Janz can argue with reason that "the metaphor [of an earth rising up] expresses a wish but hardly a confidence."[11] In recognition of the vulnerability of this wish to historical violence, the dead who speak at the poem's end are best interpreted as not promising the consolation of a new earth but a never-ending judgment of the old one. Put in another manner, the new earth that rises up in this verse exists only in the "light" of what Célan would have termed "U-topia" (*M*, 199), i.e., in the impossible expectation of an absurd messianism by which one is commanded to act as if historical shame might be overcome. The thought of this messianic "Utopia" functions much like a Kantian ideal for Célan in that its concept has a moral force to command one's resistance of the other's victimization, even as the actuality of the concept remains in question. Further, the threat of the poem's last four lines to let the "you" of its address fall into Babel emphasizes the historical crisis figured in the Shoah, a crisis in which history itself, as well as the transcendence at work in it, threatens to succumb utterly to injustice. In such a world, history will be written as if its victims had never mattered.[12] Such a crisis awakens the poetic voice both to a shame that will not be stilled and a solidarity with those whose victimization remains beyond consolation.

THE RESISTANCE OF THE DEAD TO THEIR HISTORY

For Célan, the dead of the Shoah resist their history of victimization through the shame they inspire in the inheritors of their history as these inheritors consider the disquieting vulnerability of the dead to the aggression of their mass-murderers. This powerless resistance of the Shoah's victims to their violation is not unlike what Levinas would call an ethical resistance to violence, i.e., a resistance born not out of force resisting force but of the "uncoveredness and nakedness of defenseless eyes."[13] As indicated in the preceding discussion of Célan's poem *Hinausgekrönt*, to be addressed by the annihilated of the Shoah is to confront their irremediable violation, a violation that so disturbs one's confidence that a reason can be given for it that even a recourse to eternity cannot justify such suffering. Thus one is left only with one's pathos, the undergoing in one's sensibility of a disturbance in time that defies consolation or rectification. In this way, the shame provoked in the survivor by the fragility of history's victims elicits a prophetic response on the part of those who inherit that history. In one's shame one now encounters the dead in such a manner that the very enterprise of adopting "their" history for one's own, as if their suffering can become one's own enrichment, is revealed to be abhorrent and ethically questionable. Thus Célan's lyrical address of the dead initiates a prophetic history that resists confusing one's own appropriation of the dead with the dead themselves.

In Levinas's account of historiography, on the other hand, history is characterized as the arena in which exactly such confusion can take place, in which one's appropriation of the dead becomes the identity of the dead. As discussed earlier, Levinas argues that one can only enter historiographical history as one's works are appropriated by one's survivors. This appropriation makes alien to oneself what originally was one's own. Thus in order to enter history one must lose one's own will, one's forceful resistance to violation. Historiography remains blind to the ethical resistance that emerges in the collapse of one's force, one's living. In its remembering of the dead, historiography speaks about the works of the dead and how they are appropriated by those wills inheriting the memory of the dead. The notion that one might be claimed by a vocative address that emanates from the dead is absurd for historiography—the dead, offering no active or willful resistance to their violation, can make no claim for themselves. Thus one's memory of the dead can be meaningful for the dead's inheritors only insofar as their memory of the dead finds itself within the life-projects of those who survive, those who remain caught up in their own life, their own will. For this reason, historiography is charged with the duty to dispose of the dead as a series of themes by which the living might find some information, some profit.

Levinas argues that by treating the dead as equivalent to their works, historiographical history (especially in its Hegelian and Spinozistic modes) reduces the "ipseity," the particularity, of each human will to a role in working out an abstract scheme of achievements elaborated by reason. The mood of reason, its pathos, can be characterized as an overcoming or sublating of alterity, of what is resistent to appropriation. Reason, in its desire to gather difference into similarity, justifies history in terms of its totality, of its final outcome where the various individuals comprising history find their ultimate role in the universal scheme elaborated by reason. In such an account of history, "the will of each . . . from the start consists in willing the universal or the rational, that is, in negating its very particularity."[14] In this manner the particularity of the individual who suffers history is absorbed into a political society thought merely as a system of achievements. Such a system remains blind to the outrage, as well as the shame, of the particularity of human victimization.

But the issue of the particularity of historical beings, i.e., of those beings who live and die within history, even as they escape the ability of history to absorb their particularity, can be raised only in pathetic writing that insists on distinguishing the dead from their history, their works. For such writing, the will of the individual is not subsumed in the universality of reason but functions as a surplus, a disruption, that resists the attempt of reason to justify historical suffering through the achievements of political institutions that protect human life in general. In this vein, the writings of Paul Célan provide a lyric, as well as prophetic, alternative to historiography, in which the particularity of the dead, their resistance to an acquisitive appropriation by the living, might be confronted in the pathos of shame. By evoking the shame of the Shoah's dead, Célan's poetry resists the tendency of the living to forget these dead by resisting the tendency of the living to speak about the dead, as if the dead were permanently residing in the third person where they have become an anonymous resource, the welling up of possibilities yet to be realized for those who now live.

Part Five

Sexuality/Gender/Politics

When Bruno Bosteels refers to the "text appeal" of the map, he brings into high relief a vital and provocative aspect of the postmodern and of the evolution of the cartographic metaphor. In linking the world to its ideological frame, the map seems to "embody" both the real and imaginary, in Lacanian terms; the map-sign, as material and cognitive, is a vital oxymoron. The text appeal of the map, and the politics of the body, lead us to the next section of the volume.

Virtually no issue of our day has been more heatedly discussed than sexuality and gender. For the past generation, discoveries of the natural and unnatural roles of men and women have resulted in a tumultuously evolving theoretics of sex, sexuality, and gender that has made it impossible to avoid the connection of the third term, "politics," to the first two. In this section, the politics of sexuality and gender have to do both with the more general meaning of politics, as social discourse in and through history and, to cite the passage from Terry Eagleton with which Barbara Claire Freeman begins her essay, "the way we organize our social life together," and the more specific one of hegemonic codes and their (repressive) social power.

Sexuality as a biological phenomenon has been at the root of the political since the beginning of culture itself, though only recently has this politicization of sexuality become a theme for scrutiny. Indeed, the shift from the stasis of the (generally patriarchal) premodern to the iconoclastic but still conservative modern to the more radical interrogations of the postmodern has resulted in a centralizing of the themes of sexuality and gender that has, in the last two or three decades, taken both men and women by surprise. New or revised social theory cannot avoid central discussion of this theme.

Sexuality as a biological construct is itself increasingly under interrogation, with recent genetic discoveries indicating a possible "third sex" (and possibly both a third and a fourth) accounting for the propensity on the part of many to homosexuality. These discoveries have themselves been the subject of debate within the realm of sexual and gender politics, regarding the implications of this biological "justification" of homosexuality as either empowering or marginalizing.

Such discussions blur the distinction between sexuality and gender, the former being a "neutral" biological fact, the latter a political construct embedded in the surrounding culture. When one considers the fate of Sappho, or the idea of Greek men viewing the tragic Dionysia, one realizes the historical pedigree of gender as an issue. This is not just true of Western thought and society, of course, but a virtually global phenomenon.

The three essays in this section address the nature of change with regard to sexuality and gender in particularly provocative ways. All three essays deal with the power and opportunity of seeing, speaking, and the masculine and feminine body; all three concern themselves with differing notions of *jouissance* and its incorporation and manifestation in the physical and social body.

Barbara Freeman begins with a fundamental question: what is the value of Lacan's *jouissance* for contemporary sexual and textual politics? This is a vital question, since "what one can know of *jouissance* is the very basis for ascertaining sexual difference." But this knowing, Freeman asserts, is a conceptual, masculine knowing that, as articulable, is not *jouissance*. According to Freeman, Lacan's *jouissance* is both erotic and semiotic, a surplus and a remainder, a "relationship to the Other beyond the range of the symbolic order." The feminine emerges as that which is unsaid by the patriarchal order; *jouissance* "articulates and instills a desire humanism everywhere fears and tries to exclude." Freeman explores the relational existence of woman and of existing women, showing that Lacan is very clear about what woman is for man, but not about what women are—or might be—for themselves. Feminine *jouissance*, insofar as it is articulated, becomes phallic to the extent to which it can be represented/representative.

Freeman goes on to explore St. Teresa's vision/*jouissance* and the symbolic order into which she fits, claiming that Teresa is the knowing and desiring *subject*, not the object of the male gaze, and that her writing, which anticipates Cixous's admonitions in "The Laugh of the Medusa," differs radically from Lacan's account of her, creating a fusion that erases distinctions between body and word: "here God or the Other is neither Being nor non-being but the simulacrum of an identity that displaces and resists itself." Otherness does not alienate but symbolizes, without "center." This subtle and important point will be amplified by Hwa Yol Jung's exploration of the carnival body and the relation of the feminine body to the other/Other. Freeman is particularly concerned with the vital political power, particularly in and after Lacan, associated with articulation, with the power to speak, write, and be heard/read, and the construction of gender.

Sylvia Söderlind critiques the politics of the author and critic, exploring the premodern, modern, and postmodern treatments of the theme of the Quixote as manifested from Cervantes to Borges and Kathy Acker, showing how the evolution of this figure, as written, marks the assertion, erasure, and reappearance of the author in literary, sexual, and political history. Söderlind begins with the provocative point that the authorship question in the Quixote, in terms of the author's erasure, is "not so much a cessation of his existence as a sign of ubiquity." Concentrating initially on Borges/Menard's reading of Cervantes, Söderlind shows how Borges's apocryphal critic and narrator becomes the quixotic knight, battling on the field of "literary pseudocriticism to win the favors of women"—that, indeed, Borges's narrator re-inscribes Quixote's tale into the discourse of chivalry for a new age, usurping the authority of Cervantes along the way. Then, having establishes this new pseudo-grounding in Menard, Söderlind turns her attention to Kathy Acker's *Don Quixote*, which rejects the "truth" to which history, and particularly literary history, continuously gives life. Acker, according to Söderlind, marks a new beginning for historical contextualization. Whereas for Menard plagiarism constituted a modernist triumph greater than the writing of the "original" *Quixote*, for Acker this plagiarism ("the cutting chunks out of already existing texts") is metaphorized as abortion: "impregnation by and consequent expulsion of the canonical (or mare accurately, seminal) texts of the male tradition." Just as a refusal to be a mother is a refusal to participate in history, so is a radical subversion of the canonical text. For Acker, to deny patriarchal authority is to refuse reproduction: "abortion is the only means of resistance." But abortion/nonparticipation is also therefore ritual suicide: for Acker female writers' choices are plagiarism and death.

Söderlind reveals Acker's strategy, in the transmutation of the Quixote from romance into the pornography of exploitation, as being intentionally transgressive "literary criminality." Rewriting the chivalric code and quest into pornography demonstrates, according to Söderlind, the equivalence of the imaginary and the feminine, a writing and reading from the body. Pornography is an effect, Söderlind claims, not a cause, of linguistic transformation; it is "postmodern romance."

Thus, for the postmodern, the real quest is the "joust" between writer/artist and reader/critic. Only when the critic acknowledges the artist's mastery can *jouissance* occur; only in "truly mutual consent" can the death of the author be avoided. Thus the essay becomes a kind of dance of death of the ostmodern reinvention of the author, charting the change from postmodern invisibility to a new power and structure for writing and reading.

Hwa Yol Jung extends this powerful revision of the writerly into the realm of social discourse, rooted in the corporeal and the feminine-as-other. Jung investigates "the possibility of carnal hermeneutics [Bakhtin's term], weaving Bakhtin's dialogical thought with the phenomenology of the Cartesian lived body, showing how Descartes as the canonizer of "modernity" must be overcome—the cogito transgressed, the "I-viewpoint" undermined in order to free the societal discourse of the body. Jung argues for a gestural dialectics of sound, language, and silence, showing how the development from the bodily meanings of ideograms gives way to the carnal hermeneutics of Vico, then to Heidegger's "embodied thinking," and finally to the carnal genealogy of Bakhtin, for whom consciousness itself—the "essentially human"—is a result of "material embodiment" of signs: because we exist, bodily, we are social. This social and physical base of existence means, for Bakhtin, that language, the tool of social discourse, is "overpopulated with the intentions of others."

Jung goes on to explore the development of this Bakhtinian dialectical ecology, citing Levinas's "heteronomic" subjectivity and Shoshona Felman's distinction between informative and performative dialogue, and then takes the step from the carnal and the social to the carnivalesque. Carnival hermeneutics, the nonviolent technique of social transformation, opens the possibility of the permissible destruction of social normatives, which in social discourse must be ongoing. The play of the carnivalesque leads to the valorization of the feminine, since ocularcentrism (masculine) is subverted by carnal discourse. In feminine discourse the body anchors the self in the world. "Gynesis," metamorphosed into tactility, fleshes out masculine ocularcentrism. For Jung, gynesis and the carnal hermeneutic by which it is revealed are part of the postmodern "Copernican revolution" of social thought Bakhtin's dialectics introduce. Society is, finally, a corporeal bond, Jung declares, and Bakhtin's dialectics preserve both the difference and the incommensurable. Through an acceptance of the Bakhtinian notion of the body as the core and host of all social discourse, we can come to understand the politics of gender and the role of sexuality in social development.

These three essays weave a tight pattern of concerns, through psychoanalysis and social theory to a sense of identity in social and aesthetic discourse. Their concerns are with the danger of solipsism and its antidote in the feminization of social forms, acknowledging that the "other" need not be alien, but can be, conceivably, seamlessly unified in a new politics.

14

A Union Forever Deferred: Sexual Politics After Lacan

Barbara Claire Freeman

What is the value, assuming there is any, of Lacan's theory of feminine *jouissance* for contemporary feminist sexual and textual politics? What are the politics of a Lacanian reading of femininity, and what way of re-reading Lacan does a certain political position, call it a post-humanist feminism, demand or perhaps make imperative? If, with Terry Eagleton, we define the political as "the way we organize our social life together and the power relations which this involves," do the kinds of power relations implied by a text such as *Encore* enable or disable contemporary feminist theories?[1] Inevitably, Lacan's discourse does both. And although there is always the possibility that I might "use it in order to signify something quite other than what it says," my purpose is to attempt to spell out how, and why.[2]

To be political is to make something sayable that the dominant symbolic order would prefer went unsaid, thus making it doable. A politically radical discourse might also be defined by what it allows to be symbolized, always from within the context of a specific discursive position. Aside from some important qualifications that I'll deal with later, I will argue that Lacan's distinctive contribution to feminist theory lies in his discussion of a uniquely feminine *jouissance,* for this notion impels us to say something patriarchy would prefer went unsaid, and makes sayable a desire both language and the law would disallow.[3] How, then, does Lacan's discussion of feminine sexuality empower a post-humanist feminism? More precisely, in what way is his theory of feminine *jouissance* useful, or even necessary, for feminist sexual and textual politics?

Encore, of course, is the seminar in which Lacan takes up the question of a specifically feminine *jouissance*—that moment in erotic (but I will argue perhaps also semiotic) experience that is always in excess, something over and above the phallus, which according to Lacan signifies sexual identity. There is a "*jouissance* of the body" that is "beyond the phallus," and because for Lacan *jouissance* is defined as in and of itself phallic, a *jouissance* that exceeds it is aligned with the feminine.[4] Although the woman inevitably participates in phallic sexuality, she may also partake of a sexual pleasure that is not complementary to, but supplemental of, the masculine position. It signals another order of experience (but not necessarily the ability to symbolize that experience), a "something more" (145) that stands in opposition to the solely phallic dimension. Feminine *jouissance* is a remainder, a surplus, a relationship to the Other that is beyond the range of a symbolic order that insists upon identity as the truth of being. "Radically Other" (153), it offers a site of resistance to, and the potential for a critique of, exclusively phallic notions of sexuality and sense.

For Lacan, then, feminine *jouissance* is a figure of dislocation and not of unification, a moment in which consciousness turns away from, but also towards, "itself." Lacan's decisive question is: what is involved on the side of the woman in this *jouissance* of the body, by those who are placed within the phallic function as not all? And it is precisely here that we might find something profoundly on the side of "the feminine," by which I mean what is unsaid by and always in excess of the patriarchal order. For feminine *jouissance* resists patriarchy precisely insofar as it articulates and instills a desire humanism everywhere fears and tries to exclude: for the destruction of precisely the kinds of distinctions—between self and other, male and female, possessor and possessed—upon which patriarchy and the economic arrangements that accompany it depend. What is thereby affirmed is not a subjectivity that strives for heightened individuality, unity, autonomy, or even increase of capital, but rather a surplus value—a "self," if we can call it that—that actively seeks its own consumption or consummation. In connecting it to the position of the woman (Lacan even defines the feminine relation to the phallus as that which is not totalizable, not itself, not faithful to any single identity or position, "not all"), Lacan appears to open up questions of how a specifically feminine eroticism might be written.

It is important to be precise about what Lacan means by the word *woman*, especially in light of his famous statement that "there is no such thing as *The* woman since of her essence . . . she is not all" (144). Because for Lacan the unconscious does not recognize any innate opposition between masculine and feminine, woman is neither a biological fact nor a predetermined gender. She is rather a linguistic category that denotes a specific position with respect to Being: there is something other than the Other (i.e., the unconscious), such that she is not wholly contained by it, more than only it. On the one hand, as Jacqueline Rose points out, "the feminine is constituted as a division in language, a division which produces the feminine as its negative term."[5] On the other, "there is no such thing *The* woman" because, as Ellie Ragland-Sullivan explains, she is a masculine fantasm, a category constructed by and for man, "a symptom of man's belief in a mythic, universal Woman (la femme) who will be the source of his pleasure and his truth."[6] Woman, then, is what man excludes in order to function as man. Or, as Lacan says: "there is woman only as excluded by the nature of things which is the nature of words. . . . (144). She is the signifier of the lack of the signifier, proof par excellence that something is radically missing.

Woman as "not all" is the factor that sets being beyond the limits of definition, and who thereby discloses that the all is itself "not all." She thus denotes the possibility of a specific kind of response to lack, and herein lies her political and potentially explosive force. For woman reveals that the law and the phallus that signifies it is itself not self-identical: she is the excluded term that both allows and reveals the limits of what is taken as the whole. The positioning of woman as nonessence, then, carries with it a certain questioning of the law's validity and entails, or would entail, a breakdown of the established patterns and distinctions that regulate social order. Thus what it means to speak from the position of the woman—if only existing women could speak—is both to articulate another definition of bing and to question the legitimacy of the metaphysical tradition itself. This position defines an apex of possibility. And to the extent that Lacan places such a desire on the side of the woman, he speaks in the name of the feminine and against patriarchal law.

The question of feminine *jouissance* thus makes space for the symbolization of a certain desire, one that not only discloses the law's fragility but is accompanied by a profound skepticism regarding its authority. For *woman* might also be defined by the fact that, occupying the position of "not all," she knows that the law does not exist, or at least not in the way man believes. For her the law might be best understood as an extremely effective self-parody, which in no way lessens its power to destroy. Paradoxically, we owe to Lacan, consummate theorist of the name of the father, the knowledge that there is no Father, only his name—and that the Father is always nameless.

As you might infer from the somewhat ironic turn my own discourse has taken, some major problems begin at just this point. And although my puzzlement regarding "God and the *Jouissance* of the Woman" and "A Love Letter" perhaps results from a crucial misunderstanding of Lacanian theory, I've tried to formulate a series of questions that I'd like to address in turn. In the following pages I will attempt to explore those aspects of Lacan's theory of sexual difference and feminine *jouissance* that are especially perplexing, and discuss some of the consequences for feminist theory and practice. Although it is not my intention to resolve these issues, I do hope to be clear about the questions to which they give rise, and thereby to stimulate further discussion and debate.

Let us begin with the vexed relation between "woman," a linguistic category that, since it does not participate in the universal, is designated as "not all," and existing women. What, if anything, has "the woman," who exists only as the locus of exclusion, to do with women? Although it is clear that woman, here understood as an object of exchange and desire, serves to insure the smooth functioning of the symbolic order and that her objectification aids and abets the construction of masculine subjectivity and sexuality, Lacan never asks how women relate to this construct, that is, how they relate to each other and to themselves. Lacan, in other words, is extremely lucid about what woman is for man, but not about what women are, or might be, for themselves: his sole definition of *women*, as opposed to *woman*, is "those beings who take on the status of the woman" (151). Is "woman" to be understood as the category that is excluded by the nature of words, whereas "women" are the beings positioned by that exclusion? If I am correct, it follows that, just as woman exists only as an excluded category within language, so existing women are consigned to silence. Even more allusively, Lacan remarks that "when any speaking being whatever lines up under the banner of women it is by being constituted as not all that they are placed within the phallic function" (144). Women, then, are those speaking beings who are positioned within the symbolic order as excluded from it, and who become desirable to men as a consequence of signifying that lack. But this definition does not help us understand what women signify for themselves. And the only clue Lacan offers is as much a definition of the Other as it is of women: "The Other might, somewhere, be that to which one half—since that is roughly the biological proportion—one half of speaking beings relate" (152).[7] Although, as a consequence of her exclusion, women have a privileged relation to the Other (which Lacan usually aligns with language, or, as in *Encore*, with God), this relation has significant limitations, for what women can know or say about it is radically problematic.

We have already noted that woman "has in relation to what the phallic function designates of jouissance a supplementary *jouissance*" (144), but Lacan's sole attempt to describe women's relation to it is particularly mystifying: women, he says, "hold to (*s'en tiennent*) the *jouissance* in question-none of them hold to being not all" (144).[8] Perhaps we can gloss this perplexing sentence as follows: since it is impossible for women, who are positioned as not all, to relate to what they are not (i.e., not all cannot relate to itself, since that very self is a form of non-being), *jouissance* substitutes for that to which they cannot relate, offering something they can "hold to." But it is important to ask what seems to me this crucial question: why should feminine *jouissance* not be understood precisely as the mark of a rupture in being, as that instant in which women affirm a relationship to what exceeds it? In such a reading (or rewriting) feminine *jouissance* would be understood as a radical contestation of traditional notions of Being, and its experience would put into question the truth of truth itself.

The answer lies in Lacan's theorization of the relation of woman (or women, since he makes so little distinction between them) to knowledge and language, and in his insistence that *jouissance* is exclusively corporeal, "of the body." In this regard it is particularly surprising that although he begins his influential essay "The Mirror Stage" (1949) by asserting that its experience "leads us to oppose any philosophy directly issuing form the *Cogito*" (*Écrits*, 1), in *Encore* he assumes Descartes's precept that the mind, here synonymous with language, and the body should be understood as two separate realms. For Lacan not only insists that feminine *jouissance* is "of the body," but also that "there is a *jouissance* proper to her, this 'her' which does not exist and which signifies nothing. There is a jouissance proper to her and of which she herself may know nothing, except that she experiences it-that much she does know" (145).

Especially crucial are the politics of Lacanian epistemology and with what he intends by the word *knowledge* (*connaissance*). For as he so astutely remarks in "A Love Letter," the question raised by feminine *jouissance* is precisely "to know where her knowledge (of it) is at" (158). It is, however, as if Lacan defines feminine *jouissance* as in principle unknowable, for those who experience this *jouissance* beyond the phallus are precisely those who cannot speak of it: "there is something, *jouissance,* which makes it impossible to tell whether the woman can say anything about it—whether she can say what she knows of it" (159). Indeed the question of what the subject knows or doesn't know of *jouissance* is the very basis for ascertaining sexual difference, for Lacan observes that women "don't know what they are saying, which is all the difference between them and me" (144). And furthermore, he believes "in the *jouissance* of the woman in so far as it is something more only on the condition that you screen off that *something more* until I have properly explained it" (147). Although something on the side of the feminine escapes from and exceeds the phallic function, only Lacan is in a position to explain it. But what he never explains is why he is uniquely qualified to know and articulate what women can't.

You can appreciate the double bind. Insofar as I occupy the position of the woman I can have feminine *jouissance* but can't know it, while

Lacan, occupying the position of the man, can say it but not have it: he can explain what I experience, but can't experience what he explains, and I can experience what I experience only because I can't explain it. And if I do manage to articulate *jouissance,* if I am able to position myself in relation to it such that I have knowledge of it or that it becomes an object of my knowledge, Lacan would say that what I've symbolized is no longer specifically feminine: is it the case that according to his definition, if I say it I'm a man and the *jouissance* is phallic; if I have it I'm a woman and can't say it? Should we conclude, then, that Lacan makes space for a potentially subversive eroticism only on the condition that those who "know" it can't represent it? If so, he does more than take with one hand what he gives with the other; he undercuts any possibility for a feminist sexual politics.

I would like briefly to return to my bewilderment regarding what Lacan means by *knowledge.* On the one hand, Lacan's early work, especially as exemplified by the 1957 essay "Agency of the Letter in the Unconscious," denies the possibility of any meta-language whatsoever and in so doing undercuts a definition of knowledge as synonymous with formalization, for Lacan says,"... there is no language in existence for which there is any question of its inability to cover the whole field of the signified" (*Écrits,* 150). On the other hand, the epistemological underpinnings of *Encore,* written almost twenty years later, seem to depend upon the belief in a certain meta-language, namely that of symbolic language, that privileges precisely the kind of universality the earlier Lacan appears to deny. If by the time of *Encore knowledge* has become synonymous with formal abstraction—the translation through symbolic logic of the particular into the universal—then I suspect that his definition of it has come dangerously close to the grandiose "discourse of mastery" he elsewhere critiques.[9] In other words, I do not understand the kind of "knowledge" that is in question when Lacan claims that there is a *jouissance* that women have, but "know" nothing about.

In this regard it is especially important to ask on what he bases his claim that women don't, or can't, symbolize feminine *jouissance.* Although Lacan never explains exactly why feminine *jouissance* is unknowable, I believe his answer would have to be twofold. First, given his definition of language and woman's relation to it, feminine *jouissance* is marked as feminine insofar as its experience bars any avenue to articulation. From within Lacan's theoretical framework, then, feminine jouissance is phallic (and therefore not feminine) precisely to the extent that it can be represented. Lacan's other answer is the result of long analytic experience. He's asked, he says, but women simply won't talk about it: "What gives some likelihood to what I'm arguing, that is, that the woman knows nothing of this *jouissance,* is that ever since we've been begging them—

last time I mentioned women analysts—begging them on our knees to try to tell us about it, well, not a word! We have never managed to get anything out of them" (p. 146). It is difficult to know how to read this statement. Is Lacan being provocative, waving a rhetorical red flag in the face of the women he's just insulted? If this is his strategy for getting women to talk, no wonder he's never gotten "anything out of them." Or does Lacan mean exactly what he says and simply expect us to take his word for it? In either event, he fails to question his own assumptions regarding access to language and the symbolic order. If one of the consequences of being in a marginal position with respect to the dominant order is that one is rendered silent by it, perhaps it is not merely "something in the nature of words" (or of feminine *jouissance)* that stands in the way of women's ability to symbolize a specifically feminine sexual pleasure, but patriarchal structures of oppression—to which this aspect of Lacan's thought contributes.

It is important to interpret Lacan's alleged desire to hear what women have to say of *jouissance* in the context of his treatment of Bernini's statue of St. Teresa, which he takes as irrefutable evidence that women don't "know what they experience." He says: "you only have to go and look at Bernini's statue in Rome to understand immediately that she's coming, there is no question about it. And what is her *jouissance*, her coming, from? It is clear that the essential testimony of the mystics is that they are experiencing it but know nothing about it" (p. 147). Lacan's exclusive reliance on a statue makes it difficult to take seriously the claim that he's begged women (on his knees!) to tell him "about it," but has not heard a word. For if Lacan is indeed so interested, why does he not read *St. Teresa*'s *Autobiography* (probably because he hasn't read it, Lacan doesn't notice that Bernini has changed the spelling of her name) since it would provide a perfect example of the "essential testimony" to which he presumably refers. Why does a theorist who gives such enormous privilege to language and the symbolic order rely upon the realm of the visual as evidence that woman experiences a *jouissance* she knows nothing about?[10] Can we attribute his failure to read to anything but a certain blindness, here understood as a symptom of the wish not to listen to what he does not want to hear? For St. Teresa provides an extraordinarily acute account of her experience of the relation between the all and the not all, between God and the woman, and had Lacan but read it, it might have undermined his view that woman has a *jouissance* about which she cannot speak. Here is how St. Teresa describes what Bernini represents:

> It pleased the Lord that I should sometimes see the following vision. I would see beside me, on my left hand, an angel in bodily form—a type of vision

> which I am not in the habit of seeing, except very rarely. . . . He was not tall, but short, and very beautiful, his face so aflame that he appeared to be one of the highest types of angel who seem to be all afire. . . . In his hands I saw a long golden spear and at the end of the iron tip I seemed to see a point of fire. With this he seemed to pierce my heart several times so that it penetrated to my entrails. When he drew it out, I thought he was drawing them out with it and he left me completely afire with a great love for God. The pain was so sharp that it made me utter several moans; and so excessive was the sweetness caused me by this intense pain that one can never wish to lose it, nor will one's soul be content with anything less than God. It is not bodily pain, but spiritual, though the body has a share in it—indeed a great share. So sweet are the colloquies of love which pass between the soul and God that if anyone thinks I am lying I beseech God, in His goodness, to give him the same experience.[11]

It is important to point out at least some of the ways that St. Teresa's symbolization of feminine *jouissance* contradicts Lacan's assumptions regarding it. For if, as he so astutely reminds us, "the mystic all is by no means that which is not political" (146), a careful reading of this passage may help to highlight what for feminists is useful in the attempt to theorize feminine *jouissance,* even while continuing to reveal Lacan's blindness with respect to the subject of woman.

First and foremost, St. Teresa's text resists the kinds of binarisms Lacan's work, however nuanced and subtle, takes for granted. Contrary to what Lacan assumes from looking at Bernini's statue, St. Teresa is not a passive object, merely acted upon by a phallic, penetrating other whom she experiences but knows nothing about. She is, on the contrary, the agent of her own desire. As a subject who sees the vision, she is not merely seen by it; at the same time, she experiences a relation of ecstatic surrender to that which she also envisions. Her text thus places woman in the position of knowing and desiring subject, rather than, as Lacan would have it, only as object of the male gaze. Second, her text pluralizes the oppositional modes of thought upon which Lacan relies. Just as the activity of envisioning is represented as simultaneously active and passive, so her text evidences a merger of erotic and semiotic domains that does not erase their difference. In the same way that St. Teresa conflates traditional categories of pain and pleasure ("so excessive was the sweetness caused me by this intense pain that one can never wish to lose it"), so her text reveals the speciousness of Lacan's insistence on a static opposition between visceral and linguistic registers. What St. Teresa instead describes is the experience of their inseparability and indissolubility and, as the following phrase illustrates, what she underscores is the impossibility of ascertaining where one begins and the other ends: "It is not bodily pain, but spiritual, though the body has a share in it—

indeed a great share." Nor does feminine *jouissance* lead to silence, as Lacan would have it, but rather impels linguistic expression, as if part of St. Teresa's experience includes the demand that it be written. Such a reformulation has significant implications for feminist practice: it demonstrates that part of what defines the otherness of feminine *jouissance* is that it inserts into language and the symbolic order an excess that resists the binary thinking Lacanian theory, like that of metaphysics, needs in order to perpetuate itself.

It is important, finally, to notice how radically St. Teresa's account of her relation to the Other differs from Lacan's formulation. Whereas Lacan insists that "the woman relates to the signifier of this Other, in so far as, being Other, it can only remain always Other" (151), in St. Teresa's text the Other is not only alterior, but also that to which she is intimately bound. St. Teresa does not desire her own disappearance through possession by an absolute Other, but an ecstatic fusion of self and other in which differences dissolve but neither disappear. Such an experience of the unnamable should not be understood as the search for union with an ineffable being that no name can approximate, but as the affirmation of the activity of naming and of a moment that erases distinctions between body and word, or naming and loving, while continuing to mark their place. Here God or the Other is neither being nor non-being, but the simulacrum of an identity that displaces and resists itself. The Other's alterity, then, does not stand outside of language, truth, or being, but is rather that by virtue of which its symbolization occurs. Its experience provides no center and has no site, although the moment of self-obliteration and reproduction belongs to its structure. Such are the "colloquies of love which pass between the soul and God." And that it may never be wholly known or said does not mean that nothing of it can be.

Who has the authority to say whether or not St. Teresa knows what she is talking about, or has found words adequate to convey something of what she has experienced? It seems to me, at any rate, not only that she is able to use language so that it is equal to zero and in doing so becomes equivalent to nothing at all, but that she articulates this relation in a way that does not simply return it, and us, to silence. On the one hand, her text reminds us of what Lacan says, or ought to say: that truth has no value apart from the representation of excess. But if I began by inquiring into the politics of Lacan's understanding of *jouissance,* I must conclude by questioning the paradox by virtue of which he makes a space for feminine desire only on the condition that it remain unsaid and, at least for him, unread.

15

Love and Reproduction: Plagiarism, Pornography, and Don Quixote's Abortions

Sylvia Söderlind

In an imaginary course on "Masterpieces of Western Literature" that I sometimes dream of teaching, the final exam might include the following multiple choice question:

> Who is the author of *Don Quixote*?
>
> Answer: a. Miguel de Cervantes
> b. Cid Hamete Benengeli
> c. Pierre Menard
> d. Kathy Acker

This is, of course, a trick question, but one it would be almost impossible to fail answering more or less correctly. It seems that Cervantes did indeed write *Don Quixote* in seventeenth-century Spain, though he himself claims to have bought the manuscript from the Arab Cid Hamete Benengeli. Yet according to Jorge Luis Borges, or rather his narrator-critic in "Pierre Menard, Author of the Quixote," Menard's twentieth-century fragmentary *Quixote* is infinitely richer than its predecessor. And what are we to think when a novel entitled *Don Quixote* appears in 1986, written by an American self-proclaimed punk writer named Kathy Acker?

The question of the authorship of *Don Quixote* provides a good illustration of the postmodern problematizing of questions of originality, literary property and propriety, truth claims, and the like. And it is indeed appropriate that this, probably the most sacred, text in the postmodern revisioning of the Western canon, has proved that the much-touted death of the author is not so much a cessation of his existence as a sign of his ubiquity. (In the following it will, I hope, become clear why I deliberately use the male pronoun here.)

THE MASTER IN PIECES

Even those who have not read Borges's famous piece of metacriticism are probably familiar with the story of Pierre Menard, who accomplishes the feat of recreating word for word small pieces of *Don Quixote*. Borges's fictional critic—who is the self-appointed literary executor of the equally fictional French author—states that this heroic enterprise is inspired by

> Two texts of unequal value. . . . One is that philological fragment by Novalis . . . which outlines the theme of a *total* identification with a given author. The other is one of those parasitic books which situate Christ on a boulevard, Hamlet on La Cannebière, or Don Quixote on Wall Street. (39)

While the first, romantic, approach—the identification with the author—may seem to be the one pursued by Menard, the second is the method of Kathy Acker, who places her female Quixote not on Wall Street but in a truly postmodern "zone" which is at the same time the underbelly of any big city and nowhere at all. Menard's own project is, in fact, at least according to his commentator, a little more complex than either of the two; he re-creates Quixote without ceasing to be Pierre Menard; that is, while remaining distant from the original author, yet without copying. Not being Cervantes, he is, of course, infinitely more restricted, since his "mysterious duty" (41) is to reject any versions he might come up with but the correct one. He thus has to be both Pierre Menard and Cervantes, operating a "total identification" with both self and other.

Menard's critic's essay begins with an inventory of the "visible" work left behind by Menard, which shows it to consist almost exclusively of parasitic texts: translations, transpositions, commentaries on other texts, and the like. It also contains one technical article suggesting improvements on the game of chess, which the author "proposes, recommends, discusses and finally rejects" (37). This seemingly innocuous work is the clearest case of "his resigned or ironical habit of propagating ideas which were the strict reverse of those he preferred" (42), a passing comment that illustrates a strategic affinity between Menard and Borges himself; the latter seems indeed to do just that in this parable. As the critic's praise of Menard becomes increasingly sycophantic, Borges's own impatience with his pretentious protagonist seems to grow. Although the unnamed critic may be right in announcing the prophetic nature of Menard's invention of the technique of "the deliberate anachrony and the erroneous attribution" (44), it is obvious that Borges himself deplores rather than champions such postmodern practices. While he does indeed posit Menard as the prototypical postmodern writer, it is hardly a flattering portrait.

When, in a footnote, Borges's critic-narrator dismisses the rumored existence among Menard's work of a literal translation of Quevedo's literal translation of St. Francis of Sales's *Introduction à la vie dévote* on the grounds that it has left no visible traces in Menard's library, we are immediately alerted to one of the many ironies in the text. Not only have we been told that Menard's version of the Quixote is invisible, but that "not one worksheet remains to bear witness to his years of effort" (39). Menard's intention, and the meager fruits of his labor, are communicated to the critic in letters, we are told, though never shown. When the latter juxtaposes two pages from the two *Quixote*s, his privileging of Menard's version over that of Cervantes is entirely based on his knowledge of the author's identity and intention. This is what Cervantes wrote:

> Truth, whose mother is history, rival of time, depository of deeds, witness of the past, exemplar and adviser to the present, and the future's counselor.

And here is Menard:

> Truth, whose mother is history, rival of time, depository of deeds, witness of the past, exemplar and adviser to the present, and the future's counselor. (43)

There is no doubt that the latter is infinitely richer, says the critic, since Menard's conception of history as the mother of truth, as the origin of, rather than inquiry into, reality, is much more revolutionary than Cervantes's" mere rhetorical praise of history" (43). In an age burdened by the knowledge of the inevitable fictionality of history, the idea of history as the mother of truth points directly to the postmodern problematizing of truth claims. But the truth of the matter (if I dare be so bold) is that had we encountered Menard's text without the mediation of Borges's critic; that is, had Menard's proposed text ever become visible, we would have had no trouble identifying his practice as plagiarism, a criminal offense.

The apparent championing of "erroneous attribution" becomes in the end quite paradoxical: if in fact history (which is the mother of truth) proves Menard's version to be superior to Cervantes's, what would be more erroneous: to attribute the authorship of *Don Quixote* to Menard, or to Cervantes? This is, in fact, the rather complicated question I was asking in my fictitious exam. If one is erroneous, the other must be true. The privileging of originality seems indeed to slip in through the back door here. Borges certainly has his tongue firmly planted in his cheek when he has his critic end the essay with the question, "To attribute the *Imitatio Christi* to Louis Ferdinand Céline or to James Joyce, is this not a sufficient renovation of its tenuous spiritual indications?" (44). As Paul de Man reminds us in his reading of Yeats, a grammatical question should always be suspected of a literal intent. Borges's question can only be read rhetorically if we accept the sycophantic critic's evaluation of Menard's *Quixote*. Maybe we should try to tell the dancer from the dance, and our answer to the critic's question should be an emphatic "No" according to Borges, who would no doubt reject three of the four names in my exam question (including his own creation) not only as false but as illegitimate pretenders to the authorship of his favorite book. The question at the end of Borges's parable is a good example of irony. While the narrator/critic intends it as rhetorical, the author intends it as both literal and urgent.

The claim to superiority of the later version of the story of the Knight of the Woeful Countenance finds an ironic analogue in the superiority the critic claims for his catalogue of the work of Pierre Menard over an earlier, "fallacious" one by Madame Henri Bachelier (36), for whom he seems to harbor an unmitigated contempt (as evidenced, among other things, by his omission from the otherwise scrupulous list of Menardiana of "a few vague sonnets of circumstance" written for herself, of whose existence we are only told in parentheses [38]). The critic's claim to have written the definitive version of Menard also echoes the latter's "definition" of a certain Countess de Bagnoregio in a volume

> published annually by this lady to rectify the inevitable falsifications of journalists and to present 'to the world and to Italy' an authentic image of her person, so often exposed (by very reason of her beauty and her activities) to erroneous or hasty interpretations. (38)

The sycophantic flattery of the literary authority of the countess, as well as of a certain Baroness de Bacourt, whose "unforgettable *vendredis*" (36) acquainted him with Menard, seem to indicate that this critic's own motive for rewriting Menard has to do with his desire for recognition from a woman he loves. (One might venture a guess that the critic is right in rejecting the possibility that Menard could have written even a derivative "literal translation" of *Introduction à la vie dévote*, since the mediocre poet, whose only "original" works were sonnets written to various ladies of literary society, like the mediocre critic, has no understanding of true devotion, which, like Borges's unspoken but implicit veneration for Cervantes, demands a respect for the authority of the father and for the sacredness of the original).

The analogies between Menard and his executor multiply in the course of the narrative, and the latter seems to repeat Menard's (Platonic but adoring?) relationship with his benefactress, the Countess de Bagnoregio. Borges's text itself puts the original to multiple uses: first it usurps the authority of Cervantes through Menard's act of plagiarism, then, through the critic-narrator, it reinscribes the Quixotic text in the very discourse of chivalry criticized by Cervantes by turning the critical endeavor into a romantic quest. The critic becomes the knight, fighting imaginary battles on the arena of literary pseudocriticism to win the favors of women. The hypocrisy of the critic's endeavor is revealed when he quotes, in passing, Menard's admonition that censure and praise have nothing to do with literary criticism, censure (of Madame Henri Bachelier, together with her readers—"though these be few and Calvinist, if not Masonic and circumcised" [36]), and praise (of the Countess de Bagnoregio and the Baroness de Bacourt) being, of course, exactly what he himself is engaged in. In the final analysis, Don Quixote's false view of the world is reenacted in Borges's parable of literary criticism, while the author himself subtly plays the role of Cervantes, criticizing the folly of his protagonist. Unlike Pierre Menard and his critic, Borges deplores the devaluing of originality and reveals plagiarism—reproduction instead of production—as the recourse of the mediocre mind; one might say his is a defense of the father's role as sole progenitor and authority. Borges's own love for Cervantes is true filial devotion, which respects the authority of the original—indeed, by humbly following in Cervantes's own critical footsteps, Borges emphasizes his precursor's role as original and guide—while Menard's presumed labor of love and his preposterous claim to paternity are only made possible by an aesthetics that sacrifices literary propriety and true artistry to dilettantism and hypocrisy. The villains in Borges's text are the representatives of the hypocriticism practised by the countess and the baroness, those who cannot tell the difference between a masterpiece and a purloined piece of the master, and to whom love is a question of posturing. The true heroes are not the Menards of the world but the true fathers, like Cervantes (and, implicitly, Borges himself), the very same who in the next text I discuss become the "evil enchanters" whom we still, albeit sometimes reluctantly, must love.

PLAGIARISM AS LOVE AND HATE

Borges's parable is thus, finally, a commentary on the sacredness of originality and a defense of literary paternity—a rewriting of the Bloomian relationship between author and precursor in terms of true filial devotion. But what happens to this relationship when the inheritor of the canonical text is the one whom it has relegated to the status of object? What is the relationship between the (heterosexual) woman writer and her literary fathers?

There is little obvious veneration for the original in Kathy Acker's *Don Quixote*, which looks Menardian with its collage of plagiarized fragments of other texts, all incorporated into a larger parody of the chivalric quest. Acker's version of the same fragment from Cervantes that Menard labored over indicates her parodic intent:

> If history, the enemy of time, is the mother of truth, the history of women must define female identity. The main tome on this subject or history was written by Cid Hamete Benengeli, a man. (29)

The quest here has to do with rejecting the "truth" to which mother history is continuously giving life. Acker (erroneously?) attributes the authorship of the original *Quixote* to the Arab Benengeli, after earlier having identified Arabs as liars and as lacking a concept of originality: "They write by cutting chunks out of already written texts and in other ways defacing traditions. . . . " (25). If Benengeli wrote the history of women, that history is consequently both untrue and plagiaristic; so-called historical truth must have nothing to do with women's identity. When she herself engages in cutting up other texts, she thus identifies her own authorship as just as illegitimate as Benengeli's, and implicitly, unlike Menard, renounces any claims to either originality or "truth."

The metaphor Acker uses for her own practice of "cutting chunks out of already existing texts" is the specifically female one of the abortion. When, in the beginning of the novel, somebody asks why the protagonist is having an abortion, a third party answers, "All she ever used to do was read books" (16). Later we are told that as a child she "gave [her] hand in marriage to [her] favorite book" every evening (142). It is obvious that the abortion, with all its attendant pain, is a consequence of the love/hate relationship between a female reader and the male texts that have represented her to herself. The abortion is the impregnation by and consequent expulsion of the canonical (or more accurately, seminal) texts of the male tradition.

Yet, no matter how painful, the abortion is a result of a love affair, and it involves a masochistic desire to concede to history's representations or to submit meekly to the abortionist. In an earlier text, *Blood and Guts in High School*, Acker has this to say:

> Having an abortion was obviously just like getting fucked. If we closed our eyes and spread our legs, we'd be taken care of. They stripped us of our

> clothes. Gave us white sheets to cover our nakedness. Led us back to the pale green room. I love it when men take care of me. (BG, 33)

In an interview, Acker reveals that she began copying Don Quixote because she couldn't think, while waiting to have an abortion (Friedman, 13). Contrary to the Menardian reproduction of the source text, which is—presumably—the fruit of intense labor, copying/abortion is here associated with the preempting of labor pains and the abandoning of thought and responsibility, as the knight reveals when she says:

> When a doctor sticks a steel catheter into you while you're lying on your back and you do exactly what he and the nurse tell you to; finally, blessedly, you let go of your mind. Letting go of your mind is dying. (9–10)

What you let go of in an abortion is both mind and fetus, the latter embodying the former in a perversion of the male writer's proud assertion of paternity over his brain-child/text. A woman who refuses to reproduce (the male heritage) is by definition not only childless but mindless, that is mad, relegated to the night and dead to history. The metaphor of history as mother of truth is here turned around: refusing to be a mother is refusing to participate in history.

As the romantic idea of love criticized by Cervantes turns into the sadomasochistic relationship of pornography in Acker's text, she at the same time introduces the one aspect of love that is invariably excluded from traditional pornography, in which it has no consequences (except, for real women, of course, who are themselves of no consequence to the pornographer). In Acker's text, however, with its literalization of the problem of love in the very postmodern thematics of reading and writing, reproduction is an inevitable consequence of any heterosexual love affair; abortion is the only means of resistance.

Abortion can be a passive submission, letting oneself be taken care of, which is the chivalric code's equivalent of the pornographic code's "getting fucked," or it can become a subversive action if the abortionist's weapons are turned back on him. Musing on the word *catheter*, Acker's knight reflects that it is related both to Quixote and to Kathy (thus further emphasizing the author's identification with her protagonist). Because one's identity, no matter how "false," is in the hands of those who have power over one's body (those who fuck with a catheter), the revenge is also an inevitable self-mutilation, a cutting up of the self. Since the female author has no existence outside them, the texts or representations out of which she cuts pieces are at the same time "herself." In Acker's extreme version, the abortion is a kind of ritual suicide; doomed to reproduce, the female writer's only choice is between plagiarism and death, at least as long as she desires the love of men. The difference between the Bloomian parricide and Acker's specifically female version is, of course, that the violence perpetrated in the abortion is turned directly against the writer herself and her potential offspring, and only indirectly against the fathers.

PORNOGRAPHY AND "THE FEMININE"

Acker's use of pornography, the most troubling aspect of her work to most feminist critics, may seem a paradoxical choice. Yet she chooses this genre quite deliberately for her rewriting of the chivalric quest. Because of the transgressive nature of pornography, its practitioners are commonly identified as "literary criminals," and Acker frequently refers to her own activity as piracy. Literary criminality is, especially in the wake of Kristeva's *La Révolution du langage poétique*, identified with femininity (particularly in psychoanalytic discourse, by way of the association of the imaginary with the feminine) in a way that doubly displaces real women.[1] The subversion of propriety that is the hallmark of pornography is thus inscribed in a peculiar critical position, where it is—theoretically speaking—gendered feminine, by virtue of the paradigm that identifies law with the masculine and desire with the feminine, while at the same time its representations are based on the oppression of real women. The apparent paradox resides in the coexistence of two seemingly contradictory meanings of "the feminine": on the level of the meta-language of criticism it is a metaphor for subversion, but on the level of representation it constitutes the object, that which is oppressed and forced to conform to the will of others.

Acker not only plagiarizes but indeed acts out the relationship depicted in many of her pornographic pre-texts, displacing it onto her own ambivalent relationship with the precursors whose depictions of the politics of love and sexuality may, after all, be more "real" than those allowed into the mainstream of literary history.[2] If, as critics like Susan Suleiman and Jessica Benjamin imply, ritual sexual violence is a transgression that simultaneously exceeds and acknowledges the boundaries of the self and the law, it can indeed be argued that Acker engages in a sadomasochistic relationship with her predecessors, symbolized by the two views of abortion. On the one hand, she desires masochistically to submit to the abortionist's knife, wanting to be recognized as a "good girl" (much as Menard desires the recognition of his lady readers), playing the submissive feminine role, even at the risk of "getting fucked" into mindlessness and losing herself. On the other hand, she steals the abortionist's knife, using his representations as she desires, one might say, for her sadistic pleasure, in the same way the pornographer uses women. She can only do this, however, by renouncing her own literally female authorship, by playing the masculine role of the aggressor, by engaging in cross-dressing, as it were.

While the author may wear two hats (or both the whip and the chains) or split into submissive female characters while at the same time dominating both them and their fictional masters, the ecstasy and anguish that are inherent in sadomasochistic practice are unevenly distributed in the relationship between text and reader. A female reader's particular identification with its representations places her in the position of the victim, whose body becomes the site of its considerable, albeit imaginary, violence. This reaction is not necessarily a result of a simple-minded tendency to what Suleiman calls "ultra-thematic" readings, which overlook the subversive potential of language (127), but is rather, I believe, a consequence of the fact that a writing from the body, such as Acker's, either solicits a reading from the body or risks metaphorizing it out of existence.

The current debate surrounding pornography indicates its important and ambiguous role in postmodern criticism; as the archetype of marginal or avant-garde writing, the retroactively established (anti-) canon of pornographic literature, centering on the figures of de Sade and Bataille, is frequently seen as emblematic of the preoccupations of postmodernism. But as the subversiveness of the literary avant-garde is valorized, its identification with "the feminine" becomes ever more ironic; as the term indicates, the avant-garde connotes militarism and conquest, and the misogynist character of many of its expressions (e.g., Futurism) is well documented. Not only does the current valorization of femininity remain on the level of metaphor (Kristeva's list of literary criminals, for instance, is exclusively male), but the reduction of "the feminine" to this figurative status is so pervasive as to effectively deny women their real place in literary history. Like Acker's protagonist, real women are knights errant in the a-historical night.

Most critics who have dealt with pornographic art, whether visual or verbal, agree on the violence of its representations, in which the female body is cut up, mutilated, fragmented, and in all ways violated. But it is only fairly recently that this type of transgression has come to be seen in "pornartgraphy," as Susan Gubar calls it, as an effect rather than a cause of linguistic transgression. Bataille's *L'Historie de l'oeil*, one of the crucial texts of the pornographic canon, is first and foremost about language; the representation of sexual violence, critics like Barthes (and Sontag) seem to say, is somehow secondary to linguistic transgressions. It is as if representation is an undesirable side effect or unfortunate by-product of radical language play. Only since feminist critics have begun to take an interest in this phenomenon has the problematic analogy between language and the female body that underlies it—the body as the site of linguistic violence—been brought into the discussion. For the female reader, the literal violence of the representations is hard to overlook; it is easier to reduce the other to metaphor than to assume that role for oneself.

Because of the power of the representations that she steals, then, if only to abort them, the female author who is honest enough to admit her own desire for the love of men and their texts, is doomed to reproduce, on the level of the relationship of text to reader, the same sexual hierarchy that, as a postmodernist, she claims to deconstruct within her own writing. While the postmodern critique of representation and the feminist critique of patriarchy may be analogous endeavors, their relationship may have to be reevaluated when the first is carried out in such a way—perhaps inevitably—that it nevertheless perpetuates the kinds of representations that the latter attempts to deconstruct. And although the female writer, unlike her male peers, is incapable of avoiding—indeed does not want to avoid—the literal and political implications of the sad state of affairs that makes pornography such a valuable diagnostic tool, Acker's brand of postmodernism may claim as its victim exactly the subject whose rights it professes to defend in the name of feminism.

It is significant that the relatively few women whose place in the avant-garde of postmodernism is not disputed (another one who comes to mind is Angela Carter) so often turn to pornography, while at the same time more or less subscribing to the increasingly popular genre of allegory. In allegory, Walter Benjamin claims, the relationship between the author and his/her representations is indeed analogous to that between sadist and victim (*The Origin of German Tragic Drama*). According to Susan Sontag, whose discovery of the writings of Bataille in 1966 (whether through Barthes's *Essais critiques* or not she doesn't say) introduced it as a serious object of critical study, pornography has been devalorized not only because of its taboo subject matter, but because its intent, the sexual arousal of the reader, is "at odds with the tranquil, detached involvement evoked by genuine art" (39). The readerly aesthetics of tranquility has since then been discredited with the general acceptance—among intellectuals at least, who are the readers of "pornartgraphy"—of the Barthesian advocacy of *jouissance* as the aim of the writerly text. But pornography would seem a strange anomaly in the writerly realm; aiming to activate the reader, it simultaneously leaves him (in the traditional pornographic paradigm, the reader is always male) little freedom to choose the nature of that activity. Most critics agree that even the best pornography is nothing if not single-minded (as well as single-handed, as the title of a recent book indicates—*Ces livres qu'on ne lit que d'une main*). Could the renewed critical interest in pornography be a symptom of an unconscious acknowledgement of the crucial role played by the control and manipulation of the reader in postmodernism, and/or does it indicate the realization that *jouissance* is not incompatible with manipulation? If this is so, then it is not surprising that pornography can function as a representative allegory, not only for the relationship between a female reader and her precursors but also for that between the author and the critics whose recognition he or she desires as much as do Menard and his narrator (and Borges, for that matter).

SNUFF CRITICISM AND POSTMODERN ALLEGORY

The most troubling—and potentially dangerous—aspect of literary pornography to feminists is the presumed willing submission of the victim. In *The Story of O*, which has lately replaced Bataille's as the paradigmatic text of literary pornography, O's masters insist on her consenting to her own degradation. Like the saint before God, she must will her submission to the sadist. Whether the particular explanatory paradigm used by critics to explain the phenomenon is psychoanalytic or theological—these seem to be the most frequent—the force of the erotic is seen to lie in the quest for selflessness, for the loss of subjectivity. In that respect, eroticism would seem to offer an exemplary paradigm for what is usually taken to be the crux of postmodern aesthetics—we live, as we all know, in an age where the death of the subject has superseded the death of God. Yet it is not eroticism *per se* that predominates in the postmodern avant-garde but its violent and masculinist variant, pornography. Uncomfortable as it may be, this is where we may find the answer to the question about the real status of self-loss in the postmodern allegory, of which pornography is only the most extreme form: it demands that the reader will her own submission to the mastery of the author.

While the resurgence of pornography in popular culture, particularly in the blatant and violent misogyny of many recent Hollywood movies, may be symptomatic of a backlash against feminism, the simultaneous resurgence of the genre in "high literature" (and I do not subscribe to the orthodox view of postmodernism as bridging the "great divide" between high art and popular culture) represents a backlash of another kind. It is a revenge against a critical establishment that insists on depriving the author of all control, what Borges might see as a world of Menards, a coterie of critical parasites, sycophantically vying for the readers' attention while dependent for their survival on the blood of their objects of desire—the books for which they can only admit their love after dominating them—and inherently incapable of originality. In a culture where any discourse is seen as enmeshed in power struggles, the reciprocal play on which Barthes's idea of *jouissance* claims to be predicated becomes a quest for dominance. The poststructuralist story of the death of the subject may be the critical establishment's own wish-fulfilling sadomasochistic allegory—the critic wants to usurp the authority of the author and submit the text to his own desires. (The death of the author, one might say, is a result of this kind of "snuff" criticism; consider the metaphoric presence of necrophilia in the relationship between the critic and his corpus, or the cannibalistic incorporation of pieces of the masters in the texts of Derrida, for instance.) Although many critics have declared the death of the author, none has yet proposed the death of the critic; some subjects are pronounced a great deal deader than others, and it could be argued that the deadness of the author is inversely proportionate to the aliveness of the critic.

Poststructural criticism has long tried to undo the hierarchy that designated literary texts as primary and critical commentary as secondary, but the celebration of the interdependence of host and parasite among critics who attempt to rescue their own endeavor from this derivative position is more often than not, I would argue, a cover for a much more vampiristic enterprise.[3] In a society that insists on hierarchies, and that prefers to sexualize them, the reciprocal play of reading turns into a pornographic fantasy in which the author is murdered in the name of the critic's *jouissance*. The postmodern critic is to the text as the sadist is to his object—pornography is the postmodern romance. It is against this critical assault on the subjecthood of the artist that the postmodern author so frequently seeks revenge by demanding the submission of the reader to his control. In her allegorical use of sadomasochism, Acker may thus be accurately diagnosing not only the true nature of the romance between the female author and the precursors she loves and hates, but what could be called a postmodern erotics of reading.

CRIMINAL INTENT

If Acker has shown the uncomfortable—indeed painful—consequences of the love affair between a female author and her male forebears, she has done so only to those readers for whom the motive behind her seemingly contradictory strategies of obsessive plagiarism and refusal to reproduce are visible. In other words, a reader unfamiliar with the original texts or discourses that Acker parodies—unable to put the masterpieces back together, as it were—and consequently blind to the sophisticated self-consciousness of her novel, would not be able to judge its subversive power. As in the case of Menard, critical mediation (in this case carried out by the author herself through her own meta-commentary and helped by extratextual comments on her work) is necessary for the detection of the crime. Undetected plagiarism is as paradoxical a notion as the perfect crime, and as unsatisfactory for the literary criminal who wants to be sure her illegitimate skills are recognized, admired, and, at best, loved, lest she be misunderstood. Only by detecting the motive behind the crime can the reader become an accomplice instead of a victim of the author's manipulations. We must in the end face what has been repressed since the criminalization of the "intentional fallacy" in the forties—and perpetuated in a different form in most poststructuralist criticism—and admit that not only does it, as Borges insists, matter who wrote *Don Quixote* and why, but it matters who writes, reads, and reproduces all subsequent versions of this and any other text, and why they do it the way they do. Precisely because of the threatened usurpation of their authority, postmodern writers desire even more than their predecessors to be read "correctly," but this can only happen when their (criminal?) intent is made visible—whether within or outside the text. Such a reading is reserved for a very specific readership, that same critical establishment that it is the author's intention to kill, albeit in self-defense. The lethal joust between author and critic can only be turned from a dance of death into the play of *jouissance* that will change the sadomasochistic relationship into a reciprocal recognition when the critic acknowledges the mastery of the author, and the author dares to admit his or her desire for recognition; that is, when love and desire are removed from the struggle for domination. Only when there is truly mutual consent, which is only possible when both parties are entirely conscious of each other's intent—only between mature adults, so to speak—are both free willingly—and momentarily—to submit to the mastery of the other without risking death.

16

Writing the Body as Social Discourse: Prolegomena to Carnal Hermeneutics

Hwa Yol Jung

> If we keep on speaking the same language together, we're going to reproduce the same history.
>
> —Luce Irigaray

> Aesthetics is born as a discourse of the body.
>
> —Terry Eagleton

> [P]erhaps, even if nothing else today has any future, our *laughter* may yet have a future.
>
> —Friedrich Nietzsche

PROLOGUE

Postmodern thought is marked by a rainbow coalition of many splendid things; it is a colorful polygraph. And yet carnal hermeneutics is still marginalized on its threshold.[1] The purpose of this essay is to explore the possibility of carnal hermeneutics as postmodern social discourse by intertwining Mikhail Bakhtin's dialogical thought with a phenomenology of the lived body in the backdrop of the *cogito* principle of Descartes, which became the philosophical canon of modernity.[2] Carnal hermeneutics as a postmodern project is introduced in the hopes of overcoming or transgressing the canonical institution of the *cogito* valorized as disembodied, monological, and ocularcentric: it is the mind "transcendentalized" from rather than "immanentized" in the body. As it is the act of the mind as "thinking substance" (*res cogitans*), the *cogito* is inherently monological because it is always and necessarily *ego cogito* (the "I think")—the epitome of an "invisible man" in isolation from others, both other minds and other bodies.[3] As a thinking substance, the mind is independent of the body (*res extensa*); it needs nothing more than itself to exist.[4] Once the self and the other are viewed as disembodied substances, two self-contained substances, monologism—or even solipsism in extremis—is inevitable. For Descartes, moreover, the mind as *cogito* erects the privatized, insulated, and echoless chamber of "clear and distinct ideas": the *cogito* inflicts a "reflective cramp" on the mind. Cartesian metaphysics whose epicenter is the *cogito* is identifiable with the panoptic hegemony of vision or ocularcentric metaphysics: as the product of the sovereign gaze of *kosmotheoros*, it is, as Maurice Merleau-Ponty puts it precisely, "a philosophy of reflection [*philosophie réflexive*] which identifies my being with what I think of it";[5] it is a reflective narcissism. As a matter of fact, visual metaphysics—or what Francis Bacon called philosophy's "Idols of the Theatre"—goes hand-in-hand with the monologism of the *cogito* because vision is not only isolating or distancing but also anaesthetic in denying the sociability of the (other) senses: there is a narcissism and social amnesia of and in all vision. In other words, there is an identity between the "I" and the "eye." The *cogito* is *video ergo sum*, or the mind's I is the mind's eye.[6] Heidegger contends that the "I" (or the "eye") of the *cogito* as thinking sub/stance becomes the center of thought from which the "I-viewpoint" and the subjectivism of modern thought originate: "the subjectivity of the subject is determined by the 'I-ness' (*Ichheit*) of the 'I think.'"[7] For him, the "I-viewpoint" of the Cartesian *cogito* highlights the modern age as "the age of the world picture" (*Weltbild*). Heidegger means to end once and for all the "speculative" illusion of Western metaphysics since Plato, who strove "to behold [the truth as] the eternal ideas visible in the sky."[8]

THE GENESIS OF CARNAL HERMENEUTICS

By the neologism *carnal hermeneutics*, I mean an "application"[9] of hermeneutics or interpretation theory and its procedures to the reading of the *body as social text* or *inscription in the world*, which would include such basic and diverse forms of the body's communicative performance as gesture, pantomime, dance, and boxing, as well as speech acts.[10] It is an incorporation of conceptual categories concerning all the aspects, dimensions, levels, pivots, configurations, and representations, both verbal and nonverbal, of the body's *habitus* and practice; that is, of the body politic.

Samuel Beckett, for example, is absolutely right and deep when he intimates that in language as gesture ("manual rhetoric") the spoken and the written are identical.[11] Gesture is language, simultaneously both spoken and written, because it is performance. Because it is perduring "flexion," it is called by Francis Bacon "transitory hieroglyphics."[12] We can use Joyce Carol Oates's exceptionally perceptive and engaging discussion of boxing as an exercise in carnal hermeneutics. For her, "life is a metaphor for boxing" or boxing is a scene excised and played out of life itself. In another sense, however, there is nothing like boxing. Boxing is indeed an "iconographic" text: "Life *is* like boxing in many unsettling respects. But boxing is only like boxing."[13] She writes:

> Because a boxing match is a story without words, this doesn't mean that it has no text or no language, that it is somehow "brute," "primitive," "inarticulate," only that the text is improvised in action; the language of a dialogue between the boxers of the most refined sort (one might say, as much neurological as psychological: a dialogue of split-second reflexes) in a joint response to the mysterious will of the audience which is always that the fight be a worthy one so that the crude paraphernalia of the setting—ring, lights, ropes, stained canvas, the staring onlookers themselves—be erased, forgotten. (As in the theater or the church, settings are erased by way, ideally, of transcendent action.) Ringside announcers give to the wordless spectacle a narrative unity, yet boxing as performance is more clearly akin to dance or music than narrative.[14]

From the standpoint of embodiment in extremity, moreover, the opposite of speech is not writing, but silence. What the mind is to the body, uttered speech is to silence. Not only is silence the karma of the body, but also action, that is, the body's motion is the embodiment of silence. The composer John Cage amply demonstrates that music (sound) and silence, not unlike the ancient Chinese dialectical coupling of *yin* and *yang* as complementary, are mutually implicated and enhancing. In human communication, too, silence as the hidden horizon of sound resides in the beginning, interlude, and ending of speech as verbal utterances. It also "punctuates" and thus facilitates the ongoing flow of human communication. Silence is lack of utterance or enunciation, but not lack of thought and mood, lack of words, or lack of intention to speak. As a beginning and ending of speech, it works like the "primordial" *Tao*, which is ever "silent" (unspoken) and "empty" (unwritten). In a dialogue or conversation, there is no basic opposition or incompatibility between silence and utterance. As a matter of fact, genuine dialogue demands the contact of speaking and listening as a communicative transaction. For it is a doubling or coupling of saying utterance and silent listening: one who utters and the other who listens, which are reversible or exchangeable. If there is no listening or silence, conversation would be a continuous series of monologues rather than a dialogue.

The body is not only the silent spring of language, but silence is also the body's mutiny against the abuse and misuse of language. In *Love's Body*, Norman O. Brown speaks of silence as the body's language. For silence is nothing but the word activated as flesh. "To recover the world of silence, of symbolism," he asserts, "is to recover the human body. . . . The true meanings of words are bodily meanings, carnal knowledge; and the bodily meanings are the unspoken meanings. What is always speaking silence is the body."[15] To modify his formula slightly by adding brackets around the letter "*m*" of the word *mother*: "Silence is the (m)other tongue." After the fashion of Susan Sontag, it may be said that silence, that is, the body's language, is not the "incineration," but a remedy for the "pollution" of language.[16] Silence, according to her, not only helps to attain, promote, and maximize the integrity, seriousness, and efficacy of speech but also undermines "bad speech," i.e., speech dissociated from the body or speech without feeling.

It should not escape our attention here that East Asians, whose language is characterized as the choreography of human gestures (ideography or logography), have had throughout their history the extraordinary sense of appreciating silence as a form of communication—that is, in short, carnal hermeneutics.[17] Anybody who is slightly acquainted with the Chinese ideogram would recognize it as a choreography of the body whose artistic rendition called calligraphy is the (brush) "painting" of the body as ideogram.[18] Calligraphy is a pantomimic art, somatography. It is a balletic parade in rite order that generates corporate energy—to emulate the pungent language of Marshall McLuhan. Ideograms are metaphors of the body itself. As a family of signifiers or semantemes, Chinese ideography is a conversation of gestures. For it the body is the silent spring of language whether it be spoken, written, "signed," or gesticulated.[19] Conversely, Picasso's *Swimmer* (1929) and *Acrobat* (1930) are two painted choreographs of the human body in motion or kinegraphs, which approach or perhaps surpass calligraphy.

Carnal hermeneutics is meant to be a counter-discourse because it is transgressive of and subversive to the mainstream Western philosophy of the mind, of disembodied reason.[20] It is the protestant discourse of the body that has been excommunicated for too long from the church of the mind and abandoned as an "untouchable" pariah in philosophical discourse. The body is not the site of sins, but the mind has been the site of philosophical errors. The claim that the body is the presupposed root of human coexistence and of everything that is associated with it is a denial of neither rationality nor philosophy. It only attempts to remove the mind's obstructed view of the body. It destroys the facile and false dichotomy of the mental (*res cogitans*) and the physical (*res extensa*) and overcomes physical substantialism that regards the body as substance (*res*). As the body (*soma*) does not signify the death (*sema*) of the mind, carnal hermeneutics seeks no headhunting. We may say that in it rationality stands no longer on its head, but rather on its feet. Gabriel Marcel, who influenced Merleau-Ponty's phenomenology of the lived body (*corps propre*), is irrefutable when he affirms the body as "being" in contradistinction to the body as "having" and asserts that "the problem of the reality of the body is shown to be the central problem [of human existence] and upon its solution everything else depends."[21] I am my body prior to everything else because to be anything else I first have to make use of my body. The carnal landscape is the presupposed foundation of all conceptual geography. Thus it must be pointed out that the Cartesian, rationalist definition of *conception* as categorial abstraction in isolation from the body does not do justice to its own etymology because the verb "to conceive" is, interestingly, associated with "fertility" (or fecundity) of the body in thinking with language. Etymologically, therefore, reason as con/ception is not only associative but also a markedly feminine category. Ironically, it is "conception" rather than "perception" that has a close affinity with the body, with the language of the body. "The human organism," Elizabeth Sewell declares, "thinks as a whole [*con*cretely rather than *ab*stractly], and our division of it into mind and body is the result of overemphasis on logic and intellect in near isolation which has led us into so one-sided a view of the activity of thought, so gross an underestimation of the body's forms of thought and knowledge."[22] After all, all conception—mental or physical—is corporeal: it is never incorporeal. The mind without the body is a fatal abstraction. The body is no longer the prison-house of the soul. Rather, the former is the karma of the latter. Speaking against "the despisers of the body" in *Thus Spoke Zarathustra*, Nietzsche muses over the radical notion that "body am I entirely, and nothing else; and soul is only a word for something about the body."[23] Perhaps the mind (or soul) is, for him, nothing but the circumlocution of the body. It should be said with Nietzsche, therefore, that we *exist as body*, and the body is primary to the mind.

The advent of carnal hermeneutics in modern Western thought begins with the work of Giambattista Vico.[24] His keen sense of language as an embodied phenomenon comes from his mastery of etymology. He observed that "words are carried over from bodies and from the properties of bodies to signify the institutions of the mind and spirit."[25] As for the anthropomorphization of nature by means of the body, Vico wrote:

> It is noteworthy that in all languages the greater part of the expressions relating to inanimate things are formed by metaphor from the human body

> and its parts and from the human senses and passions. Thus, head for top or beginning; the brow and shoulders of a hill; the eyes of needles and potatoes; mouth for any opening; the lip of a cup or pitcher; the teeth of a rake, a saw, a comb; the beard of wheat; the tongue of a shoe; the gorge of a river; a neck of land; an arm of the sea; the hands of a clock; heart for center (the Latins used *umbilicus*, navel, in this sense); the belly of a sail; foot for end or bottom; the flesh of fruits; a vein of rock or mineral; the blood of grapes for wine; the bowels of the earth. Heaven or the sea smiles; the wind whistles; the waves murmur; a body groans under a great weight. The farmers of Latium used to say the fields were thirsty, bore fruit, were swollen with grain; and our rustics speak of plants making love, vines going mad, resinous trees weeping. Innumerable other examples could be collected from all languages.[26]

Heidegger's reflection on the nature of thinking inheres in the tradition of Vico's carnal hermeneutics. *What Is Called Thinking?*, which is, according to Heidegger himself, "the least read" among his works alludes to *embodied thinking*. Heidegger's thought on thinking as handicraft is eloquent and unsurpassable. It reveres the combined, diatactical tradition of Democritus and Anaxogoras, who recognized the significance for humanity of the hand and the mouth, respectively. The hand is a peculiarly human institution. It signifies the humanity of man—its abyssal essence, its sensuousness, its sociability, its speaking, its thinking. Auguste Rodin's "Cathedral"—two right (rite) hands coming together—celebrates the tactile "piety" of the interhuman. In Heidegger's view, thinking, speaking, and the hand, which is always moving while being still, form a filial union. The hand is "the piety of thinking." As the hand is tactile, so are thinking and speaking and, above all, doing. Language, body, and thought are not dissociated from one another. There is no subordination of speaking to thinking, either. Only disembodied thought would subordinate the body to thinking where thinking of speaking comes before actually speaking it, i.e., the wrongheadedness of "metaphysical" thought.[27] The "thinking hand" or thinking as handiwork, of which Heidegger speaks, confers upon us the work of the hand as embodied conduct. As such, the hand is not just an "extension" of the body, but is the body incorporated. The hand is or becomes the lived body; it is an organized "corporation." Rodin's "The Thinker," which is in itself the artistic creation of two hands and the intimate sense of touch, is the exemplar of the body as organized corporation as well as embodied thinking. Thus Rainer Maria Rilke comments, "He sits absorbed and silent, heavy with thought: with all the strength of an acting man he thinks. His whole body has become head and all the blood in his veins has becomes brain."[28] In essence, Rodin's "The Thinker" symbolizes the "cathedral" of human thinking, of embodied thinking.

THE CARNAL GENEALOGY OF SOCIAL DISCOURSE

In his literary and cultural theory, Bakhtin continues and preserves—in the footsteps of Marx, William James, and Martin Buber—the prized discovery by Ludwig Feuerbach of a "Thou" which has often been hailed as the "Copernican revolution" of social thought. What (Copernican) heliocentrism is to (Ptolemaic) geocentrism in astronomy and cosmology, heterocentrism (dialogism) is to egocentrism (monologism) in social thought.[29] In Bakhtin's thought, the dialogical principle is everything. Commenting on the nature of Dostoevsky's discourse, he gives us a glimpse, brief but definitive and essential, of his dialogical principle:

> At the center of Dostoevsky's artistic world must lie dialogue, and dialogue not as a means but as an end in itself. *Dialogue here is not the threshold to action, it is the action itself.* It is not a means for revealing, for bringing to the surface the already ready-made character of a person; no, in dialogue a person not only shows himself outwardly, but he becomes for the first time that which he is—and, we repeat, not only for others but for himself as well. *To be means to communicate dialogically. When dialogue ends, everything ends.* Thus dialogue, by its very essence, cannot and must not come to an end. At the level of his religious-utopian world-view Dostoevsky carried dialogue into eternity, conceiving of it as eternal co-rejoicing, co-admiration, con-cord. At the level of the novel, it is presented as the unfinalizability of dialogue, although originally as dialogue's vicious circle.[30]

To be human is to be eternally interhuman and communicative: existence is indeed coexistence, which is fundamentally and necessarily intercorporeal and responsive.

Bakhtin's dialogical philosophy of language assumes embodiment or intercorporeality. For good reason, Katerina Clark and Michael Holquist allude to the Russian religious tradition of kenosis and speak of a Slavic Tantrism in their discussion of his translinguistics as performative utterances. *Kenosis* refers to the potential incorporation of spirituality or holiness in the body as the material subject of the world: "*consciousness itself can arise and become a viable fact only in the material embodiment of signs.*"[31] As the body is the initial insertion of the self into the world of others, other bodies, intersubjectivity is always and already intercorporeal. And it cannot be otherwise. Thus the phenomenologist Erwin W. Straus argues for the "privileged status" of the body for the existential condition of man as being in the world of other people and other things. The body is directly related to other bodies. The mind, however, is related to one body only. It is not directly related to the world, other bodies, or other minds.[32] The mind is a *relatum* only because of the body, which populates itself in the world of other people (*Mitwelt*) and other things (*Umwelt*). Only because we exist as body, we are irreducibly and inalienably social and (thus) ethical.

For Bakhtin, society as embodied is neither a collection of invisible minds nor a seriality of visible objects. The body is not an object among other objects in the world. Rather, it is an active subject, an agent: as I live my body, I am my body or I exist as my body. In other words, the body is an active inscription in the world. For Bakhtin as for Merleau-Ponty—to use the suggestive expression of Clark and Holquist—"*the body answers the world by authoring it*."[33] The idea of the lived body or the embodied self rejects the Scylla of egocentricity on the one hand and the Charybdis of anonymity on the other. Both egocentricity and anonymity misunderstand the true nature of the social or dialogical: they bring death to the social. Merleau-Ponty contended that in Sartre's thought there is no "intersubjectivity" but only "a plurality of subjects" who are held together by "the hopeless heroism of the I" and in which the Other is seen by the I as a pure negativity.[34] Similarly, Bakhtin opposes Freudian "psychologism" in favor of Marxian "socialism" because in Freudianism there is the irreconcilable antagonism between the demands of ego's instinct (pleasure principle) and the restrictions of civilization (reality principle): as Freud himself puts it concisely in *Civilization and Its Discontents*, "The liberty of the individual is no gift of civilization."[35] In comparing Freud with Bakhtin, Clark and Holquist remark: "In Freud, self is suppressed in the service of the social; in Bakhtin, self is precisely a function of the social. In Freud, the more of the other, the less of the self; in Bakhtin, the more of the other, the more of the self."[36] Bakhtin's genealogy of the social opposes the idea of both "*I* own meaning" (egocentricity) and "*no one* owns meaning" (anonymity) and opts for the "middle way" or dialogical principle: "*we* own meaning." Bakhtin's dialogism coincides with Merleau-Ponty's "fulguration of coexistence." In the "we" or the fulguration of coexistence, the self and the other are active coproducers of meaning. Thus the social is never simply "given" (*dan*) but always "conceived" or "posited" (*zadan*). "Language," Bakhtin writes, "is not a neutral medium that passes freely and easily into the private property of the speaker's intentions; it is populated—overpopulated—with the intentions of others."[37]

The "we" decenters the embodied self. As dialogue is the interplay of speaking and answering (responding), speaking without the response is monological. Thus the primacy of the response dictates the happening of a dialogue. In other words, heterocentricity or heteronomy is the soul of dialogue. In the language of Bakhtin's dialogism, therefore, the matter of "addressivity" is the regulative idea of dialogue and the logosphere. The anticipated presence of the response gives dialogue and the logosphere the assured sense of pragmaticity. Speaking of the internal dialogism of the word, Bakhtin writes:

> every word is directed toward an *answer* and cannot escape the profound influence of the answering word that anticipates. . . . Primacy belongs to the response, as the activating principle: it creates the ground for understanding, it prepares the ground for an active and engaged understanding. Understanding comes to fruition only in the response. Understanding and response are dialectically merged and mutually condition each other; one is impossible without the other.[38]

At this point we would be remiss if we fail to recognize an affinity between the structural requirement of "answerability" ("response-ability") in Bakhtin's dialogical principle and Emmanuel Levinas's ethics of proximity, which privileges the face and epitomizes human copresence or interhuman presence in terms of the structural primacy of the Other (*l'autrui*).[39] The face is indeed, according to Francis Jacques, "the most fascinating surface on earth."[40] It is the most expressive theatre of the body's performance. Like the body itself, the face is language because it is expressive flexion; its rhetoric, too, is transitory "hieroglyphics" or "ideography."

The ethics of proximity as an embodied phenomenon is characteristic of Levinas's phenomenology of the face (*visage*), which is an ethic of the "I" (ipseity) who is capable of facing (responding to) the other as "you" (alterity). The face-to-face with the other may be called an "interface." The face is indeed an ethic, a human ethic: "The epiphany of the face is ethical."[41] As the face speaks (in silence), speaks uniquely from and for each individual, it is a *de facto* ethical discourse. As such, it is an ethical hermeneutic of the body or the human as embodied. In Levinas's social ontology, which accents the primacy of the ethical, subjectivity is affirmed never for itself (i.e., never monological or egocentric) but for another (*pour l'autre*) (i.e., dialogical or heterocentric). Subjectivity comes into being as "heteronomic": "It is my inescapable and incontrovertible answerability to the other that makes me an individual 'I.'"[42] Thus the notion of responsibility or answerability that coincides with the ethical or the ethics of proximity is, first and foremost, the confirmation of the "I," which is what Levinas calls the "meontological version of subjectivity," with the face as its most basic modus. He writes, therefore, that responsibility is "the essential, primary and fundamental structure of subjectivity. For I describe subjectivity in ethical terms. Ethics, here, does not supplement a preceding existential base; the very node of the subjective is knotted in ethics understood as responsibility."[43]

Bakhtin's dialogical principle is quintessentially a linguistic principle with an ethical overtone. The anatomy of his "translinguistics" (*metalingvistika*) is unmistakably the heart of his seminal contribution to carnal hermeneutics as social discourse. In it the utterance is a molecular segment, and the word is an atomic unit, of the dialogue. It dialogizes mind and body: the uttered word becomes flesh. Because it is conceived of as verbal acts, embodied acts that are concerned with pragmatic results, Bakhtin's translinguistics may be defined as performative utterances or a parley of performances in the tradition of Vico's anatomy of language. Language is never a "prison house," but an "ecosystem" precisely because it is defined in terms of utterance as a happening of social praxis.[44] Utterance as performance is a boundless ecology of relationships both communicative and grammatological (e.g., a trilogy of the author, the text, and the reader).[45]

Performance is already a postmodern concept.[46] It is no less than theatrical/dramaturgical (Jerzy Grotowski and Richard Schechner), ethico-philosophical (John Austin and John Searle), and psychoanalytical (Sigmund Freud and Jacques Lacan). For Roland Barthes, writing (as well as reading) triggers and produces textual bliss (*jouissance*), because it is performance.[47] Richard Schechner goes so far as to say, though somewhat prematurely, that a linguistic model as applied to theatrical performance is suspect because language is "head learning," whereas performance is "body learning."[48] Grotowski's "poor theatre" emulates pantomime as its paradigm with minimal clothing (i.e., minimal masking) and the maximal economy of verbalism: "The custumes are bags full of holes covering naked bodies (i.e., 'holy bodies'); through the holes one looks directly into a torn body."[49]

Moreover, Bakhtin's translinguistics is a nexus of doing things with words in the company or copresence of others. Here it—his Slavic Tantrism, for that matter—cannot escape from but must confront Freud's psychoanalysis with its psychologism notwithstanding. In this regard, Shoshana Felman evokes the psychoanalytical sense of corporeality or the carnal dimension of language when she views speech (*parole*) as "corporeal promise" (*promesse corporelle*), which beckons a conjugal relationship between Austin's philosophy of language as speech acts and Freudian/Lacanian psychotherapeutical discourse as the "talking cure."[50] The originality of Lacan, according to Felman, lies in his dis/covery of an "irreducibly dialogic" structure in psychotherapeutical discourse and knowledge: structured like language, the unconscious is the discourse of the Other.[51] Speaking of his psychoanalytical theory, Felman stresses the fact that the "true thrust" of the psychoanalytical dialogue between the therapist and the client as "talking bodies" is illocutionary: "fundamentally, the dialogic psychoanalytic discourse is *not so much informative as it is performative*,"[52] and thus is necessarily ethical as well.

THE CARNIVALESQUE AS REBELLION

The body is not only the material and social condition of the soul's existence, but also the window, as it were, through which we peep into the inner condition of our soul—be it suffering, mourning, playing, or enjoying. There is indeed an inexorable dialogic between man's interiority and exteriority—a "double helix," so to speak. The human is the simultaneous happening of the internalization of the external and the externalization of the internal, which are chiasmic or transversal.[53] The body, which defines our existential condition in the world, is a two-dimensional, double-binded being: it is at once private and public. It interweaves and interlocks the private and the public domain.

The body's exteriority is manifested in carnival that is characteristic of man as *homo ludens*, whose body politic is unavoidably ethical as well as aesthetic, cultural, and political. Harvey Cox is unerring when he contends that the carnivalesque imagination is indispensable to the survival and periodic rejuvenation of human civilization, including its political institutions. He contends, however, that when it becomes an instrument of ideology or a particular political program, it loses its critical and creative punch and becomes shriveled into a caged bird or toothless tiger.[54]

The carnivalesque is the most radical aspect of carnal hermeneutics because it serves as a *nonviolent technique of social transformation*, radical or reformative, by the maximal display of the body. It is, for its Latin name sake, an incarnation of the festive body. It is the carnal politic *par excellence*, which is a communal celebration of festive bodies whose space is filled always with the extravagant display of vestemes and gustemes. Carnival is a parley of people as players; it is a specular pageantry. The most distinguishing characteristic of carnival is that it means to be subversive or metamorphic from the ground up and intends to preserve and perpetuate intersubjective dialogue at the same time. Carnivalization breaks up the colorless and prosaic monopoly of the established order of power. It dismantles the hierarchical by freely blending "the profane and the sacred, the lower and the higher, the spiritual and the material."[55] According to the philosophic playwright Luigi Pirandello, the Latin *humor* designates "a physical substance in the form of fluid, liquid, humidity or moisture," and humans are said to have four "humors"—blood, bile, phlegm, and melancholy.[56] And the humorist sees the world not exactly in the nude but in "shirt sleeves."[57] For Pirandello, the *principium* of humor lies in edifying "the feeling of the opposite" (*negativa*) in what we do and think. By splitting every affirmation into a negation, humor triggers and engenders the "spontaneous birth" (*ingegno*) of things. To put it more politically, humor as *negativa* uncloaks, unmasks, or exposes the "dirty bottom" of officialdom and the established regime.

As the outside is reversible to the inside, the semantics of the body is a dialogical interplay of clothing and dietetics. As for vestemes, Roland Barthes, who wears the philosophical garment of Hegel's aesthetics, goes for the clothed body because it is impossible to imagine that the body can signify anything at all without clothing. Only clothing guarantees the rite of safe passage from pure sentience to meaning.[58] Desiderius Erasmus puts the same idea differently: he regarded clothing as the second body or "the body of the body."[59] As a kind of vesteme, the fully tattooed body manifests our artistic "lust to decorate and embellish" ourselves.[60] Thomas Carlyle, too, noted the "painting" of the body—which comes before clothing—as the first "spiritual," if only "barbarous," want of humans.[61] Western travellers from Columbus to Bronislaw Malinowski had a tendency to treat the natives of the newly discovered world as "naked" and thus "primitive." The natives were "as naked in culture as they were in body."[62] Clothing thus stands for the liminal passage from savagery to civilization.

Bakhtin's work on Rabelais establishes a set of protocols for the carnivalesque, including gastronomy and gustemes. He discovers the interlocking link between the two basic human activities: eating and speaking. He speculates that "the origins of language itself may lie in the sharing of food as a primal expression of culture over nature, establishing a connection between digestion and dialogue."[63] It took the personal experience of "lean time" for Bakhtin to discover the phenomenology of dietetics as a celebration: "man's encounter with the world in the act of eating is joyful, triumphant; he triumphs over the world, devours it without being devoured himself."[64]

Leszek Kolakowski is incontrovertible when he observes that throughout ages there is an incurable antagonism between "a philosophy that perpetuates the absolute" and "a philosophy that questions accepted absolutes." In other words, the antagonism between the "priestly" and the "jesterly" are the two most general forms of intellectual culture at any given period of time in history. The former attempts to guard the absolute at any cost, while the latter is motivated by his/her distrust of the absolute or a stabilized system and wishes to deconstruct it.[65] Carnival is the "jesterly" play of difference aiming for the creation of an alternative or reversible world order. As a ludic form of subversion, it is playfully, that is, nonviolently, subversive as it intends both to destroy a "real" world and to construct a "possible" world at the same time: it indeed nonviolently deconstructs the world. Clowning dethrones the stable and established hierarchy of all kinds. In the Bruegelian and Rabelaisian themes of Bakhtin's body politic, to carnivalize the world is to dialogize it: in it carnivalization and dialogization go hand in hand. As a protest against the monological "misrule" of officialdom, carnivalesque life transgresses and transforms the canonical order of truth and the official order of reality. As Bakhtin himself writes, it

> is past millennia's way of sensing the world as one great communal performance. This sense of the world, liberating one from fear, bringing one person maximally close to another (everything is drawn into the zone of free familiar contact), with its joy at change and its joyful relativity, is opposed to that one-sided and gloomy official seriousness which is dogmatic and hostile to evolution and change, which seeks to absolutize a given condition of existence or a given social order. From precisely that sort of seriousness did the carnival sense of the world liberate man. But there is not a grain of nihilism in it, nor a grain of empty frivolity or vulgar bohemian individualism.[66]

Carnival is in brief a celebration of dialogue and community; it liberates people and brings them together and induces them to participate in communal living. Here it would be remiss if we fail to come to terms, provisionally if not conclusively, with the perceptive commentary on carnival proffered by Terry Eagleton: "Carnival is so vivaciously celebrated that the necessary political criticism is almost too obvious to make. Carnival, after all, is a *licensed* affair in every sense, a permissible rupture of hegemony, a contained popular blow-off as disturbing and relatively ineffectual as a revolutionary work of art. As Shakespeare's Olivia remarks, there is no slander in an allowed fool."[67] Eagleton, however, is only half right. Even as a licensed occurrence, carnival is a two-sided weapon: one is permission or authorization, and the other "unrestrained by law" and "disregarding accepted rules." It is then "licentious" in every sense, indeed: it is, in other words, capable of transgressing or reversing the repressive status quo by playing out fully what Arthur Rimbaud called the artist's *"dérèglement de tous les senses."*[68] *L'esprit de corps* of carnival is truly ambiguous rather than meaningless, because as the political technique of nonviolent resistance for change, it chooses to tread on the median between reticent submission and violent destruction. It is committed to practice the politics of restraint based on the sacrament of heteronomy or the uneliminable Other, which is the true soul of dialogue. In the politics of restraint out of reverence for the sanctimonious presence of the Other, the freedom to resist and rebel, too, is never absolute or autonomous, but always and necessarily relational.

Unlike revolution, which is a violent form of subversion, carnival as dialogical is the playful body in rebellion. As Bakhtin insists, the most distinguishing characteristic of violence is that it knows no laughter.[69] In both intention and result, subversion by violence brings death to dialogue whose epiphany is the Other. For it there is no alternative, because it intends to exterminate the opposition. As all prejudices and violence ensuing from them are the inevitable consequence of the intolerance of difference, there exists a radical distinction between the violence of intolerance and the laughter of tolerance.

Joyce Carol Oates, who insists that the boxer is his body and "the most profound experiences of our lives are physical events,"[70] does not hesitate to rebuke boxing as violence incarnate. Her business of speaking out against boxing is—to use the language of the French dialogical philosopher Francis Jacques—"to interrupt [*interrompre*] violence."[71] Boxers often theriomorphize themselves as "raging bulls": as Marvin Hagler says, "when I see blood, I become a bull."[72] For Oates, it is a misnomer to call boxing a blood "sport." For "[o]ne *plays* football, one doesn't *play* boxing."[73] The ultimate goal of boxing is summed up by the "young bull" Mike Tyson, when he professes that his strategy is "to drive the bone back into the brain."[74] His body-memory intends to land a deadly blow on his opponent. Boxing, furthermore, is a pure theory of power; it is an abject lesson of "power politics," *Realpolitik*. For as the boxer is his body, in boxing physical superiority is moral rectitude, i.e., might *is* right. Jean-Paul Sartre helps us define boxing as the prototype of power politics when he declares that "The upright man [i.e., the boxer] must be strong: strength is the proof of his right."[75]

In his argument against Arthur Koestler in *Humanism and Terror*, Merleau-Ponty once defended violence uncompromisingly by saying that inasmuch as we are carnal beings, we are destined to violence. Our lot is only the choice among different forms of violence. As violence is the common origin of all political regimes, insisted Merleau-Ponty, not only do "life, discussion, and political choice occur only against a background of violence," but also abstention from violence toward those who are violent is to become their accomplice.[76] In his later work *Adventures of the Dialectic*, however, Merleau-Ponty reversed himself and renounced revolutionary dialectics. He uncovers an insidious dilemma or contradiction inherent in the historical and political logic of revolution when he writes:

> Revolution become institution is already decadent if it believes itself to be accomplished. . . . There is no dialectic without opposition or freedom, and in a revolution opposition and freedom do not last for long. It is no accident that all known revolutions have degenerated: it is because as established regimes they can never be what they were as movements; precisely because it succeeded and ended up as an institution, the historical movement is no longer itself: it "betrays" and "disfigures" itself in accomplishing itself. Revolutions are true as movements and false as regimes.[77]

Nonviolence is not merely a reaction to violence, but it asserts itself as the alternative to the making of history with the intent to preserve and perpetuate intersubjective dialogue in humanity. Thus carnival's nonviolence decisively takes the side of Albert Camus's "rebel" or man in revolt, who renunciates calculated violence and eventually the totalitarian outcome of dialectical violence that ends what Merleau-Ponty calls freedom. For rebellion is a "protest against death" as well as against tyranny, brutality, terror, and servitude. Camus writes:

> Dialogue on the level of mankind is less costly than the gospel preached by totalitarian regimes in the form of monologue dictated from the top of a lonely mountain. On the stage as in reality, the monologue precedes death. Every rebel, solely by the movement that sets him in opposition to the oppressor, therefore pleads for life, undertakes to struggle against servitude, falsehood, and terror, and affirms, in a flash, that these three afflictions are the cause of silence between men, that they obscure them from one another and prevent them from rediscovering themselves in the only value that can save them from nihilism—the long complicity of men at grips with their destiny.[78]

The true rebel is the one who senses and cultivates his obligation to human solidarity with no intention of obliterating the Other. His rebellion or nonviolent subversion stands tall "midway" between silence and murder in refusing to accept being what he/she is. The rebel willingly acknowledges the dialogical interplay between the ethical principle of culpability and the epistemological principle of fallibility, whereas the revolutionary thrives on the monological absoluteness of inculpability and infallibility, however noble or ignoble his/her cause may be. Epistemological dogmatism and moral absolutism have no place in carnivalesque life because they contradict the essence of the dialogical principle that always recognizes the ever-present, porous moment and zone of ambiguity that resides between complete doubt and absolute certainty.

GYNESIS AS *JOUISSANCE*

History has by and large been the history of phallocentrism; it has erected phallocentric monuments and palaces and left their ineffaceable traces. Indeed, it may be seen as a series of unwarranted (or "phallacious") claims on "phallic sovereignty."[79] The "phallic sovereignty" of the *cogito* has held an absolute, if only visual, grip on philosophy, too.

In postmodernity the triangular nexus of body/power/knowledge, that is, the body politic—particularly, the feminine side of it—cannot be overlooked and escape our serious attention.[80] George Bellows's "Stag at Sharkey's"[81] paints boxing as a distillation of the masculine world; it

Figure 1: George Wesley Bellows, *Stag at Sharkey's* 1909.
(The Cleveland Museum of Art, Hinman B. Hurlbut Collection, 1133.22)

is a masculine social text or homotext, pure and simple. (See Figure 1.) For Joyce Carol Oates, what boxing is to masculine violence, speech is to feminine *jouissance*. Boxing for her is indeed a *dis/play* of masculinity, of specifically American masculinity: it is, as she puts it, "*[m]achismo* as sheer poetry."[82] She writes emphatically: "Boxing is for men, and is about men, and *is* men. A celebration of the lost religion of masculinity all the more trenchant for its being lost."[83] Boxing displays women's characteristic repugnance for and men's intense fascination with "bloody" violence. Mike Tyson's recent act of rape is consistent with the idea that boxing is indeed a single-edged sword of violence, which is irredeemably tragic. The fallen "hero" seems yet unaware of the deep tragedy of violence that he inflicted on his victim and himself. He is utterly confused about pseudo-homoeroticism in the ring with consensual heterosexual love-making in the bedroom.[84]

Writing the body as social discourse is a shifting concern of *écriture féminine*. Gynesis—to appropriate the neologism of Alice A. Jardine—signifies the feminine genesis of things and the valorization of the feminine.[85] In so doing, it erases the false dichotomy between the mind (*conception*) and the body (*perception*). Gynesis has *surfaced*, I think, as a keyword in postmodern thinking that is capable of redefining the human as being-in-the-world. It is a paradigmatic shifter in the "management" of postmodern philosophical discourse.

As thinking in the feminine, gynesis is an edifying attempt to combat phallocentrism and reverse sexual gerrymandering by the masculine. In the first place, gynesis as feminine genealogy intends to subvert the canonical institution of the Cartesian *cogito* as the specular theory of knowledge.[86] It is determined to overthrow the "priestly" with the "jesterly." Descartes is truly the domineering "father" or patriarch of modern Western philosophy! His *cogito* is without doubt an ocularcentric and phallocentric philosopheme. Jacques Attali boldly and sweepingly sums us his anti-ocular sentiment against the entire canon of Western philosophy since its inception when he writes: "For twenty-five centuries, Western knowledge has tried to look upon the world. It has failed to understand that the world is not for the beholding. It is for hearing. It is not legible, but audible."[87] The Cartesian dualistic hierarchy of mind and body, subject and object, the masculine and the feminine, and man and nature in terms of domination (supervision) and submission lends itself easily to racism, sexism, and anthropocentrism.[88] In the second place, gynesis as *jouissance* signifies not only the enjoyment of things carnal but also—as it is also spelled *j'ouïs sens* or "I hear meaning"—resistance against and subversion of ocularcentrism. It auscultates the "silenced voice" of the feminine, it is the *jouissance* of hearing and voicing, but not of seeing.[89] Gynesis promises to show ultimately vision's *cul-de-sac*.

The (*feminine*) body as social discourse confronts and challenges directly the idea of the "mind's I" (eye), which implies the threefold intertwined network of the mind as 1) calculative or computational, 2) egocentric, and 3) ocularcentric. The political theorist Nancy J. Hirschmann argues that what "the masculine-mind-self" is to the boy, "the feminine-body-other" is to the girl. For the boy, the self and the other are *totally separate* whereas for the girl, the self and the other are continuous.[90] Her formulation proves the point that the body—not the mind—is the living anchorage of the self in the world: with the body we are connected with the world, and without the body we are disconnected from the world. Many feminists today hold not only that women speak with a "different voice" but also that femininity is allied with the sense of touch more closely than that of sight. There is indeed a stark contrast between the voyeurism of the "mind's seeing" (eye or I) and the communal intimacy of the "body's touch" (hand, caress).[91] They contend that vision is a peculiarly phallocentric, patriarchical, and matrophobic institution, and the logic of voyeurism is uniquely a male logic. The "participatory" sense of touch valorizes gynesis, whereas "spectatorial" vision glorifies the masculine. To feminize the body politic, therefore, is to accent the sense of touch and to decenter or de-panopticize the spectre of vision in our thinking. By so doing, we loosen up the global visual grip on, and bring the communal sense of intimacy or proximity to, the world. For, as Monica Sjöö and Barbara Mor declare, "Everything touches everything in the real world."[92] Gynesis, when translated into tactility, intervenes and fleshes out masculine ocularcentrism.

Nobody is more sensitive and poignant than Luce Irigaray on these issues in developing an ethic of proximity, of "haptics."[93] As she hears it, the advocacy of the feminine is, in significant measure (*metron*), a rupture from and a revolt against the enduring "scopic regimes" of Western philosophy inclusive of the *cogito*. She writes: "Investment in the look is not privileged in women as in men. More than the other senses, the eye objectifies and masters. It sets at a distance, maintains the distance. In our culture, the predominance of the look over smell, taste, touch, hearing, has brought about an impoverishment of bodily relations. . . . The moment the look dominates, the body loses its materiality."[94] In other words, the body becomes serialized into images. To capture the essence of reality or matter by means of an anthology of images or simulacra, however, is forever a Sisyphean task. In reference to photography as the visual medium par excellence, Susan Sontag writes of image as a semblance of knowledge, a subtraction of reality, and an appearance of participation. According to her, "A photograph is pseudo-presence and a token absence."[95] To wit: image is at best but a proxy or, as Daniel J. Boorstin calls it, a "pseudo-event."[96]

EPILOGUE

In its epistemological, ethical, and political implications, Bakhtin's carnal hermeneutics stands tall with such influential and subversive social philosophers as Michel Foucault and Jürgen Habermas. Habermas is totally unaware of carnal hermeneutics and its radical implications for social philosophy. In his eagerness to refute the "philosophy of consciousness," he is blind to the body as active subject and human coexistence as necessarily intercorporeal.[97] Habermas's critical theory of society is still entrapped in the Enlightenment prison-house of disembodied reason, which willy-nilly undermines his theory of communicative action. Foucault, on the other hand, is a radical philosopher of discontinuity and a philosopher of the body politic, of the body incarcerated and abused par excellence. He is, however, ignorant of the festive, lived body, particularly of the carnivalesque side of the body politic.[98] Worst of all, moreover, Foucault's social thought is too hesitant to entertain any active role of subjectivity—including the body as active subject—without which social change or, as he calls it, "resistance" can never be authored or initiated.[99]

Bakhtin's dialogism is truly the Copernican revolution of social thought. His carnal hermeneutics as social discourse shows that human community or the ethics of proximity is first and foremost constituted as a corporeal bond and that the embodied self cannot be monologic. Although the very possibility of nonviolent social transformation must assume the embodied self as active agent, the primacy of the "we," which is the epicenter of Bakhtin's Copernican revolution, is neither reified nor magnified. It only affirms the active but decentered subject without which the self remains forever a passive onlooker, a homunculus. Bakhtin's dialogism is truly postmodern without being anti-humanist, because it is both sensitive to difference and tolerant of the incommensurable in the confirmation of human plurality.[100] It is, in essence, a communal celebration of all humanity, all embodied humanity.

Part Six

Alterity as a Strategy of Change

> In the Trinity there is, 1. ipseity; 2. alterity; 3. community.
>
> —Coleridge[1]

> There will always be an Other, or the dream of otherness. Literature is the form that dream takes in an enlightened mind.
>
> —Geoffrey Hartman[2]

Coleridge's Hegelian trinity—particularity, difference, harmony—in terms of change contains its own resistance: particularity and harmony/community, just as much as alterity/difference, contain and depend on difference for their semantic and even their semiotic existence. To recognize being is to recognize difference; to identify community is to differentiate from other communities and their traits, and to unchangingly enter the theatre of change. Change has a life of its own, as we have seen, quite apart from the developments, etiological structures, and rhetoric of history and culture. On the other hand, change is nothing (or rather *is not*) without that incorporation and repeated (re)definition. We have confronted in essay after essay in this volume the insoluble difficulties of juxtaposing language and historicity with the life of change. Such attempts result, invariably, in irresolution, alienation, otherness. Nonetheless, the writing of the self, individually and collectively, depends on our confronting and dealing with the nature and mundane reality of change. We can never (profitably) forget that at the heart of the concept of change is not just diversity, but "the state of being other," which is itself a transitional formulation caught between static and active.

In order to investigate and interrogate the state of being other and its relationship to change, and the alterity by which change manifests itself, one must inevitably relate the concept of change to conscious human life, to the signifiers by which that life is defined and experienced as such, and to the markers by which we identify the progression and condition of conscious, aesthetic life we call change. We must become, as Derrida points out at the beginning of "Otobiographies,"[3] an ear listening to "life"—that is, to writing and its difference. Derrida's text explores the relationship between autobiography and "otobiography," the plotting of the life of the ear, since it is the ear—the apparatus of reception, interpretation, and responsibility—that must "sign for" the discourse of life it "receives." All discourse, historical and otherwise, for Derrida, is signed for in its receipt in the ear of the other; therefore, all biography, as the story of life and death of the corpus (as body and as body-of-work), is for the other. Change, in the forms of transformation, translation, and even "autobiography," is a function of borderlines and thresholds of and for the other, in both the existential and deconstructive senses. And indeed, of and for alterity itself. This is the nature of the "otobiography," the life of the ear and the economy of dissemination figured by and in it. Within the otobiographical synecdoche Derrida inscribes the problem of alterity as an epistemological and, in terms of language, an ontological strategy. As Hugh Silverman points out,[4]

> The looming presence of alterity marks the difference in which Derridean writing operates, where it sets limits to itself as identity, and outlines the frame that keeps it from becoming fully other. Hence Derridean writing marks its own limits, identifies its outside, its externality, and thereby makes itself difference. (141)

The strategy of writing, for Derrida, marks it as other and yet a trace, connected and disconnected from other texts and from the integrated notion of style. Further, the Derridean notion of writing, as trace and as the site of alterity, is a perpetual differential movement.

The four essays in this final section confront the problem and the portrayal of this aporetic and dialectical conundrum, as a strategy of change, at the threshold and within the context of the postmodern.

Soraya Tlatli, in "The Intoxication of the Avant-Garde in Benjamin and Habermas," explores the theme of intoxication as liberation from the binding ethical rationality of the Kant/Habermas axis of philosophical tradition. Tlatli shows how the critical and aesthetic concentration on intoxication, for example in the surrealists, intends to "win over the energies of intoxication for the [aesthetic] revolution," citing Habermas's contention with Bataille (and by extension Benjamin). Habermas challenges the Dionysian tradition of intoxication and thus of change, since Dionysus and alterity are synonymous. Whereas for Habermas the Dionysian represents a confusion of the poetic and political spheres, this very confusion defines the aesthetic avant-garde represented by Bataille/Benjamin, for whom intoxication represents a strategic loosening of self to account for wider vision. Dionysus "redeems from the curse of identity," rescinds the principle of individuation, in the face of Habermas's Kantian critical reason, the "supreme judge of culture." Starting with Nietzsche, Tlatli shows, the avant-garde has been defined by its adversity to reason, in an aesthetics that represents a radical change in the nature of philosophy and its goals. Whereas for Nietzsche aesthetics is fruitfully released from its traditional places and transgresses the boundaries of ethics, for Habermas this is "an aesthetics of terror." Baudelaire to the Surrealists, Bataille, Foucault, Lacan, Derrida—for Habermas these, as the aesthetic avant-garde, are "the other of reason," whose declared strategy of alterity rejects identity and the principle of identity, and of any autonomous reason.

Benjamin, on the other hand, calls Nietzsche's judgment romantic reflection, in which the critic must rely on art as the writing of history, i.e., the truth of the aesthetic object and its history. For Benjamin, the movement of history is written in artistic production, which is unteleological and anti-progressive, but which—and this is anathema to Habermas—strategically fuses the poetic and the political. This fusion releases immense critical potential in language, since now the image and political action are intertwined. The intoxicated, decentered subjectivity of the avant-garde, which for Habermas is an irrational cult of "the other of reason," is for Benjamin a new possibility of creativity disconnected from any instrumentality, and therefore no longer the product of an ideological hegemonic coding. Surrealist intoxication's euphoria accents the falseness of the vapidly political, pointing the vital importance of linguistic formulation in the critical orientation of art in history and politics. Whereas Habermas cannot manage to see these historico-linguistic dimensions of the avant-garde, since his frame of reference is built on the Kantian *a priori* organization of rationality, for Benjamin the aesthetic "product" is a "snapshot" (as what he calls a "posthumous shock") of a particular historical epoch. The product, for the avant-garde, is steeped in the alterity at the heart of representation, figuration, language.

In "Foucault, Conventions, and New Historicism," David Bell approaches the theme of alterity from another point of view, still within the context of the postmodern (or here the poststructural) notion of history. Bell's theme is poaching, the dangerous invasion of rigid territoriality and hegemonic structure, in which the gaze of the master, which "eliminates adventure," responds to the invasion of an unexpected intruder. Bell shows Foucault, as a poacher on the archive of history, as intentionally strategizing the otherness of any historical research that purports to posit meaning; further, he shows Foucault, and Michel de Certeau in his critique of Foucault, as engaging the poaching metaphor as a practical work strategy as well as a theoretical one. Foucault "raids the archive," robbing it without being imprisoned nor incapacitated by its categorical strategies. In fact, Bell asserts, Foucault poaches on the archive in two ways: first he allows the archival sources to remain obscure, replacing archival identity with a structural fluidity, meandering in "uncharted" fashion through various archives, delighting in inexactitude; second, once having chosen material, Foucault hits "by chance" on what he wants in it, as though no teleological structure has been involved in the choice. In this way Foucault juxtaposes chance and system, emphasizing the importance of chance as a strategy of historical inquiry. As Bell puts it, Foucault "transforms a convention by developing a different practice"; that is, Foucault formulates a new strategy for treating history, playing with and ironizing the conformist historical urge and developing a new practice of writing history that undermines the writing of history. For Bell, however, Foucault's unconventional practice grounds itself in the most conventional of historical practice—that of clarity ("*la clarté française*")—and itself finally adheres to a convention followed and reacted to, then, by subsequent historical revisionists. Thus Foucault manipulates the "archive effect" through the strategy of poaching that has now itself been strategically institutionalized as the "new historicism." Bell illustrates this movement from practice to convention with an analysis of Stephen Greenblatt's *Shakespearean Negotiations*, which, as "second-degree poaching," according to Bell, lacks the ability to reflect on itself, its internal strategies, and new historicist effects in "American appropriation." Thus the use and abuse of (new) historical strategies for theory are revealed as naive, if powerful.

Starting from the point of view of the art historian and critic, Jeremy Gilbert-Rolfe's "Irreconcilable Similarities: The Idea of Nonrepresentation" takes a quite different stance on the nature and strategy of alterity, here as an aesthetic phenomenon. Exploring the relationship between representational and nonrepresentational painting, Gilbert-Rolfe shows how the latter, finally, "depicts" the unreal, aesthetic force rather than artistic form. Multiply interpretable, nonrepresentational art serves as the link between the "rupture of tradition" and rupture itself. Within this nonhistorical framework, Gilbert-Rolfe chronicles the theoretical response to nonrepresentational art from Michael Fried's 1965 essay "Three American Painters," in which Fried asks whether painting has withdrawn from the real or whether the real has withdrawn from painting, in this missing or avoiding the perspectival privilege accorded the modernist artist. Because it does not mediate the world of objects, Gilbert-Rolfe points out, nonrepresentational art alienates alienation and is therefore more "immediate," a sign without an articulable referent. Taking as his examples the "flattening" of Manet, the specific alienation techniques of Synthetic Cubism, and the extreme use of figure and ground in Matisse, Gilbert-Rolfe lays the groundwork for the advent of a purely spatial art of alterity.

In its complicating of the question of representation "so as to *prolong* it, not abolish it," Gilbert-Rolfe sets nonrepresentational art up as a willful strategy of "fully developed outsides" as opposed to "partially developed insides"; that is, still a representation, but now of the very thought of flow, and thus of alterity. Alterity thus becomes a strategic ploy of the artist: for Manet in the adjustment of the painted image to the condition of the sign; for Synthetic Cubism in the play of essences and aspects and the will to distill, concentrate, and essentialize; for Matisse in the play of the immediacy of another body. All of these experiments in exemplary nonrepresentationalism are linked, according to Gilbert-Rolfe, in their preoccupation with figure, and with a theory of invisibility as a strategic methodology (an "amethodology") of externals and the examination of vacantness.

This exploration leads not to a concentration on lack, however, since nonrepresentation overcomes lack, but to a theoretical concentration on a critique of completeness, displacing distance and displacement with flow and movement in a deferral, a noncapitulation to form, that invokes Derridean (as an art of signs)—or, even more centrally, with Deleuzean (as an art of the body)—alterity and thus, according to Gilbert-Rolfe, shares irreconcilable similarities with representative art. At the very limits of theory, in the nonrepresentational, "we meet with what we most desire," but discover that within the perimeters of theory we cannot name it except to demonstrate its rupture of its own tradition in being itself, not a relationality to something else, even though it continues to demonstrate the theory of representation.

Cynthia Pon, in "The Impossible Limit," reflects Gilbert-Rolfe's concerns with subject-identity and with sense—(un)certainty. Pon's central question has to do with what limit these decentering activities produce, and with what lies beyond the so-called postmodern limits of the subject. Working through a Li-Po poem, Pon explores the notion of subjectivity, figuration, and the body, pointing out that figuration is itself a limit, since a representation can never be what is represented, and the condition of representation is "disjunction" at many levels: the limits of figuration lead to the solitude of corporeality and the non-coincidence of figures, signs, and the signified. While we think of figures as discrete entities, this very thought must be omitted to establish identity and relationality; thinking of the other confirms habitation of the self.

Pon explores the Hegelian view of object-knowledge as "indifference" to being known, but shows how in this juxtaposition certainty and meaning are placed in opposition, the object now being the *in*essential element, knowledge being the essential. But this gives rise to the semantic problem of absolutes: what is spoken is no longer "true," and any "this is" involves the negation of a "this is" that becomes a "this is not." Language is truthful, therefore, insofar as it deconstructs and disfigures its own meaning. Pon points to Andrej Warminski's interpretation of Hegel in this regard, showing that Hegel must provide a fixed point from which any statement is correct, but that this point posits both an aporia and an unknowing, an "infinite sublation" of and in language. This aporia is a representation of limit that cannot be known and cannot be truth. Figuration and the dialectical indirection of language are at the center of this sublation; in the fact that figuration consists simultaneously of both entrapment and pleasure in plenitude exists the possibility of a "transmodernism" where limits are replaced by "the constant shifting of paradigms and figures" and where alterity is embedded in language and theory themselves. Like Daoism, this transmodernism does away with rational limits and concentrates on the indirection ("disfiguration") of language.

From a variety of perspectives, then, these essays look closely at the relationship of figuration to change, of paradigm shifts to the limits of representation, of stasis to alterity. Further, for all of these writers, alterity as a force is necessary for theory, an anti-(de)nominational strategy of re-openings of the theoretical discourse by which we examine and live within signs of change.

17

The Intoxication of the Avant-Garde in Benjamin and Habermas

Soraya Tlatli

In his *Philosophical Discourse of Modernity*,[1] Habermas defines Bataille's thinking with a formula that Benjamin had previously applied to surrealism: "What Benjamin affirms of the enterprise of surrealism as a whole—that it wanted to 'win over the energies of intoxication for the revolution'—Bataille also has in mind, it is the dream of an aestheticized, poetic politics, purified of all its moral elements."[2] It is important to note here the way in which Habermas adopts Benjamin's formula for his own purposes. The goal that Benjamin attributes to surrealism—'to win over the forces of intoxication for the revolution'—becomes the leading edge of Habermas's criticism of Bataille, who is found guilty of confusing the poetic and the political spheres. For Habermas, this fusion of poetics and politics comes to define the artistic and theoretical avant-garde. By analyzing the connotations of intoxication for Habermas and Benjamin, I will attempt to define two antagonistic approaches to art and, in particular, to the phenomenon of the avant-garde.

The notion of intoxication refers to a specific philosophical and mythological tradition that Habermas sets out to challenge. Intoxication is embodied in the figure of Dionysus, the god of mobility of frenzy and madness, the god who "offers radical redemption from the curse of identity, who rescinds the principle of individuation."[3] Behind the figure of Dionysus can be glimpsed the philosophy of Nietzsche, who praised this god highly. Dionysus is in fact the very emblem of the radical Nietzschean critique of modern reason's claims to autonomy.

Habermas defines modern reason according to the Kantian model, based on a distinction between the different rational legislations of theoretical reason, practical reason, and value judgment. Thus is maintained the autonomy of each judgment relative to the rational knowledge of natural phenomena, to practical decisions, and to aesthetic judgments, or judgments of taste. Each distinct sphere of activity follows the rules of validity and criteria proper to it, so that "questions of truth, of justice, and of taste (are) autonomously elaborated, that is under its own specific aspect of validity." [4] By separating the different types of judgment, Kant grounds the critical powers of reason, henceforth deemed capable of evaluating, independently and flexibly, matters of theory, of ethics, or of the beautiful. With Kant, Habermas writes that "critical reason . . . takes over the role of a supreme judge . . . in relation to culture." [5]

Just as Kantian philosophy expresses for Habermas "the modern world in an edifice of thoughts,"[6] Nietzschean philosophy contains the guiding principles of what Habermas designates the avant-garde. The concept of modern reason, defined as reason based on itself, reason that is its own justification, finds its most vehement adversary in Nietzsche. His thought challenges the autonomy of all judgment, theoretical, practical, and aesthetic. Two points will serve to sum up Nietzsche's criticism of modern reason.

First, aesthetics breaks out of its own sphere and trespasses on that of ethics. Ethical judgment is negated by aesthetics, which becomes the absolute criterion of judgment. In Nietzsche's words, "Every evil the sight of which edifies a god is justified." [7] This principle is at the origin of what Habermas calls "the aesthetics of terror," [8] an aesthetics that claims to dominate every form of action and strip it of its moral weight. The artistic avant-garde of the early twentieth century, and particularly surrealism, may be defined in terms of this Nietzschean aesthetic imperative, according to Habermas.

Second, Nietzschean philosophy calls subjectivity and the principle of individuation into question. The aesthetic experiences of the avant-garde—in Habermas' words, "dreams, fantasies, madness, orgiastic excitement, ecstasy"[9]—are similarly reduced to their philosophical principle, the Nietzschean experience of the Dionysian.

"The experience of contemporary art," affirms Habermas, "is an ingredient in the description of the Dionysian—as a heightening of the subjective to the point of self-oblivion."[10] It is undeniable that Nietzsche's philosophy fed on the artistic experience of his day, especially that of Wagner. But Habermas's reversal is less obvious. On the field of Nietzschean philosophy, he marshals and combines the most varied artistic and intellectual movements. This heterogeneous assortment includes not only the aesthetic avant-garde from Baudelaire to surrealism, but, among other thinkers, Bataille, Foucault, Lacan, and Derrida. The divergent tendencies of these individuals and movements are subsumed under the negative concept "the other of reason."[11] A central thesis of the *Philosophical Discourse of Modernity* is the following: "The aesthetic domain, as the gateway to the Dionysian, is hypostatized into the other of reason."[12] Through the avant-garde aesthetic experiences, "subject-centered reason is confronted with reason's absolute other."[13]

The shadow of Dionysus thus defines the intellectual and artistic avant-garde by explaining its singular intoxication: the abandonment of the principle of identity, the ecstatic rejection of modernity's autonomous reason.

The concept under which Habermas subsumes the avant-garde movements, which is the negation of autonomous reason, operates in his work as a primary cause, to such an extent that the reader may have the odd impression that the ultimate goal of the surrealists, as well as of Foucault, Lacan, and Derrida, was to challenge the Kantian distinction between different modes of rational legislation. In other words, when Habermas analyzes the concept of the avant-garde, he remains inside the frame of subjective judgment. It is precisely this notion of aesthetic judgment in its subjective dimension that Benjamin puts into question.

From his earliest writings, Benjamin sets himself apart from Kantian judgment, or more precisely from reflective judgment. In his dissertation, *Der Begriff der Kunstkritik in der deutschen Romantik*, Benjamin opposes Romantic criticism with Kantian reflective judgment in these terms:

> The difference between the (Kantian) concept of aesthetic judgment and the romantic reflexion is . . . easy to establish. Unlike the aesthetic judgment, romantic reflection does not proceed from a subjective reflective attitude; it is rather contained in the very form of the work and unfolds itself in criticism. . . .[14]

In contrast to reflective judgment, which is here defined solely in relation to the judging subject, art criticism is included in the form of presentation of the work itself. Art criticism, adds Benjamin, "does not take place with respect to a product, but on the contrary, within the deployment of reflection, that is, according to the deployment of reflection in a product."[15] The willingness of Romantic criticism to take into account the work in its empirical materiality is likewise the principle of the Benjaminian approach to art. In his essay on Goethe's *Elective Affinities* he develops the idea that the work contains the key to its own elucidation and borrows from the structure of the novel itself the principles of its criticism.[16]

Immanent in the noticeable distinctness of each work, art criticism must establish the relationship between the truth of the aesthetic object and history: such is the specific mode of creation that defines art criticism for Benjamin. From his earliest writings, in "Ueber das Programm der kommenden Philosophie", (1918) Benjamin makes clear his intention to correct the ahistoricity of the Kantian judging subject by developing "a philosophy truly conscious of time and history."[17] It is incumbent on art criticism to demonstrate the link between a timeless truth and the medium of history. For Benjamin, the writing of history takes place in artistic productions. This approach to art, in opposition to the subjectivity and atemporality of Kantian judgment, is crystallized most particularly in two artistic productions: baroque allegory and the surrealist image.

In his study of German *Trauerspiel*, Benjamin shows that baroque artistic productions and history reflect each other in the figure of ruin. However, his conception of history is neither theoretical nor even aesthetic, but poetic. For it is through a particular form of writing, the allegory, that Benjamin presents his own conception of history as a progress toward decline. An artistic work is no longer uniquely the reflection of its time, but expresses and reveals the movement of history. Unfinished, fragmentary, an embodiment of ruin, baroque allegory is the expression of a temporality in which history and death form a single constellation:

> In allegory the observer is confronted with the *facies hippocratica* of history as a petrified, primordial landscape. Everything about history that, from the very beginning, has been untimely, sorrowful, unsuccessful, is expressed in a face or rather in a death's head. . . . This is the heart of the allegorical way of seeing, of the baroque, secular explanation of history as the Passions of the world; its importance resides only in the stations of its decline.[18]

Benjamin expounds in this passage his vision of profane history as an endless suffering, in the double meaning of endless as without goal and without cease. He demonstrates in this way his violent opposition to the teleological conception of history as progress.[19] What is significant here, however, is that Benjamin's reading of history is based entirely on an artistic presentation and a poetic interpretation. "Allegory", he insists, "is not a playful illustrative technique, but a form of expression, just as speech is expression, and, indeed, just as writing is."[20] In other words, allegory is a necessary expression, not an artifice. And it is precisely to the extent that allegory is a mode of expression and not a ludic technique that it takes on, for Benjamin, an objective power.

It is indeed, through two different language forms—symbol and allegory—that two divergent notions of history are presented. "In the symbol," observes Benjamin, "destruction is idealized, and the transfigured face of nature is fleetingly revealed in the light of redemption."[21] The symbol derives from history conceived in its theosophic dimension, as a movement toward redemption. Benjamin's contrast between two modes of artistic production does not merely illustrate two opposing views of history; rather, these modes can be revealed only in the poetic dimension.

The critical method that is tested in the work on German *Trauerspiel* consists, then, of using a form of language as an instrument of historical analysis. Allegory is, of course, determined by its inscription in a precise historical moment, but in a more essential way it brings to its figurability a conception of history.

By the time of Benjamin's 1929 article on surrealism, his ideas had evolved. The relation with the historical past was no longer as important to him as the attempt to determine the link between the recent past—the nineteenth century—and a present dominated by the rise of fascism and communism. Henceforth it is crucial to evoke, from a historical grasp of the past, a form of awakening and criticism with respect to the present.

Benjamin's interest in surrealism is linked to this goal, for this movement in his view is situated at the border between the recent past and the immediate present. It is a snapshot of the present time, but it is not yet disengaged from the nineteenth century.

Surrealism aspires to break down the separation of the poetic and political spheres. In his article "Bewusstmachende oder rettende Kritik—Die Aktualitaet Walter Benjamins," Habermas notes that this artistic movement "could have appeared to Benjamin as a confirmation of his own theory of art."[22] But he immediately adds: "The idea of a radical politicization of art . . . has no systematic relation to his own theories of art and history." Benjamin, he concludes, "refuses to identify politics and intoxication".[23] I propose to demonstrate, on the contrary, that Benjamin's article on surrealism is at the core of his theory of art and of language.

To take the surrealist movement "for the 'artistic', 'poetic' one it superficially appears," affirms Benjamin, would be "inexcusable."[24] Conversely, surrealism allows us to avoid the inevitable misunderstanding of *l'art pour l'art*, an expression that designates both certain artistic currents that, like symbolism, demand a pure art, and a philosophical conception of the absolute autonomy of an art limited to the sphere of beautiful appearance. Indeed, it is by virtue of the surrealists' politicization of art that Benjamin finds praiseworthy "these adoptive children of the revolution."[25] But the nature of this politicization has been the object of numerous misunderstandings.

Habermas dismisses any link between Benjamin and surrealism by reason of the fusion between poetics and politics. In his *Studien zur Philosophie Walter Benjamins*, Tiedemann likewise vigorously attacks Benjamin's surrealist sympathies, in which Tiedemann detects "confusion between ethical reflection and aesthetic reflection,"[26] to which term, he does not hesitate to write, "Benjamin sacrifices the stakes of his philosophy."[27] The fact is that at no time does Benjamin espouse the political objectives of surrealism. What apparently fascinates him is, rather, the critical potential liberated by the surrealist use of language; nevertheless, he addresses his reader thus:

> To win the energies of intoxication 1for the revolution—in other words, poetic politics? We have tried that beverage. Anything rather than that! Well, it will interest you all the more how much an excursion into poetry clarifies things.[28]

To politicize art is merely to make possible another way of using language. It is not a question of "making the artist of bourgeois origin into a master of proletarian art,"[29] but of opening up, "in political action a sphere reserved one hundred percent for images.[30] This space of images is, in the case of surrealism, the product of a particular mode of enunciation. The surrealists privileged unconscious enunciation, automatic writing, spoonerisms, collective games such as Exquisite Corpse, in which the univocal meaning of language gives way to a plurality of possible meanings. In this new mode of enunciation language is no longer the product of deliberate meaning. The Surrealist experience of language liberates the creative power of language by reducing the role of the writer's subjectivity to an absolute minimum. Benjamin describes the experience this way:

> Language takes precedence. Not only before meaning. Also before the self. In the world's structure dream loosens individuality like a hollow tooth. This loosening of the self by intoxication is, at the same time, precisely the fruitful, living experience that allowed these people to step outside the domain of intoxication.[31]

This mode of enunciation is perfectly in harmony with Benjaminian criticism of instrumental language considered as a simple means of communication.[32] Contrary to Habermas's rationalist interpretation, intoxication for Benjamin does not mean the experience of a decentered subjectivity, an irrational cult of "the other of reason." It signifies a particular mode of creation that liberates potentialities inherent in language that is detached from any instrumental end, that is no longer the product of mastery.

A language free of the necessity of meaning drags men away from the rapture of intoxication to the extent that the involuntary production of images and figures of speech underlines the falseness of political set speeches filled to bursting with metaphors. Benjamin proposes to extend to the political plane the stylistic distinction between metaphor and image. "Nowhere do these two—metaphors and images—collide so drastically and irreconcilably as in politics,"[33] he states. Political metaphors are dominated by connotations of morality, stamped with a deceitful optimism; in Benjamin's words, they are like "a bad poem on springtime,"[34] in which all children are angelic and freedom is always on its way. The surrealist use of language, the production of spontaneous, immediate, unconstrained images, points up the falseness of political language of every stripe.

Benjamin sees, then, in involuntary surrealist poetry, a confirmation of his conception of art: through the forms of language in which artistic creation is expressed, the critical orientation of art with respect to historical and political reality is most clearly revealed.

This willingness to take account of the historical and linguistic dimension is precisely the blind spot of Habermas's analysis of the artistic avant-garde. Here it seems that the use of Kantian critical philosophy is inappropriate. In fact, it is the possibility of a return to a mode of autonomous judgment that determines Habermas's diatribe against the avant-garde; but this rationalist perspective lessens the impact of his argument. The point of view of Kantian transcendentalism claims to be able to account for the meaning of art and of avant-garde artistic production. But the Kantian distinction between the different types of judgment is logically necessary; it applies to any reasonable being who must recognize the autonomy of the three spheres of legislation, as well as their respective criteria of validity. The separation that Habermas tries to maintain among these spheres of activity—theoretical, practical, and aesthetic—rests on an *a priori* organization of rationality and applies to the Kantian subject, an ahistorical subject seeking a transcendental and universal organization of knowledge.

As we have seen, the Benjaminian conception of art criticism challenges this mode of judgment. The subtitle of his article on surrealism is: "The latest (*Letzte*) Snapshot of the European Intelligentsia." In a later essay on Baudelaire, Benjamin defines the snapping of the photographer this way:

> Of the countless movements of switching, inserting, pressing and the like, the snapping of the photographer has had the greatest consequences. A touch of the finger now sufficed to fix an event for an unlimited period of time. The camera gave the moment a posthumous shock, as it were.[35]

This conjunction of a brief instant in an unlimited historical time likewise defines Benjamin's aesthetic method, which grasps in poetic productions both perishable, such as allegory, and immediate, such as the surrealist image, the historical face of an epoch in a sort of "posthumous shock."

18

Foucault, Conventions, and New Historicism

David F. Bell

I shall begin with an anecdote concerning an incident that recently led me to a series of theoretical reflections on a topic I had always considered in a more or less imprecise manner, namely the notion of poaching. Not long ago I had the chance to observe an acquaintance's English mastiff. It was a rather impressive dog, as anyone who has seen a mastiff—especially for the first time—can doubtless attest. The mastiff is one of the largest dogs, and its sheer size and power can be quite overwhelming. As could be expected, I immediately inquired about its breeding origin, and my acquaintance obliged with some fascinating information. It was bred for a specific purpose: to control poachers on the property of English landowners. Consequently, traits that allowed training for a very specific type of behavior were highly prized. Those traits are quite undoglike, really. When it sees something of interest, instead of darting off to explore or chase the thing as the typical dog would do, the mastiff stops, sits, observes, and simply refuses to budge. A moment's reflection reveals this to be very useful conduct when the object is to control poachers, for the idea is most certainly not to alert them by sending a dog barking and chasing after them, thus driving them off the property to safety. On the contrary, it is much more useful and effective to immobilize them, so that they may subsequently be caught on the property, *en flagrant délit*. Detecting the presence of a poacher (defined simply as any strange person on the dog's property), a mastiff trained in the proper manner would stop moving about and remain still. When the poacher drew nearby, the mastiff would jump out, bring him or her to the ground (mastiffs weigh 150 pounds, generally), hold the victim down with a flat snout pressed against the chest (the snout was also a breeding trait specifically created for that purpose), and wait until the master arrived. Only then would the poacher be allowed to stand up, caught on the property with no means of denying his or her presence there.

I begin with these anecdotal remarks, because I would like to talk about poaching in the pages that follow, and the images conjured up by these brief observations on the breeding origin of the mastiff are significant, I think. Poaching is a dangerous, risky business that involves, in the first place, territories. Poachers make their living by venturing into terrains that do not belong to them and that have been laid out in a gridlike structure controlled by the gaze of a master, represented here by a delegate, the mastiff. Masters and owners can afford the luxury of waiting ponderously to see what may happen, because within their domains, organizations have been devised to eliminate adventure, that is, to exclude anything unexpected. Such organizations allow unforeseen events, should they occur, to be immediately discernable. The strength of the owner's strategic position is such that most of the time it will immobilize the interloper, freezing him or her in a gaze of recognition. Only the swiftest, nimblest poachers can cross into the forbidden space and make it back out without succumbing to what might seem at first to be an overwhelming force. The owner waits; poachers must venture out, move, feint, parry, thrust. They do not have the luxury of massing forces and applying them unilaterally and definitively. They can only look for an opening, dart forth quickly, and retreat before encountering the opposing force directly.

The notion of poaching is one that Michel de Certeau used when analyzing Michel Foucault's achievements in *Surveiller et punir*.[1] The following admiring and yet somewhat ironic characterization of Foucault's research "methods" mobilizes the notion at stake: "This kind of 'art' is easy to see at work. It is an art of telling: suspense, extraordinary quotations, ellipses of quantitative series, metonymical samples. . . . It also is an art of seizing the opportunity and of making a hit. . . . His reading is a poaching. Hunting through the forests of history and through our present plains, Foucault traps strange things which he discovers in a past literature. . . ."[2] De Certeau's point is that Foucault does something that is no longer recognizable as traditional history in *Surveiller et punir*. In a playful, almost ironic manner, he engages in an activity that seems to have the trappings of historical research, but which turns the archive to another use. Foucault raids the archive, but he is not interested in the patient, ponderous treatment of archival materials that is characteristic of a certain type of historical analysis since the Annales movement. In other words, Foucault wants to steal from the archive without being immobilized by a kind of classificatory activity requiring an investment that would transform him into a prisoner of the archive, into just another defender among many others of a marked-out, well-delineated territory. He does not want to become hostage to a kind of historical writing that he mimics in the beginning of *Surveiller et punir* only to refuse it and to escape from it with his treasures in a flight to avoid capture.

I am most certainly not arguing that Foucault is careless or inattentive in his use of archives. His voracious reading habits and tireless research are legendary. Moreover, he pays conscious homage to the Annales method in the incipit of *Surveiller et punir*, beginning his study of disciplinary structures in the eighteenth and nineteenth centuries by instituting what I would like to call an "archive effect." The plates that inaugurate the text in the French edition are characteristic of the tactic employed. Pretextual, figural, those plates are calculated to expose the reader to the archive even before the writing begins. The archive is there to be seen and flaunted, to serve as guarantor of the serious historical nature of the argument to follow.[3] And this "archive effect" is carried over into the first pages of the text of *Surveiller et punir*, almost entirely devoted to lengthy quotations taken from two different documents that become monuments to the two extremes of a supposedly historical development, which will be the subject of the book: the descriptions of Damien's torture, on the one hand, and the schedule of a Parisian reformatory for minors, on the other. Not only is the archive brought into the pages of the book to be seen through photographic plates, its very text is reproduced verbatim. But this homage to the archive is also a ruse, a feint, an expedition into archival territory to plunder in the hope of avoiding capture by placating authorities that are its would-be protectors.

Foucault is clearly playing with the archive in at least two different ways. First, although it is necessary to make decisions about what constitutes the archival source for the project of writing *Surveiller et punir*, it turns out to be difficult, if not impossible, to justify precisely or completely any such choices. Thus the corpus upon which Foucault bases his study must always stand outside—or at least on the fringes of—thorough methodological rationalization. When the question of his source material is posed in the interview translated into English under the title "Prison Talk," he responds as follows:

> Establishing a corpus of source data does indeed pose a problem for my research, but this is undoubtedly a different problem from the one encountered in linguistics, for example. With linguistic or mythological investigations it is first necessary to take a certain corpus, define it and establish its criteria of constitution. In the much more fluid area that I am studying, the corpus is in a sense undefined: it will never be possible to constitute the ensemble of discourses on madness as a unity, even by restricting oneself to a given country or period. With . . . prisons there would be no sense in

> limiting oneself to discourses *about* prisons; just as important are the discourses which arise within the prison, the decisions and regulations which are among its constitutive elements. . . .[4]

The parallel with structuralist methodologies so important for Foucault's intellectual formation is made explicit here. One must recall that Saussure's inaugural gesture in attempting to create a structural linguistics was to delineate what could be considered the domain of linguistic analysis and to reject as external to linguistics certain phenomena connected with language usage. "What is the integral and concrete object of linguistics?" asks Saussure at the beginning of the *Cours de linguistique générale*. "Other sciences operate on objects that are already given and that can then be considered from different points of view. Our domain is nothing like this."[5] Saussure then defines the domain that will be the object of his considerations. The allusion to mythological investigations sends the reader directly to Lévi-Strauss, who faced a problem similar to Saussure's. One need only take as an example the famous article entitled "The Structural Study of Myth" to see that one of Lévi-Strauss's fundamental issues in developing his approach to mythology is to define his corpus.[6] The following is a revealing remark that demonstrates what assumptions concerning the idea of a corpus are at work as Lévi-Strauss formulates his argument: "Our method thus eliminates a problem which has, so far, been one of the main obstacles to the progress of mythological studies, namely, the quest for the *true* version, or the *earlier* one. On the contrary, we define the myth as consisting of all its versions; or to put it otherwise, a myth remains the same as long as it is felt as such" (216–17). Defining an object of study is reduced to a gathering operation here with no inkling that this activity may, in fact, become endless because it may ultimately be boundless. Lévi-Strauss seems to think in this passage that a consensus on what might constitute versions of the same myth will be fairly straightforwardly obtained.

For Foucault's project on disciplinary technologies, such an inaugural gesture is apparently much more difficult, if not simply impossible. Foucault insists instead on the notion of fluidity. The archive for the prison book is undefined; its borders poorly marked. No territory can be ultimately delineated and become the exclusive property of the researcher working on these questions. The types of territories being studied here cannot be staked out with some definitive version of a permanent explanatory grid. Like a poacher, the researcher must meander among archives he cannot possess or master totally, where he plunders only to move on in a manner that is uncharted and destined to remain so. Foucault most certainly overestimates the possibility for a researcher in linguistics or mythology to constitute a corpus in a precise, if not to say scientific, manner. Linguistics itself in the post-structuralist age has discovered how important certain elements rejected by earlier linguistic methodologies can be for understanding language—enunciative contexts, for example. And as for the ethnological treatment of myth, the gathering of versions of myths eventually took Lévi-Strauss on a meandering path of increasing complexity that exposed him to all the theoretical aporias of ethnological thought. But Foucault exaggerates the parallel drawn with linguistics and mythology studies in order to set off and emphasize the tactical necessities, the uncharted practices he pursues in his own work. Now, I do not mean to suggest that historians, from whom Foucault also wants to separate himself, do not recognize the impossibility of completeness and preciseness when it comes to archives. I would submit, however, that they do not revel in this impreciseness, in the tactical maneuvers required by the undulating, ever-changing nature of the sources they must use. They are much more inclined to hide such ad hoc decisions, to present them as empirical necessities, and to pursue as an ideal some moment of stasis when things stop moving, frozen by the historian's gaze. Foucault, on the other hand, elevates such tactics, imposed by the things he wishes to study, to the level of something like an art form.

The second way in which Foucault plays with the archive is in the very methodology he applies once he fastens onto archival materials in search of discoveries. Let me quote one characteristic passage from the "Prison Talk" interview mentioned above to illustrate what I mean. When asked about how he discovered the text used for the dossier he published on Pierre Rivière, Foucault answers in a very interesting way.[7] The form of the question is itself extremely suggestive. The interviewer asks: "First of all, how did you come upon this astonishing text?"[8] One cannot help but call attention to the expression "come upon," denoting the surprise of a fortuitous encounter, the act of tripping over something that just happens to be in one's path. In addition, the adjective "astonishing" reinforces the impression of surprise and of the find, the hit. Foucault answers: "By chance, while systematically working through penal reports by medico-legal and psychiatric experts published in professional journals of the nineteenth and twentieth centuries" (*Power/Knowledge*, 48). The juxtapositioning of chance and systematicity here is extraordinarily evocative, it seems to me, and is a theoretical blind spot for Foucault at the moment he utters this comment. For, I would claim, the two notions of chance and systematicity are radically different, and the very presence of chance in the process of archival work is precisely what drives the Foucaldian project forward. It is not the systematic laying out of the archival material that resulted in the Pierre Rivière book, but, rather, the surprise of the find that was elevated to the status of representative moment. The importance of chance is revealed in Foucault's remark, only to be instantly covered over by a comment diverting attention toward a supposed systematicity of the research that went into the project. This kind of situation is regularly visible in Foucault's work of the period and is perfectly reminiscent of what takes place in the opening pages of *Surveiller et punir*, where the Damien document, for instance, is elevated theatrically (it is an extraordinarily theatrical document in itself) to the level of a paradigm that speaks for itself.[9]

It may seem that I have said little about convention up to this point, but the contrary is the case. What Foucault is doing in *Surveiller et punir* might well be described as an attempt to transform a convention by developing a different practice. The grounding in and systematic use of the archive characteristic of the Annales school was a convention faced by Foucault in very much the sense of the notion of convention developed by David K. Lewis. Lewis's analysis describes convention as a coordination equilibrium problem producing regularity in the behavior of members of a population when they are agents in a recurrent situation.[10] What Lewis means, simply put, is that in any given instance of a recurrent situation, everyone conforms to a certain regularity, everyone expects everyone else to conform to it, and everyone prefers to conform to it on the condition that others do so. Conventions rely on notions of expected behavior and on the idea that it is more comfortable to conform to such behavior in decision-making situations. Otherwise situations requiring decisions would become inordinately complex and lead to aleatory and therefore unsatisfactory solutions. What I am claiming is that Foucault did not use the archive in *Surveiller et punir* in the regular and expected way, but he was clearly aware of that expected usage, clearly in touch with a set of conventions that had grown up in French historical analysis over the period of the preceding decades. He was manifestly not only navigating within a region where he could expect his audience to be aware of a certain anticipated behavior, but where he could also depend on that awareness to manipulate the expectations of his readers and surprise them without creating methodological chaos.

This in itself would not be a particularly interesting observation. What makes it more intriguing is that while Foucault is attempting to change the analytic conventions of historians by developing a practice that is unconventional, or not yet conventional, the very object of his analysis is itself a series of practices that are displacing conventions, namely, the techniques of power that undercut the public discourse on penality that was supposed to found penal doctrine from the end of the Enlightenment into the nineteenth century. One could claim, I think, that Foucault is groping for a new practice of writing history in order to convey, precisely, the essence of a historical moment when a certain type of practice was itself undermining a set of existing conventions concerning penality. What if, in other words, the techniques, practices, technologies that Foucault presents as the *object* of his theory were instead the very techniques that go into building that theory, that is, were its guiding *subject*? As de Certeau remarks with great insight, "The question no longer concerns the procedures organizing social surveillance and discipline, but the procedures producing Foucault's text itself. In fact, the micro-techniques provide not only the content of the discourse but also the process of its construction."[11] The operations of the techniques/practices that Foucault "discovers" in the material he is studying are, in fact, comparable to the very techniques/practices that he mobilizes as tools for his own research and his own attempts to found a discursive practice that skirts the mastery of established conventions.

This raises some questions about Foucault's procedures that I shall not have the space to address in detail here, but that I would at least like to mention. In particular, one must call attention to the insistence in *Surveiller et punir* on the set of practices Foucault characterizes as "panoptical." Why the privilege granted to the panoptical? It could be argued that the panoptical procedures Foucault claims to unearth figure metaphorically and quite strikingly in the theoretician's, that is, Foucault's, all-seeing gaze. The penetrating look into the archive that results in the find, the hit, is ultimately comparable to the peering eye that imbues penal practice in the early nineteenth century and freezes human action in its sights. The fascination with the panoptical thus exemplifies a drift in Foucault's discursive practice from the position of the poacher back to that of the master. The foray into the archive results in a theory about the transparence and clarity sought by disciplinary techniques at the end of the eighteenth century and the beginning of the nineteenth, and, moreover, this clarity is reproduced in Foucault's own writing. The notion of clarity that these practices promote becomes, as de Certeau has argued, a *rhetoric of clarity* at the level of Foucault's own technique of argument.[12] He attempts to create a kind of narrative that ultimately aims to cover its seams, to present itself as a convincing, seductive story, persuasive because it prevents the reader from grasping the fortuitous manner in which archival finds are elevated to paradigmatic status. Foucault ultimately attempts to erase the marks of the metonymical operation he has undertaken and thereby, I would claim, in the reformulation of this rhetoric of clarity, falls back on that most ancient of French conventions, the one most pervasively imparted to every French school student, namely, the notion of the clarity of French thought and French language, *la clarté française*.

The preceding comments are not meant to disqualify Foucault's enterprise, merely to call attention to some of its underpinnings and, especially, to reveal its negotiations with a certain series of conventions, which form its backdrop. In attempting to give discursive existence to practices that are by nature non-discursive, Foucault has to address, at least implicitly—but I think he does it rather explicitly, too—the discursive conventions within which he writes. His manipulation of the "archive effect" demonstrates that he is aware of the problems he faces, and he sets out to invent a practice to deal with them, a practice that I have called poaching here, but that clearly encounters its limit in the conventional notion of *clarté*. What I would like to suggest in the final part of my argument is that this poaching, problematized by Foucault in extensive meditations in *Surveiller et punir* and in other interviews and publications dating from the same period of his writing, has, in turn, become a convention in its own right in the context of what has been called in recent years the new historicism.

Take Stephen Greenblatt's *Shakespearean Negotiations* as a first example.[13] After a vaguely Foucaldian introduction concerning power structures, the text is composed of a series of chapters all built on the same principle, namely the juxtaposition of certain archival finds with the Shakespearean text. Chapter 1: Thomas Herriot's text on the Virginia colony and Shakespeare's political plays. Chapter 2: an anecdote recounted by Montaigne concerning gender confusion in the late Renaissance and Shakespeare's comedies. Chapter 3: Samuel Harsnett's book on exorcism and Shakespeare's *King Lear*. Chapter 4: texts by Hugh Latimer and William Strachey on anxiety and Shakespeare's *Measure for Measure* and *The Tempest*. The repetitive nature of the technique employed gives it an air of conventional regularity that, in fact, belies its problematic character. But it is not just this repetitiveness that shows us we are dealing with a practice that is, in reality, no longer a practice, but a convention. It is also the lack of transcendental claims for the method. Greenblatt seems content to remain at the level of his textual juxtapositionings without any great desire to mobilize them into a more generalized questioning that might include, for example—even principally—the working through of what is involved in the implicit methods underlying the act of choosing the very archival materials he uses and inserts. What he ultimately does, it seems to me, is to lean on a practice problematized by Foucault as he was inventing it for *Surveiller et punir*, but without taking up in his (that is, in Greenblatt's) own way all the problems of tactics and maneuver within the conventions of history-writing, which were always of implicit and explicit interest for Foucault. In other words, Greenblatt seems to me to be pretending that the juxtapositioning of archival materials that was at the heart of the Foucaldian project at a certain moment needs no further justification, since it is validated simply by Foucault's success and has thus definitively entered into the possibilities of what one might call conventional critical writing. But this always depends, of course, on forgetting that for Foucault, juxtapositioning was a practice, a maneuver, a tactic in search of its own discursive theory.

It would be necessary, of course, to nuance any comparison and to identify differences in approach between Greenblatt and Walter Benn Michaels, another of the forceful proponents of new historicism. At a first level, however, their practices are similar. The book in which Michaels sets forth his own method of cultural interpretation and exhibits the elements of his adherence to Greenblatt's approach is *The Gold Standard and the Logic of Naturalism*.[14] Once again a structure of loosely joined chapters treating a variety of literary texts and cultural questions juxtaposed with little attempt to create any synthetic coherence is apparent. Michaels conducts his own raids on literary and cultural archives in a manner which inevitably recalls Foucault's pioneering work. This tactic, however, raises a series of questions related to those highlighted by Greenblatt's writing on Shakespeare. Brook Thomas formulates those questions suggestively:

> But the very dazzle of Michaels's readings creates problems for his argument as a whole. What is fascinating about them is their ability to bring together details from a variety of seemingly random social practices and to establish connections between them. As such they satisfy modernist aesthetic tastes that value a poet's ability to fuse diverse material. But placed together the essays call attention to a problem raised by Pound's *Cantos*. Relying on the modernist technique of montage, Pound hoped that the bits and pieces he juxtaposed would ultimately cohere. But they did not. Neither do the essays Michaels places next to one another under the same cover.[15]

One inevitably has the impression when reading Michaels that the tactic of juxtaposing is an end in itself, that it has become a substitute for thinking theoretically about the justifications for choices, about the context in which this procedure is devised and the theoretical turn it supposedly represents. The "dazzling" impression created by the readings suggests connections among disparate phenomena, but the ultimate synthesis that the connections imply but never fully state simply does not occur, and one is left again with bits and pieces whose presence together is never fully explained.

Fredric Jameson's recent essay on immanent criticism in the collection entitled *Postmodernism* approaches some of these problems from a different perspective, one that brings out the parallels apparent between new historicist conventional practices and the technique of structural homologies at work in structuralist analysis.[16] Jameson's exemplary new historicist text is Walter Benn Michaels's book. His diagnosis is one to which I would adhere in large part and one formulation of which I would like to quote here:

> This is also an aesthetic (or a writing convention, or mode of *Darstellung*) for which a formal rule emerges governing something like a ban or taboo on theoretical discussion and on the taking of interpretive distance from the material, the drawing up of a provisional balance sheet, the summary of the "points" that have been made. Elegance here consists in constructing bridge passages between the various concrete analyses, transitions or modulations inventive enough to preclude the posing of theoretical or interpretive questions. Immanence, the suppression of distance, must be maintained during these crucial transitional moments in such a way as to keep the mind involved in detail and immediacy. Whence, in the most successful of such artifacts, that sense of breathlessness, of admiration for the brilliance of the performance, but yet bewilderment, at the conclusion of the essay, from which one seems to emerge with empty hands—without ideas and interpretations to carry away with us. (*Postmodernism*, 188)

I would underline the centrality of two notions in this passage. First, that of convention: "an aesthetic (or a writing convention . . .)," says Jameson. The writing convention of new historicism is more than that, as Jameson suggests by equating it with an aesthetics, literally a mode of perception of the world. In other words, the convention itself expresses a fundamental theoretical take on the objects of study on which the so-called method focuses. The method turns out to be an "artifact," the second significant notion, one that seems to summarize the whole of Jameson's hesitations with respect to new historicism. An artifact is an object produced by analysis, that is, one that results from the application of analytic rules that can in some cases be sufficiently faulty to produce a false object. Here the problem seems to be that the rules are enlisted without sufficient reflection about how they function or what they mean. They are themselves artifacts capable only of producing further artifacts. As such they become aberrations destined to be swept aside as inaccurate creations once a more careful theoretical approach is devised, one that would reveal and attempt to account for the unthought practices of the previous analytic process.

What I am arguing, then, is that in the space of hardly more than a decade, a very self-conscious and experimentally savvy attempt made by Michel Foucault to finesse, one might say, the conventions of historical writing in the French mode has turned into a reigning convention in its own right as it has been mobilized by the first "classics" of new historicism. I insist in closing that Foucault's attempt to outmaneuver the conventions was itself problematic, and I trust I have stressed this point sufficiently. Running away from one convention, he runs directly into another one—perhaps the overriding convention of French culture, namely the notion of clarity. And that clarity is meant to be a persuasive, pervasive, and unquestioned effect of his argument. What is missing in new historicism, it seems to me, is a necessary reflection on the act of juxtapositioning that would confront its conventionality and attempt to deal with what its use signifies in the context of its American appropriation. Not that the convention in itself is to be condemned necessarily, but it clearly needs to be theoretically appropriated—or reappropriated. As Jameson has suggested, if we let it stand in the place of theory, then what we are giving up is the possibility of engaging in theory—a situation that, not surprisingly, is precisely the one Walter Benn Michaels has attempted at times to impose.

One might say that the writing of Greenblatt and Michaels is a sort of poaching to the second degree. Not only do they navigate in the archive in a manner that recalls Foucault's poaching, but they construct their arguments in implicit reference to a style employed by Foucault. This confusion of territories is doubtless something Foucault would have appreciated. I close with that suggestion and with a growing sense that the gaze of some mastiff is alighting on me from somewhere in this territory upon which I have trespassed.

19

Irreconcilable Similarities: The Idea of Nonrepresentation

Jeremy Gilbert-Rolfe

Nonrepresentational painting has a peculiar relationship to painting as whole. It is by definition nothing at all if it is not that which painting in general always has been and (for the most part) still is. And yet at the same time its protagonists have often been heard to claim that it is in some sense more essentially painting than is painting of any other sort. So nonrepresentational painting is an entity at once severed by definition from painting as a whole and simultaneously one that is proposed as a return to what painting most fundamentally is—or, as it were, to the fundamentals of painting as such.

The idea of the rupture, and of tradition ruptured as well as the now customary notion of tradition as a tradition of rupturing, is then a component of the idea of nonrepresentation, and I shall try now to say a few words about how this is so, and what implications it may have for any broader discussion of the limits of theory.

Art history, even when it is a history of ruptures, notoriously casts any historical sequence into a mold or mould, a cast and a fungus, of inevitability, so that the line between the dialectical and the evolutionary becomes somehow blurred. I will begin, then, by taking a very good historical argument having to do with the origins of nonrepresentation in representational painting, with a view to seeing what questions about rupture and tradition it might raise, and then turn to the possibility of the idea of nonrepresentation as one which is best seen as another idea in a series of ideas about painting, at the very least an idea that is a starting point for nonrepresentation where it is at the most an elusive possibility, and as such one among many, for a painting that seeks to represent.

Michael Fried, in his very important essay "Three American Painters," published first in 1965, describes the genesis of nonrepresentational—which he calls "nonfigurative"—painting as a sequence that passes from Manet to Synthetic Cubism to Matisse.[1] In doing so he makes a telling point which may have some bearing on the debate about nonrepresentation, in that he says that it is not clear whether one should be talking about Manet's withdrawal from the real or about the real as something that was at that time beginning *itself* to withdraw, from painting and indeed from the other mechanisms of art and culture, hitherto anchored in and dependent on a concept of the real, through which humans sought (and seek) to see the world. Fried's observation, in that it was made almost thirty years ago, seems remarkably prescient with regard to subsequent scholarship and speculation. With this in mind, I should like to address the question of Manet, Synthetic Cubism, and Matisse as forces and moments in the history of painting which in some way may be said to have prepared the ground, made a clearing in the forest, for nonrepresentation.

It makes perfect sense to see Manet's so-called "flattening" of the picture, Synthetic Cubism's assertion of the specific and alienating—in the sense of separating—conventions of pictorial space, and Matisse's extreme identification of figure and ground, as a series of preparations for a painting that would be structured through something other than an imitation of the world as it is, perhaps, known; which is to say, as an arrangement of solids and voids in which the latter signify only the absence of the former. In describing a three-stage history in which the conditions for a kind of painting that will work through (in both senses of the term) an idea of its own spatiality, Fried offers what seems to be an unarguable account.

But if one approaches the problem of representation from a slightly different point of view, and addresses the question of the relationship of the *idea* of representation to that of nonrepresentation, then quite another aspect of the matter becomes apparent: the very tradition that Fried sees as laying the ground for nonrepresentation is also one that seeks to complicate the question of representation itself in a way which would prolong it rather than abolishing it. This would by no means invalidate Fried's argument, but would complicate it in a way, and focus one's attention on nonrepresentation as the product of an act of will rather than any kind of natural consequence.

Manet's flattening of things and, less certainly, of their context may be seen as the adjustment of the painted image to the condition of the sign. The best study of this aspect of Manet's work with which I am familiar is by Penny Florence, who talks about Manet's interest in pictures and words being able to share the same space, the *Symboliste* interest in the poster and the tabloid as models of how thinking works and, as it were, how it looks.

This interest, though, is at least as much a complication of the idea of representation as it is a move away from it. It permits Manet—as it will Matisse—to posit a more fluid relationship between the human and the inanimate than would be possible in more traditional painting. As I have said elsewhere, the barmaid becomes flattened, and as this occurs she is more readily lined up with images associated with her as an object of desire: flowers, bottles, images of intoxication.[2] Specifically, her crotch is lined up with these objects. This is a complication of representation, conceivably a relocation of it, which may well mark the withdrawal of the real, of the real, even, as a withdrawing. But it doesn't imply a withdrawal from reperesentaion. On the contrary, it conceivably takes it further than it had ever been before.

Synthetic Cubism, coming after Impressionism—to which I shall return—after Cézanne, and after Analytic Cubism, undeniably asserts a space for painting that is painting's own space as opposed to the space of the world. As with Manet, I should argue that it is as much about representation as it is about passing beyond the limits of the representable. Analytic Cubism had been a movement in which, among other things, painting explored the possibilities of representation that had fascinated Manet, in Penny Florence's account of him; it had introduced collage, and in doing so had, as Fried observed in a memorable essay on the topic, introduced the idea of real space into a space alienated from the real by its insistence on its own conventionality. With regard to this insistence on its own conventionality, one would note that it took the form of combining in one painting more than one mode of representation: linear perspective on the one hand, Cézanne-like modeling on the other, to name two (and in so doing not to exhaust the list), in addition to collage. This too sounds like a complication of representation itself rather than its elimination.

Fried, in an essay that provides what is to date the best speculative explanation of the Analytic Cubists' preference for oval paintings, explains that their preoccupation with the figure, and with drawing it from more than one point of view, caused their paintings to be arranged around a vertical axis to an extent unprecedented in earlier work, and that this in its turn made it very difficult to deal with the corners of the pictorial rectangle.[3] Better, then, to eliminate them. Such an observation underlines the extent to which Synthetic Cubism was the culmination of a representational—as opposed to a nonrepresentational—endeavor. In Synthetic Cubism, a wish to distill, to concentrate and essentialize, brings painting to a point at which the gap between the image and its referent, on the one hand, and its own physical and conventional attributes, on the other, has been all but closed, although I shall say in a moment that Matisse brings them even closer, but this closure takes place in a way that redirects attention to the idea of the referent—to how it's been abstracted, in fact—rather than performing any kind of obviation of it. Synthetic Cubism is very much a matter of painting's having become a thing, but in a manner that expands or complicates its simultaneous identity as the continuation, through rupture, of painting as a describing device, as the painting *of* things. In Synthetic Cubism, painting is a thing which permits an otherwise inconceivable depiction *of* things.

It is clear that in Matisse representation strives for an even fuller identification of the objectness and conventionality of painting (which includes the conventionality of that objectness) with its subject, or more exactly with the subjectivity that has now become its subject-as-content. Matisse, for example, had his assistant wash his paintings down with turpentine each evening, in an attempt to retain maximum immediacy while still being able to work on them for a long time.

Clement Greenberg was the first to note that Jackson Pollock demolished the division of the pictorial rectangle into solids and voids by using drawing in a way that did not end up describing *forms*. In Matisse one finds representation, thirty years before nonrepresentation, identifying form with the form on which it depends, rendering it ephemeral while identifying it with the very weave of the canvas while at the same time making color—by definition a kind of formlessness—connect the woman in the painting with the objects that surround and support her, all in a context where the barely painted is further supported by a spatiality provided by the unpainted. One may say that in Matisse what is there is almost not there and is supported by that which is not there at all, which certainly sounds like an art from which the real has withdrawn and which has itself withdrawn from the solidity of the real and the tangibly apparent as opposed to the apparitional nature of subjective appearance. But it continues to be an art defined by its capacity to bring the depicted closer to the apparatus of painting without allowing it to disappear into it. It remains, like Manet's, and like Cubism, an art that *re*presents, that exists to reconstitute the world of things and a subjectivity constituted by and through them: in Manet by and through signs; in Cubism by and through essences and aspects; in Matisse by and through the idea of the immediacy of another body. Matisse above all keeps alive the domination of the pictorial space by the figure; its vitality becomes the vitality of canvas and paint—and in this sense his project is the reverse of Manet's. Although one should note, in passing, that in being in this respect the opposite of Manet, Matisse brings painting back to the signifying potential first identified with canvas when the stretcher began to replace panel painting, at which time it was felt that the weave of the canvas suggested a kind of flickering movement more suitable to the depiction of the human figure than was the flawless impassivity of gessoed wood.

Which brings me to the question of nonrepresentation, and in that to the limits of theory. The series of rupture that join Manet to Cubism to Matisse may each anticipate a fundamental departure from the figure, but at no point do they necessitate it. They are ruptures within a preoccupation with the figure and figuration. They rupture theories of representation, of what may be represented. Above all, they are theories of the representation of invisibility, of a subjectivity that believes itself to be produced by the effects resulting from its encounters with things and that, because things are always outsides that hide their interiors, are always effects identified with a world made up of the partially revealed and the immanently essential.

To make the leap to *non*representation would require a rupture within, and also away from, the tradition of painting. A rupture or a breaking away that was not implied by that tradition or that, as the observation regarding the weave of the canvas implies, could only be fully realized at the expense of that tradition—by the painted face of the canvas coming to replace the painted face to whose representation it was originally felt to be so well-suited. At the very least it would require the substitution of a kind of absolute visibility for an interest in making the invisible visible—an aesthetic, or at least a methodology (which would of course be *a*-methodological)—of outsides as opposed to one of outsides that partially reveal eternally hidden interiors. The three American painters about whom Fried wrote in his 1965 essay were Frank Stella, Kenneth Noland, and Jules Olitski, and it is to Olitski's work, a vertical (and to that extent conceivably figural) piece from 1964, that I now turn.

One can only think of Olitski's paintings in terms of surface. And in being a surface that neither veils nor reveals a form—two ways of doing the same thing—it must instead be seen as an interruption, which is placing a limit on a void. Surfaces do that, in or out of painting, when deprived of their capacity to point to what lies beyond them. A commonplace example, on which all painting is totally dependent, is the white wall. A blank white wall, in being white and blank, is far more likely to invoke an infinite spatiality than to cause one to speculate on what lies behind it. Painting has always been a space suspended in a space, which is the wall on which it hangs.

An Olitski, then, is a surface that points not to the solid but to the void even as it is very clearly no more than itself. That is to say, it possesses no ability to reconstitute within itself a memory, a reconstituted presence, of the experience of things, except in the very general sense just mentioned—where the wall is hardly a thing—and in terms of its own thingness, as a thing that to a considerable extent exists only to offer thingness in, as it were, the service of the void. Fried discusses this in terms of an idea of intensiveness that occurs in relation to the extensiveness of the pictorial rectangle.

Nonrepresentational painting changes a great deal from generation to generation, or decade to decade—or moment to moment or epoch to epoch—but the idea of nonrepresentation remains strangely consistent in certain respects.

In order to remain nonrepresentational, such painting is obliged to persist in an exploration of blankness. Its defiguration of painting reorders theories of painting not least by demonstrating the extent to which these were to begin with theories of representation, of the figure and its treatment as the place where meaning was constructed. Nonrepresentation would require a theory that was not reducible to the question of how, which is to say what part of, the figure was represented and thus made to stand for a quality, a thought, or an action, which could not otherwise be represented.

Nonrepresentation calls, as I have suggested elsewhere, for a theory of completeness rather than one of lack. The very fact that the nonrepresentational painting is not representing something means that it cannot be a depiction of a part or an aspect of a prior presence, as representation itself must be. It is difficult, therefore, to see the nonrepresentational work of art as a foregrounding of an aspect of the real, and it is therefore difficult to reduce it to the complementary discourses of history and the psychologistic, which together provide realism itself—which, in the visual arts, we now know as postmodernism—with its critical and ethical base. That would be the point at which the nonrepresentational tests the limits of art theory as we have and know it; it resists reduction to theories of the symptom.

Such a resistance is a resistance to theories of construction, by which I mean theories that want to see in terms of an abstracted space, which nonetheless continues to obey the rules of solid and void, inside and outside. In this sense to propose nonrepresentation as being in some sense irreducible to the great securities of historicism and psychologism is of course to propose for it the properties of the inhuman, and in doing so one necessarily reintroduces into the discussion of the art object from which it has been absent for many years, the idea of the beautiful, and with it that of the sublime.

To paraphrase once more remarks I have made elsewhere, nonrepresentational art reminds one of Santayana's definition—recently revived by Gilberto Perez—of beauty as pleasure considered as the property of an object.[4] And on the question of the inhuman, I have made the point that the human may strive to be beautiful but rarely succeeds, and when it does it has to live as much as an object as a subject. As an object which brings with it the idea of the not-constructed the nonrepresentational work is a work of deferral rather than depiction, and of flow and movement rather than building and balance. The surface of the painting defers to the idea of space, as the wall defers to that idea: because in its blankness it offers itself as a sign of absence (the Manet possibility, perhaps); because its whiteness offers an image of essentialized openness, light entirely uninterrupted by form (the Synthetic Cubist possibility); or because its absoluteness proposes movement of infinite speed and range (the possibility offered by a counter-example derived from Matisse, where the white wall could be seen as a surface without a weave, which in its turn reminds one that what attracted Renaissance painters of the human figure to canvas would probably have turned off their grandfathers, who wanted the infinite clarity of God, and used the smoothness of painted panel to embody it).

An art of deferral rather than depiction, of surfaces that do not give way to form—in practice obviate the search for form—of outsides that do not point to insides, obviously calls forth Derrida. And one would add, in this regard, that the irreconcilable similarities between representation and nonrepresentation are constantly reenacted at the level of nomination by the tendency of nonrepresentational painters to refer to the history of painting in the titles that they give their works, as if invoking an originally deferred possibility in the original work to which theirs has now returned. But the thinker to whom I want to turn here is not Derrida but Deleuze. In *Cinema 1* one finds the following passage, in a section dealing with the use of water in pre-war French movies:

> From this was to emerge an abstract art, in which pure movement was sometimes extracted from deformed objects by progressive abstraction, sometimes from geometrical elements in periodic transformation, a transformative group affecting the whole [*ensemble*] of space.[5]

This sounds quite close to something Fried might have said, and Deleuze ends the paragraph by saying that:

> Water had a vivid presence in American and Soviet cinema, benevolent as well as devastating; but, for better or worse, it was confronted with, and related to, organic ends. It is the French school that emancipates water,

> gives it its own finalities and makes them the form of that which has no organic consistency.[6]

In Deleuze's treatment of water in cinema one finds something like a systematic treatment of the idea of the not-constructed, the flow as an entity. As an art irreducible to the terms of the real, an art of movement and completeness—which is indeed the promise of the first stretched canvas and of the stretched canvas as such—nonrepresentation is an art of the body. But as such it is an alienation of alienation—alienation being a *sine qua non* of realism, its further alienation marking the rupture between nonrepresentation and representation—which strives to be an inorganic deferral between surface and depth, like a body of water, a surface inseparable from its volume, a body without a skeleton or a mind, an unthinking body defined by its motion, without purpose but certainly not without direction, this last a product of several countervailing tendencies, some created by its own friction.

I said earlier that I'd return to Impressionism and here, at the end, is what I have to say about it. Impressionism was a revolutionary moment in painting—the only movement, as Barnett Newman said, in which a group of painters were united solely by a technique—because of its desire to paint the world without drawing it first. To structure it through formlessness, an oxymoron which is as close as one may come to defining the ambition. Perhaps contemporary painting, no longer so close to the real, offers the possibility of thinking through (again, in both senses of the word) formlessness, a formlessness entirely identified with an object, but an object of an entirely specific (and in that sense rather unreal) sort: an object which exists only to support its surface, and where the surface exists only to be looked at. A surface to which poison is meticulously applied in order that the surface might undermine its own objectness, often through intensifying it, in order to defer to that which it is not, a spatiality.

Nonrepresentation ruptures its relationship with its own tradition by being itself, not representing, and in that by becoming irreducible to the historicist and psychologistic theories on which modernism was, to a very large extent by choice, founded. Looking elsewhere than to the limits of those theories, it finds itself at the limits of theory as such, the point at which one may not think about anything without rethinking everything. In a way obviously related to the idea of replacing the world back into the earth, nonrepresentation offers itself as one possibility among others for thinking that will be an elaborate rethinking that is more than just rethinking, and in some sense prior to it—a thinking, one might say, of deferral constantly suspended by its own activity and identity as a contemplative and intransitive as much as a transitive act. It is of course as such, as an affair of surfaces—outsides—that call for no further legitimation for themselves from an invisible interior, that nonrepresentation leads beyond the psychologistic and the historical towards the beautiful, which similarly needs no legitimation, and tends, in the final analysis, to test the limits of all theories. Which may be to say that at the limits of theory we meet what we must desire, which plays with theory and always defeats it simply because theory cannot name it, because it appears as something that was not present before: a non-representation.

20

The Impossible Limit

Cynthia Pon

This essay traces two decentering phenomena that have been associated with postmodernism: the deconstruction of subject-identity and a subjectively based knowledge; and the various engagements with, and movements toward, sense-uncertainty. A question that these decentering activities raise is whether they too entail a limit (for instance, conceptual, tactical, historical or geographical). If so, what might "transmodernism" (etymologically, the prefix suggests *over, across, beyond, through*) have to offer by way of reconstituting or permeating existing paradigms?[1] Methodologically, a reading of three texts chosen across time, space, and philosophical traditions—a T'ang poem, the first section of Hegel's *Phenomenology of Spirit,* and an excerpt from a sixth-century B.C. Daoist text, *Chuang-tzu*—may serve as one means of exploring beyond "postmodernist" limits.

The paper will proceed in the following order. First, I will trace, literally, the movement of the figures/personae in Li-po's poem, "Drinking alone under the Moon." Second, I will follow the movements and turns in Hegel's text on sense-certainty. Third, I will take a look at Chuang-tzu's play with language, which is one form of engaging between the Daoist incommunicable Truth and the limits of representation. I would like to take the movement from subjective figuration to transfigured relationship in Li-po's poem, and use it as an analogy to address the limits of representation as posed in the writings of Hegel and Chuang-tzu. The term *figuration* is used here in two senses: as non-literal representation (the bringing of forms and images before the imagination), and a second sense in which figures as personages or subjects in a discursive context tend to dominate actions and viewpoints. The movements of the three texts will show an unravelling of the link between representation and subjectivity, affecting the grip of knowledge. Finally, the various movements toward transfiguration in the three texts offer us some clues as to what may lie beyond "postmodernist limits."

In the next section of this paper, I am going to give a detailed reading of the poem, occasionally with word-for-word translation to explain the transformation of figures and their relations. Since I am reading the poem in a particular context to illustrate issues about representation and subjectivity, there will be variance from traditional interpretations of the poem.

> Flowers 花 space 間 (among the flowers) one 一 pot 壺
> of wine 酒
> Alone 獨 drinking 酌 no 無 companion 相 親 (ll. 1–2).

The poem makes use of a familiar rhetorical device in Chinese poetry—the elliptical subject. The "I" is implied but not stated except in three lines of the poem. One might speculate, for example, that the "I" is represented metaphorically and metonymically by "one pot of wine," in the space among the flowers. The space is perceived to be empty, non-relational, for "alone drinking" is reinforced by 無 相 親 "no companion" (literally "nothing/without mutual dear"). The lines describe a vast emptiness that has no reciprocity with the subject.

The elliptical subject raises the cup, invites the bright moon to join him (l. 3). The moon is visible as a result of the reflected light of the sun. The visible essence of the moon is therefore a reflection and an illusion. This distance that separates the moon from the subject's imagination and presumed knowledge of the moon—the distance between object and representation—is at the heart of the problem of figuration (which we will turn to in a moment.) If the moon accepted the invitation 邀 (l. 3), it would complete the exchange initiated by the "subject." There is also an attempt to evoke another figure in line 4, this time, the subject's shadow.

> Facing shadow 對 影 that makes 成 three people 三 人

("Facing" implies a *vis-à-vis*, reciprocal position; but the shadow's nonsubstantial status makes the threesome highly impalpable.) So far, the poem observes a sequential order with the multiplication of figures, accompanied by the multiplication of strokes from 一 "one" (pot of wine, one person/subject), to 二 "two" (相 mutual, the moon as the second intersubject), and to 三 "three" (three people, the shadow as the third intersubject), where one/ "I" is by convention the primary figure.

The attempts to set up a trilateral relationship with the moon and the shadow consequent upon the "I" do not materialize. The rhythmic stress in the next two lines lies on the negative word (不 not, 徒 merely).

The moon (As the moon) does *not* know drinking
月 既 不 解 飲
The shadow *merely* follows my body (ll. 5–6)
影 徒 隨 我 身

But for the first time in the poem, the subject "I" (我) is identified. The body of the self is affirmed curiously against the background of negation and disillusionment. The person alone is drinking. The moon is far away. The shadow is contiguous to the body, but it is the quintessential immaterial figure. The first six lines of the poem can again be read in the light of the problem of figuration. The persona (yet another figure in the literary convention) experiences frustration in the attempt to confer substance/identity to a distant or absent figure, and to him-/herself.

The moon cannot be grappled with, or touched, from the earth. One can only point at it. To personify the moon as a drinking companion, to give it a face and senses (literally prosopopeia, and hypotyposis) remains just that—a figure of "speech." It will never approach the kind of intimacy one wants, because the figure does not equal the face, the face value, and the senses (and meanings) that we give it. The figure remains elusive and resists familiarity. The moon as an astronomical body or figure is furthermore tricky because it is not what it seems. The bright, inviting surface that we see from the earth is a result of the sun's reflection. If we come close to the moon, we see it as a pock-marked, nonluminous object. There exists a discrepancy between the figure and the figured, and our "knowledge" of them both. The shadow likewise is a representative figure of the body. The shadow, whenever it occurs, is always joined to the body. It is dependent on the latter for its motions. But it is also unlike the body—a one-dimensional, matted surface that is furthermore subject to distortion. The attempt to invite the moon and the shadow to drink, to transform these figures into companions, is impossible from the perspective of the "I," given the elusive quality of these figures. The transfiguration of subjects will have to wait for a different moment in the poem, perhaps in the half-waking/half-dreaming state where reality and figuration become indistinguishable.

But before we talk about the transfiguration in the poem (with the additional sense of metamorphosis, apotheosis, and Aufhebung, which will be our links to the Hegel and *Chuang-tzu* excerpts later), there is one more figure in the poem that needs addressing. It is the figure of the self or the "I," which gives impulse to the raising and convening of other figures in the first place. The "I" identified as a pronoun or a grammatical shifter is more apparently a figure in the sense that it is an identity appropriated by a thinking and speaking subject. The "I" as figure refers to an anterior, ulterior self. But what is the self made of? Is it made up of substance, and therefore materiality is the final proof of being? Or in a different formulation: instead of speaking of a self that is composed of substance, is the self a figure for the body? In either case, physical, material being would stand as the projected end of representation. And yet the body alone does not guarantee subjectivity that is nonessential, as postmodernism has warned us. We have problems identifying a dead mass or a body living in a vegetal condition as a self, for instance. What we see in this brief rebound of questions, doubts, and suppositions is a series of referential relationships pointing restlessly among "I," self, body, and subject. None seems to be able to claim ultimate priority or status. In other words, the figuration of the "primary subject" remains a source of contention.

Figuration (whether it be in a traditional rhetorical context or in a postmodernist scene) appears to have reached a limit because figures as representations can never be what they represent. Representation exists as mediation. Representations or the figures themselves form the infinite or infinitessimal barrier between sign and the referent. There will always be a difference, a disjunction, which is the condition of representation. But if corporeal substance is taken as the final object (one hears perhaps a note of frustration here), then the problem of figuration seems paradoxically soluble. One can bypass figures and representation altogether by approaching, grasping hold of the body directly (c.f., the people that Gulliver met in his travels, who carry every object and referent on their backs—they carry themselves in this case; also Hegel's Aufzeigung, the abandonment of expression for pointing). But if we are to stay with representation, as indeed the persona in Li-po's poem has to deal with his aloneness—his body in an empty space, and the unresponsive distant figures—then figuration and its limits will have to be seen from a different angle, perhaps one where primarily the subject, self, identity, and corporeality are all seen as means of representation.

From this perspective, the embodied self, the moon and the shadow are all relegated to the same status of representational signs, material and immaterial, with no basis for priority. Li-po's poem seems to provide a reading in this direction, for from the ellipsis of the self to its assertion, *vis-à-vis* the empty figures of the moon and the shadow, there is still no sense of fulfilment. Corporeality (my body 我身) merely accentuates the solitude, the failure of coincidence between one figure and another, and between the sign and the signified. There are the body, the moon and the shadow, but they do not enter into relations, and one is not sure at this point what these representational figures signify. That is to say, the anxiety of representation still haunts the poem up to this part.

The center of the poem marks a turn toward a different understanding of the figural interplay between the self and the others. A different kind of movements and relationships is set up between the "I," the moon and the shadow, together with, or one on top of, one another.

> Momentarily 暫 accompany 伴 moon 月 on 將
> shadow 影
> Seek joy 行 樂 must 須 catch spring 及 春 (ll. 7–8)

The first of these two lines indicates a momentary *concerto* (with the multiple senses of agreement, simultaneity of action, and musical performance) of figures. Assuming the "I" is present, and together with the moon's reflected light, cast a shadow on the ground, then what we catch sight of, momentarily, is a figural composition of contiguity and imposition that is subject to change and motion. There is in fact a great sense of urgency, heightened by the awareness of time ("catch spring"). The figures must act/move 行 to seek joy.

> I 我 sing 歌 the moon 月 wanders 徘徊
> I 我 dance 舞 the shadow 影 in disarray 淩 亂 (ll. 9–10)

The trio are moving together (song and dance are composed of rhythmic waves and patterns), but each according to its own time and beat. The recovery of the "I," far from establishing a privileged figure/selfhood, is crossed by a variant sense of purpose and order (the moon wanders; the shadow is in disarray.) The Chinese syntax is particularly apt in bringing out the non-subordinate triadic relation here, for apart from the linearity (vertical or horizontal) or sequentiality of language, there is no conjunction (and no punctuation in classical Chinese) that would suggest any hierarchical causality or anteriority between the various subjects and their motions. This is different from the start of the poem when the "I" invited the moon (suggesting an active-passive relation) and gave rise to a shadow. The three figures are related by the physics of luminosity, but they are not bound by each other. Moreover, as one of the moving figures in the poem, the "I" no longer affords a stationary or ultimate viewpoint. The "I" is quite possibly drunk, and may be singing and dancing out of tune/out of step.

We have talked about how these figures compose and cross one another in unattached motions. In the last four lines of the poem, the "I," as the subject-pronoun, is once again elided, to be replaced by "together" 同 and "each" 各.

> Sober/awake 醒 時 together 同 exchange 交 joy 歡 (l. 11)

In the introduction of "together," an adverb that is an adjunct case takes the place of a personal pronoun, "I" or "we." At one moment, the three share a common identity ("together") that is not essential, that does not even point to the person as essential. "Together," the adverb, is joined to the verb, which in this case is the motion of exchanging joy. This pattern of relationship is then inverted in the next line:

> Drunk 醉 (after) 後 each 各 separates 分 散

The collective action is replaced by an impersonal pronoun, "each," and an act of dispersion. Awake or asleep, sober or drunk—these are alternate states of consciousness. If the figures come together, they do so on an equal basis; but they are also free to part, because there is *no one binding, dominating, perceiving subject*. The parallel construction of these two lines, which are mirror images of each other, enables them to be viewed as one unit. Taken imagistically, they are the compression of two phases of a ring of alternate states (awake and asleep) and movements (together and separated). The ring is then projected into infinite space and time in the final two lines of the poem.

> Forever unite 永結 in indifferent 無情 movement 遊
> Each other to meet 相 期 far across 邈 the Milky Way 雲 漢

[雲 漢 is a literary expression for the Milky Way; more literally it denotes the cloud of space, and spatial distinction.] Thus the movements of the figures, joining and separate in unattached bonds (an oxymoron), achieve a configural relation that echoes the movements of the galaxy, which is at once a diffused and gathered space in a yet larger diffused and collected space, the universe. The bodies in the galaxy, like the figures in this poem, are held together and apart by the different forces among them. Space is empty and signifying because it denotes the field of forces and the positions of these (heavenly) figures. Meanwhile the whole system of I, moon, shadow, Milky Way, and the Universe forms a pattern in motion. It is the poet's way of understanding the self in relation to other figures, and to be one, and different, with respect to the Cosmos.

Problems raised in Li-po's poem about figuration and subjective representation are not unfamiliar to the West, which also has a long tradition of grappling with language, representation, knowledge, and subjectivity. Indeed, an all-encompassing theory of representation, or the claim that everything is figure, would challenge the possibility of knowledge. Figuration that raises form and shape before our imagination is also an abstraction in the sense that it privileges particular qualities and relationships at the expense of other properties. For instance, when we say "A is B" or "A is like B" (making use of the structures of metaphor and simile, which can "in fact" be extended to many other statements not normally thought of as figurative), we already assume that A is a collectible, identifiable entity; and the same with B. The next step, which is to draw a relation between A and B, be it through metaphorical crossover, transfusion, or similitude, requires further abstraction out of qualities that are believed to make up these separate entities, and then to assimilate or "hook up" these properties. The resultant statements "A is B" or "A is like B" are clean-edged, compact, with everything seemingly tied in.

Yet at every stage much has to be left out to enable the formation of identity and relation—such is the necessity of thinking, speaking, and knowing. We cannot think and speak everything. Every time we think or speak, particular images or mental images come out in relief, while others are suppressed. It is this necessary but equally fictive or unreflective closure that a more conscious reading of figuration erupts and disrupts. The troping and fluidity of figures that lend them to constant multiplication call attention to that which is not (yet) figured, the "unknown."

The relation between representation and knowledge prompts a series of questions—what do we know about representations? Do we know anything besides representations? What do we know? How do we know? What are the basis and proof of our "knowing"? How do we "know" that we "know"? Answers to most of these questions are linked to a privileged (or grudging) I. Let us turn to one of the "founding" moments of epistemology and ontology—the Cartesian cogito ("I think, I am")—and examine its "ego" portion or basis. The cogito is tied to an "I" who, for all we know, may itself be a figure that waits to be disfigured.

The positing of the "I" is the primal act of being, thinking, and speaking, in relation to another. Statements like "I sense," "I know," or "I do not grasp," underscore a priority of subject over object, a distance between this "self" that comprehends and "the material out there." When the "I" thinks or speaks, in the words of Benveniste, "{je} est toujours *transcendant* par rapport à {tu}. Quand je sors de {moi} pour établir une relation vivante avec un être, je rencontre ou je pose nécessairement un {tu}, qui est, hors de moi, la seule {personne} imaginable." (*Problèmes de linguistique générale*, p. 232). The third person does not enter the immediate dialogue, and is put down as {non-personne}. According to Benveniste's analysis, this "I" is interchangeable in a discourse where "you" and "I" take turns in using the subjective pronoun to refer to the self. But strangely, no one really relinquishes the "I" in this context. One merely concedes the other's temporary use of it. One assumes the use of "I" immediately when one starts talking, or thinking. Even with a change in context, and one begins to use "we," the subject "I" still predominates. It is questionable then whether this transcendent "I" really steps out of the self {sors de moi} when thinking the other, or rather this thinking of the other confirms one's habitation of the self—"I am." To call something "I," "my," or "we," and the rest "you" or "the other" carries with it a centering, a privileged identification, of the "self"—"{tu} est nécessairement désigné par {je} et ne peut être pensé hors d'une situation posée à partir de {je}."[2] We assume an anchorage in the "self" that sets out to find out about, to determine, "the other." This is not so much blatant egoism or subjectivism, but a fundamental assumption of any "acquisition" or "definition" of knowledge.

What then is the relationship between knowledge and certainty? Is there a relationship? As a start, does knowledge entail sense-certainty, and vice versa? For an example of a movement toward certainty (and Warminski's essay "Reading For Example" has demonstrated that no example is innocent), let us look at the first section of Hegel's *Phenomenologie des Geistes*, "Die sinnliche Gewissheit; oder das Diese und das Meinen."[3] Hegel takes us through Wissen (knowledge), which is thought to be immediate (*unmittelbar*), but gradually sheds the content of sense-certainty to become a dual motif—*Bewusstsein* (consciousness) as the reines *Ich* (pure I) or reiner *Dieser* (pure this), and *Gegenstand* (object) as reines *Dieses* (pure this). The only truth of sense-certainty is that *"die Sache ist"* (the thing *is*). It has nothing to do with the thing's manifold relations, or qualities to itself or to others, or with the ideas that consciousness has of it. But *as we think* (*"Reflektieren wir" PhG*, 80), this essential reality (Wesen) or simple immediacy (einfache Unmittelbarkeit) turns around and marks a mediate relation—"Ich habe die Gewissheit durch ein anderes, nämlich die Sache; und diese ist ebenso in der Gewissheit durch ein anderes, nämlich durch Ich" [ibid.]. ("I have the certainty through the other, viz. through the actual fact [thing]; and this, again, exists in that certainty through an other, viz. through the I," 150).[4]

But this mediation is true only in terms of sense-cetainty (for the I to sense, to be certain, and the object to exist in sense-certainty), for the object *is*; "er [der Gegenstand] ist gleichgültig dagegen ob er gewusst wird oder nicht; er bleibt, wenn er auch nicht gewusst wird, das Wissen aber ist nicht, wenn nicht der Gegenstand ist" (*PhG*, 81). (The object is "indifferent to whether it is known or not, while the knowledge does not exist if the object is not there," 151).

Hegel's interest still lies within sense-certainty; therefore, the critical objective is not object as it exists independently, indifferently in truth, but whether the object exists in sense-certainty *als solches Wesen* (as such an essential reality) as sense-certainty gives it out to be. Essential reality or being (*Das Wesen des Dieses*) takes two forms—the here and the now. Essential being is indifferent to the actual changes of perspective—place and time (whether a person sees a tree or turns around and sees a house, and whether time changes to night or day). It is indifferent to the specificity against which the This (*Dieses*) is brought to measure. Hegel describes this being or reality as "einfach" (simple)—"und in dieser Einfachheit gleichgültig gegen das, was noch bei ihm herspielt" (*PhG*, 81). (Baillie translates the phrase as "in being this simple fact, it is indifferent to what is still associated with it" p. 152; Warminski in his essay "Reading For Example," makes much out of the word "*beiherspielen*"—*Beispiel*-exemplification, *Spiel*-play, *Byspell*-illegitimate. He translates the phrase as "indifferent to what plays to the side of it." We might even change the verb to *bei ihm herumspielen*, which would posit "This" as a fixed, immune point around which night and day, tree and house, play or shuttle.) Essential reality is simple and indifferent. This "simple" being, Hegel says, we call a universal (*ein Allgemeines*).

This universal (*die Sache ist*/it is), which is the truth of sense-certainty, is indifferent to the individual "I"s, the aggregate perspectives and meaning (*Meinung*). The problem arises when the I expresses the universal—"wir *stellen* uns . . . nicht das Allgemeine Diese . . . *vor*, aber wir *sprechen* das Allgemeine *aus*, oder wir sprechen schlechthin nicht, wie wir es in dieser sinnlichen Gewissheit *meinen*" (*PhG*, p. 82). ("We do not present before our mind in saying so the universal this . . . but we utter what is universal; in other words, we do not actually and absolutely say what in this sense-certainty we really mean" 152). What we mean as immediate, essential being, we end up, through mediation (the changes of perspective) and negation ("indifferent to what plays to the side of it"), expressing as an abstraction, a pure universal.

Sense certainty's truth thus has nothing to do with the I's meaning (*meine Meinung*). The relation between knowledge (*Wissen*) and object (*Gegenstand*) has by now undergone a reversal. The object, which was supposed to be the essential element in sense-certainty (having a concrete, independent existence), is now the unessential element (the universal). Certainty is now claimed by knowledge, the formerly unessential element: "The truth of sense-certainty lies in the object as my object, or in meaning; it is, because I know it. " ("Ihre Wahrheit ist in dem Gegenstände als *meinem* Gegenstände, oder im *Meinen* ; er ist, weil ich von ihm weiss" *PhG*, 83). In the move from "it is"—the universal in sense-certainty, indifferent to I and what I mean—to "it is, because I know it," we see the assertion of the I, which has just now been separated from the truth of sense-certainty. That subordinate clause "because I know it" explains nothing about the truth of sense-certainty. It is rather an imperious, yet feeble, attempt by the I to claim the object as my object, to lay claims to knowledge. The "proof" of the statement lies in a circular way—"I know it is because it is because. . . ." The question about sense-certainty (of a thing) is answered by a tautological glossing of "know" for "certain," ("it *is*, because *I* know it"), a conflation of two crucially different terms.

"Die sinnliche Gewissheit," Hegel follows, "ist also zwar aus dem Gegenstände vertrieben . . . noch nicht aufgehoben, sondern nur in das

Ich zurückgedrängt" (*PhG*, 83). ("Sense-certainty is thus indeed banished from the object, . . . not yet thereby done away with [*aufgehoben* which is also the word for "sublated"]; it is merely forced back into the I," 153). As we can see, the assertion "I know it" is grounded upon an individual consciousness "I," which logically has many counterparts. Hegel proceeds to demonstrate how by means of the same dialectic, the specific I is translated into the universal, indifferent "I." "Ich, dieser einzelne Ich, sage ich überhaupt, alle Ich" (*PhG*, 83). What does the translation into the universal I signify? Will the sublation of the self contribute to the sublation of sense-certainty, which has just been decreed by the "I know it"?

A comparison with the movement of subjects in Li-po's poem may be useful here. The poem begins with the elliptical subject who presumably, like the pot of wine among the flowers, occupies the center of space. He tries to create and address opposite figures, the moon, the shadow (邀 is to invite some one, a body alien to the self; 對 影 "facing shadow" suggests an opposite position.) The subject remains confined to himself, for those are subordinate figures that he raised. True universality is achieved in the poem when, in a transported reality, the I, the moon, and the shadow all become figures in their own right, who then as one, "together" 同 as well as "each" 各, indifferent to distinction and non-distinction, are united in unattached/ indifferent movements 無 情 遊.

The transfiguration in the poem is analogous to Hegel's sublation in "sense-certainty" on one point. Both are movements (Bewegungen) toward non-distinction. "Die reine Unmittelbarkeit geht also das Anderssein des Hier als Baums, welches in ein Hier, das Nichtbaum ist, das Anderssein des Jetzt als Tages, das in ein Jetzt, das Nacht ist, übergeht, oder ein anderes Ich, dem etwas anderes Gegenstand ist, nichts mehr an. Ihre Wahrkeit erhält sich als sich selbst gleichbleibende Beziehung, die zwischen dem Ich und dem Gegenstände keinen Unterschied der Wesentlichkeit und Unwesentlichkeit macht und in die daher auch überhaupt kein Unterschied eindringen kann" (*PhG*, 84). ("This pure immediacy, then, has nothing more to do with the fact of Anderssein (otherness) with Here in the form of a tree passing into a Here that is not a tree, with now in the sense of daytime changing into Now that is nighttime, or with there being an other I to whom something else is object. *Its* truth stands fast as a self-identical relation, *making no distinction of essential and non-essential, between I and object, and into which, therefore, in general, no distinction can find its way*," 155, my emphasis). But the analogy between Hegel's and Li-po's arrival at indifference stops there. Hegel's non-distinction is maintained (*behauptet*) by a "self-identical relation" (*sich selbst gleichbleibende Beziehung*) and by an assertion (*Behauptung*) that "Ich bin reines Anschauen" (*PhG*, p. 84) (which Baillie translates as:

"I am directly conscious, I intuit and nothing more, I am pure intuition; I am—seeing, looking" 155). The I refuses to turn around. It refuses to take notice of other "I"s, or an I at another time, who may see differently. Anschauung is in this case as partial and as imperious as the previous "it is, because *I* know it." Sense-certainty has not been "spirited away" by the universal I. It has to go through its own dialectics of sublation.

Certainty's dialectics has to do with the problem of language—that which is spoken is no longer (true). Sense-certainty, Hegel demonstrates, is a history of its own movement. To say "this is" always already involves the negation of "this is," and the negation of the subsequent "this is not." The third term that is arrived at/ returned to—"this is"—is no longer the immediate "this is" in the first instance; "es ist eben ein in sich Reflektiertes oder Einfaches, welches im Anderssein bleibt, was es ist: ein Jetzt [Hier], welches Absolut viele Jetzt [Hier] ist" (*PhG*, 86) ("it is a something reflected-into-self, a simple entity that remains in its otherness, what it is: a Now [Here] which is an absolute plurality of Nows [Heres]" 157).

Language turns out to be uttering what it does not mean, but Hegel has earlier said of language that it is truthful (*wahrhafterer*, more truthful than presumably imagination, *sich vorstellen*, the presenting before one's eyes), for "in ihr [die Sprache] widerlegen wir selbst unmittelbar unsere Meinung" (*PhG*, 82) ("in it [language] we ourselves refute directly and at once our own 'meaning'"). In contemporary terms, language is truthful because it always deconstructs its own meaning and truth. Such would be the truth that figuration or representation theory is after—that every figure contains its own disfigurement. This is also the way I have been trying to read Hegel's acknowledged movements (toward dialectical sublation) together with the unconscious turns (toward unknowing) in his writing on sense-certainty.

In Hegel, the deconstruction of language is the true condition of sense-certainty's sublation. But does contemporary deconstruction theory allow for this kind of sublation? Warminski offers us an exemplary reading of Hegel that denies such ultimate sublation. In "Reading For Example," Warminski equates the three processes—language, turning, and sublation (*Aufhebung*)—but with one added twist. He observes that the Hegelian Aufhebung of the singular "here" and "now" into the universal "here" and "now" "presupposes a fixed point, a posited literal meaning, against which the turning or troping can be measured" (*Diacritics*, 11, 90–91)—there is a moment at which the statement, for example, "Now is the night," must be right. Accordingly, the Hegelian *Aufhebung* "depends ultimately (undialectically) on the possibility of reading two mutually excluding meanings [because they are measured against the 'literal truth'] at once, simultaneously. . . . In short, to paraphrase too quickly, the only thing that cannot be *aufgehoben* (sublated) is *Aufhebung* (sublation) 'itself.'"[5] Warminski's reading uncovers the similarity and difference between the Hegelian method and contemporary deconstructive readings. Hegel's sublation is deconstructed on the point of the fixed, literal meaning, while rhetorical deconstruction (such as is practised by de Man) renounces the possibility of any fixed, literal meaning. But the result, inferring from Warminski's analysis, would have been the same—for both end in aporia (an unknowing, or the inability to sublate two or more mutually excluding readings). But is this how Hegel understood sublation? Hegel has provided for the relentless *Aufhebung*/turning of language when he cites the problem of *Aussprechen* (expression)—that which is spoken no longer is. Any fixed, literal meaning turns itself immediately upside down as soon as it is posited. And literal truth becomes suspect the moment it is uttered. Sublation of language and of sense-certainty will thus have to be understood as a continuous process, not as some final third term ("It is"—"It is not"—"It is").

But where does this infinite sublation or turning of language lead us? Does the aporia—the multiplication of meanings—pose another kind of limit through which there is no penetration? Are we, so to speak, stuck with signs and representations? Hegel himself tries to flee from the aporia. At the end of the section on sense-certainty, Hegel gives up language (which he says belongs to consciousness, and can never reach *das sinnliche Diese*) for Aufzeigen (to point out). "Ich zeige es auf, als ein *Hier*, das ein Hier anderer Hier, oder an ihm selbst ein einfaches Zusammen vieler Hier, d.h. ein Allgemeines ist; ich nehme so es auf, wie es in Wahrheit ist, und *statt ein Unmittelbares zu wissen, nehme ich wahr*" (*PhG*, 89, my emphasis). ("I point it out as a Here, which is a Here of other Heres, or is in itself simply many Heres together, i.e., is a universal. I take it up then, as in truth it is; and *instead of knowing something immediate*, I 'take' something 'truly', I per-ceive {*wahrnehme*, per-cipio}" 160).

In Hegel's movements of sense-certainty, certainty is finally detached from knowledge. To know or to say the truth of sense-certainty is impossible. The Hegelian solution is for the I to take something as true. I can only assert that I perceive. This is, however, an admission of unknowing, as well as of the possibility of error. "I take as true" ("*nehme ich wahr*") means that there is a great(er) possibility outside the framework of this Nehmung that things are not true. An analogy may be drawn with the stranded pilot in *The Little Prince*, who is asked to draw a sheep. Unable to do so, he draws a box instead, assuring the little prince that the sheep is safely inside the box. This taking things as true or "boxing in" curiously marks the limit of perception and of representation, with the box serving as a representation of limit itself. To continue perceiving or reading, one has to in this case get inside the box, and imagine oneself as perceiving. It is in these various senses above that the aporia (with its potential for infinite sublation) function as a limit, for one does not know, one cannot choose among the final (irreducible) representations, one has to take as (equally) true or possible. The aporia, like the box, is a representation of limit. Following the deconstruction of subject-identities and knowledge (postmodernism's contribution to the liberating project), there is the anxiety, however, that one cannot conceive of any paradigmatic shift—only representations after representations—within the box. Whether it is Hegel's *Aufzeigen* (which follows the series of egocentric assertions—"it is, because I know it," "I intuit," "I take as true") or aporia's paradoxical closing-in, because they ultimately rely on perception (*Wahrnehmung*) and illusory readings (of the sign), they remain captive and captivated, by figuration and representation. The engagement with appearances, changing representations, and destabilization of fixed meaning and identity—strategies of "postmodernism"—seem to prescribe their own boundaries. If so, can we get out of "that box"? Can the movements of *transfiguration* in Li-po's poem offer us any clue to a perspectival or paradigmatic shift?

One of the keys to transfiguration in Li-po's poem is the ring, the notion of a seamless transforming movement that unites opposite states and motions. If inquiries into knowledge, representation, and subjectivity in Hegel's "Sense-Certainty" passage and in postmodernist deconstruction risk arriving at an aporia, what might be the other half of the ring-movement? A comparison with Daoist philosophy may be helpful here, for the Daoist movement takes as its starting point the aporia. For Daoism, the genuine state is one of unknowing. Epistemology, subjects, language, and representation are considered partial compared with the unity of the Dao. Yet Daoist philosophy also runs into one difficulty—how to communicate the Dao that is incommunicable? The first line of the *Dao De Jing* points out the contradiction—"the Dao that can be spoken of is not Dao." Where do the Daoists go from here?

In Daoist philosophy, language, knowledge, and being are at odds with one another. They undermine one another's claim to authority. But instead of an anxiety that could underlie dialectical sublation, aporetic uncertainty, or representational (re)productions, Chuang-tzu's philosophy is one of play and transformation. For Chuang-tzu, language, like other mediums of expression, is both inherently limiting and inexhaustible. The multiplication of words is symptomatic of the distance from the Dao. The true state is unknowing and unspeaking. This is also the Dao that he would communicate. He will, however, make use of a "borderless language" to unravel the constraints exemplified by language. The "World" chapter in *Chuang-tzu* (the work is named after the "author") describes his words as "goblet words" that "pour out endless changes . . . with truths that never come to an end." The association with wine ("goblet") also recalls the half-sober/half-drunk song and dance in Li-po's poem. The "goblet words" are words of constant motion that refuse to be pinned down. Chuang-tzu's language plays with the conventions of language and subverts its purposes and functions, and in this sense comes close to the literary. It is full of irony and contradictions, dodging the traps in language and making use of those traps to unravel the boundaries of language.

Such traps include the distinctions of right and wrong, and the fixity 成 of subjective knowledge and desires, which are manifested in language. Chuang-tzu raises the example of an argument:

> Suppose you and I have had an argument. If you have beaten me instead of my beating you, then are you necessarily right and am I necessarily wrong? If I have beaten you instead of your beating me, then am I necessarily right and are you necessarily wrong? Is one of us right and the other wrong? Are both of us right or are both of us wrong? If you and I don't know the answer, then other people are bound to be even more in the dark. Whom shall we get to decide what is right? Shall we get someone who agrees with you to decide? But if he already agrees with you, how can he decide fairly? Shall we get someone who agrees with me? But if he already agrees with me, how can he decide? Shall we get someone who disagrees with both of us? But if he already disagrees with both of us, how can he decide? Shall we get someone who agrees with both of us? But if he already agrees with both of us, how can he decide? Obviously, then, neither you nor I nor anyone else can decide for each other. Shall we wait for still another person? (This and the following quotations from *Chuang-tzu* are taken from the second chapter, "Discussion on Making All Things Equal.")

This regulatory and arbitrary (*arbiter*, to judge) development of language forms the basis of human signification in general (and is a chief preoccupation of contemporary philosophies, such as Confucianism and Mo-ism, at the time of Chuang-tzu's writing). Chuang-tzu compares human language (which expresses the will, thoughts, and desire of a self-conceived subject) with other non-human expressions. In one of the stories in the text, Tzu-ch'i says to his student:

> You hear the piping of men, but you haven't heard the piping of earth [the sounds of nature]. Or if you've heard the piping of earth, you haven't heard the piping of Heaven!
>
> [What is the piping of Heaven?]
>
> Blowing on the ten thousand things in a different way, so that each can be itself—all take what they want for themselves, but who does the sounding?

The contrast here is between the *meaningful* expressions of human actions, emotions, and desires, and the agentless individuation of nature and the Dao. The latter is an expression of oneness that includes multitude, spontaneity, and difference without the imposition of customary meanings and order.

Like the deformed characters who more often possess the Dao than do ordinary human figures in Chuang-tzu's stories, the language that comes closer to communicating the Dao is that of irrationality and fragmentation. Chuang-tzu's own writing is said to be "at sixes and sevens; going on and on without turning around; wild and wide of the mark." Chieh Yü, one of the characters in the text, talks like a madman—his language has nothing to back it up. In many instances throughout the text, Chuang-tzu himself maintains an uncertainty about speech and reality—"Now I have just said something. But I don't know whether what I have said has really said something or whether it hasn't said something." Or in the famous story of transformation:

> Once Chuang Chou dreamt he was a butterfly, a butterfly flitting and fluttering around, happy with himself and doing as he pleased. He didn't know he was Chuang Chou. Suddenly he woke up and there he was, solid and unmistakable Chuang Chou. But he didn't know if he was Chuang Chou who had dreamt he was a butterfly, or a butterfly dreaming he was Chuang Chou. Between Chuang Chou and a butterfly there must be some distinction! This is called the Transformation of things [物 化].

These stories and statements can be seen as a radical suspension of the "I" and "meaning,"[6] and a suspension of human-centered reality or consciousness.

Chuang-tzu makes possible this radical suspension by subverting the language of logic and the imposition of rational limits, which he breaks down finally to tautological assertions ("right is right"; Hegel's "assertions" in the "Sense-Certainty" piece: I know it . . . I intuit . . . I take as true). Chuang-tzu's own discourse would go like this: "Right is right; right is not right." The use of irony and contradictory statements are ways of talking outside the conventional and delimiting frames of language. Such conventions and delimiting frames are represented, among other expressions, by "this," and "that." An ironizing critique of "this" and "that" in the second chapter in *Chuang-tzu* bears a strange echo to Hegel's attempt to sublate the "this" in "Sense-Certainty":

> Everything is its own 是 'this'/I/affirmation, and the other's 彼 'that'/you/negation. From 'this' point of view, I cannot see the other. What I affirm, I know. So I say, 'that' comes out of 'this' and 'this' depends on 'that'—which

> is to say that 'this' and 'that' give birth to each other. Life and death [also of ideas and perceptions] follow each other, death and life follow each other. What is acceptable becomes unacceptable. What causes right causes wrong, what causes wrong causes right. That is why the sage does not proceed in such a way, but illuminates all in the light of Heaven. He too recognizes a 'this,' but a 'this' which is also 'that,' a 'that' which is also 'this.' . . . So is there still a 'this' and a 'that'? Or is there no longer any 'this' and 'that'?

The voiding of distinction and valuation, and the declining to affirm one thing/position over the other—for each represents only half-truth—lead to the Daoist notion of constant changes. Life from death, death from life; true from false, false from true. All form part of the constant changes. "A state in which 'this' and 'that' no longer find their opposites is called the hinge of the Way. When the hinge is fitted into the socket, it can respond endlessly."

The use of rhetorical tricks, or disfiguration (from the perspective of rational figuration) to dispose of rational limits, is for Chuang-tzu a conduit to Dao or endless changes. Combining the two traditions that we have looked at—one moving from knowledge and sense-certainty to unknowing, and the other from unknowing to a (dis)figurative communication—does the "limit" of one complement the "limit" of another? What I see in these two very broad traditions that I have been sketching are patterns of movements that resemble the figures in Li-po's poem:

我歌月徘徊　I sing the moon wanders
我舞影凌亂　I dance the shadow in disarray
醒時同交歡　Sober together inter-joy
醉後各分散　After drunk each separates
永結無情遊　Forever unite in indifferent movement
相期邈雲漢　To meet far across the Milky Way

One might see the different movements towards sense-*un*certainty (dialectical unsublation, postmodernist deconstruction, Daoist ob-literation and transcendence) as taking part in the greater movement of knowing and unknowing as figured in Li-po's poem, where the figures are in fact language, signs, subjects, matter, even theories for or against figuration. The impulses to delve into, and go beyond, representations counteract each other ← →, but also signal a return → ← from what seems to be an impossible limit on both ends. (One cannot go beyond the existing paradigm of postmodernist representations, where the aporia is the representation of limit; and the other cannot communicate the Dao except by means of language and representations, however skewed the latter may be). Figuration, as we have seen in the two traditions above, is both entrapment and pleasure in plenitude. These two views and engagements are equally sustained in the movement of transfiguration in the poem. Here lies perhaps the possibility of "transmodernism." There are no "limits" of postmodernism (or the like) that confine or that have to be superseded, but rather the constant shifting and moving of paradigms and figures. Instead of one single movement toward knowledge or uncertainty, there are two pairs of movements that depart from each other and meet again in rings of circular motion.

Notes

INTRODUCTION

1. In Plato's *Cratylus*, 402A.

2. Odes. "The Coming of Spring."

3. We have seen how all pre-Parmenidean Greek philosophy understood change to be a condition at the core of the world, and thus of philosophy. Parmenides's thought did not eradicate the *penser de changement*, of course, but simply placed it in a different developmental frame.

4. One must note here the contradiction inherent in Parmenides's position. In the statement "all change is contradictory; therefore it does not exist," one can easily see not only the tension of opposites, but also the contradictorily impossible "is not" of change itself.

5. See my *Autoaesthetics: Strategies of the Self After Nietzsche*, Humanities Press, 1992, for development of the transgressive nature of what I call the *étrangeté*, and certainly the irony, of the Overman. Nietzsche's notion of this chimerical figure, I maintain, is always perforce a fiction, a sign, produced by the teleological transgressions of the mind (the "writerly" mind, to make Barthes's distinction).

6. "Sign, Symbol, Imaginary." In Marshall Blonsky *On Signs* (Baltimore: The Johns Hopkins University Press, 1985), 204. Lacan follows this definition with the healthy and troubling reminder that, in terms of *its* tendentiousness, the sign "presupposes the someone to whom one makes a sign of something. The shadow of this someone obscured the entry into linguistics" (204). The lurking shadow of the subject, the signifier of the signifier, cloaks the divisions in which signs begin and end.

CHAPTER 1

1. Mikhail Bakhtin, *Rabelais and His World*, translated by Helene Iswolsky (Cambridge, Mass., and London, England: The M.I.T. Press, 1968), 87.

2. *Ibid.*, 84.

3. *Ibid.*, 90–91.

4. *Ibid.*, 91.

5. *Ibid.*, 101 (my italics).

6. Henri Bergson, "Laughter," in *Comedy. An Essay on Comedy. George Meredith. Laughter. Henri Bergson.* (Garden City, New York: Doubleday Anchor Books, 1956), 64: Laughter "can travel within as wide a circle as you please: the circle remains, none the less, a closed one. Our laughter is always the laughter of a group. . . ." Bergson's definition of laughter—comprising his emphasis on "mechanical" behaviour as the primary source of a comic reaction—is a far cry from Bakhtin's accentuation of "Laughter's *universal* character," the wide-open space dominated by his carnival crowd (my italics).

7. Julia Kristeva, *Desire in Language. A Semiotic Approach to Literature and Art*. Edited by Leon S. Roudiez. Translated by Thomas Gora, Alice Jardine, and Leon S. Roudiez (Oxford: Basil Blackwell, reprinted 1984), 80 (Kristeva's italics).

8. Mircea Eliade, *Shamanism. Archaic Techniques of Ecstasy*. Translated from the French by William R. Trask (Princeton, New Jersey: Princeton University Press, Second Printing, 1974), 56.

9. William Shakespeare: *King Lear 1608 (Pied Bull Quarto). Shakespeare Quarto Facsimiles No. 1* (Oxford: At the Clarendon Press, 1964), IV, i, 6.

10. Mikhail Bakhtin, *op.cit.*, 192.

11. *Ibid.*, 194 ff. There are references to Friar John's behaviour in the episode of the "sausage war," to the thrashing of Catchpole, etc.

12. *Ibid.*, 78–79.

13. *M. Johann Mathesius Leben Dr. Martin Luthers in siebzehn Predigten*, Neu herausgegeben . . . von A. J. D. Rust (Berlin: Verlag von G. Crantz, 1841), 118: "Solcher Ostermährlein habe ich in meiner Jugend etliche gehöret, als: Da der Sohn Gottes vor die Vorburg der Hölle kam, und mit seinem Kreuze anstiess, steckten zween Teufel ihre langen Nasen als Riegel vor. Da aber Christus anklopfte, dass Thür und Angel mit Gewalt aufgingen, stiess er den beiden Teufeln ihre Nasen ab . . ."

14. Mikhail Bakhtin, *op.cit.*, 97.

15. Cf. Michel Foucault: *Folie et déraison. Histoire de la folie à l'âge classique* (Paris: Librairie Plon, 1961), 27 ff.

16. *Montaigne's Essays*, Vol. 1 (London: Dent, New York: Dutton, reprinted 1965), 345.

17. *Ibid.*, 344.

18. Cf. Helen Peters in the General Introduction to John Donne; *Paradoxes and Problems*. Edited with introduction and commentary by Helen Peters (Oxford: Clarendon Press, 1980), xv: "The Paradoxes appear to have been written in the early 1590s when Donne was a student at Thavies and Lincoln's Inns. . . ."

19. A. E. Malloch, "The Techniques and Function of the Renaissance Paradox," *SP*, 53: 2 (April, 1956), 195.

20. Cf. Northrop Frye, *Anatomy of Criticism* (New York: Atheneum, 1966), p. 40 (see also 172–75).

21. John Donne, *op.cit.*, 14.

22. Mikhail Bakhtin, *op.cit.*, 83.

23. John Donne, *op.cit.*, 14.

24. *Ibid.*, 14 (my translation).

25. *The Epigrams of Martial*, Vol. I (London: William Heinemann, etc., The Loeb Classical Library, 1919), 135.

26. According to Helen Peters in John Donne, *op.cit.*, xvi ff., two forms of literary paradox "can be identified" (xvi): 1) the *mock encomium* (cf. Erasmus's *The Praise of Folie*, published in an English translation by Sir Thomas Chaloner in 1549) and 2) the (rhetorical) presentation of an argument "against received opinion" (xvii). The second form of paradox "was reintroduced into Italy by Ortensio Lando in the sixteenth century" (p. xviii)—*cf.* Lando's *Paradossi* (1543). In one of his paradoxes Lando attempts to demonstrate that weeping is *better than laughter* ("Meglio e di piangere, che ridere," *Paradossi cioe sententie fvori del comun parere*, Venetia, 1545, fol. 38^{v}–39^{r}). Cf. the English translation of a number of Lando's paradoxes in: *The Defence of Contraries. Paradoxes against common opinion, debated in form of declamations in place of publike censure,* etc. (London, 1593). Reprinted by Da Capo Press (Amsterdam, New York, 1969).

27. John Donne, *op.cit.*, 16.

28. *Ibid.*, 16.

29. *Ibid.*, 14.

30. Cf. Mikhail Bakhtin, *Problems of Dostoevsky's Poetics*, Edited and translated by Caryl Emerson (Minneapolis: University of Minnesota Press, 1984), 124 (Bakhtin's italics).

31. Robert Burton, *The Anatomy of Melancholy*, Vol. 1 (London: Dent, New York: Dutton, reprinted 1964), 52 (Burton's italics).

32. On Kant and laughter cf. Renate Jurzik, *Der Stoff des Lachens* (Frankfurt/New York: Campus, 1985), 16 ff. In *Kritik der Urteilskraft* (1790) laughter is "only an illusion" ("blosse Täuschung," 17), but elsewhere in Kant a very *domesticated* type of laughter is provided with a somewhat limited social function (17–18). On the suppression of Easter laughter cf. Wilhelm Kosch, *Deutsches Literatur-Lexikon,* Zweite, vollständig neubearbeitete und stark erweiterte Auflage, Dritter Band (Bern: A. Francke AG Verlag, 1956), 1956.

33. Thomas Hobbes, *Leviathan* (Harmondsworth, Middlesex: Penguin Books, 1968), 125. Laughter is "caused either by some sudden act of their own, that pleaseth them; or by the apprehension of some deformed thing in another, by comparison whereof they suddenly applaud themselves."

34. William Blake, *Songs of Innocence and of Experience* (London: Oxford University Press, 1970), pl. 15.

35. *Ibid.,* pl. 6.

36. *Ibid.,* pl. 7.

37. Charles Baudelaire, *Les fleurs du mal et autres poèmes* (Paris: Garnier-Flammarion, 1964, 1989), 99–100.

38. Charles Baudelaire: *Curiosités esthétiques. L'Art romantique et autres Oeuvres critiques* (Paris: Éditions Garnier, 1962, 1983), 248:

> Le rire vient de l'idée de sa propre supériorité. Idée satanique s'il en fut jamais! Orgueil et aberration! Or, il est notoire que tous les fous des hôpitaux ont l'idée de leur propre supériorité développée outre mesure . . . Remarquez que le rire est une des expressions les plus fréquentes et les plus nombreuses de la folie.

39. *Ibid.,* 244: " . . . le Sage craint le rire, comme il craint les spectacles mondains, la concupiscence."

40. The philosopher is a somewhat exceptional case:

> Ce n'est point l'homme qui tombe qui rit de sa propre chute, à moins qu'il ne soit un philosophe, un homme qui ait acquis, par habitude, la force de se dédoubler rapidement et d'assister comme spectateur désintéressé aux phénomènes de son *moi.* Mais le cas est rare.

Ibid., 251. The philosopher attempts to *overcome* the subject-object split, but the outcome of his endeavors remains somewhat problematic. The notion of self-duplication is essential in this context. Actually, according to Paul de Man, "the notion of self-duplication or self-multiplication emerges at the end of . . . [Baudelaire's] essay as the key concept of the article . . ." (Paul de Man, "The Rhetoric of Temporality," reprinted in '*Blindness and Insight. Essays in the Rhetoric of Contemporary Criticism,* Second Edition, Revised, London: Methuen & Co., Ltd., Second printing, 1986, 212).

41. Cf. Mikhail Bakhtin, *Rabelais and His World, op.cit.*, 19, on the images of bodily life in grotesque realism: "Manifestations of this life refer not to the isolated biological individual, . . . but to the collective ancestral body of all the people."

42. Lewis Carroll, *The Annotated Alice* (Harmondsworth, Middlesex: Penguin Books, reprinted 1987), 90–91.

43. Clair Wills, "Upsetting the public: carnival, hysteria and women's texts," in Ken Hirschkop and David Shepherd (eds.): *Bakhtin and Cultural Theory* (Manchester and New York: Manchester University Press, 1989), 130.

44. Mary Russo, "Female Grotesques: Carnival and Theory," in *Feminist Studies. Critical Studies*, edited by Teresa de Lauretis (Bloomington: Indiana University Press, 1986), 221–22. The reference is to the female body as "the site" of a "desirous excess" (221).

45. *Ibid.*, 219.

46. *Ibid.*, 219. Cf. Mikhail Bakhtin, *op.cit.*, 25 (my italics).

47. Mary Russo, *op. cit.*, 219.

48. Hélène Cixous, "Castration or Decapitation?" *Signs* 7: 1 (1981), 55.

49. *Ibid.*, 55.

50. Hélène Cixous, "The Laugh of the Medusa," *Signs* 1: 4 (1976), 885.

51. Leonora Carrington, *The Seventh Horse and Other Tales* (New York: Dutton, 1988), 16.

52. *Posada's Popular Mexican Prints*, Selected and Edited, With an Introduction and Commentary, by Roberto Berdecio and Stanley Appelbaum (New York: Dover Publications, 1972), xviii. It must be stressed in this connection that Leonora Carrington wrote her story *before* she went to Mexico.

53. Leonora Carrington, *op.cit.*, 16–17.

54. *Ibid.*, 17-18.

55. Cf. Mikhail Bakhtin, *op.cit.*, 368–436.

56. Leonora Carrington, *op.cit.*, 16.

57. *Ibid.*, 18. A number of surrealist writers and painters contributed to the production of a kind of collective *novella*, "L'homme qui a perdu son squelette." (Among the contributors were Hans Arp, Marcel Duchamp, Max Ernst, and Paul Eluard.) The text was published in the magazine *Plastic/Plastique*, Nos. 4–5 (1939). Carrington wrote chapter 4: "Le squelette en vacances" (No. 5, 2–3). The "cartomancienne" is mentioned on p. 3.

58. Leonora Carrington, *The Seventh Horse, op.cit.*, 180.

59. Leonora Carrington, *The Hearing Trumpet* (London and Henley: Routledge & Kegan Paul, 1977), 141, 136.

60. Mikhail Bakhtin; *op.cit.*, 25.

61. Angela Carter, *Nights at the Circus* (London: Chatto & Windus, The Hogarth Press, 1984), 117. Cf. Buffo's "real" self-demolition in chapter 10, where he pursues Jack Walser *alias* the Human Chicken and dissolves "into a dozen Buffos, armed with a dozen murderous knives all streaming rags of blood. . . ." (178).

62. *Ibid.*, 177.

63. Søren Kierkegaard, *Either/Or*, 1 (Princeton, New Jersey: Princeton University Press, 1971), 30. Cf. *Søren Kierkegaards Papirer*, Bind III (København: Gyldendal, 1968), 199: "et Theater i Petersborg."

64. Angela Carter, *op.cit.*, 295.

65. Renate Jurzik, *Der Stoff des Lachens* (Frankfurt/New York: Campus Verlag, 1985), 107 ("Der bürgerliche Sonntagsspaziergang auf der Promenade wurde durch die Steigerung des Tempos zum Massenwettlauf"). My translation.

66. *Ibid.*, 107 (my translation).

67. *Monty Python's Flying Circus. Just the Words*, 2 (London: Methuen, Mandarin, 1990), 98 ff. This is the third series, no. 4 (9–11–72).

68. Cf. Susan Handelman, "Jacques Derrida and the Heretic Hermeneutic," in *Displacement. Derrida and After*, edited by Mark Krupnick (Bloomington: Indiana University Press, 1987), 113.

69. *The Final Foucault*, edited by James Bernauer and David Rasmussen (Cambridge, Massachusetts, and London, England: The MIT Press, 1988), vii ("An introductory note"). Cf. Didier Eribon: *Michel Foucault (1926–1984)* (Paris: Flammarion, 1989), 164, where Eribon refers to "un Foucault transformé, un homme épanoui, détendu, *rieur*" (my italics).

70. Michel Foucault, *The Order of Things* (London: Tavistock Publications, 1970), xvii. The text by Borges referred to is "The Analytical Language of John Wilkins."

71. Michel Foucault, *op.cit.*, xv, xvii.

72. Michel Foucault, *The Archaeology of Knowledge*. Translated from the French by A. M. Sheridan Smith (London: Tavistock Publications, 1972, 1974), 17 (my italics).

73. Cf. *Allen Ginsberg/William Blake. Songs of Innocence and Experience*. MGM Records(FTS3083/MGS2112). Recorded December 14th–15th, 1969.

74. The Residents: *Duck Stab*. Ralph Records (RZ-87521A). Cf. *The Residents—*

An Almost Complete Collection of Lyrics, 1972 to 1988 (Redazione/Editorial Office: STAMPA ALTERNATIVA, P.O. Box 741, 00100 ROMA CENTRO, n.d.), 68.

75. Cf. Peter Stallybrass and Allon White, *The Politics and Poetics of Transgression* (London: Methuen, 1986), 53.

76. Cf. Brian McHale; *Postmodernist Fiction* (New York and London: Methuen, 1987), 32 and *passim*.

CHAPTER 2

1. This need makes a noteworthy appearance in a science-fiction novel from the twenties that outlines the threats of the future. A strongly racist and anti-semitic tract, Hans Heyck's *Deutschland ohne Deutsche. Ein Roman von übermorgen* (Leipzig, 1929), takes place in the middle of the twenty-first century and features "noise-killers" and "*Stillschweige-Abteilungen*" as a means of escape.

2. For the broader context of silence, poetry, and modern art, see, for example, Susan Sontag, "The Aesthetics of Silence," in *Styles of Radical Will* (New York, 1970), 3–34; Ihab Hassan, *The Dismemberment of Orpheus* (New York, 1971); Christiaan L. Hart Nibbrig, *Rhetorik des Schweigens. Versuch über den Schatten literarischer Rede* (Frankfurt, 1981); Matei Calinescu, "The Silence of the Avant-Garde," in *Five Faces of Modernity* (Durham, 1987), 275–79.

3. I am quoting the poem in John Felstiner's translation; see his "The *Gilgul* of Dan Pagis: Myth, History, Silence," in *Translation Review* 32/33 (1990), 8–11; the Hebrew original and a slightly differing translation can be found in T. Carmi, Dan Pagis, *Selected Poems*, translated by Stephen Mitchell (Baltimore, 1976), 92–3.

4. Hugo von Hofmannsthal, *Ausgewählte Werke in zwei Bänden* (Frankfurt, 1957), 337–348.

5. For the context in European literature see Theodore Ziolkowski, "*James Joyces Epiphanie und die Überwindung der empirischen Welt in der modernen deutschen Prosa*," *Deutsche Vierteljahrsschrift für Literaturwissenschaft und Geistesgeschichte* 35 (1961), 594–616.

6. *Die Fackel* 1, (1899), 1f.

7. Bertolt Brecht, "*Über die Bedeutung des zehnzeiligen Gedichtes in der 888. Nummer der Fackel*" (Oktober 1933)," in *Gesammelte Werke in acht Bänden* (Frankfurt, 1967), IV, 501–503. Subsequent quotes from Brecht are from this edition.

8. For a survey see Hiltrud Gnüg, "*Gespräch über Bäume. Zur Brecht-Rezeption in der modernen Lyrik*," *Basis* 7 (1977), 89-117, and Malcolm Humble, "Brecht and Posterity: A Poem and Its Reception," *New German Studies* 14 (1986–87), 115–142.

9. For a general assessment of Brecht's position see Reinhold Grimm, *Brecht und Nietzsche oder Geständnisse eines Dichters: Fünf Essays und ein Bruchstück* (Frankfurt, 1979), 11ff., and Wolfgang Emmerich, "*Kein Gespräch über Bäume. Naturlyrik unterm Faschismus und im Exil*," in *Natur und Natürlichkeit. Stationen des Grünen in der deutschen Literatur*, edited by Reinhold Grimm and Jost Hermand (Königstein, 1981), 77–117.

10. George Steiner, *Language and Silence. Essays on Language, Literature, and the Inhuman* (New York, 1970), 123.

11. *Gesammelte Werke in fünf Bänden*, edited by Beda Allemann and Stefan Reichert (Frankfurt, 1983), II, 385. Subsequent quotes from Célan are from this edition.

12. *Poems of Paul Célan*, translated by Michael Hamburger (New York, 1988), 231; the German original reads: "*das hundert-/züngige Mein-gedicht, das Genicht*."

13. The positions of Brecht and Célan are presented with thoroughness by Theo Buck, "*Weite und Enge: Zu einer lyrischen Auseinandersetzung Célans mit Brecht*," in *Festschrift für Friedrich Beissner*, edited by Ulrich Gaier and Werner Volke (Bebenhausen, 1974), 67–89.

14. *Merkur* 13 (1959), 772.

15. Hans Magnus Enzensberger, *Gedichte 1955–1970* (Frankfurt, 1971), 162.

16. Enzensberger, *Mittelmaß und Wahn* (Frankfurt, 1988), 227.

17. *Der Untergang der Titanic* (Franfurt, 1978), 115.

18. *Titanic*, 61.

19. Walter Helmut Fritz, *Schwierige Überfahrt* (Hamburg, 1976), 64.

20. Hugo von Hofmannsthal, *Ausgewählte Werke in zwei Bänden* (Frankfurt, 1957), II, 348.

21. Fritz, *Mit einer Feder aus den Flügeln des Ikarus* (Frankfurt, 1989), 167.

22. Hans Ebeling, *Äesthetik des Abschieds. Kritik der Moderne* (München, 1989).

23. Some positions are documented in the collection *Literatur und Gesellschaft. Zur Sozialgeschichte der Literatur seit der Jahrhundertwende*, edited by Beate Pinkerneil et al. (Frankfurt, 1973).

24. One recent attempt to come to terms with writing after Auschwitz is by Günter Grass, *Schreiben nach Auschwitz. Frankfurter Poetik-Vorlesung* (Frankfurt, 1990).

25. *Kindheitsmuster* (Frankfurt, 1989). All quotes following are from this edition. The novel was first published in 1976.

26. *Sommerstück* (Frankfurt, 1989), 11. Earlier, strong formulations against the terror of usefulness and for closeness, intimacy, and aesthetic appreciation in our lives can be found in Wolf's "Büchner-Preis Rede" of 1980.

27. *Sommerstück*, 10; the warning, in keeping with Lord Chandos's experience, follows on the next page: *"Wir begannen gewahr zu werden, welchen Preis der zahlt, der auf Schönheit angewiesen ist: Er ist dem Gräßlichen ausgeliefert . . ."*

28. Hofmannsthal, II, 345.

29. At this point the investigation would have to come to terms with two very different, ambitious rehabilitations of art, Adorno's aesthetics and George Steiner, *Real Presences* (Chicago, 1989); with philosophical efforts such as by Ben-Ami Scharfstein, Erazim Kohák, or Otto Seel, to interweave human creativity, nature, and beauty; and with specific works, such as the ambiguously titled volume of poems by Jorie Graham, *The End of Beauty* (New York, 1987).

CHAPTER 3

1. Charles Jencks, *What is Post-Modernism?* (London and New York: Academy Editions and St. Martin's Press, 1986). Note that Jencks renders the term *postmodernism* with a hyphen and initial caps, as "Post-Modernism." For consistency, however, following this acknowlegement, I revert to my own standard usage.

2. *Ibid.*, 45, 47.

3. The late Thomas Lyman, Emory's eminent Romanesque art historian, told me that in conversation Portman acknowledged a debt to an actual theater: the late sixteenth-century Palladio-designed Teatro Olimpico in Vicenza, the most important Renaissance attempt to build an archeologically correct Roman theater.

4. Derrida's famous line is, *Il n'y a pas de hors-texte*. See *Of Grammatology*, translated by Gayatri Chakaravorty Spivak (Baltimore: Johns Hopkins University Press, 1976), 158.

5. I will take references to theater, spectacle, performance, the "scene," and "mise-en-scène," to be aspects of a single, multifaceted theatrical metaphor. I will not for these purposes distinguish metaphors of traditional theater from those of the contemporary form, "performance." This distinction is in any event less viable today than it was when it was first floated in the 1970s.

6. Guy Debord, *Society of the Spectacle* (Detroit: Black & Red, 1983), #15.

7. *Ibid.*, #158 and #160.

8. *Ibid.*, #160 and #1.

9. *Ibid.*, #221.

10. Jacques Derrida, "The Double Session," in *Dissemination*, translated and introduction by Barbara Johnson (Chicago: University of Chicago Press, 1981). See editor's note, p. 173.

11. *Ibid.*, 191.

12. *Ibid.*, 195.

13. *Ibid.*, 206.

14. *Ibid.*, 206.

15. *Ibid.*, 215, n.27.

16. Michel Foucault, *The Archeology of Knowledge*, translated by A. M. Sheridan Smith (New York: Pantheon Books, 1972), 207. Fredric Jameson says in his introduction to Jean-Francois Lyotard's *The Postmodern Condition: A Report on Knowledge* (Minneapolis: University of Minnesota Press, 1984), "The admission to France of such Anglo-American linguistic notions as that of Austin's 'performative' is now largely an accomplished fact (although a rather unexpected development)." While this key concept in philosophy of language is not unrelated to the concerns I pursue in this essay, "performativity" itself is not a sufficiently imagined eruption of theatrical space into discourse to warrant my including such examples in the present discussion. For a discussion of the criterion of performance in Lyotard, see Bill Readings, *Introducing Lyotard* (London and New York: Routledge, 1991), 77, 80–85, 93–97. See also Lyotard's "The Unconscious as Mise-en-scène," in Michel Benamou and Charles Caramello, *Performance in Postmodern Culture* (Madison: Coda Press, Inc., 1977), 87–98.

17. Michel Foucault, "Theatrum Philosophicum," *Language, Counter-Memory, Practice*, edited and introduced by Donald F. Bouchard, translated by Donald F. Bouchard and Sherry Simon (Ithaca: Cornell University Press and Oxford: Blackwell, 1977), 179, 196.

18. Gilles Deleuze and Felix Guattari, *Anti-Oedipus* (Minneapolis: University of Minneapolis Press, 1983), 334.

19. *Ibid.*, 55.

20. *Ibid.*, 54.

21. Jean Baudrillard, *The Mirror of Production*, translated by Mark Poster (St. Louis: Telos Press, 1975).

22. Jean Baudrillard, *Simulations*, translated by Paul Foss, Paul Patton, and Philip Beitchman (New York: Semiotext(e), Inc., 1983), 48.

23. *Ibid.*, 72.

24. Baudrillard, *Simulations*, 55, 139.

25. Françoise Collin, "Reflections on the Women's Liberation Movement,"

in *French Connections*, edited and translated by Claire Duchen (Amherst: University of Mass. Press, 1987), 142.

26. Hélène Cixous, "The Laugh of the Medusa," edited and introduced by Elaine Marks and Isabelle de Courtivron, *New French Feminisms* (New York: Schocken Books, 1981), 250, 252.

27. *Ibid.*, 254–55.

28. *Ibid.*, 262–63.

29. Hélène Cixous and Catherine Clement, *The Newly Born Woman* (Minneapolis: University of Minnesota Press, 1986). See "The Guilty One," 10–13 and 40–59.

30. *Ibid.*, "The Untenable," 147–60.

31. Luce Irigaray, *Speculum of the Other Woman* (Ithaca: Cornell University Press, 1985). These theatrical gambits are all drawn from the opening pages of "The Blind Spot of an Old Dream of Symmetry," 13–22.

32. Joan Riviere, "Womanliness as Masquerade," in *Formations of Fantasy*, edited by Victor Burgin, James Donald and Cora Kaplan. (London: Methuen, 1986).

33. Luce Irigaray, "Plato's *Hystera*," in *Speculum of the Other Woman*, 250-52.

34. *Ibid.*, 289–90.

35. *Ibid.*, 277.

36. *Ibid.*, 295–96.

37. Baudrillard, *op. cit.*, 11.

38. It is striking that Susan Rubin Suleiman and Alice Jardine, two leading feminist literary critic/theorists, have adopted theatrical forms to make theoretical statements. See Suleiman, "Metapolylogue: On Playing and Modernity," in her *Subversive Intent: Gender, Politics and the Avant-Garde* (Cambridge: Harvard University Press, 1990), 5–10; and Jardine, "in the name of the modern: feminist questions *d'après gynesis*," in Susan Sheridan, *Grafts: Feminists Cultural Criticism* (London and New York: Verso, 1988), 157–92.

39. William Saroyan, *The Time of Your Life* in *The Critics' Prize Plays*, introduced by George Jean Nathan. (Cleveland and New York: The World Publishing Company, 1945), 219.

40. Alisdair MacIntyre, *After Virtue* (Notre Dame: University of Notre Dame, 1981), 77, 27.

41. Luigi Pirandello, "Preface to *Six Characters in Search of an Author*," *Naked Masks*, edited by Eric Bentley (New York: E.P. Dutton & Co., 1952), 372–73.

42. The annual conference of the International Association for Philosophy and Literature, Montreal, May 16–18, 1991.

43. Michael Fried, "Art and Objecthood," reprinted in *Minimal Art: A Critical Anthology*, edited by Gregory Battcock (New York: Dutton, 1968), 139.

CHAPTER 4

1. Jean Baudrillard, *L'échanqe symbolique et la mort* (Paris: Gallimard, 1976). In the discussion that follows I draw especially on Part II, entitled "L'ordre des simulacres," part of which has been translated as "The Orders of Simulacra," in *Simulations*, translated by Paul Foss, Paul Patton, and Philip Beitchman (New York: Semiotexte, 1983). Subsequent references to this translation will be noted in the text with an *S* followed by the page number.

2. This is the argument of Baudrillard's *For a Critique of the Political Economy of the Sign*, translated by Charles Levin (St. Louis, Mo.: Telos Press, 1981).

3. See Jean Baudrillard, *The Mirror of Production*, translated by Mark Poster (St. Louis, Mo.: Telos Press, 1975).

4. See Jean-François Lyotard, *The Postmodern Condition*, translated by Geoff Bennington and Brian Massumi (Minneapolis: University of Minnesota, 1984), 60–67.

5. This and the quotations that follow, unless otherwise noted, are taken from "The Precession of Simulacra," which also appears in translation in *Simulations*. Originally this essay was published in Baudrillard's collection, entitled *Simulacres et simulation* (Paris: Galilee, 1981).

6. Jean Baudrillard, "The Ecstasy of Communication," translated by John Johnston in *The Anti-Aesthetic: Essays on Postmodern Culture*, edited by Hal Foster (Port Townsend, Wash.: Bay Press, 1983), 126–27.

7. Gilles Deleuze and Félix Guattari, *A Thousand Plateaus*, translated by Brian Massumi (Minneapolis: University of Minnesota Press, 1987). All subsequent quotations will be noted in the text with a *TP* followed by the page number.

8. This "inadequation" inherent to every system of signs was first noted by Claude Lévi-Strauss in his *Introduction to the Work of Marcel Mauss*, translated by Felicity Baker (London: Routledge, 1987, orig. pub. 1950), 62.

9. In her otherwise admirable *Critique, Norm and Utopia : A Study of the Foundations of Critical Theory* (New York: Columbia University Press, 1986)—to cite one example—Ceyla Benhabib ignores the simple fact that all "critique" reposes on and assumes the semiotic functioning of a doubled subject.

10. Baudrillard's discussion of Foucault and Deleuze may be found in his *Forget Foucault* (New York: Semiotexte, 1987), esp. 33–48.

11. See Baudrillard's *Les stratéqies fatales* (Paris: Grasset, 1983), 201 ff. for a discussion of "objective irony."

12. Zygmunt Bauman, *Legislators and Interpreters: On modernity, Postmodernity, and Intellectuals* (Ithaca, N.Y.: Cornell University Press, 1987), 149–187.

13. Bauman, 4.

14. Bauman, 4–5.

15. Deleuze's contribution was published under the title "A philosophical concept . . ." in *Topoi* 7; 2 (Sept., 1988), 11–12.

CHAPTER 5

1. Nonnan Malcolm, *Ludwig Wittgenstein: A Memoir* (London: Oxford University Press, 1962), 11.

2. I must note that Bartley's revised second edition endorses this view, writing that "his own original contribution was the design of the interior of the house, and citing Bernhard Leitner's work. *Wittgenstein* (La Salle, Illinois: Open Court, 1985), 118.

3. This logical precedence given to the interior structure over the exterior is first achieved with the open interior of the Rufer house (1922) mentioned above for its separation of private and public spaces. Benedetto Gravagnuolo, *Adolf Loos: Theory and Works* (New York, Rizzoli, 1982), 22.

4. *Ibid.*

5. See Bernhard Leitner, *The Architecture of Ludwig Wittgenstein* (New York: NYU Press, 1976).

6. Leitner, "Wittgenstein's Architecture," *Art Forum*, Feb. 1970, 59.

7. Leitner writes: "The building is important because it is an example of going beyond limits, because it demonstrates how enriching an unprofessional encroachment can be, and because it questions the limits of a profession that are mainly set by the very members of that profession. Wittgenstein, the philosopher, was an architect" (p. 59). Interestingly, it is precisely this judgment, made by one within the profession, that seems to have convinced Bartley to change his opinion that Wittgenstein was "just" an engineer. See his revised *Wittgenstein*, 118.

8. It should pointed out that Leitner's judgment of Wittgenstein's work, like von Wright's, derives from an explicit association with the goals of the *Tractatus*. He writes: "Wittgenstein was working on the building between his first philosophical period . . . and his second, when he taught at Cambridge. In 1918, he wrote in the preface to the *Tractatus*: 'I therefore believe myself to have

found, on all essential points, the final solution of the problems.' His architecture reflects this claim for absoluteness and rejection of compromise. It cannot be compared to the so-called 'Neue Architektur' of the same era. Important inspirations for this movement's intellectual and formal-aesthetic vocabulary were derived from new materials, new industrial processes, and a new social consciousness. Wittgenstein the philosopher shows entirely different, absolutely firm esthetics in his one practical confrontation with architecture: his philosophic posture translated into space and form" (*Wittgenstein's Architecture*, 59). What Leitner overlooks in his reading of the *Tractatus* appears to be what the Vienna Circle overlooked, namely that these reflections are about logic, not language, and, therefore, not translatable to the world of space and form. Wittgenstein was not a positivist, and the mysticism with which he ends the *Tractatus* is not contradictory. Leitner simply needs to confront his translation, his identification of an "absolutely firm esthetics" with aphorism 6.421: "It is clear that ethics cannot be put into words./ Ethics is transcendental./ (Ethics and aesthetics are one and the same.)" The uncompromising transcendental truth, then, the perfection which Leitner locates within Wittgenstein's house, according to the *Tractatus* cannot be put into space. And if the silence with which the *Tractatus* ends was to be the logic of his house nothing would have been built. For quoting an aphorism, which Engelmann also quotes in his memoir, "how things are in the world is a matter of complete indifference for the sublime. God does not reveal himself in the world" (T 6.432, translation slightly modified); not even in its details. The self-certainty that Leitner ascribes to Wittgenstein in this period, with his quotation from the preface of the *Tractatus,* is very misleading. One need simply read the preface. I'll cite the sentence that follows the one Leitner quotes: "And if I am mistaken in this belief, then the second thing in which the value of this work consists is that it shows how little is achieved when these problems are solved" (5). More importantly, to ascribe such absolute finality of solution to Wittgenstein's architecture, his interior, is to read this interior too simplistically and to prematurely delimit architecture to a set of problems in need of solution.

9. Quoted by Leitner in *The Architecture of Ludwig Wittgenstein*, 23.

10. Of course the house was furnished while Margarete lived there, in, it must be emphasized, her manner, which, judging from the few available pictures was a sparse decor of *objets d'art*, French, Chinese, and contemporary. As her sister Hermine writes: "the house fitted my sister Gretl like a glove as soon as she had furnished it in her own curious way and filled it with her personality." (Leitner, 1976, 23)

11. Quoted by Leitner in *The Architecture of Ludwig Wittgenstein*, 21.

12. Leitner, 1970, 59.

13. Leitner, 1976, 88.

14. By now our eye is so accustomed to 8' ceilings and 6' 8" doors that anything else is strikingly unusual, but the significance and use of different

sizes is not unheard of, especially prior to the modernist movement (Corbu?), which established these standards. See Christopher Alexander's *Pattern Language*. The question that needs to be asked of Wittgenstein is the appropriateness of entrance to the salon through a door of such a narrow proportioned width. Possibly it is this question of inappropriate scaling for its use that caused Hermine to remember it as "a hall-like room" (Leitner, 1976, 21).

15. Jacques Derrida opens his book *The Truth in Painting* with a "*passe-partout*," which questions the working of the frame. In this section, not quite a preface, Derrida warns against just such readings as Leitner's: "the *passe-partout* which here creates an event must not pass for a master key. You will not be able to pass it from hand to hand like a convenient instrument, a short treatise, a viaticum or even an organon or pocket canon, in short a transcendental pass, a password to open all doors, decipher all texts and keep their chains under surveillance. If you rushed to understand it in this way, I would have to issue a strong warning avertissement; this forward avertissement is not a passe-partout" (p. 12). Wittgenstein's design is not the working of an absolute logic, but merely a contingent convention of the framer's craft, and so framed is the full difficulty of that interior space that "required" raising the salon's ceiling 3 centimeters, the meeting place of public and private, the important space of sociality. To consider the problem of the space of the important salon as derivative from the framing conventions by which Wittgenstein solved the door placement is to give up the difficulties of spatial design to surface treatment, a kind of decorating that doesn't call attention to itself.

16. In a remark from 1931, collected in *Culture and Value*, Wittgenstein himself limits the importance of the *passe-partout*. He writes:

> Often, when I have had a picture well framed or have hung it in the right surroundings, I have caught myself feeling as proud as if I had painted the picture myself. That is not quite right: not "as proud as if I had painted it," but as proud as if I had helped to paint it, as if I had, so to speak, painted a little bit of it. It is as though an exceptionally gifted arranger of grasses should eventually come to think that he had produced at least a tiny blade of grass himself. Whereas it ought to be clear to him that his work lies in a different region altogether. The process through which even the tiniest and meanest blade of grass comes into being is something he has nothing to do with and knows nothing about (pp. 19–20).

One can only wonder if, in writing these lines in 1931, Wittgenstein might have thought of their pertinence to his contribution to his sister's house.

17. Benedetto Gravagnuolo writes of the house:

> But it is interesting to note that for the first time the architecture of the interior, as well, is reduced to a pure geometric simplicity, almost attaining to a unitary *Gesamtkunstwerk*. In other words, even the decoration becomes a pure play of architectural volumes and shapes. It would be difficult to deny the influence exerted over this work by the project drawn up by

Ludwig Wittgenstein for his sister Margarethe Stoneborough (in 1926, with the collaboration of Loos's pupil, Paul Engelmann).

> Quite a few formal analogies (such as the bareness of the rooms, the absolute prismatic quality of the pillars, the beams, the volumes and such details as the right-angled internal staircase) that tend to confirm this hypothesis.

However, Gravagnuolo does go on to characterize important differences between the two houses, but without referring to any particular features that mark these differences, as he does parenthetically with their similarities:

> But once again a profound difference in conceptual intent may be detected: where Wittgenstein turns the entire articulation of space into logico-philosophical calculation, Loos, on the contrary, proposes an emotive quality of "feeling oneself inside" that tends to give the interior an air of the sacred. The interior is the favored place, the sheltered place, the raison d'etre of the house (197).

While Gravagnuolo's reference to the *Tractatus* here is apt with respect to Wittgenstein's house, however unsuccessful (as will be reflected in Wittgenstein's own later philosophical writings), it is misleading in reading the complex developments of the interior of Loos's Moller house. This "air of the sacred," which he finds in the Moller interior, I find quite contrastably human, if only due to the scaling and ceiling heights. The paradigmatic sacred space is one in which entry is bared to humans. This is not at all the case with Loos's house, by Gravagnuolo's own description. It speaks to human feeling, to sheltered inhabitation, not to the anonymity of Wittgenstein's spaces, which pretend a sublimeness of proportion.

18. This is an innovation first made by Loos in the Rufer house of 1922. It is not to be found in Wittgenstein's house (despite the editor of Engelmann's memoir who, in an appendix, states that "the use of interlocking split-levels to prevent the division of the interior space into 'floors,"'(139–40)) where the division of floors is not complicated by split-levels, and where in the entranceway one meets walls rather than openings to diverse corners of the house.

19. This opening up of the interior of the house was an innovation, again, dating to the Rufer house, where Loos employs a near cubic form (10 x 10 x 12 m), in which support is provided by the four load-bearing exterior walls and a central pillar. With this structural support Loos is able to use interior walls that are only partitions and more importantly to leave out walls where traditionally they might have been placed. Even though Wittgenstein's house is four times the size of the Rufer house a similar strategy could have been employed. Yet the only area opened up through the use of pillars is the *Halle*, which in this house, quite unlike the Moller house, remains solely a formal entranceway.

20. This term was introduced by Loos's student and collaborator, H. Kulka, and so described: "Adolf Loos brought an essentially newer, loftier concept of

the space into the world: regarding space freely, planning spaces on different levels and not confined to a single story, composing related rooms into a harmonious, indivisible whole, into something that makes economical use of the space. According to their purpose and significance, the rooms are not only of different sizes but also of different heights. This enables Loos to create a larger living area with the same constructional means, since he accommodates in this manner more rooms in the same cube, on the same foundations, under the same roof, between the same enclosing walls. He makes the utmost use of the material and the building volume." (Quoted in *Raumplan versus Plan Libre*, edited by Max Risselada (New York: Rizzoli 1988), 79.

21. From Loos's "Das Prinzip der Bekleidung," quoted in Franco Borsi and Ezio Godoli, *Vienna 1900: Architecture and Design* (New York Rizzoli 1986), 153.

22. That the facade of Wittgenstein's house sticks so closely to Engelmann's sketches is evidence of this order of working from the outside, both elevation and god's eye above. In stark contrast Loos actually used dismantleable models to facilitate this working according to section, "making it possible to view simultaneously the internal distribution and the external one subordinate to it." (Gravagnuolo, 1982, 172). One can, of course, speculate that things might have been different had Wittgenstein been involved with the project from the beginning, but my sense is that Loos's lesson wouldn't have been learned in a single project, had Margarete herself been so interested.

23. This significance given to symmetry with regard to placement of windows and doors is also used as a rationale for the lighting design, as pointed out by Leitner. The irony here is that one would think that the complexities of lighting could be so simply solved. Wittgenstein's design is to place bare bulbs along the axial median of rooms, most often determining their limited number and positioning by adjacent windows. This dominant use of overhead lighting, given rooms with high ceilings, Leitner describes as "objective, homogeneous and simple, and without any directional emphasis" (1976, 99). Yet this had to have been a harsh lighting, incapable of producing the homogeneous effect that was to come with the fluorescent fixtures that we are now all accustomed to. And judging by Gunther Forg's photograph, the house's glazing leaves much of the interior dark during daylight hours, requiring artificial lighting, then, to supplement. And yet Leitner's analysis of the effect of the lighting is made only for night conditions, as otherwise he would have to take into account the effect of windows and exposure placed opposite the ceiling fixtures.

24. Argued in the above essay of 1898.

25. Probably the connection should be made explicit even at this premature point regarding this issue of the *parergon*, the frame, and Wittgenstein's picture theory of meaning. The *parergon* questions the possible congruence between the picture and reality, that such a depiction can possess a one-to-one correspondence to the world it claims to represent. In the *Tractatus* such pictures are limited to the logical space of facts (logical atomism), a delimiting that

Wittgenstein's picture theory struggles with throughout his work. As for the effacing of the parergonal in the *Tractatus*', the pertinent aphorism is: "What constitutes a picture is that its elements are related to one another in a determinate way." (T 2.14) Such a definition requires that the picture's frame be logically impervious to external effect.

26. Loos's manipulation of walls and apertures in mind of creation of space is to work parergonally. The *parergon,* which Derrida locates in his reading of Kant's *Third Critique,* precisely with respect to Kant's examples of a sculpture's garments, a building's columns, and a painting's frame, names that which works across borders, which can't be held extrinsic. The *parergon* effect is that which relates rooms and spaces in Loos's architecture in a manner that always exceeds function or rationality, which provides unexpected surprise and visual illusion for one who enters. This is the effect that Derrida maintains philosophy traditionally has sought to suppress in its philosophy of art. In *Truth in Painting* he writes of parergonality: "Philosophy wants to arraign it and can't manage. But what has produced and manipulated the frame puts everything to work in order to efface the frame effect, most often by naturalizing it to infinity, in the hands of God (one can verify this in Kant). Deconstruction must neither reframe nor dream of the pure and simple absence of the frame" (73). The design strategies employed by Wittgenstein in his house attempt just such a "naturalization" of the frame, measuring the proportion and scale of the interior, not for humanity, but for God. Wittgenstein, the philosopher of the *Tractatus,* seeks an order of clarification that can't allow the paradoxical collapse of the intrinsic/extrinsic distinction, both in his philosophy and his architecture. As Derrida goes on to say: "these two apparently contradictory gestures are the very ones—and they are systematically indissociable—of what is here deconstructed." Even the illustration Derrida places opposite the above cited text, a perspective view of receding doorways in the style of Louis XIV, stands as the archetypal framework, which Wittgenstein in his house has attempted to purify through a removal of ornamentation, in a further, modern development of the "naturalization" of the parergonal effect within the architectural interior, the view that Gunther Forg captured photographically with the barest minimum of available light.

27. It should be emphasized that the significance of this recanting by Wittgenstein of the *Tractatus,* especially as it appears in the *Investigations,* is controversial. Without really entering into its complexities, giving an inventory of Wittgenstein's changing views, it must be mentioned that such conflict opens upon the desire to treat a philosopher's work, especially an *oeuvre* like Wittgenstein's, so obviously stylistic from beginning to end, in terms of the dichotomy of radical breaks versus continuity. Wittgenstein tended to favor the first alternative, leading acceptance amongst early commentators, especially those who knew him, of talk of breaks, ruptures, and repudiations. But recent scholarship has tended to see the distance between the *Tractatus* and the *Investigations* as less exaggerated, especially with the availability of the writings of

the 30s. Anthony Kenny's work is a good example of such a reading. In the introduction to *The Legacy of Wittgenstein* he writes: "Wittgenstein tended systematically to exaggerate the inadequacies of his earlier work in a way which masks the underlying continuity of his thought even where his changes of mind were most dramatic. . . . What is attacked in Wittgenstein's later work, I maintain, is sometimes not the real *Tractatus* but a mere ghost of it. Not that Wittgenstein did not have some thoughts which he later repudiated with scorn; but they belong rather to the period of his return to philosophy in the late twenties" (ix–x).

28. This passage was first brought to my attention by Bartley's second edition of his *Wittgenstein*, where he, identifying it as Wittgenstein's "reservations," quotes it at the end of his short section on Margarete's house, but without interpretation (p. 118). Additionally, Ray Monk's recent, excellent biography on Wittgenstein cites from this quote the line: "*primordial* life, wild life striving to erupt into the open," as "a key to understanding both the purpose of his work and the direction of his life." (*Wittgenstein: The Duty of Genius* (New York: The Free Press, 1990), 490).

29. Monk, correctly I think, refers these lines to a later aphorism from 1946 concerning the limits of wisdom and the direction of a Kierkegaardian faith, a faith which is based in passion. Theory is not enough; Wittgenstein writes: "The point is that a sound doctrine need not *take hold* of you: you can follow it as you would a doctor's description.—But here you need something to move you and turn you in a new direction.—(i.e., this is how I understand it). Once you have been turned round, you must stay turned round./Wisdom is passionless. But faith by contrast is what Kierkegaard calls a passion" (C & V 53). Interestingly, Monk does not cite the architectural context of the lines from 1940 to which he gives such importance.

30. See Nicholas F. Gier, *Wittgenstein and Phenomenology: A Comparative Study of the Later Wittgenstein, Husserl, Heidegger, and Merleau-Ponty* (Albany: SUNY Press, 1981).

31. Anthony Kenny argues that "Wittgenstein's writings are now more widely read in France and Germany and other countries outside of the Anglo-American tradition;" Wittgenstein's "contribution has been neglected because more and more philosophers, especially in the United States, have attempted to model their studies on the pattern of a rigorously scientific discipline, mimicking the type of precision characteristic of mathematics, and holding up a general theory of linguistics as the ideal for philosophy of language, and an abstract system for artificial intelligence as the goal of philosophy of mind. This kind of scientism in philosophy was something which Wittgenstein abominated, and in such a climate the seeds he planted have a poor chance of flourishing growth" (*The Legacy of Wittgenstein*, vii–viii).

This striking view is supported by Stanley Cavell, who sees an important paradox in the profession. From his "Declining Decline: Wittgenstein as a Philosopher of Culture": "even when the acceptance of Wittgenstein as one of the major philosophical voices in the West since Kant may be taken for granted, it is apt to be controversial to find that his reception by professional philosophy is insufficient, that the spiritual fervor or seriousness of his writing is internal to his teaching say the manner (or method) to the substance, and that something in the very professionalization of philosophy debars professional philosophers from taking his seriousness seriously. I put this so as to bring out a structural pathos in this debarment—in philosophy's blindness to, or constricted view of, one of its masters—for various reasons" (*This New Yet Unapproachable America*, 30). As to one of these possible reasons, Cavell gives important indications in his aptly titled essay, "The Politics of Interpretation." Cavell's project of locating Emerson and Thoreau as the American source of the meaning of *ordinary* in ordinary language philosophy, his reading of Wittgenstein's, like Heidegger's, quest to bring words back home, orients what he calls his "lifetime quarrel with the profession of philosophy" (31). The problem: "to most of my colleagues the underwriting of ordinary language philosophy by transcendentalism would be about as promising as enlivening the passe by the extinct" (33). To which he adds the footnote: "In suggesting that these colleagues cannot be certain that they are right in this prediction, no more certain, at any rate, than they can be that philosophy is a science, I am appealing to this difference between the sciences and the humanities, that with the latter the past may at any time come to life, not merely as the recovery of certain neglected problems within the field but as a recovery of the field's originating preserving, authority" (33). This is the path of Wittgenstein that Cavell suggests is difficult, yet necessary, to locate. With regard to such a question of "recovery" and the climate that Cavell testifies to, one point underlined in this same article regarding his quarrel with professionalized philosophy, "the mutual shunning of the continental and the Anglo-American traditions" (31), deserves special mention in this context of Wittgenstein's recanting of his house. In the discussions with members of the Vienna Circle in 1929 the topic of Husserl and Heidegger did come up. Notably, Wittgenstein said: To be sure, I can imagine what Heidegger means by being and anxiety," and the question of "running up against the limits of language" is identified as ethics and as "indicating something" (*Wittgenstein and the Vienna Circle*, 68). Yet any such recognition on Wittgenstein's part, opening up just that dialogue that Cavell situates around the notion of "bringing words home," where the general *topos* of buildings is seen being shared between Wittgenstein, Heidegger, and Thoreau ("Declining Decline," 34-5), has been suppressed, first by World War Two and then by professional border disputes. An example: when excerpts from these discussions with the Vienna Circle first found their way into print (*Philosophical Review*, January 1965) the title and above line reflecting Wittgenstein's appreciation of Heidegger's "being and anxiety" was deleted. The full text didn't appear until two years later with the publication of the original German: *Ludwig Wittgenstein und der Weiner Kreis: Gesprache, aufzeichnet von Friedrich Waismann*, Schriften 3, edited by B.F. McGuinness (Frankfurt am Main, 1967). This censor effectively served to delay the significance of Wittgenstein's critique of his house and the importance that architecture can serve as a *topos* for his philosophy, those connections brought together, for instance, in Heidegger's "Building Dwelling Thinking" (*Poetry, Language, Thought*, 145–161). The editorial practice was exposed by Michael Murray and published as "A Note on Wittgenstein and Heidegger" in *Philosophical Review* 83 (1974), 501–3. The full German text wasn't translated until 1979.

32. This error can be seen in the just published (as I am writing this) essay by Peter Galison "Aufbau/Bauhaus: Logical Positivism and Architectural Modernism," to which I must return in more detailed critique. *Critical Inquiry* 16 (Summer 1990), 709–752.

33. The importance of the figure of the ear in Nietzsche's writing is discussed in Derrida's *The Ear of the Other*. The context is a discussion of the educated ear (certainly the meaning of Wittgenstein's comment) from Nietzsche's *On the Future of Our Educational Institutions* (1872) in which, in description of the university, he writes: "How is the student connected with the university? . . . By the ear, as a listener" (35). And Derrida asks us to: "Dream this umbilicus: it has you by the ear. It is an ear, however, that dictates to you what you are writing at this moment when you write in the mode of what is called 'taking notes.' In fact the mother—the bad or false mother whom the teacher, as a functionary of the State, can only simulate—dictates to you the very thing that passes through your ear and travels the length of the cord all the way down to your stenography. This writing links you, like a leash in the form of an umbilical cord, to the paternal body of the State" (35–6).

34. Brought under question by Wittgenstein's remarks is the founding of the edifice of modernity by Descartes upon the origin of a geometric thinking, which ultimately is employed to construct and map a new world, one radically separate from its classical predecessor. Descartes sought to invent a geometry that eliminated the possible discrepancies that Wittgenstein alludes to here. That is, analytic geometry was a system that eliminated space's "multiplicity" through a projection that left the world constructed according to its rules. The question that Wittgenstein brings up here, that of representation, was properly effaced in the seventeenth century, just at that moment when Descartes set their affect in motion. Wittgenstein's remarks here are some of the earlier indications of a critique of modernism which by this time is recognized loosely under the rubric of a postmodernism.

The requirements of an "expansible sign" that could share the phenomenological multiplicity of space, while nevertheless avoiding the temptation of an essential origin, the *Tractatus's* logical space, would be one in which the signifier/signified correlation would be called into question. This would be an historical interrogation, one that locates geometry's sign within its history. Such a critique is actually deconstruction's beginning in Derrida's analysis of Husserl's "Origin of Geometry," a reading that locates in Husserl's text the important tension within its version of the transcendental by which history, contingency, is always already found operating at its origins. Derrida writes: "But when, in the period of the crisis, history itself breaks through into phenomenology, a new space of questioning is opened, one that will be difficult to maintain in the regional limits which were so long prescribed for it" (Edmund Husserl's *Origin of Geometry: An Introduction*, 29). Historical constitution, then, renders an "expansible sign" in geometry, not due to an *eidos* of self-certainty or truth, but due to the inventiveness of the signifier, its play, by which Descartes's analysis supplanted Euclid's geometry. Derrida's critique of the sign, of its holding expression and content together, might be seen applied here to Wittgenstein's difficulty with a properly "expansible" sign. Likewise, Wittgenstein's identification of analytic geometry as providing the "correct multiplicity" (*PR*, 177) can only be accepted within the context of its deconstruction as inventive constructivism, emphasizing technical virtuosity, which built the modern world as we know it. Wittgenstein's text, here, attests to just this struggle with modern representation, with the *ethos* of Cartesian constructive geometry (see Lachterman's *The Ethics of Geometry: A Genealogy of Modernity*) whose hold on the world is only now being disassembled according to the practices of deconstruction and postmodernism.

35. The emphasis upon a word's use over its meaning can be detected as early as the *Remarks*. See especially Chapter II. An example: "14. A word only has meaning in the context of a proposition: that is like saying only in use is a rod a lever. Only the application makes it into a lever" (59). And other notable examples throughout this chapter that compare to formulations in the *Investigations*. One example from this section (also similar to one found in the *Investigations*, noted by Anthony Kenny in his book *Wittgenstein*) involves an insight formulated in the design of the door handles for his house. He writes:

> Imagine a gearbox whose lever can take four positions. Now of course it can only take three positions in succession, and that takes time; and suppose it happened that it only ever occupied one of these positions, since the gearbox was then destroyed. Wasn't it still a gearbox with four positions? Weren't the four possible?
>
> Anyone who saw it would have seen its complexity, and its complexity is only to be explained by the use for which it was intended, to which in fact it was not put. Similarly, I would like to say in the case of language: What's the point of all these preparations; they only have any meaning if they find a use. (59)

The minimal, utilitarian character of the door handles he designed were according to his own comment meant to make them invisible to all except those who were to use them. With respect to a locked latch in 1930 he wrote: "the honorable thing to do is to put a lock on the door which will be noticed only by those who can open it, not by the rest" (*C & V*, 8)

36. Wittgenstein provides a clue, also, from the *Remarks*:

> The stream of life, or the stream of the world, flows on and our propositions are so to speak verified only at instants.
>
> Our propositions are only verified by the present.
>
> So they must be so constructed that they can be verified by it. And so in some way they must be commensurate with the present; and they cannot

> be so *in spite of* their spatio-temporal nature; on the contrary this must be related to their commensurability as the corporeality of a ruler is to its being extended—which is what enables it to measure. In this case, too, you cannot say: "A ruler does measure in spite of its corporeality; of course a ruler which only has length would be the Ideal, you might say the pure ruler." No, if a body has length, there can be no length without a body—and although I realize that in a certain sense only the ruler's length measures, what can I put in my pocket still remains the ruler, the body, and isn't the length. (*PR*, 48)

37. Such a virus was reported in a letter to the editor of *Progressive Architecture* some years back.

38. These remarks and the focus of this section are drawn from the published collection entitled *Culture and Value*, selected from Wittgenstein's *Nachlass*. This work includes notes that the editor describes in the preface as "not belonging directly with his philosophical works although they are scattered amongst the philosophical texts." Left scattered, then, among the proper work, nomadic, homeless thoughts reflecting more directly Wittgenstein's life, his manner of working, his more general interests, the editor in gathering some into a published text expresses his concerns, his respects. Such separations are always difficult, and in Wittgenstein's case they are compounded by the intrinsic mixing of his aphoristic series. The editor explains: "It is not always possible to separate them sharply from the philosophical text." This certainly would be one of Wittgenstein's lessons, that a picture of philosophy with such "resolution" (as to what is the work and what is the life) would be contrary to his teaching, to the recognition that sometimes what is needed is the fuzzy picture. Yet, von Wright, needing to preserve the proprieties of the public and private (an obsession in the case of Wittgenstein's archives, especially this coded material of the *Nachlass*) exiles these very nomadic thoughts wandering through the texts to a collection, yet another text, opened this time with full security as to their difference from the philosophical work. As von Wright insists: "these notes can be properly understood and appreciated only against the background of Wittgenstein's philosophy and, furthermore, they make a contribution to our understanding of that philosophy." That is, these notes, even with the "notes of a purely 'personal' sort" excluded, provide but a frame, a decorative, culturally fitting border within which to "properly" understand Wittgenstein's philosophical world. This work, then, the editor insists is so separable from life, at least Wittgenstein's life, the external circumstances of his life, his state of mind and relations with others," i.e., his "forms of life." Such insistence in the face of Wittgenstein's lessons regarding stopping philosophy, a therapeutic goal, quite blatantly displays the work of the *parergon*, insisting on the impermeability of the frame even as what is so gathered by it includes: "It is sometimes said that a man's philosophy is a matter of temperament, and there is something in this. A preference for certain similes could be called a matter of temperament and it underlines far more disagreements than you might think" (20). Wittgenstein suggests, and the editor's notion of "purity" operative here apparently doesn't

exclude its admission, that the autobiographical can help clarify the philosophical and not simply the converse, as von Wright seeks with his frame to limit the possible connections. To admit the work of the *parergon,* the frame, requires abandoning any pretense of purity and accepting the usefulness and often necessity of the consequently fuzzy picture. This is Wittgenstein's lesson, and its difficulty ironically falls more to those who knew him than more distant readers of his text and teachings. In this connection Merleau-Ponty's comments on his interpretation of Husserl is an apt analogy: "Because for those who have known the visible Husserl the difficulties of communicating with an author are added on to those of communicating with his works. . . . Like all those near to us, Husserl present in person (and in addition with the genius' power to fascinate and to deceive) could not, I imagine, leave those surrounding him in peace. Their whole philosophical life must have lain for a time in that extraordinary and inhuman occupation of being present at the continuing birth of a way of thinking, and of helping it become objective or even exist as a communicable thought" ("The Philosopher and His Shadow," 160–1). This describes quite well the conflict surrounding current research on Wittgenstein, especially Kenny's critique cited above. Von Wright's paradox seems to hang on Derrida's assertion that "there is nothing outside the text," his inability to recognize the statement's full implications, especially for his difficult task of editing Wittgenstein's work, i.e., that such notes cannot be in any way "pure," whether autobiographical or not (see Derrida's comments in this regard on Nietzsche's text in *The Ear of the Other: "Otobiographies"*), simply due to their status as written. Reading, then, does not make such separations, always trying in its way to bring the nomadic back to the ordinary; this is Wittgenstein's lesson, certainly by the *Investigations.* And the hypothesis of the present inquiry into Wittgenstein's work is that his architecture, normally placed within the frame of autobiographic interest, does a great deal of parergonal work in clarifying the philosophical of Wittgenstein's text.

39. Certainly Wittgenstein's work evidences the difficulties of translation, literally, of carrying across, in this case the Channel, from German to English. Yet Wittgenstein continued to write in German, despite his English audience. His work's reception, then, would clearly be marked by such arrival in and through English on its way here to the new (modern) world (now postmodern?): from "*Bild*" to "picture," a move that preserves as it transforms sense, something of the context inevitably being lost. (Partially, at least, an object of this inquiry's retrieval). Optimistically, Wittgenstein suggests in this state a gain for language (its form of life?). With translation the contingency of language use makes itself apparent, indeed identified by style, opening meaning to new possibilities.

This does reject the positivist sense of "translation to a pure language by which the meaning of an expression is determined propositionally. Wittgenstein gives up such foundational views, which seek a return to an origin of sense. Rather, like Derrida, translation might better be characterized as the inevitable reading of a text to which the author from the beginning is indebted. That is, the notion of the "original" is put in question for the "translation," the two needing each other as complements. Deconstructing the notion of the original, of an original reading, of authorial intent, requires relaxing these distinctions and investing a text's meaning on its future, which always awaits the work of the translator. The concerns consequently become archaeological, political and legal, the fuller and always somewhat indefinite context of a text (see Derrida's "*Des Tours de Babel*" in *Difference in Translation*). Derrida and Wittgenstein share an enormous debt to the translator for developing the significance of their philosophy through delivering it to different language games played within and across different national borders. Derrida has emphasized that deconstruction is an American phenomenon, even as it was "originally" a French export, and his work has attempted to anticipate and be responsive to this reception, i.e., the work of the translator. (See "Deconstruction in America").

40. Many of the drawings exhibited were actually made after the projects were completed, studies which then serve to animate future projects. From the back cover of their book *Morphosis: Buildings and Projects*: "One of the unique features of the methods of design of Morphosis Architects is the way in which they use models and drawings. Unlike most architects, after a building is completed Mayne and Rotondi go back to the drawings and models, reworking and analyzing them as sources of inspiration and generation for new designs. It is through this activity of creating and recreating that the name *Morphosis* is derived."

41. See for example his treatment of color samples and measurement standards in the *Investigations*, especially *PI* I, 0.

42. Also see aphorisms 70 and 77.

CHAPTER 6

1. Descartes, "preface" to the *Principles of Philosophy*, in *The Philosophical Writings of Descartes*, trans. John Cottingham, Robert Stoothoff, Dugald Murdoch (London: Cambridge University Press, 1985), Vol. I, p. 186.

2. Friedrich Nietzsche, "*Ueber Wahrheit und Lüge im aussermoralischen Sinne*" in: *Sämtliche Werke. Kritische Studienausgabe in 15 Bänden*, ed. Giorgio Colli and Mazzino Montinari (München, Berlin, New York: De Gruyter, 1988 (2.). All further references to Nietzsche's texts refer to this edition and will be given with volume and page number only, here: I, 881. All translations from Nietzsche are my own.

3. Martin Heidegger, "The Question concerning Technology" in: *The Question Concerning Technology and Other Essays*, trans. and with an introduction by William Lovitt (New York, Cambridge: Harper 1977), p. 29.

4. Blumenberg proceeds from Husserl's understanding of metaphor as a sudden anomaly within an originally coherent mode of appearance. While a metaphor is originally rooted in the life-world, it cannot be reduced back to its

origin because the rupture is subsequently subsumed under and integrated into a higher order of normality. In order to illustrate that there is no absolute break and thus no absolute metaphor, Blumenberg quotes a verse of Matthias Claudius in which the forest is silent ["*schweigt*"] and he adds: "This is another case of the 'laughing meadow'; but in the case of the forest it is linguistically more familiar to us that one cannot see it of all the trees once one has entered into it. 'Forest' already contains a rupture of our perception. In this respect the world is a forest which we never perceive other than from within it—*in hac silva plena* says Marsilio Ficino—and which we can never see for all the trees. Just as the forest in the last instance will never dissolve itself into trees, the absolute metaphors which have been found for the world will never dissolve into properties and determinations." Hans Blumenberg, *Schiffbruch mit Zuschauer. Paradigma einer Daseinsmetapher* (Frankfurt a. M.: Suhrkamp, 1979), p. 80. Incidentally, the relationship of forest and trees in the context of phenomenology echoes in a remark by Walter Benjamin who knew the Husserl school well. Under the heading "To the Public: Please Protect and Preserve these New Plantings" he writes: "What is 'solved'? Do not all questions of our lives, as we live, remain behind us like foliage obstructing our view? To uproot this foliage, even to thin it out, does not occur to us. We stride on, leave it behind, and from a distance it is indeed open to view, but indistinct, shadowy, and all the more enigmatically entangled." Walter Benjamin, "One Way Street" in: *Reflections. Essays, Aphorisms, Autobiographical Writings*, trans. by Edmund Jephcott, ed. Peter Demetz (New York: Schocken Books, 1986), p. 67/8.

5. On the tree in Augustine see Paul G. Kuntz and Marion L. Kuntz, "The Symbol of the Tree Interpreted in the Context of other Symbols of the Great Chain of Being and the Jacob's Ladder" in: *Jacob's Ladder and the Tree of Life. Concepts of Hierarchy and the Great Chain of Being*, ed. Marion Leathers Kuntz and Paul Grimley Kuntz (American University Studies,: 1986), pp. 319–334.

6. This association of the tree and sexuality entirely determines the baroque use of the tree as an emblem. In Arthur Henkel's and Albrecht Schöne's collection of baroque emblemata where the tree fills a sizable chapter, the themes of matrimonial union and matrimonial problems seem to dominate. Even the rather sober *Zedlers Universal Lexicon* from 1733 feels obliged to inform its readers of a potential scientific basis for gendered trees in form of a theory about male and female trees which are said to maintain amorous contact in form of their roots intertwining beneath the visible surface (p.734). This aspect of the tree image is latently present still in Ferdinand Saussure's foundational work on general linguistics. Whether intentionally or not, when introducing his notion of the sign with the help of the Latin word Arbor (tree) alongside its pictorial representation, Saussure chose one of those very rare Latin nouns which belong to a masculine declination but are of female gender. In light of this Jacques Lacan's transformation of the Saussure's famous diagram of the sign into a gendered sign reveals an ironic twist.

7. Cf. Arthur Oncken Lovejoy, *The Great Chain of Being. A Study in the His-*

tory of an Idea, (Cambridge, Massachusetts a. London, England: Harvard University Press, 1936).

8. See footnote 5.

9. Cf. Frances A. Yates, "Lullism as an Art of Memory" in Frances A. Yates, *The Art of Memory* (Chicago: University of Chicago Press, 1966), p. 173–198.

10. d'Alembert, *Preliminary Discourse to the Encyclopedia of Diderot*, trans. Richard N. Schwab a. Walter E. Rex (Indianapolis: The Bobbs Merrill Company, 1963), p. 47–48.

11. On the emergence of temporalization in the natural sciences see Wolf Lepenies, *Das Ende der Naturgeschichte. Wandel kultureller Selbstverständlichkeiten in den Wissenschaften des 18. und 19. Jahrhunderts* (Frankfurt a. M.: Suhrkamp, 1978).

12. Immanuel Kant,preface to the first edition of the Critique of Pure Reason, trans. Norman Kemp Smith (New York: St. Martin's Press, 1965), p. 14 (Axxi). Translation modified.

13. Kant, Critique of Pure Reason, p. 61 (A15/B29).

14. Johann Gottfried Herder, "*Auch eine Philosophie der Geschichte*" in *Herders Werke in fünf Bänden*, ed. *Nationale Forschungs- und Gedenkstätten der klassischen deutschen Literatur in Weimar* (Berlin a. Weimar: Aufbau Verlag, 1964), Vol. II, p. 282.

15. Johann Gottfried Herder, "Auch eine Philosophie der Geschichte", p. 283.

16. Fichte, *Wissenschaftslehre* (Hamburg: Felix Meiner Verlag, 1982), p. 210. Fichte here chose the tree because it already had served Kant as an example of what an organism is (in contradistinction to a machine) in the latter parts of his Critique of Judgement.

17. Hegel, *Lectures on the Philosophy of Religion, Vol. I: Introduction and the Concept of Religion*, ed. Peter C. Hodgson (Berkley: University of California Press, 1984), p. 175. For intense reflections specifically on "Hegel's trees" see Jacques Derrida, *Glas*, trans. John P. Leavey, Jr. (Lincoln a. London: University of Nebraska Press), 1986. The index of the accompanying "GLASsary" by the translator lists several references to Derrida's discussion and it also includes the original quotations from Hegel's own texts. For a more general account of metaphoricity and philosophy see Jacques Derrida, "White Mythology: Metaphor in the Text of Philosophy" in *Margins of Philosophy*, trans. Alan Bass (Chicago: University of Chicago Press, 1982), p. 207–271.

18. Johann Georg Hamann, "*Metakritik über den Purismum der Vernunft*" in *Schriften zur Sprache*, ed. Josef Simon (Frankfurt a. M.: Suhrkamp Verlag, 1967), p. 224. The sentence appears originally in the preface of Kant's own *Critique*.

19. Hamann, p. 222.

20. Hamann, p. 222.

21. Hamann, p. 224.

22. Hamann, p.224.

23. "*-Die Entstehung verherrlichen - das ist der metaphysische Nachtrieb, welcher bei der Betrachtung der Historie wieder ausschlägt und durchaus meinen macht, am Anfang aller Dinge stehe das Werthvollste und Wesentlichste.*

[-Glorifying the origin - that is the metaphysical branch which sprouts again in the consideration of history and makes one believe that the most valuable and most essential could be found at the beginning of all things]" (II, 540).

24. "*Wir glauben etwas von den Dingen selbst zu wissen, wenn wir von Bäumen, Farben, Schnee und Blumen reden und besitzen doch nichts als Metaphern der Dinge, die den ursprünglichen Wesenheiten ganz und gar nicht entsprechen.*

[We believe to know something of the things in themselves, when we speak of trees, colors, snow and flowers, and yet we possess nothing but metaphors of those things, and they do not at all correspond to any original essences]" (I, 879).

25. I, 880.

CHAPTER 7

Earlier portions of this paper, which is part of a larger study about the theoretical and philosophical impact of texts by Jorge Luis Borges, were presented as conferences at the University of Pennsylvania (Dec. 1990), at Harvard University (Jan. 1994), and at Emory University (Feb. 1994). I would like to thank W. J. T. Mitchell for drawing my attention a long time ago to the significant frequency of the cartographic metaphor, John Carvalho for his response during the 1991 IAPL conference, José Miguel Oviedo, Peter Earle, Shelagh Lindsey, Stephen Jakobson, Joanna Morris, Oscar Barrau, and Maarten and Wouter Bosteels for their helpful suggestions, as well as David Herman and Sandra Lynn Shapshay for kindly correcting parts of the English manuscript.

1. Miguel de Cervantes Saavedra, *El ingenioso hidalgo don Quijote de la Mancha*, ed. Luis Andrés Murillo, 3 vols. (Madrid: Castalia, 1984), part 2, chapter 6. This passage, according to the narrator, is "one of the most important chapters in the entire history."

2. For the turn to territories, see for example Gilles Deleuze and Félix Guattari, *What is Philosophy?*, trans. Hugh Tomlinson and Graham Burchell (New York: Columbia University Press, 1994): "Thinking is neither a line drawn between subject and object, nor a revolving of one around the other. Rather, think-

ing takes place in the relationship of territory and the earth" (p. 85). For a return to works, see Paisley Livingston, "From Text to Work," in *After Poststructuralism: Interdisciplinarity and Literary Theory*, eds. Nancy Easterlin and Barbara Riebling, foreword Frederick Crews (Evanston, Ill.: Northwestern University Press, 1993), pp. 91–104.

3. See especially the articles in *Place and the Politics of Identity*, ed. Michael Keith and Steve Pile (London: Routledge, 1993) and in *NowHere: Space, Time and Modernity*, ed. Roger Friedland and Deirdre Boden (Berkeley: University of California Press, 1994).

4. Michel Foucault, *The Archaeology of Knowledge and The Discourse on Language*, trans. A. M. Sheridan Smith (New York: Pantheon, 1972), p. 230. Martin Heidegger's thinking in fact presents a cross-over from temporality and history to spatiality and geography. See Didier Franck, *Heidegger et le problème de l'espace* (Paris: Minuit, 1986), and Michel Haar, *The Song of the Earth: Heidegger and the Grounds of the History of Being*, trans. Reginald Lilly, foreword John Sallis (Bloomington: Indiana University Press, 1993). When in "Time and Being" (1969), *On Time and Being*, trans. Joan Stambaugh (New York: Harper & Row, 1972), Heidegger writes: "The attempt in *Being and Time*, section 70, to derive human spatiality from temporality is untenable" (p. 23), he is, according to Franck, revealing the profound reason why the earlier work necessarily must remain incomplete. From the conference "The Origin of The Work of Art" onward, then, Heidegger's thinking increasingly deals with the problematic of space (earth, world, dwelling, etc.).

5. *Mapping Ideology*, ed. Slavoj Žižek (London: Verso, 1994).

6. Andreas Huyssen, "Mapping the Postmodern," *New German Critique* 33 (1984): 10. See also Deborah Cook, "Remapping Modernity," *British Journal of Aesthetics* 30 (1990): 35–45. As Arkady Plotnitsky writes: "To use a fashionable postmodernist metaphor, postmodernism may also be *mapped* as the postmodernism of maps, whose historical or geographical decidability or even possibility, particularly as totalizing possibility, many, *but not all*, recent postmodernisms, put into question," *Reconfigurations: Critical Theory and General Economy* (Gainesville: University Press of Florida, 1993), p. 37.

7. Fredric Jameson, "Postmodernism, or The Cultural Logic of Late Capitalism," *New Left Review* 146 (1984), reprinted as the title-essay in *Postmodernism, or, The Cultural Logic of Late Capitalism* (London: Verso, 1991), pp. 44 and 54. See also Jameson's "Cognitive Mapping," in *Marxism and the Interpretation of Culture*, ed. Cary Nelson and Lawrence Grossberg (Urbana: University of Illinois Press, 1988), partially reprinted in the final section of the book on postmodernism. An important source of inspiration for Jameson is Kevin Lynch, *The Image of the City* (Cambridge: MIT Press, 1960). Other aspects of "cognitive mapping" can be found throughout Jameson's work, especially in the essay, "Modernism and Imperialism," in *Nationalism, Colonialism, and Literature*, introd. Seamus Deane (Minneapolis: University of Minnesota Press, 1990), pp. 43–66; and in

The Geopolitical Aesthetic: Cinema and Space in the World System (Bloomington: Indiana University Press, 1992). For a case-study, see Mary Hamer, "Putting Ireland on the Map," *Textual Practice* 3 (1989): 184–201. See also Timothy J. Reiss, "Mapping Identities: Literature, Nationalism, Colonialism," *American Literary History* 4 (1992): 650–77.

8. Antoine Compagnon, "Mapping the European Mind," *Critical Quarterly* 32 (1990): 4.

9. Leo Apostel and Jan Van der Veken, *Wereldbeelden: Van fragmentering naar integratie* (Kapellen: De Nederlandsche Boekhandel-Pelckmans, 1992), p. 30.

10. Michel Serres, *Atlas* (Paris: Julliard, 1994). Jorge Luis Borges, to whom I will frequently return in the following pages, also has a book called *Atlas*, with pictures by María Kodama (Buenos Aires: Sudamericana, 1984).

11. On the map as literary topos, see for example Jules Zanger, "'Harbours Like Sonnets': Literary Maps and Cartographic Symbols," *The Georgia Review* 36 (1982): 773–90. See also the special issue of *Word & Image* 4 (1988) on *Maps and Mapping*; and Mark Pietralunga, "Cartophilia in Italo Calvino's *Le città invisibili*," *Italiana 1988*, ed. Albert N. Mancini, Paolo A. Giordano, Anthony J. Tamburri (River Forest: Rosary College Italian Studies, 1990), pp. 237–49. Recent examples in North American literature include *Cartographies* by Maya Sonenberg (New York: The Eco Press, 1989), *The Art of Cartography* by J. S. Marcus (New York: Alfred A. Knopf, 1991); *Falling Off the Map: Some Lonely Places of the World* by Pico Iyer (New York: Alfred A. Knopf, 1993); and *Fathering the Map*, by Robert Pack (Chicago: University of Chicago Press, 1993). For a sampling of cartography in contemporary art, see the catalogues of recent exhibits: Lothar Baumgarten, AMERICA *Invention* (New York: Solomon R. Guggenheim Museum, 1993); *Cartographies* (Winnipeg: Winnipeg Art Gallery, 1993); *Mapping* (New York: Museum of Modern Art, 1994); *Burning Beds: Guillermo Kuitca: A Survey 1982–1994* (Columbus, Ohio: Wexner Center for the Arts, 1994). A compelling synthesis of the utopian drive behind maps can be found in Louis Marin, "Frontiers of Utopia: Past and Present," *Critical Inquiry* 19 (1993): 397–420.

12. See, in particular, Jacques Derrida, "The Double Session," *Dissemination*, trans. Barbara Johnson (Chicago: The University of Chicago Press, 1981), pp. 173–286, esp. pp. 186–87 n. 14.

13. Friedrich Nietzsche, *On the Uses and Disadvantages of History for Life*, in *Untimely Meditations*, trans. R. J. Hollingdale (Cambridge: Cambridge University Press, 1983). The "end of history" debate refers mainly to Alexandre Kojève's reading of Hegel, in *Introduction to the Reading of Hegel's Phenomenology of Mind*, ed. Allan Bloom, trans. James Nichols (New York: Basic Books, 1969). See Barry Cooper, *The End of History: An Essay on Modern Hegelianism* (Toronto: University of Toronto Press, 1984); and Julian Pefanis, "W(h)ither History," *Heterology and the Postmodern: Bataille, Baudrillard, and Lyotard* (Durham: Duke University Press, 1991), pp. 9–20. Both Hegelian and vaguely Nietzschean lines of historical argumentation are welded together in Francis Fukuyama, *The End of History and the*

Last Man (New York: Avon, 1992). For the concept of post-history, see the survey by Lutz Niethammer, with Dirk Van Laak, *Posthistoire: Has History Come to an End?*, trans. Patrick Camiller (London: Verso, 1992).

14. Michel Foucault, "Questions on Geography," in *Power/Knowledge: Selected Interviews and Other Writings 1972–1977*, ed. Colin Gordon (Brighton, Sussex: Harvester Press, 1980), p. 70. For an analysis of Foucault's geographical matrix, aside from the works of Edward Soja, see Felix Driver, "Geography and Power: The Work of Michel Foucault," in *Critical Essays on Michel Foucault*, ed. Peter Burke (Scolar Press, 1992), pp. 147–56; and Thomas Flynn, "Foucault and the Spaces of History," *Monist* 45 (1991): 165–86.

15. Georg W. F. Hegel, *The Philosophy of History*, trans. J. Sibree (Buffalo: Prometheus Books, 1991), p. 87.

16. Quoted by Brian Robinson, "The Geography of a Crossroads: Modernism, Surrealism, and Geography," in *Geography and Literature: A Meeting of the Disciplines*, ed. William E. Mallory and Paul Simpson-Housley (Syracuse: Syracuse University Press, 1987), pp. 187–88.

17. See for example Erika Fischer-Lichte, "The Shift of the Paradigm: From Time to Space? Introduction," *Proceedings of the XIIth Congress of the International Comparative Literature Association Munich 1988*, ed. Roger Bauer, Douwe Fokkema, and Michael de Graat, vol. 5 (München: Iudicium, 1990), pp. 15–18.

18. Georg Lukács, *History and Class Consciousness: Studies in Marxist Dialectics*, trans. Rodney Livingstone (Cambridge: MIT Press, 1971), p. 90. Foucault also writes that today, "our experience of the world is less that of a long life developing through time than that of a network that connects points and intersects with its own skein" ("Of Other Spaces," *Diacritics* 16 [1986]: 22).

19. Henri Lefebvre, *The Production of Space*, trans. Donald Nicholson-Smith (Cambridge: Blackwell, 1991). Edward W. Soja, *Postmodern Geographies: The Reassertion of Space in Critical Social Theory* (London: Verso, 1989). See also the recent statement by Soja, "Postmodern Geographies and the Critique of Historicism," in *Postmodern Contentions: Epochs, Politics, Space*, ed. John Paul Jones III, Wolfgang Natter, and Theodore R. Schatzki (New York: Guilford Press, 1993), pp. 113–36. Comparable to Soja's program is Derek Gregory, *Geographical Imaginations* (Cambridge: Blackwell, 1994).

20. Foucault, "Questions on Geography," pp. 69–71.

21. Soja, *Postmodern Geographies*, p. 75.

22. Jameson, *Postmodernism*, p. 52.

23. See especially the Foucauldian-inspired work of John Brian Harley, "Maps, Knowledge, and Power," in *The Iconography of Landscape. Essays on the Symbolic Representation, Design, and Use of Past Environments*, ed. Denis Cosgrove and Stephen Daniels (Cambridge: Cambridge University Press, 1988), pp. 277–

312; and "Deconstructing the Map," in *Writing Worlds. Discourse, Text & Metaphor in the Representation of Landscape*, ed. Trevor J. Barnes and James S. Duncan (London: Routledge, 1992), pp. 231–47. For a materialist perspective, see Peter Jackson, *Maps of Meaning. An Introduction to Cultural Geography* (London: Unwin Hyman, 1989).

24. Stephen S. Hall, *Mapping the Next Millenium. The Discovery of New Geographies* (New York: Random House, 1992). General accounts of cognitive or mental maps are Peter Gould and Rodney White, *Mental Maps* (New York: Penguin, 1974); Roger M. Downs and David Stea, *Maps in Minds. Reflections on Cognitive Mapping* (New York: Harper & Row, 1977); and Roger M. Downs, *Image and Environment: Cognitive Mapping and Spatial Behavior* (Chicago: Aldine, 1973). For applications to literature, see Caroline D. Eckhardt, "Recharting the Literary Map of the Americas," in *New Literary Continents*, ed. C. D. Eckhardt et al. (Whitestone, NY: Griffon, 1981), pp. 16–25, and Richard Bjornson, "Cognitive Mapping and the Understanding of Literature," *SubStance* 30 (1981): 51–62.

25. A discussion of the most typical diagrams can be found in Rolf von Eckartsberg, "Maps of the Mind: The Cartography of Consciousness," in *The Metaphors of Consciousness*, ed. Ronald S. Valle and R. von Eckartsberg (New York: Plenum, 1981), pp. 21–93. A more extensive overview is offered by Charles Hampden-Turner, *Maps of the Mind. Charts and Concepts of the Mind and its Labyrinths* (New York: Collier, 1982). Here I should also mention Freud and Lacan's attempts to describe the topology of the unconscious. For a criticism of the alliance between psychoanalysis and geography, see Derrida, "Géopsychanalyse 'and the rest of the world,'" in *Psyché. Inventions de l'autre* (Paris: Galilée, 1987), pp. 327–52.

26. See Howard F. Stein and William G. Niederland, eds., *Maps from the Mind. Readings in Psychogeography* (Norman: University of Oklahoma Press, 1989), pp. xii–xiii.

27. Deleuze and Guattari, "Geophilosophy," in *What is Philosophy?*, pp. 85–113. On the topic of spatial matrices in poststructuralism, see also Christian Ruby, *Les archipels de la différence. Foucault-Derrida-Deleuze-Lyotard* (Paris: Editions du Félin, 1989). For a philosophical reading of maps, see Christian Jacob, "Le contour et la limite. Pour une approche philosophique des cartes géographiques," in *Frontières et limites. Géopolitique, littérature, philosophie* (Paris: Editions du Centre Pompidou, 1991), pp. 143–67.

28. See especially the seminal texts "Introduction to a Critique of Urban Geography," "Report on the Construction of Situations," and "Theory of the Dérive," in *Situationist International Anthology*, ed. and trans. Ken Knabb (Berkeley: Bureau of Public Secrets, 1989). Examples of psychogeographical maps, like Guy Debord's "The Naked City," can be found on the cover of this anthology and in *On the Passage of a Few People Through a Rather Brief Moment in Time: The Situationist International 1957–1972*, ed. Elisabeth Sussman (Cambridge: MIT Press, 1991), p. 135. For an excellent study of these maps and a comparison with

Jameson, see Thomas F. McDonough, "Situationist Space," *October* 67 (1994): 59–77. A French reprint of Debord's *La société du spectacle* (Paris: Champ Libre, 1971) also reproduces a map on its cover, representing the global development of capitalism. The situationists' psychogeography, moreover, should be seen in connection with recent neo-avant-gardistic projects like the special issue of *Semiotext(e), USA: Psychotopographical Projection* (1987).

29. Alfred Korzybski, *Science and Insanity: An Introduction to Non-Aristotelian Systems and General Semantics* (Lancaster: Science Printing Press, 1933), especially the chapter "On Structure" (pp. 55–65), and the supplement, "A Non-Aristotelian System and Its Necessity for Rigour in Mathematics and Physics" (pp. 747–61). For Gregory Bateson's discussion of "map" and "territory," see "A Theory of Play and Fantasy," and "Form, Substance, and Difference," both essays in *Steps to an Ecology of Mind* (New York: Ballantine Books, 1972), pp. 177–93, and 448–66; "Every Schoolboy Knows...," in *Mind and Nature: A Necessary Unity* (New York: E. P. Dutton, 1979), pp. 30–31; and, finally, *A Sacred Unity: Further Steps to an Ecology of Mind*, ed. Rodney E. Donaldson (New York: HarperCollins, 1991), pp. 188–90, 199–200, 217–18. Most recently Wolfgang Iser has drawn upon Korzybski and Bateson for the "charting" of his literary anthropology, in "The Play of Map and Territory," *The Fictive and the Imaginary: Charting Literary Anthropology* (Baltimore: The Johns Hopkins University Press, 1993), pp. 247–50. Félix Guattari also relies on Bateson's ecology of mind in his last books, *Les trois écologies* (Paris: Galilée, 1989) and *Chaosmose* (Paris: Galilée, 1991).

30. Korzybski, *Science and Insanity*, pp. 58 and 750–51. For a criticism of the rigid polarity behind Korzybski's semantics, see William Dallman, "Of Maps, Territories, and Quanta," *Et cetera* 39 (1982): 65–70.

31. For the split of geography into the physical and the human, see Peter Haggett's *The Geographer's Art* (Oxford: Basil Blackwell, 1990). For a discussion of the distinction between *Urlandschaft* and *Kulturlandschaft*, see the classical statement by Carl O. Sauer, "The Morphology of Landscape," *University of California Publications in Geography* 2 (1925): 19–53. Insofar as "geography is based on the reality of the union of physical and cultural elements of the landscape," for Sauer "there is no place for a dualism of landscape" (p. 30). This is even more true of cartography which, without denying the fact that "the map *is not* the territory," is by definition grounded in a binding of the physical and the cultural, the material and the semiotic.

32. Martin Heidegger, "The Origin of the Work of Art," in *Basic Writings*, ed. David Farrell Krell (New York: HarperCollins, 1993), pp. 139–212. To express this counterplay, moreover, Heidegger uses the term *Riß*, whose double meaning of both "rift" and "sketch" or "outline" (*Grundriß*) offers a preliminary hint of the "map" as a way of both separating and mediating between "world" and "earth." For further comments, see Michel Haar, *The Song of the Earth*.

33. In *Text: The Genealogy of an Antidisciplinary Object* (Durham: Duke University Press, 1992), John Mowitt argues convincingly that the "text" of French

theory (Derrida, Barthes, Kristeva) does in fact emerge in answer to radical social and historical changes in the organization of disciplinary power, changes manifestly inscribed within the new object. My argument is not, however, that "sign" and "text" are impervious to socio-historical analysis, but rather that by definition the "map" is informed by a semantic and pragmatic complexity which can be shown to apply to the "sign" or "text" only through a series of stipulations of the kind found in Mowitt's book. To some extent this is also true of "discourse," although Foucault's notion engages a problematic similar to the one addressed by the spatial metaphors of "map" and "diagram." Thus, for example, in *Mapping the Language of Racism: Discourse and the Legitimation of Exploitation* (New York: Columbia University Press, 1992), Margaret Wetherell and Jonathan Potter justify the "map" metaphor in a study of "discursive practices" by invoking, among other reasons, that (1) "discourse seems insubstantial and transitory compared with the people, objects and events which furnish our world," whereas the cartographic metaphor "emphasizes that discourse does have substance, it is a material which can be explored and charted," and (2) "cultural maps and inventories keep changing," as do discursive practices (pp. 1–2).

34. Charles S. Peirce, "Logic as Semiotic: The Theory of Signs," in *Philosophical Writings of Peirce*, ed. Justus Buchler (New York: Dover, 1955), pp. 98–119. Usually, semioticians describe the map as a "diagram," which Peirce classifies as a "relational (hypo)icon." Contemporary criticisms of iconicity, however, also apply to maps, which are then increasingly seen as highly conventional signs: "symbols," in other words, rather than "icons." Finally, insofar as the map contains some type of pointing finger (a red spot, a pointing arrow, a personal pronoun, etc.) designating the viewer's position much in the same way demonstratives and shifters do, cartography also has an "indexical" constituent. Even if this element is physically or graphically absent, maps can be seen as instruments which, though thoroughly conventional, have primarily an indexical function.

35. Guy Debord, "Introduction to a Critique of Urban Geography," p. 5.

36. Louis Althusser, "Ideology and Ideological State Apparatuses (Notes towards an Investigation)," in *Lenin and Philosophy and Other Essays*, trans. Ben Brewster (New York: Monthly Review Press, 1971), p. 162. Althusser also speaks of ideology in terms of a topography (*une topique*): "A topography represents in a definite space the respective *sites* occupied by several realities: thus the economic is *at the bottom* (the base), the superstructure *above it*" (p. 135 n. 5). As Jameson writes in *Postmodernism*: "'Cognitive mapping' was in reality nothing but a code word for 'class-consciousness'—only it proposed the need for class-consciousness of a new and hitherto undreamed of kind, while it also inflected the account in the direction of that new spatiality implicit in the postmodern (which Ed Soja's *Postmodern Geographies* now places on the agenda in so eloquent and timely a fashion)" (pp. 417–18). The hypothesis of "cartography" as an answer to the question of superstructural formations is in fact already hinted

at by Althusser, for whom "the theory of the particular essence of the specific elements of the superstructure" remains, "like the map of Africa before the great explorations, a domain sketched in outline, with its great mountain chains and rivers, but most often unknown in detail beyond a few well-drawn regions" (*For Marx*, trans. Ben Brewster [London: Verso, 1979], p. 114, translation modified). Another important precursor of the marxist project of "mapping" culture is Walter Benjamin. See for example "A Berlin Chronicle," *Reflections*, trans. Edmund Jephcott (New York: Schocken Books, 1978): "I have long, indeed for years, played with the idea of setting out the sphere of life—bios—graphically on a map. First I envisaged an ordinary map, but now I would incline to a general staff's map of a city center, if such a thing existed" (p. 5).

37. Jameson, "Foreword," in *The Postmodern Condition. A Report on Knowledge*, by Jean-François Lyotard, trans. Geoff Bennington and Brian Massumi (Minneapolis: University of Minnesota Press, 1984), p. xv.

38. Althusser, *For Marx*, p. 243.

39. Most people who have grown accustomed with the *imago mundi* of the Mercator projection will at first suffer from ontological and ideological stress when they witness the unsettling "Turnabout Maps" which put Australia, Africa, or South-America no longer "down under" but "on top." For a discussion of the new Peters projection, first presented two decades ago in answer to the distortions of the Mercator projection, see Arno Peters, *The New Cartography* (New York: Friendship Press, 1983). A brief presentation of the debate can be consulted in Ward L. Kaiser, *A New View of the World. A Handbook to the World Map: Peters Projection* (New York: Friendship Press, 1987).

40. Martin Jay, *Marxism and Totality. The Adventures of a Concept from Lukács to Habermas* (Berkeley: University of California Press, 1984): "there are no easy ways to map the rugged and shifting terrain of the intellectual territory known as Western Marxism" (p. 1), but "it is to the concept of totality that we can look for a compass to help us traverse the vast and uncharted intellectual territory that is Western Marxism" (p. 14). Edward Soja follows Jay's example in using a cartographic opposition between "longitudinal" and "latitudinal" totalities, analogous to the dichotomies of diachrony and synchrony, history and society. Compare also with the title of Paul Buhle, *Marxism in the United States. Remapping the History of the American Left* (London: Verso, 1991). Finally, see also Lawrence Grossberg and Cary Nelson, "Introduction: The Territory of Marxism," in *Marxism and the Interpretation of Culture*, pp. 1–13.

41. Jameson, "Cognitive Mapping," pp. 353 and 356. I will not dwell upon the peculiar tense—something of a future anterior—in which Jameson's project is formulated ("was to have been mapped"), even though the temporality of representation, too, must be addressed by anyone intent on reshaping the model of cartographic semiosis. See also William C. Dowling, "Thinking the Totality," in his *Jameson, Althusser, Marx: An Introduction to "The Political Unconscious"* (Ithaca: Cornell University Press, 1984), pp. 38–56.

42. Jorge Luis Borges, "On Rigor in Science," *Dreamtigers*, trans. Mildred Boyer and Harold Morland, introd. Miguel Enguídanos (Austin: University of Texas Press), p. 90. According to Patrick Hughes and George Brecht, *Vicious Circles and Infinity. An Anthology of Paradoxes* (London: Penguin, 1978), pp. 65–66, Borges's story derives from Lewis Carroll. While this is confirmed by the "Emperor" and "beggar" who appear in Carroll's *Sylvie and Bruno Concluded*, the reader should also bear in mind the terminological coincidences with the fragment from Cervantes ("inclemencies," "relics"). Useful interpretations of Borges's text which I cannot discuss here include Daniel Bougnoux, "La carte et le territoire," *Vices et vertus des cercles. L'autoréférence en poétique et pragmatique* (Paris: Editions de La Différence, 1989), pp. 163–67; and Louis Marin, "L'utopie de la carte," *Utopiques: jeux d'espaces* (Paris: Minuit, 1973), pp. 291–96. In an uncharacteristic disparagement Jameson writes that examples like Borges's map "have all the vulgarity and lack of 'distinction' of Escher prints on the walls of middlebrow college students" (*Postmodernism*, p. 430 n. 60): a puzzling judgment indeed in view of the map's success in books by Jean Baudrillard, Jean-François Lyotard, Félix Guattari, and Jameson himself.

43. Borges, "Partial Enchantments of the *Quixote*," *Other Inquisitions 1937–1952*, trans. Ruth L. C. Simms, introd. James E. Irby (Austin: University of Texas Press, 1964), p. 46. The fragment is adapted from Josiah Royce, who uses the example in his discussion of infinite series and self-representative systems, "The One, the Many, and the Infinite," in *The World and the Individual*, vol. 1 (New York: Dover, 1959), pp. 504–05. Korzybski credits Royce for having pointed out this possibility of self-reflexiveness shared by cartography and language (*Science and Insanity*, pp. 58 and 751). Peirce argues against Royce with the startling but suggestive idea of a "continuous" map, in his *Collected Papers*, edited by Charles Hartshorne and Paul Weiss (Cambridge: Harvard University Press, 1934), vol. 5, p. 71.

44. As Umberto Eco shows in a witty elaboration of Borges's first text, "Map of the Empire," *The Literary Review* 28 (1985): 233–38. Moreover, according to Eco's *A Theory of Semiotics* (Bloomington: Indiana University Press, 1976), a fully rigorous map, based on the ideal of absolute correspondence, would involve what Eco calls a homomaterial congruence. Such a map would no longer be distinguishable, *as a sign*, from the territory so that every map we know, like a death mask, must *at least to some extent* be incongruent and heteromaterial (p. 257). This might be phrased as a paradoxical principle to the effect that *any efficacious map must to some extent be inadequate.*

45. Derrida, "Living On. Borderlines," p. 78. See also the memo on "Exactitude," in Italo Calvino, *Six Memos for the Next Millennium* (Cambridge: Harvard University Press, 1988), pp. 55–80.

46. See Ernest Nagel and James R. Newman, *Gödel's Proof* (New York: New York University Press, 1958): "The exploitation of the notion of mapping is the key to the argument in Gödel's famous paper" (p. 66). Gödel's commentators do not apply the theorem of incompleteness to the "mapping" process itself by

which metamathematical statements are translated into arithmetical formulas, since "the setting up of such a correspondence is the *raison d'être* of the mapping" (*Gödel's Proof*, p. 93). By contrast, Royce and Borges would stress the fact that any performance of mapping necessarily yields "a specious victory: one dragon slain only to create another" (*Gödel's Proof*, p. 58). On Gödel, incompleteness, and global maps, see also Apostel and Van der Veken, *Wereldbeelden*, pp. 48–53.

47. Lyotard, *The Postmodern Condition*, p. 55. Prior to *The Postmodern Condition*, Lyotard quotes Borges's example in a conference on Michel Butor, subsequently published in *Rudiments païens: Genre dissertatif* (Paris: Union Générale d'Editions 10/18, 1977), p. 110. There, however, Lyotard approaches a complementary interpretation of cartography on the basis of Borges's map and the Möbius strip, comparable to what I will describe in terms of Peirce's semiotics and abduction.

48. Lyotard, *The Postmodern Condition*, p. 55. For a discussion of Gödel's theorem in combination with Georges Bataille's theory of general economy and the accursed share, see Arkady Plotnitsky, *Reconfigurations: Critical Theory and General Economy*.

49. These are the words of Margaret Geller cited by Hall, who also writes: "Cosmological surveys, in a metaphoric sense, have begun to resemble the maps from a story by Jorge Luis Borges, where the map keeps growing as big as the territory it purports to map" (*Mapping the Next Millenium*, p. 366). King Louis XV is also said to have lamented that his most accurate cartographers lost more territories than his wars could possibly gain. See "Mapping and Surveying," *The New Encyclopaedia Britannica*, vol. 5 (Chicago: Encyclopaedia Britannica, 1990), p. 520.

50. Theodor Adorno in a letter to Walter Benjamin, published in *Aesthetics and Politics* (London: Verso, 1977), p. 130.

51. Terry Eagleton, *Against the Grain: Essays 1975–1985* (London: Verso, 1986), p. 80. This passage is quoted by Soja (*Postmodern Geographies*, pp. 12 and 73) and by Harley ("Deconstructing the Map," p. 239). Soja further mentions how David Harvey recognizes after his marxist turn that "he might have to pull the tightly woven rug from under himself" (*Postmodern Geographies*, p. 65). Jameson finally speaks of a "materialist reversal" which "flips over the rug" of history (*Postmodernism*, p. 359).

52. Geoffrey Bennington for example describes the "aberration" of totalizing representation: "Whenever one of a series of elements is also used transcendentally with respect to that series in order to totalize, dominate, or explain it, aberration begins." See "Aberrations: de Man (and) the Machine," in *Reading de Man Reading*, ed. Lindsay Waters and Wlad Godzich (Minneapolis: University of Minnesota Press, 1989), p. 216. As an example Bennington mentions Jameson's "untranscendable horizon" of marxism as deployed in *The Political Unconscious*: both one of a series of theories in the intellectual marketplace and the best

theory of the marketplace itself. A similar deconstructive criticism of Jameson's totalizing gesture is offered by Samuel Weber, "Capitalizing History: *The Political Unconscious*," in *Institution and Interpretation* (Minneapolis: University of Minnesota Press, 1987), pp. 40–58.

53. Derrida, "Living On. Borderlines," p. 105.

54. Jameson, *Postmodernism*, p. 51. Toward this higher and more complex level of representation, Jameson offers little more than the notion of "transcoding," with which he intends to forestall the predictable objections against the mimetic—reflective or expressive—relations marxism traditionally establishes between superstructure and base. See Jameson, *The Political Unconscious: Narrative as a Socially Symbolic Act* (Ithaca: Cornell University Press, 1981), pp. 23–58, esp. p. 40; and *Postmodernism*, pp. 393–97 and 408. Jameson also turns to Third World literature, however, in search for what he calls a "new mapping process." See "World Literature in an Age of Multinational Capitalism," in *The Current in Criticism: Essays on the Present and Future of Literary Theory*, ed. Clayton Koelb and Virgil Lokke (West Lafayette: Purdue University Press, 1986), pp. 139–58.

55. Jameson, "Imaginary and Symbolic in Lacan," *The Ideologies of Theory: Essays 1971–1986*, vol. 1 (Minneapolis: University of Minnesota Press, 1988): "The Lacanian notion of an 'asymptotic' approach to the Real, moreover, *maps* a situation in which the action of this 'absent cause' can be understood as a term limit, both indistinguishable from the Symbolic (or the Imaginary) and also independent of it" (p. 107, my emphasis). My reading here is indebted to Ph. Van Haute, *Psychoanalyse en filosofie: Het imaginaire en het symbolische in het werk van Jacques Lacan* (Leuven: Peeters, 1989), a book which not surprisingly claims to "map out" the problematic of the imaginary and the symbolic.

56. Jameson, *The Political Unconscious*, pp. 214 and 299.

57. Derrida, "The Double Session," p. 221.

58. Quoted by Julian Pefanis, *Heterology and the Postmodern: Bataille, Baudrillard, and Lyotard*, p. 118.

59. For a view of social change as the contradiction between a form and a latent content working its way to the surface, see Jameson, *Marxism and Form: Twentieth-Century Dialectical Theories of Literature* (Princeton: Princeton University Press, 1971), p. 327. Most elements of Jameson's negative or asymptotic hermeneutic which I have used for my reading of "On Rigor in Science" are gathered in this passage from *The Political Unconscious*:

> The Real is thus—virtually by definition in the fallen world of capitalism—that which resists desire, that bedrock against which the desiring subject knows the breakup of hope and can finally measure everything that refuses its fulfillment. Yet it also follows that this Real—this absent cause, which is fundamentally unrepresentable and non-narrative, and detectable only in

its effects—can be disclosed by Desire itself, whose wish-fulfilling mechanisms are the instruments through which this resistant surface must be scanned. (pp. 183–84)

60. See for example the abovementioned articles by J. B. Harley, and David Harvey, "Time and Space as Sources of Social Power," and "The Time and Space of the Enlightenment Project," in *The Condition of Postmodernity: An Enquiry into the Origins of Cultural Change* (Cambridge: Basil Blackwell, 1989), pp. 226–259.

61. Rather than an extrinsic variable, even the lack of a precise geo-historical designation is perhaps already an intrinsic part of the despotic regime of imperialism, as Kafka suggests in "The Great Wall of China": "We think only about the Emperor. But not about the present one; or rather we would think about the present one if we knew who he was or knew anything definite about him. . . . [The people] do not know what emperor is reigning, and there exist doubts regarding even the name of the dynasty" (quoted in Deleuze and Guattari, *Anti-Oedipus*, pp. 198–99).

62. Michel Foucault, *Discipline and Punish. The Birth of the Prison*, trans. Alan Sheridan (New York: Vintage, 1979); and Gilles Deleuze, "A New Cartographer (*Discipline and Punish*)," in *Foucault*, trans. Seán Hand, introd. Paul Bové (Minneapolis: University of Minnesota Press, 1988), pp. 23–44. For an earlier assessment of Foucault as a cartographer, see Ronald Hayman, "Cartography of Discourse? On Foucault," *Encounter* 47 (1976): 72–75. See also Thomas Flynn, "Foucault's Mapping of History," *The Cambridge Companion to Foucault*, edited by Gary Gutting (Cambridge: Cambridge University Press, 1994), pp. 28–46.

63. Foucault, *Discipline and Punish*, pp. 73 and 82.

64. Ibid., pp. 115, 205 and 219.

65. Ibid., p. 102.

66. Harley, "Deconstructing the Map," p. 244. For the comparison between Orwell and the Panopticon, see Maurice Blanchot, *Michel Foucault as I Imagine Him*, trans. Jeffrey Mehlman (New York: Zone Books, 1987), p. 85.

67. Jameson, *Postmodernism*, pp. 410, 272 and 401. See also Jean Baudrillard's arguments in *Forget Foucault*, trans. Nicole Dufresne (New York: Semiotext(e), 1987), about the alleged obsolescence of Foucault's concepts of power.

68. Guy Debord, *The Society of the Spectacle*, trans. Donald Nicholson-Smith (New York: Zone Books, 1994), thesis 31. In French, Debord presents "a map exactly covering the territory"; to ascribe a scale to the territory, on the contrary, already presupposes a victory of the spectacle and, hence, the impossibility of negation. From within a different tradition, Gianni Vattimo describes the "transparent society" as "a world where the norm is the exact reproduction of reality, perfect objectivity, the complete identity of map and territory," in *The Transparent Society*, trans. David Webb (Baltimore: The Johns Hopkins University Press, 1992),

p. 7. Vattimo's philosophy has recently also given way to a discussion of the question of territoriality in relation to the sacred and the secular. See, for example, Pierluigi Nicolin, "The Secularized Territory," and Michael Gold, "Sacralization of the Territory," *Casabella* 65 (1990): 4–15.

69. Lyotard writes: "Philosophy as architecture is ruined, but a writing of the ruins, micrologies, graffiti can still be done," in *Heidegger and "the jews,"* trans. Andreas Michel and Mark Roberts (Minneapolis: University of Minnesota Press, 1990), p. 43.

70. Houston A. Baker, Jr., "Local Pedagogy; or, How I Redeemed My Spring Semester," *PMLA* 108 (1993): 400–09; and Toni Morrison, *Playing in the Dark. Whiteness and the Literary Imagination* (Cambridge: Harvard University Press, 1992), p. 3. See also Lucy R. Lippard, "Mapping," *Mixed Blessings: New Art in a Multicultural America* (New York: Pantheon, 1991), pp. 3–18; and the collection of essays, *Mapping the Future: Local Cultures, Global Change*, ed. Jon Bird et al. (London: Routledge, 1993).

71. See, for example, Graham Huggan, "Decolonizing the Map: Post-Colonialism, Post-structuralism, and the Cartographic Connection," in *Past the Last Post: Theorizing Post-Colonialism and Post-Modernism*, ed. Ian Adam and Helen Tiffin (Calgary: University of Calgary Press, 1990), pp. 125–38; id., *Territorial Disputes: Maps and Mapping Strategies in Contemporary Canadian and Australian Fiction* (Toronto: University of Toronto Press, 1993); and Mahasweta Devi, *Imaginary Maps*, trans. and with a commentary by Gayatri Spivak (New York: Routledge, 1994). For a discussion, see Timothy J. Reiss, "Mapping Identities: Literature, Nationalism, Colonialism." With regard to feminism, see Annette Kolodny, "A Map for Rereading: Or, Gender and the Interpretation of Literary Texts," *New Literary History* 11 (1980): 451–67; Barbara Godard, "Mapmaking: A Survey of Feminist Criticism," in *Gynocritics. Feminist Approaches to Canadian and Quebec Women's Writing*, ed. B. Godard (Toronto: ECW Press, 1987), pp. 2–30; Amy K. Kaminsky, "Molloy's Lesbian Cartographies: Body, Text, and Geography," in *Reading the Body Politic: Feminist Criticism and Latin American Women Writers* (Minneapolis: University of Minnesota Press, 1993), pp. 96–114; Kimberlé Crenshaw, "Mapping the Margins: Intersectionality, Identity Politics, and Violence Against Women of Color," in *After Identity: A Reader in Law and Culture*, ed. Dan Danielsen and Karen Engle (New York: Routledge, 1995), pp. 332–54.

72. For an account in connection with cartography in Canadian and Australian writing, see Ian Adam, "Breaking the Chain: Anti-Saussurean Resistance in Birney, Carey and C. S. Peirce," in *Past the Last Post: Theorizing Post-Colonialism and Post-Modernism*, ed. Ian Adam and Helen Tiffin (Calgary: University of Calgary Press, 1990), pp. 79–93. See also "Writing in the Margins," "Mapping the Territory," and "Retracing the Map," in Sylvia Söderlind, *Margin/Alias: Language and Colonization in Canadian and Québécois Fiction* (Toronto: University of Toronto Press, 1991); and Helen Margaret Buss, *Mapping Our Selves: Canadian Women's Autobiography in English* (Montreal: McGill-Queen's University Press,

1993). Studies of cartography and Latin-American literature include Ester Gimbernat de González, "Mapas y texto: para una estrategia del poder," *MLN* 95 (1980): 388–99; Susan Willis, "Caliban as Poet: Reversing the Maps of Domination," in *Reinventing the Americas. Comparative Studies of Literature of the United States and Spanish America*, ed. Bell Gale Chevigny and Gari Laguardia (Cambridge: Cambridge University Press, 1986), pp. 92–105; and José Rabasa, "Dialogue as Conquest: Mapping Spaces for Counter-Discourse," *Cultural Critique* 6 (1987): 131–59. See also Walter D. Mignolo, "Putting the Americas on the Map," *Colonial Latin American Review* 1–2 (1992); id., "La lengua, la letra, el territorio," *Dispositio* 28–29 (1986): 137–60; id., "Colonial Situations, Geographical Discourses and Territorial Representations," *Dispositio* 36–38 (1989): 93–140; and Jean Franco, "Remapping Culture," *Latin American Literary Review* 40 (1992), 38–40. Undissociable from the mapping of territories is also the question of national identities; see, for example, "A Cartography for the Catalan Territory," *Lotus International* 23 (1979): 10–33.

73. Jameson, *Postmodernism*, p. 49.

74. Thomas Harrison, *Essayism. Conrad, Musil & Pirandello* (Baltimore: The Johns Hopkins University Press, 1992), p. 222.

75. See, for example, *Cartographies: Post-structuralism and the Mapping of Bodies and Spaces*, ed. Rosalyn Diprose and Robyn Ferrell (North Sydney: Allen & Unwin, 1991); and Wolfgang Natter and John Paul Jones III, "Signposts toward a Poststructuralist Geography," in *Postmodern Contentions*, pp. 165–203.

76. For example, in *Discipline and Punish*: "There can be no question here of writing the history of the different disciplinary institutions. I simply intend to map on a series of examples some of the essential techniques that most easily spread from one to another" (p. 139; cf. pp. 22–23: "Beneath the increasing leniency of punishment, then, one may map [*repérer*] a displacement of its point of application; and through this displacement, a whole field of recent objects, a whole new system of truth and a mass of roles hitherto unknown in the exercise of criminal justice"). Already prior to *Discipline and Punish*, Foucault frequently uses the expression *repérer* (variously translated as "mapping," "discerning," "mark out," etc.) to describe his method in *The Archaeology of Knowledge*, trans. Alan M. Sheridan Smith (New York: Pantheon Books, 1972), pp. 37, 41, 130–131, 203, 208, *et passim*; here, too, *quadrillage* is quite different from *repérage* and refers rather to "a reinforced police and penal framework" (p. 43). Finally, the term *repérage* (translated as "survey") also describes Foucault's unfinished project, in *The History of Sexuality: An Introduction*, trans. Robert Hurley (New York: Vintage, 1990), p. 8. The object of Foucault's analysis in this last book is described not as a "map" or "grid" (*quadrillage*) but as a "web" or "network" (*trame*) of discourses (pp. 26, 30, 34) with which "sexuality" is "harried" or "tracked down" (*traqué*) and obliged to speak the truth (pp. 20, 42, 45). A separate analysis could study the relative stability of this Foucauldian configuration of concepts, unfortunately lost whenever a translator prefers the ideal of variety over strict fidelity to the text.

77. Baudrillard, *Forget Foucault*, p. 10. Baudrillard himself uses the notion of *quadrillage*, for example, to define the urban realm through "the investment, gridding [*quadrillage*], and dismantling of all sociality by signs," and graffiti as "the hijacking [*détournement*] of the wall as the signifier of the terrorist, functional gridding [*quadrillage*] of space." See *L'échange symbolique et la mort* (Paris: Gallimard, 1976), pp. 119 and 123; *Symbolic Exchange and Death*, trans. Iain Hamilton Grant, introd. Mike Gane (London: Sage, 1993), pp. 77 and 80 (translation modified).

78. Kevin Hart, "Maps of Deconstruction," *Meanjin* 45 (1986): 107–16. Not surprisingly, Hart quotes Borges and suggests that all maps or theories "seek to be both complete and consistent but that in each case there are hidden gaps of one kind or another" (p. 110).

79 See Deleuze and Guattari, "Principle of cartography and decalcomania," in *A Thousand Plateaus*, trans. Brian Massumi (Minneapolis: University of Minnesota Press, 1987), pp. 12ff. See also Charles J. Stivale, "The Literary Element in *Mille plateaux*: The New Cartography of Deleuze and Guattari," *SubStance* 44–45 (1989): 20–34.

80. The translation is again potentially misleading insofar as Deleuze and Guattari's "tracing" (*calque*) has little in common with Derrida's "trace" (*trace*). To the contrary, rather than being "traced" to a metaphysical origin or telos, the Derridean "trace" would require a "mapping," in Deleuze and Guattari's sense. "Tracing," furthermore, fails to convey how a *calque* by definition depends upon a pre-existing original or model. Finally, as if to complicate the issue even more, Deleuze and Guattari in the French original of *What is Philosophy?* frequently use *tracer* with all the values of cartography (*carte*) and none of the tracing (*calque*).

81. Deleuze and Guattari, *A Thousand Plateaus*, p. 21. For a comparison between Deleuze and Borges, see Jean-Clet Martin, "'Le jardin aux sentiers qui bifurquent,'" *Variations: La philosophie de Gilles Deleuze* (Paris, Payot, 1993, pp. 131–46. For a hypertextual program inspired by Borges and cartography, see Stuart Moulthrop, "Reading from the Map: Metonymy and Metaphor in the Fiction of 'Forking Paths,'" in *Hypermedia and Literary Studies*, ed. Paul Delany and George P. Landow (Cambridge: MIT Press, 1991), pp. 119–32. See also George P. Landow, *Hypertext: The Convergence of Contemporary Critical Theory and Technology* (Baltimore: The Johns Hopkins University Press, 1992), p. 111.

82. Deleuze and Guattari, *A Thousand Plateaus* 14. "Blotching his map" (*tacher sa carte*) also evokes the expression *une carte de France*, argot for the *tache* or stain left on bedsheets after masturbation, the truly disseminating effects of which psychoanalysis typically traces back to the Oedipal mama-papa-pipi configuration (cf. the anti-masturbation machines described in *Discipline and Punish*).

83. Deleuze, "A New Cartographer," p. 34.

84. Deleuze, "A New Cartographer," p. 44. In a footnote of *A Thousand Plateaus* (p. 530 n. 39), Deleuze and Guattari explicitly address the differences between Foucault's analysis of "power" and their schizoanalysis of "desire," insisting upon the possibility of "lines of flight" in the panopticism of cartography.

85. Deleuze and Guattari, *Kafka: Toward a Minor Literature*, trans. Dana Polan, foreword Réda Bensmaïa (Minneapolis: University of Minnesota Press, 1986), p. 10. On the issue of Deleuze and Guattari's celebration of America in general, see Jean-Philippe Mathy, *Extrême-Occident: French Intellectuals and America* (Chicago: University of Chicago Press, 1993).

86. Deleuze and Claire Parnet, *Dialogues*, trans. Hugh Tomlinson and Barbara Habberjan (New York: Columbia University Press, 1987), p. 2 (translation modified).

87. Deleuze and Guattari, *Anti-Oedipus: Capitalism and Schizophrenia*, trans. Robert Hurley, Mark Seem and Helen R. Lane (Minneapolis: University of Minnesota Press, 1983), p. 42. In French, Deleuze and Guattari's expression may remind the reader of Roland Barthes's definition of truth as "*ce qui est à-côté*," in *Fragments d'un discours amoureux* (Paris: Seuil, 1977), p. 273. Throughout his *Dialogues*, Deleuze also stresses the difference between rhizomatic thinking, which seeks to map out lines of flight, and classical philosophy, which is always more enclined to *faire le point* than to consider what lies beside of it.

88. Friedrich Nietzsche, *Human, All Too Human*, trans. R. J. Hollingdale (Cambridge: Cambridge University Press, 1986), p. 261. With another Nietzschean quote in mind, Manfredo Tafuri also proposes to consider criticism "a deconstructive and reconstructive labor, a labor that displaces the Nietzschean 'stones' and reassembles them, which *produces* meanings by moving those already given," in *The Sphere and the Labyrinth: Avant-Gardes and Architecture from Piranesi to the 1970s*, trans. Pellegrino d'Acierno and Robert Connolly (Cambridge: MIT Press, 1987), pp. 8–9.

89. Lyotard, *Heidegger and "the jews,"* pp. 43 and 56. Similarly, Paul de Man writes that Derrida's text is "the unmaking of a construct. However negative it may sound, deconstruction implies the possibility of rebuilding," in *Blindness and Insight* (Minneapolis: University of Minnesota Press, 1983), p. 140.

90. The former often typifies deconstructive criticism in the wake of Paul de Man. With regard to the latter, see especially Gianni Vattimo, *Il concetto di fare in Aristotele* (Turin: Pubblicazioni della Facoltà di Lettere e Filosofia Università di Torino, 1961).

91. As Douglas Kellner rightly suggests in his critical overview, *Jean Baudrillard: From Marxism to Postmodernism and Beyond* (Stanford: Stanford University Press, 1989), p. 78.

92. Baudrillard, *L'échange symbolique et la mort*, p. 115 n. 1; *Symbolic Exchange and Death*, p. 86 n. 9 (translation modified). This passage recurs in "Simulacra

and Science Fiction," *Simulacra and Simulation*, trans. Sheila Faria Glaser (Ann Arbor: University of Michigan Press, 1994), p. 123.

93. Baudrillard, *Symbolic Exchange and Death*, p. 84 n. 4. For a detailed discussion of McLuhan, see also "The Implosion of Meaning in the Media," *Simulacra and Simulation*, pp. 79–86.

94. Baudrillard, *L'effet Beaubourg: Implosion et dissuasion* (Paris: Galilée, 1977), p. 41; the English translation, "The Beaubourg Effect: Implosion and Deterrence," appears in *Simulacra and Simulation*, p. 71. This does not keep Baudrillard from proposing to fill Beaubourg with "a labyrinth, a combinatory, infinite library, an aleatory redistribution of destinies through games or lotteries—in short, the universe of Borges—or even the circular Ruins, the slowed-down enchainment of individuals dreamed up by each other (not a dreamworld Disneyland, a laboratory of practical fiction)" (pp. 64–65). For a study of other references to Borges in Baudrillard's work, see Mike Gane, *Baudrillard's Bestiary: Baudrillard and Culture* (London and New York: 1991), pp. 19–25.

95. Baudrillard, *Simulacra and Simulation*, p. 1.

96. Ibid. (translation modified). In *Symbolic Exchange and Death*, Baudrillard still believes in the potential of graffiti to counter the effects of simulation with the reinjection of territoriality: "The graffitists themselves come from the territorial order. They territorialise decoded urban spaces—a particular street, wall or district comes to life through them, becoming a collective territory again" (p. 79). For *Simulacra and Simulation*, however, what is left to do is only to precipitate the disappearance of the territory: "Only what precipitates rotting, by accentuating the parodic, simulacral side of dying games of knowledge and power, has meaning" (p. 149); "What can we brandish today? No longer even the ruins of knowledge, of culture—the ruins themselves are defunct" (p. 151).

97. Baudrillard, *Simulacra and Simulation*, p. 82. The Möbius strip is a common point of reference in Baudrillard's discussion of simulation. Jameson also compares the Borges map and the Möbius strip as two emblems characteristic of the development of the sign under postmodernism. See "Periodizing the 60s," *The Ideologies of Theory*, 2 vols. (Minneapolis: University of Minnesota Press, 1988), vol. 2, p. 197.

98. Derrida, "The Double Session," *Dissemination*, p. 198.

99. Baudrillard, *Symbolic Exchange and Death*, p. 73. See also Baudrillard's most recent essay, *La pensée radicale* (Paris: Sens & Tonka, 1994): "Reality is a bitch. Contrary to what is being said about it (the real is that which resists, that against which all hypotheses shatter to pieces), reality is not very solid, or less and less so, and seems rather well-disposed to fold back in disorder" (pp. 21–22). Immediately thereafter, Baudrillard once more quotes the rotting vestiges of "On Rigor in Science," but several years of familiarity with the story have apparently given him the right to rebaptize it *The Map and the Territory* of Borges.

100. Baudrillard, *Simulacra and Simulation*, p. 6.

101. Derrida, "The Double Session," *Dissemination*, p. 208.

102. The following remarks summarize my more detailed account in "From Text to Diagram: Towards a Semiotics of Cultural Cartography," *Semiotics 1994*, ed. C. W. Spinks (forthcoming).

103. *Cartographies schizoanalytiques* (Paris: Galilée, 1989), p. 51 n. 1. This book's opening section, "Liminaire," is available in English as "Regimes, Pathways, Subjects," trans. Brian Massumi, in *Incorporations*, ed. Jonathan Crary and Sanford Kwinter (New York: Zone Books, 1992), pp. 16–37.

104. Guattari, *L'inconscient machinique: Essais de schizo-analyse* (Fontenay-sous-Bois: Recherches, 1979), p. 234 n. 28; *La révolution moléculaire* (Fontenay-sous-Bois: Recherches, 1977), p. 52 n. 1.

105. See especially "Echafaudages sémiotiques," *La révolution moléculaire*, pp. 239–84; and *L'inconscient machinique*, pp. 21–73, 205–35. Several of these essays are carelessly translated in *Molecular Revolution: Psychiatry and Politics*, trans. Janis Forman (New York: Penguin, 1984), pp. 73–107 and 120–72. In *A Thousand Plateaus*, see "The Geology of Morals," "Postulates of Linguistics," and "On Several Regimes of Signs," pp. 39–148. For an excellent commentary, see John Johnston's article in this volume.

106. See Louis Hjelmslev, *Prolegomena to a Theory of Language*, trans. Francis J. Whitfield (Madison: The University of Wisconsin Press, 1969), pp. 49–60.

107. Ibid., p. 57.

108. Eco, "A Typology of Modes of Production," *A Theory of Semiotics*, pp. 217–61.

109. See for example George W. Grace, *The Linguistic Construction of Reality* (London: Routledge, 1987), which opposes two views of language: the mapping and the reality-construction views. In *The Garden and the Map* (Urbana: University of Illinois Press, 1973), John Vernon also sees the map as exemplary of the static and dyadic paradigm of thinking, grounded in the principle of noncontradiction and the whole set of dichotomies constitutive of the Western tradition. Ironically, what Vernon labels the "map" would for Deleuze and Guattari be a "tracing" and for Eco a "replica," whereas the latter's "map" corresponds to Vernon's "garden."

110. Umberto Eco, *Semiotics and the Philosophy of Language* (Bloomington: Indiana University Press, 1986), p. 35.

111. See K. T. Fann, *Peirce's Theory of Abduction* (The Hague: Martinus Nijhof, 1970), pp. 20–21; Umberto Eco and Thomas A. Sebeok, eds., *The Sign of Three: Dupin, Holmes, Peirce* (Bloomington: Indiana University Press, 1983). Eco traces the function of this process in Borges's work in "Abduction in Uqbar," an essay

which in many ways forms the center of his answer to deconstruction, *The Limits of Interpretation* (Bloomington: Indiana University Press, 1990), pp. 152–62.

112. Eco, *A Theory of Semiotics*, p. 254.

113. Ibid., p. 245.

114. Eco, *Foucault's Pendulum*, trans. William Weaver (San Diego: Harcourt Brace Jovanovich, 1989), p. 459.

115. Eco, *Semiotics and the Philosophy of Language*, p. 45.

116. Mojdeh Baratloo and Clifton J. Balch, *Angst: Cartography*, introd. Patricia C. Phillips (New York: Lumen, 1989), pp. 5 and 12.

117. Deleuze and Guattari, *A Thousand Plateaus*, p. 5. For "a history of mapping the world ahead," see Paul Carter and David Malouf, "Spatial History," *Textual Practice* 3 (1989): 173–83.

CHAPTER 9

1. I don't refer here to Cicero's own definition of *catachresis* (or *abusio*), which seems to place it with metonymy (3.43. 169). Instead, I employ the term in the sense of a "necessary" abuse, as defined by Quintilian (a sense Cicero includes in his definition of metaphor). "By this term," writes Quintilian, "is meant the practice of adapting the nearest available term to describe something for which no actual term exists. . . . We must be careful to distinguish between *abuse* and *metaphor*, since the former is employed where there is no proper term available, and the latter when there is another term available" (8.6, 34; see also Peacham [fol.C, iiii]). Definitions of *catachresis* vary widely, and authority is difficult to trace. The Latin *abusio* is a rough translation of the Greek. Etymologically, each carries the sense of "using up" or "excessive use." (In this connection, see Derrida's discussion of *usure* in "White Mythology," a text to which the argument of the present essay owes much.) If, as Cicero claims (*Orator*, 27: 94), the term is Aristotelian, no evidence survives (see Kroll, 91–2, 94).

2. The Latin reads *Nam "gemmare vites," "luxuriem esse in herbis," "laetus esse segetes" etiam rustici dicunt*. J. S. Watson translates, "the vines are budding," "there is a luxuriancy in the grass," and "there is a bountiful crop" (236); but in English these phrases would not be considered metaphorical, and Cicero suggests that such meanings in Latin are derivative—that the concept of the "bud," for instance, derives from the metaphor of the "gem" and not the other way around. I have altered H. Rackham's translation in the Loeb edition (which reads "jewelled vines," "luxurious herbage," "joyful crops")—in the second case for the reason mentioned, and otherwise for the sake of inserting the copula, which is present or implied in the Latin.

3. See also *Rhetorica ad Herennium*: "Metaphor occurs when a word applying

to one thing is transferred to another, because the similarity seems to justify this transference" (4.34, 45).

4. See R.F. Jones, "Science and Language in England." Jones writes, "The spirit of utility, which derived its strength from the new science, and which recommended the latter to the Puritans, demanded that language be considered only a means to an end, and thus insisted [. . .] upon its subordination to the useful study of nature" (146–7). I would argue that in the rhetoric of the new science only the *insistence* upon utility was new. The Ciceronian tradition had already conceived of language as essentially a means to an end.

5. As Wilbur Samuel Howell has written (in a style that itself respects the metaphoricity of the formulations it describes), the Ramists "believed . . . that speaking is made up of logic, so far as any discourse must have subject matter and form, and is also made up of rhetoric, so far as any discourse must be clothed in words and uttered in speech" (254). For the Ramists, logic comprises the body of discourse that rhetoric may sometimes dress up in style. But we should advise caution with regard to the inclusiveness of Howell's word *speaking*. As Walter J. Ong has argued in *Ramus, Method, and the Decay of Dialogue,* Ramus conceives of the two arts as extended mental objects that, as such, occupy distinct places in the field of experience (280). In theory, at least, logic is independent of rhetoric, and thinking independent of utterance. Although the Ramist logic remains rhetorical insofar as its "method" merely reorders the topoi of the traditional "arrangement," Ramus is a precursor of Descartes insofar as he espouses the ideal of pure thought.

6. Abraham Fraunce in *The Arcadian Rhetorike* (1588), for instance, follows Talaeus in reducing the traditional catalog of tropes to dichotomized categories. That is, after separating logic from rhetoric, and putting aside grammar as well, he confers upon ornamentation a "natural" order the binary logic of which he feels no need to defend. But this methodization only marks more distinctly the separation of the two arts and the dominance of logic.

7. Cf. the statement by the Ramist John Hoskins in *Directions for Speech and Style* (c. 1599). Hoskins writes in the forward to his pupil, "The shame of speaking were small if the tongue were only disgraced by it. But as the image of the king in a seal of wax, ill represented, is not so much a blemish to the wax or the signet that sealeth it as to the king whom it resembleth, so disordered speech is not so much injury to the lips which give it forth or the thoughts which put it forth as to the right proportion and coherence of things in themselves, so wrongfully expressed." The "right orator" is "he that [. . .] apprehend[s] the consequence of things, in their truth, and utter[s] his apprehensions as truly. . . . "

8. According to Wilson, even in the beginning reason was properly joined to eloquence. In an introductory chapter, under the heading "Eloquence first geven by God, after loste by man, and laste repayred by God agayne," reason and eloquence are linked in a myth of postlapsarian cultural origin, as Wilson credits the orators with the restoration of faith and culture following the fall.

As God's "appoynted ministers," they had been given the gifts of reason and utterance, with which to "delight," "nurture" and advise men, who had become wild, cruel, foolish, and bestial: "where as Menne lyved Brutyshlye in open feldes, having neither house to shroude them in, nor attyre to clothe their backes, nor yet anye regarde to seeke their best avayle: these appoynted of God called theim together by utteraunce of speache, and perswaded with them what was good, what was badde, and what was gainefull for mankynde" (18). In Sidney's later phrase, the poet or orator was "the first light-giver to ignorance, a first nurse, whose milk by little and little enabled them to feed afterwards of tougher knowledges." In the Ciceronian tradition of Augustine, Luther, Wilson, and others, Sidney continues to view eloquence as a pleasant outward show, a shelter or clothing of reason, necessary for the sake of persuasion in a fallen world in which the will of man would otherwise serve the physical appetites.

9. In Wilson's own case, success speaks for itself. The example of the "rich snudge" is an inversion of Wilson's personal history. From humble beginnings, as the son of a yeoman of Strubby, Lincolnshire, Wilson rose through the law and Parliament to an ambassadorship and eventually to the position of Secretary of State, greatly enriching himself in the process. His oratorical skills played no small part in his success. (See Thomas J. Derrick's "Biographical Introduction," vii–lxi.)

10. Specifically, the figure of *allegory*, which Puttenham calls the "Courtly figure" (186). See note 14, below.

11. See also Puttenham's evaluation of *exergasia* (the repetition of a thought in many figures), which is "as it fareth with the bare and naked body, which being attired in rich and gorgious apparell, seemeth to the common usage of th'eye much more comely & bewtifull then the naturall" (247).

12. In Chapter XXV ("That the good Poet or maker ought to dissemble his arte, and in what cases the artificiall is more commended then the naturall, and contrariwise"), Puttenham argues that the artificial attainments of humanity constitute a natural extension of the merely natural (the vital or animal): "But what else is language and utterance, and discourse & persuasion, and argument in man, then the vertues of a well constitute body and minde, little lesse naturall then his very sensuall actions, saving that the one is perfited by nature at once, the other not without exercise & iteration?" (305).

13. Puttenham's clothing analogies more regularly and explicitly refer to the aristocracy than those of Wilson. For instance, he compares ornament to the "stone and perle, or passements of gold upon the stuffe of a Princely garment" (138).

14. This formal ambivalence regarding figurative language shows itself in the trope of allegory, "the Courtly figure," or figure of the "false semblant or dissimulation" (so called "for his duplicitie"). (Puttenham first calls allegory "the false semblant" and later "the faire semblant," as though the two adjectives

were interchangeable—as will be their equivalents for Locke.) Puttenham begins by praising allegory: "The use of this figure is so large, and his vertue of so greate efficacie, as it is supposed no man can pleasantly utter and perswade without it, but in effect is sure never or very seldome to thrive and prosper in the world, that cannot skilfully put in [use], in somuch as not onely every common Courtier, but also the gravest Counselour, yea and the most noble and wisest Prince of them all are many times enforced to use it. . . ." (186). Allegory is the highest art, but also the lowest. It is the mode of the secret, even the state secret, and of state propaganda; but it is also the mode of an hypocrisy and affectation that harm the state, as Puttenham argues at length with reference to the courts of Europe (299–302). The rhetoric of dissimulation is rhetoric *par excellence*, for rhetoric is double in its very constitution.

15. "Proper" words correspond to things and "usual" words correspond to received ideas. The "substitutive" theory of metaphor must always posit the stability of a representational or denotative language, whether that language is understood as "proper" or "usual." The rhetoricians of the sixteenth century often fail to distinguish between the two concepts of representation. The same may be said of many Baconians of the seventeenth century, including at times Bacon himself. But Locke quite clearly rejects the mystical notion that words bear any natural relation to things and speaks instead of arbitrary signs.

16. Perhaps the most famous example of such an undertaking may be found in Book III of John Locke's *Essay Concerning Human Understanding*, in which Locke calls rhetoric "the arts of fallacy" and complains of its popularity: "It is evident how much men love to deceive and be deceived, since rhetoric, that powerful instrument of error and deceit, has its established professors, is publicly taught, and has always been had in great reputation" (146). In the tradition of the Royal Society, Locke's polemic is extreme. He makes rhetoric responsible for widespread ignorance and confusion. Against rhetoric's good reputation Locke insinuates moral impropriety: "Eloquence, like the fair sex, has too prevailing beauties in it to suffer itself ever to be spoken against. And it is in vain to find fault with those arts of deceiving, wherein men find pleasure to be deceived" (147). Here eloquence is a woman, and Locke presupposes that women are vain and irrational. The vain woman paints her face and dresses smartly to deceive and please men; self-deceiving as well, she will hear only praise. At worst, she seduces men into irrationality, away from true and clear notions. The business of eloquence (here, a kind of prostitution) is to deceive, seduce—or, as Locke says of figurative speech, to "move the passions, and thereby mislead the judgment" (147). The point is the same one Puttenham makes, except that Locke's censure of figurative language is unequivocal. Moreover, Locke draws a stronger connection than Bacon does between two of Bacon's three "diseases of learning" from *The Advancement of Learning*: that of "delicate learning" (eloquence) and that of "deceit or untruth," which is "of all the rest the foulest; as that which doth destroy the essential form of knowledge; which is nothing but a representation of truth" (287). Of the latter, Bacon writes, "This vice . . . brancheth itself into two sorts; delight in deceiving, and

aptness to be deceived." Cf. Sidney's *Apology*. Sidney argues that poets and prose writers alike abuse their art when they neglect the matter of their discourse in favor of a showy "outside" of artful phrasing. Writing of the excesses of diction—neologisms, foreign words and phrases, extravagant similitudes—he employs a negative version of the classical analogy: "So is that honey-flowing matron eloquence apparelled, or rather disguised, in a courtesan-like painted affectation . . . with so far-fetched words, they may seem monsters, but must seem strangers, to any poor Englishman" (138). Sidney's treatment of rhetoric as a "disguise," in such special instances when the catachretic power of language seems too violently to disrupt customary usage, prefigures, so to speak, Locke's argument against figurative language in general. But while Sidney is concerned to censure what is foreign to what he would consider the natural poetic qualities of the English language (a kind of national propriety), Locke devotes himself to the logical purification of an instrumental language of science, a language stripped of figures.

17. In Vickers and Struever, *Rhetoric and the Pursuit of Truth*, 1–76.

18. Vickers's essay is invaluable as a corrective to the tradition of prose criticism for which R.F. Jones is largely responsible.

19. The appeal to sincerity through recourse to the plain style (or its pretended adoption) is common among Elizabethans writing in the Ciceronian tradition. (See, for example, Sidney's *Astrophel and Stella*, Sonnet 1; and Shakespeare's *Sonnets*, 83–86.) But what is a literary convention among the Elizabethans becomes an ideological weapon in the hands of the new scientists of the seventeenth century.

20. Bacon's architectural analogies also reach back toward a source. To correct the foundationless and poorly built up fabric of human reason, he proposes "to try the whole thing anew upon a better plan, and to commence a total reconstruction of sciences, arts, and all human knowledge, raised upon the proper foundations" (4). Of his method he says, "I . . . sink the foundations of the sciences deeper and firmer; and I begin the inquiry nearer the source than men have done hitherto, submitting to examination those things which the common logic takes on trust" (p. 21).

21. In Vickers, ed., *English Science, Bacon to Newton*. The gloss on "illiberal" is Vickers's.

22. For an intelligent discussion of the "theologico-political" dimensions of Sprat's work, see Joel Reed's article, "Restoration and Repression: The Language Projects of the Royal Society."

23. As Vickers writes, "it should be evident that none of the scientists connected with the Society actually wrote like an artisan, a countryman, or a merchant" (17).

24. That Jones and other modern scholars would be persuaded, too, should

be no surprise (as it indeed isn't for Vickers, who attributes the mistake only partly to faulty scholarship and partly to the biased history that the victorious Royal Society has promulgated). I follow Vickers, who notes: "In their polemics [Society members] claim to speak with a monopoly over reason, but the metaphors that some use are so violent that the reader alert to the tricks of rhetoric soon wonders whether they deceived themselves as well as hoping to deceive others" (*English Science*, 13).

CHAPTER 11

1. Birnbaum, Norman; *The Radical Renewal* (New York: Pantheon. 1988). References are in parentheses in the text.

2. I should perhaps mention that these may not in fact be the central motifs for Birnbaum himself. His central point is clear, as I shall point out, but his discussion is rather like a mosaic, dispersive rather than centripetal. It is not a dispassionate work, nor apolitical (Birnbaum is wholly engaged, in the Sartrean sense). He is perhaps more concerned with relegating the compass of American social and political critique to the past, and making the notion of renewal itself radical, rather than in renewing the radical by being programmatic. He appears to be hunting something bigger than program, and these motifs provide a certain orientation in the landscape of that hunt.

3. Lyotard, Jean-François; *The Differend*, translated by George Van den Abeele (Minneapolis: University of Minn., 1988).

4. This structural dynamic is described from four different perspectives in the following. Said, Edward; Orientalism (New York: Random House, 1979). Spivak, Gayatri; "Three Women's Texts and a Critique of Imperialism"; *Critical Inquiry* 12(1) (Fall 1985). Spivak, Gayatri; "Can the Subaltern Speak?"; in *Marxist Interpretations of Literature and Culture: Limits, Frontiers, Boundaries*. Edited by Larry Grossberg and Cary Nelson (Urbana, Illinois: University of Illinois Press, 1988). Sartre, Jean-Paul; *Anti-semite and Jew*, translated by George Becker (New York: Schoken, 1948). And Susan Griffin; *Pornography and Silence* (New York: Harper and Row, 1981).

5. See Sartre's discussion of the look in *Being and Nothingness* (New York: Washington Square Press, 1966), 340 ff.

CHAPTER 12

1. In regard to the text of *jouissance*, Barthes writes: "You cannot speak 'on' such a text, you can only speak 'in' it, *in its fashion*, enter into a desperate plagiarism, hysterically affirm the void of bliss (and no longer obsessively repeat the letter of pleasure)." Roland Barthes, *The Pleasure of the Text*, translated by Richard Miller, New York: Hill and Wang, 1975), 22. Hereafter cited in text as *PT*.

2. See the section of this paper, "The Death of the Author," for elaboration of these ideas.

3. See p. 211 of this chapter for further discussion.

4. Roland Barthes, *Writing Degree Zero,* translated by Annette Lavers and Colin Smith (New York: Hill and Wang, 1968). Originally published in French, 1953. Hereafter cited in text as *Zero.*

5. Jean-Paul Sartre, *Literature and Existentialism,* translated by Bernard Erechtman (New York: The Citadel Press, 1966). Originally published in French, 1949; originally translated to English as *What is Literature*?. Hereafter cited in text as "Sartre."

6. This is the title of the first chapter of both *Writing Degree Zero* and *What is Literature?*.

7. Susan Sontag, "Writing Itself: On Roland Barthes," in *A Barthes Reader,* edited by Susan Sontag (New York: Hill and Wang, 1982), xix, xxi.

8. William Ray, *Literary Meaning: From Phenomenology to Deconstruction* (Oxford: Basil Blackwell, 1984), 3.

9. When one asks aspiring young writers whether they have anything to say, one is asking if "something is worth the trouble of being communicated. But what do we mean by something which is 'worth the trouble' if it is not by recourse to a system of transcendent values?" (Sartre, 22).

10. Susan Sontag, Preface to *Writing Degree Zero,* xi.

11. Roland Barthes, "Authors and Writers," in *A Barthes Reader,* edited by Susan Sontag (New York: Hill and Wang, 1982), 188.

12. The examples of the post-structuralist claim that the author is dead are too numerous to mention, but see, for example, Jacques Derrida, "Tympan," in *Margins of Philosophy,* translated by Alan Bass (Chicago: University of Chicago Press, 1982), xi, where he argues that to examine authorial intention is to act as a "mechanical reader" by placing artificial limits on the text. See also his essay on "Différance" in the same volume (15), where he claims that the subject is inscribed in language. According to Derrida (as well as Barthes and Kristeva) the author is not a human subject, but a "function" of language.

Cf. Julia Kristeva, *Revolution in Poetic Language,* translated by Margaret Waller, introduced by Leon S. Roudiez (New York: Columbia Univ. Press, 1984), as well as Roudiez's introduction. Kristeva replaces the term *author* with the concept of the "writing subject." Roudiez writes, the word *author* "emphasized the conscious intent of a writer who has authority over the meaning of his work. The notion of the writing subject counters the illusions of Sartre, for instance, who asserted that no matter how far the reader might go, 'the author has gone farther than he has'" (7).

Kristeva is not denying all intentionality, but argues that consciousness is not the dominating force of writing., I would diagram Kristeva's "writing subject" as follows:

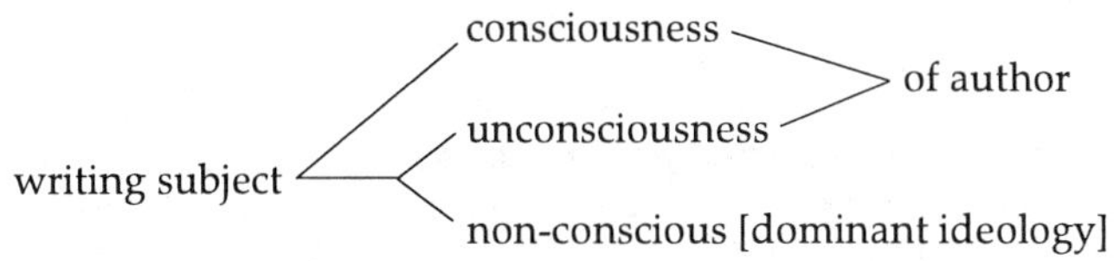

Barthes's concept of the "scriptor," which I will discuss in the next few pages of this paper, is comparable to Kristeva's "writing subject." But Barthes focuses more upon an analysis of the non-conscious forces of the text.

13. Roland Barthes, "Death of the Author," in *Image-Music-Text*, trans. Stephen Heath (New York: Hill and Wang, 1977), 143. This is repeated in Roland Barthes, *S/Z*, translated by Richard Miller (New York: Hill and Wang, 1974), 41.

14. *S/Z*, 41, 151.

15. "Death of the Author," 147.

16. *S/Z*, 211.

17. "Death of the Author," 147.

18. Roland Barthes, as quoted by Stephen Heath in a translator's note to *Image-Music-Text*, 10. Barthes's text is not identified.

19. *S/Z*, 4.

20. Roland Barthes, "From Work to Text," in *Image-Music-Text*, 163.

21. "From Work to Text," 164.

22. *PT*, 27. It is important to note that *figure* in French means both "personage" and "face." (My thanks to Hugh Silverman for pointing this out to me). This double meaning of *figure* will become significant later, since we desire the author as we desire the brush with the law—as a first layer of meaning which must be overcome.

23. See "Death," 147: "a code cannot be destroyed, only 'played off'."

24. Roland Barthes, *Roland Barthes by Roland Barthes*, translated by Richard Miller (New York: Hill and Wang, 1977), i. Hereafter cited in text as *Barthes*.

25. "We must conceive of a play in which whoever loses wins, and in which one loses and wins in every turn" (Jacques Derrida, "Différance," in *Margins of Philosophy*, 20). The point here is that the movement of différance is not a dialectical movement, an alterity of presence and absence. To use Derrida's words, it is *traces*.

What is needed is to engage in what Kristeva calls literary practice: the exploration and discovery of *possibilities* of language. This is an activity that liberates the subject from sedimented codes (Roudiez, Introduction, to *Revolution in Poetic Language*, 2).

26. "From Work to Text," 164.

27. "The play on words is based on a very simple semantic mechanism: one and the same signifier (a word) simultaneously takes two different signifieds, so that that audition of the word is divided: French appropriately calls this a *double entendre*, a double hearing." Roland Barthes, "Erte, or À la lettre," in *The Responsibility of Forms* (New York: Hill and Wang, 1985), 121.

28. See, for example, *PT*, 17, 34, 62; Barthes, 60, 117, 124.

29. *The American Heritage Dictionary of the English Language* (Boston: Houghton Mifflin, 1969). By referring to a dictionary I am not exposing the plurality of meanings, but rather a finite multiplicity (close by the *doxa*, the common usage, which is the standard used by dictionary editors). But hopefully we can overcome this limit.

30. Although it is this precision which the Barthian text undercuts.

31. Ray, 2.

32. We will see, however, that the early working out of the tension between instance and system in *Writing Degree Zero* is not completely abandoned, but rather is displaced in Barthes's later texts, since the play of meanings does not negate the instance/system tension. In fact, it is that which allows the instance and system to remain at odds with one another. Cf. Kristeva's view. Kristeva maintains a tension between instance and system in her texts, I think more so than does Barthes. See, for example, Kristeva's comments in the Preface to *Desire in Language*: "our only chance to avoid being neither master nor slave of meaning lies in our ability to insure our mastery of it (through technique or knowledge) as well as our passage through it (through play or practice). In a word, *jouissance*" (x). Kristeva appeals to an overturning of the Hegelian master-slave dialectic as an overcoming of instance and system. But Kristeva's biologism, her assertion that there are biological constraints imposed on the drive charge, seems to negate any possibility of play with the meanings of *body*. See, for example, *Revolution*, 28–29.

33. Ray, 177. Ray also notes the quotation from *S/Z* that follows.

34. Heath, 9.

35. Leon Roudiez, Introduction to *Desire in Language*, 16. Roudiez also notes that in fact there is also an English word *jouissance*, but that it is archaic and has lost the multiple connotations (most especially the sexual connotations) that the French word retains.

36. Heath, 9.

37. I conceive of the process as one that resembles Kristeva's reworking of the Hegelian dialectic, especially as worked out in her concept of negativity. in *Revolution in Poetic Language*, Kristeva writes, "while still maintaining their dualism, negativity recasts not only the thesis of *being* and *nothingness*, but all categories used in the contemplative system: universal and particular, indeterminate and determinate, quality and quantity, negation and affirmation, etc." (109).

Negativity is the fourth term of Kristeva's reworked Hegelian dialectic.

Dualisms are never synthesized, and always maintained, yet continually recast or rewoven. If we were to diagram Kristeva's model, it might be represented as pictured below:

negativity ———— 4th term
writing subject ———— 3rd term
semiotic—symbolic ———— 1st, 2nd terms

38. *Writing Degree Zero; PT*, 29, 32.

39. Roland Barthes, "Requichot and his Body," in *The Responsibility of Forms*, 281–219.

40. Sontag, "Writing Itself," xxxi.

CHAPTER 13

1. This paper uses the term *Shoah*, Hebrew for "total destruction" in the place of the more common *Holocaust*. See Emil Fackenheim, "The Holocaust: A Summing up after Two Decades of Reflection," in *Argumentum e Silentio*, edited by Amy Colin (Berlin: Walter de Gruyter, 1987), 286.

2. See Pöggeler's discussion of Célan's reception of Mallarmé in *Spur des Worts* (Freiburg: Karl Alber, 1986), 113ff. Also see Dorothee Kohler-Luginbühl, *Poetik im Lichte der Utopie* (Frankfurt am Main: Peter Lang, 1986), 154–56. Pöggeler argues that while Célan wishes to preserve Mallarmé's reticence in speaking of the mundane world, he does so in order that the tone of lament permeating the Célanian poem not become sentimental or trivial. But Pöggeler also argues that unlike Mallarmé's hermetic critic, Célan's lament would mark out in history "the difference between good and evil, the murdured and their murderers."

On the other hand, Shoshana Felman argues that Mallarmé's preoccupation with the development of arrhythmic free verse stems from his claim that revolutions fail because they change governments but not their notion of prosody. (See Shoshana Felman and Dori Laub, *Testimony*, (New York, Routledge, 1992) 19–24). In this sense, Mallarmé's preoccupation with the formal aspects of his poetry does not signal a decadent obsession with poetic effect but the setting in motion of a political and historical revolution in which the poem teaches oneself and one's fellow citizens to "reach out for what cannot be anticipated," for that which in Mallarmé's words "explodes or splits." Thus, the poem becomes an attack upon all those ways of speaking about the world that deny or cover over its transcendence of one's own experience. Certainly Célan is deeply influenced by this aspect of the Mallarméan project but resists the narrowness of a gesture that would focus upon the disruption of the poem's form in order ro effect a historical revolution. For Célan, not the form of the poem but the trajectory of its address is the central issue. The poet seeks out that particular other who lives an historical existence and for whom the poet in a manner greater than she or he can grasp is responsible.

3. Paul Célan, "Die Meridiane," in *Célan's Gesamte Werke*, edited by Bela Alleman and Stefan Reichert (Frankfurt am Main: Suhrkamp, 1983), 189 (henceforth, *M* (translation mine)).

4. As Yerushalmi has pointed out, the meaning of Hebraic history is "explored more directly and more deeply in the prophets than in the actual historical narratives," precisely because the prophetic voice is so deeply sensitive to the victimization of human beings. See Yehuda Yerushalmi, *Zakhor: Jewish History and Jewish Memory* (Seattle: University of Washington Press, 1982), 15.

5. Emmanuel Levinas, *Totality and Infinity*, translated by Alphonso Lingis (Pittsburgh: Duquesne Press, 1969), 228ff.

6. Taken from *Poems of Paul Célan*, translated by Michael Hamburger (New York: Persea Books, 1988), 186–89.

7. One should be careful to distinguish historical shame from moral guilt. Shame arises from the accusation that one has inherited a world permeated with injustice. Shame occurs when one remembers vocatively that in history humans have failed to do the good and as a result others have suffered uniquely and terribly. Unlike guilt, in which an individual confronts the self-contradiction within his or her own being that failing to respond ethically to one's neighbors implicates, shame is the self's confrontation with an exterior world in which the irremediableness of the harm suffered by other beings becomes scandalous. While the guilty conscience discovers a contradiction in his or her own being, the shameful consciousness is plagued by whether simply to be is to already be implicated in an order that is indefensibly unjust.

8. T. W. Adorno, *Aesthetic Theory*, translated by C. Lenhardt (London: Routledge and Kegan Paul, 1984), 400. I am also indebted to Alan Udoff for his thoughts on how Célan's poetry is especially responsive to the shamefulness of the Holocaust (see "On Poetic Dwelling: Situating Célan and the Holocaust," in *Argumentum e Silentio*, 335).

9. Taken from *Poems of Paul Célan*, translated by Michael Hamburger (New York: Persea Books, 1988), 208–211.

10. Paul Célan, "Ansprache Anlässlich der Entgegennahme des Literaturpreises des Freien Hasnsestadt Bremen," in *Célan Gesammelte Werke III*, 185–86.

11. Marlies Janz, *Vom Engagement absoluter Poesie: Zur Lyrik und Ästhetik Paul Célans* (Athenäum, 1976), 162.

12. Janz speaks of Célan's poetic project as the elaboration of a "Speech, which realizes (*vergegenwärtigt*) all the historical forms of human oppression." Such a speech would remain unheard in a world still enamored with the "show-horses of history."

13. Emmanuel Levinas, "Philosophy and the Idea of Infinity," *Collected Philosophical Papers: Emmanuel Levinas*, translated by Alphonso Lingis (The Hague: Martinus Nijhoff, 1987), 55.

14. Emmanuel Levinas, *Totality and Infinity*, 217.

CHAPTER 14

[An earlier version of this paper appeared in *Qui parle*.]
[I would like to thank Ellie Ragland-Sullivan for her encouragement.]

1. Terry Eagleton, *Literary Theory: An Introduction* (Minneapolis: University of Minnesota Press, 1983), 194.

2. Jacques Lacan, *Écrits: A Selection*. Translated by Alan Sheridan (New York: W. W. Norton, 1977), 155.

3. As Elizabeth Grosz so astutely reminds us, "It is not men *per se* who cause women's oppression, but rather the socio-economic and linguistic structure of the Other." See *Jacques Lacan: A Feminist Introduction* (London and New York: Routledge, 1990), 144. I thank Kevin McGrath for calling this book to my attention.

4. See especially "God and the *Jouissance* of the Woman" and "a Love Letter" in Jacques Lacan, *Feminine Sexuality: Jacques Lacan and the école freudienne*, 137–61, edited by Juliet Mitchell and Jacqueline Rose. Translated by Jacqueline Rose (New York: W. W. Norton, 1985), 145. Subsequent page references are to this edition and will be made in parentheses at the end of the quotation.

5. *Feminine Sexuality: Jacques Lacan and the école freudienne*, 55.

6. Ellie Ragland-Sullivan, *Jacques Lacan and the Philosophy of Psychoanalysis* (Urbana and Chicago: University of Illinois Press, 1987), 288.

7. *"Comment concevoir que l'Autre puisse être quelque part ce par rapport a quoi une moitié—puisqu'aussi bien c'est grossièrement la proportion* biologique—une moité des êtres parlants se réfère?" Jacques Lacan, *Encore: Le séminaire XX*, 1972–3 (Paris: Seuil, 1975), 75.

8. *"Les femmes s'en tiennent, aucune s'en tient d'être pas toute. à la jouissance dont il s'agit . . ."* *Encore*, 68.

9. In the unpublished 1969–70 seminar *L'envers de la psychanalyse* SXVIII. See Mitchell and Rose, 160–161.

10. Stephen Heath was the first Anglophone critic to mistrust Lacan's reliance upon Bernini's statue: "It might be added, moreover, as a kind of working rule that where a discourse appeals directly to an image, to an immediacy of seeing, as a point of its argument or demonstration, one can be sure that all difference is being elided, that the unity of some accepted vision is being reproduced." See "Difference," *Screen* 19.3 (1978), 53.

11. St. Teresa of Avila, *The Life of Teresa of Jesus.* Translated by and Edited by E. Allison Peers (Garden City: Image Books, 1960), 274–75.

CHAPTER 15

1. Throughout the novel, Acker's assumption of the role of outlaw is quite explicit. In the third section, "The End of the Night" (with clear echoes of Céline), she situates herself more specifically in the company of other "criminals" associated with the (mostly French) avant-garde. She has, in fact, often stated that these "literary criminals" are her true heroes. One critic, Larry McCaffery, lists as her peers: Antonin Artaud, Georges Bataille, Charles Bukowski, William Burroughs, Dada, Jean Genet, Arthur Rimbaud, the Marquis de Sade, Surrealism, the Velvet Underground, Andy Warhol, Walt Whitman, and the Sex Pistols. While McCaffery dutifully also links Acker to Emily Dickinson, Gertrude Stein, Virginia Woolf, Anaïs Nin, and (perhaps more accurately) Djuna Barnes, the argument for her place in a female tradition is much less convincing, giving the impression of an afterthought or a halfhearted concession to the demands of political correctness.

2. It is to a large extent her use of pornography that accounts for the ambivalence with which feminist critics have received Acker's texts. The discussion revolves around the question of whether pornography is purely exploitative of women or has diagnostic value as reflecting the ills of patriarchal society. Critics like Susan Sontag, Angela Carter, and Susan Suleiman tend toward the latter view, emphasizing the difference between the "moral pornography" or "pseudo-pornography" (Suleiman, 19) of those literary terrorists in the service of morality, like de Sade and Bataille, and the exploitative pornography of popular culture.

3. For a particularly enthusiastic defense of the happy interdependence between literary and critical texts, see J. Hillis Miller's "The Critic as Host."

CHAPTER 16

[This paper is part of a preliminary interrogation of carnal hermeneutics/the body politic. I wish to thank Kimberly Benston of Haverford College and Alice Benston of Emory University for their careful reading of the original version of this paper, which led me to revise it extensively. My wife Petee gave, as always, inquisitive readings.]

1. In reading *Nietzsche's Dance*, by Georg Stauth and Bryan S. Turner (Oxford: Basil Blackwell, 1988), which traces in large measure the footprints of Nietzsche's body politic in contemporary thought, we get the indelible impression that Nietzsche is the postmodern herald of carnal hermeneutics.

2. In their incomparable intellectual biography of Bakhtin, Katerina Clark and Michael Holquist speak of "Bakhtin's phenomenology of the senses" and intimate an affinity between Bakhtin's thought and the phenomenological thought of Husserl, Heidegger, and Sartre. See *Mikhail Bakhtin* (Cambridge: Harvard University Press, 1984), 70 and 94. Unfortunately, however, they fail to mention Maurice Merleau-Ponty's phenomenology, which proves to be closest to Bakhtin's thought. See the author's "Mikhail Bakhtin's Body Politic: A Phenomenological Dialogics," *Man and World*, 23 (1990), 85–99. Cf. Charles Taylor, "The Dialogical Self," in *The Interpretive Turn*, edited by David R. Hiley, James F. Bohman, and Richard Shusterman (Ithaca: Cornell University Press, 1991), 304–314, in which he evokes Bakhtin. The same must be said of Ann Jefferson's "Bodymatters: Self and Other in Bakhtin, Sartre and Barthes," in *Bakhtin and Cultural Theory*, edited by Ken Hirschkop and David Shepherd (Manchester: Manchester University Press, 1989), 152–177. Julia Kristeva is the first critic who drew our serious attention to the dialogism of Bakhtin in "Word, Dialogue, and Novel," which is the translation of the French original "Bakhtine, le mot, le dialogue et le roman" (1969). See Julia Kristeva, Chap. 3 of *Desire in Language*, edited by Leon S. Roudiez and translated by Thomas Gora, Alice Jardine, and Leon S. Roudiez (New York: Columbia University Press, 1980), 64–91. Tzvetan Todorov's recent work on Bakhtin bears "the dialogical principle" as its subtitle. See *Mikhail Bakhtin*, translated by Wlad Godzich (Minneapolis: University of Minnesota Press, 1984). For Bakhtin's dialogism among his own works, see particularly *The Dialogic Imagination*, edited by Michael Holquist and translated by Caryl Emerson and Michael Holquist (Austin: University of Texas Press, 1981).

3. Ralph Ellison's work *Invisible Man*, special thirtieth anniversary edition (New York: Random House, 1982), is a classic exploration in part of the racial implications of American society in terms of the dialectic of visibility and invisibility.

4. See José Ortega y Gasset, *Historical Reason*, translated by Philip W. Silver (New York: W. W. Norton, 1984). Ortega is critical of the Cartesian *cogito*, since it is ahistorical (timeless). Wolf Lepenies captures the ahistorical or atemporal monodology of Descartes when he writes: "Descartes's travels in time and space led him back to the philosophizing *ego*. Neither imaginary travels in the world of books nor real travels in the book of the world can provide the sound and firm knowledge necessary for the foundation of philosophy. This knowledge the philosopher can only find in himself, alone but secure in a heated room on a cold winter's day." "'Interesting Questions' in the History of Philosophy and Elsewhere," in *Philosophy in History*, edited by Richard Rorty, J. B. Scheewind, and Quentin Skinner (Cambridge: Cambridge University Press, 1984), 147. For what might be called the "postmodern" critique of Cartesianism, see particularly Dalia Judovitz, *Subjectivity and Representation in Descartes: The Origins of*

Modernity (Cambridge: Cambridge University Press, 1988) and Drew Leder, *The Absent Body* (Chicago: University Chicago Press, 1990). Leder's work is especially cogent to the development of carnal hermeneutics, because it is a phenomenological account of why and how in Cartesian philosophizing the visceral body is absent from conscious experience. Interestingly, he evokes the neo-Confucian "existential phenomenology" of Wang Yang-ming for the conceptualization of the world as "one body." The East is truly a mine field of bodily kinaesthetics. For the kinaesthetics of the body in its ecological setting, see Manfred Porkert, *The Theoretical Foundations of Chinese Medicine* (Cambridge: MIT Press, 1974). In *The Body: Toward an Eastern Mind-Body Theory*, edited by T. P. Kasulis and translated by Nagatomo Shigenori and T. P. Kasulis (Albany: SUNY Press, 1987), the Japanese philosopher Yuasa Yasuo gives us a non-dualistic account of "cultivating" the mind-body relation. Furthermore, Dōgen—who is the thirteenth-century founder of Japanese Sōtō Zen—gave the body primacy over the mind, that is, he indicated that the body is more important than the mind (*Ibid.*, 118).

5. *The Visible and the Invisible*, edited by Claude Lefort and translated by Alphonso Lingis (Evanston: Northwestern University Press, 1968), 48. The expressions *reflective cramp* and *kosmotheoros* are borrowed from Merleau-Ponty (see *Ibid.*, 57 and 113). Merleau-Ponty proposes to replace the reflective philosophy of subjectivity (or a "constituting subject") with the notion of an "instituting subject," which, in the wake of guaranteeing a common world between the self and the other, would reject the hermetically sealed self and the conception of the other as a mere "negative" of the self. See *Themes from the Lectures at the Collège de France 1952–1960*, translated by John O'Neill (Evanston: Northwestern University Press, 1970), 40.

6. See Merleau-Ponty, *The Visible and the Invisible.*, 139. "The spectacle," writes Guy Debord, "inherits all the *weaknesses* of the Western philosophical project, which undertook to comprehend activity in terms of the categories of *seeing*; furthermore, it is based on the incessant spread of the precise technical rationality that grew out of this thought. The spectacle does not realize philosophy; it philosophizes reality. The concrete life of everyone has been degraded into a *speculative* universe." *Society of the Spectacle* (Detroit: Black and Red, 1983), par. 19. For an excellent discussion of the sovereignty and autonomy of the one-sense, visionary body in the context of nineteenth-century intellectual thought, see Jonathan Crary, *Techniques of the Observer* (Cambridge: MIT Press, 1990). Richard Rorty makes a conscious attempt to avoid visual allusions in philosophizing. Edifying philosophy, as he calls it, is "the attempt to prevent conversation from degenerating into inquiry—into an exchange of views." See *Philosophy and the Mirror of Nature* (Princeton: Princeton University Press, 1979), 372. Moreover, Rorty's work is an attempt to formulate hermeneutics-centered postmodernity by overcoming epistemology-centered modernity, particularly in Descartes, Locke, and Kant. He puts it quite simply: "Hermeneutics . . . is what we get when we are no longer epistemological" (*Ibid.*, 325). In essence, Rorty's *Philosophy and the Mirror of Nature* is an "edifying" critique of the specular mindset of modernity. The French translation of it as "*l'homme spéculaire*" cap-

tures its principal task and accomplishment. For anti-ocularcentric hermeneutics, see also the author's "Martin Heidegger and the Homecoming of Oral Poetry," *Philosophy Today*, 26 (1982), 148–170.

7. See Martin Heidegger, *The Question Concerning Technology and Other Essays*, translated by William Lovitt (New York: Harper and Row, 1977), especially "The Age of the World Picture," 115–154. Cf. Walter Benjamin, "The Work of Art in the Age of Mechanical Reproduction," in *Illuminations*, edited by Hannah Arendt and translated by Harry Zohn (New York: Schocken Books, 1969), 217–251.

8. Hannah Arendt, *The Human Condition* (Chicago: University of Chicago Press, 1958), 292.

9. According to Hans-Georg Gadamer, application is an integral part of hermeneutical interpretation. See *Truth and Method*, 2nd rev. ed., revision translated by Joel Weinsheimer and Donald G. Marshall (New York: Crossroad, 1991), 308.

10. If, as Terry Eagleton says, "[a]esthetics is born as a discourse of the body," the body politic points to the postmodern direction of making the aesthetic and the political compatible. See *The Ideology of the Aesthetic* (Oxford: Basil Blackwell, 1990), 13. Cf. Maurice Merleau-Ponty, *Phenomenology of Perception*, translated by Colin Smith (New York: Humanities Press, 1962), 150: "The body is to be compared . . . to a work of art." In other words, it makes the aestheticization of politics possible as a postmodern venture. Here I have in mind Friedrich Nietzsche's *The Birth of Tragedy* as the beginning of such a venture. A seminal sociological and anthropological discussion on the use of the body is Marcel Mauss's 1934 lecture entitled "Les Techniques du corps," which was reprinted in his *Sociologie et anthropologie* (Paris: Presses Universitaires de France, 1950), 365–386 and which was translated into English by Ben Brewster as "Techniques of the Body" in *Economy and Society*, 2 (1973), 70–88. See also David Le Breton, *Anthropologie du corps et modernité* (Paris: Presses Universitaires de France, 1990), whose synopsis is found in "Body and Anthropology: Symbolic Effectiveness" (translated by Helen McPhail), *Diogenes*, 153 (1991), 85–100 and John O'Neill, *Five Bodies: The Human Shape of Modern Society* (Ithaca: Cornell University Press, 1985), and *Sociology as a Skin Trade* (New York: Harper and Row, 1972).

11. "Dante . . . Bruno. Vico . . Joyce," in Samuel Beckett *et al.*, *Our Exagmination Round His Factification for Incamination of* Work in Progress (London: Shakespeare, 1927), 11. In *Language as Gesture* (New York: Harcourt, Brace, 1952), 3, R. P. Blackmur contends that "Language is made of words, and gesture is made of motion. There is one half the puzzle. The other half is equally self-evident if only because it is an equally familiar part of the baggage of our thought. It is the same statement but the other way around. Words are made of motion, made of action or response, at whatever remove; and gesture is made of language of words. . . . When the language of words fails we resort to the language of gesture. If we stop there, we stop with the puzzle. If we go on, and

say that when the language of words most succeeds it *becomes* gesture in its words, we shall have solved the verbal puzzle with which we began by discovering one approach to the central or dead-end mystery of meaningful expression in the language of the arts." He goes on to say a little later that "gesture *is* native to language, and if you cut it out you cut roots and get a sapless and gradually rotting if indeed not a petrifying language" (*Ibid.*, 4). According to St. Augustine, gesture is the natural and universal language of all people. Because it is also cultural *habitus*, the opacity of gesture cannot be ignored. See Stephen Greenblatt, *Marvelous Possessions* (Chicago: University of Chicago Press, 1991), Chap. 4, "Kidnapping Language," 86–118. For the opacity and diversity as well as the transparency of gesture in the history of Western culture, see *A Cultural History of Gesture*, edited by Jan Bremmer and Herman Roodenburg (Ithaca: Cornell University Press, 1992) and Jean-Claude Schmitt, *La Raison des gestes dans l'Occident médiéval* (Paris: Gallimard, 1990).

12. See Thomas, "Introduction" to *A Cultural History of Gesture*, 2. Cf. Gilles Deleuze who writes that "The body is language because it is essentially 'flexion.'" *The Logic of Sense*, translated by Mark Lester and edited by Constantin V. Boundas (New York: Columbia University Press, 1990), 286.

13. *On Boxing* (Garden City: Doubleday, 1987), 4.

14. *Ibid.*, 11. Oates's ending resembles the Japanese literary technique known as *hokku*: "The fallen blossom flies back to its branch:/ A butterfly." See Marshall McLuhan and Harley Parker, *Through the Vanishing Point: Space in Poetry and Painting* (New York: Harper and Row, 1968), 37. The hermeneutical phenomenologist Paul Ricoeur establishes certain conditions in which the "understanding" of human action may be considered to be similar to text-interpretation (*Auslegung*). See "The Model of the Text: Meaningful Action Considered as a Text," *Social Research* 38, (1971), 529–562. See also Patrick A. Heelan, "Perception as a Hermeneutical Act," *The Review of Metaphysics*, 37 (1983), 61–75.

15. *Love's Body* (New York: Alfred A. Knopf, 1966), 264–265. In relating Merleau-Ponty's phenomenological thought to postmodernity, G. B. Madison notes a certain resemblance between Merleau-Ponty's later thought and Norman O. Brown's "postmodernist" thought. For Madison, it is not only "striking" but also "disconcerting." See *The Hermeneutics of Postmodernity* (Bloomington: Indiana University Press, 1988), 79–80 n. 21.

16. *Styles of Radical Will* (New York: Farrar, Straus and Giroux, 1969), 32. For her perceptive discussion of the employment of such diseases as tuberculosis and cancer as social metaphors, see *Illness as Metaphor* (New York: Farrar, Straus and Giroux, 1978). For the aesthetics of silence from a comparative perspective, see Zhang Longxi, *The Tao and the Logos: Literary Hermeneutics, East and West* (Durham: Duke University Press, 1992), Chap. 3, "The Use of Silence," 71–129. In addition to its association with the usage of language, the term *pollution* is related closely to the olfactory sense. It is the term of the environment which is social, natural, and/or racial (e.g., hygienic). As such it is socially and symbolically

loaded and regulated. In essence, it belongs to the body politic of osphresiology. Among many interesting works, see particularly Mary Douglas, *Purity and Danger* (London: Routledge and Kegan Paul, 1966) and Alain Corbin, *The Foul and the Fragrant* (Cambridge: Harvard University Press, 1986). For a general discussion of the body politic of the senses, see Diane Ackerman, *A Natural History of the Senses* (New York: Random House, 1990).

17. For a thoughtful exploration of the dialectical nexus of speech as *yang* and silence as *yin* in Chinese thought, see Lik Kuen Tong, "The Meaning of Philosophical Silence: Some Reflections on the Use of Language in Chinese Thought," *The Journal of Chinese Philosophy*, 3 (1976), 169–183. A definitive phenomenological study of the philosophical implications and ramifications of silence is found in Bernard P. Dauenhauer, *Silence* (Bloomington: Indiana University Press, 1980).

18. See the author's "Misreading the Ideogram: From Fenollosa to Derrida and McLuhan," *Paideuma*, 13 (1984), 211–227. In "The *Tao* and the *Logos*: Notes on Derrida's Critique of Logocentrism," *Critical Inquiry*, 11 (1985), 385–398, Longxi Zhang discusses the nature of the Chinese language in the context of contemporary literary criticism. For a revised and expanded version of Zhang's article, see *The Tao and the Logos*, Chap. 1, "The Debasement of Writing," 1–33. It was the American philosopher Ernest Fenollosa who became fascinated with the Chinese ideograms as a kind of "poetic alchemy," which came to be known as "etymosinology." See *The Chinese Written Character as a Medium for Poetry*, edited by Ezra Pound (San Francisco: City Lights Books, 1936). Cf. the author's "The Anatomy of Language: Vico, Joyce, and Etymosinology," *Rivista di Studi Italiani*, 4/5 (1986/1987), 211–227. Calligrammic poetry is associated closely with Guillaume Apollinaire, who was one of René Magritte's favorite writers. Interestingly, Michel Foucault speaks of the "calligram" of Magritte's "This Is Not a Pipe" as the "alphabetization" of an ideogram. He concludes that "the calligram aspired *playfully* to efface the oldest oppositions of our alphabetical civilization: to show and to name; to shape and to say; to reproduce and to articulate; to imitate and to signify; to look and to read." *This Is Not a Pipe*, translated by and edited by James Harkness (Berkeley: University of California Press, 1982), 21 (italic added).

19. The body as language is *specifically human*. It is exemplified in the language of the deaf as "sign language." The language of the deaf is "signed" rather than "written." Oliver Sacks lucidly writes of both the "ethnicity" and the "humanity" of the deaf as follows: "The study of the deaf shows us that much of what is distinctively human in us—our capacities for language, for thought, for communication, and culture—do not develop automatically in us, are not just biological functions, but are, equally, social and historical in origin; that they are a *gift*—the most wonderful of gifts—from one generation to another. We see that Culture is as crucial as Nature. . . . Sign for the deaf is a unique adaptation to another sensory mode; but it is also, and equally, an embodiment of their personal and cultural identity. For in the language of a people, Herder

observes, 'resides its whole thought domain, its tradition, history, religion, and basis of life, all its heart and soul.' This is especially true of Sign, for it is biologically unsilenceably the voice of the deaf." *Seeing Voices* (Berkeley: University of California Press, 1989), xi and 123. Cf. Carol Padden and Tom Humphries, *Deaf in America: Voices from a Culture* (Cambridge: Harvard University Press, 1988).

20. The postmodern thinker Jean-François Lyotard contends that "Everything real is rational, everything rational is real: 'Auschwitz' refutes speculative doctrine." *The Differend*, translated by Van Den Abbeele (Minneapolis: University of Minnesota Press, 1988), 179.

21. *Metaphysical Journal*, translated by Wall (London: Rockliff, 1952), 126. The anti-Cartesian Neapolitan philosopher Giambattista Vico was of the opinion that "I who think am mind and body, and if thought were the cause of my being, thought would be the cause of the body. Yet there are bodies that do not think. Rather, it is because I consist both of body and mind that I think; so that body and mind united are the cause of thought." *On the Most Ancient Wisdom of the Italians*, translated by L. M. Palmer (Ithaca: Cornell University Press, 1988), 56.

22. *The Orphic Voice* (London: Routledge and Kegan Paul, 1961), 35–36. Consonant with Lyotard's rejection of the Hegelian formula because of Auschwitz as quoted in n. 17, Terrence Des Pres observes that in the German death camps the spiritual and symbolic becomes concretized in the bodily: "In extremity man is stripped of his expanded spiritual identity. Only concrete forms of existence remain, actual life and actual death, actual pain and actual defilement; and these now constitute the medium of moral and spiritual being. Spirit does not simply vanish when sublimation fails. At the cost of much of its freedom it falls back to the ground and origin of meaning—back, that is, to the physical experience of the body. Which is another way of saying that, in extremity, symbols tend to actualize." *The Survivor* (New York: Oxford University Press, 1976), 69.

23. *The Portable Nietzsche*, edited by and translated by Walter Kaufmann (New York: Penguin Books, 1954), 146. Cf. W. B. Yeats's "Sailing to Byzantium" (1927) containing several lines that create the interesting transfusion of images concerning soul, body, and dress: "An aged man is but a paltry thing,/A tattered coat upon a stick, unless / Soul clap its hands and sing, and louder sing / For every tatter in its mortal dress, /. . ." *The Variorum Edition of the Poems of W. B. Yeats*, edited by Peter Allt and Russell K. Alspach (New York: Macmillan, 1957), 407. For Nietzsche's cultural genealogy of the body, see Eric Blondel, *Nietzsche: The Body and Culture*, translated by Seán Hand (Stanford: Stanford University Press, 1991). Nietzsche's model of the feminine is discussed in Jean Graybeal, *Language and "the Feminine" in Nietzsche and Heidegger* (Bloomington: Indiana University Press, 1990).

24. See the author's "Vico and Bakhtin: A Prolegomenon to Any Future Comparison," *New Vico Studies*, 3 (1985), 157–165.

25. *The New Science*, translated by Thomas Goddard Bergin and Max Harold Fisch (Ithaca: Cornell University Press, 1984), par. 237 (78).

26. *Ibid.*, par. 405 (129).

27. Martin Heidegger, *What Is Called Thinking?*, translated by Fred D. Wieck and J. Glenn Gray (New York: Harper and Row, 1968), 16–17. For an interesting commentary on Heidegger's conception of thinking that privileges the hand, see Jacques Derrida, "*Geschlecht* II: Heidegger's Hand," translated by John P. Leavey, Jr., in *Deconstruction and Philosophy*, edited by John Sallis (Chicago: University of Chicago Press, 1987), 161–196. For the original French text, see *Psyché: Inventions de l'autre* (Paris: Galilée, 1987), "La Main de Heidegger (Geschlecht II)," 415–451. The incomparable essayist Michel de Montaigne describes many expressive ways of the performing hands: "we require, promise, call, dismiss, threaten, pray, supplicate, deny, refuse, interrogate, admire, number, confess, repent, fear, express confusion, doubt, instruct, command, incite, encourage, swear, testify, accuse, condemn, absolve, abuse, despise, defy, provoke, flatter, applaud, bless, submit, mock, reconcile, recommend, exalt, entertain, congratulate, complain, grieve, despair, wonder, exclaim, and what not! And all this with a variety and multiplication, even emulating speech." *Works of Michel de Montaigne*, edited by O. W. Wight, Vol. 2 (New York: Hurd and Houghton, 1864), 138. For an innovative "sociology of the hand" inspired by Heidegger's insights, see David Sudnow, *Ways of the Hand* (Cambridge: Harvard University Press, 1978). For an interesting and definitive study on the healing power of the king's touch in England and France in the Middle Ages, see Marc Bloch, *The Royal Touch*, translated by J. E. Anderson (London: Routledge and Kegan Paul, 1973). Without question heremeneutics as tactile thinking is anti-ocular. See the author's "Martin Heidegger and the Homecoming of Oral Poetry" and cf. Martin Jay, "The Rise of Hermeneutics and the Crisis of Ocularcentrism," in *The Rhetoric of Interpretation and the Interpretation of Rhetoric*, edited by Paul Hernadi (Durham: Duke University Press, 1989), 55–74; "In the Empire of the Gaze: Foucault and the Denigration of Vision in Twentieth-Century French Thought," in *Foucault: A Critical Reader*, edited by David Couzens Hoy (Oxford: Basil Blackwell, 1986), 175–204; and "Scopic Regimes of Modernity," in *Vision and Visuality*, edited by Hal Foster (Seattle: Bay Press, 1988), 3–23.

28. *Rodin*, translated by Jessie Lemont and Hans Trausil (London: Grey Walls Press, 1946), 33. Cf. Albert E. Elsen, *Rodin's Thinker and the Dilemmas of Modern Public Sculpture* (New Haven: Yale University Press, 1985), 161: *The Thinker's* "powerful body signified the physical work of art, while his concentrated thought evoked the intellectual demands of the creative process."

29. Cf. Clark and Holquist, *Mikhail Bakhtin*, 244–245.

30. *Problems of Dostoevsky's Poetics*, edited by and translated by Caryl Emerson (Minneapolis: University of Minnesota Press, 1984), 252 (italics added). In the beginning was the Relation which determines and authenticates the difference between the self and the other: it is what Francis Jacques calls "*primum*

relationis" (the ontological or ontogenetic primacy of the relation). Most recently Jacques has developed the most comprehensive "dialogiques" (dialogics), or relationalist philosophy. He means to weave his ideas in and out of those of Hegel, Husserl, Buber, Levinas, and Bakhtin. See *Dialogues: Recherches logiques sur le dialogue* (Paris: Presses Universitaires de France, 1979); *L'Espace logique de l'interlocution: Dialogiques II* (Paris: Presses Universitaires de France, 1985); and *Différence et subjectivité: Anthropologie d'un point de vue relationnel* (Paris: Editions Aubier Montaigne, 1982). Only the last work has been translated into English as *Difference and Subjectivity: Dialogue and Personal Identity*, translated by Andrew Rothwell (New Haven: Yale University Press, 1991). Jacques intends to "radicalize" Bakhtin's dialogical principle by inserting "a principle of differentiation" into the structure of dialogue or interlocution: "Dialogue is only fruitful and creative (of information or meaning) if my own voice manages to achieve implicit recognition; if it is able to be disentangled at any moment by the interlocutor, but at the same time allows itself to be integrated into the progress of the conversation. As a differential reality, however, it is not heard. On this point I diverge from Bakhtin: in my view, my own voice is precisely, and only, a prerequisite of meaning and the communal pooling of meaning, a pragmatic prerequisite" (*Ibid.*, 285–286).

31. V. N. Voloshinov (Mikhail Bakhtin), *Marxism and the Philosophy of Language*, translated by Ladislav Matejka and I. R. Titunik (New York: Seminar Press, 1973), 11 (italics original). Vico, too, asserted that language as verbal acts stands at "midway between mind and body" (*The New Science*, par. 1045 [393]).

32. *Phenomenological Psychology* (New York: Basic Books, 1966), 211. In *The Body and Society* (Oxford: Basil Blackwell, 1984), Bryan S. Turner rightly contends that the social sciences have suppressed and ignored the basic fact that humans have bodies and they are bodies. Despite his contention that phenomenology is too "individualistic" to construct an adequate sociology of the body, his social ontology of the body is in significant measure phenomenologically embedded. What must be recognized and acknowledged is the insistence of phenomenological ontology that the body is the primordial mode of our being-in-the-world; that is, it is our anchorage in the world both social and natural. Only the phenomenological notion of the body as the primordial mode of our being-in-the-world can account for what Thomas Laqueur calls "sex socialized," or the body as the effects of historical and social practices. See Thomas Laqueur, *Making Sex: Body and Gender from the Greeks to Freud*, especially Chap. 6, "Sex Socialized," 193–243. For many rich and interesting topics in the cultural politics of the body in different times and different places, see *Fragments of a History of the Human Body*, edited by Michel Feher with Ramona Naddaff and Nadia Tazi, 3 parts in 3 vols. (New York: Urzone, 1989).

33. *Mikhail Bakhtin*, 175 (italics added).

34. *Adventures of the Dialectic*, translated by Joseph Bien (Evanston: Northwestern University Press, 1973), 205.

35. *The Complete Psychological Works of Sigmund Freud* (Standard Edition), translated by James Strachey (London: Hogarth Press, 1961), 21:95. For Bakhtin's critique of Freudianism, see V. N. Voloshinov (Mikhail Bakhtin), *Freudianism: A Marxist Critique*, translated by I. R. Titunik (New York: Academic Press, 1976).

36. *Mikhail Bakhtin*, 206.

37. *The Dialogic Imagination*, 294.

38. *Ibid.*, 280–282. Bakhtin is concerned with the question of "answerability" or "response-ability" in his early philosophical work: *Art and Answerability*, edited by Michael Holquist and Vadim Liapunov and translated by Vadim Liapunov (Austin: University of Texas Press, 1990).

39. As Jean-Paul Sartre puts it with brevity but forcefully: "In human societies, faces rule." *Writings of Jean-Paul Sartre*, Vol. 2: *Selected Prose*, edited by Michel Contat and Michel Rybalka and translated by Richard McCleary (Evanston: Northwestern University Press, 1974), 67. Cf. Maurice Merleau-Ponty, "The Child's Relations with Others," translated by William Cobb, in *The Primacy of Perception*, edited by James M. Edie (Evanston: Northwestern University Press, 1964), 146: "It is the simple fact that I live in the facial expressions of the other, as I feel him living in mine. It is a manifestation of what we have called, in other terms, the system 'me-and-other.'" In *Sexual Desire* (New York: Free Press, 1986), 23–24, Roger Scruton has written a focused passage about the concupiscence that the face unveils: "Why do eyes, mouth, nose and brow transfix us, when they have so little relation to the sexual prowess and bodily perfection of their bearer? The answer is simple: the face is the primary expression of consciousness, and to see *in the face* the object of sexual attraction is to find the focus which all attraction requires—the focus on another's existence, as a being who can be aware of *me*. Much has been written about the glance of love, which seems so imperiously to single out its object and so peremptorily to confront him with an intolerable choice. In truth, however, it is the glance of sexual interest that precipitates the movement of the soul, whereby two people come to stand outside the multitude in which they are presently moving, bound by a knowledge that cannot be expressed in words, and offering to each other a silent communication that ignores everything but themselves. It is as true of the glance of desire as it is of the glance of love that it concentrates into itself the whole life of the human being, constituting a direct appeal to the other to recognise my embodied existence." For the question of alterity as a postmodern theme, see Mark C. Taylor, *Altarity* (Chicago: University of Chicago Press, 1987).

40. *Difference and Subjectivity*, 148. The original French expression is "*cette surface la plus passionnante de la terre.*"

41. Emmanuel Levinas, *Totality and Infinity*, translated by Alphonso Lingis (Pittsburgh: Duquesne University Press, 1969), 199.

42. Emmanuel Levinas and Richard Kearney, "Dialogue with Emmanuel

Levinas," in *Face to Face with Levinas*, edited by Richard A. Cohen (Albany: SUNY Press, 1986), 27.

43. Emmanuel Levinas, *Ethics and Infinity*, translated by Richard A. Cohen (Pittsburgh: Duquesne University Press, 1982), 95.

44. See Clark and Holquist, *Mikhail Bakhtin*, 227.

45. For the author's discussion of the "ecological model" of *Auslegung*, see "The Edification of Oral Hermeneutics and the Ecology of the Text," in *Proceedings of the Xth Congress of the International Comparative Literature Association*, Vol. 2: *Comparative Poetics*, edited by Claudio Guillen (New York: Garland, 1985), 539–550

46. See *Performance in Postmodern Culture*, edited by Michel Benamou and Charles Caramello (Madison: Coda Press, 1977) and Henry M. Sayre, *The Object of Performance* (Chicago: University of Chicago Press, 1989). "As a medium," writes Sayre, "performance was initially intensely political in orientation" (*Ibid.*, 12). The body politic is of necessity the theatre of performance.

47. See Sayre, *The Object of Performance*, Chap. 7, "Critical Performance: The Example of Roland Barthes," 246–264. Barthes is quoted as saying that "language is a skin: I rub my language against the other. It is as if I had words instead of fingers, or fingers at the tip of my words" (260). For the indelible bond between the body and language (writing and reading) in Barthes, see John O'Neill, "Homotextuality: Barthes on Barthes, Fragments (RB), with a Footnote," in *Hermeneutics*, edited by Gary Shapiro and Alan Sica (Amherst: University of Massachusetts Press, 1984), 165–182. Speaking of the body's skin and language, torture is without question an important dimension of the body politic and carnal hermeneutics. It inscribes the "spectacle of power," and its infliction of pain is the highly visible "insignia of power." See Elaine Scarry, *The Body in Pain* (New York: Oxford University Press, 1985), Chap. 1, "The Structure of Torture: The Conversation of Real Pain into the Fiction of Power," 27–59 and Pierre Clastres, *Society against the State*, translated by Robert Hurley (New York: Zone Books, 1989), "Of Torture in Primitive Societies," 177–188.

48. *Between Theatre and Anthropology* (Philadelphia: University of Pennsylvania Press, 1985), 23. For Richard Schechner's theatrical or dramaturgical theory of performance, see also *Performance Theory*, rev. and expanded ed. (New York: Routledge, 1988). For an anthropological discussion of spoken verbal communication as performance, see Richard Bauman, *Verbal Art as Performance* (Rowley: Newbury House, 1977). Performance is defined as "a unifying thread tying together the marked, segregated esthetic genres and other spheres of verbal behavior into a general unified conception of verbal art as a way of speaking" (*Ibid.*, 5). The most celebrated and path-finding study of (Homer's) "oral poetry" as performance is Milman Parry's *The Making of Homeric Verse: The Collected Papers of Milman Parry*, edited by Adam Parry (Oxford: Clarendon Press, 1970). See also Albert B. Lord, *The Singer of Tales* (Cambridge: Harvard University Press, 1960).

I am grateful to Dennis Glew, who is my colleague and a classicist at Moravian College, for bringing Lord's work to my attention.

49. *Toward a Poor Theatre* (New York: Simon and Schuster, 1968), 64.

50. *The Literary Speech Act*, translated by Catherine Porter (Ithaca: Cornell University Press, 1983). Cf. Mary Louise Pratt, *Toward a Speech Act Theory of Literary Discourse* (Bloomington: Indiana University Press, 1977).

51. See *Jacques Lacan and the Adventure of Insights* (Cambridge: Harvard University Press, 1987), 56 *et passim*. For a discussion of pragmatic narratives in psychoanalysis, see Donald P. Spence, *Narrative Truth and Historical Truth* (New York: W. W. Norton, 1982). For a search for the intersection of (Lacan's) psychotherapeutical discourse and Bakhtin's translinguistics, see Sven Daelemans and Tullio Maranhão, "Psychoanalytic Dialogue and the Dialogical Principle," in *The Interpretation of Dialogue*, edited by Tullo Maranhão (Chicago: University of Chicago Press, 1990), 219–241.

52. *Jacques Lacan and the Adventure of Insights*, 118–119 (italics added). Cf. Merleau-Ponty, *Phenomenology of Perception*, 382–383: "My love, hatred and will are not certain as mere thoughts about loving, hating and willing; on the contrary the whole certainty of these thoughts is owed to that of the acts of love, hatred or will of which I am quite sure because I *perform* them."

53. Roy Porter writes that "It is a mark of the perduring Idealism of our culture that the 'body' side of the mind/body relationship has been neglected, or, to put the same point another way, that the major studies of the mind/body problem have been philosophical rather than material-social." "Barely Touching: A Social Perspective on Mind and Body," in *The Languages of Psyche*, edited by G. S. Rousseau (Berkeley: University of California Press, 1990), 45. Merleau-Ponty speaks of the body as "a two-dimensional being," as the "sensible sentient (*sentient sensible*) signifying the unity of the body as sentient and the body as sensible. See *The Visible and the Invisible*, Chap. 4, "The Intertwining—The Chiasm," 130–155. He goes further: "We must habituate ourselves to think that every visible is cut out in the tangible, every tactile being in some manner promised to visibility, and that there is encroachment, infringement, not only between the touched and the touching, but also between the tangible and the visible, which is encrusted in it, as, conversely, the tangible itself is not a nothingness of visibility, is not without visual existence. Since the same body sees and touches, visible and tangible belong to the same world. It is a marvel too little noticed that every movement of my eyes—even more, every displacement of my body—has its place in the same visible universe that I itemize and explore with them, as, conversely, every vision takes place somewhere in the tactile space. There is double and crossed situating of the visible in the tangible and of the tangible in the visible; the two maps are complete, and yet they do not merge into one. The two parts are total parts and yet are not superposable" (*Ibid.*, 134). Cf. *Phenomenology of Perception*, 150: "We do not merely behold as spectators the relations between the parts of our body, and correlations be-

tween the visual and tactile body: we are ourselves the unifier of these arms and legs, the person who both sees and touches them."

54. *The Feast of Fools* (Cambridge: Harvard University Press, 1969), 82.

55. Mikhail Bakhtin, *Rabelais and His World*, translated by Hélène Iswolsky (Bloomington: Indiana University Press, 1984), 285–286. Clark and Holquist speak of Rabelais as a "celebrator of the human body" (*Mikhail Bakhtin*, 295). In his "anatomy" of the "death camps," Terrence Des Pres describes graphically how the "symbolic" and the "spiritual" in the extremity of human experience lose their autonomy and get "actualized" in the "radical nakedness" of purely bodily experience. See *The Survivor* (Cf. note 22).

56. *On Humor*, translated by Antonio Illiano and Daniel P. Testa (Chapel Hill: University of North Carolina Press, 1974), 2.

57. *Ibid.*, 143.

58. *The Fashion System*, translated by Matthew Ward and Richard Howard (New York: Hill and Wang, 1983), 258.

59. See Norbert Elias, *The History of Manners*, translated by Edmund Jephcott (New York: Pantheon Books, 1978).

60. See Ernst Lehner, *Alphabets and Ornaments* (New York: Dover, 1952), xiii.

61. *Sartor Resartus* (New York: Charles Scribner's Sons, 1896 [1831]), 30.

62. Greenblatt, *Marvelous Possessions*, 95. "Within Western culture," Marianna Torgovnick observes, "the idiom 'going primitive' is in fact congruent in many ways to the idiom 'getting physical.'" *Going Primitive* (Chicago: University of Chicago Press, 1990), 228.

63. Clark and Holquist, *Mikhail Bakhtin*, 301. Without doubt Bakhtin's view is reminiscent of Nietzsche, who "conceived of eating as a basic appropriation of nature by human activity. Eating is a primary link between existing and thinking" (Stauth and Turner, *Nietzsche's Dance*, 195). Norbert Elias points out that there is a close parallel between "the 'civilizing' of eating and that of speech" as two important embodiments of socializing activity (*The History of Manners*, 116). For a fascinating discussion of "table talk" in the Renaissance, which has wide literary and sociological implications, see Michel Jeanneret, *A Feast of Words*, translated by Jeremy Whitely and Emma Hughes (Chicago: University of Chicago Press, 1991). For Mao Tse-tung, who was noted for his "scatological lyricism," the narrative of eating or not eating was the supreme function of the body politic: a revolution was not a dinner party. Here Mao is reacting against the age-old "misrule" of the gentry, which victimized the peasantry in China. See Richard H. Solomon, *A Revolution Is Not a Dinner Party* (Garden City: Doubleday, 1975). For an important discussion on orality as the body politic, see Louis Marin, *Food for Thought*, translated by Mette Hjort (Baltimore: Johns Hopkins University Press, 1989).

64. Clark and Holquist, *Mikhail Bakhtin,* 301.

65. "The Priest and the Jester," in *Toward a Marxist Humanism,* translated by Jane Ziekonko Peel (New York: Grove Press, 1968), 33–34.

66. *Rabelais and His World,* 160. In *The Art of the Novel,* translated by Linda Asher (New York: Harper and Row, 1988), 59, Milan Kundera refers to Rabelais's important "forgotten" neologism *agélaste* which comes from the Greek. Rabelais detested *agélaste* or a man who does not laugh or has no sense of humor. Mikhail Bakhtin and Michel Foucault are two of the most celebrated Nietzschean genealogists. In *The Politics and Poetics of Transgression* (Ithaca: Cornell University Press, 1986), Peter Stallybrass and Allon White view the Nietzschean study of history (i.e., genealogy) as leading to the ideal of carnival (6). For Nietzsche, according to Walter Kaufmann, "laughter becomes less a physical phenomenon than a symbol of joyous affirmation of life and of the refusal to bow before the spirit of gravity." See Friedrich Nietzsche, *Beyond Good and Evil,* translated by Walter Kaufmann (New York: Vintage, 1966), 233 n. 41. Gilles Deleuze asserts that "Those who read Nietzsche without laughing—without laughing often, richly, even hilariously—have, in a sense, not read Nietzsche at all." See "Nomad Thought" (translated by David B. Allison), in *The New Nietzsche,* edited by David B. Allison (New York: Dell, 1977), 142–149. For Bakhtin's connection to Nietzsche, see James M. Curtis, "Michael [*sic*] Bakhtin, Nietzsche, and Russian Pre-Revolutionary Thought," in *Nietzsche in Russia,* edited by Bernice Galtzer Rosenthal (Princeton: Princeton University Press, 1986), 331–354. As for Foucault, "Genealogy is history in the form of a concerted carnival." See *Language, Counter-Memory, Practice,* edited by Donald F. Bouchard (Ithaca: Cornell University Press, 1977), 161. In the radical spirit of Nietzsche, it may even be asserted that genealogy is a philosophy of the future. For, interestingly, the subtitle of his *Beyond Good and Evil,* which has suggestive references to carnival, is "Prelude to a Philosophy of the Future."

67. *Walter Benjamin or towards a Revolutionary Criticism* (London: NLB, 1981), 148.

68. Rimbaud's phrase is cited in Marshall and Eric McLuhan, *Laws of Media: The New Science* (Toronto: University of Toronto Press, 1988), 98. See also Jeanneret, *A Feast of Words,* 9. Cf. Susan Rubin Suleiman, *Subversive Intent* (Cambridge: Harvard University Press, 1990), 142–144. In *Discovering the Mind,* Vol. 2 (New York: McGraw-Hill, 1980), 62, Walter Kaufmann contends that one of Nietzsche's *personae* is "the prankster." Without this mask, Nietzsche's thought would not be "profound." By the same token, the mind, too, is dis/covered by the interruption and intervention of the body. The body measures the "profound" depth of the mind. The system of oppression and suffering leads sooner or later to resistance and rebellion. In his powerful, moving, and, by now classical essay entitled "The Power of the Powerless," Václav Havel amply vindicates the full-blown efficacy of the existential politics of resistance to totalitarianism. See *Living in Truth,* edited by Jan Vladislav (London: Faber and Faber, 1987), 36–122. He argues for choosing the existential politics of nonviolent resistance

for the sake of creating a "post-totalitarian" political order in Czechoslovakia. Havel has fully—for the moment at any rate—demonstrated the efficacy of the honored tradition of nonviolence as the way of transforming history and politics in that—to borrow the eloquent expression of Paul Ricoeur—"If non-violence is the calling of a few, it must appear to them as the duty of all. For whoever lives it and ceases to watch it from a distance, non-violence wishes to be the whole of action, wishes to make history." See *History and Truth*, translated by Charles A. Kelbley (Evanston: Northwestern University Press, 1965), 233. Moreover, Havel's politics of conscience reminds us of Henry Thoreau's spirit of civil disobedience in pronouncing jail as the only place for a just man in an unjust society. See John McGowan, *Postmodernism and Its Critics* (Ithaca: Cornell University Press, 1991), 176.

69. *Speech Genres and Other Late Essays*, edited by Caryl Emerson and Michael Holquist and translated by Vern W. McGee (Austin: University of Texas Press, 1986), 134–135.

70. *On Boxing*, 99.

71. *Difference and Subjectivity*, 88. As Jacques puts it, "The business of speech is not to break the silence but to interrupt violence" ("*Le travail de la parole n'est pas de rompre le silence mais d'interrompre la vilence*"). There is a play on *rompre* and *interrompre*: interruption means to put breaks on something with a rupture. It means to be at the threshold of radical transformation. Although they both renounce violence, there is an important difference between Oates and Jacques on the question of speech and silence. Oates rejects silence as the opposite of language signifying the death of humans. "The use of language," she declares, "is all we have to pit against death and silence." See Mary Kathryn Grant, *The Tragic Vision of Joyce Carol Oates* (Durham: Duke University Press, 1978), 164. In contrast, Jacques values silence: "Like a decision not to use violence, silence can sometimes be heroic. Far from being a mere ruse of the weak, it is a weapon, the human weapon par excellence" (*Difference and Subjectivity*, 197).

72. Oates, *On Boxing*, 18.

73. *Ibid.*, 19.

74. *Ibid.*, 75.

75. *Critique of Dialectical Reason*, Vol. 2: *The Intelligibility of History*, edited by Arlette Elaïm-Sartre and translated by Quintin Hoare (London: Verso, 1991), 24.

76. *Humanism and Terror*, translated by John O'Neill (Boston: Beacon Press, 1969), 109. For a case study of violence (revolution) as an inexorable dimension of the body politic, see Dorinda Outram, *The Body and the French Revolution* (New Haven: Yale University Press, 1989).

77. *Adventures of the Dialectic*, 39 and 207.

78. *The Rebel*, translated by Anthony Bower (New York: Alfred A. Knopf,

1956), 283–284. Earlier in 1946 Camus also wrote: "What we must defend is dialogue and the universal communication of men. Slavery, injustice, and lies are the plagues that destroy this dialogue and forbid this communication, . . . [*W*]*ords are stronger than bullets.*" *Between Hell and Reason*, translated by Alexandre de Gramont (Hanover: University Press of New England, 1991), 138–140 (italics added). Dominick LaCapra suggests that "Bakhtin's dialogical and carnivalizing rendition of dialectics provides an alternative to the totalizing incentive of speculative dialectics, and it substitutes a Rabelaisian for a Hegelian Marx." See *Rethinking Intellectual History* (Ithaca: Cornell University Press, 1983), Chap. 8, "Bakhtin, Marxism, and the Carnivalesque," 291–324 (at 315). For a persuasive account of the connection between violence and Hegel's speculative phenomenology of recognition, see Piotr Hoffman, *The Human Self and the Life and Death Struggle* (Gainesville: University Presses of Florida, 1983), Chap. 5, "Hegel on the Life and Death Struggle," 83–103; *Doubt, Time, Violence* (Chicago: University of Chicago Press, 1986), especially Chap. 2, "Time," 85–114 and "Conclusion: Violence," 117–129; and *Violence in Modern Philosophy* (Chicago: University of Chicago Press, 1989), Chap. 2, "Hegel: Logos and Violence," 73–149. It should be noted without further discussion that the phenomenology of recognition is of utmost significance for the understanding of human existence or coexistence which is both mental and bodily.

79. Alphonso Lingis speaks of "phallic sovereignty." As a phallus, a man can be seen as a sovereign sign. See *Excesses: Eros and Culture* (Albany: SUNY Press, 1983), 113 and 126.

80. It would be too pretentious for me to claim that I am a "feminist." I am only a witness to feminism as "altarity." My best friend happens to be my wife, who is a dialogical "feminist." By dialogical feminism, I mean feminism that defines man and woman as different but not as opposed. Luce Irigaray promotes the model of dialogical feminism in which the movement of history is defined—or, better, redefined—and cultivated as the joint and cooperative effort of both men and women. Jacques seems to imply what I call "dialogical" rather than "oppositional" feminism when he writes: "if the ambition of feminist protests were simply to reverse the order of things, like turning a glove inside out, the result would only be a return to the same ruinously nonrelational situation. It is no doubt too early to say whether feminist rivalry and protest is just a sign of specific unease, or a dialectical moment on the road to the double and indissociable liberation of men and women, restored to their positive difference by a viable relationship. The difficulty as I see it is as follows: when women form themselves into closed communicational communities in order to confront the supposedly closed ones of men and thereby rediscover themselves, they are not merely postponing the moment when communication with men might be resumed, but actually starting it off in a conflictual mode which merely confirms their own closure. It is relations between men and women that need to be regenerated as a matter of priority" (*Difference and Subjectivity*, 261). In dialogical feminism there is no opposition not only between spirit and body but also between the "calendar of the flesh" and the rhythm of nature. See

"Love between Us" (translated by Jeffrey Lomonaco), in *Who Comes after Subject?*, edited by Eduardo Cadava, Peter Connor, and Jean-Luc Nancy (New York: Routledge, 1991), 167–177. I might add that this is also the general model of dialogism that Bakhtin promotes. Because the human condition is irreducibly and inalienably dialogical, I am also weary of the fashionable movement of so-called "deep masculinity," which, not unlike oppositional feminism, is undialogical. Notwithstanding its seeming virtues, it is as wrong as the "separate but equal doctrine": we must stand *together* or else we perish.

81. George Bellows's "Stag at Sharkey's" first came to my attention when I took a graduate seminar with Charles Morris. It was reprinted in Morris's *Varities of Human Value* (Chicago: University of Chicago Press, 1956) in which a number of paintings were used to classify "somatotypes." Bellows's "Stag at Sharkey's" is high in dominance and low in dependence and detachment. In contrast, Pablo Picasso's "Two Harlequins" is high in detachment, with secondary strength in dependence, and low in dominance; Amedeo Modigliani's "Woman with a Necklace" is high in dependence, with secondary strength in detachment, and low in dominance; and Georges Rouault's "Christ Mocked by Soldiers" is high in dependence, with secondary strength in detachment, and low in dominance. In *The Culture of Pain* (Berkeley: University of California Press, 1991), David B. Morris discusses briefly Joyce Carol Oates's *On Boxing* (256–262), which includes Bellows's "Stag at Sharkey's."

82. *On Boxing*, 75.

83. *Ibid.*, 72. René Girard's thesis on violence and the sacred is highly pertinent to Oates's view here. Girard contends that violence is "the heart and secret soul of the sacred" and "like a raging fire that feeds on the very objects intended to smother its flames." See *Violence and the Sacred*, translated by Patrick Gregory (Baltimore: Johns Hopkins University Press, 1977), 31. The masculine violence of boxing, like war, has also specular thrills. In *The Warriors: Reflections on Men in Battle* (New York: Harper and Row, 1970), 28–32, J. Glenn Gray attends to the issue of "the delight in seeing" as one of the most enduring appeals of the battlefield: it is what the Bible terms "the lust of the eye"; it is "a primitive urge" of watching something *spectacular* that is neither familiar, nor routine, nor quotidian (e.g., the explosion of a hydrogen bomb). The delight in seeing invariably accompanies another enduring appeal of war—the delight in destruction.

84. In date rape, the pure silence of the victim's "no" is mistaken for an impure "yes," or her pure "no" is mistaken for an impure "yes." In discussing the body language of Pierre Klossowski, Gilles Deleuze puts elegantly the transfusive dilemma of speech and silence (as body language): "the pure language which produces an impure silence is a *provocation* of the mind by the body; similarly, the impure language which produces a pure silence is a *revocation* of the body by the mind" (*The Logic of Sense*, 291).

85. See Alice A. Jardine, *Gynesis* (Ithaca: Cornell University Press, 1985). For an agenda-setting discussion of feminism in the postmodern context, see

Suleiman, *Subversive Intent*, and for a variety of contemporary issues for the feminine body politic, see *The Female Body in Western Culture*, edited by Susan Rubin Suleiman (Cambridge: Harvard University Press, 1985). Dale M. Bauer discusses the feminization of Bakhtin's dialogism, particularly of its carnivalized body. See *Feminist Dialogics* (Albany: SUNY Press, 1988), especially Chap. 1, "Gender in Bakhtin's Carnival," 1–15. See also *Feminism, Bakhtin, and the Dialogic*, edited by Dale M. Bauer and Susan Jaret McKinstry (Albany: SUNY Press, 1991). The classical model for the feminist search for recognition was put forth by Simone de Beauvoir in *The Second Sex*, translated by H. M. Parshley (New York: Alfred A. Knopf, 1952). In *The Bonds of Love* (New York: Pantheon Books, 1988), Jessica Benjamin focuses on the mutual recognition between the masculine and the feminine that would avoid both "the idealization of the masculine side" and "the reactive valorization of femininity" (9).

86. For an anti-Cartesian genealogy in the context of ecophilosophy, see Morris Berman, *The Reenchantment of the World* (Ithaca: Cornell University press, 1981), and *Coming to Our Senses: Body and Spirit in the Hidden History of the West* (New York: Simon and Schuster, 1989). Cf. Alasdair MacIntyre, who writes in *Three Rival Versions of Moral Enquiry* (Notre Dame: University of Notre Dame Press, 1990), 25 that "the genealogist [e.g., Nietzsche] intended to discredit the whole notion of a canon." In *The Voice and the Eye*, translated by Alan Duff (Cambridge: Cambridge University Press, 1981), Alain Touraine identifies the "eye" with theory and the "voice" with action, respectively.

87. *Noise: The Political Economy of Music*, translated by Brian Massumi (Minneapolis: University of Minnesota Press, 1985), 3. It is no mere accident that the importance of hearing or audition is slighted in everyday academic language when we speak of "auditing" ("listening in") a course rather than "taking" it. For a seminal beginning of auditory phenomenology, see Straus, *Phenomenological Psychology*, Chap. 15, "Phenomenology of Hallucinations," 277–289. In *Philosophical Impact of Contemporary Physics* (Princeton: D. Van Nostrand, 1961), Milic Capek argues that auditory models are far better suited than visual ones to understand the development of contemporary physics. Following Husserl's phenomenology of the life-world (*Lebenswelt*), Aron Gurwitsch contends that the Galilean mathematization (geometricization) of nature is the starting point of "the ever growing alienation of the universe of physics from the world of perceptual experience." By constructing a totally abstract nature according to "algorithmic rules of operation alone," it makes "visualization" itself impossible. For Gurwitsch, therefore, the fundamental problematique of post-Galilean reason is the separation of intellectual operation from the natural world of perceptual experience. See *Phenomenology and the Theory of Science*, edited by Lester Embree (Evanston: Northwestern University Press, 1974), 48–49.

88. Cf. Leder, *The Absent Body*, 4: "One of the compelling reasons to challenge Cartesianism has to do with its far-reaching social effects. This hierarchical dualism has been used to subserve projects of oppression directed toward women, animals, nature, and other 'Others.'" The Cartesian *cogito* is both sexist

and speciesistic. To subvert it by way of the body politic is to discredit both sexism and speciesism (or anthropocentrism) at once. For what the mind is to the body, the human is to nature. In other words, the postmodernist restoration of the body entails the restoration of nature as well. The body politic is eminently *ecotopian* because it is linked to nature as flesh. The anti-Cartesian Merleau-Ponty issues a cryptic instruction to himself in his "Working Notes" in *The Visible and the Invisible*, 267: "Do a psychoanalysis of Nature: it is the flesh, the mother." In the final analysis, the homecoming of the body is also the homecoming of nature. On the question of femininity and ecology, see particularly Carolyn Merchant, *The Death of Nature* (New York: Harper and Row, 1980), and Mary Daly, *Gyn/Ecology* (Boston: Beacon Press, 1978). The term *eco-feminism* appears to have first been used by Françoise d'Eaubonne in *Le Féminisme ou la mort* (Paris: Horay, 1974). However, we should never overlook the fact that it was Simone de Beauvoir who alluded to the idea of nature as feminine with originality and profundity in *The Second Sex*. For a postmodern ecophilosophy, see the author's "Marxism and Deep Ecology in Postmodernity: From *Homo Oeconomicus* to *Homo Ecologicus*," *Thesis Eleven* 28 (1991), 86–99.

89. The double *entendre* of *jouissance* as carnal enjoyment and hearing is found in Hélène Cixous and Catherine Clément, *The Newly Born Woman*, translated by Betsy Wing (Minneapolis: University of Minnesota Press, 1986), 165–166. In a plethora of literature on the subject of feminism and anti-ocularcentrism, see particularly Evelyn Fox Keller and Christine R. Grontkowski, "The Mind's Eye," in *Discovering Reality*, edited by Sandra Harding and Merrill B. Hintikka (Dordrecht: Reidel, 1982), 207–224; E. Ann Kaplan, *Women and Film* (London: Methuen, 1982); and Carolyn Porter, *Seeing and Being* (Middletown: Wesleyan University Press, 1981). No feminist writer today is more persuasive and eloquent than Luce Irigaray in defense of feminine touch against male vision. See "The Fecundity of the Caress: A Reading of Levinas, *Totality and Infinity*, Section IV, B, 'The Phenomenology of Eros,'" in *Face to Face with Levinas*, 231–256; *This Sex Which Is Not One*, translated by Catherine Porter with Carolyn Burke (Ithaca: Cornell University Press, 1985); and *Speculum of the Other Woman*, translated by Gillian C. Gill (Ithaca: Cornell University Press, 1985). See also Edith Wyschogrod, "Doing Before Hearing: On the Primacy of Touch," in *Textes pour Emmanuel Lévinas*, edited by François Laruelle (Paris: Jean-Michel, 1980), 179–203. For the most systematic philosophical presentation of self-information in terms of hearing or listening, see David Michael Levin, *The Listening Self* (New York: Routledge, 1989). Cf. Gemma Corradi Fiumara, *The Other Side of Language: A Philosophy of Listening*, translated by Charles Lambert (New York: Routledge, 1990). The invention of the stethoscope by the French physician René-Théophile Hyacinthe Laennec in 1816 contains an interesting implication for the body politic. Because his patient was an obese female, Laennec made a cylinder out of sheets of paper in order to auscultate her heart beat. In the first place, "stethoscope" is made of the two Greek words *chest* and *seeing*. The designation of the technique of auscultating diagnosis is derived from the *visual* language of *seeing*. The condition of the patient's illness is "observed" by way of the stethoscope: the *auditory* language of hearing is translated into the *visual*

language of seeing. The language of Laennec's "sounds" became (Cartesian) "clear and distinct" ideas. This politics of language is, parenthetically, one more evidence of the masculine aristocracy of sight in Western thought since Plato and Aristotle. In the second place, since the words *observation*, *objectivity*, and *objectification* belong to the family of the optical, the use of the stethoscope "distances" and "alienates" the physician from the patient, that is, the patient becomes an object of observation in the physician's "eye." See Neil Postman, *Technopoly: The Surrender of Culture to Technology* (New York: Alfred A. Knopf, 1992), 97–101. Postman's discussion of the stethoscope is based on Stanley Joel Reiser, *Medicine and the Reign of Technology* (Cambridge: Cambridge University Press, 1978). Reiser's work is an extremely fascinating study of the impact of medical technology—such as the stethoscope, opthalmoscope, laryngoscope, X-ray, and microscope—on medical practice and health care in which "objective" in lieu of "subjective" evidence reduces personal contact and alienates the physician from the patient. Reiser's study dispels the myth that "the more the machines can take over the performing of medical functions, the more the doctor will have time to deal with his patient as a human being . . . to the benefit of both" (*Ibid.*, 229). In the context of our discussion concerning the body politic of the senses here, it is worth noting that the "visual technology" of the X-ray, for example, directly challenged the use of touch in diagnosis and the stethoscope and diagnoses based on sound. According to the prevailing sentiment of doctors, sight is a much more satisfactory agent of information than touch or hearing.

90. "Freedom, Recognition, and Obligation: A Feminist Approach to Political Theory," *American Political Science Review* 83, (1989), 1235.

91. For an account of visual dominance on Western philosophical thought, see Hannah Arendt, *The Life of the Mind*, Vol. 1: *Thinking* (New York: Harcourt Brace Jovanovich, 1971), 110ff. In *Inscribing the Other* (Lincoln: University of Nebraska Press, 1991), 20, Sander L. Gilman intimates that there is an inseparable link between racism and the body politic of the senses in the thought of the early-nineteenth-century German thinker Lorenz Oken, who regarded the "Eye-Man, the White, the European" as the highest and the "Skin-Man, the Black, the African" as the lowest in a hierarchy of the human races. For Oken (and his followers), sight is most intellectual and represents the height of aesthetic sensibility, whereas touch is least intellectual and signifies the lack of aesthetic sensibility. In essence, then, the former is "civilized" while the latter is "primitive." For Gilman's interesting discussion concerning Goethe's deconstruction of the accepted hierarchy of the senses and the sense of touch as a feminine icon, see *Ibid.*, Chap. 1, "Goethe's Touch: Touching, Seeing, and Sexuality," 29–49. In his "Editor's Introduction: Writing 'Race' and the Difference It Makes," *Critical Inquiry*, 12 (1985), 1–20, Henry Louis Gates, Jr., touches on the implicit presence of racial issues in the Western study of literature, that is, on the notion that the peoples of color (non-Europeans or non-whites) are incapable of writing which is "the visible sign of reason." For many it would be sobering to know that such giants of Western philosophy as Hume, Kant, and

Hegel are among the prejudiced believers of European superiority over the non-European world.

92. *The Great Cosmic Mother* (New York: Harper and Row, 1987), 428 (italics original). There is a famous passage in *De Rerum Natura* by Lucretius: "We smell various odors, but never see them/Approach our nostrils. We do not see heat waves;/ Our eyes cannot discern the chilling cold;/ We never see a voice. Yet all these things/ Consist of bodies that touch on our senses:/ Only a body touches and is touched." *On the Nature of Things*, translated by Palmer Bovie (New York: New American Library, 1974), 23. In his *Man and People*, translated by Willard R. Trask (New York: W. W. Norton, 1957), José Ortega y Gasset contends that "it would be a grave mistake to suppose that sight is the most important 'sense.' Even from the psycho-physiological point of view, . . . it seems more and more probable that touch was the original sense from which the others were gradually differentiated. From our more radical point of view it is clear that the decisive form of our intercourse with things is in fact touch" (72). In the hopes of building a multisensory or synaesthetic culture with an accent on tactility and media technology, which is for him nothing but an extension of the human (body), Marshall McLuhan launched the most ambitious and sweeping project of dethroning visually oriented Western thought. He attempted to retrieve or recuperate pre-literate (pre-alphabetic) acoustic space. See particularly his posthumous work, *Laws of Media*, which fashions particularly Francis Bacon, Giambattista Vico, and Karl Popper. Synaesthesis (sociability of the senses) is a "licentious" interplay of the senses. Like Helen Keller, who wrote of "hearing views," "seeing tones," and "tasting music," Jacques Lusseyran, who lost his sight in his childhood, wrote a forthright critique of the one-sided affair of the "sighted world" and eloquently spoke of synaesthesis in *And There Was Light*, translated by Elizabeth R. Cameron (Boston: Little, Brown, 1963). The early loss of sight led him to the discovery of "a new world" in which the senses of hearing and touch not only are immeasurably sharpened and heightened, but he also develops and deepens "inner seeing" and the inner "screen" of memory. I came across Lusseyran's insightful work in reading McLuhan's *Laws of Media*. For an inimitable discussion of the origins of the synaesthetic functions of the mind and the body and *thymos* (breath) as the vital source of life (e.g., speech and sense-perception) in Western thought, see Richard Broxton Onians, *The Origins of Western Thought* (Cambridge: Cambridge University Press, 1951).

93. As a part of "kinesics," "haptics" is defined as the study of how people touch each other when they talk. It is contrasted with "proxemics," which is the study of the distances people keep from each other when they talk. See Thomas, "Introduction" to *A Cultural History of Gesture*, 3.

94. Quoted in Craig Owens, "The Discourse of Others: Feminists and Postmodernism," in *The Anti-Aesthetic: Essays on Postmodern Culture*, edited by Hal Foster (Port Townsend: Bay Press, 1983), 70. Camille Paglia's *Sexual Personae* (New Haven: Yale University Press, 1990) is a celebration of phallic ocularcentrism as well as the visual personification of Western culture. In it she writes, for instance, that "[l]et us not steal from the eye to give to the ear" (34); the Venus of

Willendorf (ca. 30,000 B.C.) is "unbeautiful because art has not yet found its relation to the eye" (55); "an aesthete is one who *lives by the eye*" (60); "taste is the visible logic of objects" (60); and the transition from the Venus of Willendorf to Nefertiti (ca. 1350 B.C.) represents that from touch to sight (70–71). Both vision and tactility are bodily phenomena. On the spectrum of the senses, one is the sense of distance and the other the sense of proximity. They may stand for the (sexual) difference between the masculine and the feminine. Although Jacques Derrida contends on at least two occasions that Heidegger is indifferent to sexual difference, an argument can be made for Heidegger that there is an affinity between the ethics of care (the "helping hand") and the feminine. See Derrida and Christie V. McDonald, "Choreographies," *Diacritics*, 12 (1982), 66–76 and Derrida, "Geschlecht: Sexual Difference, Ontological Difference," *Research in Phenomenology*, 8 (1983), 65–83 whose French text is found in *Psyché*, 395–414. Cf. Page duBois, *Torture and Truth* (New York: Routledge, 1991), Chap. 14, "Women, the Body, and Torture," 145–157. In Derrida's discussion the link between Heidegger's "hand" and "sexual difference" (*Geschlechtlichkeit*) must not be overlooked. Although in Heidegger's thought *Dasein* can be "anybody" or a gender-neutral term, care (*Sorge*) is not. In *Being and Time*, translated by John Macquarrie and Edward Robinson (New York: Harper, 1962), 242, and *History of the Concept of Time*, translated by Theodore Kisiel (Bloomington: Indiana University Press, 1985), 302, Heidegger cites Hyginius's Latin fable of care (*cura*). *Cura* is the "source" (*Ursprung*) of "spirit" (Jupiter) and "body" (Earth, *humo* or *humus*). As *cura* is genderized as feminine, *Dasein* (as "*in-der-Welt-sein* and *Mitsein*) is "stamped" with care. Is not "care" (*cura*) then the "hand" that "mani/pulates" or "handles" (*Handlichkeit*) "cure"? Graybeal considers "care" as "cure" which *is* (feminine) *jouissance* (*Language and "the Feminine" in Nietzsche and Heidegger*, 125). For a discussion of caring as a feminine agenda, see Nel Noddings, *Caring: A Feminine Approach to Ethics and Moral Education* (Berkeley: University of California Press, 1984), which may be read in conjunction with Carol Gilligan's argument for the feminine as "a different voice."

95. *On Photography* (New York: Dell, 1977), 16.

96. See *The Image* (New York: Atheneum, 1962).

97. As an unswerving "guardian" of rationality, disembodied rationality, Habermas in fact disdains the body politic of such writers as Nietzsche, Bataille, Foucault, Gilles Deleuze, and Merleau-Ponty. See *The Philosophical Discourse of Modernity*, translated by Frederick Lawrence (Cambridge: MIT Press, 1987).

98. Stauth and Turner contend that "Foucault did not appear to have any genuine appreciation of the lived body within the tradition of modern phenomenology. . . . Foucault did not develop an explicit theory of embodiment" (*Nietzsche's Dance*, 191).

99. In comparing Foucault with Nietzsche, Stauth and Turner come to the conclusion that "Nietzsche, unlike Foucault, presents a view of the body which is active, reactive, and resistant rather than supine and incorporated" and that "For Nietzsche, the understanding of the importance of the body was funda-

mental to any understanding of resistance" (*Ibid.*, 17 and 66). On this score, it is no accident that feminists tend to be critical of Foucault's body politic. See, for example, Nancy Fraser, "Foucault's Body-Language: A Post-Humanist Political Rhetoric?," *Salmagundi* 61 (1983), 55–70, and Judith Butler, "Foucault and the Paradox of Bodily Inscriptions," *The Journal of Philosophy,* 86 (1989), 601–607. For the author's phenomenological critique of Foucault's formulation of the moral subject, see "The Question of the Moral Subject in Foucault's Analytics of Power," *Canadian Journal of Political and Social Theory* 11, (1987), 28–45.

100. The most celebrated passage of Jean-François Lyotard in *The Postmodern Condition*, translated by Geoff Bennington and Brian Massumi (Minneapolis: University of Minnesota Press, 1984), reads as follows: "Postmodern knowledge is not simply a tool of the authorities; it refines our sensitivity to differences and reinforces our ability to tolerate the incommensurable. Its principle is not the expert's homology, but the inventor's paralogy" (xxv).

PART SIX INTRODUCTION

1. *Table T.* (1851), 45.

2. *Beyond Formalism* (New Haven: Yale University Press, 1970), x. This epigraph serves as one of David Scott Arnold's epigraphs to his *Liminal Readings: Forms of Otherness in Melville, Joyce, and Murdoch*, which contains some very interesting liminal readings of the theme of alterity in Modernist writing. Its application to the postmodern is left to others.

3. This essay, relying on a long passage from Nietzsche's *Zarathustra*, in which the prophet confronts "an ear as big as a man," is the initial part of *The Ear of the Other*, the English version of which is edited by Professor Christie V. McDonald, who of course organized the conference of the International Association for Philosophy and Literature, from which this volume is extracted and of which it stands as a representative, as the ear of the other.

4. "Merleau-Ponty and Derrida: Writing on Writing" (141). In *Ontology and Alterity in Merleau-Ponty*, edited by Galen A. Johnson and Michael B. Smith (Evanston, Ill.: Northwestern University Press, 1990), 130–141. This volume contains much of interest to any investigation of the relationship between contemporary views of alterity and the issues of style, writing, text, and the politics of alterity.

CHAPTER 17

1. J. Habermas, The Philosophical Discourse of Modernity, translated by Frederick Lawrence (Cambridge: Polity Press, 1987); hereinafter cited as PDM.

2. *PDM*, p. 220.

3. *Ibid.*, 93.

4. *Ibid.*, 19. For a detailed analysis of the autonomy of each of the cultural and rational spheres, see J. Habermas, "Die Moderne—ein unvollendes Projekt" in *Kleine Politische Schriften I–IV* (Frankfurt: Suhrkamp, 1981), 454.

5. *Ibid.*, 19.

6. *Ibid.*, 19.

7. Nietzsche, *On The Genealogy of Morals* (New York, 1969), 69. Cited in *PDM.*, 398.

8. *PDM.*, 100.

9. *Ibid.*, 306.

10. *Ibid.*, 93.

11. *Ibid.*, 96.

12. *Ibid.*, 96.

13. *Ibid.*, 94. According to Habermas the "aesthetic, body-centered experiences of a decentered subjectivity" constitute "the modern origin of aesthetic experience heightened in avant-garde fashion." (*PDM*, p. 306–307). For an interesting examination of the ambiguous function of aesthetics in Habermas's theory of modern rationality, see Claude Piché, "Art and Democracy in Habermas," in *Writing the Politics of Difference*; edited by H. J. Silverman, (New York: SUNY, 1991), 265–274.

14. *Der Begriff der Kunstkritik in der deutschen Romantik*, (Frankfurt: Suhrkamp, 1973), 82. With polemic intent, Benjamin frequently opposes the romantic concept of immanent critique to the contemporary understanding of art critique. The romantic notion of "art critique, he states, is radically opposed to the contemporary understanding of the essence of art criticism, for its main goal is not to state a judgment, but . . . to fulfill, to systematize the work of art itself." (72). Benjamin later adds: "Whereas, according to our contemporary concepts, art criticism proceeds from a factual knowledge and an evaluation of the work of art, the romantic concept of critique differentiates itself from any particular and subjective aesthetic appreciation" (74). My translation.

15. *Ibid.*, 74.

16. "Goethes Wahlverwandtschaften," in *Illuminationen* (Frankfurt: Suhrkamp, 1977).

17. "Ueber das Programm der kommenden Philosophie," in *GS* 2(1), 160.

18. *The Origin of German Tragic Drama*, translated by John Osborne (London: New Left Books, 1977), 166.

19. For a critique of the positive concept of history see: "Theses on the Philosophy of History," in *Illuminations*, (edited by Hannah Arendt, H. Zohn, (New York: Schocken Books, 1969).

20. *The Origin of German Tragic Drama*, 162.

21. *Ibid.*, 166.

22. "Bewusstmachende oder Rettende Kritik: Die Aktualitaet Walter Benjamins" in *Zur Aktualitaet Walter Benjamins*, edited by S. Unseld (Frankfurt: Suhrkamp, 1972), 214. My translation.

23. *Ibid.*, 215. My translation.

24. "Surrealism, the Last Snapshot of the European Intellingentsia," in *Reflections: Aphorisms, Essays and Autobiographical Writings*, Peter Demetz, translated by Edmund Jephcott (New York: Harcourt, Brace, Jovanovich, 1978), 177; hereinafter cited as *Surrealism*.

25. *Ibid.*, 180.

26. Rolf Tiedemann, *Studien zur Philosophie Walter Benjamins* (Frankfurt: Suhrkamp, 1973), 146. My translation.

27. *Ibid.*, 152.

28. *Surrealism*, 190.

29. *Ibid.*, 191.

30. *Ibid.*, 191.

31. *Ibid.*, 179.

32. C.f. "On Language as Such and on the Language of Man", in *Reflections*, *op.cit.*, 314–333. The surrealist image and the baroque allegory share some common features according to Benjamin. In allegory "word . . . and sound are emancipated from any traditional meaning (. . .) In its individual parts, fragmented language has ceased merely to serve the process of communication. . . ." in *The origin of German Tragic Drama*, *op.cit.*, 207–208. For surrealism, "language only seemed itself where sound and image, image and sound interpenetrated with automatic precision and such felicity that no chink was left for the penny-in-the-slot called 'meaning'". *Surrealism*, 178–179. On the relationship between Benjamin's conception of allegory and avant-garde art, see Peter Burger, *Theory of the Avant-Garde*, translated by Michael Shaw (Minneapolis: University of Minnesota Press, 1984), 68–73.

33. *Surrealism*, 191.

34. *Ibid.*, 190.

35. *Charles Baudelaire: A Lyric Poet in the Era of High Capitalism*, translated by Harry Zohn (London: New Left Books, 1973), 132.

CHAPTER 18

1. Michel Foucault, *Surveiller et punir; naissance de la prison* (Paris: Gallimard, 1975).

2. Michel de Certeau, *Heterologies; Discourse of the Other*, translated by Brian Massumi (Minneapolis: University of Minnesota Press, 1986).

3. The choice made by Foucault's American editor to place the illustrations in the middle of the text simply misses the point.

4. Michel Foucault, *Power/Knowledge: Selected Interviews and Other Writings 1972–1977*, edited by Colin Gordon, translated by Colin Gordon, Leo Marshall, John Mepham, and Kate Soper (New York: Pantheon Books, 1980), 38.

5. Ferdinand de Saussure, *Cours de linguistique générale*, edited by Tullio de Mauro (Paris: Payot, 1975), 23. The translation is my own.

6. Claude Lévi-Strauss, "The Structural Study of Myth," in *Structural Anthropology* (New York: Basic Books, 1963), 206–31.

7. *Moi, Pierre Rivière, ayant égorgé ma mère, ma soeur et mon frère. . . : un cas de parricide au XIXe siècle*, presented by Michael Foucault (Paris: Gallimard/Julliard, 1973).

8. Foucault, *Power/Knowledge*, 48.

9. The art of making the archive speak is one that Jacques Rancière worked to develop during the same period, although his projects came to fruition slightly later. See *La nuit des prolétaires* (Paris: Fayard, 1981) and *Le maître ignorant: cinq leçons sur l'émancipation intellectuelle* (Paris: Fayard, 1987).

10. See David K. Lewis, *Convention: A Philosophical Study* (Oxford: Basil Blackwell, 1986).

11. *Heterologies*, 189–90.

12. *Heterologies*, 191–92.

13. Stephen Greenblatt, *Shakespearean Negotiations: The Circulation of Social Energy in Renaissance England* (Berkeley: University of California Press, 1988).

14. Walter Benn Michaels, *The Gold Standard and the Logic of Naturalism: American Literature at the Turn of the Century* (Berkeley: University of California Press, 1987).

15. Brook Thomas, *The New Historicism and Other Old-Fashioned Topics* (Princeton: Princeton University Press, 1991), 132.

16. Fredric Jameson, *Postmodernism, or, The Cultural Logic of Late Capitalism* (Durham: Duke University Press, 1991).

CHAPTER 19

1. Michael Fried, *Three American Painters* (Cambridge, Mass.: Fogg Art Museum, 1965).

2. See my "Edouard Manet and the Pleasure Problematic," *Arts Magazine* (February 1988), 43. Both that essay and the present one also appear in Gilbert-Rolfe, *Beyond Piety* (New York: Cambridge University Press, 1995).

3. Fried recalls making this point as I have described it here, but does not recall where he made it. He thought it was in "Three American Painters," which it isn't. I recall reading it but have been unable to find it. It exists, but in a factual limbo of some sort.

4. Gilberto Perez, "Bell Bottom Blues," *The Nation* (Feb. 18th., 1991), 211.

5. Gilles Deleuze, *Cinema 1, The movement-image,* trans. H. Tomlinson and B. Habberjam (Minneapolis: University of Minnesota, 1986), 43.

6. *Ibid.*, 150.

CHAPTER 20

1. A shorter version of this essay was presented in the panel "From Postmodernism to Transmodernism: Cross-Cultural Perspectives," at IAPL—Montréal.

2. Émile Benveniste, *Problèmes de linguistique générale* (Paris: Gallimard, 1966) 228.

3. All references marked as *PhG* followed by a page number are to: G. W. F. Hegel, *Phenomenologie des Geistes,* edited by Johannes Hoffmeister (Hamburg: Felix Meiner, 1952).

4. English translations are provided in parentheses after the German quotations. Translations of extended quotations and page references are taken from G. W. F. Hegel, *The Phenomenology of Mind,* translated by J. B. Baillie (New York: Humanities Press Inc, 1977).

5. *op cit.*, 91.

6. Cf. the pun in Hegel's title of the section we just read: "Sense-Certainty; or the This and Meaning [*Meinen*—My meaning]."

Bibliography

Acker, Kathy. *Blood and Guts in High School*. New York: Grove Press, 1978.

Ackerman, Diane. *A Natural History of the Senses*. New York: Random House, 1990.

Adam, Ian. "Breaking the Chain: Anti-Saussurean Resistance in Birney, Carey, and C. S. Peirce." *WLWE*. Fall 1989. Vol. 29 #2. 11–22

———. *Don Quixote*. New York: Grove Press, 1986.

d'Alembert, Jean de Rond. *Preliminary Discourse to the Encylopedia of Diderot*, trans. Richard N. Schwab a. Walter E. Rex (Indianapolis: The Bobbs Merrill Comapny, 1963).

Alexander, Christopher. *A Pattern Language*. New York: Oxford University Press, 1977.

Apostel, Leo, and Jan Van deer Veken. *Wereldbeelden: Van fragmentering naar ingtegratie*. Kapellen: De Nederlandsche Boekhandel/Pelckmans, 1992.

Bacon, Francis. *The New Organon and Related Writings*. Ed. Fulton H. Anderson. Indianapolis: The Liberal Arts Press, 1960.

———. *The Works of Francis Bacon*. Vol. 3. James Spedding, Robert Leslie Ellis, and Douglas Denon Heath, eds. London: Longmans & Co, 1887.

Bakhtin, Mikhail. *The Dialogic Imagination*. Ed. Michael Holquist. Trans. Caryl Emerson and Michael Holquist. Austin: University of Texas Press, 1981.

———. *Problems of Dostoevsky's Poetics*, Ed. and trans. Caryl Emerson. Minneapolis: University of Minnesota Press, 1984.

———. *Rabelais and His World*. Trans. Helene Iswolsky. Cambridge, Mass. and London, England: The M.I.T. Press, 1968.

Bann, Stephen. "The Truth in Mapping." *Word and Image* 4 (1988), 498–509.

Baratloo, Mojdeh, and Clifton J. Balch. *Angst: Cartography*. New York: Lumen, 1989.

Barthes, Roland. *Le bruissent de la langue*. Paris: Seuil, 1984.

———. *Essais Critiques*. Collection of Tel Quel. Paris: Seuil, 1964.

———. *Fragments d'un discourse amoureux*. Paris: Seuil, 1977.

———. *Le Plaisir du texte*. Collection of Tel Quel. Paris: Seuil, 1973.

Bartley, William W. *Wittgenstein*. Second ed. La Salle, Ill.: Open Court, 1985.

Bataille, Georges. *L'Histoire de l'oeil*. Paris: Pauvert, 1973.

Baudelaire, Charles. *Curiosités esthétiques. L'Art romantique et autres oeuvres critiques*. Paris: Éditions Garnier, 1962, 1983.

———. *Les fleurs du mal et autres poèmes*. Paris: Garnier-Flammarion 1964, 1989.

Baudrillard, Jean. "The Ecstacy of Communication." Trans. John Johnston. In *The Anti-Aesthetic: Essays on Postmodern Culture*. Ed. Hal Foster. Port Townsend, Wash.: Bay Press, 1983.

———. *L'échange symbolique et la mort*. Paris: Gallimard. 1976.

———. *For a Critique of the Political Economy of the Sign*. Trans. Charles Levin. St. Louis: Telos Press 1981.

———. *Forget Foucault*. New York: Semiotext(e), 1987.

———. *The Mirror of Production*. Trans. Mark Poster. St. Louis: Telos Press, 1975.

———. *Selected Writings*. Ed. Mark Poster. Stanford: Stanford University Press, 1988.

———. *Simulations*. Trans. Paul Foss, Paul Patton, and Philip Beitchman. New York: Semiotext(e), 1983.

Bauman, Zygmunt. *Legislators and Interpreters: On Modernity, Postmodernity, and Intellectuals*. Ithaca: Cornell University Press, 1987.

Benhabib, Ceyla. *Critique, Norm, and Utopia: A Study of the Foundations of Critical Theory*. New York: Columbia University Press, 1986.

Benjamin, Andrew, ed. *The Lyotard Reader*. Oxford: Basil Blackwell, 1989.

Benjamin, Jessica. "The Bonds of Love: Rational Violence and Erotic Domination." In *The Future of Difference*. Ed. Hester Eisenstein and Alice Jardine. New Brunswick and London: Rutgers University Press, 1980.

Benjamin, Walter. *The Origin of German Tragic Drama*. Trans. John Osborne. London: NLB, 1977.

———. "Geschichtsphilosophische Thesen." *Ausgewälte Schriften*. ed. Th. Adorno, Frankfurt: Suhrkamp, 1955.

———. *Reflections. Essays, Aphorisms and Autobiographical Writings*, trans. Edmund Jephcott, ed. Peter Demetz (New York: Schocken Books, 1986).

Bennington, Geoffrey. "Aberrations: de Man (and) the Machine." In *Reading de Man Reading*. Eds. Lindsay Waters and Wlad Godzich. Minneapolis: University of Minnesota Press, 1989.

Bergson, Henri. "Laughter," in *Comedy: An Essay on Comedy [by] George Meredith*. By Wylie Sypher. Garden City, New York: Doubleday Anchor Books, 1956.

Bernauer, James, and David Rasmussen, eds. *The Final Foucault*. Cambridge, Mass., and London, England: The MIT Press, 1988.

Bjornson, Richard. "Cognitive Mapping and the Understanding of Literature." *SubStance* 30(1981): 51–62.

Blake, William. *Songs of Innocence and of Experience*, London: Oxford University Press, 1970.

Blanchot, Maurice. *Michel Foucault as I Imagine Him*. Trans. Jeffrey Mehlman. New York: Zone Books, 1987.

Blondel, Eric. *Nietzsche: The Body and Culture*. Trans. Seán Hand. Stanford: Stanford University Press, 1991.

Bloom, Harold. *The Anxiety of Influence: A Theory of Poetry*. Oxford: Oxford University Press, 1973.

Blumenberg, Hans. *Schiffbruch mit Zuschauer. Paradigma einer Daseinsmetapher* (Frankfurt a. M.: Suhrkamp, 1979).

Boelhower, William. "Inventing America: A Model of Cartographic Semiosis." *Word and Image* 4(1988): 475–97.

Borges, Jorge Luis. *Biblioteca personal (prólogos)*. Madrid: Alianza, 1988.

———. "Magias parciales del Quijote." *Obras completas*. Vol. 2, Buenos Aires: Emece, 1974–1989.

———. "Pierre Menard, Author of the *Quixote*." Trans. James E. Irby. In *Labyrinths: Selected Stories and Other Writings*. New York: New Directions, 1964.

———. "Del rigor en la ciencia." *El Hacedor*. In *Obras Completas*. Barcelona: Emecé, 1989.

Bougnoux, Daniel. "La carte et le territoire." In *Vices et vertus des cercles: L'auto-référence en poétique et pragmatique*. Paris: La Différance, 1989.

Boyle, Robert. *Selected Philosophical Papers of Robert Boyle*. Ed. M. A. Stewart. New York: Barnes & Noble, 1979.

Brecht, Bertolt. "Über die Bedeutung des zehnzeiligen Gedichtes in der 888. Nummer der Fackel (Oktober 1933)." In *Gessemlte Werke in acht Bänden*. Frankfurt: Suhrkamp 1967.

Buck, Theo. "Weite und Enge: Zu einer Lyrischen Auseinanderstzung Celans mit Brecht." In *Festschrift für Friedrich Beissner*. Eds. Ulrich Gaier and Werner Volke. Bebenhausen; Rotsch 1974.

Burton, Robert. *The Anatomy of Melancholy*. Vol. 1. London: Dent; New York: Dutton. Reprinted 1964.

Calinescu, Matei. "The Silence of the Avant-Garde." In *Five Faces of Modernity*. Durham, North Carolina: Duke University Press, 1987.

Calvino, Italo. *Six Maps for the Next Millennium*. Cambridge, Mass.: Harvard University Press, 1988.

Carmello, Charles. *Performance in Postmodern Culture*. Madison, Wisconsin: Coda Press, 1977.

Carrington, Leonora. *The Hearing Trumpet*. London and Henley: Routledge & Kegan Paul, 1977.

———. *The Seventh Horse and Other Tales*. New York: Dutton, 1988.

Carroll, Lewis. *The Annotated Alice*. Harmondsworth, Middlesex: Penguin Books. Reprinted 1987.

Carter, Angela. *Nights at the Circus*. London: Chatto & Windus, The Hogarth Press, 1984.

———. *The Sadeian Woman: An Exercise in Cultural History*. London: Virago Press, 1979.

Cavell, Stanley. *This New Yet Unapproachable America*. Albuquerque: Living Batch Press, 1989.

Célan, Paul. *Gesammelte Werke in fünf Bänden*. Ed. Beda Allemann and Stefan Reichert. Frankfurt: Suhrkamp 1983.

———. *Poems of Paul Célan*. Trans. Michael Hamburger. New York: Persea Books 1988.

Cervantes Saavedra, Miguel de. *El ingenioso hidalgo don Quijote de la Mancha*. Ed. Luis Andrès Murillo. Madrid: Castalia, 1984.

Cicero. *Cicero on Oratory and Orators*. Trans. J. S. Watson. Carbondale: Southern Illinois University Press, 1970.

———. *De Oratore, Book III*. Trans. H. Rackham. Cambridge, Mass: Harvard University Press, 1968.

———. *Orator*. Ed. Wilhelm Kroll. Berlin: Weidmannsche, 1913.

Cixous, Hélène. "Castration or Decapitation?" *Signs* 7, no. 1 (1981).

———. "The Laugh of the Medusa," *Signs* 1, no. 4 (1976).

———. "The Laugh of the Medusa." In *New French Feminisms*. Ed. Elaine Marks and Isabelle de Courtivron. New York: Schocken Books, 1981.

Cixous, Hélène, and Catherine Clement. *The Newly Born Woman*. Minneapolis: University of Minnesota Press, 1986.

Clark, Katerina, and Michael Holquist. *Mikhail Bakhtin*. Cambridge: Harvard University Press, 1984.

Collin, Françoise. "Reflections on the Women's Liberation Movement." In *French Connections*. Ed. and trans. Claire Duchen. Amherst: University Massachusetts Press, 1987.

Compagnon, Antoine. "Mapping the European Mind." *Critical Quarterly* 32.2(1990): 4.

———. *La seconde main ou le travail de la citation*. Paris: Editions du Seuil, 1979.

Corbin, Alain. *The Foul and the Fragrant*. Cambridge, Mass.: Harvard University Press, 1986.

Crary, Jonathan. *Techniques of the Observer*. Cambridge, Mass.: MIT Press, 1990.

D'Alembert, Jean. *Discours Preliminaire d'encyclopedie* [1751]. Paris: A. Colin, 1929.

Dauenhauer, Bernard P. *Silence*. Bloomington: Indiana University Press,1980.

Debord, Guy. *Society of the Spectacle*. Detroit: Black and Red, 1983.

De Certeau, Michel. *Fabula mistica*. Bologna: Il Mulino, 1987.

———. *Heterologies: Discourse On the Other*. Trans. Brian Massumi. Minneapolis: University of Minnesota Press, 1986.

———. *The Writing of History*. Trans. Tom Conley. New York: Columbia University Press, 1988.

Deleuze, Gilles, and Feliz Guattari. *Anti-Oedipus*. Minneapolis: University of Minnesota Press, 1983.

———. *Qu'est-ce que la philosophie?* Paris: Minuit, 1991.

———. *A Thousand Plateaus*. Trans. Brian Massumi. Minneapolis: University of Minnesota Press, 1987.

Deleuze, Gilles, and Claire Parnet. *Dialogues*. Trans. Hugh Tomlinson and Barbara Habberjan. New York: Columbia University Press, 1987.

———. "A New Cartographer (*Discipline and Punish*)." In *Foucault*. Trans. Seàn Hand. Minneapolis: University of Minnesota Press, 1988.

Derrida, Jacques. "The Double Session." In *Dissemination*. Trans. Barbara Johnson. Chicago: University of Chicago Press, 1981.

———. *The Ear of the Other: Otobiography, Transference, Translation*. Trans. Peggy Kamuf. Ed. Christie McDonald. New York: Schocken Books, 1985.

———. *Edmund Husserl's Origin of Geometry: An Introduction*. [1962]. Trans. John P. Leavey, Jr. Stony Brook, New York: Nicolas Hays, 1978.

———. "How to Avoid Speaking: Denials." Trans. Ken Frieden. In *Languages of the Unsayable: The Play of Negativity in Literature and Literary Theory*.

Edited by Sanford Budick and Wolfgang Iser. New York: Columbia University Press, 1989.

———. "Living on Borderlines." In *Deconstruction and Criticism*. Ed. Harold Bloom, et al. New York: Continuum, 1990.

———. *Of Grammatology*. Trans. Gayatri Chakravorti Spivak. Baltimore: The Johns Hopkins University Press, 1976.

———. *Psyché: Inventions de l'autre*. Paris: Galilée, 1987.

———. "Des Tours de Babel." In *Difference in Translation*. Ed. Joseph F. Graham. Ithaca, New York: Cornell University Press, 1985.

———. *The Truth in Painting*. Trans. Geoffrey Bennington and Ian McLeod. Chicago: University of Chicago Press, 1987.

———. "White Mythology: Metaphor in the Text of Philosophy." In *Margins of Philosophy*. Trans. Alan Bass. Chicago: University of Chicago Press, 1982.

Des Pres, Terrence. *The Survivor*. New York: Oxford University Press, 1976.

Descartes, René. *Discours de la Methode*. Paris: J. Vrin, 1966.

———. *The Philosophical Writings of Descartes*, trans. John Cottingham, Robert Soothoff, Dugald Murdoch (London: Cambridge University Press, 1985).

———. *Principles of Philosophy*. Lewiston, New York: E. Mellen Press, 1988.

Diprose, Rosalyn, and Robyn Ferrell, eds. *Cartographies: Post-structuralism and the Mapping of Bodies and Spaces*. North Sydney: Allen and Unwin, 1991.

Douglas, Mary. *Purity and Danger*. London: Routledge and Kegan Paul, 1966.

Eagleton, Terry. *Against the Grain: Essays 1975–1985*. London: Verso, 1986.

———. *Literary Theory: An Introduction*. Minneapolis: University of Minnesota Press, 1983.

Ebeling, Hans. *Ästhetik des Abschieds. Kritik der Moderne*. München: 1989.

Eckartsberg, Rolf von. "Maps of the Mind: The Cartography of Consciousness." In *The Metaphors of Consciousness*. Ed. Ronald S. Valle and R. von Eckartsberg. New York: Plenum, 1981.

Eckhardt, Caroline D. "Recharting the Literary Map of the Americas." In *New Literary Continents*. Ed. C. D. Eckhardt, et al. Whitestone, New York: Griffon, 1981.

Eco, Umberto. *Foucault's Pendulum*. Trans. William Weaver. San Diego: Harcourt Brace Jovanovich, 1989.

———. *The Limits of Interpretation*. Bloomington: Indiana University Press, 1990.

———. "Map of the Empire." *The Literary Review* 28(1985): 233–38.

———. *Semiotics and the Philosophy of Language*. Bloomington: Indiana University Press, 1986.

———. *A Theory of Semiotics*. Bloomington: Indiana University Press, 1976.

Eliade, Mircea. *Shamanism. Archaic Techniques of Ecstasy*. Trans. William R. Trask. Princeton, New Jersey: Princeton University Press, Second Printing, 1974.

Ellison, Ralph. *Invisible Man*. New York: Random House, 1982.

Enzenberger, Hans Magnus. *Der Untergang der Titanic*. Frankfurt: Suhrkamp 1978.

———. *Gedichte 1955–1970*. Frankfurt: Suhrkamp 1971.

———. *Mittelmass und Wahn*. Frankfurt: Suhrkamp 1988.

Eribon, Didier. *Michel Foucault (1926–1984)*. Paris: Flammarion, 1989.

Fichte, Johan Gottlieb *Wissenschaftslehre*. Hamburg: F. Meiner, 1984.

Foster, Hal. *Out of Site: A Social Criticism of Arthitecture*. Ed. Diane Ghirardo. Seattle: Bay Press, 1991.

Foucault, Michel. *The Archaeology of Knowledge*. Trans. A. M. Sheridan Smith London: Tavistock Publications, 1972, 1974.

———. *The Archaeology of Knowledge*. Trans. A. M. Sheridan Smith. New York: Pantheon Books, 1972.

———. *Discipline and Punish: The Birth of the Prison*. Trans. Alan Sheridan. New York: Vintage, 1979.

———. *Folie et déraison. Histoire de la folie à l'âge classique*. Paris: Librairie Plon, 1961.

———. *Microfisica del potere*. Turin: Einaudi, 1977.

———. *The Order of Things*. London: Tavistock Publications, 1970.

———. *L'ordine del discorso*. Turin: Einaudi, 1972.

———. "Of Other Spaces." *Diacritics* 16(1986): 22–27.

———. *Power/Knowledge: Selected Interviews and Other Writings 1972–1977*. Ed. Colin Gordon. Brighton, Sussex: The Harvester Press, 1980.

———. "Theatrum Philosophicum." In *Language, Counter-Memory, Practice*. Ed. Donald F. Bouchard. Trans. Donald F. Bouchard and Sherry Simon. Ithaca: Cornell University Press. 1977.

———. *This is Not a Pipe*. Trans. and ed. James Harkness. Berkeley: University of California Press, 1982.

Fraunce, Abraham. *The Arcadian Rhetorike* (1588). Ed. Ethel Seaton. Oxford: Basil Blackwell, 1950.

Fried, Michael. "Art and Objecthood." Reprinted in *Minimal Art: A Critical Antology*. Ed. Gregory Battcock. New York: E. P. Dutton and Co., 1968.

Friedman, Ellen G. "A Conversation with Kathy Acker." *Review of Contemporary Fiction* X(1990): 12–22.

Fritz, Walter Helmut. *Mit einer Feder aus den Flügeln des Ikarus*. Frankfurt: Fischer Taschenbucher, 1989.

———. *Schwierige Überfahrt*. Hamburg: Hoffman und Campe, 1976.

Frye, Northrop. *Anatomy of Criticism*. New York: Atheneum, 1966.

Gier, Nicholas F. *Wittgenstein and Phenomenology: A Comparative Study of the Later Wittgenstein, Husserl, Heidegger, and Merleau-Ponty*. Albany: SUNY Press, 1981.

Ginsberg, Allen. *Allen Ginsberg/William Blake. Songs of Innocence and Experience*. MGM Records(FTS3083/MGS2112). Recorded December 14th–15th, 1969.

Gnüg, Hildrud. "Gespräch über Bäume. Zur Brecht-Rezeption in der modernen Lyrik." *Basis* 7(1977): 89–117.

Godard, Barbara. "Mapmaking: A Survey of Feminist Criticism." In *Gynoscritics: Feminist Approaches to Canadian and Quebec Women's Writing*. Ed. B. Godard. Toronto: ECW Press, 1987.

González, Ester Gimbernat de. "Mapas y texto: para una estrategia del poder." *MLN* 95(1980): 388–99.

Grass, Günter. *Schreiben nach Auschwitz. Frankfurter Poetik-Vorlesung*. Frankfurt: Luchterhand 1990.

Gravanuolo, Benedetto. *Adolf Loos: Theory and Works*. New York: Rizzoli, 1982.

Graybeal, Jean. *Language and "the Feminine" in Nietzsche and Heidegger*. Bloomington: Indiana University Press, 1990.

Grimm, Reinhold. *Brecht und Nietzsche: oder Geständnisse eines Dichters: Fünf Essays und ein Bruchstück Stationen des Grünen in der deutschen Literatur*. Ed. Reinhold Grimm and Jost Hermand. Frankfurt: Suhrkamo, 1981.

Grosz, Elizabeth. *Jacques Lacan: A Feminist Introduction*. London and New York: Routledge, 1990.

Grumley, John E. "Michel Foucault: Anti-totalizing Scepticism of Totalising Prophesy?" In *History and Totality: Radical Historicism from Hegel to Foucault*. London: Routledge, 1989.

Guattari, Felix. *Cartographies schizoanalytiques*. Paris: Galilée. 1989.

———. *Psychanalyse et transversalité: Essai d'analyse institutionnelle*. Paris: François Maspero, 1974.

Gubar, Susan. "Representing Pornography." In *For Adult Users Only: The Dilemma of Violent Pornography*. Ed. Susan Gubar and Joan Hoff. Bloomington: Indiana University Press, 1989.

Habermas, Jurgen. "The Entwinement of Myth and Enlightenment: Max Horkheimer and Theodor Adorno." In *The Philsophical Discourse of Modernity: Twelve Lectures*. Trans. Frederick G. Lawrence. Cambridge, Mass.: MIT Press, 1987.

Haggett, Peter. *The Geographer's Art*. Oxford: Basil Blackwell, 1990.

Hall, Stephen S. *Mapping the Next Millenium: The Discovery of New Geographies*. New York: Random House, 1992.

Hamer, Mary. "Putting Ireland on the Map." *Textual Practice* 3(1989): 184–201.

Hampden-Turner,Charles. *Maps of the Mind: Charts and Concepts of the Mind and Its Labyrinths*. New York: Collier, 1982.

Handelman, Susan. "Jacques Derrida and the Heretic Hermeneutic." In *Displacement, Derrida and After*. Ed. Mark Krupnick. Bloomington: Indiana University Press, 1987.

Harley, J. B. *The Iconography of Landscape. Essays on the Symbolic Representation, Design, and Use of Past Environments*. Eds. Denis Cosgrove and Stephen Daniels. Cambridge: Cambridge University Press, 1988.

———. *Writing Worlds. Discourse, Text, and Metaphor in the Representation of Landscape*. Eds. Trevor J. Barnes and James S. Duncan. London: Routledge, 1992.

Harrison, Thomas. *Essayism, Conrad, Musil, and Pirandello*. Baltimore: The Johns Hopkins University Press, 1992.

Hart, Kevin. "Maps of Deconstruction." *Meanjin* 45(1986): 107–16.

Hart Nibbring, Christiaan L. *Rhetorik des Scheigens. Versuch über den Schatten literarischer Rede*. Frankfurt: Suhrkamp 1981.

Harvey, David. "The Experience of Space and Time." In *The Condition of Postmodernity*. Oxford: Basil Blackwell, 1989.

Hayman, Ronald. "Cartography of Discourse? On Foucault." *Encounter* 47.6(1976): 72–75.

Heidegger, Martin. *Poetry, Language, Thought*. Trans. Albert Hofstadter. New York: Harper and Row, 1971.

Hegel, Johann Friedrich Wilhelm. *Lectures on the Philosophy of Religion*, ed Peter C. Hodgson (Berkley: University of California Press, 1984).

Heidegger, Martin. *The Question concerning Technology and Other Essays*, trans. and with an introduction by William Lovitt (New York a. Cambridge: Harper, 1977).

Herder, Johann Gottfried. *Herders Werke in fünf Bänden*, ed. Nationale Forschungs- und Gedenkstätten der klassischen deutschen Literatur (Berlin u. Weimar: Aufbau Verlag, 1964).

Heyck, Hans. *Deutschland ohne Deutsche. Ein Roman von übermorgen*. Leipzig: L. Staackman Verlag 1929.

Hobbes, Thomas. *Leviathan*. Harmondsworth, Middlesex: Penguin Books, 1968.

Hofmannsthal, Hugo von. *Ausgewählte Werke in zwei Bänden*. Frankfurt: Fischer 1957.

———. *Literatur und Gesellschaft. Zur Sozialgeschichte der Literatur seit der Jahrhundertwende*. Ed. Beate Pinkerneil, et al. Frankfurt: Fischer 1973.

Hoskins, John. *Directions for Speech and Style* (c.1599). Ed. Hoyt H. Hudson. Princeton: Princeton University Press, 1935.

Howell, Wilbur Samuel. *Logic and Rhetoric in England, 1500–1700*. Princeton: Princeton University Press, 1956.

Huggan, Graham. "Decolonizing the Map: Post-Colonialism, Post-structuralism, and the Cartographic Connection." In *Past the Last Post: Theorizing Post-Colonialism and Post-Modernism*. Eds. Ian Adam and Helen Tiffin. Calgary: University of Calgary Press, 1990.

Humble, Malcolm. "Brecht and Posterity: A Poem and Its Reception." *New German Studies* 14(1986–87): 115–42.

Hutton, Patrick H. "The History of Mentalities: The New Map of Cultural History." *History and Theory* 20(1981): 237–59.

Huyssen, Andreas. "Mapping the Postmodern." *New German Critique* 33(1984): 10.

Hwa Yol Jung. "The Anatomy of Language: Vico, Joyce, and Etymosinology." *Rivista di Studi Italiani* 4/5(1986–1987): 211–27.

———. "Martin Heidegger and the Homecoming of Oral Poetry." *Philosophy Today* 26(1982): 148–170.

———. "Mikhail Bakhtin's Body Politic: A Phenomenological Dialogics." *Man and World* 23(1990): 85–99.

———. "Misreading the Ideogram: From Fenellosa to Derrida and McLuhan." *Paideuma* 13(1984): 211–27.

———. "Vico and Bakhtin: A Prolegomenon to Any Future Comparison." *New Vico Studies* 3(1985): 157–65.

Irigaray, Luce. *Speculum of the Other Woman*. Ithaca: Cornell University Press, 1985.

Jackson, Peter. *Maps of Meaning: An Introduction to Cultural Geography*. London: Unwin Hyman, 1989.

———. *The Ideologies of Theory: Essays 1971–1986*. Minneapolis: University of Minnesota Press, 1988.

———. *Marxism and the Interpretation of Culture*. Ed. Cary Nelson and Lawrence Grossberg. Urbana, Ill.: University of Illinois Press, 1988.

———. Foreword. *The Postmodern Condition: A Report on Knowledge*. By Jean-François Lyotard. Trans. Geoff Bennington and Brian Massumi. Minneapolis: University of Minnesota Press, 1984.

———. "Postmodernism, or the Cultural Logic of Late Capitalism." *New Left Review* 146(1984): 84.

Jardine, Alice. "In the name of the modern: feminist questions *d'après gynesis*." *Grafts: Feminist Cultural Criticism*. Ed. Susan Sheridan. London and New York: Verso, 1988.

Jay, Martin. *Marxism and Totality: The Adventures of a Concept from Lukács to Habermas*. Berkeley: University of California Press, 1984.

Jefferson, Anne. "Bodymatters: Self and Other in Bakhtin, Sartre and Barthes." In *Bakhtin and Cultural Theory*. Ed. Ken Hirschkop and David Shepherd. Manchester, England, and New York: Manchester University Press, 1989.

Jencks, Charles. *What is Post-Modernism?* London and New York: Academy Editions and St. Martin's Press, 1986.

Johnson, Barbara. *The Critical Difference*. Baltimore: The Johns Hopkins University Press, 1981.

Jones, Richard Foster. "Science and Language in England of the Mid-Seventeenth Century." In *The Seventeenth Century: Studies in the History of English Thought and Literature from Bacon to Pope*. Ed. R.F. Jones. Stanford: Stanford University Press, 1965.

Judovitz, Dalia. *Subjectivity and Representation in Descartes: The Origins of Modernity*. Cambridge: Cambridge University Press, 1988.

Jurzik, Renate. *Der Stoff des Lachens*. Frankfurt/New York: Campus Verlag, 1985.

Kaiser, Ward L. *A New View of the World. A Handbook to the World Map: Peters Projection*. New York: Friendship Press, 1987.

Kant, Immanuel. *Critique of Pure Reason*, trans. Kemp Smith (New York: St. Martin's Press, 1965).

Kant, Emmanuel. *Critique of Pure Reason*. Trans. F. Max Muller. Garden City, New York: Anchor Books, 1966.

Kariel, Henry S. *The Desperate Politics of Postmodernism*. Amherst: The University of Massachusetts Press, 1989.

Kenny, Anthony. *The Legacy of Wittgenstein*. Oxford: Blackwell, 1984.

Kierkegaard, Søren. *Either/Or*. Vol. 1. Princeton, New Jersey: Princeton University Press, 1971.

Kolodny, Annette. "A Map for Rereading: Or, Gender and the Interpretation of Literary Texts." *New Literary History* 11(1980): 451–67.

Korzybski, Alfred. *Science and Sanity: An Introduction to Non-Aristotelian Systems and General Semantics*. Lakeville: International Non-Aristotelian Publishing Co, 1958.

Kosch, William. *Deutsches Literatur-Lexikon, Zweite, vollständig neubearbeitete und stark erweiterte Auflage*. Dritter Band. Bern: A. Francke AG Verlag, 1956.

Kraus, Karl. *Die Fackel* 1 (1899): 1f.

Kristeva, Julia. *Desire in Language. A Semiotic Approach to Literature and Art*. Ed. Leon S. Roudiez. Trans. Thomas Gora, Alice Jardine, and Leon S. Roudiez. Oxford: Basil Blackwell. Reprinted 1984.

———. *La Révolution du langage poe'tique*. Paris: Seuil, 1974.

Kulka, H. *Raumplan versus Plan Libre*. Ed. Max Risselada. New York: Rizzoli, 1988.

Kunz, Marion L., and Paul G. eds, *Jacob's Ladder and the Tree of Life. Concepts of Hierarchy and the Great Chain of Being*, (American University Studies, 1986).

Lacan, Jacques. *Ecrits: A Selection*. Trans. Alan Sheridan. New York: W. W. Norton, 1977.

———. *Encore: Le séminaire XX 1972–73*. Paris: Seuil, 1975.

———. *Feminine Sexuality: Jacques Lacan and the école freudienne*. Eds. Juliet Mitchell and Jacqueline Rose. Trans. Jacqueline Rose. New York: W. W. Norton, 1985.

Lachterman, David. *The Ethics of Geometry: A Genealogy of Modernity*. New York: Routledge, 1989.

Lang, Berel. "Postmodernism in Philosophy: Nostalgia for the Future, Waiting for the Past." In *Literature and the Question of Philosophy*. Ed. Anthony J. Cascardi. Baltimore: The Johns Hopkins University Press, 1987.

Leder, Drew. *The Absent Body*. Chicago: University of Chicago Press, 1990.

Leitner, Bernard. *The Architecture of Ludwig Wittgenstein*. New York: New York University Press, 1976.

Lepenies, Wolf. *Das Ende der Naturgeschichte. Wandel kultureller Selbstverständlichkeiten in den Wissenschaften desn 18. und 19. Jahrhunderts* (Frankfurt a. M.: Suhrkamp, 1978).

Lévi-Strauss, Claude. *Introducion to the Work of Marcel Mauss*. Trans. Felicity Baker. London: Routledge, 1987.

Lik Kuen Tong. "The Meaning of Philosophical Silence: Some Reflections on the Use of Language in Chinese Thought." *The Journal of Chinese Philosophy* 3(1976): 169–83.

Locke, John. *An Essay Concerning Human Understanding*. 2 vols. Ed. Alexander Campbell Fraser. New York: Dover, 1959.

Lovejoy, Arthur Oncken. *The Great Chain of Being. A Study in the History of an Idea*, (Cambridge, Massachussetts and London: Harvard University Press, 1936).

Lozano, Jorge. *El discurso historico*. Madrid: Alianza, 1987.

Lyotard, Jean-François. *The Differend*. Trans. George Van Den Abbeele. Minneapolis: University of Minnesota Press, 1988.

———. "Glose sur la résistance." In *Le postmoderne expliqué aux enfants: correspondance 1982–1985*. Paris: Galilée, 1986.

———. *Heidegger and "the jews"*. Trans. Andreas Michel and Mark Roberts. Minneapolis: University of Minnesota Press, 1990.

———. *The Postmodern Condition: A Report on Knowledge*. Trans. Geoffrey Bennington and Brian Massumi. Minneapolis: University of Minnesota Press, 1984.

———. "Réécrire la modernité." *L'inhumain: Causeries sur le temps*. Paris: Galilée, 1988.

MacIntyre, Alisdair. *After Virtue*. Notre Dame: University of Notre Dame Press, 1981.

Makower, Jack and Laura Bergheim. *The Map Catalog: Every Kind of Map and Chart on Earth and Even Some Above It*. New York: Vintage, 1986.

Malcolm, Norman. *Ludwig Wittgenstein: A Memoir*. London: Oxford University Press, 1962.

Malloch, A. E. "The Techniques and Function of the Renaissance Paradox." *SP* 53, 2 (April, 1956): 195.

de Man, Paul. *Allegories of Reading: Figural Language in Rousseau, Nietzsche, Rilke, and Proust*. New Haven: Yale University Press, 1979.

———. *Blindness and Insight*. Minneapolis: University of Minnesota Press, 1983.

———. "Phenomenality and Materiality in Kant." In *The Textual Sublime: Deconstruction and Its Differences*. Eds. Hugh J. Silverman and Gary Aylesworth. Albany: SUNY Press, 1990.

———. "The Rhetoric of Temporality." Reprinted in *Blindness and Insight. Essays in the Rhetoric of Contemporary Criticism*. Second ed. London: Methuen & Co., Ltd., Second printing, 1986.

Marcel, Gabriel. *Metaphysical Journal*. Trans. Bernard Wall. London: Rockliff, 1952.

Marin, Louis. "L'utopie ed la carte." *Utopiques: jeux d'espaces*. Paris: Minuit, 1973.

Martial. *The Epigrams of Martial* Vol. 1 London: William Heinemann, etc., The Loeb Classical Library, 1919.

Massumi, Brian. "Revolutionary sidestepping is called 'transversality.'" In *A User's Guide to Capitalism and Schizophrenia: Deviations from Deleuze and Guattari*. Cambridge Mass.: MIT Press, 1992.

McCaffery, Larry. "The Artists of Hell: Kathy Acker and 'Punk' Aesthetics." In *Breaking the Sequence: Women's Experimental Fiction*. Ed. Ellen G. Friedman and Miriam Fuchs. Princeton: Princeton University Press, 1989.

McHale, Brian. *Postmodernist Fiction*. New York and London: Methuen, 1987.

Merleau-Ponty, Maurice. *Themes from the Lectures at the Collège de France 1952–1960*. Trans. John O'Neill. Evanston: Northwestern University Press, 1970.

———. *The Visible and the Invisible*. Trans. Alphonso Lingis. Ed. Claude Lefort. Evanston: Northwestern University Press, 1968.

Miller, J. Hillis. "The Critic as Host." In *Deconstruction and Criticism*. Ed. Harold Bloom. New York: Seabury Press, 1979.

Monk, Ray. *Wittgenstein: The Duty of Genius*. New York: The Free Press, 1990.

Montaigne. *Montaigne's Essays* Vol. 1. London: Dent: New York: Dutton, Reprinted 1965.

Monty Python's Flying Circus. Just the Words. Vol. 2. London: Methuen, Mandarin, 1990.

Murray, Michael. "A Note on Wittgenstein and Heidegger." *Philosophical Review* 83(1974): 501–503.

Nagel, Ernest, and James R. Newman. "The Idea of Mapping and Its Use in Mathematics." In *Gödel's Proof*. New York: New York University Press, 1958.

Nietzsche, Friedrich. *Human, All-too-human*. Trans. R. J. Hollingdale. Cambridge: Cambridge University Press, 1986.

———. *On the Future of Our Educational Institutions*. Trans. J. M. Dennedy. New York: Macmillan, 1924.

———. *The Portable Nietzsche*. Trans and ed. Walter Kaufmann. New York: Penguin Books, 1954.

———. *Sämtliche Werke. Kritische Studienausgabe in 15 Bänden*, ed. Giorgio Colli and Mazzino Montinari (München a. Berlin: De Gruyter, 1988, 2.).

———. *Werke*. Trans. and ed. Girgio Colli and Mazzoni Montinari. Berlin: de Gruyter, 1967–.

Norris, Christopher. *What's Wrong with Postmodernism, Critical Theory, and the Ends of Philosophy?* Baltimore: The Johns Hopkins University Press, 1990.

Ortega y Gasset, José. *Historical Reason*. Trans. Philip W. Silver. New York: W. W. Norton, 1984.

———. "'Interesting Questions' in the History of Philosophy and Elsewhere." In *Philosophy in History*. Ed. Richard Rorty, J. B. Scheewind, and Quentin Skinner. Cambridge: Cambridge University Press, 1984.

Padden, Carol, and Tom Humphries. *Deaf in America: Voices from a Culture*. Cambridge Mass.: Harvard University Press, 1988.

Pagis, Dan. "The *Gilgul* of Dan Pagis: Myth, History, Silence." Trans. John Felstiner. In *Translation Review* 32/33(1990): 8–11.

Peacham, Henry. *The Garden of Eloquence* (1577). ed. R.C. Alston. Mensten, England: The Scolar P, Ltd., 1971.

Peirce, C. S. "The Criterion of Validity in Reasoning." In *Philosophical Writings*. Ed. Justus Buchler. New York: Dover, 1955.

Peters, Helen. *General Introduction to John Donne: Paradoxes and Problems*. Ed. by Helen Peters Oxford: Clarendon Press, 1980.

Peters, Arno. *The New Cartography*. New York: Friendship Press, 1983.

———. *Space and Time: Their Equal Representation as an Essential Basis for a Scientific View of the World*. New York: Friendship Press, 1985.

Pietralunga, Mark. "Cartophilia and the Pietic Imagination: Map Consciousness in Italo Calvino's *Le città invisibili*." *Italiana 1988*. Ed. Albert N. Mancini, Paolo A. Giordano and Anthony J. Tamburri. River Forest, Ill.: Rosary College Italian Studies 4, 1990.

Pirandello, Luigi. "Preface to *Six Characters in Search of An Author*." In *Naked Masks*. Ed. Eric Bentley. New York: E. P. Dutton and Co., 1952.

Ponzio, Augusto. *Il filosofo e la tartaruga*. Ravenna: Longo, 1990.

———. *Man as a Sign: Essays on the Philosophy of Language*. Ed. S. Petrilli. Berlin and New York: Mouton de Gruyter, 1990.

Porkert, Manfred. *The Theoretical Foundations of Chinese Medicine*. Cambridge Mass.: MIT Press, 1974.

Posada. *Posada's Popular Mexican Prints*. Ed. and trans. Roberto Berdecio and Stanley Appelbaum. New York: Dover Publications, 1972.

Pound, Ezra, ed. *The Chinese Written Character as a Medium for Poetry*. San Francisco: City Lights Books, 1936.

Puttenham, George. *Arte of English Poesie* (1589). Ed. Gladys Dodge Willcock and Alice Walker. Cambridge: Cambridge University Press, 1936.

Quintilian, Marcus Fabius. *Institutio Oratoria*. 4 vols. Trans. H.E. Butler, M.A. Cambridge, Mass.: Harvard University Press, 1976.

Rabassa, José. "Dialogue as Conquest: Mapping Spaces for Counter-Discourse." *Cultural Critique* 6(1987): 131–59.

Ragland-Sullivan, Ellie. *Jacques Lacan and the Philosophy of Psychoanalysis*. Urbana and Chicago: University of Illinois Press, 1987.

Readings, Bill. *Introducing Lyotard*. London and New York: Routledge, 1991.

Réage, Pauline. *The Story of O*. Trans. Sabine d'Estrée. New York: Ballantine Books, 1965.

Reed, Joel. "Restoration and Repression: The Language Projects of the Royal Society." *Studies in Eighteenth-Century Culture* Ed. Leslie Ellen Brown and Patricia Craddock. 19(1989): 399–412.

Rivière, Joan. "Womanliness as Masquerade." In *Formations of Fantasy*. Eds. Victor Burgin, James Donald, and Cora Kaplan. London: Methuen, 1986.

Robinson, Brian. "The Geography of a Crossroads: Modernism, Surrealism, and Geography." In *Geography and Literature: A Meeting of the Disciplines*. Eds. William E. Mallory and Paul Simpson-Housley. Syracuse: Syracuse University Press, 1987.

Rorty, Richard. *Philosophy and the Mirror of Nature*. Princeton: Princeton University Press, 1979.

Rossi-Landi, Ferruccio. *Metodica filosofica e scienza dei segni*. Milan: Bompiani, 1985.

———. *Significato, comunicazione e parlare comune*. Second Ed. Venice: Marsilio, 1980.

Royce, Josiah. "The One, the Many, and the Infinite." In *The World and the Individual*. New York: Dover, 1959.

Ruby, Christian. *Les archipels de la différances: Foucault-Derrida-Deleuze-Lyotard*. Paris: Editions du Félin, 1989.

Russo, Mary. "Female Grotesques: Carnival and Theory." In *Feminist Studies; Critical Studies*. Ed. Teresa de Lauretis. Bloomington: Indiana University Press, 1986.

Sacks, Oliver. *Seeing Voices*. Berkeley: University of California Press, 1989.

Saroyan, William. *The Time of Your Life*. In *The Critics' Prize Plays*. Intro. George Jean Nathan. Cleveland and New York: The World Publishing Company, 1945.

Sauer, Carl O. "The Morphology of Landscape." *University of California Publications in Geography* 2(1925): 19–54.

Schopenhauer, Arthur. *Werke in Zwei Banden*. Munchen and Wien: Hanser, 1977.

Sewell, Elizabeth. *The Orphic Voice*. London: Routledge and Kegan Paul, 1961.

Shakespeare, William. *King Lear 1608 (Pied Bull Quarto). Shakespeare Quarto Facsimiles No. 1*. Oxford: At the Clarendon Press, 1964.

Shapiro, Gary. *After the Future: Postmodern Times and Places*. Albany: SUNY Press, 1990.

Sidney, Sir Philip. *An Apology for Poetry*. Ed. Geoffrey Shepherd. Manchester: Manchester University Press, 1980.

Soja, Edward. *Postmodern Geographies: The Reassertion of Space in Critical Social Theory*. London: Verso, 1989.

Sontag, Susan. "The Pornographic Imagination." In *Styles of Radical Will*. New York: Farrar, Stauss, and Giroux, 1969.

———. *Styles of Radical Will*. New York: Farrar, Strauss, and Giroux, 1970.

Sprat, Thomas. *History of the Royal Society* (1667). Ed. Jackson I. Cope and Harold Witmore Jones. St. Louis: Washington University Studies, 1958.

St. Teresa of Avila. *The Life of Teresa of Jesus*. Ed. and trans. E. Allison Peers. Garden City: Image Books, 1960.

Stallybrass, Peter and Allon White. *The Politics and Poetics of Transgression*. London: Methuen, 1986.

Stauth, Georg, and Bryan S. Turner. *Nietzsche's Dance*. Oxford: Basil Blackwell, 1988.

Stea, David. *Maps in Minds: Reflections on Cognitive Mapping*. New York: Harper and Row, 1977.

Steiner, George. *Language and Silence. Essays on Language, Literature, and the Inhuman*. New York: Atheneum, 1970.

Sulieman, Susan Rubin. "Pornography, Transgression, and the Avant-Garde: Bataille's *Story of the Eye*." In *The Poetics of Gender*. Ed. Nancy K. Miller. New York: Columbia University Press, 1986.

———. *Subversive Intent: Gender, Politics, and the Avant-Garde*. Cambridge Mass.: Harvard University Press, 1990.

Taylor, Charles. "The Dialogical Self," In *The Interpretive Turn*. Ed. David R. Hiley, James F. Bohman, and Richard Shusterman. Ithaca: Cornell University Press, 1991.

Taylor, Mark C. "Back to the Future." In *Postmodernism—Philosophy and the Arts*. Ed. Hugh J. Silverman. New York: Routledge, 1990.

Todorov, Tzvetan. *Mikhail Bakhtin*. Trans. Wlad Godzich. Minneapolis: University of Minnesota Press, 1984.

Uspensky, Boris A. *Storia e semiotica*. Milan: Bompiani, 1988.

Vattimo, Gianni. *La società transparente*. Milan: Garzanti, 1989.

Vernon, John. *The Garden and the Map: Schizophrenia in Twentieth-Century Literature and Culture*. Urbana: University of Illinois Press, 1973.

Vickers, Brian, ed. *English Science, Bacon to Newton*. Cambridge: University Press, 1987.

———. "The Royal Society and English Prose Style: A Reassessment." In *Rhetoric and the Pursuit of Truth: Language Change in the Seventeenth and Eighteenth Centuries*. Los Angeles: William Andrews Clark Memorial Library, UCLA., 1985.

Vico, Giambattista. *The New Science*. Trans. Thomas Goddard Bergin and Max Harold Fisch. Ithaca: Cornell University Press, 1984.

———. *On the Most Ancient Wisdom of the Italians*. Trans. L. M. Palmer. Ithaca: Cornell University Press, 1988.

Willis, Susan. "Caliban as Post: Reversing the Maps of Domination." In *Reinventing the Americas: Comparative Studies of Literature of the United States and Spanish America*. Eds. Bell Gale Chevigny and Gari Laguardia. Cambridge: Cambridge University Press, 1986.

Wills, Clair. "Upsetting the public: carnival, hysteria and women's texts." In Eds. *Bakhtin and Cultural Theory* Ken Hirschkop and David Shepherd, Manchester and New York: Manchester University Press, 1989.

Wilson, Thomas. *Arte of Rhetorique* (1553). Ed. Thomas J. Derrick. New York: Garland, 1982.

Wittgenstein, Ludwig. *Ludwig Wittgenstein und der Weiner Kreis: Gesprache, aufzeichnet von Friedrich Waismann*. Shriften 3. Ed. B. F. McGuinness. Frankfurt am Main, 1967.

———. *Tractatus Logico-philosophicus*. London: Routledge and Kegan Paul, 1933, 1949.

Wolf, Christa. *Kindheitsmuster*. Darmstadt: Luchterhand, 1979.

———. *Sommerstück*. Darmstadt: Luchterhand, 1989.

Wood, David, ed. *Writing the Future*. London: Routledge, 1990.

Yasuo, Yuasa. *The Body: Toward an Eastern Mind-Body Theory*. Ed. T. P. Kasulis. Trans. Nagatomo Shigenori and T. P. Kasulis. Albany: SUNY Press, 1987.

Yates, Frances A. *The Art of Memory* (Chicago: University of Chicago Press, 1966).

Yeats, W. B. *The Variorum Edition of the Poems of W. B. Yeats*. Ed. Peter Alt and Russell K. Alspach. New York: Macmillan, 1957.

Yourcenar, Marguerite. *Mémoires d'Hadrien*. Paris: Gallimard, 1974.

Zanger, Jules. "'Harbours Like Sonnets': Literary Maps and Cartographic Symbols." *The Georgia Review* 36 (1982): 773–90.

Zedlers Universallexikon, 1733.

Zhang, Longxi. *The Tao and the Logos: Literary Hermeneutics, East and West*. Durham: Duke University Press, 1992.

Ziolkowski. "James Joyces Epiphanie und die Überwindung der empirischen Welt in der modernen deutschen Prosa." *Deutsche Vierteljarhsschrift für Literaturwissenschaft und Geistesgeschichte* 35 (1961): 594–616.

Zukin, Sharon. "Postmodern Urban Landscapes: Mapping Culture and Power." In *Modernity and Identity*. Eds. Scott Lash and Jonathan Friedman. Cambridge: Basil Blackwell, 1992.

Index